Lecture Notes in Artificial I

Subseries of Lecture Notes in Compute

Edited by J. G. Carbonell and J. Siekman

Lecture Notes in Computer Science

Edited by G. Goos, J. Hartmanis and J. van Leeuwen

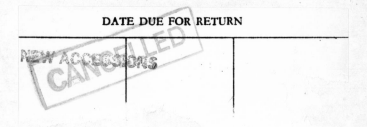

Springer
Berlin
Heidelberg
New York
Barcelona
Budapest
Hong Kong
London
Milan
Paris
Santa Clara
Singapore
Tokyo

Stefan Wermter   Ellen Riloff
Gabriele Scheler (Eds.)

Connectionist, Statistical and Symbolic Approaches to Learning for Natural Language Processing

Springer

Series Editors

Jaime G. Carbonell
School of Computer Science, Carnegie Mellon University
Pittsburgh, PA 15213-3891, USA

Jörg Siekmann
University of Saarland
German Research Center for Artificial Intelligence (DFKI)
Stuhlsatzenhausweg 3, D-66123 Saarbrücken, Germany

Volume Editors

Stefan Wermter
Department of Computer Science, University of Hamburg
Vogt-Koelln-Straße, D-22527 Hamburg, Germany

Ellen Riloff
Department of Computer Science, University of Utah
Salt Lake City, UT 84112, USA

Gabriele Scheler
Department of Computer Science, Technical University of Munich
Arcisstr. 21, D-80290 Munich, Germany

Cataloging-in-Publication Data applied for

Die Deutsche Bibliothek - CIP-Einheitsaufnahme

**Connectionist, statistical and symbolic approaches to learning for natural language
processing** / Stefan Wermter ... (ed.). - Berlin ; Heidelberg ; New York ; Barcelona ;
Budapest ; Hong Kong ; London ; Milan ; Paris ; Santa Clara ; Singapore ;
Tokyo : Springer, 1996
  (Lecture notes in computer science ; Vol. 1040 : Lecture notes in artificial intelligence)
  ISBN 3-540-60925-3
NE: Wermter, Stefan [Hrsg.]; GT

CR Subject Classification (1991): I.2.6, I.2.7, I.2.1, I.2, J.5

ISBN 3-540-60925-3 Springer-Verlag Berlin Heidelberg New York

© Springer-Verlag Berlin Heidelberg 1996
Printed in Germany

Typesetting: Camera ready by author
SPIN 10512554   06/3142 – 5 4 3 2 1 0   Printed on acid-free paper

Preface

The purpose of this book is to present a collection of papers that represents a broad spectrum of current research in learning methods for natural language processing, and to advance the state of the art in language learning and artificial intelligence. The book should bridge a gap between several areas that are usually discussed separately, including connectionist, statistical, and symbolic methods.

In order to bring together new and different language learning approaches, we held a workshop at the International Joint Conference on Artificial Intelligence in Montreal in August 1995. Paper contributions were selected and revised after having been reviewed by at least two members of the international program committee as well as additional reviewers. This book contains the revised workshop papers and additional papers by members of the program committee.

In particular this book focuses on current issues such as:

- How can we apply existing learning methods to language processing?
- What new learning methods are needed for language processing and why?
- What language knowledge should be learned and why?
- What are the similarities and differences between different approaches?
- What are the strengths of learning as opposed to manual encoding?
- How can learning and manual encoding be combined?
- Which aspects of system architectures have to be considered?
- What are successful applications of learning methods in various fields?
- How can we evaluate learning methods using real-world language?

We believe that this selection of contributions is a representative snapshot of the state of the art in current approaches to learning for natural language processing. This is an extremely active area of research that is growing rapidly in interest and popularity. Systems built by learning methods have reached a level where they can be applied to real-world problems in natural language processing and where they can be compared with more traditional encoding methods. The book will provide a basis for discussing various learning approaches to support natural language processing. We hope that this collection will be stimulating and useful for all interested in the areas of learning and natural language processing.

January 1996

Stefan Wermter
Ellen Riloff
Gabriele Scheler

ORGANIZING COMMITTEE

Stefan Wermter, University of Hamburg, Germany
Ellen Riloff, University of Utah, USA
Gabriele Scheler, Technical University Munich, Germany

INVITED SPEAKERS

Eugene Charniak, Brown University, USA
Noel Sharkey, Sheffield University, UK

PROGRAM COMMITTEE

Jaime Carbonell, Carnegie Mellon University, USA
Joachim Diederich, Queensland University of Technology, Australia
Georg Dorffner, University of Vienna, Austria
Jerry Feldman, ICSI, Berkeley, USA
Walther von Hahn, University of Hamburg, Germany
Aravind Joshi, University of Pennsylvania, USA
Ellen Riloff, University of Utah, USA
Gabriele Scheler, Technical University Munich, Germany
Stefan Wermter, University of Hamburg, Germany

ACKNOWLEDGMENTS

We would like to thank Katja Hillebrand, Uwe Jost, Alexandra Klein, Eva Landmann, Manuela Meurer, Jens-Uwe Möller, and Volker Weber from the University of Hamburg for their important help and assistance during the preparations of the workshop and the book. Furthermore, we would like to thank Tony Cohn, the IJCAI-95 workshop chair, and Carol Hamilton at AAAI for their cooperation. We would like to thank Alfred Hofmann and Anna Kramer from Springer for the effective cooperation. Finally, we thank the participants of the workshop and the contributors to this book.

Table of Contents

Statistical Approaches

Symbolic Approaches

Learning Approaches for Natural Language Processing

Stefan Wermter[1] and Ellen Riloff[2] and Gabriele Scheler[3]

[1] University of Hamburg, Dept. of Computer Science, 22527 Hamburg, Germany
[2] University of Utah, Dept. of Computer Science, Salt Lake City, UT 84112, USA
[3] Technical University Munich, Dept. of Computer Science, 80290 Munich, Germany

Abstract. The purpose of this chapter is to provide an introduction to the field of connectionist, statistical and symbolic approaches to learning for natural language processing, based on the contributions in this book. The introduction has been split into three parts: (1) neural networks and connectionist approaches, (2) statistical approaches, and (3) symbolic machine learning approaches. We will give a brief overview of the main methods used in each field, summarize the work that is presented here, and provide some additional references. In the final section we will highlight important general issues and trends based on the workshop discussions and book contributions.

1 Introduction

In the last few years, there has been a lot of interest and activity in developing new approaches to learning for natural language processing [66, 52, 80, 24, 11, 39]. Various learning methods have been used, including connectionist methods/neural networks, statistical methods, symbolic machine learning algorithms, genetic methods, and various hybrid approaches.

In general, learning methods are designed to support automated knowledge acquisition, fault tolerance, and plausible induction. Using learning methods for natural language processing is especially important because learning is an enabling technology for many language-related tasks, such as speech recognition, spoken language understanding, machine translation, and information retrieval. Furthermore, learning is important for building more flexible, scalable, adaptable, and portable natural language systems.

A complete survey of all research in the field of connectionist, statistical, and symbolic approaches to learning for natural language processing cannot be our goal in this chapter. The field has grown much too large already. In fact, such a survey could easily fill a textbook of its own. However, as an aid to the reader, we will set the stage for the contributions in this book. We have organized the book and this survey chapter into three parts for connectionist, statistical, and symbolic learning approaches. In each of the three parts of this chapter, we will give (1) a brief introduction to the general approach, (2) a description, categorization and discussion of the paper contributions, and (3) some pointers to further work.

2 Connectionist Networks and Hybrid Approaches

2.1 Introduction

Recently, artificial neural networks and connectionist networks[4] have received a lot of attention as computational learning mechanisms for natural language processing [66, 52, 24, 2, 80]. There exist many different architectures for connectionist networks. For instance, feedforward networks are useful because of their universal function approximation qualities [34, 16]. While feedforward networks can represent only a fixed length input, recurrent networks can represent variable length input [23, 40, 61]. Most connectionist networks can be trained with a specific learning rule based on the network architecture and the units used.

Connectionist networks have been shown to model successfully a whole variety of language learning tasks [60, 72, 45, 32]. In addition, the combination or integration of connectionist networks with statistical and symbolic representations is an important field for natural language processing [33, 22, 79, 76, 80]. From the viewpoint of knowledge engineering, it might be efficient to encode well-known rules rather than learning them from scratch. From the viewpoint of cognitive behavior, it is interesting to explore human symbolic reasoning for natural language processing based on neural architectures. We speak of a hybrid connectionist approach either if several different connectionist networks are integrated or if connectionist networks are integrated with symbolic or statistical methods.

2.2 Connectionist Approaches for Syntax and Semantics

In this book, the work described by Sharkey and Sharkey argues for a separation of learning and representation. They trained a simple recurrent network with sequences generated by a finite state grammar with bidirectional links. An analysis showed that the networks had a restricted capability to encode embeddings. Then a constructive method was used to improve the performance of the network. Incorrect predictions were identified and hidden units responsible for these predictions were found. A new retraining phase for these incorrect predictions followed and led to better prediction performance. This work might lead to the incremental development of special neural network architectures which cannot be built easily without constructive methods.

The underlying motivation of the approach taken by Lawrence, Fong, and Giles is to explore whether a neural network can exhibit the same discriminatory power for grammaticality as linguists have claimed to exist in universal principles and learned parameters. They have compared different neural network algorithms and symbolic machine learning algorithms. Recurrent Elman networks provided the best discriminatory performance on training and test sets.

---

[4] The terms artificial neural networks and connectionist networks are often used in a similar manner, both refer to networks which are based on very rough computational models of biological neurons.

The authors claim that the Elman network has learned a state machine which can discriminate between grammatical and ungrammatical sentences while other learning algorithms like feedforward models, decision trees, and nearest neighbor algorithms have only learned to find closest matches.

Hayward, Tickle, and Diederich focus on a detailed analysis of rule representation in a single connectionist network. A network is trained with simple sentences using an extension of the cascade correlation algorithm. The task is to learn which combinations of noun – verb – noun combinations are grammatical. Usually little emphasis is put on extracting the rules from a network. In this approach it is demonstrated that simple rules can be extracted from a Cascade network. While the training corpus is relatively simple, this is one of the few papers which focuses on the explanation of connectionist representations and the possible extraction of rules.

The work presented by Scheler uses supervised learning for the construction of classification functions from semantic representations to overt grammatical categories, and interpretation functions from texts to semantic representations. Semantic representations consist of a set of atomic, logically interpretable features which are grounded in cognitive representations. They can be derived automatically from surface coding of texts with sufficient accuracy to provide grammar checking for definiteness of English noun phrases. The results are considerably better than a "naive" approach which classifies surface encodings directly. With this work the difficult issue of providing logical interpretations for real texts automatically has been confronted and a general solution using connectionist learning methods has been presented.

Winiwarter, Schweighofer, and Merkl explore the use of unsupervised learning techniques for knowledge acquisition in concept and document spaces. In particular unsupervised learning in Kohonen feature maps is adapted to cluster legal text segments. This unsupervised learning method was applied to cluster full text documents of court decisions and it could be shown that most similar documents fell into similar regions.

2.3 Hybrid Approaches for Spoken Language

Spontaneously spoken language can be very erroneous. At the acoustic level, phonemes or words may be incorrectly analyzed, and restarts, interjections, pauses, repairs, and repetitions often occur. Furthermore, sentences may be grammatically or semantically incorrect. In general, it is hardly possible to encode all necessary knowledge in fault-tolerant rules. Connectionist networks have been examined for spoken language analysis due to their support of learning and fault-tolerance. The integration of connectionist approaches with symbolic approaches has also been explored.

The approach described by Weber and Wermter tackles the analysis of spoken language in the hybrid connectionist architecture SCREEN. Based on a speech recognizer, spontaneously spoken sentences are processed. Feedforward and recurrent connectionist networks for semantic and syntactic analysis are used wherever possible, but symbolic techniques are also used in a restricted manner for the control of different networks and for simple rules which always hold. The focus in this chapter is on improving the analysis of noisy and ungrammatical spoken sentences by integrating acoustic, syntactic, and semantic knowledge. Furthermore, it is shown that a flat analysis using connectionist learning supports a robust and fault-tolerant analysis of spoken language.

The hybrid symbolic/connectionist architecture SKOPE for spoken Korean by Lee and Lee uses connectionist learning in Time Delay networks, primarily in the speech component. Time-delay networks offer a method of learning a sequence of events. The morphological and syntactical components are based on table-driven parsing techniques and spreading activation respectively. In general, Lee and Lee argue for the combination of connectionist speech learning with symbolic language encoding.

Geutner and colleagues combine different learning approaches for translating spoken natural language between English, German, and Spanish[5]. Within their JANUS system, statistical hidden Markov models and connectionist Time Delay Networks are explored at the speech recognition level. Subsequently, a concept spotter, a statistical LR parser and a connectionist parser are examined to provide an interlingua-like language description for the translation. A main point within the JANUS system is that multiple learning strategies are explored in a complementary manner to make hand-coded language representations unnecessary.

2.4 Genetic Approaches

The paper by Smith and Witten describes a genetic algorithm for the induction of natural language grammars. The genetic learning algorithm works on logical s-expressions which can represent context free grammars without recursion. Starting with a random population of different potential grammars for a given first string, only those which parse the string are part of the initial population. If a new string is added, reproduction operators combine two different grammars from the current population. Furthermore, additional mutation operators can replace leaf or internal nodes in a grammar in order to provide more variation in the search space of possible grammars. Although relatively few, small sentences are used for genetic learning, this approach is a new interesting alternative since it is also frequency-based and robust.

2.5 Further Work

There are a large number of important references in the field of connectionist natural language processing and we cannot hope to be complete or comprehensive. However, in order to provide some pointers to start with, we will very briefly list some of the important references. For a fundamental early

---

[5] This paper could also be grouped into the statistical section. However, because of the many different learning strategies used and due to the focus on spoken language it was placed in the group of hybrid approaches for spoken language.

paper about connectionism in general one could start with [25, 51]. Architectural issues of connectionist and hybrid connectionist systems are discussed in [68, 22, 23, 40, 61, 3, 21, 52, 19, 56, 80]. Some representative references for semantic and syntactic analysis with connectionist networks can be found in [38, 50, 60, 75, 70, 79]. For references on cognitively oriented connectionist natural language processing some references are [14, 78, 69, 42, 12].

3 Statistical Approaches

3.1 Introduction

With the recent trend for learning in natural language processing, statistical methods have gained new popularity, and are being applied to new domains. They are usually characterized by using large text corpora and performing some analysis which uses primarily the text characteristics without adding significant linguistic or world knowledge [5, 11, 48]. Text corpora that have been built include the still widely used Brown corpus [27], and newer corpora such as the LOB corpus [28] and the Penn treebank [49].

Annotation of corpora with part-of-speech tags or parse trees has been a focus of corpus-based language analysis. Additional important application areas of statistical techniques to written natural language are thesaurus-building (or lexical clustering) and probabilistic grammar learning. Statistical techniques that have been used for these tasks are n-gram techniques, unsupervised clustering and hidden Markov models (e.g. [71, 44]). A special case is grammar induction, which uses context-free grammars in addition to probabilistic information from texts.

3.2 Probabilistic Grammar Induction and Disambiguation

In this book, Ersan and Charniak present a system for syntactic disambiguation using probabilistic information on word classes derived from the Wall Street Journal corpus. They show how the improved parser can be used to extract data on verb case-frames and noun-preposition and adjective-preposition combinations. This is achieved by identifying occurrences of particular syntactic combinations in the parses, which are counted and passed through a probabilistic filter. Precision and recall for the resulting combinations are evaluated with respect to an English dictionary. This statistical work is particularly interesting since it addresses the important question what is learned in probabilistic language representations.

Hogenhout and Matsumoto also collect general statistics on the occurrence of semantic classes in the application of grammar rules. That is, the syntactic word class information is augmented by the probability of a semantic class in the application of a single rule within a context-free grammar. This probability is calculated by the Inside-Out algorithm with certain smoothing parameters.

Semantic classes are defined by reference to a standard thesaurus. The probabilities of the classes were used to improve ambiguity resolution within a handwritten grammar. Experiments conducted on the Japanese EDR corpus show a statistically significant improvement on parsing accuracy (sentence and bracket accuracy) for the incorporation of probabilistic semantic class information.

Fong and Wu describe a model for learning probabilistic link grammars. Link grammars are highly-lexicalized context-free grammars where individual words can be linked via labeled arcs. The probabilities of the links are estimated using an expectation maximization training method. After training and subsequent pruning, the learned representation contains grammatical rules as sets of simple disjuncts and probabilities. This approach was tested with two artificial corpora of short simple sentences to demonstrate the learning behavior. It could be shown that the perplexity of the described model is lower than a comparable probabilistic link model as well as a bigram model.

Prepositional phrase attachment has been a major problem for structural analysis of natural language. Franz describes a statistical approach to learning prepositional phrase attachment based on categorial features. A loglinear model is described which consists of a contingency table for recording the frequency of certain feature combinations as well as a loglinear model for smoothing the frequency counts for zero occurrences. The Brown corpus and Wall Street Journal corpus were used for training and testing. The results are slightly worse than human performance but better than simple heuristics like right association. Learning in this statistical model is simple but can be applied efficiently to a large number of training and test instances.

3.3 Part-of-speech Tagging and Probabilistic Word Classes

Grünwald uses a greedy minimum description length (MDL) approach to cluster words in semantic-syntactic classes, based on a subset of the Brown corpus. According to the MDL principle, learning is defined as reducing the total length of a set of data (measured in bits) by introducing a theory which can generate certain data, and thus serves as an abbreviation of the data set. The implementation uses a "greedy" learning mechanism, i.e. decreasing the total description length in each step. As a result, a number of the derived word classes are given. The advantage of the MDL approach in comparison with a simple n-gram technique is the availability of a stopping criterion for learning, which prevents overfitting of the data.

The approach by Mast and colleagues offers a new application area, namely the classification of dialog acts. Dialog acts describe a spoken dialog at a higher level using shallow understanding with labels like "accept", "reject", "request-suggestion". State-dependent semantic classification trees and statistical polygrams are used to acquire a classification of sentences according to their respective dialog acts. German and English dialogs were labeled and used for this task. It is argued that polygrams are preferable to the decision tree methods for dialog act classification.

Selective sampling is a technique for selecting only particularly informative unlabeled training examples for subsequent labeling and training. Engelson and Dagan describe an approach for selective sampling applied to probabilistic part-of-speech tagging. Using an implicit model, the current training data is used to evaluate the uncertainty for classifying an additional training example. Examples with a larger uncertainty for classification are particularly good training examples for labeling and training. Since labeling large corpora is very expensive, time-consuming work, the technique of selective sampling could allow systems to work with much larger corpora.

3.4 Further Work

The classical applications in natural language processing are part-of-speech tagging [46, 15, 18], and lexical extraction for various information retrieval tasks [13, 77, 35, 30, 73]. This has recently been extended to anaphora resolution [8], text alignment [41], grammar induction [6] and statistical machine translation [59, 7]. Statistical analysis has also been used in speech recognition [4], which is however not the main focus of the present volume.

4 Symbolic Approaches

4.1 Introduction

Symbolic approaches to learning encompass a wide variety of machine learning techniques. Many inductive learning algorithms have been developed in the machine learning community, such as decision tree algorithms [63, 65] and conceptual clustering [26]. Explanation-based learning [17, 53] is another type of symbolic learning that pushes training examples through a domain theory to create generalized examples for future use. Case-based learning techniques [31, 62] and analogical reasoning methods [10] try to map new situations onto previously encountered situations to find the best solution. There are also a wide variety of rule-based approaches to concept learning.

Information extraction (IE) is a relatively new subfield of natural language processing that has received a lot of attention recently because of the message understanding conferences (MUCs) [57, 58]. The MUCs have encouraged researchers to work on real-world text (e.g., newswire articles) and to develop practical methods, and have been instrumental in bringing together NLP researchers from a variety of areas towards a common goal. There has also been growing interest in developing trainable IE systems that can use learning methods to increase their portability to new domains; some of these systems are mentioned in the next section.

4.2 Information Extraction

One of the main challenges in information extraction research is developing methods and systems to acquire the necessary knowledge bases automatically. Huffman has developed one such system, LIEP, which learns dictionaries of extraction patterns. LIEP attempts to find relationships between constituents that have been tagged as relevant by a user. One of the distinguishing features of LIEP is that the underlying sentence analyzer, ODIE, parses sentences "on-demand" by attempting to verify syntactic relationships only when asked to do so. LIEP hypothesizes syntactic relationships between constituents and asks ODIE to determine whether the relationships are plausible. This approach chooses among competing patterns using empirical feedback on a training corpus and can generalize existing patterns when the same syntactic relationships are identified in a new context.

Hastings describes the CAMILLE lexical acquisition system which was originally developed to learn word meanings for an information extraction system. CAMILLE infers the meanings of new words based on semantic constraints provided by the surrounding context and a concept hierarchy. This paper explains why different learning strategies are used for nouns and verbs, and discusses implications for related research in knowledge representation, cognitive modeling, and evaluation.

Riloff discusses the application of learned extraction patterns to problems in text classification. The AutoSlog dictionary construction system learns extraction patterns automatically using an annotated training corpus and the learned patterns have been shown to be effective for information extraction. This paper presents experiments in three domains which show that the extraction patterns created by AutoSlog are also useful for text classification. These results demonstrate that AutoSlog's dictionaries represent important domain concepts and that information extraction dictionaries can be useful for other natural language processing tasks as well.

The CRYSTAL system by Soderland and colleagues automatically learns information extraction patterns. CRYSTAL is an automated dictionary construction tool that uses an annotated training corpus and a concept hierarchy to generate extraction patterns. The produced extraction patterns are tested on a training corpus to ensure they satisfy a minimum error tolerance threshold. This paper discusses the issues of creating an appropriate training corpus and domain ontology, the expressiveness of its learned patterns, and its search control strategy.

4.3 Inductive Learning Algorithms

Many researchers are taking advantage of inductive learning methods developed in the machine learning community and are applying them to problems in natural language processing. A good example of this type of work is the application of the C4.5 decision tree algorithm to anaphora resolution by Aone and Bennett. Newspaper articles annotated with discourse information are given to C4.5 as training instances. Aone and Bennet use 66 features to represent each training instance; the feature values are determined automatically during text processing. Their paper presents a series of experiments using different parameter combinations (such as anaphoric chaining, anaphoric type identification, and confidence factors) in the context of a full information extraction system, and compares the performance of the learning system with hand-coded knowledge sources.

Cardie promotes the view that all ambiguity problems in NLP can be recast as classification tasks and presents a general architecture for embedding machine learning techniques in natural language processing systems. The Kenmore framework is composed of a text corpus, a sentence analyzer, a human supervisor, and a machine learning algorithm. In the acquisition phase, texts are parsed by the sentence analyzer to produce training cases, which are then annotated by a human and presented to the machine learning algorithm as training data. Cardie describes experiments with Kenmore for several ambiguity problems using a hybrid nearest-neighbor/decision tree learning system embedded in an information extraction system.

Learning is also used in the ALT-J/E system for the acquisition of hierarchical semantic knowledge, presented by Yamazaki, Pazzani and Merz. An inductive learning method (FOCL) is first used to learn translation rules whose disjunctions are clustered to form the semantic hierarchy. The frequency of co-occurring terms in a disjunction of rules measures the similarity of terms for the semantic hierarchy. Then the average linkage method for clustering is applied to build the hierarchy. The experimental results showed that learning or updating semantic hierarchies improves the accuracy of learning translation rules.

Moulinier and Ganascia describe the application of an inductive learning system, CHARADE, to the problem of text categorization. Given an attribute-value representation of training examples, this system generates k-DNF rules that cover the positive training examples but not the negative examples. This paper contrasts CHARADE with decision-tree learning algorithms and compares the performance with previously reported results for a decision tree algorithm and a Bayesian classifier on the Reuters categorization corpus. Additional experiments also illustrate the role that redundancy can play in learning effective rule sets.

Inductive logic programming (ILP) is currently a hot topic in machine learning circles, so it is not surprising to see ILP being applied to problems in natural language processing. Zelle and Mooney describe CHILL, an inductive logic programming system, and use it to learn search-control rules for parsing operators. They compare CHILL's performance with that of a naive ILP program that generates a parser without search-control rules. Both systems perform well on a small data set of case-role mapping assignments, but CHILL was much more successful at parsing a larger data set from the Penn Treebank corpus. The paper also discusses how CHILL can be used to generate database queries from sentences.

Mooney and Califf use inductive logic programming to tackle the problem of learning past tenses of English verbs. Their system, FOIDL, induces first-order decision lists that represent rules associated with past tense formation. Key properties are that this system uses only intensional rather than extensional background definitions and does not need explicit negative examples. FOIDL is compared with FOIL [64], IFOIL, and previously reported results.

4.4 Analogical, Rule-based, and Explanation-based Learning

Federici, Pirrelli, and Yvon use analogical-based learning techniques to learn how to pronounce words. The center of their approach is the representation of paradigmatic nodes and links for core components of words that are the same orthographically and phonologically. The paradigmatic nodes are viewed as analogical islands that are generally reliable. This approach is compared with another analogy-based system without paradigms, a decision tree system, and an instance-based learner.

Osborne investigates the role that punctuation might play in learning grammar rules. Osborne's learning system generates grammar rules using a model-based approach to filter out rules that are not consistent with the model and to revise rules so that they become consistent with the model. Since punctuation symbols are often used in natural language to delimit modifiers, separate phrases, and disambiguate sentence structure, Osborne contends that including them in a language model could improve a system's ability to learn an effective grammar.

Joshi and Srinivas describe the application of explanation-based learning (EBL) to speed up the performance of a parser. Their parser is based on an LTAG (Lexicalized Tree Adjoining Grammar) formalism. As input, the learning system uses a parsed corpus that contains dependency and phrase structure information. The learning algorithm is then used to generalize the parses, so that the generalized parses can be used for subsequent sentences. Experimental results show that using the EBL system can substantially reduce the time required for parsing.

A rule-based approach for acquiring compound nouns automatically is described by Jacquemin. He argues that even though there are lexicons available that contain important terms for some domains (e.g., many technical domains), there will always be a need to learn new terms as knowledge evolves. This paper describes a system that begins with a dictionary of terms for a domain and uses a set of rules to infer new terms as they are encountered in text. The rules represent patterns that rewrite the original terms in a different form by recognizing coordinations (e.g., conjunctions formed from the original terms), insertions (new words inserted between the original words), and permutations (e.g., a compound noun transformed into a prepositional phrase). Jacquemin also discusses how conceptual links can be assigned to the new terms and presents empirical results from a medical corpus.

Kaneda and colleagues propose a learning model to support machine translation in the ALT-J/E framework. Verb selection is among the most important problems in machine translation. Their system learns to find appropriate English verbs for Japanese verbs based on the verbs and their semantic case role fillers. Instead of using existing translation examples, they argue that a carefully selected number of hand-made translation rules together with some existing translation examples provides better guidance to the learning model.

Hahn, Klenner, and Schnattinger take a formal approach to concept learning by presenting a terminological representation language. This language is a formalism to support learning the meanings of new words based on predefined knowledge and surrounding context. This approach depends on a large knowledge base of predefined concepts for the domain and associated background knowledge. A key feature of the formalism is that it supports the generation of multiple hypotheses and uses its knowledge sources to sift through and assess competing hypotheses.

4.5 Further Work

To learn more about information extraction techniques and systems, see [47, 36]. Several systems have been developed recently that learn dictionaries for information extraction, such as [43, 67, 74]. Some older systems that incorporated symbolic learning techniques with natural language processing include [1, 29, 9, 37]. Explanation-based learning has also been previously applied to NLP (e.g., see [55]), and rule-based learning techniques have been used to extract information from on-line dictionaries and build knowledge bases automatically [54, 20].

5 Summary and Discussion of General Issues

In this section we step back from the analysis of specific approaches and summarize what we consider to be general issues and trends in the field of learning for natural language processing based on the contributions in this volume and the discussions at the workshop.

5.1 Flat Analysis and Learning

First, there is an important relationship between learning and the underlying representations. In general, the connectionist, statistical, and symbolic approaches described in this volume use flat representations rather than deeply structured representations to support learning. Learning approaches often focus on syntactic/semantic tagging, classification and feature extraction rather than syntactic/semantic analysis using e.g. highly structured HPSG grammars.

5.2 Comparative Evaluation of Different Learning Methods

It is important and necessary to compare different learning approaches according to their strengths and weaknesses. We have seen several examples for such an evaluation of different learning approaches in this volume. It would be interesting to extend such comparisons within the field of learning natural language processing.

5.3 Learning Language Problems from the Real World

We see an important trend emerging for using real-world data for the learning algorithms in language processing. Several years ago, in the communities of natural language processing, connectionism, and machine learning, many smaller "toy" problems or domains were used. However, now that many corpora, lexica, and knowledge bases are available, this opens up many possibilities for further research on learning language in real-world problems and domains.

5.4 Hybrid Approaches for Complex Tasks

In some cases, however, the tasks get so complex that it might not be possible to choose a single best learning technique. This is the case for problems like learning to translate spoken language to another language, where many different modules have to be involved to attack such complex problems. Here we cannot expect that evaluation tests to identify a generally best learning method will succeed. Rather, individual modules can be evaluated and many different learning methods might be useful; sometimes combined with manually-encoded knowledge if it is available. For such complex problems like speech translation or interactive information extraction, the question of a desired hybrid learning architecture is very important and many different connectionist, statistical and symbolic methods may prove useful for solving complex tasks.

References

1. J. R. Anderson. Induction of Augmented Transition Networks. *Cognitive Science*, 1:125–157, 1977.
2. J. A. Barnden and K. J. Holyoak, editors. *Advances in connectionist and neural computation theory*, volume 3. Ablex Publishing Corporation, Norwood, New Jersey, 1994.
3. L. Bookman and R. Sun. Integrating neural and symbolic processes. *Connection Science*, 5:203–204, 1993.
4. H. A. Bourlard and N. Morgan. *Connectionist Speech Recognition*. Kluwer, Boston, 1993.
5. E. Brill. *A Corpus-Based Approach to Language Learning*. PhD thesis, University of Pennsylvania, 1993.
6. T. Briscoe and J. Caroll. Generalised probabilistic LR parsing of natural language (corpora) with unification-based grammars. Technical Report TR 224, Computer Laboratory, University of Cambridge, UK, England, June 1991.
7. P.J. Brown, S. Della Pietra, V. J. Della Pietra, F. Jelinek, J. D. Lafferty, R. L. Mercer, and R. S. Roossin. A statistical approach to machine translation. *Computational Linguistics*, 16(2):79–85, 1990.
8. J. D. Burger and D. Connolly. Probabilistic resolution of anaphoric reference. In *Probabilistic Approaches to Natural Language*, AAAI Fall Symposium, 1992. AAAI Press.
9. J. G. Carbonell. Towards a self-extending parser. In *Proceedings of the Seventeenth Meeting of the Association for Computational Linguistics*, pages 3–7, 1979.

10. J. G. Carbonell. Derivational analogy: a theory of reconstructive problem solving and expertise acquisition. In *Machine Learning: An Artificial Intelligence Approach*. Morgan Kaufmann, San Mateo, CA, 1986.

11. E. Charniak. *Statistical Language Learning*. MIT Press, Cambridge, MA, 1993.

12. M. H. Christiansen. The (non)necessity of recursion in natural language processing. In *Proceedings of the 14th Annual Conference of the Cognitive Science Society*, pages 665–670, Indiana University, Bloomington, 1992.

13. K. Church and P. Hanks. Word association norms, mutual information and lexicography. *Computational Linguistics*, 16(1), 1990.

14. G. W. Cottrell. A model of lexical access of ambiguous words. In S. I. Small, G. W. Cottrell, and M. K. Tanenhaus, editors, *Lexical Ambiguity Resolution*, pages 179–194. Morgan Kaufmann, San Mateo, CA, 1988.

15. D. Cutting, J. Kupiec, J. Pedersen, and P. Sibun. A practical part-of-speech tagger. In *Proceedings of the Third Conference on Applied Natural Language Processing*, pages 133–140, 1992.

16. G. Cybenko. Approximation by superposition of a sigmoidal function. *Mathematics of Control, Signals and Systems*, 2:303–314, 1989.

17. G. DeJong and R. Mooney. Explanation-based learning: an alternative view. *Machine Learning*, 1:145–176, 1986.

18. S. J. DeRose. Grammatical category disambiguation by statistical optimization. *Computational Linguistics*, 14(1), 1988.

19. J. Diederich. An explanation component for a connectionist inference system. In *Proceedings of the Ninth European Conference on Artificial Intelligence*, pages 222–227, Stockholm, 1990.

20. W. Dolan, L. Vanderwende, and S. D. Richardson. Automatically deriving structured knowledge bases from on-line dictionaries. In *Proceedings of the First Conference of the Pacific Association for Computational Linguistics*, pages 5–14, 1993.

21. G. Dorffner, editor. *Neural Networks and a New AI*. Chapman and Hall, London, UK, 1995.

22. M. G. Dyer. Symbolic neuroengineering for natural language processing: a multi-level research approach. In J. A. Barnden and J. B. Pollack, editors, *Advances in Connectionist and Neural Computation Theory, Vol.1: High Level Connectionist Models*, pages 32–86. Ablex Publishing Corporation, Norwood, NJ, 1991.

23. J. L. Elman. Finding structure in time. *Cognitive Science*, 14:179–221, 1990.

24. J. Feldman. Structured connectionist models and language learning. *Artificial Intelligence Review*, 7(5):301–312, 1993.

25. J. A. Feldman and D. H. Ballard. Connectionist models and their properties. *Cognitive Science*, 6:205–254, 1982.

26. D. H. Fisher. Knowledge acquisition via incremental conceptual clustering. *Machine Learning*, 2:139–172, 1987.

27. W. N. Francis and H. Kucera. *Manual of Information to Accompany a Standard Corpus of Present-day Edited American English*. Brown University, Department of Linguistics, 1979.

28. R. Garside, G. Leech, and G. Sampson. *The Computational Analysis of English: A Corpus-Based Approach*. Longman, 1983.

29. R. H. Granger. FOUL-UP: A program that figures out meanings of words from context. In *Proceedings of the Fifth International Joint Conference on Artificial Intelligence*, pages 172–178, 1977.

30. G. Grefenstette. *Explorations in Automatic Thesaurus Discovery*. Kluwer, Boston, 1994.

31. K. Hammond. CHEF: A model of case-based planning. In *Proceedings of the Fifth National Conference on Artificial Intelligence*, pages 267–271, 1986.

32. J. Henderson. Connectionist syntactic parsing using temporal variable binding. *Journal of Psycholinguistic Research*, 6, 1994.

33. J. A. Hendler. Marker passing over microfeatures: towards a hybrid symbolic connectionist model. *Cognitive Science*, 13:79–106, 1989.

34. K. Hornik, W. Stinchcombe, and H. White. Multilayer feedforward networks are universal approximators. *Neural Networks*, 2:359–366, 1989.

35. J. Hughes and E. Atwell. Automatically acquiring a classification of words. In *Proceedings of the IEEE Colloquium on Grammatical Inference*, 1993.

36. P. Jacobs and L. Rau. SCISOR: extracting information from on-line news. *Communications of the ACM*, 33(11):88–97, 1990.

37. P. Jacobs and U. Zernik. Acquiring lexical knowledge from text: a case study. In *Proceedings of the Seventh National Conference on Artificial Intelligence*, pages 739–744, 1988.

38. A. N. Jain. Generalization performance in PARSEC - a structured connectionist parsing architecture. In J. E. Moody, S. J. Hanson, and R. P. Lippmann, editors, *Advances in Neural Information Processing Systems 4*, pages 209–216. Morgan Kaufmann, San Mateo, CA, 1992.

39. D. Jones, editor. *New Methods in Language Processing*. University College London, 1995.

40. M. I. Jordan. Attractor dynamics and parallelism in a connectionist sequential machine. In *Proceedings of the Eighth Conference of the Cognitive Science Society*, pages 531–546, Amherst, MA, 1986.

41. M. Kay and M. Röscheisen. Text-translation alignment. *Computational Linguistics*, 18(2), 1993.

42. G. Kempen and T. Vosse. Incremental syntactic tree formation in human sentence processing: a cognitive architecture based on activation decay and simulated annealing. *Connection Science*, 1 (3):273–290, 1989.

43. J. Kim and D. Moldovan. Acquisition of semantic patterns for information extraction from corpora. In *Proceedings of the Ninth IEEE Conference on Artificial Intelligence for Applications*, pages 171–176, 1993.

44. J. Kupiec. Robust part-of-speech tagging using a hidden Markov model. *Computer Speech and Language*, (6):225–242, 1992.

45. S. C. Kwasny and K. A. Faisal. Connectionism and determinism in a syntactic parser. In N. Sharkey, editor, *Connectionist Natural Language Processing*, pages 119–162. Lawrence Erlbaum, 1992.

46. G. Leech, R. Garside, and E. Atwell. The automatic grammatical tagging of the LOB corpus. *ICAME News*, 7:13–33, 1983.

47. W. G. Lehnert and B. Sundheim. A performance evaluation of text analysis technologies. *AI Magazine*, 12(3):81–94, 1991.

48. D. M. Magerman. Natural language parsing as statistical pattern recognition. Technical Report PhD thesis, Stanford University, 1994.

49. M. Marcus, B. Santorini, and M. Marcinkiewicz. Building a large annotated corpus of English: the Penn treebank. *Computational Linguistics*, 19(1), 1993.

50. J. L. McClelland and A. H. Kawamoto. Mechanisms of sentence processing: assigning roles to constituents. In J. L. McClelland and D. E. Rumelhart, editors, *Parallel Distributed Processing*, volume 2, pages 272–326. MIT Press, Cambridge, MA, 1986.

51. J. L. McClelland, D. E. Rumelhart, and G. E. Hinton. The appeal of parallel distributed processing. In D. E. Rumelhart and J. L. McClelland, editors, *Parallel Distributed Processing*, volume 1, pages 3–44. MIT Press, Cambridge, MA, 1986.

52. R. Miikkulainen. *Subsymbolic Natural Language Processing*. MIT Press, Cambridge, MA, 1993.

53. T. M. Mitchell, R. Keller, and S. Kedar-Cabelli. Explanation-based generalization: a unifying view. *Machine Learning*, 1:47–80, 1986.

54. S. Montemagni and L. Vanderwende. Structural patterns vs. string patterns for extracting semantic information from dictionaries. In *Proceedings of the Fourteenth International Conference on Computational Linguistics*, pages 546–552, 1992.

55. R. Mooney and G. DeJong. Learning Schemata for Natural Language Processing. In *Proceedings of the Ninth International Joint Conference on Artificial Intelligence*, pages 681–687, 1985.

56. M. Mozer and P. Smolensky. Using relevance to reduce network size automatically. *Connection Science*, 1 (1):3–16, 1989.

57. *Proceedings of the Fourth Message Understanding Conference*, Morgan Kaufmann, San Mateo, CA, 1992.

58. *Proceedings of the Fifth Message Understanding Conference*, Morgan Kaufmann, San Francisco, CA, 1993. Morgan Kaufmann.

59. S. Nirenburg, J. Beale, and I. Domashnev. A full-text experiment in EBMT. In Daniel Jones, editor, *New Methods in Language Processing*. University College London, 1995.

60. J. B. Pollack. On connectionist models of natural language processing. Technical Report PhD thesis, Technical Report MCCS-87-100, New Mexico State University, Las Cruces, NM, 1987.

61. J. B. Pollack. Recursive distributed representations. *Artificial Intelligence*, 46:77–105, 1990.

62. B. W. Porter, R. Bareiss, and R. C. Holte. Concept learning and heuristic classification in weak-theory domains. *Artificial Intelligence*, 45, 1990.

63. J. R. Quinlan. Induction of decision trees. *Machine Learning*, 1:80–106, 1986.

64. J. R. Quinlan. Learning logical definitions from relations. *Machine Learning*, 5(3):239–266, 1990.

65. J. R. Quinlan. *C4.5: Programs for Machine Learning*. Morgan Kaufmann, San Mateo, CA, 1992.

66. R. G. Reilly and N. E. Sharkey. *Connectionist Approaches to Natural Language Processing*. Lawrence Erlbaum Associates, Hillsdale, NJ, 1992.

67. E. Riloff. Automatically constructing a dictionary for information extraction tasks. In *Proceedings of the Eleventh National Conference on Artificial Intelligence*, pages 811–816. AAAI Press/The MIT Press, 1993.

68. D. E. Rumelhart, G. E. Hinton, and R. J. Williams. Learning internal representations by error propagation. In D. E. Rumelhart and J. L. McClelland, editors, *Parallel Distributed Processing*, volume 1, pages 318–362. MIT Press, Cambridge, MA, 1986.

69. D. E. Rumelhart and J. L. McClelland. PDP models and general issues in cognitive science. In D. E. Rumelhart and J. L. McClelland, editors, *Parallel Distributed Processing*, volume 1, pages 110–146. MIT Press, Cambridge, MA, 1986.

70. G. Scheler. Learning the semantics of aspect. In D. Jones, editor, *New Methods in Language Processing*. University College London Press, 1995.

71. H. Schütze and Y. Singer. Part-of-speech tagging using a variable context Markov model. In *Proceedings of the Connectionist Models Summer School*, pages 122–129, Boulder. CO, 1993.

72. N. E. Sharkey. A PDP learning approach to natural language understanding. In I. Alexander, editor, *Neural Computing Architectures*, pages 92–116. North Oxford Academic, 1989.

73. F. Smadja. From n-grams to collocations: an evaluation of Xtract. In *Proceedings of 20th Meeting of the Association for Computational Linguistics*, 1991.

74. S. Soderland, D. Fisher, J. Aseltine, and W. Lehnert. CRYSTAL: inducing a conceptual dictionary. In *Proceedings of the Fourteenth International Joint Conference on Artificial Intelligence*, pages 1314–1319, 1995.

75. M. F. St. John and J. L. McClelland. Learning and applying contextual constraints in sentence comprehension. *Artificial Intelligence*, 46:217–257, 1990.

76. R. Sun. Robust reasoning: integrating rule-based and similarity-based reasoning. *Artificial Intelligence*, pages 241–295, 1995.

77. J. Veronis and N. M. Ide. Word sense disambiguation with very large neural networks extracted from machine readable dictionaries. In *Proceedings of the Thirteenth International Conference on Computational Linguistics*, 1990.

78. D. L. Waltz and J. B. Pollack. Massively parallel parsing: a strongly interactive model of natural language interpretation. *Cognitive Science*, 9:51–74, 1985.

79. S. Wermter and V. Weber. Learning fault-tolerant speech parsing with SCREEN. In *Proceedings of the National Conference on Artificial Intelligence*, pages 670–675, Seattle, USA, 1994.

80. S. Wermter. *Hybrid Connectionist Natural Language Processing*. Chapman and Hall, London, UK, 1995.

Separating Learning and Representation*

Noel E. Sharkey and Amanda J.C. Sharkey

Department of Computer Science

University of Sheffield, UK.

Abstract

Two of the most promising aspects of connectionist natural language research have been (i) the use of powerful statistical learning techniques to model language learning and (ii) the development of new representational theories. Often the two are treated together; some part of a grammar is induced by a net and the subsequent representations are analysed for the maintenance of structural information. In this chapter, representation and learning are treated separately. A simple recurrent net trained on a bidirectional link grammar showed severe limitations in its ability to handle embedded sequences. Then, after an analysis of the problem, a constructive method was used to develop representations, using the same SRN architecture, that exhibited the potential to correctly recognise embeddings of any length. These findings illustrate the benefits of the study of representation, which can provide a basis for the development of novel learning rules.

Over the last decade, neural computing research has been highly renowned for the development of statistical "learning" techniques. In the realm of "pure" learning theory there have been many impressive proofs of the capabilities of different types of learning rule. For example, White (1992) and colleagues have proven that backpropagation learning algorithm (which implements a type of non-linear multiple regression) will, universally, approximate any static function given unbounded resources. It is partly because of these learning abilities that there has been considerable research on the induction of language skills from experimenter-defined linguistic environments (for reviews see Sharkey & Reilly, 1992; Sharkey, 1992; and more recent issues of the journal, Connection Science).

[0]We are grateful to ESRC Grant No R-000-22-1133 for funding this research, and to Stuart Jackson for running the simulations, and for his contribution to the development of the ideas on which this work is based.

This has led, unsurprisingly, to an interest in the connectionist modelling of aspects of language learning and language acquisition (e.g. Plunkett and Marchman, 1991; Rumelhart and McClelland, 1986; Elman, 1990; 1991).

However, it is not just the use of learning rules that has led to the popularity of connectionist modelling of language processes. What separates connectionism from other statistical methods is that connectionist models combine statistical learning with various theories of representation. For example, the first paper on Backpropagation (Rumelhart, Hinton, & Williams, 1986) focused on how the networks automatically developed "internal representations" of the training task. And this was quickly followed by analyses of the representations for particular tasks (e.g. Hinton, 1986; Sejnowski & Rosenberg, 1986).

By the late 1980s, early 1990s, much of the debate in cognition and connectionism centered around whether or not there were novel connectionist representations (e.g. Smolensky, 1988) and, if so, whether they were sufficient to support the cognitive architecture (e.g. Fodor & McLaughlin, 1990). These arguments culminated in van Gelder's (1990) notion of a new type of connectionist functionally compositional representation typified by the representations developing in Pollack's (1990) RAAM networks (c.f. Sharkey, 1991 for a review and typology of connectionist representations).

One of the most important developments since then has been the demonstration of the *useability* of connectionist representations. Although even standard statistical methods in natural language processing can be said, in some sense, to develop representations (Charniak, 1995), it is their useability that separates connectionist from standard statistical representations. That is, useable representations are those that can be passed between different connectionist modules (Sharkey & Sharkey, 1992) or that can be systematically transformed (or manipulated) in tasks such as active/passive transformations (Chalmers, 1990), English to Spanish translation (Chrisman, 1991), necessary inference (Blank, Meeden, & Marshall, 1992), and manipulation of logic formulae (Niklasson & Sharkey, 1992)[1]

The representational questions addressed in this chapter are somewhat different. The previous research cited above has been concerned with the learning of representations. In this paper we separate the two and focus

---

[1]More recently this work has led to a debate about what level of systematicity uniquely connectionist representations can obtain. Hadely (1994), for example, has argued that such representation can only exhibit what he calls *weak* systematicity. However, Niklasson and his associates (e.g. Niklasson & van Gelder, 1994) have shown, that connectionist internal representations exhibit a form of *strong* systematicity.

on what a particular type of net *can* represent rather than what it can learn to represent. Previous work (e.g. Denker *et. al*, 1987) has shown that there may be easy solution to problems that Backpropagation cannot learn in a standard feedforward network. In this chapter, we examine a problem in the temporal dynamics of natural language processing that has proved difficult for a Simple Recurrent Network (Elman, 1989) to learn; namely the problem of embedded sequences.

In the remainder of this chapter we shall first briefly review the modelling of the temporal aspects of natural language processing and discuss research on the problem of sequence embedding. Second, we present a learning experiment that shows up a limitation of SRN learning and we diagnose the problems by introducing *prediction space analysis*. Finally, a constructive method is applied to show that although SRNs do not *learn* it, there is a representational solution to the problem of sequence embedding.

1   Modelling the Sequential Nature of Language

One of the problems faced by the modellers of the early and mid 1980s was how to represent the temporal characteristics of language with artificial neural nets. The artificial neural nets used had only feedforward connections and thus could not preserve a memory of prior inputs. Although some methods were used to get around problems of sequentiality such as assemblies or frames (Hinton, 1981; McClelland and Rumelhart, 1981), moving input windows (Sejnowski and Rosenberg, 1986), and Wickelfeatures (Rumelhart and McClelland, 1986), these amounted to using the input space as fixed width memory buffer.

A seemingly natural step forward has been to augment feedforward network architecture with recurrent or feedback links that preserve a *fading* memory of the past. One of the most popularly used recurrent nets for modelling language, developed by Elman (1988), is the Simple Recurrent Net (SRN) as illustrated in Figure 1. The task of the SRN is to learn to predict the legal successors of the current input (e.g. as in grammar recognition). This approach has yielded many successes both in simple grammar learning (e.g. Servan-Schreiber, Cleeremans, & McClelland, 1991; and in creating appropriately structured lexical representations (e.g. Elman, 1990). Moreover, the SRN has been used to model a wide range of psychological findings on implicit learning (Cleeremans, 1993).

In work that introduced the SRN, Elman (1988) generated 10,000

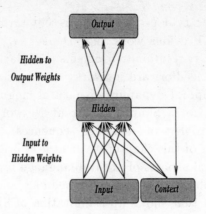

Figure 1: A simple recurrent net (SRN) showing recurrent links from the hidden units to the input. As each element of a sequence, such as a sentence, is presented on the input units (at time *t*), the previous hidden unit representation (at time *t-1*) is copied onto the context units in the input stream.

monoclausal two and three word sentences using 29 lexical items, and presented these to an SRN. After training, as each word was input, the net's predictions reflected the expected frequencies of occurrence of legal successors. This prediction was made on the basis of the current input word, together with the previous hidden unit state. Although the individual words had no internal structure (other than that occasioned through the use of a randomly assigned 31 bit vector, where each word was represented by a different bit), analysis of the hidden unit representations indicated that the SRN had discovered several major categories of words. Hierarchical cluster analysis of the hidden unit activations showed that the net had developed representations for the input patterns that reflected information about the possible sequential ordering of the inputs[2]. This suggested that the net contained the knowledge that the lexical category VERB followed the lexical category NOUN. Similarly, the verb category was broken down into those verbs which require a direct object and those for which a direct object is optional.

In subsequent research, Elman (1991) showed that SRNs could be used to predict successive, legitimate words occurring in sentences gener-

---

[2]But see Sharkey & Jackson, 1994 on the problems associated with the relationship between Euclidean distance measures, such as cluster analysis, of hidden unit space and the actual Computational space of networks

ated from a phrase structure grammar, shown in Table 1, presented one word at a time to the network. Both simple monoclausal sentences, eg **(John feeds dogs)**, and complex multiclausal sentences, eg **(Dog(who boys feed) hears girl)** and the more complex e.g. **(Boys (who girls (who dogs chase) see) hear)** can be generated from the grammar. In order to make the appropriate predictions the net has to be able to handle agreement, argument structure, and sequential dependencies across embedded phrases; arguably it has to *induce* the grammar from which the sentences were generated. The results suggest that the net had learned to represent abstract grammatical structure. For example, when presented with a subject noun, the net correctly predicted a verb which agreed with the number of the subject noun (ie singular/plural), even when a relative clause intervened. In addition, given a particular noun and verb, the net was shown to correctly predict the class of the next transition allowed by the grammar. The main limitation that emerged from these studies was that the sequential dependencies began to degrade after about three levels of embedding. Interestingly, good performance on the complex sentences was only achieved when an *incremental learning* regime was adopted. When Elman (1991) trained an SRN on data sets with progressively higher proportions of the multiclausal sentences (typically, there progression went from 0% to 25% to 75% to 100%), the SRN then *was* able to learn the more complex multiclausal sentences it had previously been unable to learn.

S →	**NP VP '.'**
NP →	**PropN ‖ N — N RC**
VP →	**V (NP)**
RC →	*who* **NP VP** — *who* **VP (NP)**
N →	*boy — girl — cat — dog*
	boys — girls — cats — dogs
PropN →	*John — Mary*
V →	*chase — feed — see — hear — walk — live —*
	chases — feeds — sees — hears — walks — lives

Table 1: Phrase structure grammar used by Elman (1991).

In a systematic follow-up of Elman's (1988) work, the SRN was employed by Servan-Schreiber, Cleeremans and McClelland (1991). Using sequences of letters, rather than words, they trained an SRN on examples generated from a simple finite state grammar (FSG). In one experiment

the FSG was used to generate 60,000 strings to train an SRN. After training, the SRN was tested on a set of 70,000 new examples and correctly
recognised all of the grammatical strings. This led to the conclusion that
the SRN had learned to be a perfect recogniser for the finite state grammar. Further experiments looked at the ability of the SRN to keep track
of long distance sequential dependencies. Servan-Schreiber *et al.* devised
a finite state grammar in which the last letter was contingent on the first
(ie if the first letter was P, so was the last, and if the first letter was T, so
was the last). However, when the embedded subgrammars between these
points were the same, regardless of initial letters, the net was unable to
differentially predict the last letter. When the contingencies within the
embedded grammars were altered (by changing the transition probabilities so that they depended on the first letter), performance improved for
short embeddings, but deteriorated to chance level when the embeddings
were more than 5 elements long.

2 Extending Long Range Sequential Capabili-
ties of SRNs.

In this section of the chapter, we report on experiments designed to examine the embedding limitation of SRNs in most simple interesting grammars. Then we take a constructive approach to show that the SRN architecture (detached from the learning method) is capable of representing
long sequential dependencies.

2.1 Learning a Grammar with a Bidirectional Link

The real problem of extending the long range sequential capabilities of
SRNs lies in their limitations with respect to embedded sequences. This
study concerns the induction of a simple finite state grammar with a
bidirectional link between two of its nodes as shown in Figure 2. This is
referred to here as FSG_{bi}.

Because FSG_{bi} contains a bidirectional link, it can be used to generate
an unbounded number of other unique sequences with any number of
embedded C's between nodes 2 and 4. In the study, reported here, FSG_{bi}
was used to generate 5 separate training sets, each incorporating different
numbers of embedded C sequences (c.f. Table 2, where the training sets
are designated as T1, T2 and so on). Using a 5(3)-3-5 SRN architecture,
five populations of 10 SRN's each, were trained using the data sets shown

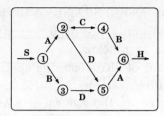

Figure 2: A finite state grammar (FSG_{bi}) with a *bidirectional link* between nodes 2 and 4.

in Table 2. The mean number of cycles to learn for each population is shown at the bottom of Table 2.

	T1	T2	T3	T4	T5
	SACB	SACB	SACB	SACB	SACB
	SADA	SADA	SADA	SADA	SADA
	SACCCB	SACCCB	SACCDA	SACCDA	SACCDA
	–	SACCCCCB	–	SACCCB	SACCCB
	–	–	–	–	SACCCCDA
Means	61716 (4)	-(0)-	86727(8)	12252(1)	-(0)-

Table 2: The training sets for FSG_{bi}, as used in a bidirectional link study with the mean training times and the number of converging SRNs, out of 10, in parentheses ().

The mean training time results at the bottom of Table 2 show that sequences with 3 embedded **C**s, such as T1 (4 converged) and T4 (1 converged) are difficult to learn. Moreover, the SRNs do not learn sequences with more than 3 embedded **C**s as in T2 and T5. This aligns with the results from testing all of the converged nets on novel sequences containing at least 4 embedded **C**s. They all break down at 4. Thus, this seems to be the limit of the long range sequential dependencies that the SRNs with 3 hidden units can develop. This also concurs with the findings of Servan-Schreiber *et al.* for a more complex grammar.

An extensive analysis of the SRNs, using generalisation testing and prediction space analysis (see below), revealed two main general problems for SRNs attempting to learn FSG_{bi}: (i) SRNs learn specific path information (by which we mean that they learn the specific sequences in the training set and not all of the legal alternatives); (ii) as the number of embedded elements increases, SRNs tend to cluster similar input elements together in hidden unit space regardless of context. Each of these problems is dealt with in turn below.

The first problem, that of SRNs learning specific path information, is shown in the generalisation examples in Table 3. The two SRNs trained on T1 and T4 were tested on the sequences **SACCCCB** and **SAC-CCCCCB**. Table 3 shows, in the FSG_{bi} *requirements* column, the predictions that a perfect FSG recogniser would make. Both SRNs produce correct responses for the sequence **SACCCB**, which was part of their training sets. However, they do not make the same predictions as each other or as FSG_{bi} (the requirements column). They have extracted specific path information from the training data, as opposed to learning to predict all legal successors. The disadvantage of such specific path information shows up in the generalization performance of the two SRNs for the **SACCCCB** sequence. It causes the SRNs to loose their way and fail on the longer embedded **C** sequences.

FSG_{bi} requirements	SRN trained on T1		SRN trained on T4	
	SACCCB	**SACCCCCB**	**SACCCB**	**SACCCCCB**
S → AB	S → AB	S → AB	S → AB	S → AB
A → CD	A → CD	A → CD	A → CD	A → CD
C → CB	C → CB	C → CB	C → CB	C → CB
C → CD	C → C	C → C	C → CD	C → CD
C → CB	C → B	C → B	C → B	C → B
C → CD	B → H	C → CD	B → H	C → CD
C → CB	–	C → AB	–	C → B
B → H	–	B → D	–	B → H

Table 3: The generalization performance of an SRN trained on T1 and of one trained on T4. The → symbol means 'predicts'.

It should be noted that this is an unavoidable general problem for all SRNs learning grammars with such bidirectional links. For example, regardless of the number of embedded **C**s that an SRN is trained on (and learns), the final **C** will only ever be trained to predict **B**. Thus any extension to the number of embedded **C**s in the test is doomed to failure.

The second problem is that of clustering similar input elements together in hidden unit space regardless of context as embedding length increases. In order to understand this problem we needed to visualise the computational properties of SRNs. Thus we developed a geometric analysis method which we next describe. The method is an elaboration of decision space analysis (e.g. Sharkey & Sharkey, 1993; Sharkey, Sharkey, & Jackson, 1994). Since the SRN operates by predicting the next input, the application of the new geometric model is called *prediction space analysis*. Prediction space diagrams for SRNs trained on a finite state grammar are shown in Figures 3 and 4.

There are two parts to constructing a prediction space. In the first part, the input sequences are plotted as *trajectories* through hidden unit space as shown in Figure 3, where hidden unit space is bounded between 0 and 1 with one axis for each hidden unit. The input at time t is plotted in hidden unit space by $\mathbf{h}_{t+1} = f(\mathbf{x}, \mathbf{h}_t)$, where $\mathbf{h}$ is hidden unit vector with real values ranging between 0 and 1, $\mathbf{x}$ is an input vector, and $f(x) = 1/1 + e^{-x}$. This procedure is carried out for every input in an input sequence and the resulting points are joined by a dashed line to form a trajectory through hidden unit space as shown in Figure 3 (this is much easier to read on a computer where the individual cubes can be rotated in any direction).

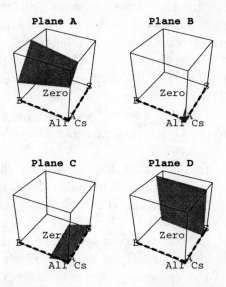

Figure 3: A prediction space analysis of an SRN that failed to converge on FSG_{bi}, T2. All planes but only the SACCCCB trajectory are shown. The prediction planes are labelled.

In the second part, each vector of weights to an output unit is used to draw a *prediction plane*, H, through hidden unit space as shown in Figure

3 (Plane A). The plane for an output unit is given by $w_0 + xw_1 + yw_2 + zw_3 = \theta$, where the w_i are the weights to an output unit, w_0 is a bias weight, xyz are the hidden unit values to be derived, and θ is a threshold value above which the output on a unit becomes 1. The relationship between each $f(\mathbf{x})$ and all of the planes determines what the current input predicts. Thus, for example, the plane for the unit responsible for predicting **A** as output can be calculated on the basis of the set of trained weights. The plane can then be drawn in the hidden unit space, where it can be seen that hidden unit representations of inputs that fall on its positive side will output an **A**, and those that fall on the negative side will not[3].

The prediction space diagram shown in Figure 3 is of one sequence trajectory through the prediction space for an SRN that *failed* to learn the T2 training set, containing the **SACCCCB** sequence. The diagram shows the hidden units trajectory for the required predictions **ACCCCB**. There are four diagrams, one for each of the prediction planes, for the sake of clearer visualisation. Each diagram contains a different prediction plane as indicated in the plot lables. Now the problem of the clustering similar input elements together in hidden unit space regardless of context as embedding length increases, can be demonstrated.

In Figure 3, all of the **C**s are located in the lower front right vertex of the hidden unit cube. The SRN will correctly predict **C** in all cases (Figure 3 (Plane C) shows the cluster of **C** points on the +1 side of the C plane). However, it will *not* correctly predict the alternate **D** and **B** on each traversal of the **C** link because it is on the zero side of all of the C and D planes.

What is required for this task is that the values of the context units are sufficiently different on each traversal to enable the trajectory to "bounce" a point back and forth across the D and B planes, given a sequence of embedded **C** inputs. The problem is that, as the sequence of **C** inputs increases in length, the context units lose their discriminative capacity, that is, backpropagation tries to treat all input **C**'s in the same fashion, works against what the grammar requires the context units to do, and homogenises all embedded input **C**'s. The required "bouncing" behaviour can be seen in Figure 4, for the SRN trained to convergence on T1. The figure shows the trajectory for the sequence SACCCB. However, as

---

[3] Prediction space analysis can be used most obviously for visualising SRNs with 3 hidden units. However, it is also possible to extend the method to SRNs with more hidden units by using principal components analysis to reduce the dimensionality of hidden unit space. The prediction planes can then be projected in the principal component subspace.

discussed above, this SRN has a generalisation problem because it has extracted specific path information. The problem can be seen for the third **C**, which is the +1 side of the B plane but on the zero side of all of the others.

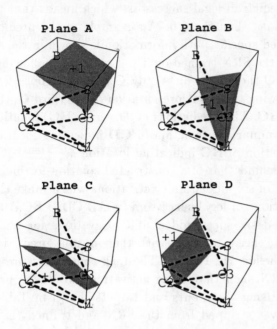

Figure 4: A prediction space analysis of an SRN trained to convergence on FSG_{bi}, T1. All planes but only the SACCCB trajectory are shown. Note that for Plane C, the second **C** is on the +1 side of the plane - this is ambiguous from the figure but is the best orientation available.

The question to be addressed here is, is the problem with the representational capacity of the SRN with 3 hidden units or is it with the backpropagation learning rule? In other words, can the SRN represent what it cannot learn? This is tackled by using constructive methods to find a representation for FSG_{bi}. If the problem can be overcome through the use of constructive methods, this implies that the problem is not attributable to a limited representational capacity as a result of using only 3 hidden units, but is due to backpropagation failing to find the necessary distinct representations.

2.2 Constructing Representations for the Bidirectional Link

The total number of different predictions for an SRN trained on FSG_{bi} is 6 regardless of the number of traversals of the **C** link (ie AB,CD,D,BC,A and H). However, SRNs often learn specific path information instead of learning to predict all legal successors, which means that they make different predictions than these 6. An example of the predictions of a net that has learned specific path information is shown in the second column of Table 3 for the SRN trained on T1. Essentially, following presentation of the second **C** the net predicts only **C** instead of both legal successors, **CD**, and following the input presentation of the third **C**, the net predicts **B** instead of **BC**. The predictions (**CD** versus **BC**) identify the location within the grammar; a prediction of **CD** indicating location 2 in Figure 2, and a prediction of **BC** indicating location 4.

The idea behind that of a constructed solution for bidirectional links is to find a set of six hidden unit activations which make the six different output predictions of legal successors (ie AB,CD,D,BC,A and H). It was possible to find six such hidden unit activations for one of the SRNs trained on T1; these, together with their output predictions are shown in Table 4, labelled **H1** to **H6**. The task then was to retrain the lower half of the SRN such that these activations would be produced where appropriate. Using the inputs and targets shown in Table 5, the input weight layer was stripped from the SRN and trained (as a single layer net) on the 6 'correct' hidden unit vectors, (with a 8-3 architecture, to a tolerance of 0.01). The weights from this single layer network were then placed back into the SRN trained on T1.

Hidden		Output
H1	→	AB
H2	→	CD
H3	→	CB
H4	→	A
H5	→	D
H6	→	H

Table 4: A set of hidden unit activations that make the required predictions.

The resulting SRN performed well on subsequent tests, demonstrating the effectiveness of this Constructive Solution. Performance was assessed

Constructive Solution for FSG_{bi}		
Input	Target	Prediction
S # $\rightarrow$	H1	AB
A H1 $\rightarrow$	H2	CD
C H2 $\rightarrow$	H3	CB
C H3 $\rightarrow$	H2	CD
B H3 $\rightarrow$	H6	H
D H2 $\rightarrow$	H4	A
A H4 $\rightarrow$	H6	H
B H1 $\rightarrow$	H5	D
D H5 $\rightarrow$	H4	A

Table 5: The training sets used to train a single layer perceptron on the 'bouncing behaviour'.

through testing on two extensive test sets sets: (i) an embedded **C** sequence of the form **SA** {80,001 **C**'s } **B**, and (ii) **SA** { 80,0000 **C**'s } **DA**. For both training sets, the Constructed SRN correctly predicted all legitimate successors in all cases. Thus the generalisation performance on FSG_{bi} was perfect even for the extremely embedded **C** sequences of 80,000 elements.

Conclusions

In our introduction, we pointed to research on the (re)useability of connectionist representations in different domains. This chapter extends the research by showing an example of the usefulness of separating representation and learning. The studies reported here show that an SRN architecture can be used to represent the solution for a bidirectional link grammar that the SRN could not learn. Prediction space analyses were used to diagnose the learning problem that the SRN was facing and subsequent construction injected the required representations into the net. This is a promising result for the study of connectionist representation and the developing connectionist theory of cognition. However, it shows some of the limits of current statistical learning theory. The next step must be to analyse the representational properties of SRNs in more detail and to devise learning algorithms that will deliver these representations.

References

Blank, D.S., Meeden, L.A., & Marshall, J.B. (1992) Exploring the symbolic/subsymbolic continuum : A case study of RAAM. In J.Dinsmore, (Ed) *The Symbolic and Connectionist Paradigms: Closing the Gap*, Lawrence Erlbaum Associates.

Chalmers, D.J. (1990) Syntactic transformations on distributed representations. *Connection Science*, 2(1), 53-62.

Charniak, E. (1995) Learning syntactic disambiguation through word statistics and why you should care about it, Paper presented to the IJCAI-95 Workshop on New Approaches to Learning for Natural Language Processing,August

Chrisman, L. (1991) Learning recursive distributed representations for holistic computation. *Connection Science* 3.4, 345-366.

Cleeremans, A. (1993) *Mechanisms of implicit learning: Connectionist models of Sequence Processing*. MIT Press; London, England.

Denker, J., Schwartz, D., Wittner, B., Solla, S., Howard, R., Jackel, L., & Hopfield, J. (1987) Large automatic learning, rule extraction, and generalisation. *Complex Systems*, 1, 877-922.

Elman, J.L. (1988) Finding structure in time (Tech. Rep. No. 8801) San Diego, CA: University of California, Center for Research in Language.

Elman, J.L. (1990) Finding structure in time. *Cognitive Science*, 14, 179-211.

Elman, J.L. (1991) Distributed representations, simple recurrent networks and grammatical structure. *Machine Learning*, 7, 195-225.

Fodor, J.A. & McLaughlin, B.P. (1990) Connectionism and the problem of systematicity: why Smolensky's solution doesn't work. *Cognition*, 35, 183-204

Fodor, J.A. & Pylyshyn, Z. (1988) Connectionism and cognitive architecture: A critical analysis. *Cognition*, 28, 3-71.

Hadley, R. F., (1994), Systematicity in Connectionist Language Learning, In *Mind and Language*, vol. 9, no. 3, Blackwell Publishers.

Hinton, G.E., (1981) Implementing semantic networks in parallel hardware. In G.E. Hinton & J.A. Anderson (Eds) *Parallel models of associative memory*. Hillsdale, N.J.: Lawrence Erlbaum Associates Inc. 161-187.

Hinton, G.E. (1986) Learning distributed representations of concepts. *Proceedings of Eighth Annual Conference of the Cognitive Science Society*

McClelland, J.L. & Rumelhart, D.E. (1981) An interactive activation model of context effects in letter perception: Part 1. An account of basic findings. *Psychological Review*, 88, 375-407.

Niklasson, L. & Sharkey, N.E. (1992) Connectionism and the issues of compositionality and systematicity. In R.Trappl (Ed) *Cybernetics and Systems*. Dordrecht: Kluwer Academic Press.

Niklasson, L.F. & van Gelder, T. (1994) Can connectionist models exhibit non-classical structure sensitivity. *Proceedings of the Cognitive Science Society*, pp 664-669.

Plunkett, K., & Marchman, V.A. (1991) U-shaped learning and frequency effects in a multi-layered perceptron: Implications for child language acquisition. *Cognition*, 38, 43-102.

Pollack, J. (1990) Recursive distributed representations. *Artificial Intelligence*, 46, 77-105.

Rumelhart, D.E., Hinton, G.E., and Williams, R.J. (1986) Learning internal representations by error propogation, In D.E. Rumelhart and J.L. McClelland, *Parallel Distributed Processing: Explorations in the microstructure of cognition, Vol 1: Foundations*, MIT Press: Cambridge, MA, chapter 8.

Rumelhart, D.E., McClelland, J.L., & the PDP Research Group (1986) On learning the past tenses of English verbs. In D.E. Rumelhart & J.L. McClelland (Eds) *Parallel Distributed Processing: Explorations in the microstructure of cognition. Vol 1.* Cambridge, MA: MIT Press

Sejnowski, T.J., & Rosenberg, C. (1986) NetTalk: A parallel network that learns to read aloud. Tech. Rep. JHU-EECS-86-01, Johns Hopkins University.

Servan-Schreiber, D., Cleeremans, A., & McClelland, J.L. (1991) Graded state machines: The representation of temporal contingencies in simple recurrent networks. *Machine Learning*, 7, 161-193.

Sharkey, N.E. (1991) Connectionist representation techniques. *Artificial Intelligence Review*, 5, 143-167.

Sharkey, N.E. (Ed) (1991) *Connectionist Natural Language Processing*. Oxford:Intellect and Kluwer.

Sharkey, N.E. and Jackson, S.A. (1994) An Internal report for Connectionists In R. Sun and L. Bookman (Eds) *Computational Architecture's Integrating Neural and Symbolic Processes*. Kluwer: MA, 223-244

Sharkey, N.E. & Reilly, R.G. (1992) Connectionist Natural Language Processing In R.G. Reilly and N.E. Sharkey (Eds) *Connectionist Approaches to Natural Language Processing*. Lawrence Erlbaum Associates: Hillsdale, N.J. pp 1-9.

Sharkey, N.E. & Sharkey, A.J.C. (1992) A modular design for connectionist parsing. Connectionism and Natural Language Processing. M.F.J.

Drosaers & A. Nijholt (Eds) *Proceedings of Workshop on Language Technology 3*, Twente, 87-96.

Sharkey, N.E. & Sharkey, A.J.C. (1993) Adaptive generalization. *Artificial Intelligence Review* **7**, 313-328.

Sharkey, N.E., Sharkey, A.J.C, and Jackson, S.A. (1994) Opening the black box of Connectionist Nets: Some lessons from Cognitive Science, *Computer Standards and Interfaces*, 16, 279-293

Smolensky, P. (1988) On the proper treatment of connectionism. *The Behavioural and Brain Sciences*, 11.

van Gelder, T. (1990) Compositionality: A Connectionist variation on a classical theme. *Cognitive Science*, 14, pp 355-364.

White, H. (1992) *Artificial Neural Networks: Approximation and Learning theory*. Blackwell. Oxford.

Natural Language Grammatical Inference: A Comparison of Recurrent Neural Networks and Machine Learning Methods

Steve Lawrence, Sandiway Fong, C. Lee Giles*

lawrence@elec.uq.edu.au, {sandiway,giles}@research.nj.nec.com

NEC Research Institute, 4 Independence Way, Princeton, NJ 08540

Abstract. We consider the task of training a neural network to classify natural language sentences as grammatical or ungrammatical, thereby exhibiting the same kind of discriminatory power provided by the Principles and Parameters linguistic framework, or Government and Binding theory. We investigate the following models: feed-forward neural networks, Frasconi-Gori-Soda and Back-Tsoi locally recurrent neural networks, Williams and Zipser and Elman recurrent neural networks, Euclidean and edit-distance nearest-neighbors, and decision trees. Nonneural network machine learning methods are included primarily for comparison. We find that the Elman and Williams & Zipser recurrent neural networks are able to find a representation for the grammar which we believe is more parsimonious. These models exhibit the best performance.

1 Motivation

1.1 Representational Power of Recurrent Neural Networks

Natural language has traditionally been handled using symbolic computation and recursive processes. The most successful stochastic language models have been based on finite-state descriptions such as n-grams or hidden Markov models. However, finite-state models cannot represent hierarchical structures as found in natural language[2] (Pereira, 1992). In the past few years several recurrent neural network (RNN) architectures have emerged which have been used for grammatical inference. RNNs have been used for several smaller natural language problems, eg. papers using the Elman network for natural language tasks include: (Stolcke, 1990; Allen, 1983; Elman, 1984; Harris and Elman, 1984; John and McLelland, 1990). Neural network models have been shown to be able to account for a variety of phenomena in phonology (Gasser and Lee, 1990; Hare, 1990;

---

* Steve Lawrence is also with Electrical and Computer Engineering, University of Queensland, St. Lucia 4072, Australia. Lee Giles is also with the Institute for Advanced Computer Studies, University of Maryland, College Park, MD 20742.

[2] The inside-outside re-estimation algorithm is an extension of hidden Markov models intended to be useful for learning hierarchical systems. The algorithm is currently only practical for relatively small grammars (Pereira, 1992).

Touretzky, 1989a; Touretzky, 1989b), morphology (Hare et al., 1989; MacWhinney et al., 1989) and role assignment (Miikkulainen and Dyer, 1989; John and McLelland, 1990). Induction of simpler grammars has been addressed often - eg. (Watrous and Kuhn, 1992; Giles et al., 1992) on learning Tomita languages. There has been some interest in learning more than regular grammars with RNNs. Jordan and others (Pollack, 1990; Berg, 1992; Sperduti et al., 1995) have used recursive auto-associative distributed memories (RAAMs) in RNNs. Others (Das et al., 1992; Sun et al., 1993; Zeng et al., 1994) have used RNNs tied to external trainable stacks. The grammars learned were not large. Our task differs from these in that the grammar is considerably more complex. Recently large regular grammars have been learned by RNNs (Giles et al., 1995; Clouse et al., 1994). However, these grammars have unusual properties when implemented as sequential machines in the sense that they have little logic.

It has been shown that RNNs have the representational power required for hierarchical solutions (Elman, 1991), and that they are Turing equivalent (Siegelmann and Sontag, 1995). The RNNs investigated in this paper constitute complex, dynamical systems. Pollack (Pollack, 1991) points out that Crutchfield and Young (Crutchfield and Young, 1989) have studied the computational complexity of dynamical systems reaching the onset of chaos via period-doubling. They have shown that these systems are not regular, but are finitely described by indexed context-free-grammars. Several modern computational linguistic grammatical theories fall in this class (Joshi, 1985; Pollard, 1984).

1.2 Language and Its Acquisition

Certainly one of the most important questions for the study of human language is: How do people unfailingly manage to acquire such a complex rule system? A system so complex that it has resisted the efforts of linguists to date to adequately describe in a formal system (Chomsky, 1986)? Here, we will provide a couple of examples of the kind of knowledge native speakers often take for granted.

For instance, any native speaker of English knows that the adjective *eager* obligatorily takes a complementizer *for* with a sentential complement that contains an overt subject, but that the verb *believe* cannot. Moreover, *eager* may take a sentential complement with a non-overt, i.e. an implied or understood, subject, but *believe* cannot:[3]

> *I am eager John to be here   I believe John to be here
> I am eager for John to be here *I believe for John to be here
> I am eager to be here   *I believe to be here

Such grammaticality judgments are sometimes subtle but unarguably form part of the native speaker's language competence. In other cases, judgment falls not on acceptability but on other aspects of language competence such as interpretation.

---

[3] As is conventional, we use the asterisk to indicate ungrammaticality in these examples.

Consider the reference of the embedded subject of the predicate *to talk to* in the following examples:

> John is too stubborn for Mary to talk to
> John is too stubborn to talk to
> John is too stubborn to talk to Bill

In the first sentence, it is clear that *Mary* is the subject of the embedded predicate. As every native speaker knows, there is a strong contrast in the co-reference options for the understood subject in the second and third sentences despite their surface similarity. In the third sentence, *John* must be the implied subject of the predicate *to talk to*. By contrast, *John* is understood as the object of the predicate in the second sentence, the subject here having arbitrary reference; in other words, the sentence can be read as *John is too stubborn for some arbitrary person to talk to John*. The point we would like to emphasize here is that the language faculty has impressive discriminatory power, in the sense that a single word, as seen in the examples above, can result in sharp differences in acceptability or alter the interpretation of a sentence considerably. Furthermore, the judgments shown above are robust in the sense that virtually all native speakers will agree with the data.

In the light of such examples and the fact that such contrasts crop up not just in English but in other languages (for example, the *stubborn* contrast also holds in Dutch), some linguists (chiefly Chomksy (Chomsky, 1981)) have hypothesized that it is only reasonable that such knowledge is only partially acquired: the lack of variation found across speakers, and indeed, languages for certain classes of data suggests that there exists a fixed component of the language system. In other words, there is an innate component of the language faculty of the human mind that governs language processing. All languages obey these so-called universal principles. Since languages do differ with regard to things like subject-object-verb order, these principles are subject to parameters encoding systematic variations found in particular languages. Under the innateness hypothesis, only the language parameters plus the language-specific lexicon are acquired by the speaker; in particular, the principles are not learned. Based on these assumptions, the study of these language-independent principles has become known as the Principles-and-Parameters framework, or Government-and-Binding (GB) theory.

In this paper, we ask the question: Can a neural network be made to exhibit the same kind of discriminatory power on the data GB-linguists have examined? More precisely, the goal of the experiment is to train a neural network from scratch, i.e. without the bifurcation into learned vs. innate components assumed by Chomsky, to produce the same judgments as native speakers on the sharply grammatical/ungrammatical pairs of the sort discussed above.

The remainder of the paper is organised as follows. In Sect. 2 we introduce our dataset and describe our problem. In sections 3 to 6 we describe the models used and our experimental methodology. We present our results in Sect. 7 and discuss techniques we used to improve the results in Sect. 8. Full details on a successful simulation are given in Sect. 9 and we draw conclusions in Sect. 10.

2 Data

Our primary data consists of 552 English positive and negative examples taken from an introductory GB-linguistics textbook by Lasnik and Uriagereka (Lasnik and Uriagereka, 1988). Most of these examples are organized into minimal pairs like the example *I am eager for John to be here/*I am eager John to be here* that we have seen earlier. We note here that the minimal nature of the changes involved suggests that our dataset may represent an especially difficult task. Due to the small sample size, the raw data was first converted (using an existing parser) into the major syntactic categories assumed under GB-theory. Table 1 summarizes the parts-of-speech that were used.

Table 1. Parts-of-speech

Category	Examples
Nouns (N)	*John, book* and *destruction*
Verbs (V)	*hit, be* and *sleep*
Adjectives (A)	*eager, old* and *happy*
Prepositions (P)	*without* and *from*
Complementizer (C)	*that* or *for* as in *I thought* that ... or *I am eager* for ...
Determiner (D)	*the* or *each* as in the *man* or each *man*
Adverb (Adv)	*sincerely* or *why* as in *I sincerely believe* ... or Why *did John want* ...
Marker (Mrkr)	possessive *'s, of,* or *to* as in *John's mother, the destruction* of ..., or *I want* to *help* ...

The part-of-speech tagging represents the sole grammatical information supplied to the neural network about particular sentences in addition to the grammaticality status. A small but important refinement that was implemented was to include subcategorization information for the major predicates, namely nouns, verbs, adjectives and prepositions. (Our experiments showed that adding subcategorization to the bare category information improved the performance of the neural networks.) For example, an intransitive verb such as *sleep* would be placed into a different class from the obligatorily transitive verb *hit*. Similarly, verbs that take sentential complements or double objects such as *seem, give* or *persuade* would be representative of other classes.[4] Flushing out the subcategorization requirements along these lines for lexical items in the training set

---

[4] Following classical GB theory, these classes are synthesized from the theta-grids of individual predicates via the Canonical Structural Realization (CSR) mechanism of Pesetsky (Pesetsky, 1982).

resulted in 9 classes for verbs, 4 for nouns and adjectives, and 2 for prepositions. Examples of the input data are shown in Table 2. We note here that tagging was done in a completely context-free manner. Obviously, a word, e.g. *to*, may be part of more than one part-of-speech. The tagger being part of a larger parsing system is capable of assigning the correct parts-of-speech, but no disambiguation was done to provide a greater challenge.

Table 2. Examples of part-of-speech tagging

Sentence	Encoding	Grammatical Status
I am eager for John to be here	n4 v2 a2 c n4 v2 adv	1
	n4 v2 a2 c n4 p1 v2 adv	1
I am eager John to be here	n4 v2 a2 n4 v2 adv	0
	n4 v2 a2 n4 p1 v2 adv	0

3   Experimental Methodology

We divide the data up into a training set and a test set. A window of a fixed number of symbols is used as input to the models and the width of this window is varied for different simulations. The window is moved from the start to the end of each sentence in temporal order, and a classification is obtained at the final step. For those models which cannot form internal states, it does not make sense to use an input window which is smaller than the length of the sentence, although we do present some results in this case for comparison purposes.

For input to the neural networks and nearest-neighbor models, the 23 part-of-speech symbols were encoded into a fixed length window made up of segments containing eight separate inputs, corresponding to the classifications noun, verb, adjective, etc. Sub-categories of the classes were linearly encoded into each input in a manner demonstrated by the specific values for the noun input: Not a noun = 0, noun class 1 = 0.5, noun class 2 = 0.667, noun class 3 = 0.833, noun class 4 = 1. The linear order was defined using our judgment of the similarity between the various sub-categories. Two outputs were used in the neural networks, corresponding to grammatical and ungrammatical classifications. A confidence criteria was used: $y_{max} \times (y_{max} - y_{min})^5$. There is some contradiction in the data due to the ambiguity of the part-of-speech conversion. We decided to remove the contradictory data for the results presented here.

It is important to ask whether results are statistically significant. Our results are based on multiple training/test set partitions and multiple random seeds (for

---

[5] For an output range of 0 to 1 and softmax outputs.

those models which use them). We equalised the number of positive and negative examples in the training and test sets in order to ensure that the models cannot produce results based on the ratio of positive to negative examples. We have also used a set of Japanese control data. Japanese is at the opposite end of the language spectrum when compared to English and we expect a model trained on the English data to perform poorly on the Japanese data. Indeed, all models attain 50% or less correct classification on average for the Japanese data.

More details can be found in Sect. 9 and (Lawrence et al., 1995).

4 Nearest-Neighbors

In the nearest-neighbors technique, the nearest-neighbors to a test sentence are found using a similarity measure. The class of the test sentence is inferred from the classes of the neighbors. We investigated the following similarity measures:

1. *Euclidean distance.* The neighbors are found based on their Euclidean distance from the test sentence in the space created by the input encoding ($\sqrt{\sum_{i=1}^{n}(y_i - d_i)^2}$). As expected, models with a small temporal window did not achieve significantly greater than 50% correct classification. However, models with a large temporal window (near the size of the longest sentences) achieved up to 65% correct classification on average.
2. *Edit distance.* In edit-distance computation a cost is assigned for inserting, deleting, and substituting symbols in a sequence. Dynamic programming can be used to calculate the cost of transforming one sequence into another [6]. We were unable to attain greater than 55% correct classification on average for the test set. Although we expect careful selection of the cost table to improve performance, analysis of the operation of the method leads us to believe that it will never obtain very good performance[7].

5 Decision Trees

For comparison purposes, we tested the C4.5 decision tree induction algorithm by Ross Quinlan (Quinlan, 1993). Decision tree methods construct a tree which

---

[6] Sequences of length zero up to the actual sequence length are considered. The following equations are used iteratively to calculate the distances ending in the distance between the two complete sequences. i and j range from 0 to the length of the respective sequences and the superscripts denote sequences of the corresponding length. For more details see (Kruskal, 1983).

$$d(\mathbf{a}^i, \mathbf{b}^j) = \min \begin{cases} d(\mathbf{a}^{i-1}, \mathbf{b}^j + w(a_i, 0)) & \text{deletion of } a_i \\ d(\mathbf{a}^{i-1}, \mathbf{b}^{j-1}) + w(a_i, b_j) & b_j \text{ replaces } a_i \\ d(\mathbf{a}^i, \mathbf{b}^{j-1}) + w(0, b_j) & \text{insertion of } b_j \end{cases}$$

[7] Consider how to define the cost for deleting a noun without knowing the context in which it appears.

partitions the data at each level in the tree based on a particular feature of the data. C4.5 only deals with strings of constant length, hence we used an input window corresponding to the longest string. We expect that significantly more data would be required to match the performance of the RNNs due to the position dependence created by the fixed input window. We used the standard settings in the C4.5 package for pruning, etc. We obtained 60% correct classification performance on the test data on average.

6 Neural Networks

Our primary interest was to train an RNN to form internal states in order to create an automata which may describe the grammar in a more parsimonious manner, and hence generalise better to unseen examples. However, we tested feedforward networks with time delayed inputs for comparison as well. We tested the following models: Multi-layer perceptron (MLP), Frasconi-Gori-Soda (FGS), Back-Tsoi FIR, Williams and Zipser, and Elman neural networks. A brief description of each model follows

1. *Multi-layer perceptron.* The output of a neuron is computed using[8]

$$y_k^l = f \left(\sum_{i=0}^{N_{l-1}} w_{ki}^l y_i^{l-1} \right) \qquad (1)$$

2. *Frasconi-Gori-Soda locally recurrent networks.* A network with local feedback connection around the hidden nodes as described in (Frasconi et al., 1992).
3. *Back-Tsoi FIR.* A multi-layer percepton network with an FIR filter and a gain term included in every synapse as described in (Back and Tsoi, 1991).
4. *Williams and Zipser.* A fully connected recurrent network where all nodes are connected to all other nodes as described in (Williams and Zipser, 1989).
5. *Elman (Elman, 1990; Elman, 1991).* A recurrent network where each hidden layer node has a feedback connection to all other hidden layer nodes. The feedback connections are trainable and we use full backpropagation through time for training instead of the truncated version used by Elman.

The size of the neural networks (the number of hidden nodes) was determined based on the goal that the networks should be large enough to learn the training data in a reasonable time but no larger (larger networks lead to easy creation of a lookup table by the model and poor generalization - this is known as overfitting).

---

[8] where y_k^l is the output of neuron k in layer l, N_l is the number of neurons in layer l, w_{ki}^l is the weight connecting neuron k in layer l to neuron i in layer $l-1$, $y_0^l = 1$ (bias), and f is commonly a sigmoid function.

7 Results

Initially, partial success was only obtained with models employing a large temporal input window. We were unable to train the networks using a small temporal window although it is theoretically possible. We experienced difficulty because the gradient descent search technique used became stuck in local minima. We are interested in training RNNs with small temporal input windows because these are the only networks which are forced to form internal states in order to learn successfully - they are forced to look for solutions which may be more parsimonious and generalize better. After adding techniques designed to avoid local minima we were able to train an RNN with sequences of the last two words as input to give 100% correct classification on the training data. This performance was obtained with an Elman RNN. Generalization on the test data resulted in 74% correct classification on average. This is better than the performance obtained using any of the other methods, however it is still quite low. The available data is quite sparse and we expect increased generalization performance as the amount of data increases (as well as increased difficulty in training). Additionally, the dataset has been hand-designed by GB linguists to cover a range of grammatical structures and it is likely that the separation into the training and test sets creates a test set containing many grammatical structures that are not covered in the training set.

Tables 3 and 4 summarize the results obtained with the various methods. The locally recurrent networks (Frasconi-Gori-Soda, Back-Tsoi) did not perform significantly better than the standard multi-layer perceptron. Using a large temporal input window, the neural network models were able to attain 100% correct classification performance on the training data and 65% correct classification on the test data. The nearest-neighbor and decision tree methods did not exceed this performance level. Using a small temporal input window, no model except the Elman RNN exceeded 55% correct classification on the test data. The Elman network was able to attain 74% correct classification on the test data and the W&Z network was able to attain 71%. In order to make the number of weights in each architecture approximately equal we have used only single word inputs for the W&Z model but two word inputs for the others. This reduction in dimensionality for the W&Z network improved performance.

8 Gradient Descent

We have used backpropagation-through-time [9] (Williams and Zipser, 1990) to train the globally-recurrent networks [10] and the gradient descent algorithm described by the authors for the FGS and Back-Tsoi FIR networks. The error

---

[9] Backpropagation-through-time extends backpropagation to include temporal aspects and arbitrary connection topologies by considering an equivalent feedforward network created by unfolding the recurrent network in time.

[10] Real-time (Williams and Zipser, 1989) recurrent learning was also tested but did not show any significant convergence for our problem.

Table 3. Percentage correct classification for the training data.

TRAIN	large window	small window
MLP	100	55
FGS	100	56
BT-FIR	100	56
Elman	100	**100**
W&Z	100	**92**

Table 4. Percentage correct classification for the test data.

TEST	large window	small window
Edit-distance	55	N/A
Euclidean	65	55
Decision trees	60	N/A
MLP	63	54
FGS	65	59
BT-FIR	64	54
Elman	65	**74**
W&Z	59	**71**

surface of a multilayer network is generally non-convex, non-quadratic, and often has large dimensionality. We found the standard gradient descent algorithms to be impractical for our problem. We employed the techniques described below for improving convergence. Although these techniques are heuristic and reduce the elegance of the solution, they are motivated by analysing the operation of the algorithm and are applicable to many other problems.

1. Detection of Significant Error Increases. If the NMSE increases significantly during training then the network weights are restored from a previous epoch and are perturbed to prevent updating to the same point. We have found this technique to increase robustness of the algorithm when using learning rates large enough to help escape local minima, particularly in the case of the Williams & Zipser network.

2. Target outputs. Target outputs were 0.1 and 0.9 using the logistic activation function and -0.8 and 0.8 using the *tanh* activation function. This helps avoid saturating the sigmoid function. If targets were set to the asymptotes of the sigmoid this would tend to: a) drive the weights to infinity, b) cause outlier data to produce very large gradients due to the large weights, and c) produce binary outputs even when incorrect - leading to decreased reliability of the confidence measure.

3. Stochastic updating. In stochastic update parameters are updated after each pattern presentation, whereas in true gradient descent (often called "batch" updating) gradients are accumulated over the complete training set. Batch update attempts to follow the true gradient, whereas stochastic is similar to adding noise to the true gradient - this noise can help the algorithm avoid local minima. We found that stochastic update produced significantly better results.

4. Learning rate schedule. Relatively high learning rates are typically used in order to help avoid slow convergence and local minima. However, a constant learning rate results in significant parameter and performance fluctuation during the entire training cycle such that the performance of the network can alter significantly from the beginning to the end of the final epoch. Moody and Darkin have proposed "search then converge" learning rate schedules of the form (Darken and Moody, 1991): $\eta(t) = \eta_0 / (1 + t/\tau)$ where $\eta(t)$ is the learning rate at time t, η_0 is the initial learning rate, and τ is a constant. We have found that the learning rate during the final epoch still results in considerable parameter fluctuation[11] and hence we have added an additional term (see section 9) to further reduce the learning rate over the final epochs. We have found the use of learning rate schedules to improve performance considerably.

In addition to these techniques, we also tried the following, but were unable to obtain improved performance.

1. Sigmoid functions. Symmetric sigmoid functions (eg. tanh) often improve convergence over the standard logistic function. For our particular problem we found the difference was minor.

2. Sectioning of the training data. We investigated dividing the training data into subsets. Initially, only one of these subsets was used for training. After 100% correct classification was obtained or a pre-specified time limit expired, an additional subset was added to the "working" set. This continued until the working set contained the entire training set. These trials were performed with the data ordered alphabetically, which enabled the networks to focus on the simpler data first. Elman suggests that the initial training constrains later training in a useful way (Elman, 1991). The use of sectioning has consistently decreased performance in our case.

3. Cost function. The relative entropy cost function has received particular attention (Haykin, 1994) and has a natural interpretation in terms of learning probabilities (Kullback, 1959). We investigated using both quadratic ($E = \frac{1}{2}\sum_k (y_k - d_k)^2$) and relative entropy cost functions ($E = \sum_k [\frac{1}{2}(1+y_k) \, log\frac{1+y_k}{1+d_k} + \frac{1}{2}(1-y_k) \, log\frac{1-y_k}{1-d_k}]$): where y and d correspond to the actual and desired output values, and k ranges over the outputs (and also the patterns for batch

---

[11] NMSE results which are obtained over an epoch involving stochastic update can be misleading. We have been surprised to find quite significant difference in these on-line NMSE calculations compared to a static calculation even if the algorithm appears to have converged.

update). We found the quadratic cost function to provide better performance. A possible reason for this is that the use of the entropy cost function leads to an increased variance of weight updates and therefore decreased robustness in parameter updating.

9 Simulation Details

Full details for the best performing model, the Elman network, are given below. For the remaining models, variations in specific implementation details (eg. the number of hidden nodes) did not make a significant difference. The results reported in this paper are for an initial learning rate of 0.2 and 20 hidden nodes.

The network contained three layers including the input layer. The hidden layer contained 20 nodes. Each hidden layer node had a recurrent connection to all other hidden layer nodes. The network was trained for a total of 1 million stochastic updates. All inputs and outputs were within the range zero to one. Bias inputs were used. The best of 50 random weight sets was chosen based on training set performance. Weights were initialised as shown in Haykin (Haykin, 1994). Targets outputs were 0.1 and 0.9 using the logistic output activation function. The quadratic cost function was used. The search then converge learning rate schedule used was $\eta = \dfrac{\eta_0}{\frac{n}{N/2} + \frac{c_1}{max\left(1, (c_1 - \frac{max(0, c_1(n - c_2 N))}{(1-c_2)N}\right)}}$ where $\eta =$ learning rate, $\eta_0 =$ initial learning rate $= 0.2$, $N =$ total training epochs, $n =$ current training epoch, $c_1 = 50$, $c_2 = 0.65$. The training set consisted of 373 non-contradictory examples. The English test set consisted of 100 non-contradictory samples and the Japanese test set consisted of 119 non-contradictory samples. 74% correct classification was obtained on the English test set and 53% correct classification was obtained on the Japanese test set. The total training time was around 4 hours on a Sun Sparc 10 workstation.

10 Conclusions

We investigated the use of feed-forward neural networks, Frasconi-Gori-Soda and Back-Tsoi locally recurrent neural networks, Williams and Zipser and Elman recurrent neural networks, Euclidean and edit-distance nearest-neighbors, and decision trees for classifying natural language sentences as grammatical or ungrammatical, thereby exhibiting the same kind of discriminatory power provided by the Principles and Parameters linguistic framework, or Government-and-Binding theory. From best to worst performance, the architectures are roughly: Elman, W&Z, FGS, Euclidean distance nearest neighbors, MLP, C4.5 decision trees, and edit-distance nearest neighbors. Theoretically, a W&Z network with the same number of nodes should have at least the same representational power as an Elman network, yet the Elman network provides better performance. Investigation shows that this is due to the more complex error surface of the W&Z architecture.

Are the methods really learning anything? Nearest-neighbors, decision trees, feedforward networks do not learn parsimonious representations of the grammar - they work by finding statistically close matches in the training data. They are expected to require a much larger amount of data for similar performance. On the other hand, recurrent neural networks do learn a grammar. 100% correct classification of the training data is not possible using only a small temporal input window without forming internal states.

We have shown that both Elman and W&Z recurrent neural networks are able to learn an appropriate grammar for discriminating between the sharply grammatical/ungrammatical pairs used by GB-linguists. The recurrent neural networks considered here posses the required representational power for the task considered. However, difficulty lies in finding the optimum parameters (weights). The standard training algorithms were unable to find a solution to our problem. We were able to find a solution by adding techniques aimed at improving the convergence of the training algorithm.

Current generalisation performance is not very high, however, the results appear significant considering the nature of the dataset (sparse and grammatical structures differ between the training and test sets). We plan to generate more data - we expect better generalization performance, however we also expect training to be more difficult. Hence, we need to continue to address the convergence of the training algorithms. We believe that the basic assumptions of smoothness in the required function approximation and the nature of parameter updating provide opportunities for improvement (as demonstrated by the techniques described within). The grammar learnt by the recurrent networks could be extracted and examined (Giles et al., 1992; Watrous and Kuhn, 1992). Further progress can be made by continuing to address the convergence of the backpropagation algorithm. However, we envisage a point after which advances will depend on considering the connectionist treatment of hierarchical representations.

References

Allen, R. B. (1983). Sequential connectionist networks for answering simple questions about a microworld. In *5th Annual Proceedings of the Cognitive Science Society*, pages 489–495.

Back, A. and Tsoi, A. (1991). FIR and IIR synapses, a new neural network architecture for time series modeling. *Neural Computation*, 3(3):375–385.

Berg, G. (1992). A connectionist parser with recursive sentence structure and lexical disambiguation. In *Proceedings AAAI*, pages 32–37.

Chomsky, N. (1981). *Lectures on Government and Binding.* Foris Publications.

Chomsky, N. (1986). *Knowledge of Language: Its Nature, Origin, and Use.* Prager.

Clouse, D., Giles, C., Horne, B., and Cottrell, G. (1994). Learning large DeBruijn automata with feed-forward neural networks. Technical Report CS94-398,

Computer Science and Engineering, University of California at San Diego, La Jolla, CA.

Crutchfield, J. P. and Young, K. (1989). Computation at the onset of chaos. In Zurek, W., editor, *Complexity, Entropy and the Physics of Information*. Addison-Wesley, Reading, MA.

Darken, C. and Moody, J. (1991). Note on learning rate schedules for stochastic optimization. In *Neural Information Processing Systems 3*, pages 832–838. Morgan Kaufmann.

Das, S., Giles, C., and Sun, G. (1992). Learning context-free grammars: Limitations of a recurrent neural network with an external stack memory. In *Proceedings of The Fourteenth Annual Conference of the Cognitive Science Society*, pages 791–795, San Mateo, CA. Morgan Kaufmann Publishers.

Elman, J. (1990). Finding structure in time. *Cognitive Science*, 14:179–211.

Elman, J. (1991). Distributed representations, simple recurrent networks, and grammatical structure. *Machine Learning*, 7(2/3):195–226.

Elman, J. L. (1984). Structured representations and connectionist models. In *6th Annual Proceedings of the Cognitive Science Society*, pages 17–25.

Frasconi, P., Gori, M., and Soda, G. (1992). Local feedback multilayered networks. *Neural Computation*, 4(1):120–130.

Gasser, M. and Lee, C. (1990). Networks that learn phonology. Technical report, Computer Science Department, Indiana University.

Giles, C., Horne, B., and Lin, T. (1995). Learning a class of large finite state machines with a recurrent neural network. *Neural Networks*. In press.

Giles, C., Miller, C., Chen, D., Chen, H., Sun, G., and Lee, Y. (1992). Learning and extracting finite state automata with second-order recurrent neural networks. *Neural Computation*, 4(3):393–405.

Hare, M. (1990). The role of similarity in hungarian vowel harmony: A connectionist account. Technical Report CRL Tech report 9004, Centre for Research in Language, University of California, San Diego.

Hare, M., Corina, D., and Cottrell, G. (1989). Connectionist perspective on prosodic structure. Technical Report CRL Newsletter Volume 3 Number 2, Centre for Research in Language, University of California, San Diego.

Harris, C. L. and Elman, J. L. (1984). Representing variable information with simple recurrent networks. In *6th Annual Proceedings of the Cognitive Science Society*, pages 635–642.

Haykin, S. (1994). *Neural Networks, A Comprehensive Foundation*. Macmillan, New York, NY.

John, M. F. S. and McLelland, J. L. (1990). Learning and applying contextual constraints in sentence comprehension. *Artificial Intelligence*, 46:5–46.

Joshi, A. K. (1985). Tree adjoining grammars: how much context-sensitivity is required to provide reasonable structural descriptions? In D. R. Dowty, L. K. and Zwicky, A. M., editors, *Natural Language Parsing*. Cambridge University Press, Cambridge.

Kruskal, J. B. (1983). An overview of sequence comparison. In Sankoff, D. and Kruskal, J. B., editors, *Time Warps, String Edits, and Macromolecules: The*

Theory and Practice of Sequence Comparison. Addison-Wesley, Reading, Massachusetts.

Kullback, S. (1959). *Information Theory and Statistics.* Wiley, New York.

Lasnik, H. and Uriagereka, J. (1988). *A Course in GB Syntax: Lectures on Binding and Empty Categories.* MIT Press, Cambridge, MA.

Lawrence, S., Giles, C. L., and Fong, S. (1995). On the applicability of neural network and machine learning methodologies to natural language processing. Technical Report UMIACS-TR-95-64 and CS-TR-3479, Institute for Advanced Computer Studies, University of Maryland, College Park MD 20742.

MacWhinney, B., Leinbach, J., Taraban, R., and McDonald, J. (1989). Language learning: cues or rules? *Journal of Memory and Language*, 28:255–277.

Miikkulainen, R. and Dyer, M. (1989). Encoding input/output representations in connectionist cognitive systems. In Touretzky, D. S., Hinton, G. E., and Sejnowski, T. J., editors, *Proceedings of the 1988 Connectionist Models Summer School*, pages 188–195, Los Altos, CA. Morgan Kaufmann.

Pereira, F. (1992). Inside-outside reestimation from partially bracketed corpora. In *Association for Computational Linguistics, ACL 92.*

Pesetsky, D. M. (1982). *Paths and Categories.* PhD thesis, MIT.

Pollack, J. (1990). Recursive distributed representations. *Artificial Intelligence*, 46:77–105.

Pollack, J. (1991). The induction of dynamical recognizers. *Machine Learning*, 7:227–252.

Pollard, C. (1984). *Generalised context-free grammars, head grammars and natural language.* PhD thesis, Department of Linguistics, Stanford University, Palo Alto, CA.

Quinlan, R. (1993). *C4.5: Programs for Machine Learning.* Morgan Kaufmann, San Mateo, California.

Siegelmann, H. and Sontag, E. (1995). On the computational power of neural nets. *Journal of Computer and System Sciences*, 50(1):132–150.

Sperduti, A., Starita, A., and Goller, C. (1995). Learning distributed representations for the classification of terms. In *Proceedings of the International Joint Conference on Artificial Intelligence*, pages 509–515.

Stolcke, A. (1990). Learning feature-based semantics with simple recurrent networks. Technical Report TR-90-015, International Computer Science Institute, Berkeley, California.

Sun, G., Giles, C., Chen, H., and Lee, Y. (1993). The neural network pushdown automaton: Model, stack and learning simulations. Technical Report UMIACS-TR-93-77, Institute for Advanced Computer Studies, University of Maryland, College Park, MD.

Touretzky, D. S. (1989a). Rules and maps in connectionist symbol processing. Technical Report CMU-CS-89-158, Carnegie Mellon University: Department of Computer Science, Pittsburgh, PA.

Touretzky, D. S. (1989b). Towards a connectionist phonology: The 'many maps' approach to sequence manipulation. In *Proceedings of the 11th Annual Conference of the Cognitive Science Society*, pages 188–195.

Watrous, R. and Kuhn, G. (1992). Induction of finite-state languages using second-order recurrent networks. *Neural Computation*, 4(3):406.

Williams, R. and Zipser, D. (1989). A learning algorithm for continually running fully recurrent neural networks. *Neural Computation*, 1(2):270–280.

Williams, R. and Zipser, D. (1990). Gradient-based learning algorithms for recurrent connectionist networks. In Chauvin, Y. and Rumelhart, D., editors, *Backpropagation: Theory, Architectures, and Applications*. Erlbaum, Hillsdale, NJ.

Zeng, Z., Goodman, R., and Smyth, P. (1994). Discrete recurrent neural networks for grammatical inference. *IEEE Transactions on Neural Networks*, 5(2):320–330.

Extracting Rules for Grammar Recognition from Cascade-2 Networks.

Ross Hayward, Alan Tickle & Joachim Diederich

Neurocomputing Research Centre
Queensland University of Technology
2 George Street Brisbane
Queensland Australia.

Abstract. Any symbolic representation of how a neural network decides on a particular classification is important, not only for user acceptance but also for rule refinement and network learning. This paper describes a decompositional rule extraction technique which generates rules governing the firing of individual nodes in a feedforward neural network. The technique employs heuristics to reduce the complexity in searching for rules which explain the behaviour of a neural network trained with sparsely coded data. The hidden and output units within the constructed networks are considered to represent distinct rules which govern the classification of patterns. A symbolic representation of the complete network can be gained from aggregation of these rules. Since the algorithm is not constrained to a particular network architecture, we focus on a comparison of the rule sets gained from networks constructed using the Cascade 2 algorithm and multi-layer perceptrons trained using backpropagation. The specific networks of interest are those trained to recognise if simple fixed length sentences are grammatically correct.

1 Introduction

Rule extraction from neural networks provides a mechanism for explaining the knowledge acquired during the network training process. Without such a mechanism a neural network must simply remain an axiom of the subject under consideration. An explanation of how or why a particular classification has been made on an instance from a problem domain has a variety of uses. It is important for increasing user confidence, providing new knowledge, and evaluating weaknesses that may exist within training data from a problem domain.

The aim of this paper is to employ a new rule extraction technique to examine network architectures and training conditions that yield optimal solutions for a natural language problem. The problem domain we consider must be difficult enough to require one or more hidden units within the trained networks as we are concerned with how the internal structure of the networks interact to classify an instance. The problem however, must be relatively simple in the rules that classify an instance to provide a clear comparison between the rules obtained from networks with different internal structure. We use the Lap algorithm to extract rules at the level of individual units from within each separate neural network trained with a simple Natural Language problem. Specifically the problem is to recognise sentences which are grammatically correct. (This problem is adapted from Elman, J.L. 1991). The training data consists of all possible combinations of several words in the format *Noun Verb Noun* where each word can exist in either their singular or plural form and where both nouns are optional. The verbs used are divided into three separate categories: those verbs requiring a direct object, those verbs optionally requiring a direct object and those verbs not requiring a direct object. For example, the sentences: *girl sees John*, *girls see John* and *girls live* are classified as grammatically correct while *girl see John, girls sees John* and *girls lives* are not. This is a simple but interesting problem since although it is possible to make distinctions between noun and verb, there are more complex dependencies as to which type of nouns and verbs make up a grammatically correct sentence.

1.1 Network Learning

The networks employed for comparison are either Multi-Layer Perceptrons (MLPs) or Cascade 2 networks. The most significant difference between the two network types is that the Cascade 2 algorithm dynamically adds units to the network during training whereas the structure of an MLP is established prior to training.

The original Cascade correlation algorithm (Fahlman & Lebiere 1990) is unique in the way it constructs networks and the Cascade 2 algorithm is only marginally different. It involves training a single layer network until the reduction in the overall network error becomes insignificant indicating a local minimum or relatively flat surface has been found in the weight space. During the training process a pool of candidate units is maintained which are fully connected from the input and hidden layers. The weights into and out of the candidate units are initially selected at random and altered as each of the units is trained to approximate the error of the original network. After candidate training stagnates, that is, none of the candidate units are making appreciable gains in matching the network error, the best candidate unit is added to the hidden layer of the network. This involves freezing its input weights and negating the weights into the output layer. Training the weights into the output layer begins again and the process is repeated until an acceptable overall error is achieved.

The fact that the weights into each of the hidden units are fixed in a Cascade network means that every pattern presented to the network during training will have a constant associated output from each of the hidden units. Figure 1 shows how the addition of hidden units in a Cascade network can be considered as generating an extra input dimension for an output unit. This reduces the overall error in classifying the patterns. An equivalent description of the Cascade algorithm is to say that it repeatedly trains a single layer network with a larger input space. The Cascade network is similar to multilayer feed forward network in that the hidden units locate distinguishing features in each pattern but differs in that the normal multilayer networks distribute the feature detection over all the hidden units at once. The goal within Cascade 2 of inserting hidden units into the network is to reduce the overall network error by a maximum amount. Hence rules governing the activation of these units might be expected to yield strong classification abilities.

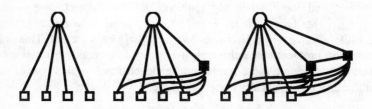

Fig. 1. Each additional hidden unit added to the network introduces a new dimension for output unit training

1.2 Rule Extraction

Rule extraction techniques can be divided into three basic categories; learning, eclectic or transparent (Andrews, Diederich & Tickle 1995). Learning techniques treat the network as a black box, constructing rules using conventional learning algorithms based on the classification results gained from the network. This can provide a rule set with classification capabilities equivalent to the network, but fails to provide any information about the distribution of knowledge in the network and how this knowledge is used to classify instances from the problem domain. Rules formed in this case may be artificial, and not entirely reflect *how* the network classifies. Recent studies have shown that although this type of approach may at first seem efficient, the complexity is actually exponential in the number of inputs to the network. (Golea, 1995)

The transparent or decompositional approach extracts rules at the level of individual input and output units by examining the corresponding weights and activation. The overall network rules are an aggregation of the rules extracted at the individual unit level. These methods are computationally expensive and have been constrained to approximating hidden units with binary threshold units (Cravin & Shavlik, 1994). This is somewhat problematic for these methods as it can be shown that the XOR problem can be solved by a neural network whose single hidden unit has activation levels of less than 0.5 in a range of 0 to 1 for all possible input patterns. Rules predicting the activation of a node with this type of behaviour are not only difficult to express in some logical form, but are also difficult to combine into rules that describe the overall network classification.

The eclectic approach is a combination of both the transparent and learning methods. It uses information about weighted links within the network together with information gained from the presentation and classification of patterns by the network to construct a rule set

1.3 Localist Representation of Data

The Lap algorithm uses information from the problem domain to reduce the search through weight space to locate rules for a given unit. The algorithm expects that each attribute in a pattern from the problem domain can only have a single value. To represent this in the problem domain each input to the network must be either 0 or 1, and one and only one input within an attribute may have a value of 1. This is localist at the input level of the network as it requires that each input unit represent a distinct value from the problem domain. Of the input units used to represent an attribute, each unit must individually represent a single feature which the attribute may have.

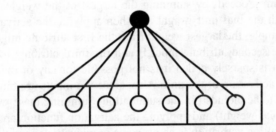

Fig. 2 Each attribute, represented by a rectangular box, defines several input units such that for any pattern presented to the network only one of the units in an attribute will have a value of 1.

2 The Lap Algorithm

The LAP algorithm makes extensive use of the fact that sparsely coded data may only have one value per attribute for any pattern, and that patterns from the problem domain consist of binary values. These heuristics significantly reduce the size of the search that must conducted through weight space to formulate rules. The aim of the algorithm is to identify sets of inputs to a unit that will provide an activation greater than some desired value at the units output. For example, assume a network consisting of twelve inputs and that the inputs (which we will represent with uppercase letters A to L) represent three attributes, each attribute able to assume one of four values:

Attribute 1	A	B	C	D
Attribute 2	E	F	G	H
Attribute 3	I	J	K	L

If a unit is trained with instances from the problem domain and its activation is constrained to be in the range 0 to 1 for any pattern presented to its input. The Lap algorithm locates the sets of inputs that are required to be 1 for a desired minimum activation at a particular unit. In the current example, a network unit might be required to have an activation of at least F. In this case application of the Lap algorithm may generate a clause:

if an input pattern has (A OR B) AND E values then the units activation > F

This implies that if the third attribute of a pattern has any value I, J, K or L, the level of activation will be maintained or increased since the attribute is not part of the given rule. If the pattern has a value of D and not (A or B) then the activation level of the unit will be lower than F.

The Lap algorithm proceeds by summing the largest of the weights within each of the attributes with the bias unit weight and then applying the activation function to the total. For example, the largest weight from the first attribute might be associated with input A, the second attribute input E and the third attribute for input I. Since the input domain is sparsely coded it is not possible for any of the other inputs to contribute to the activation of the unit. Also, since the inputs are binary valued only the weights need to be included in the summation. Summing these weights (with the inclusion of the bias weight) and applying the activation function provides the units' output. If the resulting activation is above some previously defined threshold F, then one of the attributes is chosen and the next largest weight in that attribute used in calculating the activation. The previous weight from that attribute discarded. This process continues until the calculated activation level drops below the threshold F if smaller weights are used in the summation from *any* of the attributes. The values discarded after each summation then indicate the values and attributes required to construct a rule which guarantees the activation of the unit will be at least F. Since there must be one value for each attribute, the rules are of the form of a conjunction of disjunctions. If an attribute can have any of its possible values and the activation level is still greater than F, then the disjunction for that attribute is omitted from the rule as the term is trivially true.

The technique is most efficient when there is a clearly dominant weight within each attribute. The worst case occurs when any of the values within any of the attributes will cause the unit to have an activation greater than F. A simple alteration to the algorithm can be made to locate rules that ensure that a units activation is not greater than some predetermined value. This is done by summing the smallest of the weights within each attribute with the bias weight and ensuring that the activation generated by this sum is not greater than the predetermined value.

```
(* Recursive Lap procedure *)

LET Value_i := A data structure containing the weight of, and a reference to, input i.
LET ValueList_j = A list of Value_i associated with attribute j sorted by Value_i weight
LET InputArray = An array of all ValueList_j
LET F = The required activation level of the unit.

PROCEDURE extract(InputArray) : BOOLEAN

LET weighted_sum := sum of the maximum weights from each ValueList_j
                        in InputArray and the bias weight

IF activation(weighted_sum) < F THEN
    (* Activation of unit is below desired value *)
    RETURN FALSE;
ELSE
    FOR each ValueList_j IN InputArray DO
            IF the number of elements in ValueList_j > 1 THEN
                    (* Test if a smaller weight will still allow desired value *)
                    LET MaxValue := the Value_i in ValueList_j containing
                                        the largest weight (* List head *).
                    REMOVE MaxValue from ValueList_j
                    IF extract(InputArray) = FALSE THEN
                            (* Restore MaxValue *)
                            ADD MaxValue to ValueList_j
                            INCREMENT attributes_checked
                    END
            ELSE
                    INCREMENT attributes_checked
            END
    END
    IF attributes_checked = total number of attributes THEN
            (* No other weight combinations in the remaining Values_i        *)
            (* will provide an activation > F than the current maximums       *)

            Remove the Value_i with the maximum weight from each ValueList_j
                    in InputArray
            Form a rule from the remaining Values_i in InputArray
            (* Using set subtraction for positive rules *)
            Save Rule
    END
    RETURN TRUE
END
END (*PROCEDURE*)
```

2.1 Aggregation of Unit Rules

The goal of the rule extraction process is to express the rules representing the output of the network in terms of the rules found for each unit. Given that the Lap technique can provide a minimum activation level for an individual unit that receives input solely from the network input units, we must explore the possibility that several of the inputs may be from other hidden units. The Lap algorithm requires that each input to a unit is binary valued and this can not be assumed if the inputs are from hidden units with sigmoidal activation functions. To overcome this problem the activation of the hidden units is sparsely coded into distinct ranges. When extracting rules from subsequent units in the network, an input from a hidden unit is translated into multiple inputs. Rules are then extracted to provide a minimum activation for each range. This significantly adds to the complexity of the rule extraction technique both in maintaining rules for certain activation levels and conversion of a single weighted link between units to a sparsely coded multiple link.

3 A Natural Language Task

We used the Lap algorithm to investigate how a simple language problem is encoded by a MLP with a single hidden layer trained with backpropagation and networks generated with the Cascade-2 algorithm. The problem is the classification of fixed length sentences into the classes of being either grammatically correct or incorrect. Each sentence is constructed using the three lexical attributes and associated values shown in Table 1 in the form *Noun Verb Noun*, for example *John sees girl*. All of the possible 96 three word sentences were constructed, sparsely coded and each represented by a 14 dimensional binary vector. The *no-word* value was included since the rule extraction technique requires that attributes within a pattern must have a value. The task is novel in that it involves complex dependencies between the values of each attribute in a simple sentence. Not only does the network need to recognise how subject nouns must agree with their verbs it must also distinguish between verbs requiring a direct object, verbs where a direct object is optional and verbs where a direct object is not allowed.

Table 1 Sentence attributes and their associated values

Attribute	Value
Noun 1	John, girl, girls, no-word
Verb	see, sees, live, lives, feed, feeds
Noun 2	John, girl, girls, no-word

The task was to compare the rules extracted from the networks at both the individual unit level and at the network level. We conducted experiments using three categories of networks:

- Networks generated with the Cascade 2 algorithm using 48-fold cross-validation. This entailed constructing each of the 48 networks using the entire training set less two randomly selected patterns from the input space.

- Networks generated with the Cascade 2 algorithm using the complete training set.

- MLPs containing 2,3,4,5 and 6 hidden units trained with the complete data set

The networks were trained by using a target output of 1 if the sentence was grammatically correct and 0 otherwise. The hidden and output units in all the networks contained asymmetric sigmoidal activation functions. With the exception of the MLP with two hidden units, all the networks converged to give a root mean square error of approximately 0.02 in classifying each pattern. The smallest error an MLP network was able to achieve with two hidden units was approximately 0.17 which only correctly classified 97% of the sentences. In the case of the Cascade networks generated using the full training set, only a single hidden unit was ever required to solve the problem. Cascade networks constructed using cross validation however required between one and three hidden units. These networks yielded root mean square errors (averaged over all 48 networks) of 0.036 and 0.345 for the training and validation patterns respectively. The large error in classifying the validation patterns is due to the Cascade 2 algorithm having a tendency to produce networks which overfit the training data. The Lap algorithm was applied to each of the networks in the above three categories and rules obtained for the hidden and output units. Each rule predicting whether the activation of its associated unit will be greater than 0.5.

3.1 Results

Each network constructed by the Cascade 2 algorithm containing a single hidden unit yielded an identical rule set. The results of the rule extraction process on the hidden node in these cases are given in Table 2. Each row defines values the attributes must have to enable the unit to have an activation greater than 0.5. Cells in the tables containing *any* indicate that the attribute can have any of its possible values and the rule will still be valid.

The values which the attributes and hidden node are required to have for the output unit to have an activation greater than 0.5 are shown in Table 3. By substituting the rules obtained for the hidden unit into the results obtained for the output unit, rules classifying the grammar in terms of the input attributes are constructed (Table 4).

Table 2 Rules indicating the activation of the hidden unit will be greater than 0.5

Noun 1	Verb	Noun 2
girls	lives, see, feed	any
girls, John, girl	lives	no-word
girls	lives, see, live, feed	no-word

Table 3 Rules indicating the grammar is correct in terms of the hidden unit activation and values from the input space.

Noun1	Verb	Noun 2	Hidden Unit Activation
girl, John	sees	any	any
girl, John	sees, feeds	John, girl, girls	any
girl, John	any	any	>0.5
any	sees, feeds, see, live	any	>0.5
any	sees, feed, see, live, feeds	John, girl, girls	>0.5

Table 4 Rules indicating the grammar is correct in terms of attributes from the input space by aggregating rules in Table 2 and Table 3.

Noun 1	Verb	Noun 2
girl, John	sees, feeds	John, girls, girl
girl, John	sees	any
girl, John	lives	no-word
girls	see	no-word
girls	see, feed	John, girls, girl
girls	live	no-word

While the rules representing the hidden unit give no indication as to whether or not the grammar is correct, they do provide information which when combined with the rules for the output unit is capable of making a correct classification. The rules demonstrate a complex dependence of the output unit on the activation of the hidden unit. A simple example that demonstrates this is that none of the sentences beginning with the noun *no-word* are grammatically correct. The output unit does not directly depend on whether the first word of the sentence being classified is *no-word*, but does depend on the hidden unit having an activation greater than 0.5 in those cases. The hidden unit will only have such an activation provided *no-word* is not the first word of the sentence.

The rules for individual units extracted from the MLP with three hidden units are presented in a similar manner in Table 5 and Table 6. The Tables 2 through 6 contain clauses for the minimal architectures which could be achieved for both network types which correctly classify the sentences. If the two architectures are indeed minimal then the Cascade network has enabled information to be encoded in a much more efficient manner for decompositional rule extraction as there are simply less hidden units from which to extract rules. The Lap algorithm also located 13 clauses from the MLP which classify an instance from the problem domain, but only yielded 8 clauses from the Cascade network which achieve the same effect. It is also interesting to note that 31 weighted links were required in the Cascade network compared to 49 in the MLP.

Table 5 Rules describing when the hidden units will have an activation greater than 0.5 in a multi-layer perceptron.

Unit	Noun1	Verb	Noun2
Hidden 1	girls, no-word	feeds,live, lives, see	any
	girls	feeds,feed,lives,see,live	no-word
	any	feeds	no-word
Hidden 2	no-word	feed,live, lives, see	any
	no-word, girl John	live, see, feed	any
	no-word	live,sees,lives,feed,see	girl, girls, John
	no-word, girl John	feed,live, lives, see	girl, girls, John
Hidden 3	no-word	live	any
	any	live	no-word

Table 6 Rules indicating the multilayer perceptron will have an activation greater than 0.5 and correctly classify the sentence

Hidden Unit 1 activation	Hidden Unit 2 activation	Hidden Unit 3 activation
<0.5	<0.5	any
<0.5	any	>0.5
any	<0.5	>0.5

Table 7 indicates the number of clauses obtained from the MLPs trained using backpropagation. The rows in the table correspond to a particular network having the indicated number of hidden units. The number of clauses extracted from the units within the networks are evenly distributed between the hidden units as one would expect when employing the backpropagation algorithm for training. However, the total number of clauses for each network does seem to increase with the number of hidden units within the network. It should be noted that the network with two hidden units only managed to classify 96.8% of the patterns.

Table 7 The number of clauses extracted from the units of MLPs with 2 3 4 5 and 6 hidden units

Units	Output	hidden1	hidden2	hidden3	hidden4	hidden5	hidden6
2	1	5	6				
3	3	3	4	2			
4	3	2	5	2	3		
5	6	2	2	3	1	4	
6	10	7	3	5	2	3	4

Table 8 The number of Cascade networks constructed using cross validation with the average number of clauses extracted from each unit

Number of hidden units	Number of networks	Number of unique rule sets	Average number of clauses in output	Average number of clauses hidden 1	Average number of clauses hidden 2	Average number of clauses hidden 3
1	23	1	5	3		
2	11	7	8.3	2.3	2	
3	14	14	17	1.9	2.14	3.2

The results of extracting rules from the Cascade networks trained using cross validation are given in Table 8. Of the 48 networks constructed, 23 contained a single hidden unit. All of these 23 networks yielded an identical rule set to the one obtained when the networks were trained on the complete data set. Networks requiring two hidden units had 7 unique rule sets for the 11 networks constructed while the 14 networks with 3 hidden units generated a unique rule set for each network. By unique we mean that the rules extracted from the individual units contained different clauses. The results obtained indicate a relationship between the number of clauses required to describe the behaviour of a network and the network overfitting the training patterns from the problem domain. The rules describing the classification ability of an entire network may not be unique. No attempt was made to aggregate the rules describing the behaviour of individual units into rules describing the overall behaviour of a network due to the complexity of the task.

3.2 Conclusion

The complexity of current rule extraction techniques confines their use to small problems and the Lap algorithm is no exception to this. However, the algorithm does have some redeeming features. It can be employed irrespective of the network architecture and generate rules describing various levels of activation of single network units. Minor modifications to the algorithm can be made so that the rules extracted from a single unit correspond to a negated form of the rules extracted using the original algorithm. In this case the algorithm will be most efficient when each attribute has a value with a dominantly more negative weight than other values within the same attribute and will degrade to a worst case when no possible input pattern will provide an activation smaller than that required.

The language problem has provided an example which clearly shows how the internal structure of networks, combined with the activation levels of individual units interact to classify instances from a problem domain. Using this example we were also able to examine how the Cascade 2 algorithm behaves when using incomplete data sets. In general the behaviour was quite good with 23 of the 48 networks constructed providing the same rule set that could be obtained from a Cascade network trained on the complete data set. The comparison between the rules extracted for the MLPs and Cascade networks indicated that the Cascade network was able to represent information in a much more efficient manner than the MLPs. This may have been due to the problem domain under consideration or the manner in which the networks trained, that is, the particular solution that was eventually located in the weight space. Both the network architectures provided an increase in the number of clauses with an increase in the number of hidden units within the networks. This indicates that more specific features are being located in the training patterns than are necessary for classification. This overfitting can be avoided by employing a termination set of patterns which are not used during training. If the network error increases in classifying these patterns at any time during training, the network is assumed to be overfitting the training data. This method was not employed here as we have focused on how the rule sets change with a decrease in the generalisation capability of the networks.

References

Andrews R., Diederich J., Tickle A: A Survey and Critique of Techniques for Extracting Rules from Trained Neural Networks, To appear in Knowledge Based Systems, (Ed: Li Min) (1995)

Andrews R. and Geva S.,: Rule extraction from a constrained error backpropagation MLP, Automated Reasoning Research Report CIT-94-20. (1994)

Cravin M. and Shavlik J., (1994) "Using Sampling and Queries to Extract Rules from Trained Neural Networks.", Machine Learning Proceedings of the 11th International Conference (San Francisco, CA).

Elman J.L.,: Distributed Representations, Simple Recurrent Networks, and Grammatical Structure. Machine Learning 7 (1991) 195-225

Fahlman S. & Lebiere C.,: The Cascade-Correlation Learning Architecture, in Advances in Neural Information Processing Systems 3 (R. Lippman, J Moody, and D. Touretzky, eds) San Mateo (1990) 190-196.

Fu. L.,: Rule Generation from Neural Networks IEEE Transactions on Systems, Man, and Cybernetics. 24 (1994) 1114-1124

Golea, M. Personal Communication. (1995)

Rummelhart, D.E.; Hinton, G.E. and Williams, R.J.,:Learning Internal Representations by Error Propagation." In: Rumelhart, D.E.; McClelland, J.L., (Eds.): Parallel Distributed Processing. Vol .: Foundations, Cambridge Mass.:The MIT Press. (1986)

Towell G. and Shavlik J.,: The extraction of Refined Rules From Knowledge Based Neural Networks. Machine Learning 13 (1993) 71-101

Generating English Plural Determiners from Semantic Representations: A Neural Network Learning Approach

Gabriele Scheler

FG KI/Kognition
Institut für Informatik
TU München
D-80290 München
scheler@informatik.tu-muenchen.de

Abstract. In this paper, we present a model of grammatical category formation, applied to English plural determiners. We have identified a set of semantic features for the description of relevant meanings of plural definiteness. A small training set (30 sentences) was created by linguistic criteria, and a functional mapping from the semantic feature representation to the overt category of indefinite/definite article was learned. The learned function was applied to all relevant plural noun occurrences in a 10000 word corpus. The results show a high degree of correctness (97%) in category assignment. We can conclude that the identified semantic dimensions are relevant and sufficient for the category of definiteness. We also have the significant result that actually occurring uses of plural determiners can be accounted for by a small set of semantic features. In a second experiment, we generated plural determiners from textually derived semantic representations, where the target category was removed from the input. Because texts are semantically underdetermined, these representations have some degree of noise. In generation we can still assign the correct category in many cases (83%). These results can be improved in various ways. It is finally discussed, how these results can be applied to practical NLP tasks such as grammar checking.

1   Introduction

In this paper we present a learning approach to the generation of an obligatory grammatical category, namely the category of definiteness/indefiniteness in English. In any human language there is a number of grammatical distinctions which are specific to that language and for which hard and fast rules concerning the use of the corresponding morphological or lexical expressions can not be determined. These grammatical distinctions comprise the language-specific categories of tense, mood, aspect, cases, nominal classifiers and determiners, etc. They usually correspond to basic cognitive classifications and the logic of these categories has in some cases been explored in great detail ([7]). However, relating the logical form of a sentence to its overt expression is a difficult and error-prone task, for which heuristics are hard to find (cf. [2],[5]).

In this work, we show how an assignment function for definiteness of English plural nouns could be learned, which has been tested on a 10000-word corpus.

The basic methodology consists of devising a set of semantic dimensions which correspond to the logical distinctions expressed by a certain grammatical category. In the case of definite determiners, we have chosen the dimensions of givenness (i.e. type of anaphoric relation), of quantification, of type of reference (i.e. predication or denotation), of boundedness (i.e. mass reference or individual reference) and of collective agency. The different logical forms of the sentences can be represented by a set of sentential operators, which are defined in first-order logic. These sentential operators can be used as atomic semantic features, which are consequently sufficient in representing the logical meaning of a sentence with respect to the chosen semantic dimensions.

An empirical question that can be answered by generation experiments is whether the resulting semantic representations are indeed sufficient for the generation of a particular grammatical category. Another question of practical importance is whether these semantic representations can be derived from running text by automatic methods and what results we can achieve in using automatically generated semantic representations for category assignment.

The paper is structured as follows: In the next section, we discuss the semantic dimensions that have been used and their relation to logical formulations of cognitive content. Then we present the methodology and the results from the learning of a mapping function from semantic representation to the grammatical category. We show how we can extract semantic features from a surface coding of running text (without the target category) and present the results of the category assignment from this automatically generated semantic representation. We discuss the context of this research and applications to grammar checking and machine translation. The main results are summarized in the conclusion.

2 Semantic dimensions and features

The goal in this section is to define a set of semantic features that capture the meaning of plural determiners in English and relate to cognitive operations and cognitive representations by way of logical definitions. This approach has been explained in detail in [17]. The main idea is to 'ground' atomic semantic features by treating them as unary operators in first-order logic, and define them with reference to a logical ontology and cognitive primitives. Features can be ordered into *dimensions* of logically mutually exclusive features.

In this paper, certain dimensions have been selected with the goal of finding a set of semantic features which is sufficient to explain the uses of definite/indefinite determiners in any text.

The use of logical definitions is threefold:

- they provide an abstract description of the cognitive level
- the basic conceptual primitives are identified
- semantic features are grounded

First-order logic is seen as a tool for a meta-theory of cognition. It is presumably not an adequate cognitive representation per se. However, we believe that any cognitive representation must bear an identifiable relation to its logical formulation. We do not present full logical forms or logical definitions for semantic features here. For the most part, the logic of the semantic features that are used here has been defined before (see below), and we can refer to that work.

2.1 Generalized quantification

An obviously relevant semantic dimension concerns the type of quantification of the noun phrase. According to the concept of generalized quantification [4], we distinguish between

- **num** quantifier with an explicit quantity, e.g. four, five etc.
- **some** an unspecified quantity, which constitutes a small percentage
- **most** an unspecified quantity, which constitutes a large percentage
- **all** universal quantification, constrained with respect to the discourse setting, e.g. *He talked to the ladies* (*the ladies* are "all ladies" in the current discourse setting).
- **general** universal quantification, unconstrained with respect to discourse, but pragmatically constrained (i.e. nearly all, in general, disregarding exceptions, e.g. *Women know these things*).

2.2 Anaphoric relation

The type of anaphoric relation concerns the contrast between given and new referents in discourse. There are also noun phrases which refer to objects not previously introduced explicitly, but which are textually implied. For a theory of discourse referents and co-reference relations we refer to [7]. In general, types of anaphoric relations are relative to the method of anaphoric solution.

Co-reference can be realized through synonymic relations (*snuff-boxes – such banalities*) or indicated syntactically (*they were like duellists*), or some combination thereof. A textual implication must be resolved by a specific lexical knowledge base. For instance, part-whole relations or incorporated objects constitute indirect anaphoric relations. Examples for the first type are nouns which designate a part of an object, such as *end, limitation, corner*, as in *moustache with stiff waxed ends, the limitations of the policeman mentality, the corners of his lips*. Objects which are lexically implied in verbs occur in phrases such as *say words to that effect, state in words*, or *snap disdainful fingers*. It is possible to represent the different types of anaphoric relation by a scalar value which gives a measure of the "distance" to an antecedent, e.g. number of relations traveled in a lexical knowledge base. However in the absence of a system for anaphoric relation assignment, a threefold distinction into new-given-implied may be used.

- **given** noun phrase with a co-referring antecedent
- **implied** noun phrase which refers to an object implied by a lexical relation
- **new** noun phrase that introduces a new referent

2.3 Reference to Discourse Objects

A basic distinction in the reference of noun phrases concerns the complementary notions of denotation and predication. Noun phrases may be used to pick out a specific discourse object, or to introduce a new one, but they are often also used merely to designate a quality or property. An example for this distinction is *She was one of the foremost writers of detective fiction* where *writer* is used denotationally (it co-refers with *she*), and *detective fiction* is used predicatively, i.e. does not refer to a particular object.

- **denotation** noun phrase that denotes an object term in discourse (e.g., *He was walking about in the park*)
- **predication** noun phrase that denotes a property in discourse (where a property is a one-place relation of a discourse object) (e.g., *It's more a park than a garden*)

This distinction, which is explicit in a logical representation, is often not as clear-cut in a real text. Difficult cases, taken from the text (s. 3.1), are for instance:

101. You'll find Anderson there with the four GUESTS.
102. None of those people can be CRIMINALS.
103. MURDERERS look and behave very much like everybody else.
104. He suspected that these people were MURDERERS.
105. MURDERERS are often hearty.
106. Mere MEN being in charge, we've got to be careful.
107. 'MEN - MEN,' sighed Mrs Oliver.

Again, things might be easier, if we had a scale of discourse prominence: Discourse prominence could be either defined with respect to the cognitive/ logical representation, i.e. the status of an object in the discourse representation as central, peripheral or not referring, if we had a corresponding theory of discourse objects. Or it may be a measure that is only practically defined from textual analysis, i.e. using syntactic clues such as subject/object, use of descriptive adjectives, "be", numerals, determiners, possessive pronouns etc. Instead of two concepts, predication and denotation, we would get scalar or fuzzy concepts. For instance, in this case, 102 is 'very predicative', 101 is 'very referential', 106 is 'somewhat referential', 103 'mostly predicative' etc.

2.4 Boundedness

Boundedness of reference is a phenomenon that is attested both in the verbal and the nominal domain (cf. [12], [8]). Mass reference or reference to substances can be defined by invariance under partition (part of X = subset of X), while piecewise reference or reference to individuals does not allow partitioning without change of designation (part of X = constituting object of X).

- **mass** reference to an unbounded quantity of one kind (e.g., *a Lovely Young Thing with tight poodle CURLS*)
- **pieces** reference to a collection of individuals (e.g., *Those dreadful police-women in funny HATS who bother people in parks!*)

2.5 Agentive involvement

Plural noun phrases which have agentive meanings can refer to a set of individuals, each of which performs an individual action, or to a set of individuals which collectively performs one action. A further discussion and full logical axiomatization of boundedness and agentive involvement can be found in (cf. [9], [10]).

- **collective** a plural noun referring to set of individuals and a common action (e.g., *The two girls sang a duet.*)
- **distributive** a plural noun referring to a set of objects and individual actions (e.g., *Four people brought a salad to the party.*)

These features are primarily defined for agentive constructions, where the plural noun phrase acts as a subject. They may be seen to carry over to other constructions, where an action is associated with a set of objects, such as *She wrote chatty ARTICLES on The Tendency of the Criminal; Famous Crimes Passionnels; Murder for Love vs. Murder for Gain.* Here *articles* is collective, as all articles together are on the named subjects. Compare this to e.g., *She has written the ARTICLES The Tendency of the Criminal; Famous Crimes Passionnels and Murder for Love vs. Murder for Gain.* We have used the dimension of agentive involvement in the extended sense here.

3 From semantic features to morphological expression

The question that has been investigated by the first experiment is the adequacy of a semantic representation for noun phrases which consists of the semantic dimensions and individual features given in section 2. In particular, we wanted to know how a functional assignment that has been learned by a set of linguistically chosen examples carries over to instances of the relevant phenomenon in real texts.

3.1 Method

In order to answer this question, we use the method of supervised learning by back-propagation, as implemented in the SNNS-system (cf.[20]). Supervised learning requires to set up a number of training examples, i.e. cases, where both input and output of a function are given. From these examples a mapping function is created, which generalizes to new patterns of the same kind.

We created a small training corpus for typical occurrences of bare plurals and definite plurals. 30 example sentences were taken from an English grammar

([18]). For each example, a semantic feature representation was created. This consists of a number of features from the list given above. For each semantic dimension, a feature value was set referring to the logical interpretation of the sentence. Sometimes a certain dimension was not applicable which resulted in a neutral value (∗) for that dimension. Examples are given in Table 1. The sym-

He gives wonderful PARTIES.
`new general predication pieces *`
`indef`
The MUSICIANS are practicing a new piece.
`given all reference pieces collective`
`def`
They were discussing BOOKS and the theater.
`new general predicative mass *`
`indef`

Table 1. Examples from the training set: Sentences, semantic representations, and grammatical category

bolic descriptions were translated into binary patterns by using 1-of-n coding. The assignment of the correct output category consisted in a binary decision, namely, definite plural or bare (indefinite) plural.

We wanted to know how such a set of training examples relates to the patterns found in real texts. Accordingly, we tested the acquired classification on a narrative text, ("Cards on the table" by A. Christie), for which the first 5 chapters were taken, with a total of 9332 words. Every occurrence of a plural noun without a possessive or demonstrative pronoun formed part of the dataset. Modification by a possessive pronoun (*my friends*), or a demonstrative pronoun (*those people*) leads to a neutralization of the indefiniteness/definiteness distinction as expressed by a determiner. Generating possessive or demonstrative pronouns is beyond the goals of this research. As a result, there were 125 instances of definite or bare plural nouns. For these test cases, another set of semantic representations was manually created.

3.2 Results

The mapping from semantics to grammatical category for the example sentences could be learned perfectly, i.e. any semantic representation was assigned its correct surface category (cf. Table 2).

This success in learning can be explained by the careful selection of semantic features which describe the relevant semantic dimensions of a surface category such as definiteness.

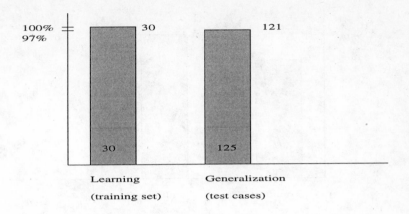

Table 2. Mapping from semantic representation to output category

The learned classifier was then applied to the cases derived from the running text.

Again, a high percentage of correctness (97 %) could be achieved (cf. Table 2). This result is remarkable, as we did not expect to be able to describe each occurrence of a plural noun by this rather small set of 5 dimensions and 15 features. Rather we had anticipated difficulties for a number of examples which seemed somehow idiosyncratic or 'idiomatic' in their use. Examples that had been set aside as idiomatic were almost always assigned correctly.

The few remaining misclassifications have also been examined (s. below). They are due to stylistic peculiarities, as in 45 and 89. Also, two sentences involving numerals were not classified correctly. This has probably not been sufficiently covered by the training set.

45 INTRODUCTIONS completed, he gravitated naturally to the side of Colonel Race.
given all predication mass collective
89 I held the most beautiful CARDS yesterday.
new some predication pieces *
94 He saw four EXPRESSIONS break up - waver.
implied num predication pieces distributive
118 Yes. That's to say, I passed quite near him THREE TIMES.
implied num predication pieces *

We also compared results from generalization of the special training set with generalization from a random selection of training cases from the actual text. The results are given in Table 3.

We see that we need less examples to find the mapping function from a semantic representation to morphological expression when we select a set of

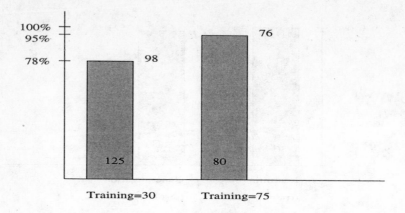

Table 3. Generalization from randomly selected text cases

training examples by linguistic criteria than just picking random examples. An English grammar thrives to capture all uses of a specific grammatical category irrespective of its frequency. This proves to be an asset in learning a mapping function that will generalize well to a real text.

We get comparable results only when we use app. 50 % of the whole set for training. As the absolute numbers are small, this may not seem to be of much importance for practical NLP. However, when we consider learning the whole set of grammatical categories in a natural language, this finding may be of practical importance.

3.3 Discussion

We have achieved to learn a generation function from semantic representations with remarkably few wrong assignments. The remaining problems with functional assignment which are due to stylistic variation are less than we expected, but they may go beyond an analysis in terms of semantic-logical features.

It seems that a small number of examples is sufficient to fix the generation function properly. Accordingly, a learning situation of few example sentences which contains the most frequent and/or the decisive patterns may fix the important points of the function. We can use in principle a sampling method (cf. [3]), or a linguistic principle of selection (which in the ideal case should be the same thing.)

In this case, we have set up patterns of 15 binary features. Of these different features within a dimension are mutually exclusive, i.e. do not co-occur. On the other hand, sometimes a certain dimension is not used in the representation of a noun phrase. This makes a theoretical number of app. 750 different patterns, i.e. constellations of semantic features. This is a size that is beyond explicit rule coding; consequently attempts to handle syntax-semantic mapping by rule creation did not achieve coverage of real texts beyond handling of selected examples ([6, 5]). Once a generation function has been learned, a function of this size may be implementable by a lookup table, at least if we just use binary features.

Not all of the theoretically possible patterns may occur, and only a subset will be frequent. For instance, our sample of 125 patterns contains 59 different patterns. It should be stressed that learning of a binary classification function is not restricted to neural network approaches. Supposedly any pattern classifier such as decision trees ([11]), adaptive distance classification ([13, 14]), or statistical supervised clustering methods can do it. A comparison of different methods in this respect is beyond the scope of this paper.

4   Generation from noisy input

For the goal of cognitive modeling it is interesting to look at the kind of semantic representations necessary to explain attested morphological categories and their use. For practical purposes, however, semantic representations cannot be manually created. They have to be derived from running text by automatic methods. This is a goal that is not easy to reach.

First of all, texts are semantically underdetermined. They do not contain all the information present in a speaker's mind that corresponds to a full logical representation. Fortunately, these logical representations are highly redundant for the selection of a grammatical category, so that a noisy representation is often sufficient for practical NLP tasks such as text understanding, machine translation or grammar checking. Secondly, there remains the problem of how to represent or *code* a text such as to derive a maximum of semantic information from it.

In this paper we wanted to look at the possibility of using a neural network learning approach to syntax-semantics mapping for *grammar checking*, i.e. the automatic correction of the definiteness category in a running text. This could be a valuable feature in a foreign language editor.

The main idea is to provide a slot-value representation of surface-accessible textual features and use that representation as input to the learning of the interpretation function. In this case, we have created surface representations for the core of a sentence (NP – VP – NP), or for nominal phrases with prepositional phrases attached. Both types constitute the immediate local context for the plural noun phrases, and both can be represented by the same slots and values. This approach means to leave out a lot of textual detail, and extract only specific information into the surface representation which is needed for further semantic processing. We have called this way of doing deep textual analysis *vertical modularity* (cf. [16]) to distinguish it from the more usual approach of processing morphology, syntax, lexical semantics and sentential semantics in horizontal layers. In particular, we have used slots for

- head noun
- modifiers of the head noun
- predicate or preposition
- dependent noun
- modifiers of the dependent noun

Values in the slots were lexical classes for head noun, predicate and dependent noun (e.g., perceptual_entity, physical_object, body_part, person,communication) taken from a small working dictionary, and grammatical classes for modifiers (e.g., adjective, numeral,demonstrative, singular, plural).

Some examples are given in Table 4.

```
3 VOICES drawled or murmured.
perceptual_entity * plural qu action * * * *

4 in aid of the London HOSPITALS.
event * singular indef prep institution desc_adj plural qu

5 a Lovely Young Thing with tight poodle CURLS.
object desc_adj singular indef prep body_part desc_adj plural qu

7 He wore a moustache with stiff waxed ENDS.
body_part * singular indef prep part desc_adj plural qu
```

Table 4. Examples for surface textual coding

In order to investigate the possibilities of grammar checking, we left out the definiteness category for the target noun phrase, i.e. substituted *indef/def* by *qu*. For this experiment we have used a set of 81 randomly chosen examples from the running text.

This representation is fairly primitive in that it needs a fixed length of inputs, incorporates a dictionary look-up for lexical items which is not supported by a full English dictionary, i.e. a full and consistent ontology, and uses only few of the syntactical, morphological and lexical information available. An improved method of surface coding is currently being investigated ([1]). As this experiment is expected to be a harder problem than the former one, we used cross-validation for learning rather than the usual distinction of training and test cases. Cross-validation is a preferable statistical method for limited data sets (cf. [19]), it means that we learn 80 examples in each run and generalize to the remaining one. This is repeated 81 times so that we get generalization figures for all 81 cases.

The results for learning and for generalization are given in Table 5. Data on 'noisy' assignments (between 1 – 4 errors) are also given.

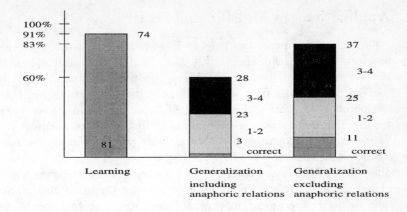

Table 5. Mapping from encoded surface text to semantic representation

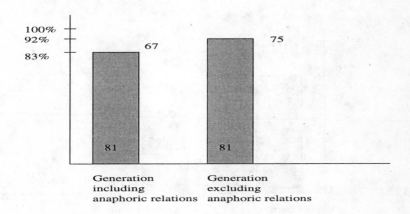

Table 6. Generation from automatically derived semantic representations

These results amount in an average of 4.1 errors per pattern, where 15 bits had to be set. When we use these noisy patterns as input to the learned generation function (cf. Table 6), we find that we can still assign 83% correctly. This is due to the fact that the semantic representation is often redundantly explicit, not all of the features are needed to set an output category correctly. However it is clear from the surface coding, which is restricted to the local context of a single sentence that the dimension of anaphoric relation cannot be learned successfully. We excluded that dimension from the interpretation and generation task by annotating the surface representation with the correct anaphoric relation. Consequently, results improved as seen in Tables 5 and 6.

5 Applications in Multilingual NLP

The main task of this paper has been to identify a set of semantic features for the description of the definiteness category in English and apply it to instances of plural nouns in a real text. A possible application to grammar checking has been spelled out in the former section. The results lead us to expect that with the development of a more sophisticated textual coding, we may have a practical tool for checking and correcting definiteness of English plural nouns.

We may raise the question whether a direct pattern completion approach to grammar checking may not be equally promising. I.e. given a surface text encoding without the target category, we may try to learn the correct category as a classification of surface sentences. We have used the same surface encoding as in the previous experiment and provided the output category for the training cases. To make the results comparable, we have used cross-validation again. The best results were achieved with a hidden layer of 20 units (i.e. a 53-20-2 net). The results of this approach are given in Table 7.

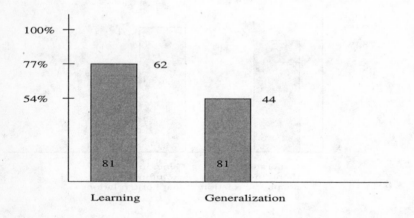

Table 7. Determiner Selection as Classification of Surface Sentences

We see that the results are approximately at chance level. Using the more complicated route of creating semantic representations first and generating from them proves to be considerably better. Both approaches could benefit from a better textual encoding. Yet a representation that is created from an example set of a particular task will probably not be as good as a semantic representation that is task-independent and grounded in cognition.

The results from all these experiments are not conclusive yet in deciding whether full semantic representations will eventually be better for practical applications than mere textual matching.

We have formerly applied a similar approach to the interpretation and generation of verbal aspects in an interlingual approach, i.e. a machine translation application (cf.[15]). In that case using a full semantic representation improved results by about 20% compared to a direct matching of source language surface representation and target language aspectual category.

The work reported here can also be used for multilingual interpretation and generation. This is especially interesting for languages without nominal determiners, such as Japanese or Russian. In these cases other grammatical information that is provided in the surface coding, e.g. Japanese particles with topic/comment contrast combining the agentive/givenness dimensions and Japanese word order and nominal classifiers, can be used to set the semantic features of the intermediate, interlingual representation. Generation of an English determiner can then be handled by the unilingual learned generation function.

The history of machine translation and message understanding has shown that mere surface scanning and textual matching approaches tend to level off as they have no capacity for improving performance beyond a certain percentage. In contrast, using explicit semantic representations which can be linked to cognitive models provides a basis for both human language understanding and practical NLP. Using semantic representations has additional advantages for interactive systems both for grammar checking and machine translation. The additional plane of semantic representation allows a system to assess the validity of a given decision and frame a question in other cases. Systems which require a high quality of performance will certainly have to incorporate an interactive component.

6   Conclusion

Two main questions have been raised in the introduction:

(a) Are semantic feature representations sufficient in explaining the use of morphological categories in real texts?
(b) Can semantic representations be derived from running text by learning methods and what performance do we get in generation from automatically derived semantic representations?

Both questions can be answered affirmatively with some restrictions especially concerning the quality of the automatically derived semantic representation. Further work needs to be done on surface textual coding to improve the learning of the interpretation function. However, learning semantic representations is a significant improvement in efficiency and performance over former rule-based methods.

We have also compared this approach to a direct textual categorization approach for the task of checking the use of a determiner. The results of using the cognitively more adequate method including semantic representations were considerably better. The grounding of representations in logical semantics and cognition should be an asset in developing high-quality NLP systems. A major result of this research is that mapping from surface to semantic representation is a viable approach for practical NLP tasks when we use a learning method to create the mapping function.

References

1. Stefan Bauer. Entwicklung eines Eingabe-Taggers für lexikalisch-syntaktische Information. Diploma thesis, Technische Universität München, Lehrstuhl Brauer, November 1995.
2. W. Brauer, P. Lockemann, and H. Schnelle. Text Understanding – The Challenges to Come. In O. Herzog and C.-R. Rollinger, editors, *Text Understanding in LILOG*, Springer, 1991, pp. 14–32.
3. Ido Dagan and Sean Engelson. Committee-based sampling for training probabilistic classifiers. *(this volume)*, 1995.
4. P. Gärdenfors, editor. *Generalized Quantification*. North-Holland, 1990.
5. O. Herzog and C.-R. Rollinger, editors. *Text Understanding in LILOG*, Springer, 1991.
6. Jerry R. Hobbs, Mark E. Stickel, Douglas E.Appelt, and Paul Martin. Interpretation as abduction. *Artificial Intelligence*, 63:69–142, 1993.
7. Hans Kamp and Uwe Reyle. *From Discourse to Logic: Introduction to Modeltheoretic Semantics of Natural Language, Formal Logic and Discourse Representation*. Studies in Linguistics and Philosophy. Kluwer, 1993.
8. Manfred Krifka. *Nominalreferenz und Zeitkonstitution im Deutschen*. Wilhelm Fink, 1989.
9. Godehard Link. First order axioms for the logic of plurality. In J. Allgayer, editor, *Processing Plurals and Quantifications*. CSLI Notes, Stanford, 1991.
10. Godehard Link. Plural. In A. von Stechow and D. Wunderlich, editors, *Handbuch Semantik*. De Gruyter, 1991.
11. J.R. Quinlan. *C 4.5 - Programs for Machine Learning*. Addison-Wesley, 1995.
12. Gabriele Scheler. Zur Semantik von Tempus und Aspekt, insbesondere des Russischen. Magisterarbeit, LMU, München, April 1984.
13. Gabriele Scheler. The use of an adaptive distance measure in generalizing pattern learning. In I. Aleksander and J. Taylor, editors, *Artificial Neural Networks 2*, North Holland, 1992, pp. 131–135.
14. Gabriele Scheler. Feature selection with exception handling using adaptive distance measures. Technical Report FKI-178-93, Technische Universität München, Institut für Informatik, July 1993.
15. Gabriele Scheler. Machine translation of aspectual categories using neural networks. In J. Kunze and H. Stoyan, editors, *KI-94 Workshops. 18. Dt. Jahrestagung für Künstliche Intelligenz*, 1994, pp. 389–390.
16. Gabriele Scheler. Learning the semantics of aspect. In Daniel Jones, editor, *New Methods in Language Processing*. University College London Press, 1996.
17. Gabriele Scheler and Johann Schumann. A hybrid model of semantic inference. In Alex Monaghan, editor, *Proceedings of the 4th International Conference on Cognitive Science in Natural Language Processing (CSNLP 95)*, 1995.
18. A.J. Thompson and A.V. Martinet. *A Practical English Grammar*. Oxford University Press, 1969.
19. Sholom M. Weiss and Casimir A. Kulikowski. *Computer Systems That Learn*. Morgan Kaufmann, 1991.
20. Andreas Zell et al. *Snns User Manual v. 3.1*. Universität Stuttgart: Institute for parallel and distributed high-performance systems, 1993.

Knowledge Acquisition in Concept and Document Spaces by Using Self-organizing Neural Networks

Werner Winiwarter[1], Erich Schweighofer[2], Dieter Merkl[3]

[1] Department of Information Engineering, University of Vienna,
Liebiggasse 4/3, A-1010 Vienna, Austria
email: ww@ifs.univie.ac.at
[2] Institute of Public International Law, University of Vienna
Universitätsstraβe 2, A-1090 Vienna, Austria
email: erich.schweighofer@univie.ac.at
[3] Institute of Software Technology, Vienna University of Technology
Resselgasse 3/188, A-1040 Vienna, Austria
email: dieter@ifs.tuwien.ac.at

Abstract. Exploratory data analysis seems to be a good tool for the acquisition and representation of the inherent knowledge in legal texts. The main difficulty besides the necessary input is the analysis of the various text and document structures. In our prototype CONCAT we use neural network technology to learn about the relations within the concept and document space of an existing domain. The results are quite encouraging because with existing input data a usable representation of the knowledge space can be obtained.

1 Introduction

Exploratory data analysis seems to be a good tool for the representation of the inherent knowledge in legal texts. Existing legal information retrieval systems do not satisfy the demands of lawyers because they provide only a syntactic representation of the legal data (e.g. statutes, treaties, court decisions or literature). Advanced formalisations of legal knowledge exist in the form of legal expert systems or conceptual information retrieval systems. The main drawback of these systems is the very high development cost. Therefore our approach deals with the problem of automatic knowledge acquisition. Our main assumption in the design of the prototype CONCAT is that the relevant information is represented in a special terminology, document structure or text patterns. We want to formalize in this way the expert knowledge about legal language. Lawyers have formed definite concepts of human beings, objects, and processes by use of methods of abstraction and logic thinking. A major prerequisite for such research is that the necessary input data is restricted to existing and easily available information and can be refined by the user itself. A knowledge base with such rules has to be developped for a specific legal text corpora. At the present state of research the emphasis is on the dedection of the appropriate representation of legal concepts. We want to analyse automatically each concept representation with regard to its connotations and form a meaning space of the concept. The connotation analysis is based on the interpretation of the contexts of the individual legal terms which are represented as vectors. We adapted this model to the computation of a document space for text corpora.

2 Related Work

Conceptual information retrieval systems use knowledge representation techniques in order to encode the semantics of legal concepts [Cross85, Bing87]. The legal domain is mapped to a knowledge scheme: semantic networks [Paice91], conceptual graphs [Dick91], concept frames [Hafner81], diagnostic expert systems [Merkl92], object-oriented programming [Mital91] or also neural networks [Belew87, Bench-Capon93, Rose89, Rose93]. The usefulness of conceptual information retrieval systems has been proven but the bottleneck of knowledge acquisition remains like in the case of the traditional approach to legal knowledge representation in the form of intellectually produced thesauri or classifications [Blair90].

As large text corpora are now available in the legal field the techniques from natural language understanding could provide some help. However, the arising restrictions are even more severe. Only small so-called question-answering systems have been built [Jacobs90]. Legal texts would require a very intense and time-consuming linguistic analysis which is illusory at this moment. The 1990s have witnessed a resurgence of interest in empirical and statistical methods of language analysis [Church93]. The text analysis as the data-intensive approach to language is a pragmatic tool that is well suited to meet the requirements of broad coverage of legal text. Three questions have to be faced: Choice of appropriate text structures (documents, concepts or word patterns), necessary knowledge input to the learning algorithm and similarity computation. These parameters are interchangeable. A good similarity computation could diminish the necessary input or problems of "good" word patterns.

In the 1960s and 1970s much work has been done on the computation of similarities between documents and queries by using the vector space paradigm [Salton83]. Interesting adaptations of the standard model are the Generalized Vector Space Model (GVSM) [Wong87] and Extended Boolean Logic [Salton89]. This model was used with relevance feedback to rank documents with quite good results [DeMulder94]. A more promising approach seems to be the contextual representation of legal concepts which was proposed by Schweighofer and Winiwarter within the KONTERM project [Schweighofer93a]. The standard vector space model is used to capture the main meaning of the legal term. This approach is characterized by the assumption that the analysis of legal texts should begin with the expert knowledge of lawyers about legal knowledge [Schweighofer93b, Merkl94]. As terms can have numerous variations an extension to automatic linguistic analysis of the observed variations would be very useful [Jaquemin94]. Salton also extended his model by local vector similarity operations [Salton94].

The KONTERM approach can be easily merged with the techniques of exploratory data analysis of computational linguistics. It is inappropriate in the legal field not to consider the existing knowledge about the legal language and emphasize on the computation of co-occurrences [Rajman92, Schütze94] or an association thesaurus [Jing94]. The use of simple linguistic analysis seems to be very promising [Gelbart93, Konstantinou93].

As the exploratory data analysis leads more or less to the detection and use of text patterns, the high potential of neural networks should be further examined. Artificial neural networks could give an answer to the very important question how much time-consuming input or refinement of the model to a particular text corpus is really necessary.

3 Generation of Vectors

As basis for the similarity computation we transformed the document texts as well as the document descriptions to vectors. Figure 1 summarises the individual steps of the applied process model.

The document texts are transformed to sequential word lists. By making use of a lemmatising module these sequential lists are then converted to a word index. The lemmatising module is designed to take care of important morphological phenomena, that is, spelling errors, vowel-gradation, inflexions, and suffixes.

This simple linguistic analysis has to be supplemented by some adaptations to the text corpus. For large texts we removed all words except significant nouns. This time-consuming task can be omitted if neural nets are used for similarity analysis.

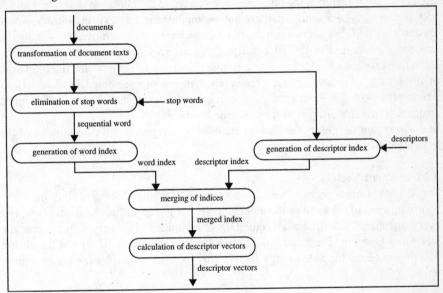

Fig. 1. Process model

3.1 Descriptor Vectors

The necessary input in the form of knowledge on legal terminology determines the further analysis. The documents are indexed by use of the thesaurus entries which results in an index containing the postings for the individual descriptor occurrences. The user is not restricted to the use of simple descriptors but can also apply synonyms and compound descriptors to the representation of the domain knowledge.

By merging the word and the descriptor index, the contexts of the descriptor occurrences are extracted and represented by vectors D_i according to the vector space model of information retrieval [Salton83]:

$$D_i = (TERM_{i1}, TERM_{i2}, ..., TERM_{in}).$$

As weighting function we used binary indexing so that $TERM_{ik} = 1$ if the word k

($1 \leq k \leq n$) is present in the context of the descriptor occurrence and $TERM_{ik} = 0$ otherwise. Thus, the vectors D_i capture the context meaning as a function of the absence or presence of certain words.

The similarity between two different occurrences of a descriptor is expressed by the number of words that are present in both contexts, that is, the number of vector components which equal 1 in both descriptor vectors. We used the symmetric coefficient of Dice as similarity measure [Salton83].

The coefficient represents exactly the percentage of words which the two contexts D_i and D_j have in common. Therefore, the value range is the interval [0, 1], the value equals 0 if the two vectors are completely different and equals 1 if they are identical.

According to the similarity values the descriptor occurrences are clustered by use of a quick partition algorithm that creates non-hierarchical disjunctive clusters [Panyr87]. The similarity value of each pair of descriptor occurrences is compared with a given threshold. If the similarity exceeds the threshold and one of the two occurrences is already a cluster member, the other one is appended to the cluster in question. Only if both participants of a similar pair are not yet included in any existing cluster, a new cluster is created. In a second run duplicate cluster entries are removed by joining the concerned clusters. Finally, all descriptor occurrences not captured so far by the clustering process are added as single element clusters. To simplify the interpretation of the results of clustering, the created clusters are supplemented by descriptions which represent the descriptor connotations and are created from the five most frequent words that are part of the concerned contexts.

In the next step the descriptor clusters are used for a representative description of the individual documents.

3.2 Document Vectors

For the document vectors we did not use the whole document but only the approximation in the form of the automatically computed document description. For every document description a vector DD_i is computed. The only difference is the weighting function. The descriptor terms take the value range [0, 9] and the cluster description terms the value range [0, 1]. This in order to emphasize the descriptor terms.

4 Connectionist Approach

Artificial neural network models consist of many simple, neuron-like processing elements called neurons or units. These units interact by using weighted connections. Data processing with artificial neural networks may roughly be described as activating a set of dedicated units, i.e. input units, and then propagating activation along the weighted connections until another set of dedicated units is reached, i.e. output units. The state of the output units is used as the result of the neural network. Learning rules specify the way in which the weighted connections have to be adapted in order to improve the performance of the artificial neural network. With regard to the learning process we identify at least two different paradigms: supervised learning and unsupervised learning [Hinton89, Rumelhart86]. Within our approach we utilise an artificial neural network adhering to the unsupervised learning paradigm, namely self-organising feature maps [Kohonen82, Kohonen89, Kohonen90]. The architecture of self-organising feature maps consists of a layer of input units and a grid of output units. In the case of our application we used a two-dimensional plane of output units. Each output unit is connected to its topological neighbours and is assigned a so-called weight vector which is of the same dimension as the input data. The crucial steps of the learning process can be described as follows.

(1) Random selection of one input vector x.

(2) Selection of the winning unit i by using the Euclidean distance measure. In this formula w_i (w_j) denotes the weight vector assigned to output unit i (j).

$$i: \|w_i\text{-}x\| <= \|w_j\text{-}x\|, \text{ for all output units } j$$

(3) Adaptation of the weight vectors w_j in the neighbourhood of the winning unit i at learning iteration t. The strength of the adaption is determined with respect to a so-called learning rate eps(t) which starts with an initial value in the range of [0, 1] and decreases gradually during the learning process to 0. The scalar function $delta_{i,j}(t)$ determines the amount of adaption dependent on the neighbourhood relation between the winning unit i and unit j which is currently under consideration. Generally, the weight vectors of units which are in close neighbourhood to the winning unit are adapted more strongly than weight vectors which are assigned to units that are far away from the winning unit. This so-called neighbourhood function has to guarantee that at the end of the learning process only the weight vector which is assigned to the winning unit is adapted. Obviously, with these two restrictions on the learning rate and the neighbourhood function the learning process will terminate.

$$w_j(t+1)=w_j(t)+eps(t)*delta_{i,j}(t)*[x\text{-}w_j]$$

(4) Repeat steps (1) through (3) until no more changes to the weight vectors are observed.

The outcome of the learning process of self-organising feature maps results in a clustering of related input data in topologically near areas within the grid of output units. The repetition of this adaption during the numerous presentations of input vectors makes the formation of areas possible which consist of output units specialised to regularities in the feature vectors of the various input data.

5 Evaluation

As test environment for our approach we used documents from the European Community law database CELEX.

5.1 Descriptors

The test database for descriptors consisted of 41 text segments of documents. The text material - terms with context windows - was produced as retrieval result from a search in the CELEX database for the term 'neutrality'. We selected 'neutrality' because this concept is a very good example of a term with several meanings. By intellectual separation we achieved clusters of the various context related meanings of the term neutrality which represented the comparison module for our automatic analysis, see Figure 2.

Due to space restrictions we can present only the various groups and the CELEX numbers of the documents. We specify each document by its CELEX number. Furthermore, each cluster is labelled by a short descriptive term. Note that several segments of one document are designated by using capital letters, e.g. /A, /B, etc.

- Neutrality of States (STATE): 992E2408, 990H0306, 989H0195, 987H0184, 987H0183, 982H0240
- Fiscal neutrality:
  - Neutrality of the value-added tax system (VAT): 389L0465, 385L0361, 381Y0924(10), 367L0227/A, 367L0227/B, 690C0097, 690C0060, 690C0035
    - deduction of residial VAT (RES_VAT): 689J0159/A, 689J0119
    - import turnover tax (IMP_VAT): 689C0343
    - parent companies and subsidiaries of different member States (SUB_VAT): 390L0435
  - spirits (SPIRITS): 689C0230
  - CO_2/energy tax (EN_TAX): 392D0180
  - sugar sector (SUGAR): 390B0354
  - non-discrimination in matters of taxation (NON_DISC): 689J0159/B, 689J0011/A
- Neutrality of competition:
  - Neutrality of common rules for the allocation of slots at Community airports (SLOTS): 393R0095/A, 393R0095/B, 393R0095/C, 393R0095/D
  - Neutrality of the Community eco-management and audit scheme (ENVIRON): 393R1836, 392R0880
  - Neutrality of the tariff structures in the combined transport of goods (TRANSPORT): 393D0174/A, 393D0174/B, 393D0174/C
  - Neutrality of computer reservation systems for air transport services (AIR_SERV): 391R0083, 388R2672
- Neutrality of the research programmes of the Joint Research Centre (RESEARCH): 392D0274
- Neutrality of anti-dumping duties (ANTI_DUMP): 392R0738
- Chemical neutrality:
  - oil seeds (OIL): 386R2435
- Neutrality of the customs valuation system:
  - customs value of goods (CUSTOMS): 689J0011/B
- Conjunctural neutrality (CONJUNCT): 385D105.1
- Cost-neutrality (COST): 385D105.3
- Budgetary neutrality (BUDGET): 380Y1231(06)

Fig. 2. Intellectual separation

The efficient clustering algorithm of KONTERM produces sound results. The clusters can be seen as types of the concept that are described automatically. A shortcoming of KONTERM is the sensitivity to the correct adjustment of the parameters (i.e. list of stop words, threshold value). However, multiple clustering with different parameters can be a useful support for the analysis of a term. The outcome of the clustering algorithm is represented in Figure 3. For each cluster we give the consecutive number of the text segment as well as its corresponding CELEX number. Furthermore, we provide the cluster description which consists of the ten most frequent words that are contained in the respective contexts.

During our experiments self-organising feature maps are trained with the descriptor vectors as input data. The length of these vectors is about 500 components. Therefore, we perform a projection from a very high dimensional input space onto a two-dimensional output space by means of the self-organising map.

The most obvious difference to the statistical approach is that the neural network does not produce clusters but maps. The advantage of such maps is a better description of the relationships between the various connotations of a concept which can be described by using well-known geographical terms:

Hills: Strong concentration of document segments with the same meaning,

Plateaux: Loose set of document segments with similar meanings,

```
1 41 NEUTRALITY
/1/11/  393R1836, 392R0880
MEMBER, STATES, COMPOSITION, COMPETENT, BODIES, INDEPENDENCE, PROVISIONS,
THIS, REGULATION, CONSISTENT
/2/3/4/  393D0174/A, 393D0174/B, 393D0174/C
APPLICATION, TARIFF, STRUCTURE, PRINCIPLE, INCOME, RAILWAY, COMPANIES,
CERTAIN, ROUTES, ADJUSTMENTS
/5/15/18/21/22/27/  992E2408, 990H0306, 989H0195, 987H0184, 987H0183, 982H0240
QUESTION, NO, COUNCIL, AUSTRIAN, COMMISSION, BONDE, IRISH, UNILATERAL,
DECLARATIONS, WRITTEN
/6/7/8/9/  393R0095/A, 393R0095/B, 393R0095/C, 393R0095/B
MEMBER, STATES, AIRPORT, PRINCIPLE, NO, RESPONSIBLE, TRANSPARENCY,
DISCRIMINATION, CERTAIN, REQUIREMENT
/14/20/  391R0083, 388R2672
PARTICULAR, NO, BASIS, CONDITIONS, ORDER, DISCRIMINATION, SUBJECT, REGARDS,
SYSTEMS, CO-OPERATION
/19/30/31/33/  389L0465, 367L0227/A, 367L0227/B, 690C0060
TAX, VALUE, ADDED, SYSTEMS, PRODUCTION, DISTRIBUTION, MEMBER, STATES,
PROVISIONS, SERVICES
/28/35/36/37/38/  381Y0924, 689J0159/A, 689J0159/B, 689J0119, 689J0011
MEMBER, STATES, TAX, COMPETITION, VAT, REMISSION, EXPORTATION, GOODS,
COMMON, RESPECT
The other remaining clusters consist of only one single document:
392D0274, 392R0738, 392D0180, 390L0435, 390B0354, 386R2435, 385L0361, 385D0105/A,
385D0105/B, 380Y1231, 690C0097, 690C0035, 689J0011/B, 689C0343, 689C0230
```

Fig. 3. Clusters obtained by using a statistical approach

Valleys: Document segments with meaning elements of several groups,
Region: Neighbourhood relationship between hills and plateaux.
A note on the graphical representation of the final maps which are given in Figure 4 below is in order. The graphical representation contains as many entries as there are output units in the artificial neural network. Thus, every entry corresponds to exactly one unit of the self-organising feature map. Each entry is further assigned either the CELEX number of a text segment or a dot. The appearance of a label denotes the fact that the corresponding unit exhibits the highest activation level with regard to the input vector corresponding to this CELEX number. Therefore, this unit is the winning unit. On the contrary, a dot appears in the final map if none of the input vectors is assigned to the corresponding unit. In other words, the respective unit does not exhibit the highest activation level for any input vector. Due to the limited space in the figures the CELEX number of only one text segment is shown even in the case where more than one text segment is assigned to an output unit. The other text segments are given as footnotes. In order to ease comparison we give the short mnemonic description for each CELEX number as they are introduced above.
Note that the topological arrangement of the labels is an indication for the similarity of the corresponding text segments. However, the distance of the labels in terms of the two-dimensional surface cannot be used as an exact metric of semantic similarity. The neural network produces good hills (e.g. neutrality of the common rules for the allocation of slots at Community airports, neutrality of states) comparable to the clusters of the statistical analysis but also some interesting plateaux (e.g. fiscal neutrality or neutrality and environment). A region can be seen including the

meanings fiscal neutrality, cost neutrality, budgetary neutrality, and conjunctural neutrality.

Although the interpretation of the neural network is more difficult than the statistical approach, the main advantage remains that the tuning of the model (stop word list, threshold value) is not necessary.

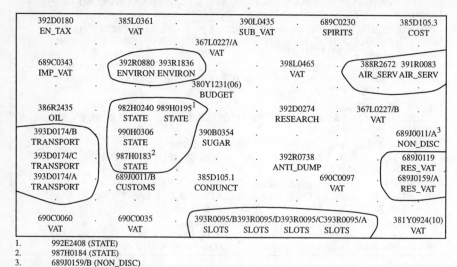

392D0180 EN_TAX	.	385L0361 VAT	.	.	390L0435 SUB_VAT	.	689C0230 SPIRITS	.	385D105.3 COST
				367L0227/A VAT	.	.	.		.
689C0343 IMP_VAT	.	392R0880 393R1836 ENVIRON ENVIRON	.	.	398L0465 VAT	.	388R2672 391R0083 AIR_SERV AIR_SERV	
		.	380Y1231(06) BUDGET	.	.	.		
386R2435 OIL	.	982H0240 989H0195[1] STATE STATE	.	.	392D0274 RESEARCH	.	367L0227/B VAT	
393D0174/B TRANSPORT		990H0306 STATE	.	390B0354 SUGAR	.	.	.	689J0011/A[3] NON_DISC	
393D0174/C TRANSPORT	.	987H0183[2] STATE	.	.	392R0738 ANTI_DUMP	.	689J0119 RES_VAT	
393D0174/A TRANSPORT	.	689J0011/B CUSTOMS	.	385D105.1 CONJUNCT	.	690C0097 VAT	.	689J0159/A RES_VAT	
690C0060 VAT	.	690C0035 VAT	.	393R0095/B 393R0095/D 393R0095/C 393R0095/A SLOTS SLOTS SLOTS SLOTS				381Y0924(10) VAT	

1.   992E2408 (STATE)
2.   987H0184 (STATE)
3.   689J0159/B (NON_DISC)

Fig. 4. Final map without elimination of stop words

5.2 Documents

The test environment for our approach is a database consisting of 75 full text documents of court decisions from the European Community law database CELEX. The thesaurus is taken from the lexicon :SUBjects of CELEX which contains some 250 descriptors, more or less corresponding to the major chapters of the treaties and areas of Community activity. Only few descriptors are added to this list. The automatically produced document description [Schweighofer93a] is transformed to a weighed document vector. The descriptor terms get the value range [0, 9] and the cluster description terms the value range [0, 1]. This document vector is the input to the neural network.

Some remarks about the quality of the thesaurus are in order. The indexation in the lexicon in CELEX is of rather poor quality because of the low number of descriptors and the stress on the area of Community activity. Although the automatic indexation is paramount to the intellectual one some inconsistences remain which can be easily resolved by adding more descriptors.

The length of these vectors is about 630 components. As mentioned above, each output unit in the artificial neural network is assigned to the CELEX number and a short mnemonic description.

The documents of the European Court of Justice cover the following main topics:

    * Supremacy of Community law (SUPR)

    * Direct applicability of Community law (APPL)

* Direct effect of secondary legislation (EFFECT)
* Questions concerning the European Parliament (seat, conciliation, locus standi) (EP)
* Questions concerning the relationship between public international law and Community law (treaty-making power of the European Community, effect of treaties in Community law) (INT LAW)
* Non-contractual liability of the European Community (LIAB)
* Fundamental human rights (RIGHTS)
* Legal base chosen for a legal act (BASE)
* Legal status of regions (REGION)
* Safeguard clauses (SAFE)

The map as depicted in Figure 5 shows good hills concerning the non-contractual liability of the European Community, questions concerning the European Parliament, the relationship between public international law and Community law as well as human rights. A good region is formed by the hills concerning direct applicability of Community law and direct effect of secondary legislation. Shortcomings are some "run-aways" which are due to the poor thesaurus and the merge of descriptors concerning the legal questions (e.g. direct applicability of Community law) and the area of Community activity (e.g. agriculture).

6 Conclusion

This paper shows the potential of neural networks in combination with statistical methods for learning by using exploratory data analysis of legal texts. Such an approach can only be sucessful if easily available data can be matched against a specific text corpus. Neural networks can produce quite useable maps of descriptor and document spaces automatically. Yet, the interpretation of the final maps demonstrated to be more laborious because of the different paradigm of presentation, improved visualization is subject to ongoing work. However, the outcome of the experiments are quite encouraging already at the moment. The next step will concern the extension of the input material to simple syntactic constructs. The knowledge base can be refined by our prototype to a good representation of the relevant knowledge in a given text corpus. Thus, this knowledge base would be a good tool for information extraction and consequently useful for automatic knowledge acquisition within the legal domain.

Acknowledgements

This research is funded by the Jubiläumsfonds of the Oesterreichische Nationalbank (research project no. 4941). We thank the Office for Publications of the European Communities for providing us with the documents.

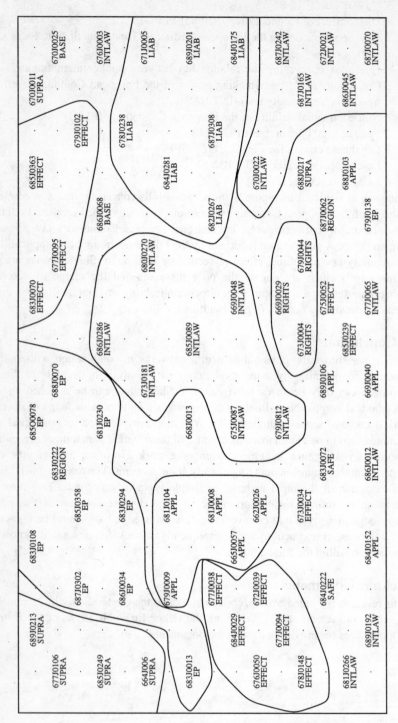

Fig. 5. Final map of documents of the European Court of Justice

References

BELEW, R.K. (1987): A Connectionist Approach to Conceptual Information Retrieval. In: Proc. Int. Conf. on Artificial Intelligence & Law. Baltimore: ACM Press.

BENCH-CAPON, T. (1993): Neural Networks and Open Texture. In: Proc. Int. Conf. on Artificial Intelligence & Law. Baltimore: ACM Press.

BING, J. (1987): Designing Text Retrieval Systems for Conceptual Searching. In: Proc. Int. Conf. on Artificial Intelligence & Law. Baltimore: ACM Press.

BLAIR, D.C./MARON, M.E. (1990): Full-Text Information Retrieval: Further Analysis and Clarification. In: Information Processing & Management, Vol. 26, No. 3.

CHURCH, K.W./MERCER, R.L. (1993): Introduction to the Special Issue on Computational Linguistics Using Large Corpora. In: Computational Linguistics, Vol. 19, No. 1.

CROSS, G.R./deBESSONET, C.G. (1985): Representation of Legal Knowledge for Conceptual Retrieval. In: Information Processing & Management, Vol. 21, No. 1.

DE MULDER, R.V./VAN NOORTWIJK, C. (1994): A System for Ranking Douments According to their Relevance to a (Legal) Concept, In: Proc. Int. Conf. RIAO, New York.

DICK, J.P. (1991): Representation of Legal Text for Conceptual Retrieval. In: Proc. Int. Conf. on Artificial Intelligence & Law. Baltimore: ACM Press.

GELBART, D./SMITH, J.C. (1993): FLEXICON: An Evaluation of a Statistical Ranking Model Adapted to Intelligent Legal Text Management. In: Proc. Fourth Int. Conf. on Artificial Intelligence and Law. Baltimore: ACM.

HAFNER, C.D. (1981): An Information Retrieval System Based on a Computer Model of Legal Knowledge. Ann Arbor: UMI Research Press.

HINTON, G. (1989): Connectionist Learning Procedures. In: Artificial Intelligence, Vol. 40.

JACOBS, P.S./RAU, L.F. (1990): SCISOR: Extracting Information from On-line News. In: CACM, Vol. 33, No. 11.

JACQUEMIN, C. (1994): FASTR : A Unification-Based Front-End to Automatic Indexing. In: Proc Int Conf RIAO, New York.

JING, Y./CROFT, W.B. (1994): An Association Thesaurus for Information Retrieval. In: Proc. Int. Conf. RIAO. New York.

KOHONEN, T. (1982): Self-organized formation of topologically correct feature maps. In: Biological Cybernetics, Vol. 43.

KOHONEN, T. (1989): Self-Organization and Associative Memory. Springer: Berlin.

KOHONEN, T. (1990): The Self-Organizing Map. In: Proc. of the IEEE, Vol. 78, No. 9.

KONSTANTINOU, V./SYKES, J./YANNOPOULOS, G.N. (1993): Can Legal Knowledge Be Derived from Legal Texts? In: Proc. Fourth Int. Conf. on Artificial Intelligence and Law. Baltimore: ACM.

MERKL, D./SCHWEIGHOFER, E./WINIWARTER, W. (1994): CONCAT - Connotation Analysis of Thesauri Based on the Interpretation of Context Meaning. In: Proc. 5th Int. Conf. on Database and Expert Systems Applications. Berlin: Springer.

MERKL, D./TJOA, A M./VIEWEG, S. (1992): BRANT - An Approach to Knowledge Based Document Classification in the Information Retrieval Domain. Proc. Int. Conf. on Database and Expert Systems Applications. Wien: Springer.

MITAL, V./STYLIANOU, A./JOHNSON, L. (1991): Conceptual Information Retrieval in Litigation Support Systems. In: Proc. Int. Conf. on Artificial Intelligence & Law. Baltimore: ACM Press.

PAICE, C.D. (1991): A Thesaural Model of Information Retrieval. In: Information Processing & Management, Vol. 27, No. 5.

PANYR, J. (1987): Vektorraum-Modell und Clusteranalyse in Information Retrieval-Systemen. In: Nachr. Dok., Vol. 38. (in German).

RAJMAN, M./BONNET, A. (1992): New Tools for Text Analysis: Corpora-Based Linguistics. In: 1st Annual Conference of the Association for Global Strategic Information. Bad Kreuznach.

ROSE, D.E./BELEW, R.K. (1989): Legal Information Retrieval: A Hybrid Approach. In: Proc. Int. Conf. Artificial Intelligence and Law. Baltimore: ACM.

ROSE, D.E. (1993): A Symbolic and Connectionist Approach to Legal Information Retrieval. Hillsdale, N.J.: Lawrence Erlbaum.

RUMELHART, D.E./McCLELLAND, J.L. (1986): Parallel Distributed Processing - Explorations in the Microstructure of Cognition. Cambridge, Mass.: MIT Press.

SALTON, G. (1989): Automatic Text Processing: The Transformation, Analysis, and Retrieval of Information by Computer. Reading, Mass.: Addison-Wesley.

SALTON, G./ALLAN, J. (1994): Automatic Text Decomposition and Structuring. In: Proc. Int. Conf. RIAO, New York.

SALTON, G./McGILL, M.J. (1983): Introduction to Modern Information Retrieval. New York: McGraw-Hill.

SCHÜTZE, H./PEDERSEN, O. (1994): A Cooccurrence-Based Thesaurus and Two Applications to Information Retrieval. In: Proc. Int. Conf. RIAO. New York.

SCHWEIGHOFER, E./WINIWARTER, W. (1993a): Legal Expert System KONTERM - Automatic Representation of Document Structure and Contents. In: Proc. Int. Conf. on Database and Expert Systems Applications. Berlin: Springer.

SCHWEIGHOFER, E./WINIWARTER, W. (1993b): Refining the Selectivity of Thesauri by Means of Statistical Analysis. In: Proc. Third Int. Congress on Terminology and Knowledge Engineering. Cologne: Indeks Verlag.

WONG, S.K.M./ZIARKO, W./RAGHAVAN, V.V./WONG, P.C.N. (1987): On Modeling of Information Retrieval Concepts in Vector Spaces. In: ACM Trans. on Database Systems, Vol. 12, No. 2.

Using Hybrid Connectionist Learning for Speech/Language Analysis

Volker Weber and Stefan Wermter

University of Hamburg
Department of Computer Science
22765 Hamburg, Germany
{weber|wermter}@informatik.uni-hamburg.de

Abstract. In this paper we describe a *screening* approach for *speech/ language analysis* using *learned, flat* connectionist representations. For investigating this approach we built a hybrid connectionist system using a large number of connectionist and symbolic modules. Our system SCREEN[1] learns a flat syntactic and semantic analysis of incremental streams of word hypothesis sequences. In this paper we focus on techniques for improving the quality of pruned hypotheses from a speech recognizer using acoustic, syntactic, and semantic knowledge. We show that the developed architecture is able to cope with real-world spontaneously spoken language in an incremental and parallel manner.

1 Introduction

Processing real-world spontaneously spoken language in computational models causes more problems than the analysis of written texts since spontaneous language is often irregular, faulty and heterogeneous. Besides the "noise" produced by a human speaker (interjections, pauses, repetitions, repairs, restarts, etc.) there is also noise induced by the faulty output of the speech recognizer. In this article we will describe an approach which combines real-world speech and language processing based on a hybrid connectionist learning system.

Several connectionist learning techniques have been used for text analysis in the past. McClelland, Kawamoto and Miikulainen used connectionist learning for case role analysis [9, 12]. Syntactic tagging with a connectionist learning approach has been studied by Hanson and Kegl [4]. Furthermore, Elman and Mozer examined sequence processing [3, 13], McMillan, Mozer, Towell, and Shavlik dealt with rule induction [10, 15] and Wermter investigated a scanning understanding of complex phrases [25]. These connectionist approaches concentrated on *written text* while our approach in this paper deals with real-world *spontaneously spoken language* analysis. Only recently there has been more interest in speech/language integration [5, 8, 16, 17, 18]. However most approaches have not yet explored *connectionist learning* techniques of *flat* syntactic and semantic representations for improving the quality of speech/language analysis.

---

[1] Symbolic Connectionist Robust EnterprisE for Natural language

Different techniques have to be used for analyzing spoken language than for analyzing text. In particular, we consider the following general properties as important for analyzing spoken language.

Learning: Spontaneous language is often irregular. Therefore it is difficult to design rules which are able to cope with unrestricted real-world spontaneous language utterances. Therefore, we decided to use learning techniques which are able to generalize. Another advantage of a learning approach is that a system built for a specific domain can be ported easier to another domain.

Fault-tolerant processing: Connectionist learning approaches are able to cope with irregularities. Since spontaneous language contains phenomena like repairs, interjections, pauses, repetitions, false starts, ungrammatical constructions, and unforeseeable semantic constructions it is necessary to deal with them in a fault-tolerant manner. Some local irregularities can be dealt with by the inherent fault-tolerance of connectionist learning models while other often occurring irregularities can benefit from the design of specialized error-detection modules.

Flat screening analysis: Since spontaneous language utterances possess very different constructions it is difficult to design a high level interpretation which is general enough to cover all utterances. Therefore, the interpretation level should be rather close to a *flat* syntactic and semantic analysis for the integration with speech recognition since a deep interpretation level is too restrictive for faulty spontaneous language.

Based on these principles we designed and implemented the incremental and parallel hybrid connectionist architecture SCREEN for speech/language integration [23]. It uses a large number of connectionist networks but also a number of symbolic modules for rather simple tasks (like for instance the comparison of two words). Connectionist networks support learning, fault-tolerance, and flat screening analysis that we identified as being essential for the integration of speech/language analysis.

Current speech-recognizers compute word hypotheses which form a word graph. The huge number of paths through a word graph often exceeds the computational capacities for further syntactic and semantic analysis. Therefore the search space of a word graph has to be pruned. This can be done with an acoustic score computed by the speech recognizer. Unfortunately the acoustic score alone does not give enough evidence for good sentence hypotheses. Flat syntactic and semantic analysis provides additional knowledge for testing whether a given path is syntactically or semantically more plausible than another one in order to reduce the search space of good hypotheses which have to be interpreted.

SCREEN is a new hybrid connectionist system for the flat syntactic and semantic analysis of spontaneous speech. First we have explored the feasibility of dealing with spontaneous language using transcripts [20, 23]. After these preliminary successful case studies with transcripts we extended the SCREEN system to processing streams of word hypotheses generated by a speech recognizer. In this paper we describe the system architecture, give a description of the flat representations, point out the advantages of a screening analysis for improving the quality of hypotheses, and provide a detailed analysis of the running system.

2 From acoustics to flat syntactic and semantic analysis

2.1 The output of a speech recognizer

Acoustic signals are transformed to word hypotheses by a speech recognizer. Current speech recognizers produce many different word hypotheses for an acoustic signal. Typically the output of a speech recognizer is a list of word hypotheses (table 1) which represent a word graph (figure 1). The list consists of a start-time and an end-time in seconds, the recognized German word (in this paper with its literal English translation), and an acoustic score which gives the acoustic plausibility in the range from 0.0 (unplausible) to 1.0 (plausible).

The word graph can be constructed from the word hypotheses by connecting a word hypothesis with end-time X with an immediately following word hypothesis with start-time X+0.01s. For instance, the first word hypothesis in table 1 "#PAUSE#" (end-time 0.14s) can be connected with the word hypothesis "schönen" or "schön" ("fine"; start-times 0.15s). In table 1 and figure 1 we have chosen a rather small list of word hypotheses to be able to show the full word graph and to illustrate the principle of improving the quality of sentence hypotheses with flat syntactic and semantic knowledge. Usually word graphs are much bigger and the necessity for pruning is much more obvious.

start time	end time	word hypothesis		score by speech-recognizer
0.00	0.14	#PAUSE#		4.074477e-16
0.15	0.44	schönen	(fine)	8.200215e-15
0.15	0.44	schön	(fine)	8.200215e-15
0.45	0.62	bis	(until)	1.479265e-13
0.63	0.83	dann	(then)	7.858106e-17
0.63	0.83	sollen	(should)	1.900592e-17
0.63	0.84	dann	(then)	6.550429e-17
0.63	0.87	sollen	(should)	4.126975e-17
0.63	0.87	dann	(then)	8.347788e-17
0.84	1.02	drauf	(on)	1.626915e-17
0.85	0.87	<NIB>	not recognized	5.582233e-30
0.88	1.02	auf	(good)	4.482144e-17
1.03	1.57	Wiedersehen	(bye)	1.168121e-14
1.58	3.04	#PAUSE#		7.456669e-09

Table 1. Word hypotheses for sentence "Fine, until then, good bye". Note that for illustration and didactic reasons we have chosen an extremely simplified word graph with a small number of word hypotheses.

Following the edges of the word graph we can build sentence hypotheses. There are plausible hypotheses like "Schön bis dann auf Wiedersehen" ("Fine until then good bye") or syntactically and semantically implausible ones like

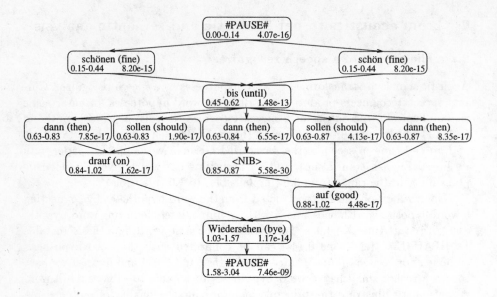

Fig. 1. Word graph for the word hypotheses from table 1.

"Schönen bis sollen drauf Wiedersehen" ("Fine until should on bye"). However both sentence hypotheses have an average acoustic score of about 2.4e-14 per word hypothesis so that the acoustic score does not give enough evidence for favoring a particular sentence hypothesis. Furthermore, this example illustrates that the syntactic and semantic processing has to be fault-tolerant to cope with such unforeseeable irregular input.

2.2 Flat syntactic and semantic analysis

For dealing with faulty spontaneous input we decided to use a flat syntactic and semantic representation (see figure 2 for a simple example of flat representations). We use 13 different syntactic categories for representing words (**N**oun, prono**U**n, ad**J**ective, **V**erb, **A**dverb, p**R**eposition, **C**onjunction, **D**eterminer, nu**M**eral, **I**nterjection, **P**ast participle, pause (**/**), and **O**ther) and 20 different semantic categories (statements of being (**IS**), having (**HAVE**), meeting (**MEET**), moving (**MOVE**), and **AUX**iliary; **SUG**gestions, **SEL**ections, and **UTTER**ances; **PHYS**ical, **ABS**tract, and **ANIM**ate objects; time or location points (**HERE**), Sou**RC**es, and **DEST**inations; **LOC**ation and **TIME**; Negati**O**ns, agreements (**YES**), and **QUEST**ions; unspecific semantics (**NIL**)). Furthermore, we use 8 abstract syntactic and 17 abstract semantic categories for the analysis at the phrase level. Since the flat syntactic and semantic analysis is learned, the approach does not crucially rely on these particular categories [24]. A more detailed description of these categories and flat syntactic and semantic analysis can be found in previous work [20, 23].

		Schön (Fine)	bis (until)	dann (then)	auf (good)	Wiedersehen (bye)
Basic	syntax	adjective	preposition	adverb	preposition	noun
	semantics	yes	here	time	nil	nil
Abstract	syntax	modus group	prepositional group		prepositional group	
	semantics	confirmation	time at		miscellaneous	

Fig. 2. Utterance with its flat representations. Note that the categories refer to the German utterance and cannot correspond correctly to the literal English word translation in all cases.

3 Architecture for speech/language integration

For fault-tolerant incremental speech processing and flat language analysis we developed the SCREEN system. The system currently contains six main parts. The parts are the *speech construction part* for constructing sentence hypotheses from word hypotheses delivered by a speech-recognizer, the *speech evaluation part* for computing syntactic and semantic plausibilities needed for choosing the best sentence hypotheses, the *category part* for flat syntactic and semantic analysis at the word and phrase level, the *correction part* for detecting and dealing with often occurring errors (repairs) in spontaneous language, the *subclause part* for detecting subclauses, and finally the *case frame part* for providing case frame representations of an utterance.

All parts consist of several modules which are either connectionist or symbolic. All modules communicate via a common message structure and allow parallel and incremental processing. The communication mechanism does not distinguish between symbolic and connectionist modules and is the basis for integration in our hybrid connectionist architecture SCREEN. The main goal in SCREEN is to push connectionist learning and a flat screening analysis as far as possible in order to provide fault-tolerant processing.

In previous work we gave a detailed description and analysis of the category part for flat syntactic [23] and semantic analysis [20] as well as the correction part [19] so that we will not go into details of the syntactic and semantic analysis here. In this article we will explain and discuss the new speech-related parts (speech construction part and speech evaluation part) within the general architecture.

3.1 Speech construction part

The speech construction part forms the interface between the speech recognizer[2] and the flat screening analysis[3]. Therefore the incremental stream of incoming

---

[2] Currently we use word hypotheses provided by our project partners at the University of Karlsruhe and the University of Hamburg.

[3] The speech recognizer and the speech construction part communicate via the INTARC/ICE communication environment [1].

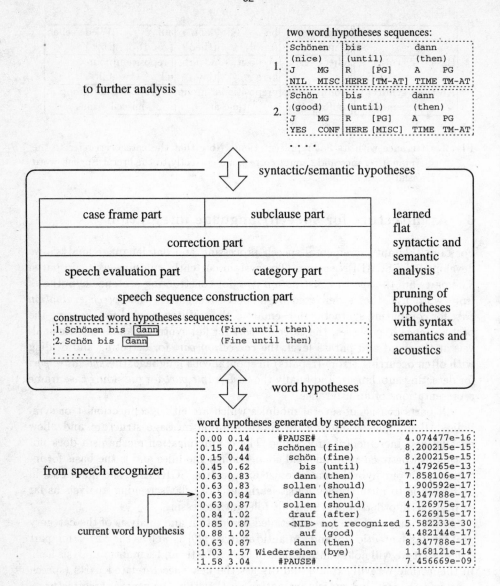

Fig. 3. Overview of the SCREEN system with example word hypotheses from tab.1.

word hypotheses is combined to an incremental stream of sentence hypotheses (see figure 3). These incremental partial sentence hypotheses become part of SCREEN's hypothesis space. The hypothesis space is pruned based on a combination of the acoustic plausibility (given by the speech recognizer), the syntactic plausibility, and the semantic plausibility (computed by modules of the speech evaluation part, see section 3.3). A sentence hypothesis may be dropped from the

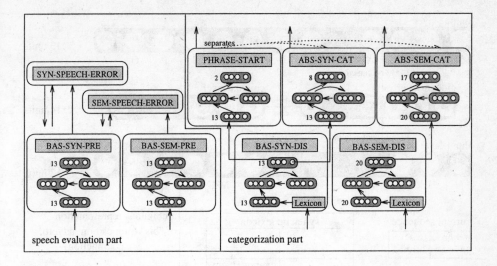

Fig. 4. Overview of the speech evaluation and categorization parts.

hypothesis space if its plausibility is too low or if it cannot be completed by any of the observed word hypotheses from the speech recognizer. The speech construction part combines the processing of individual sentence hypotheses with the parallel computation of competitive sequence hypotheses in the hypothesis space.

3.2 Categorization part

The computation of the syntactic and semantic plausibility of a partial sentence hypothesis depends on the basic syntactic disambiguation (BAS-SYN-DIS) and the basic semantic disambiguation (BAS-SEM-DIS). These disambiguations are also input for the abstract categorization modules which compute a phrase delimiter (PHRASE-START), abstract syntactic phrase categories (ABS-SYN-CAT), and abstract semantic phrase categories (ABS-SEM-CAT). Furthermore the output of the disambiguation is input to the prediction modules of the speech evaluation part.

The disambiguation in the modules BAS-SYN-DIS and BAS-SEM-DIS is based on simple recurrent networks and a syntactic and semantic lexicon (see figure 5). The current word of a sentence hypothesis is retrieved from the lexicon with its potentially ambiguous representation. The ambiguous representation is input to the network. The category of the unit with the highest activation in the output layer is chosen as the disambiguated category of the current word. The context layer from the previous disambiguations allows previous words to influence the current sentence hypothesis.

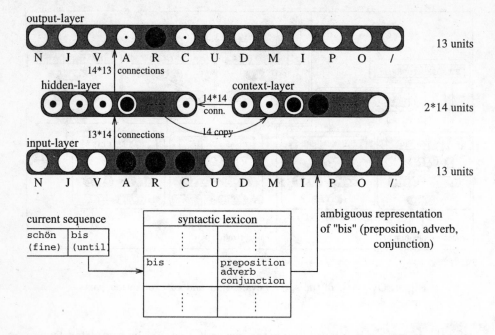

Fig. 5. Basic syntactic disambiguation for the sentence hypothesis "Schön bis ···" ("Fine until ···").

3.3 Speech evaluation part

The speech evaluation part computes the incremental syntactic and semantic plausibility of a sentence hypothesis. It uses the modules SYN-SPEECH-ERROR, SEM-SPEECH-ERROR, BAS-SYN-PRE, and BAS-SEM-PRE (see figure 6). The output of the BAS-SYN-PRE (resp. BAS-SEM-PRE) module is a vector of plausibilities for the prediction of categories. For instance the categories **N**oun, **D**elimiter, and nu**M**eral are very plausible to follow "bis" ("until") in figure 7 while **A**dverb, **I**nterjection, **P**ast participle, and **O**ther are less plausible but still possible. For computing a syntactic (resp. semantic) sentence plausibility based on possible category plausibilities we need to select a particular category. Since BAS-SYN-DIS (resp. BAS-SEM-DIS) disambiguates the categories we take the plausibility of the prediction vector for that category, which was found by the disambiguation network. This selection is done by SYN-SPEECH-ERROR for the syntactic sentence plausibility and by SEM-SPEECH-ERROR for the semantic sentence plausibility. If the syntactic category of the occurring current word is among the predicted syntactic categories at the directly preceding word, then this sentence hypothesis is considered plausible, otherwise implausible.

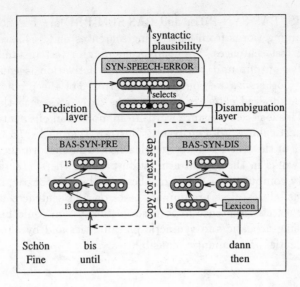

Fig. 6. Computing the syntactic plausibility for a sentence hypothesis.

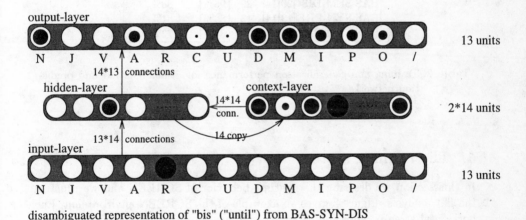

disambiguated representation of "bis" ("until") from BAS-SYN-DIS

Fig. 7. Basic syntactic prediction for the sentence hypothesis "Schön bis ···" ("Fine until ···"). The basic syntactic categories were explained in section 2.2.

4 Improvement in the hypothesis space

In this section we illustrate the performance of learning a flat basic syntactic and semantic disambiguation and prediction. The overall performance for training and test sets is illustrated in table 2. The results for BAS-SYN-DIS,

BAS-SEM-DIS, BAS-SYN-PRE, and BAS-SEM-PRE are based on a training set of 813 training words from 64 training sentences and 1543 test words from 120 unknown test sentences. We count a training or test instance as assigned correctly if the output unit with the maximal activation is equal to the desired category; otherwise we count it as an error. For the prediction networks we count if the desired category is within the categories with the highest five activations. This is necessary since words from more than one syntactic category can follow a particular word. Our results illustrate that 85%–97% of the training and 72%–89% of the test set have been learned. This performance allows us to use these networks in the speech evaluation part for the syntactic and semantic plausibility computation. Based on these combined acoustic, syntactic, and semantic plausibilities, first preliminary tests on 184 sentences show that the quality of the selected sentence hypotheses of the system could be increased by about 30% using acoustic and syntactic plausibilities and by about 50% using acoustic, syntactic, and semantic plausibilities.

Module	No. of units			correct assignments	
	I	H	O	train	test
BAS-SYN-DIS	13	14	13	97%	89%
BAS-SEM-DIS	20	14	20	95%	83%
BAS-SYN-PRE	13	14	13	89%	81%
BAS-SEM-PRE	20	14	20	85%	72%

Table 2. Training and generalization performance for disambiguation and prediction networks

5   The running system

In this section we describe the runtime behavior of SCREEN and we illustrate the flat analysis. Figure 8 gives an example of the SCREEN environment. Each horizontal stream represents a single sentence hypothesis from the hypothesis space. If there are more hypotheses in the hypothesis space than can be displayed they can be made visible by using the vertical scroll bar. The horizontal scroll bar is used for sentence hypotheses which are longer than the current display. The buttons allow the system to be stopped at a particular step for a deeper analysis of the system results.

Each word hypothesis of a sentence hypothesis is represented by a number of units. These units represent the flat syntactic and semantic analysis and the confidence for the sentence up to the current word. While the displayed units only show the highest activation for a categorization their contents can be inspected in more detail by a mouse click to a displayed unit. Then a zoom window occurs which displays all output units for a categorization (see bottom of figure 8).

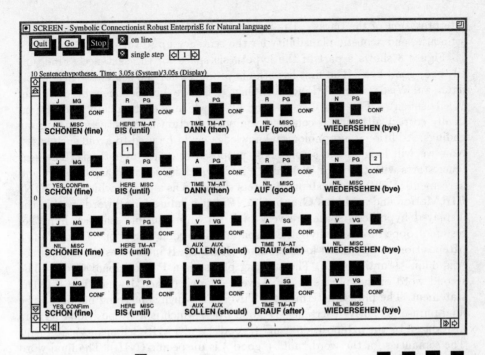

Fig. 8. Snapshot for sentence "Fine, until then, see you". Note that the categories refer to German rather than English. The abbreviations are: AdJective, pReposition, Adverb, Noun, Verb; Modus Group, Preposition Group, Verb Group, Special Group; **NIL** or unspecific semantic, **HERE** time or location, **TIME** object, **YES** or agreement, **AUX**iliary statement; **MISC**ellaneous, TiMe-**AT**, **CONFIRM**ation. The white boxes in the second displayed sentence are zoomed and shown below the SCREEN window. The abbreviations for the right zoom window are: Overall plausibility for the **SEQU**ence up to the current word, **SYN**tactical resp. **SEM**antical plausibility, acoustic score from the **SPEECH**-recognizer.

For each word hypothesis there are five activations as square boxes and one as vertical bar. If a word starts a new phrase the vertical bar is filled; its length corresponds to the activation for the phrase-delimiter detector. The upper left box shows the basic syntactic category for the word, the lower left the basic semantic category. The upper right box shows the abstract syntactic category for a phrase; the lower right the abstract semantic category for a phrase. Based on previous experiments [21, 22] it is advisable to take the leftmost abstract syntactic category of a phrase as final syntactic interpretation for the whole phrase and the rightmost semantic abstract category of a phrase as final semantic interpretation of the phrase. The rightmost box shows the combined syntactic, semantic, and acoustic plausibility for the sentence up to the current word.

Figure 8 shows a part of the hypothesis space for the sentence "Fine, until then, good bye". The first hypothesis produced for the sentence "Schön, bis dann, auf Wiedersehen" ("Fine, until then, good bye") is "Schönen, bis dann, auf Wiedersehen" ("Fine, until then, good bye") which is syntactically and semantically correct although it contains a minor inflection incorrectness in German endings. Additional morphological knowledge could be used to avoid such cases. Now we will look at the second best proposed sentence hypothesis. The sentence starts with the word "Schön" ("Fine") which is identified as adJective and agreement (**YES**). The system interprets this word as a phrase which is a **CON-FIRM**ation and a **M**odus **G**roup. **CONF**idence values for all words within the displayed hypothesis space are very high since implausible sentence hypotheses are dropped from the hypothesis space. The second word "bis" ("until") is a p**R**eposition and a time or location point (**HERE**). It introduces the new phrase "bis dann" ("until then"). The starting phrase is a **P**repositional **G**roup. The second word of this phrase is the **A**dverb "dann" ("then") which is a **TIME**-statement. The phrase determines a Ti**M**e-**AT** which something happens. The final phrase is "auf Wiedersehen" ("good bye") which is a **P**repositional **G**roup introduced by the p**R**eposition "auf" ("good") and a **MISC**ellaneous-statement. The semantics for the word "auf" ("good") is unspecific (**NIL**). The final word "Wiedersehen" ("bye") is found to be a **N**oun also with unspecific semantics (**NIL**) in this domain since it belongs to a **MISC**ellaneous "politeness formula".

6 Discussion and related work

Learning: Our system differs from symbolic parsers, like for instance that of Mellish [11], and structured connectionist parsers, like that of Howells [6], in its ability to learn. As we have pointed out learning is essential for processing faulty real-world spontaneous language. Learning reduces knowledge engineering, avoids the design of a rule base and increases the portability of a system.

Fault-tolerance: Fault tolerance is extremely important for spoken language analysis because of spontaneity, irregularity and unforeseen input. Since the number of occurring errors and unforeseen constructions is unrestricted, a system must be able to deal with them without breaking. SCREEN possesses an explicit fault-tolerance represented by the modules of the correction part as well as an implicit fault-tolerance based on the inherent fault-tolerance and the similarity-based processing of connectionist networks [14].

Screening analysis with flat representations: We have developed and implemented a screening approach to speech/language analysis with a modular hybrid connectionist architecture. The system does a flat fault-tolerant syntactic analysis and semantic analysis of real-world spontaneous language. Within the screening approach we use a flat learned, fault-tolerant interpretation. The screening analysis is the basis for further analysis, for instance flat translation, functional grammar analysis as well as for the syntactic and semantic improvement of the hypothesis space.

The *related work* that is probably closest to ours is the PARSEC system [7]. PARSEC is a hybrid connectionist system and part of the speech translation system JANUS [17]. The aim of PARSEC is to generate case role representations based on sentences. It possesses several connectionist modules which trigger symbolic transformation rules. In contrast SCREEN offers also the opportunity of explicit fault tolerance in the correction part and SCREEN works on an incremental stream of real-world word hypotheses rather than manually transcribed sentences [7].

Hybrid Architecture: SCREEN is one of the first modular hybrid connectionist systems which integrate speech and language processing by using learned connectionist flat representations. We try to use connectionist networks wherever possible but also use symbolic processing wherever necessary. The system control structure and the message passing have been implemented symbolically as well as several small modules for simple equality tests. The connectionist modules have a symbolic interface and use a general message structure for communication. Therefore from the outside of the modules there is no difference between symbolic and connectionist modules. Modular hybrid architectures in other approaches have also been proven to be useful for common sense reasoning [14] and hybrid text processing [25].

Parallelism: Parallel processing is possible at different levels. First, there is the inherent parallelism of connectionist networks within the modules. Second, at the module level there are many modules running in parallel. Finally, sentence hypotheses in the hypothesis space can be processed in parallel.

Incrementality: Our approach is designed for incremental analysis. That is, we start the analysis with the first incoming word hypotheses from the speech recognizer. This allows us to integrate knowledge from the flat syntactic and semantic analysis for improving the hypothesis space. Therefore it is possible to reduce the hypothesis space at very early stages. The incremental analysis also allows SCREEN to start with further processing as early as possible.

7 Conclusions

We have described SCREEN, a hybrid connectionist system for incremental spoken language analysis. We have shown that flat connectionist analysis can be used to improve the choice of good sentence hypotheses. The system is based on the key principles of *learning, fault-tolerant processing*, and *flat screening* analysis. Based on the concepts in SCREEN we argue for a hybrid solution for the integration of speech and language processing. We use connectionist networks wherever possible and symbolic computation wherever necessary. The learned representation makes it easy to port the system to other corpora and domains. The fault-tolerance allows SCREEN to deal with irregularities generated by a human or a speech recognizer. Furthermore, the flat representations provide a new basis for speech/language processing, and support the acoustic, syntactic and semantic processing of real-world spoken utterances.

Acknowledgments

This research was funded by the German Research Association (DFG) under contract DFG Ha 1026/6-2 and by the German Federal Ministry for Research and Technology (BMBF) under Grant #01IV101A0. We would like to thank S. Haack, M. Löchel, M. Meurer and M. Schrattenholzer for their work on SCREEN. Special thanks to U. Sauerland for his work on the speech construction and evaluation parts.

References

1. J. W. Amtrup. ICE: INTARC communication environment. User guide and reference manual. VM-Techdok 14, Universität Hamburg, November 1994.
2. J. W. Amtrup, A. Hauenstein, C. Pyka, V. Weber, S. Wermter. An outline of the Verbmobil project with focus on the work at the University of Hamburg. In P. Mc Kevitt, ed., *Proceedings of the AAAI-94 Workshop on Integration of Natural Language and Speech Processing.* Seattle, Washington, USA, August 1994.
3. J. L. Elman. Finding structure in time. *Cognitive Science*, 14(2):179–211, 1990.
4. S. J. Hanson, J. Kegl. PARSNIP: A connectionist network that learns natural language grammar from exposure to natural language sentences. In *Proceedings of the 9th Annual Conference of the Cognitive Science Society*, pp. 106–119. Seattle, Washington, 1987.
5. A. Hauenstein, H. H. Weber. An investigation of tightly coupled time synchronous speech language interfaces using a unification grammar. In *Proceedings of the AAAI-94 Workshop on the Integration of Natural Language and Speech Processing.* Seattle, Washington, 1994.
6. T. Howells. VITAL: A connectionist parser. In *Proceedings of the 10th Meeting of the Cognitive Science Society*, pp. 18–25. Montreal, Canada, 1988.
7. A. N. Jain. Generalization performance in PARSEC - a structured connectionist parsing architecture. In J. E. Moody, S. J. Hanson, R. R. Lippmann, eds., *Advances in Neural Information Processing Systems 4*, pp. 209–216. Morgan Kaufmann, San Mateo, CA, 1992.
8. D. Jurafsky, C. Wooters, G. Tajchman, J. Segal, A. Stolcke, N. Morgan. Integrating experimental models of syntax, phonology, and accent/dialect in a speech recognizer. In *Proceedings of the AAAI-94 Workshop on the Integration of Natural Language and Speech Processing.* Seattle, Washington, July/August 1994.
9. J. L. McClelland, A. H. Kawamoto. Mechanisms of sentence processing: Assigning roles to constituents of sentences. In J. L. McClelland, D. E. Rumelhart, The PDP research group, eds., *Parallel Distributed Processing: Explorations in the Microstructure of Cognition*, vol. 2., Psychological and Biological Models, chapter 19, pp. 272–331. MIT Press, Cambridge, MA, 1986.
10. C. McMillan, M. C. Mozer, P. Smolensky. Rule induction through integrated symbolic and subsymbolic processing. In J. E. Moody, S. J. Hanson, R. P. Lippmann, eds., *Advances in Neural Information Processing Systems 4*, pp. 969–976. Morgan Kaufmann, San Mateo, CA, 1992.
11. C. S. Mellish. Some chart-based techniques for parsing ill-formed input. In *Proceedings of the 27th Annual Meeting of the Association for Computational Linguistics*, pp. 102–109, 1989.

12. R. Miikkulainen. *Subsymbolic Natural Language Processing. An integrated model of scripts, lexicon and memory.* MIT Press, Bradford Book, Cambridge, MA, 1993.

13. M. C. Mozer. Neural net architecture for temporal sequence processing. In A. Weigend, N. Gershenfeld, eds., *Predicting the future and understanding the past.* Addison-Wesley Publishing, Redwood City, CA, February 1993.

14. R. Sun. *Integrating Rules and Connectionism for Robust Common Sense Reasoning.* Wiley and Sons, New York, 1994.

15. G. Towell, J. W. Shavlik. Interpretation of artificial networks: Mapping knowledge-based neural networks into rules. In J. E. Moody, S. J. Hanson, R. R. Lippmann, eds., *Advances in Neural Information Processing Systems 4*, pp. 977–984. Morgan Kaufmann, San Mateo, CA, 1992.

16. W. von Hahn, C. Pyka. System architectures for speech understanding and language processing. In G. Heyer, H. Haugeneder, eds., *Appl.Ling.* Wiesbaden, 1992.

17. A. Waibel, A. N. Jain, A. McNair, J. Tebelskis, L. Osterholtz, H. Saito, O. Schmidbauer, T. Sloboda, M. Woszczyna. JANUS: Speech-to-speech translation using connectionist and non-connectionist techniques. In J. E. Moody, S. J. Hanson, R. R. Lippmann, eds., *Advances in Neural Information Processing Systems 4*, pp. 183–190. Morgan Kaufmann, San Mateo, CA, 1992.

18. N. Ward. An approach to tightly-coupled syntactic/semantic processing for speech understanding. In *Proceedings of the AAAI-94 Workshop on the Integration of Natural Language and Speech Processing.* Seattle, Washington, 1994.

19. V. Weber, S. Wermter. Artificial neural networks for repairing language. In *Proceedings of the 8th International Conference on Neural Networks and their Applications.* Marseilles, FRA, December 1995.

20. V. Weber, S. Wermter. Towards learning semantics of spontaneous dialog utterances in a hybrid framework. In J. Hallam, ed., *Hybrid Problems, Hybrid Solutions — Proceedings of the 10th Biennial Conference on AI and Cognitive Science*, pp. 229–238. Sheffield, UK, 1995.

21. S. Wermter, M. Löchel. Connectionist learning of flat syntactic analysis for speech/language systems. In M. Marinaro, P. G. Morasso, eds., *Proceedings of the International Conference on Artificial Neural Networks*, vol. 2, pp. 941–944. Sorrento, Italy, 1994.

22. S. Wermter, U. Peters. Learning incremental case assignment based on modular connectionist knowledge sources. In P. Werbos, H. Szu, B. Widrow, eds., *Proceedings of the World Congress on Neural Networks*, vol. 4, pp. 538–532. San Diego, CA, 1994.

23. S. Wermter, V. Weber. Learning fault-tolerant speech parsing with SCREEN. In *Proceedings of the 12th National Conference on Artificial Intelligence*, vol. 1, pp. 670–675. Seattle, Washington, 1994.

24. S. Wermter, V. Weber. Artificial neural networks for automatic knowledge acquisition in multiple real–world language domains. In *Proceedings of the 8th International Conference on Neural Networks and their Applications.* Marseilles, FRA, December 1995.

25. S. Wermter. *Hybrid Connectionist Natural Language Processing.* Chapman and Hall, London, UK, 1995.

SKOPE: A Connectionist/Symbolic Architecture of Spoken Korean Processing*

Geunbae Lee and Jong-Hyeok Lee

Department of Computer Science & Engineering
Pohang University of Science & Technology
San 31, Hoja-Dong, Pohang, 790-784, Korea
gblee@vision.postech.ac.kr

Abstract. Spoken language processing requires speech and natural language integration. Moreover, spoken Korean calls for novel processing methodology due to its linguistic characteristics. This paper presents SKOPE, a connectionist/symbolic spoken Korean processing engine, emphasizing that: 1) connectionist and symbolic techniques must be selectively applied according to their relative strength and weakness, and 2) linguistic characteristics of Korean must be fully considered for phoneme recognition, speech and language integration, and morphological/ syntactic processing. The design and implementation of SKOPE demonstrates how connectionist/symbolic hybrid architectures can be constructed for spoken agglutinative language processing. Also SKOPE presents many novel ideas for speech and language processing. Phoneme recognition, speech morphological analysis, and syntactic analysis experiments show that SKOPE is a viable approach for spoken Korean processing.

1 Introduction

Spoken language processing challenges for integration of speech recognition into natural language processing, and must deal with multi-level knowledge sources from signal level to symbol level. The multi-level knowledge integration and handling increase the technical difficulty of both the speech and the natural language processing. In the speech recognition side, the recognition must be at phoneme-level for large vocabulary continuous speech, and the speech recognition module must provide right level of outputs to the natural language module in the form of not single solution but many alternatives of solution hypotheses. The n-best list [5], word-graph [14], and word-lattice [13] techniques are mostly used in this purpose. The speech recognition module can also ask the linguistic scores from the language processing module in a more tightly coupled bottom-up/top-down hybrid integration scheme [15]. In the natural language side, the insertion,

---

* This research was partially supported by KOSEF and ETRI. The SKOPE's various modules were programmed by our students: the phoneme recognition module by Kyunghee Kim, the morphological analysis module by ByungChang Kim & Wonil Lee, and finally the syntax analysis module by Wonil Lee.

deletion, and substitution errors of continuous speech must be compensated by robust parsing and partial parsing techniques, e.g. [3]. Often the spoken languages are ungrammatical, fragmentary, and contain non-fluencies and speech repairs, and must be processed incrementally under the time constraints [12].

Most of the speech and natural language systems which were developed for English and other Indo-European languages neglect the morphological processing, and integrate speech and natural language at the word level [4, 1]. Often these systems employ a pronunciation dictionary for speech recognition and independent dictionaries for natural language processing. However, for the agglutinative languages such as Korean and Japanese, the morphological processing plays a major role in the language processing since these languages have very complex morphological phenomena and relatively simple syntactic functionality. Unfortunately even the Japanese researchers apply degenerated morphological techniques for the spoken Japanese processing [6, 17]. Obviously degenerated morphological processing limits the usable vocabulary size for the system, and word-level dictionary results in exponential explosion in the number of dictionary entries. For the agglutinative languages, we need sub-word level integration which leaves rooms for general morphological processing.

The spoken language processing calls for multi-strategic approaches in order to deal with signal level as well as symbol level information in a symbiotic and unified way. Recent development of connectionist speech recognition [11] and connectionist natural language processing [18] shed lights on the connectionist/symbolic hybrid models of spoken language processing, and some of the researches are already available for English and other Indo-European languages [23, 22]. We feel that it is the right time to develop connectionist/symbolic hybrid spoken languages processing systems for the agglutinative languages such as Korean and Japanese.

This paper presents one of such endeavors, SKOPE (Spoken Korean Processing Engine) that has the following unique features: 1) The connectionist and symbolic techniques are selectively used according to their strength and weakness. The learning capability, fault-tolerant property, and ability of simultaneous integration of multiple signal-level sources make the connectionist techniques suitable to the phoneme recognition from the speech signals, but the structure manipulation and powerful matching (binding) properties of the symbolic techniques are the better choices for the complex morphological processing of Korean. However, the parallel multiple constraint relaxation capability of the connectionist techniques are applied together with the symbolic structure binding techniques for the syntactic processing. 2) The linguistic characteristics of Korean are fully considered in phoneme recognition, speech and language integration, and morphological/syntactic processing. 3) The SKOPE provides multi-level application program interfaces (APIs) which can utilize the phoneme-level, the morpheme-level, and the syntactic structure-level services for several applications such as spoken language interface, voice information retrieval and spoken language translation.

We hope the experience of SKOPE development provide viable answers to some of the open questions to the speech and language processing, such as 1) how learning and encoding can be synergetically combined in speech and language processing, 2) which aspects of system architecture have to be considered in spoken language processing, especially in connectionist/symbolic hybrid systems, and finally 3) what are the most efficient way of speech and language integration, especially for agglutinative languages.

2   Characteristics of Spoken Korean

This section briefly explains the linguistic characterists of spoken Korean before describing the SKOPE system. In this paper, Yale romanization is used for representing the Korean phonemes. 1) A Korean word, called *Eojeol*, consists of more than one morphemes with clear-cut morpheme boundaries. 2) Korean is a postpositional language with many kinds of noun-endings, verb-endings, and prefinal verb-endings. These functional morphemes determine the noun's case roles, verb's tenses, modals, and modification relations between Eojeols. 3) Korean is a basically SOV language but has relatively free word order compared to the rigid word-order languages, such as English, except for the constraints that the verb must appear in a sentence-final position. However, in Korean, some word-order constraints do exist such that the auxiliary verbs representing modalities must follow the main verb, and the modifiers must be placed before the word (called head) they modify. 4) The unit of pause in speech (which is called *Eonjeol*) may be different from that of a written text (an Eojeol). The spoken morphological analysis must deal with an Eonjeol since no Eojeol boundary can be provided in the speech. 5) Phonological changes can occur in a morpheme, between morphemes in an Eojeol, and even between Eojeols in an Eonjeol. These changes include consonant and vowel assimilation, dissimilation, insertion, deletion, and contraction.

3   The SKOPE Architecture

The above spoken Korean characteristics and the relative strength and weakness of symbolic/connectionist techniques result in the general SKOPE architecture which is shown in figure 1. The architecture consists of three different but closely interrelated modules: phoneme recognition, (error-corrective) morphological analysis, and syntactic analysis module. The phoneme recognition module processes the signal-level information, and changes it to the symbol-level information (recognized phoneme sequences). The morphological analysis begins the primitive language processing, and connects the speech recognition to the language processing at the phoneme-level. The syntactic analysis module finishes the language processing[2], and produces the domain independent syntac-

---

[2] We believe that the semantic and pragmatic processing should be integrated into the domain knowledge for *practical application under the current NLP technology*, so we excluded the semantic and pragmatic processing from our general model.

tic structures for application systems. The following subsections briefly describe each module.

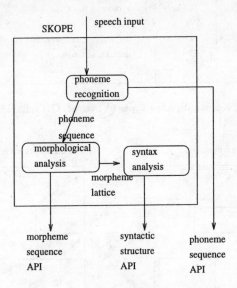

Fig. 1. The spoken Korean processing engine architecture. The architecture has two-level interfaces between modules: phoneme sequence and morpheme lattice for efficient and generalized speech and natural language integration.

3.1 Diphone-Based Connectionist Phoneme Recognition

The phoneme recognition is performed by developing the hierarchically organized group of TDNNs (time delay neural networks) [21]. Considering the signal characteristics of the Korean phonemes, we define diphones as new sub-word recognition units (phoneme-like units). The defined diphones are shown in figure 2, and are classified into four different types. The diphones have the co-articulation handling features similar to the popular triphones [9] but are much fewer in numbers. Figure 3 shows the architecture of the component TDNNs in the phoneme recognition module. The whole module consists of total 19 different TDNNs for recognition of the defined Korean diphones. The top-level TDNN identifies the 18 vowel groups of diphones (we re-classified the total 618 diphones into 18 different groups according to the vowels that are contained in the diphones). The 18 different sub-TDNNs recognize the target diphones. For the training of TDNNs, we manually segment the digitized speech into 200 msec range (which includes roughly left-context phoneme, target diphone, and right context phoneme), and perform 512 order FFTs and 16 step mel-scaling [21] to get the filter-bank coefficients. Each frame size is 10 msec, so 20 (frames) by 16 (mel-scaling factor) values are fed to the TDNNs with the proper output

diphone types	diphone numbers	diphone examples
V	21	a, o, wu, i, u, ye, ...
C1V	378	ha, sa, ka, la, ma, kha, ...
VC2	147	an, am, eng, em, wun, in, ...
C2C1	72	ngs, nn, ngt, ngh, ...

Fig. 2. Four different Korean diphone types (V: vowel, C1: syllable-first consonant, C2: syllable-final consonant)

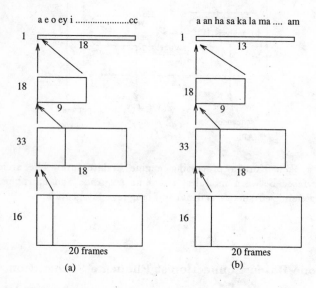

Fig. 3. (a) The TDNN architecture for the vowel group identification. Note the cc group contains no vowels. (b) The architecture of sub-TDNNs for /a/ vowel group. The other 17 sub-TDNNs have the same architecture, but different number of output units according to the number of diphones in each of the vowel group.

symbols, that is, vowel group name or target diphone names. After the training of each TDNN, the phoneme recognition is performed by feeding 200 msec signals to the vowel group identification network and subsequently to the proper diphone recognition network. The 200 msec signals are shifted by 30 msec steps and continuously fed to the networks to process the continuous speech in a spoken Korean pause unit, *Eonjeol*. The final outputs are sequence of diphones for each 200 msec range in 30 msec intervals.

3.2 Error-Corrective Morphological Analysis

Unlike conventional morphological analysis for text inputs, SKOPE morphological analysis starts with the recognized diphone sequences which contains insertion, deletion, and substitution speech recognition errors. The conventional morphological analysis procedure [19] - morpheme segmentation, morphotactics modeling, and orthographic rule (or phonological rule) modeling, must be augmented and extended to cope with the unreliable diphone sequences: 1) The conventional morpheme segmentation is extended to deal with the diphone sequences that have speech recognition errors and between-morpheme phonological changes as well as irregular conjugations during the segmentation, 2) the morphotactics modeling is extended to cope with the complex verb-endings and noun-endings in Korean, and 3) the orthographic rule modeling is combined with the phonological rule modeling to correctly transform the diphone transcriptions (phonetic spelling) to orthographically spelled morpheme sequences.

The central part of the morphological analysis lies in the dictionary construction. In our dictionary, each phonetic transcription of single morpheme has a separate dictionary entry. Figure 4 shows the unified dictionary both for speech and language processing (called morpheme-level phonetic dictionary) with three different morpheme entries ci-wu, l, swu. The extended morphological analysis

phonetic transcription header	original morpheme	left morphological connectivity	right morphological connectivity	left phonemic connectivity	right phonemic connectivity
ci-wu	ci-wu	regular verb	regular verb	'c' sound no-change	'wu' sound no-change
l	l	adnominalizing verb-ending	adnominalizing verb-ending	'l' sound no-change	'l' sound no-change
sswu	swu	bound-noun	bound-noun	's' sound change to 'ss'	'wu' sound no-change

Fig. 4. The morpheme-level phonetic dictionary for ci-wu (delete), l (adnominalizing verb-ending), and swu (bound-noun).

is based on the well-known tabular parsing technique for context-free language [2] and augmented to handle the Korean phonological rules and speech recognition errors in the diphone sequence inputs. Figure 5 shows the extended error-corrective morphological analysis process. The example diphone sequence was obtained from the input speech ci-wul-$sswu$ (meaning: can/cannot be removed), and the morphological analysis produces ci-wu+l+swu (remove+ ADNOMINAL+ BOUND-NOUN), where '+' is the morpheme boundary, and '-' is the syllable boundary. Using the example, each morphological analysis step: morpheme segmentation, morphotactics modeling and phonological/orthographic modeling will be explained in turn. The morpheme segmentation is basically performed using the Viterbi search-based lexical decoding to recover the possible errors in

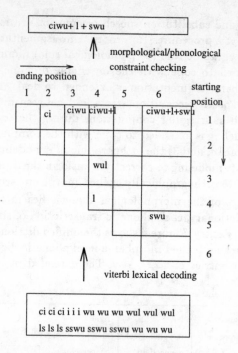

Fig. 5. Morphological parsing of the speech diphone sequences (from top: output morpheme sequence in an *Eonjeol*, triangular parsing table, input diphone sequences). More explanations will follow.

the diphone sequences. For Viterbi search, the phonetic transcription headers for each morpheme in the dictionary are converted into diphone transcription headers, and each converted header is turned into a simple HMM (hidden markov model). The converted HMMs for each morpheme headers are organized into a tree structure for efficient search. The HMMs are the simplest ones which have only left-to-right and self-transitions. Figure 6 shows the tree-structured HMMs for the diphone transcribed morpheme headers. Additional diphone nodes (the dark circles) are deliberately inserted for the inter-morpheme co-articulation modeling. The transition probability in each HMM is defined:

$$a_{ij} = \begin{cases} \alpha & i = j \\ \frac{1-\alpha}{N} & i \neq j \wedge d^t = s_i \wedge d^{t+1} = s_j \\ 0 & \text{otherwise} \end{cases}$$

where a_{ij} is a transition probability from state i to state j, N is the number of all possible transitions from state i. d^t is a diphone observable at time t, and s_i is a diphone at state i. This model assigns self-transition probability α and left-to-right transition probability $\frac{1-\alpha}{N}$. All other transition probabilities are zeros. In each state, the diphone emission probabilities are defined:

$$b_i(k) = \begin{cases} \beta & d_k = s_i \\ \frac{1-\beta}{M} & \text{otherwise} \end{cases}$$

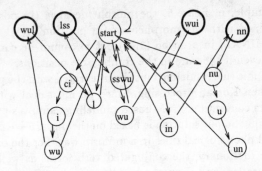

Fig. 6. Diphone transcribed headers for the morpheme *ciwu, l, swu, iss, nun*. In each node, if the path from the root completes a morpheme, a pointer leads to the corresponding morpheme entry in the dictionary. The darker nodes designate the inserted diphones for smooth inter-morpheme co-articulation modeling. The self-transition for each node is left out except the root for figure simplicity.

where $b_i(k)$ is a probability of producing diphone d_k at state i, and M is the number of all the diphones in the model minus one. We adjust α and β experimentally, and the flexible adjustment helps to cope with the insertion and deletion errors in the diphone sequences. The Viterbi search with the tree-structured HMM dictionary headers segments out all the possible morphemes in the given diphone sequences, and we enroll all the segmented morphemes into the triangular table to the proper positions. For example, in figure 5, morphemes such as *ci (carry), ci-wu (delete), l (adnominal verb-ending), wul (cry), swu (bound-noun)* are segmented and enrolled in the table position (1,2), (1,3), (4,4), (3,4), (5,6). The position (i,j) designates the starting and ending position of each morpheme in the given input *Eonjeol*.

After the viterbi lexical decoding, we need to check the morphological and phonological constraints for all the enrolled morphemes in the table, and this process is called morphotactics and phonological modeling. The morphotactics modeling is necessary in order to combine only legal morphemes into an *Eojeol* (Korean word), and the process is performed by morpheme-connectivity checking. Since Korean has well developed postpositions (noun-endings, verb-endings, prefinal verb-endings) which play as grammatical functional morphemes, we must assign each morpheme proper part-of-speech (POS) tags for the efficient connectivity checking. Our more than 300 POS tags which are refined from the 13 major Korean lexical categories are hierarchically organized, and contained in the dictionary (in the name of morphological connectivity, see figure 4). In case of idiomatic expressions, we place multiple-morpheme-expressions directly in the dictionary as a single unit for efficient search, where two different POS tags are necessary for the left and the right morphological connectivity. For single morpheme, the left and the right POS tags are always same. The separate morpheme-connectivity-matrix (sometimes, it is called morpheme-adjacency-matrix) indicates the legal POS tag combinations, so the morphotactics modeling is performed using the POS tags (in the dictionary) and morpheme-connectivity-matrix. For example, in figure 5, the morpheme *ciwu* (in position (1,3)) can be legally combined with the morpheme *l* (in position (4,4)) to make *ciwu+l* (delete+ADNOMINAL, in position (1,4)) but *ci* cannot be combined with *wul* to make *ci+wul* even if they are in the combinable positions.

The orthographic rule modeling must be integrated with the phonological rule modeling in spoken Korean processing. Since we must deal with the erroneous speech inputs, the conventional rule-based modeling requires so many number of rule applications [8]. So our solution is based on the declarative modeling of both orthographic and phonological rules in a uniform way. For the orthographic rule modeling, in our dictionary, the conjugated verb forms as well as the original verb forms are enrolled, and the same morphological connectivity information is applied for both original verb forms as well as the conjugated ones. The phonological rule modeling is also accomplished declaratively by having the separate phonemic connectivity information in the dictionary (see figure 4). The phonemic connectivity information for each morpheme declares the possible phonemic changes in the first (left) and last (right) positioned phonemes in the morpheme, and the phoneme-connectivity-matrix indicates the legal sound combinations in Korean phonology using the defined phonemic connectivity information. For example, in figure 5, the morpheme *l* can be combined with the morpheme *swu* during the morpheme connectivity checking even if *swu* is actually pronounced as *sswu* (see the input in figure 5). The phoneme-connectivity-matrix supports the legality of the combination of *l* sound with *ss* sound. This legality comes from the Korean phonology rule *glotalization* (one form of consonant dissimilation) stating that *s* sound becomes *ss* sound after *l* sound. In this way, we can declaratively model all the major Korean phonology rules such as (syllable-final consonant) standardization, consonant assimilation, palatalization, glotalization, insertion, deletion, and contraction.

3.3 Table-Driven Connectionist/Symbolic Syntax Analysis

The error-corrective morphological analysis produces the morphologically analyzed (segmented and stem reconstructed) morpheme sequences. Since there are usually more than one analysis results due to the errors of speech recognition process, the outputs are usually organized as morpheme lattice. For the seamless integration of the morphological analysis with the syntax analysis, we employ the same table-driven control for the syntax analysis as well as the morphological analysis.

We extend the category formation and functional application rules in the previous categorial unification grammar[24, 20] to deal with the word order variations in Korean:

- if category a $\in$ C, then a $\in$ C'
- if category a $\in$ C', and category set S $\in$ C', then a/S $\in$ C' and a\S $\in$ C'

where S is an unordered set of categories.

- left cancellation: a_i b\{$a_1, a_2, \ldots, a_n$\} results in b\{$a_1, a_2, \ldots, a_{i-1}, a_{i+1}, \ldots, a_n$\}

– right cancellation: $b/\{a_1, a_2, \ldots, a_n\}\ a_i$ results in $b/\{a_1, a_2, \ldots, a_{i-1}, a_{i+1}, \ldots, a_n\}$

The syntax analysis is performed by interactive relaxation (spreading activation) parsing on the categorial grammar where the position of the functional applications are controlled by a triangular table. The original interactive relaxation parsing [7] was extended to provide efficient constituent searching and expectation generation through positional information provided by categorical grammar and triangular table. Figure 7 shows table-driven interactive relaxation parsing. The interactive relaxation process consists of the following three steps

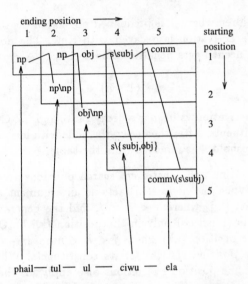

Fig. 7. Table-driven interactive relaxation parsing of a categorial grammar. The input sentence is *phai-l-tul-ul ciwu-ela* (delete the files). Only single morpheme chain and only one sense for each morpheme is shown as input for clear illustration. The *subj*, *obj*, *comm* indicate *np[subj]*, *np[obj]*, *s[command]*, respectively. The table contains only the nodes that participate in the final parse trees.

that are repetitively executed: 1) add nodes, 2) spread activation, and 3) decay.

add nodes Grammar nodes (syntactic categories from the dictionary) are added for each sense of the morphemes when the parsing begins. A grammar node which has more activation than the predefined threshold Θ generates new nodes in the proper positions (to be discussed shortly). The newly generated nodes search for the constituents (expectations) which are in the appropriate table positions, and are of proper function applicable categories. For example, in figure 7, when np\np(2,2) fires, it generates np(1,2). The generated np(1,2) searches for the constituents np(1,1) to be combined with np\np(2,2).

spread activation The bottom-up spreading activation is as follows:

$$n \times \rho \times a \times \frac{a_i{}^2}{\sum_{j=1}^{n} a_j{}^2} \qquad (1)$$

where predefined portion ρ of total activation a is passed upward to the node with activation a_i among the n parents each with node activation a_j. In other words, the node with large activation gets more and more activation, and it gives an inhibition effects without explicit inhibitory links [16]. The top-down spreading activation uniformly distributes:

$$\rho' \times a \qquad (2)$$

among the children where ρ' is predefined portion of the source activation a. **decay** The node's activation is decayed with time. The node with less constituents than needed gets penalties plus decays:

$$a \times (1 - d) \times \frac{Ca}{Cr} \qquad (3)$$

where a is an activation value, d is a decay ratio, and Ca, Cr is the actual and required constituents. After the decay, the node with less activation than the predefined threshold Φ is removed from the table.

The node generation and constituent search positions are controlled by the triangular table. When the node a(i,j) acts as an argument, it generates node only in the position (k,j) where $1 < k < j$, and the generated node searches for the constituents (functors) only in the position (k,i-1). Or when the node is generated in the position (i,k) where $j < k < number - of - morphemes$, it searches for the position (j+1,k) for its constituents. When the node acts as a functor, the same position restrictions also apply for the node generation and the argument searching. The position control combined with the interactive relaxation guarantees an efficient, lexically oriented, and robust syntax analysis of spoken languages.

4   Implementation and Experiments

The SKOPE was fully implemented in UNIX/C platform, and have been extensively tested in practical domains such as natural language interface to operating systems. The phoneme recognition module targets 1000 morpheme continuous speech, currently speaker dependent due to the short of standard speech database for Korean. The unified morpheme-level phonetic dictionary has about 1000 morpheme entries and compiled into a tree structure. The morpheme-connectivity-matrix and phoneme-connectivity-matrix are encoded with the more than 300 special Korean POS (part-of-speech) symbols.

This section demonstrates the SKOPE's performance in continuous diphone recognition, error-corrective morphological analysis, and syntax analysis experiments. For the continuous diphone recognition experiment, we generated about

5500 diphone patterns from the 990 Eojeol patterns (66 Eojeols, 15 times pronunciation) for the training of TDNNs. In the performance phase, the new 2600 test Eojeol patterns (260 Eojeol, 10 times pronunciation) are continuously shifted with 30 msec step, and generate 7772 test diphone patterns disjoint from the training patterns. Figure 8-a shows the continuous diphone recognition performance. The *correct* designates that the correct target diphones were spotted in the testing position, and the *delete* designates the other case. The *insert* designates that the non-target diphones were spotted in the testing position. To compare the ability of handling continuous speech, we also tested the diphone recognition using the hand-segmented test patterns with the same 7772 target diphones. Figure 8-b shows the segmented diphone recognition performance. Since the test data are already hand-segmented before input, there are no insertion and deletion errors in this case. The fact that the segmented speech performance is not much better than the continuous one (93.8% vs. 93.4%) demonstrates the diphone's suitability to handling the continuous speech.

(a) continuous diphones

	total	correct	delete	insert
pattern size (rec. rate)	7772	7259 (93.4%)	513 (6.6%)	3000 (38.6%)

(b) segmented diphones

	vowel group	sub-TDNNs average	total average
rec. rate	94.8%	98.2%	93.8%

Fig. 8. (a) Continuous diphone recognition versus (b) segmented diphone recognition

For the morphological analysis performance, we used the same 990 Eojeol patterns to train the phoneme recognition module, and the 2600 Eojeol patterns to test the morphological analysis performance directly from the speech input. Figure 9 shows the results.

	total	correct	deleted	inserted
number of morphemes	4266	3440 (80.6%)	826	902

Fig. 9. Morphological analysis from continuous speech signals. The table indicates that, among the total 4266 morphemes in 2600 Eojeol patterns, the 80.6% are correctly recognized and analyzed, and 19.4% cannot be analyzed for deletion errors. The 902 spurious morphemes are also generated due to the speech insertion errors.

This experiment shows that most of the morphological errors are propagated from the incorrect (deleted) or spurious (inserted) phoneme recognition results. To see the pure performance of the morphological and syntactic analysis modules assuming no speech recognition error, we artificially made the phoneme lattices by mutating the correctly recognized phoneme sequences according to the phoneme recognizer's confusion matrix. Each phoneme lattice was made to contain at least one correct recognition result, so the phoneme recognition performance is assumed to be perfect except the artificially made insertion errors (mutations). In this way, we made 6 or 7 lattices for each of the 50 sentences, altogether 330 phoneme lattices. The average phoneme alternatives per single correct phoneme in the lattice are 2.3, and average sentence length is 31 phonemes. This means there are average 2.3^{31} phoneme chains in each lattice. The used sentences are natural language commands to UNIX [10] and are fairly complex which have one or two embedded sentences or conjunctions. Figure 10 shows the morphological and syntactic analysis results for these artificially made phoneme lattices. For the syntactic level interactive relaxation, we used the following parameters (which are experimentally determined): upward propagation portion ρ 0.05, downward propagation portion ρ' 0.03, decay ratio d 0.87, the node generation threshold Θ 0.51, and the node removal threshold Φ 0.066.

	total sentences	correctly analyzed sentences
morphological	330	330
syntactic (1-best)	330	117 (35.5%)

Fig. 10. The morphological and syntactic analysis from the artificially made phoneme lattices.

The morphological analysis was perfect as shown in the table. Since the phoneme lattice was made to contain at least one correct phoneme recognition result, the morphological analysis must be perfect as long as the morpheme is enrolled in the dictionary and the connectivity information can cover all the morpheme combinations. This was possible due to the small number of test sentences (50 sentences). This results verify that most of the morphological analysis errors from real speech input are actually propagated from the phoneme recognition errors as discussed before. However, the syntax analysis results are marginal here since we only count the single best scored tree, and we don't use yet any semantic features in the analysis. The syntax analysis failures mainly come from 1) the insertion errors (artificial mutations) in the phoneme lattices[3], which result in ambiguous morpheme lattice, and finally produce redundant syntax trees, and 2) the inherent structural ambiguities in the sentence. These failures should be

---

[3] Recall we generated average 2.3 phonemes per single correct phoneme.

greatly reduced if we generate n-best scored parse trees, and let the semantic processing module select the correct ones.

5 Conclusions and Future Works

This paper explains the design and implementation of spoken Korean processing engine, which is a connectionist/symbolic hybrid model of spoken language processing by utilizing the linguistic characteristics of Korean. The SKOPE model demonstrates the synergetic integration of connectionist and symbolic techniques by considering the relative strength and weakness of two different techniques, and also demonstrates the phoneme level speech and language integration for general morphological processing for agglutinative languages. Besides the above two major contributions, the SKOPE architecture has the following unique features in spoken language processing: 1) the diphones are newly developed as a sub-word recognition unit for connectionist Korean speech recognition, 2) the morphological and syntactic analysis are tightly coupled by using the uniform table-driven control, 3) the phonological and orthographic rules are uniformly co-modeled declaratively, and 4) the table-driven interactive relaxation parsing and extension of the categorial grammar can provide robust handing of word-order variations in relatively free word-order languages. Currently, we are developing applications on top of our SKOPE, including Korean/Japanese speech-to-speech translation system and intelligent natural language interface agent for UNIX operating system.

References

1. M. Agnas, H. Alshawi, I. Bretan, D. Carter, K. Ceder, M. Collins, R. Crouch, V. Digalakis, B. Ekholm, B. Bamback, J. Kaja, J. Karlgren, B. Lyberg, P. Price, S. Pulman, M. Rayner, C. Samuelsson, and T. Svensson. Spoken language trnaslator: first year report. Technical Report ISRN SICS-R-94/03-SE, Swedish Institute of Computer Science and SRI International, 1994.

2. A.V. Aho and J. D. Ullman. *The theory of parsing, translation, and compiling, Vol 1: parsing.* Prentice-Hall, Englewood Cliffs, NJ, 1972.

3. P. Baggia and C. Rullent. Partial parsing as a robust parsing strategy. In *Proceedings of the ICASSP-93*, 1993.

4. M. Bates, R. Bobrow, P. Fung, R. Ingria, F. Kubala, J. Makhoul, L. Nguyen, R. Schwartz, and D. Stallard. The BBN/HARC spoken language understanding system. In *Proceedings of the ICASSP-93*, 1993.

5. Y. Chow and R. Schwartz. The n-best algorithm: An efficient procedures for finding top N sentence hypothesis. In *Proceedings of the second DARPA workshop on speech and natural language*, Los Altos, CA, 1989. Morgan Kaufmann Publishers, Inc.

6. T. Hanazawa, K. Kita, S. Nakamura, T. Kawabata, and K. Shikano. ATR HMM-LR continuous speech recognition system. In *Proceedings of the ICASSP-90*, 1990.

7. T. Howells. Vital: A connectionist parser. In *Proceedigns of the tenth annual conference of the cognitive science society*, pages 18–25, 1988.

8. K. Koskenniemi. Two-level model for morphological analysis. In *Proceedings of the 6th International Joint Conference on Artificial Intelligence*, 1983.

9. K. F. Lee. *Automatic speech recognition*. Kluwer Academic Publishers, Inc., 1989.

10. W. Lee and G. Lee. From natural language to shell-script: A case-based reasoning system for automatic unix programming. *Expert systems with applications: An international journal*, 9(2), 1995 (in press).

11. R. Lippmann. Review of research on neural networks for speech recognition. *Neural Computation*, 1, 1989.

12. W. Menzel. Parsing spoken language under time constraints. In *Proceedings of 11th Europenan conference on artificial intelligence*, 1994.

13. H. Murveit, J. Butzberger, V. Digalakis, and M. Weintraub. Large-vocabulary dictation using SRI's Decipher speech recognition system: progressive search techniques. In *Proceedings of the ICASSP-93*, 1993.

14. M. Oerder and H. Ney. Word graphs: An efficient interface between continuous-speech recognition and language understanding. In *Proceedings of ICASSP-93*, 1993.

15. D. Paul. A CSL-NL interface specification. In *Proceedings of the second DARPA workshop on speech and natural language*, Los Altos, CA, 1989. Morgan Kaufmann Publishers, Inc.

16. J. Reggia. Properties of a competition-based activation mechanism in neuromimetic network models. In *Proceedings of the IEEE first international conference on neural networks*, 1987.

17. Hidefumi Sawai. TDNN-LR continuous speech recognition system using adaptive incremental TDNN training. In *Proceedings of the ICASSP-91*, 1991.

18. N. Sharkey. *Connectinist natural language processing: Readings from connection sciencee*. Intellect: Oxford, UK, 1992.

19. R. Sproat. *Morphology and computation*. The MIT Press, 1992.

20. H. Uszkoreit. Categorial unification grammars. In *Proceedings of the COLING-86*, pages 187–194, 1986.

21. A. Waibel, T. Hanaazawa, G. Hinton, K. Shikano, and K. Lang. Phoneme recognition using time-delay neural networks. *IEEE Transactions on Acoustics, Speech and Signal Processing*, 37(3):328 – 339, 1989.

22. A. Waibel, A. Jain, A. McNair, J. Tebelskis, L. Osterholtz, H. Saito, O. Schmidbauer, T. Sloboda, and M. Woszcayna. JANUS: Speech-to-speech translation using connectionist and non-connectionist techniques. In Moody, Hanson, and Lippman, editors, *Advances in neural information processing systems 4*. Morgan Kaufmann, 1992.

23. S. Wermter and V. Weber. Learning fault-tolerant speech parsing with SCREEN. In *Proceedings of the AAAI-94*, 1994.

24. H. Zeevat. Combining categorial grammar and unification. In Reyle and Rohrer, editors, *Natural language parsing and linguistic theories*, pages 202–209. 1988.

Integrating Different Learning Approaches into a Multilingual Spoken Language Translation System*

P. Geutner[1], B. Suhm[2], F.-D. Buø[1], T. Kemp[1], L. Mayfield[2],
A. E. McNair[2], I. Rogina[1], T. Schultz[1], T. Sloboda[1],
W. Ward[2], M. Woszczyna[1] and A. Waibel[1,2]

[1] Karlsruhe University (Germany)
[2] Carnegie Mellon University (USA)
Interactive Systems Laboratories

Abstract. Building multilingual spoken language translation systems requires knowledge about both acoustic models and language models of each language to be translated. Our multilingual translation system JANUS-2 is able to translate English and German spoken input into either English, German, Spanish, Japanese or Korean output. Getting optimal acoustic and language models as well as developing adequate dictionaries for all these languages requires a lot of hand-tuning and is time-consuming and labor intensive. In this paper we will present learning techniques that improve acoustic models by automatically adapting codebook sizes, a learning algorithm that increases and adapts phonetic dictionaries for the recognition process and also a statistically based language model with some linguistic knowledge that increases recognition performance. To ensure a robust translation system, semantic rather than syntactic analysis is done. Concept based speech translation and a connectionist parser that learns to parse into feature structures are introduced. Furthermore, different repair mechanisms to recover from recognition errors will be described.

1   Introduction

Our multilingual spoken language translation system JANUS-2 [2, 3] evolved from the previous JANUS [1] system which was able to process syntactically well-formed read speech within a certain domain and a limited vocabulary of 500 words. JANUS-2 processes spontaneous human-to-human dialogs in a scheduling domain where the vocabulary – depending on the language – may vary between

* Our German recognition engine, developed at the University of Karlsruhe, is part of the VERBMOBIL project and VERBMOBIL systems developed under BMBF funding. The Spanish speech translation module has been developed at Carnegie Mellon University under project ENTHUSIAST funded by the US Government. Other components are under development in collaboration with partners of the C-STAR Consortium.

2000 and 3000 words. The JANUS-2 system provides a framework under which complementary speech translation system components from different projects, like VERBMOBIL [4], ENTHUSIAST and the C-STAR Consortium [5], can be integrated and compared. Currently, English and German spoken input can be translated into either English, German, Spanish, Japanese or Korean output. Work is in progress to add Spanish and Korean as input languages.

We will propose a data-driven learning approach for automatic codebook adaptation based on amount and distribution of data to improve the acoustic models within the speech recognizer. Second, a method for automatically increasing and adapting a phonetic dictionary will be introduced. Moreover, a statistically based approach is combined with linguistic knowledge to create morpheme-based language models. Also a new approach towards robust translation of spoken language will be presented. We briefly describe a parsing and translation approach based on an interlingua text (ILT), where an interlingua is intended to be a language-independent representation of meaning. Besides, the functionality of a connectionist parser that learns to parse into feature structures is shown. Finally, we report on efforts to detect erroneous system output and provide interactive methods to recover from such errors.

2 JANUS Overview

2.1 Data Collection

Data collection to establish a large database of spontaneous human-to-human negotiation dialogs in English and German has started about 18 months ago. In the meantime, several sites in Europe, the US and Asia have adopted the scheduling task under several research projects and funding sources. Since the same calendars and data collection protocols are used the data elicited shares the same domain and procedural constraints.

Table 1 summarizes the current status of data collection. Since scheduling utterances typically consist of more than one sentence, there is already more data available for English scheduling than ATIS [3]. More data collection will establish databases in size at least comparable to ATIS for all languages.

2.2 System Overview

The main system modules are speech recognition, parsing, discourse processing, and generation of target language output. Each module is language-independent in the sense that it consists of a general processor that applies independently specified knowledge about different languages.

The recognition module decodes the speech in the source language into a list of sentence candidates, represented either as a word lattice or N-Best list. At the core of the machine translation components is a language independent

---

[3] The approximately 18000 utterances in English scheduling correspond to some 30000 sentences.

Table 1. Comparison of databases

English Scheduling		
	dialogs	words
recorded	1984	505 K
transcribed	1826	460 K
German Scheduling		
	dialogs	words
recorded	734	158 K
transcribed	534	115 K
Spanish Scheduling		
	dialogs	words
recorded	340	79 K
transcribed	256	70 K
ATIS3		
transcribed	n/a	250 K

representation of meaning (ILT), which is extracted from the recognizer output by the parsing module. As last step, this language independent representation is sent to the generator to be translated into any of the target languages. Figure 1 shows the system architecture.

After parsing, a discourse processor can be used to put the current utterance in the context of previous utterances. Based on the current discourse state, speech and natural language processing system components can be integrated to resolve parsing ambiguities and dynamically adapt the vocabulary and language model of the recognizer.

We explore several approaches for the main processes. We are experimenting with TDNN's, MS-TDNN's [6], MLP's, LVQ [7] and HMM's [8, 15] for acoustic modeling. We are using n-grams, word clustering, automatic phrase detection [9] and morpheme-based approaches for language modeling [17]. Statistically trained skip parsing [10, 11], neural net parsing [12] and concept spotting parsing [13] are being applied for extracting the meaning. Also statistical models as well as plan inferencing for identification of the discourse state [14] are being used. This multi-strategy approach leads to improved performance with appropriate weighting of the output from each strategy.

2.3 Recognition Performance Analysis

The baseline JANUS-2 recognizer can be described as follows:

- *Preprocessing*: LDA on melscale fourier spectrum and additional acoustic features (power, silence)
- *Acoustic modeling*: LVQ-2 or phonetically tied SCHMM, explicit noise models

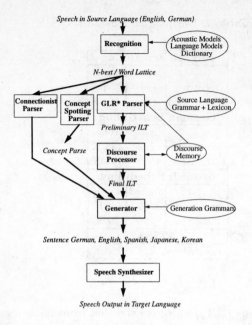

Fig. 1. System architecture

– *Decoder*: Viterbi search as first pass, followed by a word-dependent N-Best search, standard word bigram language model, word lattice output

Current recognition results on the English, German and Spanish Spontaneous Scheduling Task (ESST, GSST, SSST) can be seen in Table 2.

The low absolute recognition accuracies are due to the challenging nature of human-to-human spontaneous speech. Recent evaluations on the Switchboard task confirm that human-to-human dialogs are much more difficult to recognize than human-machine spontaneous speech (like ATIS). Current state-of-the-art systems achieve word accuracies between 30% and 50% on the Switchboard database.

Perplexities range between 35 and 90 for ESST, SSST and GSST, and somewhat over 100 for Switchboard. Additionally, human-to-human dialogs are significantly more disfluent [11]. Large variations in speaking rates and strong coarticulation between words contribute considerably to the difficulty of recognizing human-to-human spontaneous speech.

Table 2. JANUS-2 recognition performance

	ESST	GSST	SSST
Word Accuracy	66%	69.9%	61%

3 Different Learning Approaches

The following three sections will describe efforts and results of improving the recognition component along its major knowledge sources: acoustic models [15], dictionary [16] and language models [17].

3.1 Data–Driven Codebook Adaptation

The performance of a parametric classifier is always dependent on the adequacy of the underlying model assumptions. In speech recognition with HMM-based systems, usually the model assumption for the distribution of the data in feature space is the sum of N multivariate gaussian distributions. Whereas this model assumption can be shown to cover all possible distributions, this holds only if the number of gaussians is chosen correctly. Mainly governed by practical concerns, in most speech recognition systems this number is often chosen to be the same power of 2 for each of the different phonemes that have to be modelled, meaning that a fixed number of codebook vectors is assigned to each of the phonemes. However, as the available training data differs between phonemes, and the size of the feature space covered by the different phonemes varies greatly, constant codebook size leads to suboptimal allocation of resources.

We therefore suggest methods aimed at automatic optimization of the number of parameters for the semi-continuous phonetically tied HMM used in JANUS-2. We have developed [15] two different algorithms to adapt the codebook size of each phoneme according to the amount and the distribution of the training data similar to [18]. Basically, both algorithms start with one gaussian and during training the amount of parameters is incremented until some quality criterion determines when to stop the process of increasing the codebook size. We compared a *variance* criterion based on the average distance between data points and their nearest codebook vector with a *prediction* criterion which tries to capture how well the modeling of the recognizer can predict unseen data.

Table 3 compares recognition accuracies and codebook sizes of the baseline models with models automatically adapted using the variance and prediction criterion. As can be seen, the more efficient parameter allocation when adapting codebook sizes leads to significant error reduction if the same number of parameters is used. Furthermore, the number of parameters can even be reduced by 60% with still better performance than the baseline system.

Table 3. Results for codebook adaptation (GSST)

Model	Codebook Size	Word Accuracy
baseline	4600	66.9%
variance	4201	69.9%
prediction	1677	67.8%

3.2 Dictionary Learning

Due to the enormous variability in spontaneous human-to-human dialogs, creating adequate dictionaries with alternative pronunciations is crucial [19]. However, hand tuning and modifying dictionaries is time consuming and labor intensive. Pronunciations of a word should be chosen according to their frequency and also modifications of the dictionary should not lead to higher phonetic confusability after retraining. Therefore we have proposed [16] a data-driven approach to improve existing dictionaries and automatically add new words and pronunciation variants whenever needed.

The learning algorithm requires transcriptions for the whole training set and a phoneme confusability matrix of the speech recognizer used. First, phonetic transcriptions for all appearances of each word are generated by the help of a phoneme recognizer. Then, variants which are infrequent or which would lead to erroneous training of confusable phonemes are eliminated. Finally, the acoustic models are retrained allowing for the newly acquired pronunciations variants.

As can be seen in Table 4, our algorithm for adapting and adding phonetic transcriptions to a dictionary improves the recognition accuracy of the decoder significantly and, for a context independent recognition system, leads to performance that is comparable to the context dependent results (cf. Table 3). The baseline decoder for these experiments uses 69 context independent phoneme models. Evaluation using context dependent models is in progress.

Table 4. Results for dictionary learning (GSST)

Dictionary	Word Accuracy
baseline	61.7%
adapted	65.6%

3.3 Morpheme–Based Language Models

Comparing various languages like English, Spanish and German, it can be easily seen that German and Spanish differ from English by an outstanding number of inflections and compound words. Due to this fact dictionaries for morphologically rich languages grow much faster with increasing database size, compared to English (cf. Figure 2). One way to limit this growth with an increasing amount of training data is to use smaller base units than words within the recognition process.

Concerning German, three different ways of word decomposition have been evaluated:

1. strictly morpheme-based decomposition, e.g.:
   - weggehen $\rightarrow$ weg-geh-en[1]
     (*to go away*)
   - Spracherkennung $\rightarrow$ Sprach-er-kenn-ung
     (*speech recognition*)
2. decomposition in root forms:
   - weggehen $\rightarrow$ weggeh@
     (*to go away*)
   - Dialoge $\rightarrow$ Dialog@
     (*dialogs*)
3. combination of strictly morpheme-based decomposition and root forms:
   - weggehen $\rightarrow$ weg-geh@
     (*to go away*)

Table 5 shows dictionary size and recognition accuracy using the respective decomposition methods, based on 250 GSST dialogs. As can be seen, all decomposition methods reduce vocabulary size. The impact on recognition accuracy is small, but the morpheme-based approach outperforms the open-vocabulary baseline system. The only small improvement may be due to the fact that the acoustic confusability increases when using smaller recognition units and thus deteriorates the gain in the language model. In a real application, however, this reduction in vocabulary growth leads to a reduction of new words, thus reducing the word error rate, and smaller dictionaries also accelerate recognition speed significantly. Further research will focus on finding more efficient and acoustically less confusable decompositions automatically, and also test the impact on translation.

4 Speech Translation

We are developing various translation schemes like a generalized robust LR parser [10], statistical grammar inference, a concept based translation approach [13] and a connectionist parsing approach [12]. In this paper the two latter will be described.

---

[1] Hyphens are used for clarification purposes as decomposition markers only and do not appear in the actual German spelling.

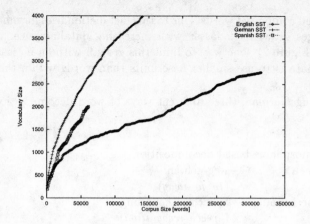

Fig. 2. Vocabulary growth

Table 5. Comparison of decomposition methods (GSST)

	Dictionary	Accuracy
Baseline (closed-vocabulary)	3085	66.9%
Baseline (open-vocabulary)	3062	64.7%
Morphemes	2204	65.8%
Root Forms	3062	63.5%
Combined	2998	65.1%

4.1 Concept Based Speech Translation

The basic premise of the concept based approach is that the structure of the information conveyed is largely independent of the language used to encode it. Our system tries to model the information structures inherent in a task, e.g. the scheduling task, and the way these structures are represented through words in various languages. This system is an extension of the Phoenix Spoken Language System [20]. It uses the Phoenix parser to parse input into slots of semantic frames, and then uses these frames to generate output in the target language.

The Parser. Unlike individual words, semantic units used in a task domain are not language specific. Based on transcriptions of scheduling dialogs, we have developed a set of fundamental semantic units in our parse which represent the different concepts a speaker would use. For instance, a typical *temporal* token could have *date* as subtoken, which could in turn consist of *month* and *day* subtokens. The *temporal* token could be part of a statement of unavailability.

In contrast to previous speech translation systems, we presently don't perform syntactic analysis. Speaker utterances, as decoded by the recognizer, are parsed into semantic chunks which are concatenated without grammatical rules. This approach is particularly well suited to parsing spontaneous speech, which is often ungrammatical and subject to recognition errors. This approach is more robust than requiring well-formed input and the reliance on syntactic cues provided by short function words such as articles and prepositions.

The Generator. The generation component of the system is a simple left-to-right processing of the parsed text. The translation grammar consists of a set of target language phrasings for each token, including lookup tables for variables like numbers and days of the week. When a lowest-level token is reached in tracing through the parse, a target language representation is created by replacing tokens with templates for the parent token, according to the translation grammar. The result is a meaningful, although terse translation, which emphasizes communicating the main point of an utterance. An example is illustrated in Fig. 3.

Original utterance:

  THAT SATURDAY I'M NOT SURE ABOUT BUT YOU SAID
  YOU MAY BE BACK IF YOU THINK YOU'LL BE BACK
  THIS SUNDAY THE TWENTY EIGHTH I COULD SEE
  YOU AFTER ELEVEN AM ON THAT IF YOU'RE BACK

Translated:

Saturday that's not so good for me Sunday the twenty eighth works for me after eleven a.m. (ENGLISH)

El sábado no me va demasiado bien pero el domingo veintiocho me va bien después de las once de la mañana. (SPANISH)

Samstag könnte ich nur zur Not aber Sonntag der achtundzwanzigste geht bei mir ganz gut nach elf Uhr morgens. (GERMAN)

Fig. 3. Translation example

Results. We have implemented this system for bi-directional translation between English, German and Spanish in our scheduling task. Table 6 shows the performance of parser and subsequent generator on transcribed data. Evaluation of the system based on speech decoded by the JANUS-2 recognizer is still underway.

One disadvantage of this approach is the telegraphic and repetitive nature of the translations. This could be overcome by providing multiple translation options for individual tokens in the target language module, different levels of politeness, etc. However, at present we feel that it is sufficient for intelligible communication.

Table 6. End–to–End evaluation on transcribed data

	Parsed from		Translated into
	token	utterance	utterance
English	95.6%	90.0%	90.2%
German	92.4%	89.6%	87.3%
Spanish	88.8%	58.3%	82.2%

4.2 Connectionist Parser

Alternatively to a slot based parser, also a connectionist parser can be used. The major drawback of connectionist parsers, compared with symbolic parsers, has been the lack of detailed linguistic information in the output. We present a connectionist natural language parser that learns to produce feature structures [21, 22, 23], the most frequently used representation scheme in computational linguistics. The most outstanding advantage of this parser is its capability of learning complex feature structures, by automatically splitting the overall problem into several small classification tasks which are learnable (Divide and conquer). Each of these smaller tasks is then learned by a separate backpropagation network, using constructive learning. Constructive learning ensures an optimal network architecture, being as small as possible and achieving the highest possible performance.

Parser principle. The parser consists of three main parts:

1. *The Chunker*, composed of three networks, splits an input sentence into chunks. The first network finds regular expressions, such as numbers. Numbers are classified as being ordinal or cardinal numbers. They are presented as words to the following networks. The next network arranges words to phrases. The third network puts together phrases to clauses. In total, we get four levels of chunks: words, phrases, clauses and sentences.
2. *The Linguistic Feature Labeler* attaches features and feature values (if applicable) to these chunks. There is a classifier for each feature, which finds zero or one atomic value. Since there are many features, each chunk may get none, one or several pairs of feature and atomic values. As a feature normally only occurs at a certain chunk level, the classifier is specialized to decide on a particular feature at a particular chunk level. This specialization prevents the learning task from being too complex.

3. *The Chunk Path Finder* determines how a chunk relates to its parent chunk. It has one classifier per chunk level and chunk path element.

The following English sentence will illustrate the work of the parser:

Can you meet in the morning

The Chunker segments the sentence before passing it to the Linguistic Feature Labeler, which adds semantic labels (shown in **boldface** below):

```
(((speech-act *suggest)
  (sentence-type *query-if))
 ((frame *free))
  ((                              can))
 (((frame *you))
  (                               you))
  ((                              meet))
 ((frame *special-time))
  (                               in)
  (((specifier definite))         the)
  (((time-of-day morning))        morning)))
```

The Chunk Path Finder then adds paths, where appropriate (shown in **boldface**):

```
([]((  speech-act *suggest)
  ( sentence-type *query-if))
 ([]( frame *free))
  ([]([]                          can))
  ([who](( frame *you))
   ([]                            you))
  ([]([]                          meet))
  ([when](( frame *special-time))
   ([]                            in)
   ([](( specifier definite))     the)
   ([](( time-of-day morning))    morning)))
```

Converting this into feature structure, we get the following semantic feature structure (ILT):

```
(((speech-act *suggest)
  (sentence-type *query-if)
  (frame *free)
  (who ((frame *you)))
  (when ((frame *special-time)
         (specifier definite)
         (time-of-day morning)))))
```

Based on this ILT representation, utterances in the target language can be generated.

5 Handling Unreliability

Since a speech translation system involves interaction between two human users, the system should provide methods for adaptive recovery from misrecognitions, miscommunication and mistranslations. First results in this direction are described here.

We have developed a speech interface for repairing recognition errors by simply respeaking or spelling a misrecognized section of an utterance. While much speech "repair" work has focused on repairs within a single spoken utterance [24], we are concerned with the interactive repair of errorful recognizer hypotheses [25].

5.1 Identifying Errors

To be able to repair an error, its location has to be determined first. We pursue two strategies to identify misrecognitions as subpieces of the initial recognizer hypothesis.

The *automatic subpiece location* technique requires the user to respeak only the errorful subsection of the (primary) utterance. This (secondary) utterance is decoded using a vocabulary and language model limited to substrings of the initial erroneous hypothesis. Thus, the decoding identifies the respoken section in the hypothesis. Preliminary testing showed that the method works poorly if the subpiece to be located is only one or two words long. However, this drawback is not severe since humans tend to respeak a few words around the error.

A second technique uses *confidence measures* to determine for each word in the recognizer's hypothesis whether it was misrecognized. First, we applied a technique similar to Ward [26], which turns the score for each word obtained during decoding into a confidence measure by normalizing the score and using a Bayesian updating technique based on histograms of the normalized score for correct and misrecognized words. Since we found this not to work well on our English scheduling task, we are currently developing different methods to compute confidence measures based on decoder, language model and parse scores.

5.2 Robust Speech Repair

After locating and highlighting erroneous sections in the recognizer hypothesis, misrecognitions are corrected.

The *spoken hypothesis correction* method uses N-Best lists for both the initial utterance and the respoken section. The N-Best list for the highlighted section of the initial utterance is rescored using scores from decoding the secondary utterance. Depending on the quality of the N-Best lists, most misrecognitions can be corrected.

The *spelling hypothesis correction* method requires the user to spell the highlighted erroneous section. A spelling recognizer decodes the spelled sequence of letters. By means of a language model we restrict the sequence of letters to alternatives found among the N-Best from the located section.

To date, we have evaluated our methods over sentences from the Resource Management task. Table 7 shows the improvements in sentence accuracy, based on recordings from one speaker of the February and October 1989 test data. We selected a subset of erroneous utterances; therefore the accuracy of the baseline system is significantly lower than the 94% performance our system achieves on the whole test set. The results indicate that repeating or spelling a misrecognized subsection of an utterance can be an effective way to repair recognition utterances.

Table 7. Improvement of sentence accuracy by repair

No Repair (baseline)	63.1%
Respeak	83.8%
Spell	88.5%
Respeak + Spell	89.9%

6 Conclusions

We described JANUS-2, our multilingual spoken language translation system. We introduced different learning approaches that reduce hand-tuning efforts, yield better word accuracy and even accelerate recognition speed. All of these techniques can be applied in several languages and help making significant advances towards building a multilingual translation system for spontaneous human-to-human dialogs. Beyond recognition of spontaneous speech JANUS-2 provides a framework for investigating important areas like robust parsing, machine translation of spoken language and developing methods to recover from recognition and parsing errors.

7 Acknowledgements

The German speech recognition engine was funded by grant 413-4001-01IV101S3 from the German Federal Ministry of Education, Science, Research and Technology (BMBF) as a part of the VERBMOBIL project. The English and Spanish speech translation components were funded in part by grants from the Advanced Research Project Agency, the US Government, Siemens Corporation and ATR Interpreting Telecommunications Research Labs of Japan. We gratefully acknowledge their support. The views and conclusions contained in this document are those of the authors.

References

1. L. Osterholtz, A. McNair, I. Rogina, H. Saito, T. Sloboda, J. Tebelskis, A. Waibel and M. Woszczyna: *Testing Generality in JANUS: A Multi-Lingual Speech to Speech Translation System.* Proc. ICASSP 92, vol. 1, pp. 209-212

2. M. Woszczyna, N. Coccaro, A. Eisele, A. Lavie, A. McNair, T. Polzin, I. Rogina, C.P. Rose, T. Sloboda, M. Tomita, J. Tsutsumi, N. Aoki–Waibel, A. Waibel and W. Ward: *Recent Advances in JANUS: A Speech Translation System.* Proc. EUROSPEECH 93, vol. 2, pp. 1295-1298

3. B. Suhm, P. Geutner, T. Kemp, A. Lavie, L. Mayfield, A.E. McNair, I. Rogina, T. Sloboda, W. Ward, M. Woszczyna and A. Waibel: *JANUS: Towards Multilingual Spoken Language Translation.* DARPA Speech and Natural Language Workshop 1994

4. W. Wahlster: *Verbmobil: Translation of Face-To-Face Dialogs.* DFKI, November 1993

5. C-STAR - Consortium for Speech Translation Research: *Organization and Goals.* Unpublished Notes, München, June 1994

6. H. Hild and A. Waibel: *Speaker-Independent Connected Letter Recognition With a Multi-State Time Delay Neural Network.* Proc. EUROSPEECH 93, vol. 2, pp. 1481-1484

7. O. Schmidbauer and J. Tebelskis: *An LVQ based Reference Model for Speaker–Adaptive Speech Recognition.* Proc. ICASSP 92, vol. 1, pp. 441-445

8. I. Rogina and A. Waibel: *Learning State–Dependent Stream Weights for Multi–Codebook HMM Speech Recognition Systems.* Proc. ICASSP 94

9. B. Suhm and A. Waibel: *Towards Better Language Models for Spontaneous Speech.* Proc. ICSLP 94, vol. 2, pp. 831-834

10. A. Lavie and M. Tomita: *GLR* - An Efficient Noise-skipping Parsing Algorithm for Context-free Grammars.* Proceedings of Third International Workshop on Parsing Technologies, 1993, pp. 123–134

11. B. Suhm, L. Levin, N. Coccaro, J. Carbonell, K. Horiguchi, R. Isotani, A. Lavie, L. Mayfield, C. Pennstein-Rosé, C. Van Ess-Dykema and A. Waibel: *Speech–Language Integration in a Multi–Lingual Speech Translation System.* Workshop on Integration of Natual Language and Speech Processing, AAAI-94, Seattle

12. F.-D. Buø, T.-S. Polzin and A. Waibel: *Learning Complex Output Representations in Connectionist Parsing of Spontaneous Speech.* Proc. ICASSP 94, vol. 1, pp. 365-368

13. L. Mayfield, M. Gavalda, W. Ward and A. Waibel: *Concept-Based Speech Translation*. Proc. ICASSP 95, vol. 1, pp. 97-100
14. C. Penstein Rosé and A. Waibel: *Recovering From Parser Failures: A Hybrid Statistical/Symbolic Approach*. to appear in "The Balancing Act: Combining Symbolic and Statistical Approaches to Language" Workshop at the 32nd Annual Meeting of the ACL, 1994
15. T. Kemp: *Data-Driven Codebook Adaptation in phonetically tied SCHMMS*. Proc. ICASSP 95, vol. 1, pp. 477-479
16. T. Sloboda: *Dictionary Learning: Performance through Consistency*. Proc. ICASSP 95, vol. 1, pp. 453-456
17. P. Geutner: *Using Morphology towards better Large Vocabulary Speech Recognition Systems*. Proc. ICASSP 95, vol. 1, pp. 445-448
18. U. Bodenhausen: *Automatic Structuring of Neural Networks for Spatio-Temporal Real-World Applications*. Ph.D thesis, University of Karlsruhe, June 1994
19. J.-L. Gauvin, L.-F. Lamel, G. Adda and M. Adda-Decker: *The LIMSI Continuous Speech Dictation System: Evaluation on the ARPA Wall Street Journal Task*. Proc. ICASSP 94, vol. 1, pp. 557-560
20. W. Ward: *Understanding Spontaneous Speech: The Phoenix System*. Proc. ICASSP 91, vol. 1, pp. 365-367
21. G. Gazdar, E. Klein, G.K. Pullum, and I.A. Sag: *Generalized Phrase Structure Grammar*. Blackwell Publishing, Oxford, England and Harvard University Press, Cambridge, MA, USA, 1985
22. R. Kaplan and J. Bresnan: *Lexical-functional grammar: A formal system for grammatical representation*. In *The Mental Representation of Grammatical Relations*, pp. 173-281. The MIT Press, Cambridge, MA, 1982.
23. C. Pollard and I. Sag: *An Information-Based Syntax and Semantics*. CSLI Lecture Notes No.13, 1987.
24. C. Nakatani and J. Hirschberg: *A Speech–First Model for Repair Identification in Spoken Language Systems*. Proc. of the ARPA Workshop on Human Language Technology, March 1993
25. A.-E. McNair and A. Waibel: *Improving Recognizer Acceptance through Robust, Natural Speech Repair*. Proc. ICSLP 94, vol. 3, pp. 1299-1303
26. S.-R. Young and W. Ward: *Learning New Words from Spontaneous Speech*. Proc. ICASSP 93, vol. 2, pp. 590-591

Learning Language Using Genetic Algorithms

Tony C. Smith and Ian H. Witten

Department of Computer Science, University of Waikato, Hamilton, New Zealand
Email tcs@cs.waikato.ac.NZ; phone: +64 (7) 838–4453; fax: +64 (7) 838–4155

Abstract. Strict pattern-based methods of grammar induction are often frustrated by the apparently inexhaustible variety of novel word combinations in large corpora. Statistical methods offer a possible solution by allowing frequent well-formed expressions to overwhelm the infrequent ungrammatical ones. They also have the desirable property of being able to construct robust grammars from positive instances alone. Unfortunately, the "zero-frequency" problem entails assigning a small probability to all possible word patterns, thus ungrammatical n-grams become as probable as unseen grammatical ones. Further, such grammars are unable to take advantage of inherent lexical properties that should allow infrequent words to inherit the syntactic properties of the class to which they belong.

This paper describes a genetic algorithm (GA) that adapts a population of hypothesis grammars towards a more effective model of language structure. The GA is statistically sensitive in that the utility of frequent patterns is reinforced by the persistence of efficient substructures. It also supports the view of language learning as a "bootstrapping problem," a learning domain where it appears necessary to simultaneously discover a set of categories and a set of rules defined over them. Results from a number of tests indicate that the GA is a robust, fault-tolerant method for inferring grammars from positive examples of natural language.

1 Introduction

Grammatical inference is the gradual construction of a correct grammar based on a finite set of sample expressions. In general, the training set may contain both positive and negative examples from the language under study. However, in the case of natural languages, it is widely held that children learn a grammar from positive instances alone, and that parents tend not to offer overt correction during the learning process. This proves problematic as it is known to be impossible to infer a correct grammar from positive instances only [5].

Probabilistic approaches offer a solution to this problem by allowing frequent, well-formed expressions to statistically overwhelm the infrequent ungrammatical ones. More precisely, probabilities for word combinations (n-grams) are derived in accordance with their observed frequencies. Parsing from models constructed in this way can thus be made more efficient than standard Phrase Structure Grammars (PSGs), which must treat all possible strings as equiprobable. Examples of frequency-based grammars include Probabilistic Context-Free Grammars

(PCFGs) [2], which assign a probability to each string such that the probabilities of all strings sum to one, and Hidden Markov Models (HMMs) [11, 7], which assign a probability to each string such that the probabilities for all strings of a given length sum to one.

Inductive methods for constructing such grammars derive probabilities for each of their transitions by recording frequencies for n-grams garnered from the training set. As the training set will not contain all possible n-grams of the language, some means for assigning probabilities to unobserved transitions must be incorporated. Solutions to this so-called "zero-frequency problem" usually entail assigning a small but equal probability to all unseen patterns. The result, however, is that ungrammatical n-grams become as probable as unseen grammatical ones.

A further difficulty with such models is that they will assign lower probabilities to transitions involving infrequent words than to those involving more common words of the same syntactic category. For this reason they are unable to take advantage of any lexical properties known to be characteristic of the language.

The extent of these limitations can be reduced by applying frequency analysis to the lexical categories of a tagged text. However, recent work indicates that grammar induction is an instance of a "bootstrapping problem" [4, 13], a learning domain where it appears necessary to simultaneously discover a set of categories and a set of rules defined over them. That is, lexical tagging for the purpose of inferring syntactic structure should not be constrained by existing notions of syntactic categories—the rules and categories must be derived together.

This paper outlines a grammar induction method that incorporates the frequency-based conditioning aspects of probabilistic techniques while supporting the notion of language learning as a bootstrapping problem. The approach uses a genetic algorithm (GA) to adapt hypothesis grammars toward more effective models of the language under study—in this case, English.

Following the approach of evolutionary programming [15], a population of grammars is allowed to evolve for a fixed number of generations before any culling decisions are made. In this way, apparent shortcomings that arise from a single adaptation are given a chance to reveal possible longer term benefits. Grammars are represented as LISP AND-OR s-expressions, and evolution is achieved using standard GA techniques for tree transformations [1]. Individual grammars are selected for reproduction and mutation in proportion to their size. The strength of the population as a whole is measured by its ability to parse the training set.

The GA is statistically sensitive in that the utility of frequent patterns is reinforced during the random selection of tree nodes. The more often a given node can account for substrings within training expressions, the more likely it will persist as a recurring feature in subsequent generations of grammars. Its presence in a large number of candidate grammars thereafter gives it a higher probability of continued selection.

The view that language learning is a bootstrapping process is supported because lexical categories emerge as nodes most efficient at capturing regularities in the training set. For example, an inferred structure in which an OR-node of nouns is followed by an OR-node of verbs is a more efficient generalisation of the combinatoric capacity of these words than is an OR-node whose arguments are all possible sequences combining one noun and one verb. By using grammar size as a measure of fitness, the most simple representation has the best chance of being carried forward into the next generation.

2 Grammar Induction Using Genetic Algorithms

Genetic algorithms are an analogue of natural selection. They adapt principles of reproduction, mutation and "survival of the fittest" to evolve successively better generations of computer programs for a particular task. For grammar induction, the "chromosome" is usually a context-free grammar whose fitness is measured by its ability to cover (i.e. parse, accept, generate, etc.) a training set of sample strings. Reproduction is simulated by dissecting two disparate grammars at suitable, randomly chosen points and joining the first half of one grammar with the second half of the other, and similarly joining the remaining halves. Mutation occurs by changing any single randomly chosen symbol of a grammar with another symbol taken randomly from the set of symbols for the language.

Some effort has been directed towards applying GAs to the inference of context-free grammars. Koza [6] outlined a GA for detecting exons of length 5 within DNA. After 35 generations, the resulting 61-node tree was 100% successful at identifying all exons in a segment of 1000 nucleiotide bases. Wyard [16] devised a genetic algorithm for the language of correctly balanced nested parentheses which successfully inferred a concise correct grammar from 20 test strings in just 3 generations. Wyard also constructed a GA for inferring the more complex language of all strings containing equal numbers of a's and b's, but was unable to produce a successful grammar due to the model becoming stuck in a local maximum.

In developing a genetic algorithm for inferring a context-free grammar description for a more complex language such as English, aspects of prior successful GA models were retained while those of failed attempts were avoided. Koza's successful exon identifier represented a grammar as a logical s-expression using AND, OR and NOT, while Wyard's failed "a-b language" recogniser used the more traditional Chomsky Normal Form (CNF). Many CNF grammars trivially translate into logical s-expressions. For example, the CNF grammar

$$
\begin{array}{lll}
\text{S} & \Rightarrow \text{NP VP} \\
\text{NP} & \Rightarrow \text{Det N} \\
\text{VP} & \Rightarrow \text{V} & \text{NP} \\
\text{Det} & \Rightarrow \text{a} & \| & \text{the} \\
\text{N} & \Rightarrow \text{dog} \| & \text{cat} \\
\text{V} & \Rightarrow \text{saw} \| & \text{bit}
\end{array}
$$

expands to

$$S \Rightarrow \text{Det N V} \quad \text{Det N}$$
$$\text{Det} \Rightarrow \text{a} \quad \| \quad \text{the}$$
$$\text{N} \Rightarrow \text{dog} \| \text{cat}$$
$$\text{V} \Rightarrow \text{saw} \| \text{bit}$$

which has the following equivalent s-expression

(AND (OR **a the**)(OR **dog cat**)(OR **saw bit**) (OR **a the**)(OR **dog cat**))

This representation is not a true s-expression in that the AND symbol is used to indicate catenation, and thus imposes a strict ordering on its arguments. The OR symbol indicates that any one of the operands may substitute for the complete node, and thus imposes no ordering. This representation is used throughout the rest of the paper.

Recursive CFGs cannot be translated to s-expressions in this way, thus our decision to use s-expressions as the representation has certain limitations. However, it is quite difficult to develop an efficient evaluation function for recursive grammars. First, a breadth-first parser would be needed for testing grammars, adding a great deal of additional computation to the evaluation process. S-expressions are easily tested bottom-up, allowing more time for the evolutionary search. Second, simplistic evolution on recursive CFGs permits the constant threat of infinite looping in the form of, say, $S \Rightarrow S$, and thus requires additional constraints in testing for fitness. Because the training set consists of finite length strings, the resulting s-expressions are a clean, simple intermediate representation from which questions about recursive substructure can be addressed at a later time. Furthermore, questions such as whether English allows infinite center embedding (e.g. "the cheese that the mouse that the cat ... chased ate smelled.") or merely embedding to a fixed depth indicate that the issue of a recursive natural language grammar has not yet been fully resolved.

In a further step towards simplification, we limit the set of operators to just AND and OR. It is worth noting that NOT is seldom included in CFG formulations anyway. In addition, n-ary AND and OR expressions are rendered in their binary equivalents to simplify many of the GA functions.

3 The Evolutionary Process

The GA proceeds from the creation of a random population of diverse grammars based on the first sample string. The vocabulary of the expression is added to an initially empty lexicon of terminal symbols, and these are combined with randomly chosen operators in the construction of a candidate grammar. A NULL symbol is also included in the lexicon to support the possibility of optionally omitted constructs within a grammar. If the candidate grammar can parse the first string, it is admitted into the initial population. Figure 1 shows two possible grammars for "the dog saw a cat".

Early experiments in which initial grammars were constructed in a completely random manner often took a considerable amount of time to produce even a

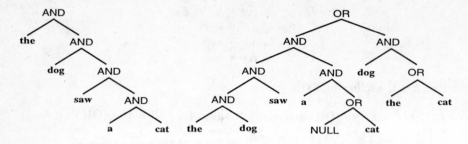

Fig. 1. Two sample grammars for "the dog saw a cat".

single grammar capable of parsing the first expression. Constraints, such as a maximum depth for nesting of randomly constructed nodes, were subsequently placed on the grammar-generator to guide it towards suitable grammars more quickly. Additional simplification steps include the substitution of (OR **x x**) and (AND **x** NULL) with just **x** to preempt unnecessary steps during parsing. Also, in keeping with Mauldin's [8] suggestion for maintaining diversity, duplicate grammars are always removed from the population.

3.1 Reproduction

At each presentation of a new sample string, the GA adds any new vocabulary items to the set of terminal symbols. Two grammars from the existing population are randomly chosen for "sexual" reproduction. Selection is carried out in inverse proportion to a grammar's size. That is, grammars with fewer nodes are given a higher probability than those with a larger number of nodes, under the assumption that smaller grammars are more effective.

A single, randomly selected node from one parent is exchanged with one from the other parent to produce two offspring. If an offspring is able to parse at least one string from the training set it is added to the existing population, otherwise it is discarded. The process is non-destructive so the parents also persist. Figure 2 shows parents and offspring from one reproductive event.

3.2 Mutation

Parallel to reproductive events, another grammar is also randomly selected for mutation. Selection here is done in direct proportion to a grammar's size (i.e. a larger grammar is more likely to be selected than a smaller one) under the assumption that a larger grammar is not adding to the fitness of the population as a whole. Moreover, a larger size indicates the presence of extraneous nodes which further implies a greater capacity to benefit from mutation. A single node is chosen randomly from the grammar. If it is a leaf node, it is replaced with a randomly selected terminal symbol (possibly the NULL terminal) from the lexicon. If it is an internal node, it is replaced with the complement operator.

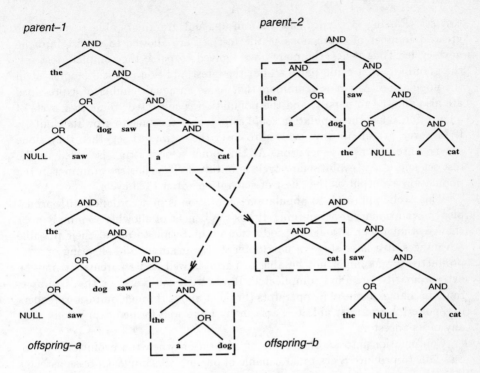

Fig. 2. Reproduction via node exchange.

The mutated grammar is added to the existing population if it can parse at least one of the test strings. Its original form is also allowed to persist.

GAs traditionally assign probabilities to both reproduction and mutation. Mutation is often given a low probability (presumably) to allow the adaptation procedures to play the greater part in dictating the direction of the evolutionary process. The primary function of mutation is to reduce the possibility of becoming stuck in a local maximum, though this is not always successful if culling decisions are made too early. We needed a method of adding newly acquired lexical items into the population of grammars. One option is to simply add a conjunctive representation of the new sentence as a disjunctive option at the root of one or all grammars. However, this was seen as too strong an intervention in the adaptative process. We decided on the more passive approach of allowing new words to be swapped in during a mutation. Because new words would be given the same chance of selection as all other vocabulary items, mutation was allowed to occur frequently so that the population did not flounder too long in its search for a correct grammar.

3.3 Fitness

Adaptation occurs in cycles of a fixed number of reproductions and mutations. After each cycle, all grammars are tested for their ability to parse the existing test set. Parsing is carried out bottom-up, and grammars able to parse the greatest number of expressions in the test set are allowed to persist into the next cycle. Thus if no grammars have evolved to parse the complete test set, the grammars that could parse all but the latest addition will still be present in the population. Any new grammars that parse an equal number of expressions are also allowed to persist, and the population is subjected to another cycle of adaptation. Thus the population could conceivably continue to grow indefinitely. If, however, grammars have evolved to cover the entire test set, then they alone survive into the next generation. At this point a new string is added to the test set and a new evolutionary cycle is initiated. The shortest grammar in the population is output as the "best-of-generation" after each cycle.

This cyclic approach to population adaptation is in accordance with principles of evolutionary programming. It has the benefit of allowing seemingly poor changes that occur through reproduction or mutation to reveal their possible advantages at a later stage of development. For example, the offspring of a reproductive event might not be able to parse as well as its parents. It may be extraordinarily large and complicated. However, it could also be that a simple, random change in one of its operators (brought about through mutation) renders it a powerful grammar able to parse many more well-formed expressions than any of its ancestors.

Continuation into another cycle of adaptation when the evolutionary process fails to produce a grammar capable of parsing all sample expressions helps limit the number of new concepts that must be learned at any one time. Unlike Wyard's algorithm which incorporated partial parses into the fitness evaluation, incremental adaptation ensures the evolution of at least one completely successful grammar before any culling decisions are made.

4 Results

A series of experiments were devised to examine the behaviour of the GA. The first test sought to compare the GA's response to a small subset of English. A population of 10 randomly constructed grammars was generated for the sentence "the dog saw a cat", the best (i.e. smallest) of which was the following 13 node s-expression.

(AND (AND (AND **the dog**)(AND **saw** (OR (OR **cat** NULL) **a**))) **cat**)

The decision to start with 10 grammars is arbitrary, intended merely to avail the algorithm of some initial diversity.

The sentence "a dog saw a cat" was added to the training set and the initial population was allowed to evolve for one cycle of 25 generations. The cycle length was arrived at through trial and error. Successful grammars were often found in one or two generations, but a larger period allowed a wider exploration of the search space and a better chance for the emergence of more efficient grammars.

Five correct grammars resulted from the first cycle, the best of which was

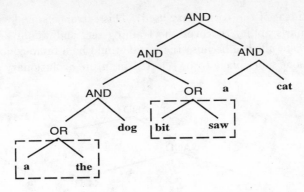

Fig. 3. Lexical categories emerge in OR nodes.

(AND (AND (AND (OR **a the**) **dog**) (AND **dog saw**)) (AND (OR **a
the**)**cat**))

This grammar has grouped the determiners into a single disjunctive node—a
desirable result from a grammar induction system. It has also fortuitously copied
the determiner node into the direct object noun phrase, and thus has inferred a
new string.

The sentence "the dog bit a cat" was added to the training set to see if a similar grouping effect could be achieved for main verbs. The population obtained
from the previous cycle was evolved for another 2 cycles (50 generations) before
it developed any grammars that could parse all three test strings. The best of
the two successful grammars was this 13-node grammar

(AND (AND (AND (OR **a the**) **dog**)(OR **bit saw**))(AND **a cat**))

and its corresponding tree is shown in Fig. 3. As was hoped, the verbs have
emerged within a single node, though the serendipitous determiner node in the
object noun phrase has been lost in the process.

Finally, the sentence "the cat saw a cat" was added to the training set to see
if nouns would also group together. After 3 cycles (75 generations), 22 grammars
evolved that could parse the complete test set. The shortest of these,

(AND (AND (AND (OR **a the**) (OR **bit** (OR **cat dog**)))(OR (OR **bit** (AND
a dog)) **saw**)) (AND **a cat**))

has successfully collapsed the nouns of the subject noun phrase under a single
node. The corresponding tree for this grammar is shown in Fig. 4. From the four
training expressions, four additional well-formed sentences have been inferred:
"a cat saw a cat", "a cat bit a cat", "a dog bit a cat", and "the cat bit a cat".
Even so, two aspects have emerged that weaken the grammar's overall appeal.
First, the word "bit" has been erroneously incorporated into the set of subject
nouns (the fact that consequent sentences might be argued as grammatical is

simply an accident of the vocabulary used). This extraneous node adds nothing to the grammar's ability to cover the training set, and would be removed if enough time were allowed because the result would be a more concise grammar and therefore one more likely to be selected in future evolutionary steps.

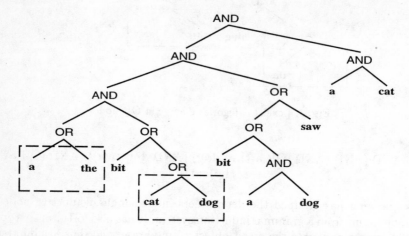

Fig. 4. The grammar after four sample strings.

Second, the direct object noun phrases "a dog" and "a cat" have been distributed between two dissociated nodes. This also is the result of an inadequate amount of evolutionary time, as the seemingly obvious advantage of

$$(AND \; a \; (OR \; dog \; cat))$$

over

$$(OR \; (AND \; a \; dog)(AND \; a \; cat))$$

has not yet emerged. To increase the combinatoric cost of failing to generalise the object nouns, we added the strings "the dog saw a mouse" and "a cat chased the mouse" to the training set in two successive cycles. The best grammar obtained from the additional 100 generations is shown in Fig. 5 and, as expected, the additional complexity of the training set has led the GA toward a more effective generalisation of syntactic components—including the emergence of the $S \Rightarrow NP$ VP general form often used in stochastic context-free grammars for English.

4.1 Robustness

A second experiment was designed to examine the extent to which the order of presentation affects the resulting grammar. Specifically, we wanted to see whether the $S \Rightarrow NP \; VP$ sentence form emerges as a natural consequence of the algorithm and training set irrespective of the order chosen for the sample strings.

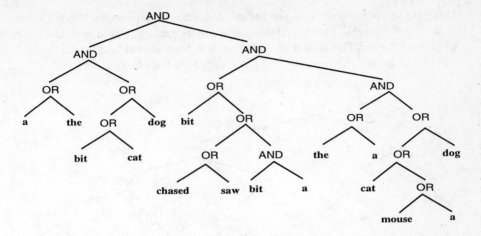

Fig. 5. A $S \Rightarrow NP\ VP$ structure emerges after 6 sample strings.

The training set was reordered in such a way as to create a different presentation sequence while maintaining the principle of minimum information change.

As before, an initial population of 10 grammars was randomly constructed for the first sentence—in this case "the dog saw a mouse". A second sentence, "the dog saw a cat", was added to the training set and, after one evolutionary cycle, two grammars evolved that were able to cover both sentences. A new string, "a dog saw a cat", was added and three grammars were found after three cycles. One cycle was sufficient to find three grammars that could accommodate "the cat saw a cat", while "a cat chased the mouse" required six cycles before a grammar capable of parsing the complete training set was found. Finally, "the dog bit a cat" was added, and after two cycles the following 43 node grammar emerged as the best of the final population.

(AND (AND (AND (OR (OR (OR cat a) mouse) the)(OR (OR cat (OR dog the)) (OR mouse cat)))(OR NULL (OR bit saw)))(AND (OR NULL chased) (AND (OR (OR (OR NULL mouse) a) the) (OR (OR mouse cat) (OR dog the)))))

The nouns, verbs and (to a lesser extent) determiners within this grammar have distilled into their corresponding lexical categories as separate disjunctive nodes. However, the full grammatical structure (too large to depict here) reveals that the verb category has been split between what might be viewed as the noun phrase and verb phrase structures.

Given this cleft category, and the knowledge that the sample strings could be covered by a 23 node grammar[1], we decided to let the population evolve through an additional five cycles without adding anything to the training set.

---

[1] A minimal grammar for the specified training set must have 2 determiners and 2 nouns in the subject noun phrase, 3 main verbs, 2 determiners and 3 nouns in the object noun phrase—giving a total of 12 leaf nodes. The number of internal nodes

This gave the population a chance to find more efficient representations for some of the substructures. Figure 6 shows the 31 node grammar produced after the additional cycles. The split verb category has been united and, apart from 4 extraneous nodes, the desired $S \Rightarrow NP\ VP$ structure has emerged intact.

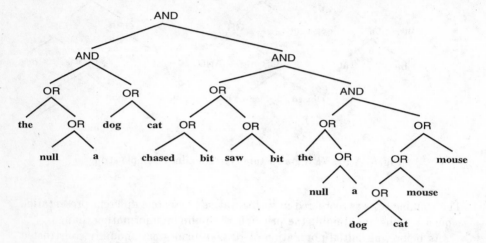

Fig. 6. Various presentation sequences yield $S \Rightarrow NP\ VP$ structure.

4.2 Effectiveness

Earlier, we mentioned that many CNF grammars translate into s-expressions. The reverse is also possible. If we perform this transformation on the grammar shown in Fig. 6, using nonterminal symbols commonly found in natural language PSGs to stand in for some of the expanded nodes, the following rules are obtained.

$$
\begin{array}{lll}
S & \Rightarrow NP1 & VP \\
NP1 & \Rightarrow Det & N1 \\
VP & \Rightarrow V & NP2 \\
NP2 & \Rightarrow Det & N2 \\
Det & \Rightarrow the & \parallel\ null\ \parallel a \\
N1 & \Rightarrow dog & \parallel\ cat \\
N2 & \Rightarrow N1 & \parallel\ mouse \\
V & \Rightarrow chased & \parallel\ bit\ \parallel saw
\end{array}
$$

This description differs in detail only slightly from the grammar presented as an example of CNF earlier in the paper. The redundant nodes have been eliminated from the verb and noun substructures under the assumption that

---

in a binary tree is exactly one less than the number of leaf nodes, thus the minimal grammar has 23 nodes.

binary disjunctions can easily be "flattened" into nodes of arbitrary arity, at which point repeated terminal symbols could be dropped.

The seemingly persistent occurrence of extraneous nodes may be an inherent penalty paid for the over-use of mutation. This could perhaps be remedied if another method for introducing new vocabulary items could be found. In fact, finding an alternate method is not merely desirable but essential. As the size of the vocabulary grows, the probability that any one lexical item is selected during mutation decreases proportionately. Experimentation with larger training sets reveals that while the evolutionary process moves quickly in the earliest stages, when small generalisations produce large payoffs, it is easily bogged down when it must "mutate in" a new terminal symbol obtained by a random probe into a large lexicon.

The discrepancies and limitations brought on by frequent mutation, however, do not necessarily invalidate the grammar itself because

> ... the very elegance and simplicity of [an inferred grammar] is rather more evidence *against*, than evidence for, it being the grammar our brain is built to use ... [since] adaptations are typically *not* maximally efficient engineering solutions to the problems they solve. ([3], pp. 145–146)

That slight perturbations are so often present in inferred grammars, irrespective of the approach adopted for their construction, is the consequence of building a description based on facts rather than speculation or intuition [14]. Grammar induction as a whole seems to be bringing an end to the view that a good grammar will generate all and only the grammatical strings of a language [3].

5   Discussion

Recent years have seen a great deal of interest and activity in developing new approaches to learning for natural language processing. A variety of connectionist models have been devised that are apparently able to learn the underlying structure of a subset of English expressions [12]. While it is often difficult to assess the quality of a model within the resulting multi-dimensional maps, progress towards representation in classical terms is being made [9], and the full benefit of connectionist techniques may gradually become more apparent.

Symbolic approaches have long been the principal methodology for grammar induction. In general, they seek to characterize language structure through basic pattern recognition techniques, and have proven quite useful when applied to artificial languages such as the L-strings of graphics programming [10]. However, repeating patterns of more than four or five words are uncommon in samples of natural language, thus models produced in this way tend to be insufficient for processing novel sentences even when very large corpora are used for training. In addition, unlike connectionist models, frequent patterns do not reinforce the model any more than infrequent ones. Once a concept is learned, it tends to persist unchanged throughout the training period.

Statistical models attempt to circumvent problems arising from novel word patterns by assigning small probabilities to all unseen n-grams. But ungrammatical patterns are consequently viewed as being just as likely as unseen grammatical ones and, because any possible word combination must be assigned some probability, the model eventually degenerates to a complete graph. Even so, this comprehensive nature of statistical models makes them extremely robust when processing novel expressions. In addition, frequently observed n-grams reinforce learned concepts, and the resulting model can greatly assist processing tasks, such as parsing, by directing searches to more likely solutions first.

The GA described in this paper is a compromise between these three approaches. Like connectionism, it is an adaptive process whereby the model is gradually conditioned by the training set. Recurring patterns help to reinforce partial inferences, but intermediate states of the model may include incorrect generalisations that can only be eradicated by continued evolution. This is not unlike the developing grammar of a child which includes mistakes and overgeneralisations that are slowly eliminated as their weaknesses are made apparent by increasing positive evidence.

Like statistical methods, a GA is sensitive to pattern frequency. The more often a learned concept can account for substrings of the sample expressions, the more likely it will persist as a recurring feature in subsequent generations of the model. From an evolutionary programming perspective, the presence of a concept in a large proportion of models in the population also gives it a higher probability of continued survival.

Processors using the grammar produced by this GA do not have explicit access to the frequencies used in its construction and thus are not able to take advantage of this information for processing tasks. The output of the GA is instead a grammar that, as has been shown, is easily translated into the CNF representation typical of symbolic learners. Such grammars can in principle be incorporated into any existing processor that uses CNF grammars.

The current restriction to non-recursive CFGs could be relaxed by allowing nodes to contain pointers to existing substructures in the grammar, though steps must be taken to ensure that the resulting graph is acyclic. Alternatively, persistent nodes could be replaced by nonterminals that point into a pool of useful substructures. Such a pool might even be subject to its own cycles of reproduction and mutation. These, and a number of other possible improvements, are currently being investigated. As it stands, the GA is an effective, fault-tolerant method for grammar induction, one which merits further development.

References

1. Bickel, A. S., and Bickel, R. W. 1987. Tree structured rules in genetic algorithms. In Davis, L., ed., *Genetic Algorithms and Simulated Annealing*. Pittman.
2. Charniak, E. 1993. *Statistical language learning*. Massachusetts: MIT Press.
3. Devitt, M., and Sterelny, K. 1987. *Language and Reality: An Introduction to the Philosophy of Language*. Oxford: Blackwell.

4. Finch, S., and Chater, N. 1992. Bootstrapping syntactic categories using statistical methods. In Daelemans, W. & Powers, D., ed., *Background and Experiments in Machine Learning of Natural Language*, 229–236. Tilburg, NL.: ITK.

5. Gold, E. M. 1967. Language identification in the limit. *Information Control* 10:447–474.

6. Koza, J. R. 1992. *Genetic Programming*. MIT Press.

7. Kupiec, J. M. 1989. Augmenting a hidden markov model for phrase-dependent word tagging. In *Proceedings of the 1989 DARPA Speech and Natural Language Workshop*, 92–98. Philadelphia: Morgan Kaufmann.

8. Mauldin, M. L. 1984. Maintaining diversity in genetic search. In *Proceedings of the National Conference on AI*, 247–250. AAAI.

9. Moisl, H. 1992. Connectionist finite state natural language processing. *Connection Science* 4(2):67–91.

10. Nevill-Manning, C. G.; Witten, I. H.; and Maulsby, D. L. 1994. Compression by induction of hierarchical grammars. In Storer, J. A., and Cohen, M., eds., *Proceedings of the Data Compression Conference*, 244–253. Los Alamitos, California: IEEE Press.

11. Rabiner, L., and Juang, B. H. 1993. *Fundamentals of speech recognition*. Prentice Hall.

12. Rager, J., and Berg, G. 1990. A connectionist model of motion and government in chomsky's government-binding theory. *Connection Science* 2(1 & 2):35–52.

13. Smith, T. C., and Witten, I. H. 1995. Probability-driven lexical classification: A corpus-based approach. In *Proceedings of PACLING-95*.

14. Stich, S. 1980. Grammar, psychology, and indeterminacy. In Block, N., ed., *Readings in Philosophy of Psychology, Volume 2*. London: Methuen and Co. 208–222. reprint.

15. Wijkman, P. A. I. 1994. A framework for evolutionary computation. In *The Third Turkish Symposium on Artificial Intelligence and Neural Networks*.

16. Wyard, P. 1991. Context free grammar induction using genetic algorithms. In *Proceedings of the 4th International Conference on Genetic Algorithms*, 514–518.

A Statistical Syntactic Disambiguation Program and What It Learns

Murat Ersan and Eugene Charniak*

Department of Computer Science, Brown University
Providence, RI 02912-1910

Abstract. We describe a program that uses statistical information on word-usage to perform syntactic disambiguation, and show that the use of this information significantly improves performance. The bulk of the paper, however, attempts to answer the question: what did the program learn that would account for this improvement? We show that the program has learned many linguistically recognized forms of lexical information, particularly verb case frames and prepositional preferences for nouns and adjectives. We also show that viewed simply as a learner of lexical information the program is also a success, performing slightly better than hand-crafted learning programs for the same tasks.

1 Introduction

Work in statistical language processing typically gathers statistics on some aspects of natural language use, applies the statistics to a natural-language task, and then shows that using the statistics improves task performance. Thus such research fits within a broad construction of language-learning work — a program is exposed to some data and improves its performance thereby. From a learning point of view, however, one is left less than completely satisfied: if this is learning, it seems to be of a trivial sort, even though the tasks and programs may be complicated indeed.

Some of the reasons behind the dissatisfaction can be exposed by asking exactly what the program has learned. There are simple answers to this question. Obviously the program learned how to perform some task better; or again, it learned the particular statistical properties of language decreed by the model employed. But these answers seem to beg the question. Is there some non-trivial way to characterize what has been learned?

In this paper we describe a particular program that gathers statistics on word usage and uses these statistics to help syntactically disambiguate sentences. We briefly describe this program and how the statistics help it pick the correct syntactic structure. However, the bulk of the paper is an attempt to give a nontrivial description of what the program has learned. We show that it has learned many of the sorts of lexical facts linguistics knows and loves: verb case frames and noun/adjective prepositional preferences in particular. Furthermore, we show

---

* This research was supported in part by NSF grant IRI-9319516.

that, simply viewed as a learning program, its performance is comparable to or perhaps slightly better than the best special-purpose verb case-frame learner of which we are aware. (We know of no programs for extracting noun/adjective preposition preferences with which to compare our system.)

2 Statistical Syntactic Disambiguation

English sentences typically have many legal syntactic parses. The problem of syntactic disambiguation is picking from these the parse intended by the author. In this section we describe a system for syntactic disambiguation. We keep the description simple because our concern here is not the system per se, but rather what the system learned that made possible its improved performance. See [6] for a more complete description of the program and its underlying theory.

From a statistical point of view syntactic disambiguation is formalized as finding the most probable parse of the sentence. One comparatively simple version of this ideas uses the notion of a probabilistic context-free grammar (PCFG). A PCFG is a grammar in which each rule has an associated probability that is to be interpreted as the probability of using that particular rule given that one needs to expand a constituent of the corresponding type (i.e., the probability of using vp → v np given one needs to expand a vp). The probability of a complete parse in such a system is simply the product of the probabilities of all the rules used in the parse. There are efficient algorithms for finding the parse with the highest probability, and one might then choose that parse as one's best guess for the correct (intended) parse.

Unfortunately, PCFGs serve only to distinguish between common and uncommon constructions. They do not offer much help if things get at all complicated. For example, Figure 1 shows what one of our PCFGs produced as its analysis of the sentence "Speaking to a group of bankers President Reagan said profits rose." While many things are wrong here, let us consider two in particular. First, notice the prepositional phrase (pp), "of bankers President Reagan said profits." A key mistake was to create a pp consisting of the preposition "of" followed by a sentence (the "complement" of the pp). Now some prepositions do take sentences as their complements ("because" is a good example) but "of" hardly ever does so. Unfortunately, our program does not know this. It only knows that in general sentential pp's are less common than nominal ones. Presumably the system would have a better chance of finding the correct parse were it to know, not just the relative probability of pp rules, but their probability for a given preposition, or, as we shall call it, the probability of the rule given the head of the phrase.

Similarly, note in Figure 1 the putative np "bankers President Reagan." We know that while "President" is a plausible modifier of "Reagan," "bankers" is not. Again, if the system knew this it would presumably parse better.

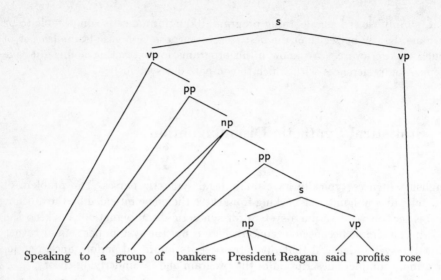

Fig. 1. A sentence badly parsed by a PCFG

2.1 The Model

What we observed in the previous section, then, is the need to augment our PCFG grammar with more detailed lexical information. To do this we devised the system shown in Figure 2. Starting with a body of text (the corpus), we collect statistics on how individual words are used to create the "statistical database." These statistics are then used by a parser to parse new sentences (the "test data") and the "parsing results" tell us how well our new parser works. (For the moment we ignore the lower portion of the diagram.)

Now let us consider in slightly greater detail the kinds of statistics collected in the database. Figure 3 gives a parse for the sentence "Sheep dogs pulled the sleds over rocks." Each constituent, such as the np for "Sheep dogs," is marked with both its part of speech (in this case np) and its *head*. The head of a constituent is the "central" word of the phrase, "dogs" in the case at hand. More generally, the head of a noun phrase is typically the main noun in the phrase, the head of a verb phrase is the main verb, the head of a prepositional phrase is the preposition, etc. So besides the np we just looked at, we see that the head of the verb phrase "pulled sleds over rocks" is the main verb "pulled," while the head of the prepositional phrase "over rocks" is the preposition "over."

In our comments about the parse in Figure 1 we noted that we could have done better had we kept track of the kinds of rule used to expand individual prepositions; to use our new terminology, we want to keep track of the rule used for each possible head of the constituent. Again, when we noted that "bankers" is an unlikely modifier of "Reagan," we were commenting that "bankers" is a poor subconstituent of a constituent headed by "Reagan." Thus our statistics keep track of such things. Figure 4 shows some statistics gathered from the example

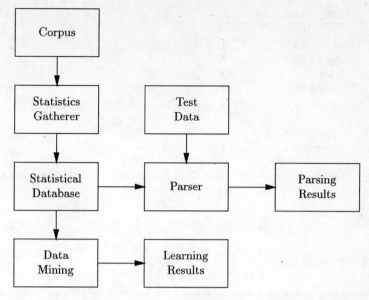

Fig. 2. Gathering, using, and analyzing lexical statistics

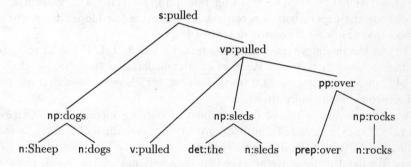

Fig. 3. Phrase marker for "Sheep dogs pulled the sleds over rocks."

in Figure 3. We see there that the preposition "over" is the head of a pp that uses the rule pp → prep np and that the noun "sleds" is a subconstituent of a phrase headed by "pulled." The "count" in Figure 4 indicates how often we have seen the relationship in question. In our example each relation was seen exactly once. When processing a large corpus the counts are summed over all of the sentences.

Actually, things are more complicated than Figure 4 lets on. First, the data collected by this system is more detailed than shown here. For instance, distinctions between subjects and objects of verbs, ignored in our example, are captured in the real data. Also, we have assumed here that there is only one parse for this sentence, while in reality sentences have multiple parses. However, techniques for handling this obstacle are well known (see, e.g., [7]) and we do not go into

Head	Rule/Subhead	Count
pulled		
	s → np vp	1
	vp → v np pp	1
	dogs	1
	sleds	1
	over	1
over		
	pp → prep np	1
	rocks	1

Fig. 4. Portion of the statistics for "Sheep dogs pulled the sleds over rocks."

them here.

2.2 The Experiment

The system was run using data collected by parsing 36 million words of *Wall Street Journal* (WSJ) text provided by the ACL Linguistics Data Collection Initiative (ACL-LDCI). (For more on this data, see [11].) The grammar used throughout the experiment is a context-free grammar developed from work on context-free grammar induction described in [4, 5].

To test the model we used sentences from parsed ACL-LDCI WSJ text, none of which is used in training. We restricted consideration to sentences that use the 5400 most common words from this corpus, which were those that appeared in the corpus 500 or more times.

We take as the principal measurement of parsing success bracket-crossing accuracy (henceforth called simply *accuracy*): the percentage of bracketing found in the model's most probable parse that do not cross the bracketing in the LDCI parses. We like this measure because it is relatively insensitive to disagreements about the structures a grammar should assign. However, we are cognizant of its deficiencies; when used alone it can be made artificially high by certain tricks. Thus to keep ourselves honest we also report *recall*: the percentage of bracketing found in the LDCI parse that were also in the model's most probable parse. However, we judge the significance of the results solely in terms of the accuracy measure.

We compare these measures for three models:

1. The full model as described earlier ("complete")
2. The model using only the PCFG probabilities ("PCFG")
3. A model assuming uniform right-branching parses ("right branching").

In a right-branching model each word is assumed to start a new constituent that ends at the end of the sentence, e.g., (The (girl (went (to (the park)))))), which has an accuracy of .75. English is close to being completely right branching, so "right branching" is generally considered a good "dumb" benchmark.

The major parsing results are shown in Table 1. The picture painted by these figures is reasonably clear. While assuming pure right branching only gives an accuracy of only 57.2%, we get 84.9% accuracy for a PCFG using none of the word statistics, and 91.1% accuracy for the model using all of our statistical information. This latter figure represents a 41.1% reduction in the number of bracket-crossing errors when compared to the pure PCFG. This is consistent with other work using statistics on lexical information such as [1, 9].

Table 1. Syntactic disambiguation results

Probability Model	Percent Accuracy	Error Reduction	Percent Recall
Complete	91.1	41.1	80.8
PCFG	84.9		76.1
Right Branching	57.2		67.2

3 Verb Case Frames

We now turn to the question of what the system described above actually learned. We took as our initial hypothesis that it had, in fact, learned at least some of the lexical information commonly of interest in linguistic discussions. To test this hypothesis we applied "data-mining" techniques to the statistical database that drove the parsing system, as outlined in Figure 2. That is, if the system had in fact learned this information, it ought to be reasonably easy to extract it from the statistical data already extant. Or, to put it another way, we ought to be able to reuse our system as an automatic collector of lexical information.

In our first experiment we attempted to collect verb case-frame information automatically from our data. Verb case frames are defined as the types of syntactic arguments a verb can take. These syntactic arguments can be in the form of objects, prepositional phrases, infinitives, etc. For example, the verb *abandon* is followed either by a noun phrase or by a noun phrase and a prepositional phrase.

Yesterday they abandoned the project. (Case frame: np)
He abandoned himself to despair. (Case frame: np_p)

There have already been a few attempts at learning verb case frames from corpora. Brent [2, 3] has tried to extract this information from both untagged and tagged corpora. Similarly, Manning [10] generated case-frame lists for verbs from untagged corpora. To make our results compatible, we tried to follow Manning whenever possible. In particular, since different dictionaries supply different kinds of case frames for verbs, we used the verb case frames Manning used as specified in Table 2.

Table 2. The sixteen verb case frames employed in our system

Number	Case Frame	Explanation
1	iv	Intransitive verb
2	np	Transitive verb
3	dtv	Ditransitive verb
4	that	That complement
5	np_that	Object followed by that complement
6	wh	Wh-clause complement
7	np_wh	Object followed by wh-clause
8	inf	Infinitive complement
9	np_inf	Object followed by infinitive
10	ing	-ing participle complement
11	np_ing	Object followed by -ing participle
12	adj	Adjective used as a complement
13	np_adj	Object followed by adj complement
14	adj_inf	Adj complement followed by inf
15	p	Prepositional phrase
16	np_p	Object followed by a preposition

3.1 Identification of Case Frames

The system first identifies the verbs, next gathers the statistics on various case frames, and finally identifies which case frames for a verb appear to be statistically significant.

Because we parse the corpus, we can identify a word as a verb if it is the head of a verb rule (i.e. a rule that expands a verb phrase vp.) This is a straightforward and simple procedure when compared with Brent's technique for verb detection by which anything that occurs both with and without the suffix -ing in the text is considered a potential verb, and if a potential verb is not preceded by a determiner or a preposition other than *to*, it is taken as a verb.

The grammar used to parse the WSJ corpus contains 1209 rules for expanding verb phrases. These rules are mapped into our verb case frames. The verb rules that contain adverbs are treated as if they contained no adverbs, e.g. the rule vp → v adv pp is mapped to the case frame in which a verb takes a prepositional phrase, i.e. p. If a rule contains punctuation marks or connecting words such as "and", only the part of the rule up to the punctuation mark or connecting word is taken into consideration, e.g. the rule vp → v np and vp is classified as a transitive verb rule. Because our case frames do not have anything after a preposition, the verb rules having nonterminals after a preposition are treated as if the preposition were the last nonterminal of the rule. Pronouns that appear in the rules are considered nouns, e.g. the rule vp → v pron np is mapped to the rule vp → v np np, i.e. ditransitive. Finally, some rules cannot be associated with our case frames, because of either the complexity of the rules or errors in the grammar. The probability mass of these rules, however, is less than 2% of all the rules.

We then go through our statistical data looking at each rule associated with a particular verb, as in Figure 4. If we have been able to associate that rule with a particular case frame, the count for that rule is added to the count for the appropriate verb/case-frame pair. When all of the statistics for a particular verb have been processed, the data is filtered to determine which case frames appear to be statistically significant.

3.2 Filtering

Some of the case frames identified by our program are the actual case frames of the verb, while some are wrong ones due to a mistake in the tagger or parser or to other causes, such as prepositional phrases that are not actual arguments of the verb. So the raw results have to be filtered and the actual case frame assignments distinguished from the wrong ones.

The filtering method used here is the one proposed by Brent [2]. This method assumes that B_s is the estimated upper bound on the probability that the program assigns a wrong case frame to a verb token. Assume that a verb occurs m times in a corpus, and n of those times is classified as having a certain case frame. The B_s values are used to calculate the probability that all these n assignments are wrong. This probability is bounded by

$$\sum_{i=n}^{m} \binom{m}{i} B_s^i (1 - B_s)^{m-i} \tag{1}$$

In our case, n indicates the counts for each case frame, m is the total number of occurrences of the verb assigned to any case frame, and $\binom{m}{i}$ is the i-combination of m elements.

If the probability that all n assignments are false is low, then the probability that at least one of them is correct is high. So if the above sum is less than some confidence level (in our system $C = 0.02$) then we assume that the case-frame assignment is correct.

Each case frame has its own B_s value, since the probability that a case-frame assignment is wrong changes from frame to frame. For example, the tagger and parser we used are more likely to make mistakes that generate extra p frames than any other frame. All the B_s values have been set empirically.

3.3 Evaluation

The *Oxford Advanced Learner's Dictionary* (OALD) [8] is used for testing the results of the program. The case frames learned by the program and the case frames in OALD do not have a direct correspondence, so OALD's 51 case frames are mapped into our 16 case frames. Then the machine-readable version of OALD is used to extract all the verbs and their case frames automatically. That version of OALD has separate entries for the different forms of verbs (e.g., abandon, abandoned, abandoning, and abandons), so each verb form that appears in our data can be directly compared to the dictionary.

The comparison program outputs, for each verb in our data, the correct case frames that our system generated, the extra ones (those not in the OALD but generated by our program) and the missing ones (those in OALD but not generated by our program).

Our system can be evaluated using two kinds of measurements: *precision*, the ratio of the correct case frames generated by our system to all the case frames generated by our system, and *recall*, the ratio of the correct case frames generated by our program to all the case frames the dictionary supplies. Among the most common verbs of the WSJ corpus, 30 were chosen randomly to be used in the evaluation. These verbs are different from those used by Manning, because the contexts of the corpora are different.

Table 3. Comparison with previous verb-case-frame work

	precision (%)	recall (%)
combined verb forms	92	52
original program	87	58
Manning's system	90	43

We achieved 87% precision and 58% recall. As mentioned previously, different forms of a verb are evaluated separately. Then the information about them is combined. To do this, we first grouped the different forms of every verb. Next, for each group the aggregate rule counts were calculated. As seen in Table 3, this had the effect of increasing precision and decreasing recall. What happened, intuitively, is that combining verb forms increased the number of times we saw any particular verb so the number of times we needed to see a case frame went up as well. It seems that many case frames were only observed in one (or a few) forms of the verb and these were deleted by the binomial filter.

Table 3 compares the results of our system to those generated by Manning. It can be seen that both systems achieve almost the same precision, and our system has slightly better recall. Brent's systems, on the other hand, was able to learn only six case frames (np, dtv, that, np_that, inf, np_inf). Table 4 shows the case frames our system generated for the group of verbs used in the evaluation: the table lists the number of correct case frames generated by our program, the number of wrong case frames, and the number of case frames of the verb. Additionally, the final column shows the incorrect case frames generated by our program.

4 Prepositions

The grammatical rules of English require particular prepositions after particular nouns and adjectives, some of which are obligatory and some optional. Examples of these kinds of noun-preposition and adjective-preposition pairs are: "frontier between", "head of", "interested in", "glad about", etc. We tried to determine

Table 4. Comparison of verb case frame results with OALD

Verb	# Right	# Wrong	Out of	Wrong case frames
abandon	2	0	2	
admit	3	1	7	iv
agree	2	0	5	
aim	1	0	5	
announce	2	0	3	
ask	4	0	9	
calculate	3	0	5	
decide	4	0	8	
delay	3	1	4	np_p
determine	3	0	7	
employ	1	1	2	p
engage	2	0	7	
fear	3	0	6	
gain	2	1	5	np_inf
hear	5	0	9	
join	3	0	4	
learn	3	0	7	
look	2	0	7	
make	4	0	9	
measure	3	1	4	wh
pick	2	0	3	
plunge	2	0	4	
prepare	3	0	4	
project	3	0	4	
provide	2	0	4	
retire	3	0	3	
rise	1	2	3	np, np_inf
study	3	0	6	
watch	5	0	8	
withdraw	3	0	4	
TOTAL	82	7	158	

both obligatory and optional prepositions, though not the distinction between obligatory and optional.

The program that finds obligatory or optional prepositions attached to nouns starts by identifying the prepositions and nouns. We identify nouns as words that head noun rules, and similarly for prepositions. As mentioned previously, we already have the information about which preposition is attached to which word in the corpus. (Figure 4 shows the preposition "over" as attached to the verb "pulled." The principle is the same for prepositions attached to nouns and adjectives.) Using this information, we find the prepositions attached to each noun and their counts. Next this raw data is filtered to get rid of the rare prepositions and errors that could have occurred during the tagging and parsing process.

The filter used at this stage is the same as the one used in filtering verb case frames, i.e., the binomial filter. However, this time all prepositions are assigned the same B_s value, 0.01. This value is found experimentally. In the binomial filter m is the number of total occurrences of a particular noun and n is the number of times it appears with a specific preposition. Those that pass the filter are considered correct noun-preposition pairs.

The same procedure is followed to determine the prepositions for adjectives.

4.1   Evaluation

To evaluate the results of the programs, a group of nouns and adjectives was chosen randomly among the most common nouns and adjectives that take prepositions. This time, however, the evaluation was done by hand, since no on-line source on this type of prepositional information could be found. We used the OALD (which does not have the information on prepositions on-line) to evaluate our results. A problem arose in the evaluation because the dictionaries were not concise and complete in listing the prepositions that can be used with nouns and adjectives; instead the dictionary lists prepositions that can be attached to the nouns but in example sentences new prepositions are introduced. Also, some prepositions that we believe correct do not appear in the dictionary: e.g. price *of*, offer *of*, house *of*. Therefore we make two different evaluations: one takes into account only those prepositions that appear in the dictionary, and another (called *self evaluation*) also allows those prepositions we believe correct. Table 5 displays the precision and recall for both nouns and adjectives.

Table 5. Precision and recall according to the dictionary and self evaluation

	precision (%)	recall (%)
self evaluation (nouns)	87	55
dictionary evaluation (nouns)	70	45
self evaluation (adjs)	80	71
dictionary evaluation (adjs)	65	67

We believe that a high precision for both nouns and adjectives has been achieved. Tables 6 and 7 display our results on the small set of nouns and adjectives used in the evaluation. In these tables we show for each noun/adjectve the number of correct (as judged by the self-evaluation method) prepositions generated by our program, the number and types of wrong prepositions generated by our program, and the toal number of prepositions for the word. The prepositions that do not appear in the dictionary but were classified as correct in the self-evaluation results are listed in the final column.

5 Conclusion

We described a system that learned to better determine the correct parse of a sentence by parsing a large amount of text and gathering statistics on the properties of particular lexical items. The use of these statistics resulted in a 41% decrease in the number of parsing errors.

We then looked more closely at exactly what the system had learned by collecting these statistics and found that it had, at least in part, learned many of the lexical relations that linguists consider important. In particular, we looked at the statistical database produced by the original system and extracted from it verb case-frame information. The resulting data is comparable to that provided by special-purpose systems for collecting this data. We also extracted data on the prepositions used by various nouns and adjectives. In this case we did not have a prior hand-written system against which we could compare, but the results seem convincing nevertheless.

References

1. Bod, A. Rens, Using an annotated language corpus as a virtual stochastic grammar. In *Proceedings of the Eleventh National Conference on Artificial Intelligence*, Menlo Park: AAAI Press/MIT Press (1993) 778-783
2. Brent, Michael R., Automatic acquisition of subcategorization frames from untagged text. In *Proceedings of the 29th Annual Meeting of the Association for Computational Linguistics* (1991) 209–214
3. Brent, Michael R. and Berwick, R. C., Automatic acquisition of subcategorization frames from tagged text. In *Proceedings of the 4th DARPA Speech and Natural Language Workshop* (1991) 342–345
4. Carroll, Glenn and Charniak, Eugene, Two experiments on learning probabilistic dependency grammars from corpora. In *Workshop Notes, Statistically-Based NLP Techniques*, AAAI (1992) 1-13
5. Charniak, Eugene and Carroll, Glenn, Context-sensitive statistics for improved grammatical language models. In *Proceedings of the Twelfth National Conference on Artificial Intelligence*, Menlo Park: AAAI Press/MIT Press (1994) 728-733
6. Charniak, Eugene, *Parsing with context-free grammars and word statistics.* Technical Report CS-95-28, Department of Computer Science, Brown University (1995)
7. Charniak, Eugene, *Statistical Language Learning.* Cambridge: MIT Press (1993)
8. Hornby, A. S., *Oxford Advanced Learner's Dictionary of Current English.* Oxford: Oxford University Press. 3rd ed. (1985)
9. Magerman, David M., Statistical decision-tree models for parsing. In *Proceedings of the 33rd Annual Meeting of the Association for Computational Linguistics* (1995) 276-283
10. Manning, Christopher D. Automatic acquisition of a large subcategorization dictionary from corpora. In *Proceedings of the 31st Annual Meeting of the Association for Computational Linguistics* (1993) 235-242
11. Marcus, Mitchell P., Santorini, Beatrice, and Marcinkiewicz, Mary Ann, Building a large annotated corpus of English: the Penn treebank. In *Computational Linguistics* **19** (1993) 313-330

Table 6. Comparison of noun-preposition couples with OALD

Nouns	# Right	# Wrong	Out of	Wrong prepositions	Assumed correct
account	1	1	3	for	
acquisition	2	0	2		
agreement	2	0	5		on
amount	1	0	1		
bank	2	0	2		in
bid	1	0	2		
board	1	0	1		
business	2	0	4		in
chairman	1	0	1		
companies	3	1	3	that	in
control	1	0	3		
court	2	0	2		in
decline	2	0	2		
demand	2	0	3		
exchange	2	1	3	in	
group	1	0	1		
growth	2	0	2		
head	1	0	5		
index	1	0	1		
line	3	0	6		
lot	1	0	3		
market	2	0	2		
meeting	3	0	4		in, with
member	1	0	1		
number	1	0	2		
offer	2	0	2		
operations	2	0	3		in
part	1	0	2		
president	1	0	1		
price	3	0	4		in
quarter	1	1	1	from	
sale	2	0	3		in
share	2	1	3	from	
stake	1	0	2		
unit	1	1	1	in	
value	1	1	3	at	
TOTAL	47	7	86		

Table 7. Comparison of adjective-preposition couples with OALD

Adjective	# Right	# Wrong	Out of	Wrong prepositions	Assumed correct
adequate	1	0	2		
afraid	1	0	2		
available	2	0	3		
aware	1	0	2		
capable	1	0	1		
cautious	1	1	2	in	
compatible	1	0	1		
consistent	1	0	1		
different	3	0	4		in
difficult	1	0	1		
due	1	1	3	out	
eager	1	1	1	in	
enthusiastic	1	0	2		
familiar	1	0	2		
fearful	2	0	2		
guilty	1	1	2	in	
highest	3	1	3	for	of, since, in
impossible	1	0	2		
larger	2	0	2		of, than
responsible	1	0	1		
same	1	2	1	for,in	
skeptical	2	0	2		
suitable	1	0	2		
typical	1	1	1	in	
TOTAL	32	8	45		

Training Stochastic Grammars on Semantical Categories

Wide R. Hogenhout and Yuji Matsumoto

Nara Institute of Science and Technology, 8916-5 Takayama-cho, Ikoma-shi, Nara 630-01, Japan

Abstract. The evaluation of systems that parse natural language, on the basis of a score like bracketing accuracy or sentence accuracy, on an unseen text is becoming an important issue in grammar building and parsing. The statistical induction of grammars and the statistical training of (hand written) grammars are ways to attain or improve a score, but a stochastic grammar does not reflect the often stereotypical use of words depending on their semantical categories, often referred to as selectional restrictions or semantical patterns.

We present an algorithm that collects probabilities reflecting the way semantical categories are interacting with the rules of the grammar, combining the probability of a grammar rule and the probability of a semantical class. This method does not depend on any specific grammar or set of semantical categories, so it can be used on (almost) any existing system. We present experimental results that show our method gives a considerable improvement over regular stochastic grammars.

1 Introduction

In recent years there is an increasing interest in evaluation methods for natural language parsers, and the bracketing accuracy, sentence accuracy (Viterbi score) or other scores on an unseen test set from a corpus is becoming more and more important, see for example [2, 18]. This has stimulated a new approach to grammar building: building the grammar by hand, based on a corpus, and training it statistically. For example, the project described in [3] is based on this method, making the Viterbi consistency the main criterion for changes to the grammar. Another approach which has recently been receiving attention is grammar induction, see for example [33].

At the same time many practical natural language systems use 'semantical patterns' or 'selectional restrictions' to resolve syntactical ambiguities. These terms are basically different ways of saying that words are more likely to appear in a certain context, for example most types of machines are a likely object of *to switch on*, but not a likely object of *to write*. Being able to do this automatically has proved to be very important in practical systems, because working out such knowledge by hand is extremely labour-intensive and therefore expensive. Furthermore, this is a major hurdle when porting a system to a new domain.

In [17] a method is presented for automatic acquisition of such 'semantical patterns'. The idea is that phrases like *John eats a cake* are translated to patterns like (human,subject,consume) and (food,object,consume), which can be of help in syntactical disambiguation. This is not a statistically based method, finding the probabilities for all possible patterns, but one that produces a list of patterns without probabilities. A problem with this method is the limited size of the list that was produced. Also, the method only produces the tuples and does not indicate how to apply them. Many sentences have more than one ambiguity, so these patterns have to be combined in some way.

We have developed an algorithm that automatically collects statistical data about the way semantical categories are used in relation to a grammar. Starting from a grammar, which has been build by hand, and a classification of the words used in the corpus, the algorithm collects probabilities for the semantical classes, or to be more exact the probability that a word from a certain class will be used at a certain point in the analysis of a sentence.

The same algorithm can be used for grammar induction, but the experiments we present in this paper relate to the training of a hand-written grammar.

As for the patterns we use, you can think of the same sort of relations (verb-subject, etc.) as the earlier example, but consider the following sentence from the LOB corpus [22, 23] :

When shortage of labour is one of the main checks on our scope
for increasing output rapidly, the case for making separate
assessments seems particularly strong.

One of the problems here is that the word *rapidly* may be attached to *increasing* and to *is*. This is the same ambiguity as in the sentence *He told me to do it rapidly*, where it is not clear whether the speaking was rapid or something should be done rapidly.

We counted 84 occurrences of the adverb *rapidly* modifying a verb, and of those 84 occurrences 7 are with the verb *to increase* (8.3%), against zero for the verb *to be*. Since we are interested in working with semantical categories, we replaced the verbs with their category in the 1000 bottom categories of Roget's Thesaurus. Now the effect becomes even stronger: of all occurrences 50% are covered by 6 categories, and the category that *to increase* falls into in the example above, covers 22.6%. We will show how to obtain such (or similar) information automatically, and how to apply it when a sentence contains many ambiguities.

We would like to emphasize that this method does not only cover adverbs. We collect general statistics on the occurrence of semantical classes for nonterminals in the grammar, which relates to all possible sorts of ambiguity.

2 The Patterns

The algorithm works on a context free grammar, on which we impose no restrictions. (Later we will discuss the possibility of imposing a particular restriction.) Using this a *head* should be selected for every left-hand-side nonterminal in the grammar. For rules leading to a terminal this is easy; we simply take the semantical category of the word as the head. For all other rules it is necessary to indicate which head of the right-hand-side nonterminals is selected as head for the left-hand-side nonterminal. For example the rule $VP \to \underline{VP} \quad PP$ indicates that the verb phrase on the left selects the head of the underlined verb phrase as it's own head. Thinking of the parse tree, every node selects the head of one of it's children as it's own head. We do not put any conditions on which nonterminal should select which head, so the grammar builder can make the choice that gives the best results.

The next step is to make an identifier (say a number) for all rules in the grammar and for the semantical categories. If the rule above has number 132, we could find the pattern (132,#person,#eat), where #person and #eat indicate the category for *person* and *to eat* respectively.

3 The Algorithm

The algorithm we use is based on the Inside Outside Algorithm. We will not discuss the Inside Outside Algorithm or give any proofs here, for a good introduction to these techniques in natural language processing see [6] or [3]. In a nutshell, we replace the probability of a rule with the probability of a pattern, consisting of a rule and certain semantical categories.

This algorithm can be combined easily (and efficiently) with chart parsing, see [24], and we will assume it is in this article. We will therefore give the equations in terms of edges (from the chart) rather than nonterminals. Every edge must contain the number of the applied rule, and the head-categories of the edges that were used to produce it. It also indicates which head-category is selected as the head-category of the edge itself. Together with the usual information (nonterminal and position in sentence) this contains a pattern as we described it.

When reading the equations, note that the notions of inside probability and outside probability relate to edges rather than nonterminals. This is caused by the possibility of (unresolved) multiple word senses, which cause different edges. This means it is possible that two edges are covering the same fragment and have the same nonterminal, but are not the same because they have different head-categories.

3.1 Notation

We number the rules in the grammar and we write rule number x as R_x. When the left hand side nonterminal of rule x is p we write R_x^p. We also distinguish the edges by numbering them and write edge number k as e_k. When edge e_k was produced with rule x we write e_k^x. If edge e_k was produced with rule x and received head-categories $A = (a_1, a_2, ..., a_n)$ we write $e_k^{x,A}$. Note that n is usually not higher than 2.

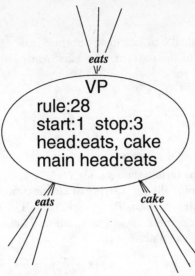

Fig. 1. Edge with additional information for the verb phrase in the sentence *[John] eats cake*, rule 28 is $VP \rightarrow V \quad N$

When the edges $e_{c1}...e_{cn}$ having head-categories $A = (a_{c1}...a_{cn})$ can be used to produce edge e_k with rule x we write $\{e_{c1}...e_{cn}\} \rightarrow e_k^{x,A}$.

We calculate the inside and outside probabilities of edges. We write this as $I(e)$ and $O(e)$ respectively. We will also be using the probability of a pattern, associated with an edge:

$$P(R_x, A) = P(R_x, (a_1, a_2, ..., a_n))$$

Note that we require head-categories to be in the right order; pattern $(R_x, (a, b))$ is not the same as $(R_x, (b, a))$.

3.2 Initial Estimation

The algorithm iteratively calculates the probabilities of patterns using a count of the number of times these patterns are used in the corpus, and reestimates this count using the probabilities. To get this process going we need an initial estimation. We use the following equation for the initial count for a pattern from a sentence w in the corpus:

$$C_{\text{initial}}^w(R_x, A) = \frac{\text{number of times } e^{x,A} \text{ is used in parses of w}}{\text{number of alternative parses of w}}$$

This allows us to calculate the initial probabilities, much in the same way as the original Inside Outside Algorithm.

$$P_{\text{initial}}(R_x^p, A) = \frac{\sum_{w \in \text{corpus}} C_{\text{initial}}^w(R_x^p, A)}{\sum_{y, B, w \in \text{corpus}} C_{\text{initial}}^w(R_y^p, B)}$$

Using this probability we can start the reestimation process.

3.3 Reestimation

The inside probability is calculated like in the normal Inside Outside Algorithm, but taking the probability of the pattern that is associated with the edge rather than the probability of the rule.

$$I(e_k^{x,A}) = \sum_{\{e_{c1}, e_{c2}, \ldots, e_{cn}\} \to e_k^{x,A}} P(R_x, A) \prod_{i=1}^{n} I(e_{ci})$$

The inside probability for terminals is simply $I(e^{x,A}) = P(R_x, A)$. This allows us to calculate all inside probabilities, starting at the bottom and working to the top. Then we start calculating the outside probabilities. The outside probability of every edge with the start symbol should be made 1. The outside probabilities of lower edges now then be calculated with

$$O(e_k) = \sum_{\{e_{c1}, \ldots, e_{cn}\} \cup \{e_k\} \to e_q^{x,A}} O(e_q^{x,A}) P(R_x, A) \prod_{i=1}^{n} I(e_{ci}) \ .$$

The probability of the whole sentence is calculated by taking the inside probabilities of all edges with the start symbol as nonterminal together:

$$P(w) = \sum_{e: \text{ nonterminal is S}} I(e) \ .$$

Now we can reestimate the count a pattern receives. We estimate the probability of the edge by multiplying the inside and outside probability for every occurrence, dividing the sum by the probability of the sentence using

$$C^w(R_x, A) = \frac{1}{P(w)} \sum_{e_k^{x,A}} O(e_k) I(e_k) \ .$$

Dividing this by the total of the nonterminal gives us the new probabilities, allowing us to iterate the calculation.

$$P_{\text{new}}(R_x^p, A) = \frac{\sum_{w \in \text{corpus}} C^w(R_x^p, A)}{\sum_{y, B, w \in \text{corpus}} \frac{1}{P(w)} \sum_{p: e_k^{y,B}} O(e_k) I(e_k)}$$

Here $p : e_k^{y,B}$ means we sum over all edges that were constructed with a rule that has p as left hand side nonterminal.

We stop the iteration of the algorithm when the change in the entropy after each iteration becomes very small.

4 Changing the Algorithm

The algorithm as explained in the previous paragraph is only possible on large amounts of data. Even if the corpus is large we might, in some cases, be faced with sparse data for particular patterns. This means it is desirable to smooth the data in some way.

The maximum number of right-hand-side nonterminals that should be used in a rule (this is a possible limitation to the grammar) depends on the number of categories that have been defined. If this is a small number, the maximum could perhaps be larger, but for the time being we assume that no rule has more than two right-hand-side nonterminals.

For rules with one right-hand-side nonterminal the problem is not so serious, so we will focus on rules with two. We calculate the counts and probabilities of all patterns as the algorithm indicates, but when we use the probability (particularly for reestimation), we take

$$P_{\text{smooth}}(R_x, (a, b)) \stackrel{\text{def}}{=} P_{\text{left}}(R_x, a) + P_{\text{right}}(R_x, b)$$

where P_{left} and P_{right} are

$$P_{\text{left}}(R_x, a) \stackrel{\text{def}}{=} \sum_i P(R_x, (a, i))$$

and

$$P_{\text{right}}(R_x, b) \stackrel{\text{def}}{=} \sum_i P(R_x, (i, b)) \ .$$

We can also simulate a probabilistic grammar by taking

$$P_{\text{plain}}(R_x, A) = \sum_{i,j} P(R_x, (i, j)) \ .$$

We can now also use a combination of P, P_{smooth} and P_{plain}. Let $\lambda = (\lambda_1, \lambda_2, \lambda_3)$ be a vector such that $\lambda_1 + \lambda_2 + \lambda_3 = 1$, then

$$P_{\text{combined}}(R_x, A) \stackrel{\text{def}}{=} \lambda_1 P_{\text{plain}}(R_x, A) + \lambda_2 P_{\text{smooth}}(R_x, A) + \lambda_3 P(R_x, A) \ .$$

The observation we would like to make now is that we can change the algorithm while it is running: after making a number of iterations with, say, $\lambda = (0, 0.5, 0.5)$, we can change the vector and continue with $\lambda = (0.5, 0.5, 0)$. We can even make a sequence like
$$\lambda = (0, 0, 1)(0, 0.1, 0.9)(0, 0.15, 0.85)(0, 0.2, 0.8) \text{ (etc.)}$$
At this point it may not be clear why it makes sense to do this, but from initial experiments we noticed that changing the order gives different results. It therefore might make sense to try to find a good performing order.

5   Reducing Parameters

For a grammar with many rules and many categories the number of parameters that has to be trained can become quite big, requiring a big training corpus. In the first place, the number of categories should be in balance with the size of the corpus. A big corpus can train for many categories, a small corpus allows only few categories. Calculating the number of parameters is of course straightforward.

A more drastic way of reducing the number of parameters, is using only P_{smooth}, and collecting data on the heads independent from each other. This takes away the relations between heads of right-hand-side nonterminals, but it strongly reduces the number of sentences that are needed in the training phase. (For n rules with two heads and m categories, the number of parameters is reduced from $n * m^2$ to $n * m * 2$.)

As another possible step towards reducing the number of parameters, we can select which rules of the grammar should be trained with many categories. Those should be rules that are used much, and that play a role in disambiguation. Rules that are not related to frequent ambiguity problems, or rules for which little data is available, should perhaps not be trained on categories. This can be solved by making their probability constant for all categories, effectively turning them into the sort of rule that is used in a usual PCF.

6   Multiple Senses

Using a set of semantical categories we will obtain more than one category for many words, this often represents various meanings or senses, and we will have to deal with this problem in some way. The most simple solution (which we already mentioned while explaining the algorithm) is creating edges for every sense. This means different categories are treated as different parses.

This is feasible for a small amount of ambiguity (the algorithm will now award the most frequent possibility) but for sentences with many words with various categories it puts very (too) much weight on the algorithm. This can be avoided by applying (partial) sense tagging. Approaches like [38, 35, 15] are very useful for this task. Note that the baseline system as suggested by [11], giving 75% correct, might be good enough for our purposes. We do not require total disambiguation, we just need the amount of ambiguity to be reduced.

However, for these reasons we expect that the algorithm will work better within a specific domain than for general language, because semantical categories can often be defined more easily in a domain.

Semantical categories can be indifferent towards part of speech (like Roget's Thesaurus) or be differentiated by part of speech before further classification (like for example WordNet). This method can be used for both types of categories.

If the latter type is used, it is possible (but not necessary) to put a further restriction on the grammar; namely that a nonterminal should always select a head with the same part of speech. This restricts the number of possible patterns. The most practical solution is perhaps to do this with most rules, and allow exceptions only where necessary.

7 Experiments

In this section we will describe an experiment we conducted to compare the results of a hand-written, statistically trained grammar using the method described here with the results of the same grammar trained by the normal Inside-Outside Algorithm.

We conducted experiments on about 5000 Japanese newspaper sentences from the EDR corpus [21]. We used a hand-written grammar developed in the Ph.D. research of Dr. T. Fuchi [10], in combination with the JUMAN morphological processor, see [28], and the SAX parser, see [27].

The EDR corpus contains sentences from (general) Japanese newspapers. It gives morphological information (separation into words, part of speech tags), semantical tags for the words, a bracketing for the sentence (without nonterminals) and other information which we did not use. It would seem logical to use the semantical tags in the EDR corpus, and we did try to do so in experiments. But we found in our experiments that we obtained better results with an independent thesaurus. The results presented here have been obtained using the Japanese Bunruigoihyo thesaurus [31].

For more details about these experiments, such as about the difference between EDR semantic tags and Bunruigoihyo classes, see [20].

7.1 The Sense Tagging

The EDR gives a non-ambiguous class for most words, but the problem we had with these classes was that many are not placed in the ontology, forcing us to classify many words as 'undefined.' Using an independent thesaurus we were faced with the problem of word sense ambiguity, but we did have a complete ontology covering all classes.

The method we used for resolving word-sense ambiguity was very simple. We selected a suitable number of high-level nodes that could serve as semantical classes. If all senses of a word are under one selected node, we can select that node. If not, we select the node that covers the highest number of senses (the idea behind this is, that this might well be the most frequent class). If several selected nodes cover the same number of senses and there is no other selected node with more senses, we choose one at random.

This method is very naive, but we evaluated a set of tags and concluded that about 80% was correct. This is not a particularly good score, and it therefore shows that you do not need very sophisticated word-sense tagging to gain from this method. We expect the results to improve if the precision of sense tagging becomes higher.

We used 10 categories. The Bunruigoihyo thesaurus does not have separate ontologies for different parts of speech, so this is quite a low number. But it is important to note that the probabilities are conditioned on rules, which in most cases means it is also conditioned on a part of speech since many rules always have a headword with the same part of speech. Therefore the behavior effectively depends on the part of speech of the headword.

7.2 Parsing and Evaluation

We have run the parser on sentences from the EDR corpus that were no longer than 25 Japanese characters. The grammar produced one or more parses for 84% of the sentences. As evaluation criterion we used the brackets from the EDR corpus, considering sentences that contained one or more *crossing errors* as wrong. This has a few drawbacks:

- Sometimes the EDR corpus and the grammar had different style of bracketing. Neither of the two was wrong, but there were crossing brackets.
- The EDR corpus bracketing contains errors and sometimes what appears to be inconsistencies.

We decided do discard the sentences for which every parse contained a crossing error against the treebank. We ended up using the following two groups of sentences: 4568 sentences were used for training, 600 sentences (not in the training set) were used for testing. We measured both the sentence accuracy (percentage of sentences that contained no crossing error), and bracketing accuracy (percentage of bracket pairs in the parses that make no crossing error) for the selected parses. The grammar performed a complete bracketing, but we nevertheless measured bracket recall (percentage of bracket pairs in treebank matched by a bracket pair in the parse) as well.

7.3 The Results

We used smoothing as described earlier, using a vector λ with three values that add up to one. Notice that if the first value is 1 and the other two 0, the algorithm behaves like the normal Inside Outside algorithm, simulating a regular stochastic grammar. Table 1 gives the results. The first is a normal stochastic grammar, the second represents the model without smoothing. The third only uses smoothing (therefore treats the headwords as independent) and the last one indicates the best mix we found.

The differences in accuracy are statistically significant between the first (regular stochastic grammar) and the others. The difference is also significant between the second (no smoothing) and the last model. But the difference between the second and the third, and between the third and the fourth, is not statistically significant.

One very consistent result we found is that the scores are better when the first vector (for the rule probability) is set to 0. The rule probability has a negative influence and results are better when it is ignored completely.

Table 1. Results from experiment with Bunruigoihyo

Smoothing Vector	Sentence Accuracy	Br. Accuracy	Br. Recall
$\lambda = (1, 0, 0)$	40.8 %	93.35 %	92.31 %
$\lambda = (0, 0, 1)$	52.3 %	94.55 %	93.74 %
$\lambda = (0, 1, 0)$	55.0 %	94.91 %	94.13 %
$\lambda = (0, .6, .4)$	57.8 %	95.10 %	94.27 %

8 Related Research

Stochastic grammars: See [6] for an introduction to statistical techniques in natural language processing, including the Inside Outside Algorithm, and [3] for a description of the 'IBM-Lancaster approach' to treebanking and statistical training of corpus-based hand-written grammars.

The Inside Outside Algorithm was introduced by [1]. We did not use the Inside Outside Algorithm for grammar induction in our experiments, but see for example [29] and [33] for work on this problem. Another paper discussing the algorithm and applications in speech recognition is [25]. See also [7].

Other statistical techniques in syntactical disambiguation: Research on syntactical disambiguation often focuses on specific structures like preposition attachment or noun collocations, which differs from our approach in that we are seeking a complete framework for solving ambiguity, rather than focusing on one specific problem. Examples of such work are [5, 37], and [9, 19] for work specific to preposition attachment.

Other experiments on disambiguating using statistics have been reported in for example [35, 34, 32, 30].

We already mentioned the method in [16, 17], which focuses on similar relations as we do, although in quite a different way. In [36] a technique for acquiring semantic collocations is presented. (We will not discuss the work on collocations in general).

Recently methods avoiding the use of a context free grammar have also been suggested, such as in [4] and [26].

Sense tagging: Research to the problem of automatic sense tagging and general results on tagging corpora have been published in [38, 35, 15, 14, 34]. There has been an interest in using bilingual methods as well, see for example [8, 13].

Related issues like constancy of senses with relation to collocations or discourse are discussed in for example [39] and [12].

The evaluation criteria for such tagging systems are problematic because humans are not very consistent in their sense distinctions. These problems are discussed in [11].

9 Conclusion

We have presented an algorithm which automatically collects data on how semantical categories are interacting with a grammar, by processing a corpus. It can be used on any grammar and with any set of semantical categories (except perhaps that the grammar should not have too many nonterminals in a rule), so it does not depend on a specific system.

We have chosen a type of pattern that reflects the use of language, and at the same time can be processed on a realistic scale. It gives not only the probability of the rules, but the probability of patterns including rules and semantical categories, reflecting the way these are used in the corpus.

These patterns can also be used to evaluate a sentence as a whole, and the most likely analyses can be selected by combining the probabilities. This is an aspect which has often been ignored in approaches aiming at 'selectional restrictions' or 'semantical patterns'.

We claim this is a timely development because grammars written by hand based on a corpus and trained statistically are beginning to show the potential for realistic applications. The discovery of richer information about the right way to interpret sentences can increase the score of such grammars on unseen text.

Our experiments show that using these patterns, the performance of a regular context free grammar can be improved strongly. This shows that semantical patterns can be learned by a grammar in this way, even though patterns usually don't make sense to people. It also shows that it is not necessary to have a specially designed grammar, the grammar we used was designed for general use and we did not alter it.

It also proves that a very simple word sense tagging can be sufficient to bring about a considerable improvement. It is quite possible that results would be better still if the sense tagging would be done more carefully.

References

1. J. K. Baker. Trainable grammars for speech recognition. *Speech Communication Papers for the 97th Meeting of the Acoustical Society of America*, pages 547–550, 1979.
2. E. Black, S. Abney, D. Flickenger, C. Gdaniec, R. Grishman, P. Harrison, D. Hindle, R. Ingria, F. Jelinek, J. Klavans, M. Liberman, M. Marcus, S. Roukos, B. Santorini, and T. Strzalkowski. A procedure for quantitatively comparing the syntactic coverage of English grammars. In *Proceedings of the Workshop on Speech and Natural Language, Defense Advanced Research Projects Agency, U.S. Govt.*, 1991.
3. E. Black, R. Garside, and G. Leech. *Statistically-Driven Computer Grammars of English: The IBM/Lancaster Approach*. Rodopi, 1993.
4. R. Bod. Using an annotated corpus as a stochastic grammar. In *Proceedings of the Sixth Conference of the European Chapter of the Association for Computational Linguistics*, pages 37–44, 1993.

5. N. Calzolari and R. Bindi. Acquisition of lexical information from a large textual Italian corpus. In *Proceedings of the 13th International Conference on Computational Linguistics (COLING-90)*, pages 54–59, 1990.

6. E. Charniak. *Statistical Language Learning*. MIT Press, 1993.

7. E. Charniak and G. Carroll. Two experiments on learning probabilistic grammars from corpora. In *Workshop Notes, Statistically-Based NLP Techniques, AAAI*, pages 1–13, 1992.

8. I. Dagan, A. Itai, and U. Schwall. Two languages are more informative than one. In *Proceedings of the 29th Annual Meeting of the Association for Computational Linguistics*, pages 130–137, 1991.

9. D. Fisher and E. Riloff. Applying statistical methods to small corpora: Benefiting from a limited domain. In *Working Notes, Fall Symposium Series, AAAI*, pages 47–54, 1992.

10. Takeshi Fuchi. *New Means to Analyze Japanese Morphemes and Dependency Structure and Formalization of Rules to Derive Implied Meanings*. PhD thesis, Tokyo University, 1994. in Japanese.

11. W. A. Gale, K. W. Church, and D. Yarowsky. Estimating upper and lower bounds on the performance of word-sense disambiguation programs. In *Proceedings of the 30th Annual Meeting of the Association for Computational Linguistics*, pages 249–256, 1992.

12. W. A. Gale, K. W. Church, and D. Yarowsky. One sense per discourse. In *Proceedings of the 4th DARPA Speech and Natural Language Workshop*, pages 233–237, 1992.

13. W. A. Gale, K. W. Church, and D. Yarowsky. Using bilingual materials to develop word sense disambiguation methods. In *Theoretical and Methodological Issues in Machine Translation*, pages 101–111, 1992.

14. W. A. Gale, K. W. Church, and D. Yarowsky. Work on statistical methods for word sense disambiguation. In *Working Notes, Fall Symposium Series, AAAI*, pages 54–60, 1992.

15. W. A. Gale, K. W. Church, and D. Yarowsky. A method for disambiguating word senses in a large corpus. *Computers and the Humanities*, 26:415–439, 1993.

16. R. Grishman, L. Hirschman, and N. T. Nhan. Discovery procedures for sub-language selectional patterns: Initial experiments. *Computational Linguistics*, 12(3):205–216, 1986.

17. R. Grishman and J. Sterling. Acquisition of selectional patterns. In *Proceedings of the 14th International Conference on Computational Linguistics (COLING-92)*, pages 658–664, 1992.

18. P. Harrison, S. Abney, E. Black, D. Flickenger, C. Gdaniec, R. Grishman, D. Hindle, R. Ingria, M. Marcus, B. Santorini, and T. Strzalkowski. Evaluating syntax performance of parser/grammars of English. In *Proceedings of the Workshop on Evaluating Natural Language Processing Systems, Association for Computational Linguistics*, 1991.

19. D. Hindle and M. Rooth. Structural ambiguity and lexical relations. In *Proceedings of the 29th Annual Meeting of the Association for Computational Linguistics*, pages 229–236, 1991.

20. W. R. Hogenhout. Enrichment of models for stochastic grammars: Semantical categories. Master's thesis, Nara Institute of Science and Technology, 1995.

21. Japan Electronic Dictionary Research Institute, Ltd. *EDR Electronic Dictionary Technical Guide*, 1994.

22. S. E. Johansson, E. Atwell, R. G. Garside, and G. N. Leech. The Tagged LOB Corpus: User's Manual. Technical report, Norwegian Computing Centre for the Humanities, 1986.

23. S. E. Johansson, G. N. Leech, and H. Goodluck. Manual of information to accompany the Lancaster-Oslo/Bergen Corpus of British English, for use with digital computers. Technical report, Department of English, University of Oslo, 1978.

24. M. Kay. Algorithm schemata and data structures in syntactic processing. Technical Report CSL-80-12, XEROX PARC, 1980.

25. K. Lari and S. J. Young. Applications of stochastic context-free grammars using the Inside Outside Algorithm. *Computer Speech and Language*, 5:237–257, 1991.

26. D. M. Magerman. Statistical decision-tree models for parsing. In *Proceedings of the 33d Annual Meeting of the Association for Computational Linguistics*, 1995.

27. Yuji Matsumoto and R. Sugimura. A parsing system based on logical programming. In *Proceedings of the 10th International Joint Conference on Artificial Intelligence*, pages 671–674, 1987.

28. Yuuji Matsumoto et al. *Japanese Morphological Analysis System JUMAN Manual Version 2.0*, 1994. Nara Institute of Science and Technology Technical Report, NAIST-IS-TR94025 (in Japanese).

29. F. Pereira and Y. Schabes. Inside Outside reestimation from partially bracketed corpora. In *Proceedings of the 30th Annual Meeting of the Association for Computational Linguistics*, pages 128–135, 1992.

30. F. Pereira and N. Tishby. Distributional similarity, phase transitions and hierarchical clustering. In *Working Notes, Fall Symposium Series, AAAI*, pages 108–112, 1992.

31. National Language Research Institute Publications. *Word List by Semantic Principles (Bunruigoihyou)*. Shuei Shuppan, 1964. in Japanese.

32. P. Resnik. Wordnet and distributional analysis: a class-based approach to lexical discovery. In *Workshop Notes, Statistically-Based NLP Techniques, AAAI*, pages 54–64, 1992.

33. Y. Schabes, M. Roth, and R. Osborne. Parsing the wall street journal with the inside-outside algorithm. In *Proceedings of the Sixth Conference of the European Chapter of the Association for Computational Linguistics*, pages 341–347, 1993.

34. H. Schütze. Context space. In *Working Notes, Fall Symposium Series, AAAI*, pages 113–120, 1992.

35. H. Schütze. Word sense disambiguation with sublexical representations. In *Workshop Notes, Statistically-Based NLP Techniques, AAAI*, pages 109–113, 1992.

36. S. Sekine, J. Carroll, S. Ananiadou, and Jun'ichi Tsujii. Automatic learning for semantic collocation. In *Third Conference on Applied Natural Language Processing, Association for Computational Linguistics*, pages 104–110, 1992.

37. F. Smadja. From n-grams to collocations: An evaluation of Xtract. In *Proceedings of the 29th Annual Meeting of the Association for Computational Linguistics*, pages 279–284, 1991.

38. D. Yarowsky. Word-sense disambiguation using statistical models of Roget's categories trained on large corpora. In *Proceedings of the 14th International Conference on Computational Linguistics (COLING-92)*, pages 454–460, 1992.

39. D. Yarowsky. One sense per collocation. In *Human Language Technology, Workshop Proceedings*, pages 266–271, 1993.

Learning Restricted Probabilistic Link Grammars

Eva Wai-man Fong   Dekai Wu

HKUST
Department of Computer Science
University of Science & Technology
Clear Water Bay, Hong Kong

Abstract. We describe a language model employing a new *headed-disjuncts* formulation of Lafferty *et al.*'s (1992) probabilistic link grammar, together with (1) an EM training method for estimating the probabilities, and (2) a procedure for learning some simple lexicalized grammar structures. The model in its simplest form is a generalization of n-gram models, but in its general form possesses context-free expressiveness. Unlike the original experiments on probabilistic link grammars, we assume that no hand-coded grammar is initially available (as with n-gram models). We employ *untyped* links to concentrate the learning on lexical dependencies, and our formulation uses the *lexical* identities of heads to influence the structure of the parse graph. After learning, the language model consists of grammatical rules in the form of a set of simple disjuncts for each word, plus several sets of probability parameters. The formulation extends cleanly toward learning more powerful context-free grammars. Several issues relating to generalization bias, linguistic constraints, and parameter smoothing are considered. Preliminary experimental results on small artificial corpora are supportive of our approach.

1 Introduction

Although finite-state language models, in particular the linguistically simplistic trigram model, have occupied a predominant position in statistical language modeling, a context-free grammar formalism, with its enhanced ability to model center embeddings and long-distance dependencies, has the potential of outperforming the simpler models, given sufficiently constrained learning techniques for estimating the parameters reliably. We are studying *probabilistic link grammars*, a relatively new context-free grammar formalism with the desirable property of being highly lexicalized (Lafferty *et al.* 1992). In our models, the grammar rules (in the form of *disjuncts*) are induced in addition to their probabilities. We have extended the original probabilistic link grammar model to suit our purpose, and also made a number of revisions to better capture word associations and resolve the sparse data problem.

There have been attempts in learning stochastic context-free grammars (Lari & Young 1990, Jelinek *et al.* 1992), but the perplexities of these language models have so far been well above that of trigram language models (Brown *et al.* 1992). Newer approaches have focused on the more constrained context-free formalisms, such as dependency grammars (Carroll & Charniak 1992) and link grammars (Lafferty *et al.* 1992). Link grammar has the additional attraction of being highly lexical. Lexicality is a desirable feature since it enables the grammar to condition its predictions more accurately upon the specific identities of words, rather than general categories which are less informative. (In fact, lexicality accounts for the relative efficacy of n-gram language models compared with traditional context-free grammars.)

In this paper, we shall describe a novel approach to induce a restricted class of probabilistic link grammars which employs maximum-likelihood estimation from incomplete data. The training algorithm employed falls in the general class of EM algorithms (Baum 1972, Dempster *et al.* 1977). We shall also address issues such as appropriate parameter initialization, use of a suitable bias, and linguistic constraints to guide generalization.

2 Background

2.1 Link Grammar

Our point of departure is Lafferty *et al.*'s (1992) probabilistic model of link grammar. Link grammar is a relatively new context-free formalism for natural language proposed by Sleator & Temperley (1991). It does not have explicit constituents and possesses a high degree of lexicalization. In link grammar, a sequence of words is in the language if there exists at least one valid *linkage* for the words. Words (vertices) are connected by *links* (labelled arcs), and a linkage is valid if the resulting graph is connected and planar with arcs drawn above the words, and at most one arc connects a given pair of words. Figure 1 shows a link grammar parse (linkage) for an English sentence.

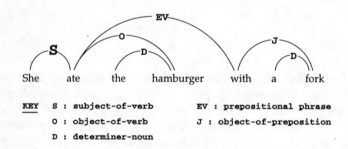

KEY S : subject-of-verb   EV : prepositional phrase
     O : object-of-verb   J : object-of-preposition
     D : determiner-noun

Fig. 1. A link grammar parse

Rules in link grammar are in the form of *disjuncts*, where each disjunct corresponds to a usage of the word, or a particular way of satisfying its requirements. A disjunct comprises two ordered lists of connector names: the *left list* (connectors that link to the left of the current word) and the *right list* (connectors that link to the right of the current word). A disjunct is denoted as:

$$((L_1, L_2, \cdots, L_m) (R_n, R_{n-1}, \cdots, R_1))$$

which is equivalent to:

$$(L_1 \,\&\, L_2 \,\&\, \cdots \,\&\, L_m \,\&\, R_1 \,\&\, R_2 \,\&\, \cdots \,\&\, R_n)$$

There exists an efficient top-down link grammar parsing algorithm, presented in Sleator & Temperley (1991). The probabilistic model of link grammar proposed in Lafferty *et al.* (1992) was based on this top-down parsing algorithm.

2.2 Probabilistic Link Grammar

The basic operation of link grammar is *linking*. Here we use the term *link* to refer to a 7-tuple (W, d, O, L, R, l, r), where the word W with its disjunct d is linked to (at least one of) the words L and R via the connectors l and r. Thus a link depends on two connectors, a right connector and a left connector, say l and r, of two words L and R (L to the left of R) respectively. These connectors are roughly analogous to a nonterminal which is to be rewritten for a phrase structure grammar. A word W with its disjunct d is produced given the previously generated words and disjuncts. An *orientation* is also chosen for the link by deciding whether d links to l, to r, or to both l and r. (Hereafter, we use the random variable O to represent the orientation of a link. The possible values for O are $\leftarrow$, $\rightarrow$ and $\leftrightarrow$.)

The particular model in Lafferty *et al.* (1992) makes the simplifying assumption that a (W, d, O)-tuple is generated only based on the words nearest to the left and right that have already appeared, L and R, together with the associated connectors l and r. Thus the set of model parameters is

$$P(W, d, O | L, R, l, r).$$

Since each word in a sentence is generated exactly once, there is only one link probability $P(W, d, O | L, R, l, r)$ for each word. In an N-word sentence $W_1, W_2, ..., W_N$, a *linkage* (or a parse) is a set of N links $\{(W, d, O, L, R, l, r)_i\}$, and the probability of a linkage Γ is a product of N factors, together with an initial disjunct d_1 of word W_1:

(1) $$P(S, \Gamma) = P(W_1, d_1) \prod P(W, d, O | L, R, l, r)$$

The probability of a sentence S is the sum of the probabilities of all its linkages, and thus we have:

$$P(S) = \sum_{\Gamma} P(S, \Gamma)$$

Under this model, the probability of a linkage does not depend on the order of traversal of the links – a given linkage only maps to one order in which the links are traversed, that order according to the top-down link grammar parsing algorithm. In this way, the derivation of a parse is not hidden and so does not need to be trained.

Note that the set of model parameters $P(W, d, O | L, R, l, r)$ may be rewritten as

$$P(W | L, R, l, r) P(d | W, L, R, l, r) P(O | d, W, L, R, l, r).$$

As this implies a huge set of conditional probabilities which may be impossible in practice for any training algorithm to form reliable estimates of them, these probabilities were approximated in Lafferty *et al.* (1992) as

$$P(W, d, O|L, R, l, r) \approx P(W|L, R, l, r)P(d|W, l, r)P(O|d, l, r).$$

An EM-based training algorithm, in the spirit of the Inside-Outside algorithm (Baker 1979), was used for estimating the model parameters. The set of rules (disjuncts) need to be coded manually.

3   A Framework for Learning Untyped-Link Grammars

We now describe our framework for inducing probabilistic link grammars, assuming that no *a priori* hand-coded grammar is available. We discuss first our representational constraints, then the learning procedure.

3.1   Expressiveness Constraints

An *a priori* grammar would constrain the legal disjuncts for each word to some predetermined set. In the absence of such constraints, it is necessary to restrict the space of allowed disjuncts by other means. We imposed the following two conditions.

Bounded number of connectors If no limit is placed on the number of connectors in a disjunct, the search space would be infinite, and learning would not be possible. On studying linkage patterns of sentences by means of Sleator and Temperley's (non-probabilistic) link grammar (Sleator & Temperley 1991), we observe that most words would not be linked to many words in a given sentence. In particular, it is rare for words to need disjuncts with more than three connectors on either of the left and right connector lists (with the exception of very complex sentences and disjuncts having multi-connectors [1], which are not addressed in this basic model). Therefore, we postulate that a large portion of the sentences can be parsed using only the relatively simple disjuncts, that is, those disjuncts with a small number of connectors.

To make learning feasible, we need to restrict the number of possible disjuncts under our framework. We use the number of connectors in disjuncts to form our framework, and restrict our attention to those disjuncts with a maximum number of N left and N right connectors, where N is specified as a parameter to the learning algorithm.

Untyped links To further reduce the space of possible disjuncts, we made the simplification of allowing for only one type of link. Since the number of disjuncts is exponential in the order of the number of link types, learning would be extremely difficult without this restriction. A more complex model, with a large number of link types corresponding to different relationships between the connected words, generally possesses greater power in modeling the data in full. However, the complexity of the model would increase the

---

[1] connectors that are endpoints of more than one link

dimension of learning, making it easy for the generalization process to get stuck in local maxima, and hard to obtain reliable estimates of the model parameters.

Notice that our restriction is somewhat analogous to context-free bracketing grammars which possess only a single type of nonterminal, except that the link grammar formulation still allows lexical constraints to be expressed. The resulting language model supports more abstract structural dependencies than pure n-gram models, but without losing the lexicality advantages of n-grams.

3.2 Learning Procedure

Learning proceeds in three stages:

1. Initialize probabilities
2. Train on corpus
3. Prune disjuncts

Initialization Since EM only guarantees convergence to local maxima instead of a globally maximal solution, it is important that the parameter estimation process starts with good initial estimates. We used windowed trigram probabilities for initializing the parameters $P(W|L, R, l, r)$.

Training We have studied two variants of EM training. The original method is described in Lafferty *et al.* (1992). Our new formulation for the headed-disjuncts model is described in Section 6.

Pruning At the end of the EM estimation process, disjuncts with very low probabilities are pruned and the probability values are renormalized. Manual analysis of the parses produced by the induced grammar confirmed that pruning improves the quality of the generalization by reducing the number of parses for a sentence and boosting probabilities of the more promising linkages. Disjunct pruning can be applied to each iteration of the parameter estimation process to speed up generalization, provided that the threshold is set at a suitable level. The success of this greedy strategy depends on the choice of the pruning threshold and the sensitivity of the results to this value. To avoid omitting useful disjuncts, we have chosen to prune the low probability disjuncts only at the end of the training process.

4 Problems with Lafferty *et al.*'s Formulation

For our initial experiments with the learning procedure, we employed the same probabilistic approximations as in Lafferty *et al.*'s (1992) original formulation, which we refer to hereafter as the LST model. However, under these approximations, we were unable to obtain satisfactory results (see Sections 8–10). Inspection revealed several factors that contributed to the low performance.

Dependence on link type information With the untyped links that make learning feasible, the model parameters—$P(W|L, R, l, r)$, $P(d|W, l, r)$ and $P(O|d, l, r)$—become less predictive, since the type of word association usually gives some clue about the word that is being generated next. For instance, the probability of linking the noun dog to the preceding article the would be high if it is expecting a determiner-noun relationship in its disjunct being currently considered, but would be extremely low if it is looking for a word to fulfill the object-of-verb relationship. However, an untyped-link model does not distinguish between these two cases, and both are assigned the same parameter values. Thus it would be more difficult for the learning process to generalize well without information about the types of the links.

Sensitivity to sparse data Results for the LST model have not been reported in literature, and they would also depend on how the link types are classified. However, on analyzing the model parameters, we find that the model is extremely prone to the *sparse data problem*, due to its huge number of parameters some of which are not normalized and thus contain redundancies. We are particularly concerned with the set of probabilities $P(W|L, R, l, r)$, which may not be apt for modeling word correlations.

As an illustration, consider the association between the words the and ball. Instead of parameters involving just the two associated words, we also need a third word to make up the parameter $P(W|L, R, l, r)$. Temporarily ignoring the connector types, we need parameters of the form $P(\text{the } |L, \text{ball})$, where L is a word in the vocabulary, to model the determiner-noun relationship between the and ball, instead of just the single parameter $P(\text{the } | \text{ball})$. Suppose we are able to deduce from the training corpus the probabilities

$$P(\text{the } | \text{ hit ball}),$$
$$P(\text{the } | \text{ kick ball}),$$
$$P(\text{the } | \text{ throw ball}),$$
$$P(\text{the } | \text{ have ball}),$$
$$P(\text{the } | \text{ to ball}).$$

But these are not going to be of use when we are given sentences with phrases containing the ball but are not covered in the above, e.g. The new chairman is on the ball. It would be rare that a corpus contains all the possible words that can occur with a binary association between two other words. Thus the problem of insufficient training data is exaggerated.

Insensitivity to orientations Furthermore, we noticed that under this probabilistic framework it is difficult to model the exact associations between words. Given two words, L and R, there are three ways, i.e. *orientations*, in which they generate a word W, where $(L < W < R)$: W may be linked to L, to R, or to both of them. All three orientations will be assigned the same values for $P(W|L, R, l, r)$ and $P(d|W, l, r)$, though perhaps a different $P(O|d, l, r)$. However, the first two parameters, namely the word probabilities and disjunct probabilities, are exactly the more influential ones, from which we observe a much greater variance and also predictive power.

Whereas the deficiency of link types can be avoided by finding the right link types and then the disjuncts either manually or by some clustering method, before or after the link structures are induced, the other two problems may be tackled by reformulating the probabilistic model.

5 Formulation of the Headed-disjuncts Model

In reformulating the probabilistic model, our objective is to incorporate the orientation factor into the probabilities for choosing a word and a disjunct in the linking process, while at the same time reducing the size of the parameter space.

Recall that the parameters of probabilistic link grammar are the set of *link probabilities*

$$P(W, d, O|L, R, l, r) =$$
$$P(W|L, R, l, r)P(d|W, L, R, l, r)P(O|d, W, L, R, l, r)$$

which were approximated by

$$P(W|L, R, l, r)P(d|W, l, r)P(O|d, l, r).$$

On the other hand, we can also rewrite $P(W, d, O|L, R, l, r)$ as

$$P(O|L, R, l, r)P(W|L, R, l, r, O)P(d|W, L, R, l, r, O)$$

which makes it easier to capture the true association between W, L and R.

The first of these parameters, $P(O|L, R, l, r)$, may be approximated by $P(O|l, r)$, since knowing the identities of the words L and R may not be of much help in predicting the orientation for linking them to a word, without knowing which word they are linking to.

Therefore, we have

$$P(W, d, O|L, R, l, r) =$$
(2) $$\qquad P(O|l, r)P(W|L, R, l, r, O)P(d|W, L, R, l, r, O).$$

For our untyped-link model, a connector is either present or NIL. This has implications on the values of $P(O|l, r)$, as shown in Table 1. The case for l and r both present needs

Table 1. Relationship between orientation and connectors l and r

l	r	Orientation allowed
present	NIL	$\leftarrow$
NIL	present	$\rightarrow$
present	present	$\leftrightarrow, \leftarrow$

a bit of explanation. In the parsing algorithm, linking to the left and linking to the right are intentionally made assymetric to avoid overcounting. Since the $\rightarrow$ orientation is allowed only when l is NIL, we have only two possible orientations when both l and r are not NIL. The only orientation probabilities that need to be estimated are $P(\leftrightarrow |l, r)$ and $P(\leftarrow |l, r)$ where both l and r are not NIL.

By including the orientation into the conditional probabilities $P(W|L, R, l, r, O)$ and $P(d|W, L, R, l, r, O)$, it is possible to capture details on the choice of words and disjuncts associated with the different orientations, while at the same time reducing the size of the parameters.

In deriving a formula for P_w, we consider three cases, each corresponding to an orientation. For the orientations where W is linked with one of L and R, we may simply omit the unlinked word from the conditional probability, as it does not play a role in generating W. For the orientation $\leftrightarrow$, whereby W is linked to both L and R (we may think of this as W is generated by both L and R), we can derive the following expression, assuming L, l and R, r are independent:

$$P(W|L, R, l, r) = \frac{P(W|L, l)P(W|R, r)}{P(W)}$$

Thus we may approximate $P(W|L, R, l, r, O)$ by

$$(3) \qquad P(W|L, R, l, r, O) \approx
\begin{cases}
P(W|L, l) & if\, O = \leftarrow \\
P(W|R, r) & if\, O = \rightarrow \\
\dfrac{P(W|L, l)P(W|R, r)}{P(W)} & if\, O = \leftrightarrow
\end{cases}$$

Similarly, we can derive an expression for P_d as follows:

$$(4) \qquad P(d|W, L, R, l, r, O) \approx
\begin{cases}
P(d|W, L, l) & if\, O = \leftarrow \\
P(d|W, R, r) & if\, O = \rightarrow \\
\dfrac{P(d|W, L, l)P(d|W, R, r)}{P(d|W)} & if\, O = \leftrightarrow
\end{cases}$$

The prime parameters that we need to estimate for the model are thus: $P(W|L, l)$, $P(W|R, r)$, $P(d|W, L, l)$, $P(d|W, R, r)$, $P(d|W)$, and $P(W)$, where $P(W)$ is equivalent to the unigram probabilities which are independent of our model and can be computed before the parameter estimation process.

We note that the parameters in the revised model, are in the order of bigrams, whereas the parameters $P(W|L, R, l, r)$ in the original probabilistic model are in the order of trigrams. We may achieve further economy in the number of model parameters by using $P(d|W, l)$ and $P(d|W, r)$ instead of $P(d|W, L, l)$ and $P(d|W, R, r)$, but we believe that the latter set would be more representative of the underlying probabilistic events, especially for an untyped-link model.

For initializing the parameters $P(W|L, l)$ and $P(W|R, r)$, we can make use of *windowed* bigram probabilities, distorted by *mutual information* scores so that links between highly correlated words are preferred.

We call this formulation the *headed-disjuncts* model (henceforth HD), because the disjunct preferences of each word in the sentence are influenced by its lexical heads.

6 EM Estimation for the Headed-disjuncts Model

The parameter estimation process of the revised model is similar to that of the LST model. The inside and outside probabilities are computed in the same top-down manner, but with the link probabilities $P(W, d, O|L, R, l, r)$ decomposed in a different way, as described in Equations 2, 3, and 4.

After calculating the inside and outside probabilities of a sentence, the training algorithm proceeds with updating the counts for the parameters. The complexity of the training algorithm is $O(D^3 N^3)$, where D is an upper bound on the number of disjuncts of an arbitrary word in the grammar, and N the number of words in the sentence. The counts that we need to obtain for estimating the model parameters are shown in Table 2. Since this revised model separates the treatment of the word and disjunct

Table 2. List of Counts to be computed for HD Model

Parameter estimated	Counts needed
$P(W|L, l)$	$Count(W, L, l), Count(L, l)$
$P(W|R, r)$	$Count(W, R, r), Count(R, r)$
$P(d|W, L, l)$	$Count(d, W, L, l), Count(W, L, l)$
$P(d|W, R, r)$	$Count(d, W, R, r), Count(W, R, r)$
$P(d|W)$	$Count(d, W), Count(W)$

probabilities for the different orientations, the calculations for the associated counts also differ. For instance, we only increment $Count(W, L, l)$ for linkages in which W and L are connected, that is, the orientation is either $\leftarrow$ or $\leftrightarrow$ when we link W to L and some other word R to the right.

In the formulas for counts that follow, we let

$$P_L = P(\leftarrow |l, r)\, P(W|L, l)\, P(d|W, L, l) \times$$
$$P_I(L, W, l\triangleright, \triangleleft left[d])\, P_I(W, R, right[d], r)$$
$$P_R = P(\rightarrow |l, r)\, P(W|R, r)\, P(d|W, R, r) \times$$
$$P_I(L, W, l, left[d])\, P_I(W, R, right[d]\triangleright, \triangleleft r)$$
$$P_{LR} = P(\leftrightarrow |l, r) \times$$
$$\frac{P(W|L, l)P(W|R, r)}{P(W)} \frac{P(d|W, L, l)P(d|W, R, r)}{P(d|W)} \times$$
$$P_I(L, W, l\triangleright, \triangleleft left[d])\, P_I(W, R, right[d]\triangleright, \triangleleft r)$$

$$Count(W, L, l) = P(S)^{-1} \sum_{R > W, r} P_O(L, R, l, r) \times$$

$$\sum_{d \in D(W)} \{P_L + P_{LR}\}$$

$$Count(W, R, r) = P(S)^{-1} \sum_{L < W, l} P_O(L, R, l, r) \times$$

$$\sum_{d \in D(W)} \{P_R + P_{LR}\}$$

$$Count(d, W, L, l) = P(S)^{-1} \sum_{R, r} P_O(L, R, l, r) \times$$

$$\{P_L + P_{LR}\}$$

$$Count(d, W, R, r) = P(S)^{-1} \sum_{L, l} P_O(L, R, l, r) \times$$

$$\{P_R + P_{LR}\}$$

$$Count(d, W) = P(S)^{-1} \sum_{L, R, l, r} P_O(L, R, l, r) \times$$

$$\{P_L + P_R + P_{LR}\}$$

$$Count(L, l) = P(S)^{-1} \sum_{R, r} P_O(L, R, l, r) \, P_I(L, R, l, r)$$

$$Count(R, r) = P(S)^{-1} \sum_{L, l} P_O(L, R, l, r) \, P_I(L, R, l, r)$$

7 Regularization Issues

7.1 Generalization Bias

We would like our grammar induction process to produce generalizations that favor simpler linkages, following Occam's razor. We implement this preference by adding to the counts computed from the original corpus a set of virtual counts which follow a predetermined distribution favoring simpler disjunct categories in the complexity hierarchy (Table 3). This is analogous to augmenting the input space with a set of input vectors containing a specified distribution of certain features. In our case, these features are the counts for disjuncts used in valid linkages. The bias helps guide the learning process toward the correct solution space.

7.2 Linguistic Constraints

On analyzing the preliminary experiment results, we found that determiners (such as a, an, the, his, her, etc.) have been causing confusion to the learning process. Traditional linguistic schools usually regard determiners as *modifiers* of their *head* nouns, which may in turn be modifiers of some other words in the sentence, such as the

Table 3. Disjunct complexity in ascending order, for a maximum of 2 connectors

Rank	Disjunct configurations	
1	$((l_1)$ NIL$)$	$($NIL $(r_1))$
2	$((l_1)(r_1))$	
3	$((l_1, l_2)$ NIL$)$	$($NIL $(r_1, r_2))$
4	$((l_1, l_2)(r_1))$	$((l_1)(r_1, r_2))$
5	$((l_1, l_2)(r_1, r_2))$ $((l_1, l_2)(r_1, r_2))$	

main verb.[2] Since in English a determiner always appears to the left of its associated noun, it can only be connected with a noun to the right. Obviously a determiner in English does not have disjuncts with one or more left connectors. This is an example of using linguistic knowledge to limit the number of disjuncts to be considered when constructing hypothetical linkages in the grammar induction process.

We remark that the linguistic constraints we may introduce into the learning process are language dependent; different languages generally require different sets of applicable linguistic constraints. A small number of constraints is usually effective in pruning a large number of invalid hypotheses and helps the induction process concentrate on the remaining hypotheses which are likely to lead to a grammar that possesses a greater amount of linguistic flavor. Of course, this is based on our hypothesis that linkages conforming to linguistic theories tend to yield better language models.

7.3 Smoothing

Obtaining reliable estimates of the parameters has always been a fundamental issue for probabilistic language models. We have used windowed N-grams to smooth our model parameters. The smoothed estimates are given by

$$\tilde{P}(W|L, l) = \gamma^{-1} \delta_l(W)[\lambda P(W|L) + (1 - \lambda)P(W|L, l)]$$
$$\tilde{P}(W|R, r) = \gamma^{-1} \delta_r(W)[\lambda P(W|R) + (1 - \lambda)P(W|R, r)]$$

where

$$\delta_l(W) = \begin{cases} 1, & W \text{ has a disjunct that can link to } l \\ 0, & \text{otherwise} \end{cases}$$

$$\delta_r(W) = \begin{cases} 1, & W \text{ has a disjunct that can link to } r \\ 0, & \text{otherwise} \end{cases}$$

and γ is a normalizing constant. λ takes on values between 0 and 1, and it can be estimated from the training data to maximize the predictive power of the resulting distribution. For many natural language tasks, simply assigning a reasonable constant value to λ can yield satisfactory performance.

---

[2] Whether a determiner or the associated noun should be the head is still controversial. But for the purpose of predicting word co-occurrences and grammar induction, we consider the traditional approach to be more suitable.

8 Experimental Setup

The aim of the experiments is to test the viability of our approach and facilitate analysis of the behaviour of the learning procedure, and hence corpora comprising relatively short and simple sentences are suitable. As we were unable to locate available simple English corpora, we have constructed two experimental English corpora (see Table 4). We generated parameters for both the LST and HD models, as well as for the bigram model. Since the number of hypotheses the training algorithm needs to consider grows

Table 4. Particulars of corpora used in experiments

Corpus	# Sentences	Vocabulary Size	Max. Length	Training	Testing
A	320	57	8	80%	20%
B	600	92	8	80%	20%

exponentially with the maximum number of connectors allowed in a disjunct, we set the limit of two left and two right connectors in the disjuncts for experimental purpose. We expect this would be adequate for most of our training and testing data which contain relatively short English sentences and few adjectives[3]. The threshold for pruning disjuncts has been set to 0.001.

We have also used the following linguistic constraints to guide the induction process:

- *determiners* have no left connectors and have only one right connector in their disjuncts;
- *verbs* have at least one left connector (for connecting to the subject). This left connector should link to a special WALL word in imperative sentences;
- *prepositions*, when they appear in lowercase, have exactly one left connector in their disjuncts.

These constraints are simple to formulate, and can largely reduce the number of possibilities needed to be considered during the induction process.

9 Parsing Results

We first evaluated our probabilistic models by comparing the resulting parse structures and their derivation probabilities. These parses (or linkages) were generated by a probabilistic link grammar parser, which read in a set of probabilistic grammar rules,

---

[3] We have purposely selected sentences without two consecutive adjectives modifying a noun, since that would necessitate disjuncts with greater than two left connectors for the noun. Sleator and Temperley introduced the notion of *multiconnectors* which can be linked to more than one connector (Sleator & Temperley 1991), but this has not been incorporated into any probabilistic model we are aware of.

and output for each input sentence all its valid linkages together with their derivation probabilities.

Our evaluation criterion is the *correctness of parsing*. For each sentence in the test set, linkages (parse structures) that score the highest probabilities in each of the models are compared. A linkage which resembles the parse by humans is preferred to one which does not.

In our evaluation, we classify the mostly likely parse (i.e. one with the highest derivation probability) to be *correct* if it is the same as a parse (in link grammar) which a human would give for the sentence. Since a linkage which is not exactly correct may still contribute to good probability evaluations, we allow for a class of *acceptable* linkages, which contains the correct linkages as well as those with only minor deviations from the correct one which the human evaluator regards as tolerable. We restrict an acceptable linkage to differ from a correct parse by at most one misplaced, or extraneous, link. An example of an acceptable, but not exactly correct, linkage is shown in Figure 2. Linkages that are not acceptable are classified as *wrong*.

Acceptable linkage:

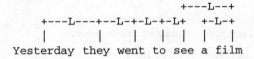

Correct linkage:

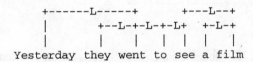

Fig. 2. Examples of acceptable and correct linkages.

We also carried out the above evaluation for the top three scoring linkages for each sentence in the test set. In this case, a sentence is regarded as having been parsed correctly if at least one among these three is a correct linkage for the sentence.

We observed that the HD approximation yields superior performance to the LST approximation under this evaluation criterion.

Table 5. Parsing correctness (measured using the most likely parse)

Model	% correct parses	% acceptable parses
LST	46.0	60.0
HD	68.75	85.9

Table 6. Parsing correctness (measured using the 3 most likely parses)

Model	% correct parses	% acceptable parses
LST	47.6	63.4
HD	85.9	92.2

10 Perplexity Results

The predictive accuracy of language models is often compared by evaluating their *perplexities* with respect to some common test data. For the same data set, a smaller perplexity measure implies a better model.

Perplexities with respect to our two corpora are computed for each of our probabilistic link grammar models, as well as the bigram model. The results are shown in Table 7. Since corpus B contains a larger number of sentences, the perplexity values

Table 7. Model comparison using perplexity measures

Corpus	Bigram	LST	HD
A	25.09	48.90	28.41
B	32.64	39.94	17.89

computed are more reliable. The HD model is superior to the bigram model according to the perplexity measures for corpus B and comparable for corpus A. Note however that the bigram perplexities are supplied for reference and are not directly comparable, because the corpora are too small to compensate for the larger number of parameters in the link grammar models. More significantly, for both corpora, the HD approximation yields significantly better predictive measures than the LST approximation.

11 Conclusion and Future Work

We believe that trend for probabilistic grammar models is towards increased *expressiveness* (as in the context-free formalism), *constrainedness* (as in dependency grammar and link grammar), and *lexicality* (as in link grammar and lexicalized tree-adjoining grammar).

In our work, we studied the viability of inducing probabilistic link grammars from corpora. The original model probabilistic link grammar proposed by Lafferty *et al.* (1992) was simplified to the untyped-link case with a limit on the number of connectors in the disjuncts, to make learning the grammar rules feasible. Later on, we also made some revisions to the probabilistic model in order to better capture word associations and to address the sparse data problem. We have also addressed a number of issues in improving the generalization process.

To test the viability of our approach, we have conducted experiments using English corpora of limited vocabulary and relatively simple sentences. Though our preliminary experiments are not on a very large scale, they are supportive of our approach. We are planning to conduct experiments for corpora of substantial sizes, to yield more representative perplexity measures.

The next step is to extend our grammar induction approach to deal with real corpora with larger vocabularies and more complex sentences. Learning can start with the short and simple sentences and proceed incrementally to the more complex sentence structures, coupled with the introduction of more complex disjuncts.

Acknowledgements

We are grateful to John Lafferty for explaining details of his probabilistic link grammar model; to Li Deng and Dit-Yan Yeung for valuable comments.

References

BAKER, JAMES K. 1979. Trainable grammars for speech recognition. In *Speech Communication Papers for the 97th Meeting of the Acoustic Society of America*, ed. by D. H. Klatt & J. J. Wolf, 547–550.

BAUM, LEONARD E. 1972. An inequality and associated maximization technique in statistical estimation for probabilistic functions of Markov processes. *Inequalities*, 3(1):1–8.

BROWN, PETER F., STEPHEN A. DELLA PIETRA, VINCENT J. DELLA PIETRA, JENNIFER C. LAI, & ROBERT L. MERCER. 1992. An estimate of an upper bound for the entropy of English. *Computational Linguistics*, 18(1):31–40.

CARROLL, GLENN & EUGENE CHARNIAK. 1992. Learning probabilistic dependency grammars from labelled text. In *AAAI Fall Symposium on Probabilistic Approaches to Natural Language*, 25–32, Cambridge, MA. Proceedings to appear as AAAI technical report.

DEMPSTER, A. P., N. M. LAIRD, & D. B. RUBIN. 1977. Maximum likelihood from incomplete data via the EM algorithm. *Journal of the Royal Statistical Society B*, 39:1–38.

JELINEK, FREDERICK, JOHN D. LAFFERTY, & ROBERT L. MERCER. 1992. Basic methods of probabilistic context-free grammars. In *Speech Recognition and Understanding: Recent Advances, Trends, and Applications*, Nato ASI Series, Vol. F75, 345–360. Springer Verlag.

LAFFERTY, JOHN D., DANIEL SLEATOR, & DAVY TEMPERLEY. 1992. Grammatical trigrams: A probabilistic model of link grammar. In *AAAI Fall Symposium on Probabilistic Approaches to Natural Language*, 89–97, Cambridge, MA. Proceedings to appear as AAAI technical report.

LARI, K. & S. J. YOUNG. 1990. The estimation of stochastic context-free grammars using the inside-outside algorithm. *Computer Speech and Language*, 4:35–56.

SLEATOR, DANIEL & DAVY TEMPERLEY. 1991. Parsing English with a link grammar. Technical Report CMU-CS-91-196, Dept. of Computer Science, Carnegie Mellon University.

STAROSTA, STANLEY. 1991. Dependency grammar and monostratal transfer. In *2nd Japan-Australia Joint Symposium on Natural Language Processing*.

Learning PP Attachment from Corpus Statistics

Alexander Franz

Center for Machine Translation
Carnegie Mellon University
Pittsburgh, PA 15213
amf@cs.cmu.edu

Abstract. One of the main problems in natural language analysis is the resolution of structural ambiguity. Prepositional Phrase (PP) attachment ambiguity is a particularly difficult case. We describe a robust PP disambiguation procedure that learns from a text corpus. The method is based on a loglinear model, a type of statistical model that is able to account for combinations of multiple categorial features. A series of experiments that compare the loglinear method against other strategies are described. For the difficult case of three possible attachment sites, the loglinear method predicts PP attachment with significantly higher accuracy than a simpler procedure that uses lexical association strengths. At the same time, on general newswire text, the accuracy of the statistical method remains 10% below the performance of human experts. This suggests a limit on what can be learned automatically from text, and points to the need to combine machine learning with human expertise.

1 Introduction

The resolution of structural ambiguity is a problem that has to be addressed by every natural language analysis system. One of the most difficult types of structural ambiguity is Prepositional Phrase (PP) attachment. An example, identifying the main constituents of the sentence, is shown below.

[$_{\text{Verb Phrase}}$ Adjust [$_{\text{Noun Phrase}}$ the beam focus] [$_{\text{PP}}$ with the calibration tool]].

Should the PP *with the calibration tool* be attached to the verb *adjust*, perhaps representing an instrument for the action? Or should it be attached to the Noun Phrase *the beam focus*, perhaps because it forms a part of it? We present a statistical model of PP attachment that uses a number of features to learn how to make the most likely attachment decision. Before this work is described in detail, the next section summarizes previous approaches to the PP attachment problem.

1.1 Syntactic Principles for Ambiguity Resolution

Early work on Human Sentence processing resulted in a number of syntactic principles for structural disambiguation. [11] proposed two simple principles of human parse preference:

Minimal Attachment. Construct a parse tree that has as few nodes as possible.

Late Closure (or **Right Association**). Attach new material to the lowest possible node.

In practice, the effect of these principles depends on the exact grammar rules that are assumed. More importantly, the proper attachment of a PP is often determined by the meaning of the constituents that are involved — syntactic principles alone are not sufficient.

1.2 Semantic Rules

The traditional Artificial Intelligence approach based on "commonsense semantics" used manually-constructed semantic inheritance hierarchies and frame-based semantic representations with semantic slot-filler constraints for structural disambiguation.

The ABSITY system [15] is a good example. ABSITY used a mechanism called the *Semantic Enquiry Desk* for structural disambiguation, including PP attachment. Hirst employed a frame-based representation system losely based on Montague's higher order intensional logic. In making attachment decisions, the Semantic Inquiry Desk implemented the following semantic principles:

Verb-guided Preferences. An attachment is favored if it obeys verb-guided preferences, as stated in the case slots of the frame corresponding to the verb. Cases may be "compulsory", "preferred", or "unpreferred".

Plausibility. An attachment is preferred if it is plausible. Plausibility is determined by "slot restriction predicates". Alternatively, following the "Exemplar Principle", objects or actions are considered plausible if "the knowledge base contains an instance of such an object or action, or an instance of something similar".

As many developers of large-scale natural language analysis systems have discovered, the commonsense semantics approach is fraught with difficulty. Hand-crafted semantic hierarchies are brittle, narrow in scope, and difficult to extend and keep internally consistent. Manually tuning such knowledge bases for the purpose of ambiguity resolution is a labor-intensive process that becomes difficult as the knowledge base grows larger, with diminishing returns on knowledge engineering efforts.

2 Learning PP Attachment from Text

In the last few years, attention has turned to methods for ambiguity resolution that learn from text corpora. This section highlights some recent results in order to set the scene for the experiments involving the loglinear method.

2.1 Lexical Associations

[10] introduced the notion of *lexical preferences* for ambiguity resolution, and [14] described a method for learning lexical preferences for PP attachment from a text corpus. Like all other recent corpus-based studies, Hindle & Rooth only addressed the pattern of a Verb followed by a Noun Phrase and a Prepositional Phrase, where the problem is simplified by only considering the head words. This is illustrated below.

[$_{\text{Verb}}$ Adjust] the beam [$_{\text{Noun}_1}$ focus] [$_{\text{Preposition}}$ with] the calibration [$_{\text{Noun}_2}$ tool].

Hindle & Rooth used 13 Million words of AP Newswire stories, which were processed with a POS tagger and Hindle's robust FIDDITCH parser. The corpus yielded 2.6 million NPs, and 223,000 verb-noun-preposition cases. (There were also additional verb or noun cases without prepositions, or with only one attachment site.) These cases were used to build a table of bigram counts, where each bigram is a pair of verb-preposition, noun-preposition, or verb/noun without a preposition. To obtain these bigrams, the prepositions were assigned to either the verb or the noun. Then, Maximum Likelihood estimates were used to derive the following probabilities:

$P_{\text{verb-attach}}(\text{preposition}|\text{verb,noun})$
$P_{\text{noun-attach}}(\text{preposition}|\text{verb,noun})$

The probabilities for specific nouns and verbs were smoothed with each preposition's observed frequency of noun attachment and verb attachment in general, $\frac{f(N,p)}{f(N)}$ and $\frac{f(V,p)}{f(V)}$. The attachment decision was then based on the log likelihood ratio between the probabilities for verb and noun attachment.

The model was evaluated on 880 verb-noun-preposition triples. 67% of the PPs were attached to the noun (i.e. in accordance with the principle of Right Association). Human judges on the triples obtained accuracy rates of 85%-88%. The lexical association procedure had an average accuracy rate of 80%.

2.2 Class-based Generalization

Hindle and Rooth's work estimated lexical association strengths between verbs/nouns and prepositions, so their sample space consisted of the cross-product of the set of nouns/verbs and the set of prepositions. It seems intuitively plausible that the objects of the PPs contain some disambiguating information, but adding the PP objects would mean enlarging the sample space to the cross-product of the set of verbs/nouns, the set of prepositions, and the set of nouns. Hindle & Rooth's lexically-based probability estimation scheme would not work over such a large sample space.Two subsequent studies solved this problem by coarsening the sample space by grouping words together into word classes.

[18] describes a series of experiments that included the prepositional objects. The nominal synonym sets from WORDNET were used to provide the word classes. Both the attachment site and the prepositional object are placed into a semantic or *conceptual* class, and the relative strengths of the conceptual association between the classes via the preposition are estimated from a text corpus.

Resnik & Hearst used the parsed Wall Street Journal (WSJ) texts from the Penn Treebank [16]. The model was evaluated on 174 test cases. Hindle & Rooth's lexical association strategy on this data achieved 81.6% accuracy, while Resnik & Hearst's conceptual association strategy obtained an average accuracy of 77.6%. When the two methods were combined by choosing the conceptual strategy if its confidence was above a threshold, and else the lexical association strategy, overall accuracy rose to 82.2%.

Another study that used class-based generalization was reported in [17]. In this experiment, the classes were derived automatically with a Mutual Information clustering procedure [5]. The method used features that correspond to exact word matching on any of the four head words (Verb, $Noun_1$, Preposition, $Noun_2$), and class membership of a head word.

An automatic procedure was used to select the most informative subset of all the possible features; peak performance was obtained with around 200 features. These features were combined in a maximum entropy model. Using the parsed WSJ corpus, trained on 20,000 PP cases, and evaluated on 3,000 cases, the model achieved 81.6% accuracy. A second experiment was performed on IBM computer manuals that were annotated by the University of Lancaster. Here, after training on 8,000 PP cases, an evaluation on 900 PP cases showed 84.1% accuracy. Finally, Ratnaparkhi et al. compared their maximum entropy method to decision trees using the same features, and found that the decision tree procedure had lower accuracy: 77.7% on WSJ texts, and 79.5% on the computer manuals.

3 Learning PP Attachment

We will now turn to the experiments involving the loglinear method. The premise of these experiments is that it is necessary to combine lexical and syntactic features to resolve PP attachment ambiguity. The method is based on a loglinear model, since that is a type of statistical model that is able to combine a number of categorial features. The advantage of using a loglinear model is that it takes into account the effects of *combinations* of feature values, as well as the main effects of individual feature values.

3.1 Overview of Modeling Procedure

Training and evaluation of the loglinear method for involves the following steps:

1. Training samples and a pool for random sets of evaluation samples are chosen from the Penn Treebank.
2. Exploratory data analysis is performed in order to determine relevant features, their possible values, and an approximation of their interactions.
3. The feature values for each PP case in the training data are determined. This results in a feature vector for each training sample.
4. The feature vectors are cross-classified in a contingency table.
5. The contingency table is smoothed with a loglinear model.
6. Conditional probabilities P(attachment|features) from the smoothed contingency table are used to predict PP attachment for a series of random sets of PP cases from the evaluation pool. Performance statistics are kept.

The following sections describe each step in more detail.

3.2 Features

The first step was to examine some PPs in the training corpus, and to determine an initial set of features for PP attachment disambiguation. This resulted in the following set of features.

PREPOSITION. Possible values of this feature include one of the more frequent prepositions in the training set, or the value *other-prep*. The set of frequent prepositions contains the following: *about, across, after, against, among, around, as, at, before, between, by, during, for, from, in, into, like, of, on, over, per, since, through, to, toward, under, upon, with, within, without*.

VERB-LEVEL. Lexical association strength between the verb and the preposition. (This is described in detail below.) Note that this is estimated without a general verb/noun skewing term as used by Hindle & Rooth.

NOUN-LEVEL. Lexical association strength between the noun and the preposition. (Further details below.) Note that this is estimated without a general verb/noun skewing term.

NOUN-TAG. Part of speech of the nominal attachment site. This is included to account for correlations between attachment and syntactic category of the nominal attachment site, such as "PPs disfavor attachment to proper nouns".

NOUN-DEFINITENESS. Does the nominal attachment site include a definite determiner? This feature is included to account for a possible correlation between PP attachment to the nominal site and definiteness, which was derived by Hirst from Crain & Steedman's principle of presupposition minimization.

PP-OBJECT-TAG. Part of speech of the object of the prepositional phrase. Certain types of PP objects favor attachment to the verbal or nominal site. For example, temporal PPs, such as "in 1959" where the prepositional object is tagged CD (cardinal), favor attachment to the VP, because it is more likely to have a temporal dimension.

The association strengths for VERB-LEVEL and NOUN-LEVEL were measured using the Mutual Information between the noun or verb, and the preposition. Mutual Information provides an estimate of the magnitude of the ratio between two measures:

1. The probability of observing the verb or noun together with an attached prepositional phrase with a certain preposition, i.e. the joint probability P(verb/noun,preposition).
2. The probability of observing both the noun or verb and the prepositional phrase assuming that the two events are independent, i.e, P(verb/noun)P(preposition).

The probabilities were derived as Maximum Likelihood estimates from all PP cases in the training data. That is, the probabilities were estimated as follows, were $f(x)$ is the frequency of event x that was observed in the training sample:

$$(1) \quad P(\text{verb},\text{preposition}) \approx \frac{f(\text{verb},\text{preposition})}{\text{Number of verb tokens}}$$

$$(2) \quad P(\text{noun},\text{preposition}) \approx \frac{f(\text{noun},\text{preposition})}{\text{Number of noun tokens}}$$

(3) $P(\text{noun}) \approx \dfrac{f(\text{noun})}{\text{Number of noun tokens}}$

(4) $P(\text{verb}) \approx \dfrac{f(\text{verb})}{\text{Number of verb tokens}}$

(5) $P(\text{preposition}_{\text{verb}}) \approx \dfrac{f(\text{preposition attached to any verb})}{\text{Number of verb tokens}}$

(6) $P(\text{preposition}_{\text{noun}}) \approx \dfrac{f(\text{preposition attached to any noun})}{\text{Number of noun tokens}}$

Then, the Mutual Information values for nouns and prepositions were computed as follows:

(7) $\text{MI}(\text{noun,preposition}) = \dfrac{P(\text{noun,preposition})}{P(\text{noun})P(\text{preposition}_{\text{noun}})}$

And the Mutual Information values for verbs and prepositions were computed similarly:

(8) $\text{MI}(\text{verb,preposition}) = \dfrac{P(\text{verb,preposition})}{P(\text{verb})P(\text{preposition}_{\text{verb}})}$

The Mutual Information values were ordered by rank. Then, the association strengths were categorized into eight levels (A-H), depending on percentile in the ranked Mutual Information values. For example, the top two percentiles of the noun-preposition Mutual Information values were assigned level A, the third through tenth percentiles were assigned level B, and so on.

3.3 The Loglinear Model

A loglinear model is a statistical model of the effect of the features and their combinations on the cell counts in a contingency table. A contingency table is an array with one dimension for each feature. During training, each cell in the contingency table records the frequency of data with the appropriate combination of feature values. Then, a loglinear model is used to smooth the cell counts, in order to "obtain cell estimates for every cell in a sparse array, even if the observed count is zero" [2].

The model is called "loglinear" because its mathematical form is a linear combination of the logs of cell counts. Let $m_{ijk...}$ be the expected cell count for cell $(i, j, k, ...)$. The general form of a loglinear model is as follows:

(9) $\log m_{ijk...} = u + u_{1(i)} + u_{2(j)} + u_{3(k)} + u_{12(ij)} + u_{...} + ...$

In Formula 9, u is the mean of the logarithms of all the expected counts, $u + u_{1(i)}$ is the mean of the logarithms of the expected counts at level i of the first feature, $u + u_{2(j)}$ is the mean of the logarithms of the expected counts at level j of the second feature, and so on. In other words, the term $u_{1(i)}$ represents the deviation of the expected cell counts at level i of the first feature from the grand mean u. A loglinear model provides a way to estimate expected cell counts that depend not only on the main effects of the features, but also on the interactions between features. This is achieved by adding "interaction terms" to the model. For example, the term $u_{12(ij)}$ represents the effect of the combination of the ith level of the first variable and the jth level of the second variable. For further details, see [1].

3.4 Estimating Cell Counts

The expected cell counts $\hat{m}_{ijk...}$ are estimated using the *iterative proportional fitting* algorithm [Deming and Stephan, 1940]. The interaction terms in the loglinear models represent constraints on the estimated expected marginal totals. Each of these marginal constraints translates into an adjustment scaling factor for the cell entries. The iterative procedure has the following steps:

1. Start with initial estimates for the estimated expected cell counts. For example, set all $\hat{m}_{ijk...} = 1.0$.
2. Adjust each cell entry by multiplying it with the scaling factors. This moves the cell entries towards satisfaction of the marginal constraints.
3. Iterate through the adjustment steps until the algorithm converges and the maximum difference ϵ between the marginal totals observed in the sample and the estimated marginal totals reaches a certain minimum threshold, e.g. $\epsilon = 0.1$.

In this way, the cell counts are smoothed by the application of the interaction terms specified in the loglinear model. The smoothed contingency table is then used to obtain the conditional probability distribution P(attachment|features), which is used to predict the PP attachment.

3.5 Experimental Data and Evaluation

Training and evaluation data was obtained from the Penn treebank. All 1.1 million words of parsed text in the Brown Corpus, and 2.6 million words of parsed WSJ articles, were used. Most instances of PPs that are attached to VPs and NPs were extracted. This resulted in 82,000 PP cases from the Brown Corpus, and 89,000 PP cases from the WSJ articles. Verbs and nouns were lemmatized to their root forms if the root forms were attested in the corpus. If the root form did not occur in the corpus, then the inflected form was used. For example, the verb *relegate* does not occur in its uninflected form, but always occurs as the past participle *relegated*, usually forming the collocation *relegated to* (and few times *relegated for*).

All the PP cases from the Brown Corpus, and 50,000 of the WSJ cases, were reserved as training data. The remaining 39,000 WSJ PP cases formed the evaluation pool. In each experiment, performance was evaluated on a series of 25 random samples of 100 PP cases from the evaluation pool.

This evaluation scheme has two advantages. First, this scheme avoids the fallacy of simply maximizing performance on a fixed evaluation set. Second, the average accuracy figures that are usually reported in the literature indicate the accuracy to which a given method will converge if repeated a large number of times. But such average figures do not indicate the variance of the method — how likely are individual outcomes to stray from the average, and how far will they stray? Variance is an important consideration, since, in an application, one is concerned with the behavior of the method on rather small samples, such as individual written sentences or spoken "dialog turns". Evaluating a series of small samples gives an indication of the variance.

In this study, boxplots are used to summarize the performance of the PP attachment method over a series of test samples. The data points are arranged in a vertical line from the lowest to the highest number. The box is drawn between the *quartiles*; that is, it includes the central 50% of the data points. The middle value or *median* is indicated by a line across the box. The whiskers are drawn from the ends of the box for a distance of 1.5 times the interquartile range. Any data points that fall outside this range are considered outliers, and are indicated by separate marks.

4   Experimental Results: Two Attachments Sites

All previous work on automatic PP attachment disambiguation has only considered the pattern of a verb phrase containing an object, and a final prepositional phrase. This leads to two possible attachment sites, the verb and the object of the verb. This pattern is usually further simplified by considering only the heads of the possible attachment sites, corresponding to the sequence "Verb Noun$_1$ Preposition Noun$_2$".

The first set of experiments concerns this pattern. There are 53,000 such cases in the training data, and 16,000 such cases in the evaluation pool. A number of methods were evaluated on this pattern according to the 25-sample scheme described in Section 3.5 above. The results are shown in Figure 1. In this figure, each boxplot corresponds to the series of accuracy results obtained with one attachment disambiguation strategy. The following sections describe this series of experiments in detail.

4.1   Baseline: Right Association

Prepositional phrases exhibit a tendency to attach to the most recent possible attachment site; this is referred to as the principle of "Right Association". For the "V NP PP" pattern, this means attaching to the noun phrase. This strategy is simple to implement, and it is used here as the baseline. On the evaluation samples, a median of 65% of the PP cases were attached to the noun phrase. This is labeled "Right Association" in Figure 1.

4.2   Results of Lexical Association

The "lexical association" strategy of Hindle & Rooth was described in Section 2.1 above. This method was reimplemented to provide a comparison against the loglinear method. In the reimplementation, the probabilities were estimated from all the PP cases in the training set. Since the corpora are bracketed, it was possible to estimate the lexical associations with much less noise than Hindle & Rooth, who were working with unparsed text. The median accuracy for the reimplementation of Hindle & Rooth's method was 81%. This is labeled "Hindle & Rooth" in Figure 1.

4.3   Results of the Statistical Model

Next, the loglinear method was evaluated. Based on the set of features listed in Section 3.2 above, different feature sets and different interaction terms for the loglinear model were implemented. The model that obtained the highest accuracy used the following features: PREPOSITION, VERB-LEVEL, NOUN-LEVEL, and NOUN-DEFINITENESS. This included all second-order interaction terms in the loglinear model. This method achieved a median accuracy of 82%; it is labeled "Loglinear Model" in Figure 1.

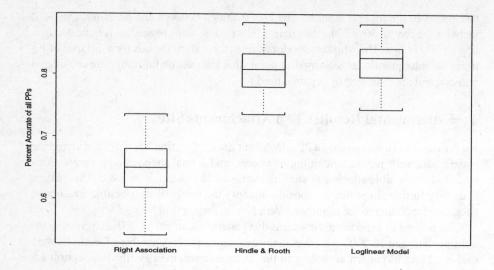

Fig. 1. PP attachment accuracy for two possible attachment sites. The figure compares three different strategies for performing automatic PP attachment. Each boxplot corresponds to a series of 25 random samples, with each sample containing 100 PPs.

4.4 Discussion

As is clear from the boxplot, the results of the loglinear model are very similar to the results of Hindle & Rooth's lexical association strategy. The median for the loglinear model is about one percent higher, and the spread of the loglinear evaluation samples is a little bit smaller, but the range is very similar. Overall, there is no significant difference between the two strategies.

5 Experimental Results: Three Attachment Sites

On the pattern with two possible attachment sites, the loglinear method did not perform better than the lexical association strategy. But in actual text, there are often more than two possible attachment sites for a prepositional phrase. For this reason, a second series of experiments was carried out that investigated different PP attachment strategies for cases with more than two possible attachment sites.

5.1 Additional PP Patterns

As suggested by [13], the "Verb NP PP" case might be relatively easy because the two possible attachment sites differ in syntactic category, and therefore might have very different kinds of lexical preferences. This is clearly true for some prepositions. For example, statistically speaking, most PPs with *of* attach to nouns, and most PPs with *to*

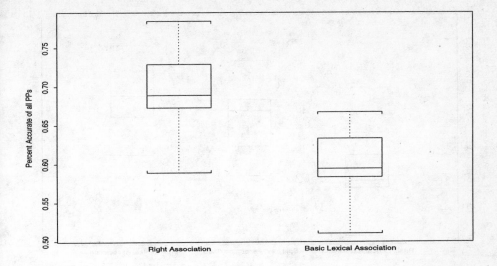

Fig. 2. PP attachment accuracy results for three possible attachment sites. The diagram compares the strategies of "Right Association" and "Lexical Association" for automatic PP attachment. Each boxplot corresponds to a series of 25 random samples, with each sample containing 100 PPs.

and *by* attach to verbs. Thus, a more realistic test of automatic PP attachment procedures should include two attachment sites that have the same syntactic category.

One possible pattern that fulfills this criterion would be two verbs followed by a prepositional phrase, i.e. "Verb$_1$ Verb$_2$ PP". However, there are rather few instances of this pattern in the corpus. Furthermore, this pattern probably exhibits a strong tendency towards right association; that is, most PPs would attach to Verb$_2$.

Another possible pattern that would include syntactically homogeneous possible attachment sites is "Noun$_1$ Noun$_2$ PP". However, most cases in the corpus where a prepositional phrase is preceded by two possible nominal attachment sites occur inside a verb phrase. In this case, the verb should also be considered as a possible attachment site. Thus, the pattern "Verb Noun$_1$ Noun$_2$ Preposition Noun$_3$" was selected for the second series of experiments. There were 28,000 such cases in the training data, and 8000 cases in the evaluation pool.

5.2 Baseline: Right Association

As in the first set of experiments, a number of methods were evaluated on the three attachment site pattern with 25 samples of 100 random PP cases. The results are shown in Figures 2–4. The baseline is again provided by attachment according to the principle of "Right Attachment" to the most recent possible site, i.e. attachment to Noun$_2$. A median of 69% of the PP cases were attached to Noun$_2$. This is labeled "Right Association" in Figure 2.

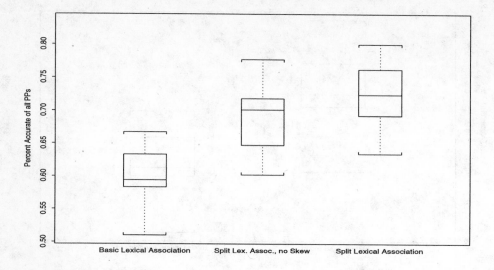

Fig. 3. PP attachment accuracy for three possible attachment sites. The figure compares three different strategies for performing automatic PP attachment based on lexical associations. Each boxplot corresponds to a series of 25 random samples, with each sample containing 100 PPs.

5.3 Results of Lexical Association

Next, the lexical association method was evaluated on this pattern. First, the method described by Hindle & Rooth was reimplemented by using the lexical association strengths estimated from all PP cases. The results for this strategy are labeled "Basic Lexical Association" in Figure 2. This method only achieved a median accuracy of 59%, which is worse than always choosing the rightmost attachment site. Of course, Hindle & Rooth's method was not designed for the case of three attachment sites, so these results should not be taken as a criticism of Hindle & Rooth's approach, but only as an indication that a method that only uses lexical association strength is not sufficient for this pattern. These results also suggest that Hindle & Rooth's scoring function worked well in the "Verb Noun$_1$ Preposition Noun$_2$" case not only because it was an accurate estimator of lexical associations between individual verbs/nouns and prepositions which determine PP attachment, but perhaps also because it accurately predicted the general verb-noun skew of individual prepositions.

5.4 Results of Enhanced Lexical Association

The direct application of the lexical association strategy to the pattern with three attachment sites resulted in rather low accuracy. It seems intuitively plausible that this pattern calls for a combination of a structural feature with lexical association strength. To implement this, Hindle & Rooth's method was modified to estimate attachments to the verb, first noun, and second noun separately. This resulted in estimates that combine

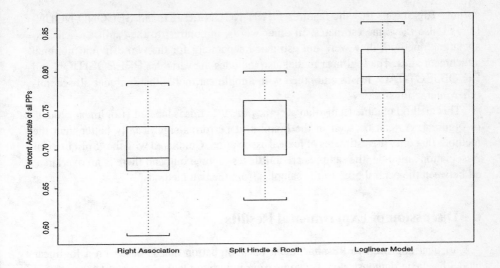

Fig. 4. Summary of PP attachment accuracy results for three possible attachment sites. Each boxplot corresponds to a series of 25 random samples, with each sample containing 100 PPs.

the structural feature directly with the lexical association strength. The modified method performed much better than the original lexical association scoring function, but it still only obtained a median accuracy of 72%. This is labeled "Split Lexical Association" in Figure 3, which compares three different lexical association strategies for the pattern with three attachment sites.

It is possible that the general skewing terms $\frac{f(N,p)}{f(N)}$ and $\frac{f(V,p)}{f(V)}$ used by Hindle & Rooth to smooth the lexical association estimates were overwhelming the individual lexical associations. To test this possibility, a strategy using three-way split lexical association estimates without the smoothing terms was also evaluated. This method, labeled "Split Lex. Assoc., no Skew" in Figure 3, performed worse than the three-way split estimation procedure, obtaining a median accuracy of 70%.

5.5 Results of the Loglinear Model

The relatively low accuracy of the basic lexical association strength strategy on the "Verb Noun Phrase Noun Phrase Prepositional Phrase" pattern with three possible attachment sites indicates that this pattern calls for combining structural and lexical sources of evidence.

To achieve this, various loglinear models that combine different subsets of the features listed in Section 3.2 were implemented. The highest accuracy was obtained by a loglinear model that includes the variables VERB-LEVEL, FIRST-NOUN-LEVEL, and SECOND-NOUN-LEVEL. These features use the same Mutual Information-based measure of lexical association as the previous loglinear model for two possible attachment sites, which were estimated from all nominal and verbal PP attachments in the corpus. This means that the features FIRST-NOUN-LEVEL and SECOND-NOUN-LEVEL use the same estimates; in other words, in contrast to the "split Lexical Association" method, they were not estimated separately for the two different nominal attachment sites. The loglinear model also includes the variables PREPOSITION and PP-OBJECT-TAG. It was smoothed with a loglinear model that includes all second-order interactions.

This method obtained a median accuracy of 79%; this is labeled "Loglinear Model" in Figure 4. As can be seen in the boxplot, it performs significantly better than the methods that only use estimates of lexical association. Compared with the "Split Lexical Association" method, the samples are a little less spread out, and there is no overlap at all between the central 50% of the samples from the two methods.

6 Discussion of Experimental Results

A statistical approach to PP attachment disambiguation that is based on a loglinear model has been demonstrated. By comparing it with the lexical association strategy, it was shown that this method is able to combine lexical and syntactic clues; this suggests that it is also applicable to other problematic types of structural ambiguity.

The main results for the pattern with three possible attachment sites are summarized in Figure 4. The Lexical Association strategy with split nominal attachment site estimates does not perform well on the more difficult pattern with three possible attachment sites. The statistical method, which uses a loglinear model to combine a number of different features, and so provides probability estimates based on the *combinations* of different features, predicts attachment with significantly higher accuracy, achieving a clear separation between the central 50% of the evaluation samples.

The simpler "Verb Noun Phrase Prepositional Phrase" pattern with two syntactically different attachment sites yielded a null result: The loglinear method did not perform significantly better than the lexical association method. This might mean that the results of the lexical association method cannot be improved by adding other features. (It is also possible that the features that could result in improved accuracy were not identified in this study.)

6.1 Accuracy of Evaluation Data

The PP attachments in the Penn Treebank are not completely accurate. As noted by [14], there are some types of prepositional phrases for which it is not possible to identify the correct attachment site, since there is little discernible difference in meaning between different attachments. This means that in the ideal case, an automatic procedure should be evaluated only on sentences for which there is a clearly identifiable correct attachment. If it is not possible to prepare such evaluation data, and a corpus such as the Penn Treebank is used as the gold standard, then the target should not be 100% accuracy, but a lower figure that reflects the presence of some undecidable PP cases in the evaluation data.

There has been one study that evaluated the accuracy of the attachments in the Penn Treebank on sentences for which human experts were able to identify a correct attachment. Starting with 300 random sentences from the Penn Treebank, [17] found that three human treebanking experts agreed on 274 PP attachments. Thus, the experts did not agree on almost 9% of the PP cases. Judged against the gold standard of the 274 PP attachments agreed upon by three human experts, the Penn Treebank had an error rate of 4%.

6.2 Comparison against Human Performance

Some previous studies have investigated the performance of humans on PP attachment tasks. If random sentences with "Verb NP PP" cases from the Penn treebank are taken as the gold standard, then [14] and [17] report that human experts using only head words obtain 85%-88% accuracy. If the human experts are allowed to consult the whole sentence, their accuracy judged against random Treebank sentences rises to approximately 93%. Perhaps this figure could be taken as the target for automatic PP attachment procedures evaluated against random sentences from the Penn Treebank.

On the "Verb NP PP" pattern, the loglinear model achieved a median accuracy of 82%. Compared with the results of the studies using human treebanking experts, there remains an accuracy gap of 3%-6%, which remains a challenge for future work. And, if the experts are allowed to consult the whole sentence, the accuracy gap rises to about 11%. (Note that these figures should only be taken as an approximation; it is difficult to compare accuracy rates from different studies.)

The results reported in this study were obtained on Wall Street Articles, which are stylistically homogeneous, but still somewhat broad in scope compared to more tightly circumscribed domains. The results reported in [17] and [19] suggest that accuracy would be higher if the loglinear method was trained and evaluated on text from a more restricted domain.

The results show that there is still a performance gap between human experts and the automatically trained procedure. Perhaps future research will show how the accuracy of the statistical learner can eb raised by taking into account additional aspects of the context.

7 Acknowledgments

Thanks to R. W. Oldford for CL-TO-S, a package to call S (a precursor to S-PLUS) from COMMON LISP. CL-TO-S was obtained from STATLIB, an archive of statistical software, papers, datasets, and mailing list digests. STATLIB (http://lib.stat.cmu.edu/) is maintained by Mike Meyer at CMU.

References

1. Alan Agresti. *Categorical Data Analysis*. John Wiley & Sons, New York, 1990.
2. Y. M. Bishop, S. E. Fienberg, and P. W. Holland. *Discrete Multivariate Analysis: Theory and Practice*. MIT Press, Cambridge, MA, 1975.
3. Lois Boggess, Rajeev Agarwall, and Ron Davis. Disambiguation of Prepositional Phrases in automatically labelled technical text. In *AAAI-91*, pages 784–789, 1991.
4. Eric Brill and Philip Resnik. A rule-based approach to Prepositional Phrase attachment disambiguation. In *Proceedings of COLING-94*, pages 1198–1204, 1994.
5. Peter F. Brown, Vincent J. Della Pietra, Peter V. deSouza, and Robert L. Mercer. Class-based n-gram models of natural language. *Computational Linguistics*, 18(4):467–480, 1990.
6. Stephen Crain and Mark J. Steedman. On not being led up the garden path: The use of context by the psychological syntax processor. In David R. Dowty, Lauri Karttunen, and Anrnold M. Zwicky, editors, *Natural Language Parsing*, pages 320–358, Cambridge, UK, 1985. Cambridge University Press.
7. W. E. Deming and F. F. Stephan. On a least squares adjustment of a sampled frequency table when the expected marginal totals are known. *Ann. Math. Statis*, (11):427–444, 1940.
8. Richard O. Duda and Peter E. Hart. *Pattern Classification and Scene Analysis*. John Wiley & Sons, New York, 1973.
9. Stephen E. Fienberg. *The Analysis of Cross-Classified Categorical Data*. The MIT Press, Cambridge, MA, second edition edition, 1980.
10. M. Ford, J.W. Bresnan, and R. Kaplan. A competence-based theory of syntactic closure. In Joan W. Bresnan, editor, *The Mental Representation of Grammatical Relations*, Cambridge, MA, 1982. MIT Press.
11. Lyn Frazier. *On Comprehending Sentences: Syntactic Parsing Strategies*. PhD thesis, University of Massachusetts, Amherst, MA, 1979.
12. Lyn Frazier. Sentence processing: A tutorial review. In M. Coltheart, editor, *Attention and Performance XII*, pages 559–586, Hillsdale, NJ, 1987. Lawrence Erlbaum.
13. Ted Gibson and Neal Pearlmutter. A corpus-based analysis of psycholinguistic constraints on PP attachment. In Charles Clifton Jr., Lyn Frazier, and Keith Rayner, editors, *Perspectives on Sentence Processing*. Lawrence Erlbaum Associates, 1994.
14. Donald Hindle and Mats Rooth. Structural ambiguity and lexical relations. *Computational Linguistics*, 19(1):103–120, 1993.
15. Graeme Hirst. *Semantic Interpretation and the Resolution of Ambiguity*. Cambridge University Press, Cambridge, 1986.
16. Mitchell P. Marcus, Beatrice Santorini, and Mary Ann Marcinkiewicz. Building a large annotated corpus of English: The Penn Treebank. *Computational Linguistics*, 19(2):313–330, 1993.
17. Adwait Ratnaparkhi, Jeff Rynar, and Salim Roukos. A maximum entropy model for Prepositional Phrase attachment. In *ARPA Workshop on Human Language Technology*, Plainsboro, NJ, March 8-11 1994.
18. Philip Resnik and Marti Hearst. Structural ambiguity and conceptual relations. In *Proceedings of the Workshop on Very Large Corpora*, pages 58–64, 1993.
19. Eiichiro Sumita, Osamu Furuse, and Hitoshi Iida. An example-based disambiguation of Prepositional Phrase attachment. In *Fifth International Conference on Theoretical and Methodological Isues in Machine Tranlation*, pages 80–91, Kyoto, Japan, 1993.
20. Greg Whittemore, Kathleen Ferrara, and Hans Brunner. Empirical study of predictive powers of simple attachment schemes for post-modifier Prepositional Phrases. In *Proceedings of ACL-90*, pages 23–30, 1990.

A Minimum Description Length Approach to Grammar Inference

Peter Grünwald*

CWI, P.O. Box 4079, 1009 AB AMSTERDAM, The Netherlands

Abstract. We describe a new abstract model for the computational learning of grammars. The model deals with a learning process in which an algorithm is given an input of a large set of training sentences that belong to some unknown grammar. The algorithm then tries to infer this grammar. Our model is based on the well-known *Minimum Description Length Principle*. It is quite close to, but more general than several other existing approaches. We have shown that one of these approaches (based on *n*-gram statistics) coincides exactly with a restricted version of our own model. We have used a restricted version of the algorithm implied by the model to find classes of related words in natural language texts. It turns out that for this task, which can be seen as a 'degenerate' case of grammar learning, our approach gives quite good results. As opposed to many other approaches, it also provides a clear 'stopping criterion' indicating at what point the learning process should stop.

1 Introduction

In this paper we construct an algorithm that has as its sole input a *training text*, that is, a very large fragment of a natural language text in for example English. It should then output grammatical rules underlying this language; so in this case, English grammar rules. Thus learning takes place using positive examples only – possibly including noise. No explicit negative example is ever given. Approaches along these lines are commonly called [8] 'Grammatical Inference'. It should immediately be noted that there are severe limits to the grammatical inference approach: we will simply use context-free grammars and the fact that they are not capable of fully capturing natural language grammars is just one of many weaknesses of the approach [8]. Nevertheless, it will turn out to be interesting to see just how far one can get with such an abstract approach.

Our algorithm is based on the *Minimum Description Length* (MDL) *Principle*, introduced in its present form by Rissanen [10]. The original ideas behind this very general principle stem from R.J. Solomonoff. In his landmark 1964 paper [11] they were already applied to grammar inference. In the next two sections we will give a very short introduction to the MDL Principle and to how it can be

---

* E-mail: pdg@cwi.nl. Partially supported by the European Union through Neuro-COLT ESPRIT Working Group Nr. 8556, and by NWO through NFI Project AL-ADDIN under Contract number NF 62-376.

used for grammar induction. Section 4 discusses our approach, first describing its algorithmic aspects and then explaining how we compute description lengths. The reader who wants to see first what this approach leads to before worrying about the details may want to have a look at Sect. 5 first, where we discuss the results of some experimental data we obtained with an implementation of our algorithm. Section 6 compares our model to some others and discusses whether our approach makes sense from a linguist's point of view. The paper ends with some concluding remarks.

2 The MDL Principle

One of the basic ideas of Solomonoff's theory of induction[2] [11] is that 'learning' can, under the right circumstances, be seen as 'finding a shorter description of the observed data'. Here one views learning as finding a hypothesis that explains some observed data and makes predictions about data yet unseen. The MDL Principle, introduced in its present form by J. Rissanen [10], is a principle of statistics that is explicitly based upon Solomonoff's ideas. It goes as follows:

MINIMUM DESCRIPTION LENGTH PRINCIPLE. *The best theory to explain a set of data is the one which minimizes the sum of*

1. *the length, in bits, of the description of the theory;*
2. *the length, in bits, of the data when encoded with the help of the theory.*

The general idea here is that an 'empty' theory (the words 'theory' and 'hypothesis' will be used interchangeably here) which does not give any clue as to the sort of data we are dealing with, has no predictive value whatsoever. On the other hand, a theory that describes all of the data perfectly is very much restricted by the data and therefore does not really generalize. Therefore, it has no predictive value either. We have to find some trade-off, and in the next section we will see in a practical setting that the total description length can become much smaller using such a trade-off.

3 Grammar Learning and the MDL Principle

Consider three grammars that can account for a given natural language text [11]:

the promiscuous grammar This is an 'empty' grammar: given an input alphabet (vocabulary) of words, it accepts every concatenation of them as a sentence. Of course, it is a hopeless overgeneralization.

the ad hoc grammar This grammar accepts exactly all the sentences it has seen so far, but no single different sentence. Of course, it is a hopeless undergeneralization.

---

[2] See [9] for a good introduction to Solomonoff's theory.

the 'right' grammar

This is just a context-free grammar of English as can be found in several textbooks. In a sense, it is the best generalization we can arrive at within the context free grammar framework.

Now consider the description length we arrive at if we want to reproduce the entire training text of length (i.e. the number of words) L, where we may choose L to be much larger than the description length of the right grammar. From the MDL point of view, here the training text fulfills the role of the *data*, and the grammar the role of the *theory*:

The promiscuous grammar (which has a very short description size of course) says nothing at all about the example sentences that have been seen so far; so in order to reproduce these sentences, we must list them all explicitly. The ad hoc grammar (which has a description size of about L) completely describes the training text (provided we have written down and numbered the production rules $S \rightarrow <$ sentence $>$ in the same order as in the training text). The ad hoc grammar thus provides a data description of size approximately 0 but a grammar description of size approximately L. The total description lengths for both the ad hoc and the promiscuous grammar are of size about L. The right grammar however makes for a much smaller description of the data, while it has a fixed theory size. Therefore its total description length will be much lower than L, provided our training text is long enough. To see why this is so, one must appreciate the *constraining* function of a grammar:

Suppose the first word of a sentence has turned out to be an interrogative pronoun (like *where*, *who*, etc.). The grammar now predicts that the next word can *only* be a verb[3]! If we suppose that about 1/4 of all different words in natural language are verbs, this means that, given a vocabulary of size n, we need to reserve about $\log n - 2$ bits for this word. This is 2 less than the $\log n$ we would need for the unique specification of this word without the help of a grammar.

Each regularity of this kind helps to reduce the description length for some words in the training text. Therefore, the longer the training text, the bigger the savings will be. We have made use of regularity in the training text in order to shorten its description. The shortest description possible is the one that makes use of all the regularity that may be found at all – and for large training texts this can only be a grammar similar to the one we were looking for [11]!

Note that we have now found a *criterion* to find out if learning has occurred (we arrive at a shorter description length of theory+data given the theory), but we have not yet given any guidelines as to *how* learning should take place. Trying to keep things as abstract as possible, we will use the description length for that, too. Simply trying out all grammars that are consistent with a given text and

---

[3] Of course, this is not entirely true ('What *the* ... does this research lead to??'). But we will see in section 6 that the fact that the next word will be a verb *with high probability* can already be used to reduce the description length of the training text.

picking the one that yields the shortest description is infeasible. Therefore we adopted a 'greedy' approach: One starts with a set of possible hypotheses, the *hypothesis space* $\mathcal{H}$ (consisting of all grammars that could account for a given training text. E.g., the set of all context free grammars). One picks one of the hypotheses $h \in \mathcal{H}$ as the current one, and one has *operators* transforming the current hypothesis into another hypothesis $h' \in \mathcal{H}$. At each step, one performs the operation that yields the highest immediate decrease in description length (of the new hypothesis plus the data given this new hypothesis). If no such operation is possible any more, learning stops, and the current hypothesis is output as the 'best' one. Of course one may get stuck in 'local minima' using this approach. In the following section we look at the choices that have to be made and the details that have to be filled in if one wants to turn such a greedy approach into a *practical* model.

4 Our Approach

The Algorithm

The input to our algorithm is a training text $t_1^L = t_1 t_2 \ldots t_L$. L is the total length of the training text; t_i stands for the i-th word of the training text. We have an alphabet $\mathcal{W}$ of different (distinct) words, and we will index the elements w of $\mathcal{W}$ from 1 to $|\mathcal{W}|$. So for each i, $1 \leq i \leq L$, there is exactly one j, $1 \leq j \leq |\mathcal{W}|$, such that $t_i = w_j$.

Given t_1^L, the algorithm tries to build a grammar covering it. It does so in a bottom-up way. We define a *partial grammar* $\mathcal{C}$ as a set of context-free grammar rules for a training text, but not necessarily with a starting symbol. Thus correct sentences may be partially parsed, but sometimes not be completely reduced to the non-terminal *Sentence*. In [6] we make the notion of 'partially parsing' precise. One can describe $\mathcal{C}$ in a somewhat non-standard way as a set of classes $c \in \mathcal{C}$. For each class c there is exactly one corresponding 'non-terminal' c'. The class then is the set of production rules with this non-terminal on the left-hand-side. There are two basic operations: the merge operation or *merge* for short and the construction operation or *construct* for short.

If two productions c_l and c_k are merged, then they disappear from $\mathcal{C}$ and are replaced by a new class c_n that contains the union of the grammar rules in c_l and c_k, with all left-hand sides replaced by c_n'. For example, suppose for the moment we have arrived at a $\mathcal{C}$ with $|\mathcal{C}| = 10$ and $c_5 = \{c_5' \rightarrow c_6' c_7' | c_2'\}$ and $c_4 = \{c_4' \rightarrow c_3'\}$. Now if we merged c_5 and c_4, we would arrive at a new class $c_{new} = \{c_{new}' \rightarrow c_6' c_7' | c_2' | c_3'\}$ and we would remove c_5 and c_4 from $\mathcal{C}$ and then re-index $\mathcal{C}$ so as to incorporate c_{new}. Because it simplifies the notation, we will often write this step as if we would let the merged classes continue to exist and simply increase the number of classes by one. In our example, this means that we would introduce a new class $c_{11} = \{c_{11}' \rightarrow c_5' | c_4'\}$. Notice that this yields an equivalent new partial grammar; but we will see later that when computing the description length, it is important to keep in mind that a merge really *decreases* the number of classes by one in stead of increasing them, as the simpler notation wrongly suggests.

If two classes c_l and c_k are constructed, then a new class c_m is formed containing just one production rule: $c_m = \{c'_m \rightarrow c'_l c'_k\}$. The basic functioning of our algorithm is shown in Fig. 1.

---

1 **ASSIGN** ONE SEPARATE CLASS TO EACH DIFFERENT WORD THAT OCCURS IN THE TRAINING TEXT: $c_1 := \{c'_1 \rightarrow w_1\}$, $c_2 := \{c'_2 \rightarrow w_2\}$ ETC. TOGETHER THESE CLASSES FORM THE INITIAL PARTIAL GRAMMAR $\mathcal{C}$.

2 **COMPUTE** THE TOTAL DESCRIPTION LENGTH OF THE TRAINING TEXT WHICH IS THE SUM OF THE DESCRIPTION LENGTH OF THE TRAINING TEXT *given* THE SET OF CLASSES $\mathcal{C}$ AND THE DESCRIPTION LENGTH OF THE SET OF CLASSES $\mathcal{C}$ ITSELF.

3 **COMPUTE** FOR ALL PAIRS OF CLASSES $c_i, c_j \in \mathcal{C}$: THE *difference* IN DESCRIPTION LENGTH THAT WOULD RESULT FROM A MERGE OF THESE TWO CLASSES RESULTING IN A NEW CLASS $c_n = \{c'_n \rightarrow c'_i | c'_j\}$.

4 **COMPUTE** FOR ALL PAIRS OF CLASSES $c_i, c_j \in \mathcal{C}$: THE *difference* IN DESCRIPTION LENGTH THAT WOULD RESULT FROM A CONSTRUCTION OF A NEW CLASS $c_m = \{c'_m \rightarrow c'_i c'_j\}$.

5 **IF** THERE ARE ONE OR MORE OPERATIONS FOR WHICH THE NEW DESCRIPTION LENGTH WOULD BE SMALLER THAN THE OLD ONE, **PERFORM** THE OPERATION THAT YIELDS THE SHORTEST NEW DESCRIPTION LENGTH AND **CONTINUE** AT STEP 2.

6 **ELSE** STOP THE EXECUTION.

Fig. 1. the basic algorithm

How to Compute the Description Length

We must come up with a method that defines a description length DL in an exact manner for all possible training texts and all possible grammars (i.e. all possible $\mathcal{C}$). We can do this using a *code* that defines a unique representation for each different training text. We want our code to be *dense*[4], i.e. each sequence of codewords defines a training text t_1^L and no two different sequences of codewords define the same t_1^L. The idea is now that we use our partial grammar $\mathcal{C}$ in such a way that it can be seen as such a code; but information theory [5] teaches

---

[4] If we do not use a dense code, the nice theoretical result of the equivalence between a restricted version of our approach and another one (Sect. 6), does not hold any more.

us that in order to arrive at an ideal code (i.e. a code that yields the shortest possible representation (description) of the training text) we need to keep track also of the frequencies of occurrence of the classes in C for a given t_1^L.

Furthermore, in order to make the construct and merge operations really capable of reducing the DL, we must somehow incorporate in our code the basic fact about grammars discussed before: the earlier words (classes) in a sentence (parse tree) partially determine the words (classes) that may follow. Only if our code can make use of these dependencies, can construct and merge operations really reduce the DL.

In our approach, we let each class (i.e. non-terminal) determine a *distribution* on all classes that may be its direct successors. By using a distribution instead of some hard rule of the form 'c_j may follow c_i; c_k may not' we automatically handle noise in the training text. For a class c_i we arrive at the distribution of its successors by counting, for all j, $1 \leq j \leq |C|$ the number of times we encounter that class c_i turns out to be followed by class c_j while parsing t_1^L according to our grammar C. This determines a set of parameters χ_{ij}. Notice that if we normalized χ_{ij} by dividing it by a constant for all j (keeping i fixed), such that $\sum_{1 \leq j \leq |C|} \chi_{ij} = 1$, then we could regard the set of all χ_{ij} as a crude estimate of a kind of probability distribution. If our training text were representative of its underlying language, then we might view this distribution as giving the conditional probability that, given that at some point in some parse tree of some natural language text of the same language as t_1^L, we have encountered non-terminal c_i', the next non-terminal we encounter will be c_j'.

Two things should be noted here. First, we use only dependencies between one (non-) terminal and its immediate successor here, thereby making our approach related to those using 2-gram statistics [1]; we will see however in Sect. 6 that, at least theoretically, our approach can very well handle long-term dependencies. Second, the 'number of times c_j follows c_i while parsing t_1^L according to $C(t_1^L)$' and thus the set of parameters χ_{ij}, is only well-defined if C is *unambiguous* while of course, interesting grammars may very well be ambiguous; we will further discuss this issue in Sect. 7.

Actually Computing the Description Length

More formally, we define a *2-gram stochastic partial grammar* for a training text t_1^L as a tuple:

$$\mathcal{G} = <\mathcal{C}, \mathcal{P}_1, \mathcal{P}_2> . \tag{1}$$

Both $\mathcal{P}_1$ and $\mathcal{P}_2$ are sets of parameters. They are dependent on both t_1^L and $\mathcal{C}$, so they may also be seen as functions of them. $\mathcal{C}$ is a partial grammar as defined before. Notice that $\mathcal{C}$ defines a *shortest possible parse* of t_1^L which we will write as $\mathcal{C}(t_1^L)$. This means that if one parses t_1^L according to $\mathcal{C}$ in a bottom-up fashion, one arrives at a string of classes $u_1^{L'}$ where $L' \leq L$. If $\mathcal{C}$ is unambiguous, as we assume here, then it determines a *unique* way to parse t_1^L into a string that is as short as possible, so $\mathcal{C}(t_1^L)$ is well-defined. Due to restrictions on the size of this chapter, we will have to use words in the definitions of $\mathcal{P}_1$ and $\mathcal{P}_2$. It should be noted that if one introduces the right notations, one can express all these definitions in a purely mathematical fashion [6]. In order to define $\mathcal{P}_1$ and $\mathcal{P}_2$, we first have to define their contents (we have to be really precise now. We used χ_{ij} to explain the general idea, but it turns out that we cannot use just one kind of parameter here - we need to make a distinction between two quite different sorts of parameters θ_{ij} and ν_{ij}):

$\theta_{ij} = $ *number of times c_j follows c_i in $C(t_1^L)$* .

$\nu_{ij} = $ *number of times production $c_i' \to \dots \mid \dots \mid c_j' \mid \dots \mid \dots$*
  is used to replace c_j' by c_i' in the bottom-up parsing process
  that reduces t_1^L to $C(t_1^L)$.

$\mathcal{P}_1 = \{\theta_{ij} \mid c_i c_j \, appears \, in \, C(t_1^L)\}$.

$\mathcal{P}_2 = \{\nu_{ij} \mid \{c_i' \to \dots \mid \dots \mid c_j' \mid \dots \mid \dots\} \in \mathcal{C}\}$.

To turn $\mathcal{G}$ into a code (description) of t_1^L, we now turn to information theory [5]. Each $\mathcal{G}$ determines an ideal (Shannon-Fano) code to encode a training text. For our purposes, it is not necessary to explicitly construct this code; in stead, it is enough only to compute the number of bits $DL(t_1^L \mid \mathcal{G})$ it would take to encode training text t_1^L using this ideal code for $\mathcal{G}$. It should be clear that the two terms of the right-hand side of the following equation provide just the information needed to encode t_1^L in such a way that it can be completely reproduced:

$DL(t_1^L \mid \mathcal{G}) = $ *number of bits it takes to encode at all positions in the string*
  $C(t_1^L)$ *what class is the next one*
  $+$ *the number of bits it takes to encode all choices that must*
  be made on which production to apply when generating t_1^L
  back from $C(t_1^L)$

$$= \mathbf{H_1}(\mathcal{P}_1) + \mathbf{H_2}(\mathcal{P}_2) \ . \tag{2}$$

$\mathbf{H_1}$ and $\mathbf{H_2}$ can be seen as entropy-like functions on $\mathcal{P}_1$ and $\mathcal{P}_2$ respectively. For explicit expressions, the reader is referred to [6]. Suffice it to say here that to arrive at an expression for the first term, one should realize that $\mathcal{P}_1$ can be viewed as describing the parameters of a stationary ergodic Markov Chain; after some normalizing, the definitions of the entropy of such a chain [5] can be used for quick computation of the first term of (2). Regarding the second term, we may interpret each class as a 'source' (in the sense of information theory) that can emit any of the productions in the class as outputs. $\mathcal{P}_2$ determines the entropy of this source (class). From the set of entropies of all classes, one can easily compute the second term of (2).

The total description length is of course given by

$$DL(t_1^L) = DL(t_1^L \mid \mathcal{G}) + DL(\mathcal{G}) \ .$$

We have just computed the first term. Now for the second. From (1) we see that we can split this term up as follows:

$$DL(\mathcal{G}) = DL(\mathcal{C}) + DL(\mathcal{P}_1) + DL(\mathcal{P}_2) \ .$$

C is a set of grammar rules. Notice that for a natural language this should have some fixed length. On the other hand, we can take L about as large as we want. Therefore, from some L onwards, $DL(C)$ will be neglectably small as compared to $DL(t_1^L \mid G)$, as this latter term does grow with increasing L. For this reason, we will neglect $DL(C)$ in our computation.

On the other hand, $DL(\mathcal{P}_1)$ and $DL(\mathcal{P}_2)$ *do* grow as our training text increases in size. To see why this is so, one should realize that the *range* of each θ_{ij} increases as L increases (theoretically θ_{ij} can range from 0 to $L-1$). Therefore, the number of bits required to specify all θ_{ij} increases too; it takes about $O(\log L)$ bits. The same reasoning holds for $DL(\mathcal{P}_2)$. We will omit the exact definitions for $DL(\mathcal{P}_1)$ and $DL(\mathcal{P}_2)$ here, but it should be clear by now that they can easily be constructed.

5 Some Results

We have made an initial implementation of the algorithm just described and let it run on the 'Brown Corpus' [7], a huge sample of rather modern American English. In order for the algorithm to work within the limits of available computer power, some adjustments had to be made; details about this can be found in [6][5]. An important one is the fact that we used as training text not the full Brown corpus, but the reduction of the Brown corpus to just those sentences *all* words of which are among the 10000 most frequent words in the corpus. We named our reduced training text 'Brown 10000'. Also, classes of the form $\{c_i' \to w_i\}$ were allowed to be the operands of merges and constructs only if w_i was among the 450 most frequent words.

Just Merging

First, we will discuss the results of running a restricted version of our algorithm, namely one in which only merges and no constructs are allowed. In this case, the algorithm yields a C each element of which is of the form $c_n = \{c_n' \to w_i|w_j|w_k|\ldots\}$; as c_n' is used in no right-hand side of any production, one may view a class simply as a set of words now. Then 'grammar inference' degenerates into finding classes (hence the name!) of syntactically and/or semantically related words, a task for which automatic procedures have often been proposed before [1, 4].

Figures 2, 3 and 4 show the results of running this algorithm on 'Brown 10000'. The first figure shows the total description length of the training text after each merge. One can see that in the beginning it goes down quite rapidly, each merge clearly giving a more compact description of the training text. Then, at some point (after about 160 merges), the merge operation does not really 'help' any more and the description length starts to rise again. If one does not

---

[5] The algorithm discussed there differs somewhat from the one we present here, but the necessary adjustments are the same.

stop the algorithm, it continues until all 450 words are in one class and the DL is *very* high (we stopped after 310 merges). Figure 3 gives a more fine-grained picture showing the three terms that sum to $DL(t_1^L)$: $DL(\mathcal{G})$, $\mathbf{H_1}(\mathcal{P}_1)$ and $\mathbf{H_2}(\mathcal{P}_2)$. This decomposition clarifies what exactly goes on here: as more merges take place, the number of parameters decreases: if we only allow merges, the *effective* number of classes decreases by one after each merge, so there are less θ_{ij} to store. Then describing $\mathcal{P}_1$ takes less bits and $DL(\mathcal{G})$ decreases. As for explaining the form of the other two curves, we refer to [6] where we prove a theorem that $\Delta\mathbf{H_2}(\mathcal{P}_2) \geq -\Delta\mathbf{H_1}(\mathcal{P}_1)$ for each possible $\mathcal{C}$.

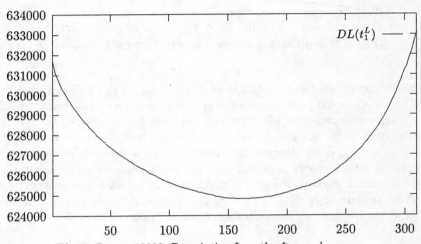

Fig. 2. Brown 10000: Description Length after each merge

Figure 4 focuses on the 'best' situation: it shows so-called *dendrograms* [4] of a (representative) part of the class structure that has been arrived at after 160 merges, when the description length is smallest. In a dendrogram a vertical link between two words means that they have been merged together, the two horizontal lines that start out from the middle of a vertical line and end into the two edges of another vertical line more to the left indicate a merge between two classes. The farther to the left, the higher the number of steps the algorithm has already performed. Words that are not connected are not in the same class. We would say that the results speak for themselves.

Grammar Rules

If we do allow constructs to happen, there arises a problem in computing ΔDL, the difference in description length that would result from a construct of two classes c_i and c_j. We would have to compute this difference for all pairs of classes in $\mathcal{C}$ and this simply takes too much time. In our current implementation, we used

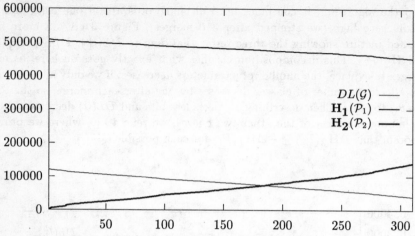

Fig. 3. Brown 10000: Description Length Terms after each merge

an easily computable heuristic approximation to ΔDL due to Solomonoff [11]. Unfortunately, we do not arrive at very good rules using this approximation (the reader who wants to see these rules nevertheless is referred to [6]). Rule constructing in its present simple form does not really work very well. It is not clear at this point whether the approximation is simply not good enough, whether a totally greedy approach does not work well or whether our training corpora do not contain enough internal structure to make 'sensible' grammar rules worthwhile. In relation to this latter conjecture it should be noted here that in experiments with *toy grammars* much better grammar rules were formed.

6 Related Approaches

Our approach is an extension to and a more exact version of Solomonoff's original one. However, there is also a clear relation to the many statistical approaches to word classification. We will give a detailed comparison to the one that seems most similar to ours:

A Generalization of a Statistical (ML) Approach

Brown *et al.* [1] give an approach to word classification based on 2-grams and the Maximum Likelihood (ML) Principle, a very common tool in statistics. In [6], we explicitly prove that our approaches reduces to Brown *et al.*'s if one 1) 'forbids' constructs and lets only merges take place (as we did in our first experiment) and 2) neglects the term of the description length of the theory $DL(\mathcal{G})$ and only looks at the description length of the data $DL(t_1^L \mid \mathcal{G})$. To give at least some idea of why this should be so: if all hypotheses one takes into

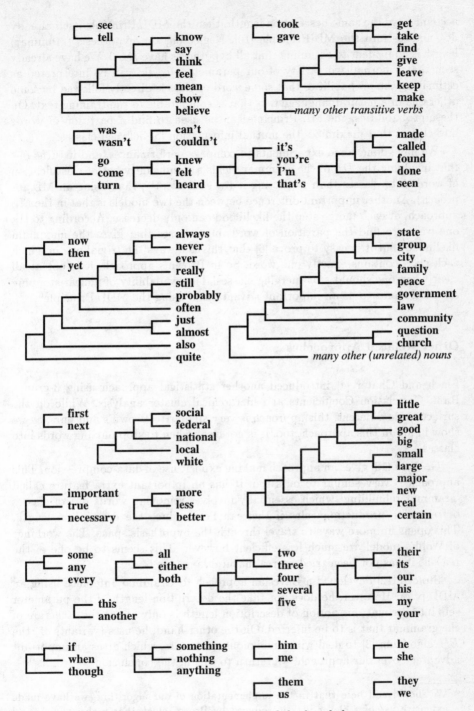

Fig. 4. Brown 10000: some of the found classes

account have the same description length, then the MDL Principle itself already degenerates into the ML Principle [10]. Neglecting the hypothesis (grammar) length is equivalent to assuming that all hypotheses have DL 0. We have already seen that a normalized variety of our parameters θ_{ij}, ν_{ij} can be interpreted as estimating the probabilities that some word or class is directly followed by some other one in a natural language text that is comparable to the training text. On these probabilities, the ML Principle can be used to find a partition of words into classes that maximizes the mutual information [5] between classes.

We have done some experiments to compare performances, and it turns out that involving the DL of the grammar yields a significantly better classification of words into classes than neglecting it (or equivalently, than using an ML approach). Another important difference between the two models is that in the ML approach, at each merge step the likelihood can only decrease. According to [1], one wants to find the partition of words into classes that gives the maximum likelihood, but it is easy to prove [6] that this is always the trivial one in which each class contains exactly one word. So in Brown's approach, it is not at all clear when one should *stop* merging classes! The availability of a clear stopping criterion seems to us an important advantage of using the MDL Principle[6].

Other Related Approaches

Finch and Chater [4] introduced another statistical approach using 3-grams, Rank Correlation Coefficients and hierarchical cluster analysis. While on the surface quite different, this approach is very similar to Brown's and ours, as we show in [6]. In this approach, too, it is not clear when to stop putting words into classes.

G. Wolff [13] gives an approach making explicit use of data-compression. This approach is very similar to ours too. It has an important extra feature called 'grammar rebuilding' which essentially involves removing words out of classes or removing production rules if this can help reduce the description length. This opens up more ways to travel through the hypothesis space. The workings of Wolff's model are much less efficient however. This seems to be one of the reasons it has not been tried on real natural language texts.

Stolcke [12] developed a Bayesian approach to Grammar Inference using an MDL prior. However, he does not take the description length of the parameter sets into account; his notion of description length is only about the *structure* of the grammar that is to be inferred. On the other hand, he uses (variants of) the *EM*-algorithm [3] to deal with ambiguous grammars, which gives an important advantage over our approach; we return to this in the conclusion.

---

[6] We should add here that in the implementation of our algorithm, we have made extensive use of a clever idea introduced by Brown *et al.* that makes their - and our - algorithm considerably more efficient than it would be under a straightforward implementation.

Linguistic Aspects

As we have remarked before, our approach only exploits dependencies between (non-) terminals and their immediate successors in the training text and in the parse tree. Of course, we know since Chomsky [2] that dependencies between words within a sentence may be of arbitrary distance. In a corpus-based probabilistic approach like ours it gets even worse, because the probability of a word occurring on one sentence is influenced by words occurring many sentences earlier. But notice that, at least in theory, our approach can cope with this in a peculiar manner: it starts out with only 2-gram dependencies. But as the algorithm performs more and more constructs, longer and longer parts of a sentence get treated as one single entity. Then the algorithm also considers the direct successors of this entity, thereby implicitly employing long-range dependencies. On the other hand, the question remains whether a greedy approach like ours can ever find the *right* long-range dependencies by starting out with only very short-range dependencies. It could very well be that repeated constructs, even of a more sophisticated kind than ours, will always lead C into a 'local minimum' at which some (construct-) grammar rules that reduce the DL have been found, but not those from which the algorithm can continue to construct more general grammar rules.

7 Conclusion and Future Work

On the practical side, we have seen that a greedy MDL-based approach to clustering words in classes works quite well, though the direct extension of this approach to the construction of simple grammar rules with more than one symbol on the right-hand side does not lead to very good results.

On the theoretical side, we have seen that several existing models both of grammar inference and of word classification can be seen as restricted versions of a more general model based on the MDL Principle, and we have introduced a clear stopping-criterion for the 'greedy algorithms' used in these models.

Apart from the problems with 'constructs', there is still another important problem with our approach, a problem that comes in two guises:

1 class per word The words of the input alphabet are *partitioned* into classes. But in natural language, a word often belongs to more than one 'class'.

Ambiguity The description length of the training text given $\mathcal{G}$ is, as it stands, only well-defined if $\mathcal{G}$ is unambiguous, i.e. (partially) parsing t_1^L according to $\mathcal{G}$ does not yield more than one shortest concatenation of classes. But many interesting context-free grammars are ambiguous at some point.

In fact, the first point made above can be seen as a special case of the second point, namely the case when we use the restriction of our algorithm that performs only merges. We are currently studying the EM-algorithm and other techniques used by Stolcke [12] in order to try to resolve this problem.

8 Acknowledgements

The author wishes to thank his supervisor Prof. Dr. Ir. P.M.B. Vitányi for many useful remarks on his Master's Thesis. Further thanks are due to Mark Steijvers and Jeroen van Maanen for many useful discussions.

References

1. P.F. Brown, V.J. Della Pietra, P.V. deSouza, J.C. Lai, and R.L. Mercer. Class-based n-gram models of natural language. *Computational Linguistics*, 18:467–479, 1992.
2. N. Chomsky. *Syntactic Structures*. Mouton, The Hague, 1957.
3. A. Dempster, N. Laird, and D. Rubin. Maximum likelihood from incomplete data via the EM algorithm. *Journal of the Royal Statistical Society, Series B*, 34:1–38, 1977.
4. S. Finch and N. Chater. A hybrid approach to the automatic learning of linguistic categories. *AISB Quarterly*, 78:16–24, 1991.
5. R.G. Gallager. *Information Theory and Reliable Communication*. Wiley, New York, 1968.
6. P.D. Grünwald. Automatic grammar induction using the MDL Principle. Master's thesis, Free University of Amsterdam, Amsterdam, 1994.
7. H. Kučera and W. Francis. *Computational Analysis of Present Day American English*. Brown University Press, 1967.
8. P. Langley. Machine learning and grammar induction. *Machine Learning*, 2:5–8, 1987. Editorial of special issue on language learning.
9. M. Li and P.M.B. Vitányi. *An introduction to Kolmogorov complexity and its applications*. Springer-Verlag, 1993.
10. J. Rissanen. A universal prior for integers and estimation by minimum description length. *Ann. Statist.*, 11:416–431, 1982.
11. R.J. Solomonoff. A formal theory of inductive inference, part 1 and part 2. *Inform. Contr.*, 7:1–22, 224–254, 1964.
12. A. Stolcke. *Bayesian Learning of Probabilistic Language Models*. PhD thesis, ICSI, Berkeley, 1994.
13. J.G. Wolff. Language acquisition, data compression, and generalization. *Language and Communication*, 2:57–89, 1982.

Automatic Classification of Dialog Acts with Semantic Classification Trees and Polygrams *

Marion Mast and Heinrich Niemann and Elmar Nöth and Ernst Günter Schukat-Talamazzini

Lehrstuhl für Mustererkennung, Universität Erlangen-Nürnberg, Martensstr. 3, D-91058 Erlangen, {mast,niemann,noeth,schukat}@informatik.uni-erlangen.de, Phone: +49 9131 85 7799, Fax: +49 9131 303811

Abstract. This paper presents automatic methods for the classification of dialog acts. In the VERBMOBIL application (speech-to-speech translation of face-to-face dialogs) maximally 50 % of the utterances are analyzed in depth and for the rest, shallow processing takes place. The dialog component keeps track of the dialog with this shallow processing. For the classification of utterances without in depth processing two methods are presented: Semantic Classification Trees and Polygrams. For both methods the classification algorithm is trained automatically from a corpus of labeled data. The novel idea with respect to SCTs is the use of dialog state dependent CTs and with respect to Polygrams it is the use of competing language models for the classification of dialog acts.

Keywords: automatic learning, dialog act classification, hidden polygram models, polygrams, semantic classification trees.

1 Introduction

The VERBMOBIL-System delivers translations of spontaneous speech in negotiation dialogs. The current scenario is that two participants (with German and Japanese mother tongue respectively) want to find a date for a business meeting. They speak English unless they don't know how to express the next utterance in English. In this case they press the VERBMOBIL button and continue in their mother tongue. VERBMOBIL will then deliver a translation.

The system does not act as a participant of the dialog like in information retrieval dialogs (e.g. in the ATIS domain) but keeps track of the ongoing dialog. When VERBMOBIL is activated the system has to:

- recognize the words of the actual utterance
- make a linguistic analysis

* This work was funded by the German Federal Ministry of Education, Science, Research and Technology (BMBF) in the framework of the Verbmobil Project under Grant 01 IV 102 H/0. The responsibility for the contents of this study lies with the authors. The authors wish to thank R. Kuhn for providing the SCT software.

- update the dialog history
- generate an English translation and
- create speech output by speech synthesis

When VERBMOBIL is not activated some of these tasks can be omitted. The dialog component has to fulfill 4 major tasks (see [AMR95]):

- provide contextual information for other VERBMOBIL-components,
- predict the next admissible dialog acts which are needed e.g. for the recognition component,
- follow the dialog when VERBMOBIL is inactive which means both participants speak English and no translation is needed and
- control clarification dialogs between VERBMOBIL and its users.

The work presented here concerns the third of these tasks: maximally 50 % of the utterances are analyzed in depth and for the rest shallow processing takes place. This is done by the segmentation and classification of the dialog acts. The dialog acts are classified with semantic classification trees (SCTs), which are trained automatically. Another method for the classification of dialog acts are polygrams.

2   Dialog Component

The dialog is seen as a sequence of dialog acts, and the dialog model in figure 1 describes admissible sequences of dialog acts (see [Mai94]). The dialog consists of:

- an *introduction phase* in which the participants greet, if necessary introduce each other and introduce the dialog goal (appointment scheduling)
- a *negotiation phase* in which the participants negotiate a date for a business meeting and
- a *closing phase* in which the result of the negotiation can be repeated and confirmed, and the dialog ends or the participants change to another dialog goal (this can be a date for another meeting).

The edges in the model correspond to dialog acts and the nodes to dialog states. The model consists of 5 dialog states. One further state models deviations from this model. This state can be reached from any of the other states. After the deviation (e.g. a clarification subdialog) has been processed, the dialog jumps back to the state from which the deviation state has been reached.

The dialog component (see [AMR95]) consists of 3 modules. The *finite state machine* provides an efficient and robust implementation of the dialog model. It checks the consistency of the uttered dialog acts with the dialog model. The *statistical layer* is an information-theoretic model (similar to language models for dialog acts) which is used for the prediction of dialog acts. The *dialog planner* keeps track of the plans of the users which means constructs and updates a discourse history. Plans are divided up into the different phases like negotiation

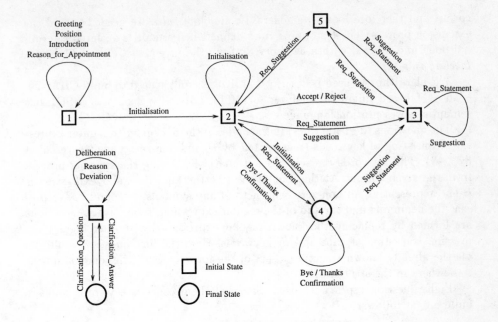

Fig. 1. The Dialog Model

and clarification. The planning process works top-down, which means that high level goals are divided into subgoals. This process ends with dialog acts as basic subgoals which can be identified from the utterances. To follow the plans of the users, the system has to identify the dialog acts.

3 Semantic Classification Trees

Classification trees are decision trees for the classification of patterns, where the decisions are made up by rules. They process the given textual information of a sequence of symbols $w = w_1 \ldots w_m$ of varying length m. The specific rules for a given task and the order of their application were trained automatically based on a corpus unlike in conventional rule based systems, where the rules are hand coded.

The structure of a binary classification tree is characterized by a binary *splitting rule* in each nonterminal node. Terminal nodes are labeled with a category and/or a scoring vector. For the automatic training of a classification tree splitting, stopping and labeling rules are needed in addition to a training corpus (see [Kuh92]). The binary splitting rules are YES-NO-questions. To avoid an overexpansion of the tree, which means that it is totally adapted to the training corpus and therefore looses its generality, *stopping rules* are needed to end the expansion process. These stopping rules define when a node is declared a terminal node and labeled with a category $\mathcal{C}_\kappa$ from the inventory $\{\mathcal{C}_1, \ldots, \mathcal{C}_K\}$ by a *labeling rule*.

The algorithm we used is described in [Kuh92] and is used to build CHANEL – an SCT-based linguistic analyzer for ATIS. CHANEL generates a SQL-like semantic representation language.

The questions (decision rules) in the nodes of the SCT refer to regular expressions consisting of keywords (represented by v) and non-zero gaps (represented by "+"). The keywords are selected automatically during the training process from the given corpus. At the root of the tree the known regular expression is $<+>$, representing all non-zero sequences of any symbols. "$<$" and "$>$" represent the beginning and the end of the regular expression, respectively. Questions are formed by replacing the known regular expression by another regular expression consisting of gaps and/or keywords. E. g. the first question could be: "Is the already known structure $<+>$ of the form $<+v+>$, i.e. does v appear somewhere in the structure?"

Eight question types were used. Seven of them concern keywords and are build e.g. as follows:

- *Join*: they "join" the edges of a gap together; they are of the type "Is the + equal to v?" (v is set to every item in the vocabulary during the training phase)
- *More*: they establish that there is one or "more" symbol v in a gap; they are of the type "Is the + of the form + M(v) +, where M(v) can be of the form v, vv, or $v + v$, and there is no v on either side of the M() within the original +".

One question is about the length of the utterance.

The rule which selects the best question or decides that it should be a leaf node is based on an impurity measure I, where the impurity

- is always non-negative,
- takes a maximum value for a node containing equal proportions of all possible categories,
- is zero for a node containing only one of all possible categories.

Therefore in node T a question is chosen which maximizes ΔI.

The algorithm uses the Gini criterion as measure of impurity which always lies between 0 and 1. If T is a certain node and $f(j \mid T)$ is the proportion of items in the node that belong to category j, then the Gini impurity $I(T)$ of the node is defined as

$$I(T) = \sum_{j \neq k} f(j \mid T) f(k \mid T) = 1 - \sum_j f^2(j \mid T) \tag{1}$$

For the growing of the tree a strategy with two stages is used. First a much to large tree is grown using a simple stopping rule, e.g. that each terminal node contains fewer than N items (N close to 1) or the maximum value of ΔI is 0. Then the tree is pruned from the leaves upwards using an independent data set. Thereafter the tree is expanded on this second data set and pruned on the first. This process is iterated until two successive pruned trees are identical (a prove that this must be is found in [GRD91]).

In figure 2 a part of an SCT trained with the algorithm described in [Kuh92] for the VM-application is given. The categories which are classified are the dialog acts in the dialog model (see figure 1).

Each terminal node is labeled with a dialog act and corresponds to a keyword pattern, which is build up by the positively answered questions on the path from the root. E.g. node 21 is labeled with category 'Bye'. Node 23 points at a subtree (which is not given due to space limitations). In each nonterminal node the keyword pattern of the so far positively answered questions is expanded by a question.

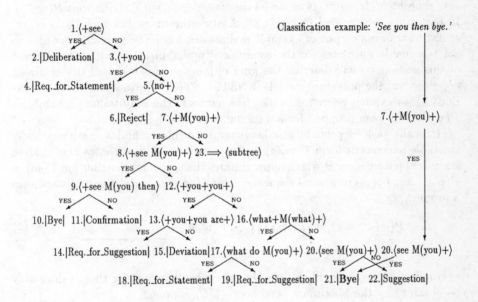

Fig. 2. Part of a classification tree for 16 dialog acts and an exemplary classification; the tree was trained automatically from 80 % of the English dialogs

4 Classification with Polygrams

Direct application of Bayes rule is an alternative approach to identify the dialog act category of a given word sequence. Bayes rule selects that particular label

κ^* for classification which maximizes the a posteriori probability

$$P(\mathcal{C}_\kappa \mid \boldsymbol{w}) = \frac{P(\boldsymbol{w}, \mathcal{C}_\kappa)}{P(\boldsymbol{w})} = \frac{P(\boldsymbol{w} \mid \mathcal{C}_\kappa) \cdot P(\mathcal{C}_\kappa)}{\sum_{\lambda=1}^{K} P(\boldsymbol{w} \mid \mathcal{C}_\lambda) \cdot P(\mathcal{C}_\lambda)} \qquad (2)$$

of the input text. In the above equation, $P(\boldsymbol{w}, \mathcal{C}_\kappa)$ may be interpreted as the (joint) probability distribution of a two-stage, discrete random process. In the first stage, a dialog act category $\mathcal{C}_\kappa$ is selected from the inventory $\{\mathcal{C}_1, \ldots, \mathcal{C}_K\}$ according to the a priori probability distribution $P(\mathcal{C}_\kappa)$, $\kappa = 1, \ldots, K$. In the second stage, a word sequence $\boldsymbol{w} = w_1 \ldots w_m$ of varying length m is produced; this second generation process is controlled by the conditional production probabilities $P(\boldsymbol{w}|\mathcal{C}_\kappa)$, where κ denotes the category index selected before.

Estimates for the parameters $P(\mathcal{C}_\kappa)$ may be easily obtained from a training corpus by computing the relative frequencies of word strings in category κ. The actual problem, however, is to model the class-dependent distributions $P(\boldsymbol{w}|\mathcal{C}_\kappa)$. In our study, we decided to create stochastic grammars. For each $\mathcal{C}_\kappa$, a representative training corpus of example realizations has to be provided in order to get reasonable estimates for the conditional probabilities $P(\boldsymbol{w}|\mathcal{C}_\kappa)$. In the rest of this section we will describe the kind of language models used in our dialog act classifier: the polygram models [KNST94, STKN94]. Note that in the equations below explicit reference to the class names in the conditional probabilities $P(\boldsymbol{w}|\mathcal{C}_\kappa)$ has been dropped for notational convenience.

It is the task of probabilistic language modeling to find a mathematically tractable parametric form $P(\boldsymbol{w}|\boldsymbol{\Theta})$ together with reliable estimates $\hat{\boldsymbol{\Theta}}$ of its free statistical parameters $\boldsymbol{\Theta}$ which approximates the true joint distribution $P(\boldsymbol{w}) = P(w_1 \ldots w_m)$ of a given word sequence. This expression can be decomposed into a product

$$P(w_1 \ldots w_m) = P(w_1) \cdot \prod_{n=2}^{m} P(w_n \mid \underbrace{w_1 w_2 \ldots w_{n-2} w_{n-1}}_{\text{word history}}) \qquad (3)$$

of conditional n-gram probabilities. In principle, estimates for these values may be obtained by the Maximum Likelihood (ML) approach

$$\hat{P}(w_n \mid w_1 \ldots w_{n-1}) = \frac{\#(w_1 \ldots w_{n-1} w_n)}{\sum_v \#(w_1 \ldots w_{n-1} v)} = \frac{\#(w_1 \ldots w_n)}{\#(w_1 \ldots w_{n-1})} \qquad (4)$$

where $\#(\cdot)$ denotes an operator that counts the word n-gram occurrences in the training data. However, since the estimate (4) becomes rapidly unreliable with increasing order n, the word history in Eq. (3) has to be restricted to a few recent words. A language model that is exclusively based on word histories of duration $n-1$ is referred to as n-gram model [Jel90]. In practice, only bigram models

$$P(\boldsymbol{w}) = P(w_1) \cdot \prod_{n=2}^{m} P(w_n \mid w_{n-1}) \qquad (5)$$

or trigram models

$$P(\boldsymbol{w}) \; = \; P(w_1) \cdot P(w_2|w_1) \cdot \prod_{n=3}^{m} P(w_n \mid w_{n-2}w_{n-1}) \qquad (6)$$

can be robustly trained.

The situation improves as soon as lower order statistics are recruited in order to smooth higher order ones. Consequently, the polygram model approximates the true conditional n-gram distributions by successively reducing the word history and computing a convex combination

$$\tilde{P}(w_n \mid w_1 \ldots w_{n-1}) \; = \; \lambda_0 \cdot \frac{1}{L} \; + \; \lambda_1 \cdot \hat{P}(w_n) \; + \; \lambda_2 \cdot \hat{P}(w_n|w_{n-1})$$

$$+ \; \sum_{i=2}^{n} \lambda_i \cdot \hat{P}(w_n \mid w_{n-i+1} \ldots w_{n-1}) \qquad (7)$$

of the related ML estimates. The interpolation weights λ_i are usually assumed dependent on some statistics of the word history $w_1 \ldots w_{n-1}$. Our choice was to create a functional dependence based on the essential width

$$\eta \; = \; \max \left\{ \nu \mid \#(w_{n-\nu} \ldots w_{n-1}) > 0 \right\} \qquad (8)$$

of the n-gram context. The weight vectors defined this way can be systematically optimized with respect to a cross validation data set using the EM algorithm [JM80]. In contrast to the nonlinear recursive "back-off" procedure in [Kat87] the polygram model enables smoothing of conditional n-grams with a low but non-zero number of occurrences, too; moreover, the (linear) interpolation weights are systematically designed in order to maximize the model-dependent validation set likelihoods.

It is evident from the zerogram component $1/L$ of the interpolation formula (7) (where L denotes the size of the vocabulary) that the smoothed probabilities $\tilde{P}(\cdot)$ will get positive values even if the higher order ML estimators disappear. As a consequence, we may evaluate the right hand side of the decomposition formula (3) without artificially cutting down the word histories of conditional n-grams provided the ML estimators in Eq. (4) are replaced by the smoothed counterparts in Eq. (7). Thus, a polygram language model can be expected to capture even long-spanning contextual dependences among the words of an utterance, provided the training corpus is sufficiently large and representative.

Note that this language model is required to store the complete set of training data statistics; the frequencies of all word polygrams (i.e. unigrams, bigrams, trigrams, and so forth) observed at least once in the training material are involved in the probability computations. In order to bound the complexity of the model, a certain maximum length N of n-grams considered in the interpolation formula should be set.

5 Data

For the training of SCTs and polygrams a classified set of utterances is needed. In VERBMOBIL German and English appointment scheduling dialogs were recorded and transcribed. Non-speech phenomena like breathing and noises (e.g. paper rustle) were removed from the transcription. 214 German and 56 English dialogs were labeled with the dialog acts occurring in the dialog model (see figure 1, approximately 6000 German and 1600 English dialog acts). For a description of all used dialog acts see [Mai94].

6 Results

6.1 Classification with SCTs

For the classification of dialog acts different SCTs were grown. First one SCT for the classification of all dialog acts for the English and German data, respectively, was trained. Therefore, 80 % of the labeled data were used for training and the remaining 20 % for testing the SCT (training set $\neq$ test set). In figure 2 a part of the classification tree for the English data is given. For the classification of 16 dialog acts a recognition rate of 46 % and 59 % for the German and English data was reached, respectively. The better results for the English data could be influenced by the more uniform scenario for the English dialogs. The German dialogs were recorded at 3 sites and the scenario slightly differed. In some dialogs private appointments were scheduled, in others business appointments. This can influence the dialog structure and the realization of utterances (see [KM93]). The results show a tendency for the most frequently occurring dialog acts to be best recognized. This is due to the still insufficient amount of training data.

Classification of the dialog acts for each dialog state: In each state of the dialog model (see figure 1) only a subset of all dialog acts can follow. Therefore, for each dialog state one SCT is grown which classifies only the (in this state) possible dialog acts. The recognition rates for each dialog state are given in figure 3 (The outgoing edges for state 2 and 4 are the same).

6.2 Classification with Polygrams

For both languages, eight polygram classifiers were trained. Each classifier involved 16 competing language models, one for each dialog act category. The order, i.e. the maximum allowable context length N of the polygram models ranged from $N = 1$ to $N = 8$. As with the classification trees, 80 % of the training data was used to build the models, and 20 % was used as independent test set. The partitioning of the material was the same in both experiments.

The recognition rates that could be achieved with polygrams are indicated in figure4. For the larger sized German corpus, the maximum recognition performance of 68.7 % correct decisions was obtained using the pentagram model, i.e.,

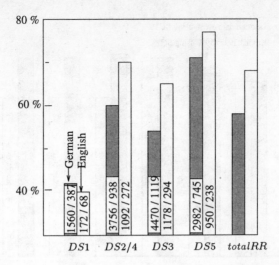

Fig. 3. Recognition rates for each dialog state (DS1-DS5), that is, one SCT per dialog state. The numbers are the samples in the test / training set.

N-gram statistics up to an order of $N = 5$. In contrast, the trigram performance (67.3 %) for the considerably smaller English corpus could not be improved further by increasing the model order.

It is interesting to observe that near-optimum recognition rates (67.1 % and 67.0 %, respectively) are already attainable with a simple bigram classifier. Moreover, even the unigram-based dialog act labeling, which completely ignores word order and thus essentially amounts to score the input utterance by a words-in-a-bag strategy, enables correct identification by a rate of roughly 60 %.

These findings suggest – in fact confirm our expectation – that word identity is much more important in our task than phrase structure. The rapid saturation of recognition rate with respect to the model order gives some evidence that higher order interactions among adjacent words play a minor role. However, one can suspect that dialog act categories are often triggered by associations of word tuples which are widely scattered over the input text positions. A mathematical model that deals with long-spanning contextual effects is described in [STHKN95].

7 Conclusion and Future Work

In the VERBMOBIL-system shallow processing takes place when the user doesn't need a translation. In these phases the dialog module tracks the ongoing dialog. The dialog planner constructs and updates the dialog history based on the recognized dialog acts.

This paper presents two methods – SCTs and polygrams – for the automatic classification of dialog acts. The classification algorithms don't need input from

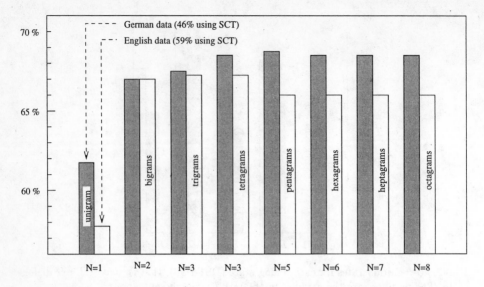

Fig. 4. Recognition rates for polyphone classifiers of different orders

syntax and semantics. The algorithms classify the utterances based on the textual representation. For the training of these algorithms a corpus of utterances – labeled with dialog acts – is needed.

For the classification of 16 dialog acts recognition rates with SCTs of 46 % and 59 % for the German and English data are reached, respectively. If a classification tree for each dialog state – classifying all dialog acts which can follow in this state – is trained, the recognition rates are 58 % and 68 %, respectively.

The recognition rates with polygrams are even better (see figure 5). For the German data a maximum of 69 % (with pentagrams) and for the English data a maximum of 67 % (with trigrams) was reached. Remarkable is that:

- with SCT the classification of the English data works better than of the German data, with polygrams it's vice versa.
- the polygrams are generally working better than the SCTs for this classification problem.
- polygrams even regarding only bi- or trigrams result in an almost optimal recognition rate.

7.1 SCTs Including Prosodic Information

Improvement of these results could be reached by the integration of prosodic features for the classification process. In [Fis94] prosodic information was integrated in the SCT-Algorithm to find phrase boundaries in utterances. In this case the SCT is based not only on the textual information given by an utterance

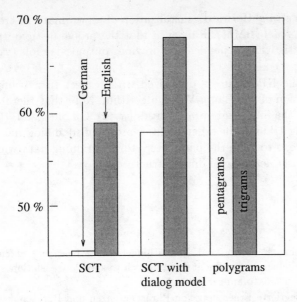

Fig. 5. Recognition rates for SCTs with and without the dialog model and polygrams.

but also uses prosodic features for the classification. In the training phase questions about keywords and prosodic features can be learned. This could also be helpful for the classification of dialog acts. Useful prosodic features are *sentence mode* and *accentuation*.

For the segmentation of turns into utterances the SCT-Algorithm could be used as well. For this classification problem prosodic information especially prosodically marked phrase boundaries are even more important. First experiments show that utterance boundaries coincide with phrase boundaries in 96 %.

7.2 Hidden Polygram Models

The results indicate that application of Bayes rule using competing polygram models performs considerably better in dialog act classification than SCTs. Moreover, it becomes evident from figure 3 that additional improvement can be gained if the structural restrictions of the dialog model are exploited during analysis.

It is thus a promising idea to develop an integrated probabilistic model of dialog-driven word production. The *Hidden Polygram Model* (HPM) is a mathematical device which describes a two-stage random process:

- The particular dialog act categories are selected according to a probabilistic finite state machine $(\boldsymbol{\pi}, \boldsymbol{A})$ with a vector $\boldsymbol{\pi}$ of initial probabilities π_i and a matrix $\boldsymbol{A}$ of transition probabilities a_{ij}.
- Each time a dialog state has been occupied, a sequence of words is produced. This second process, in turn, is controlled by a state-dependent polygram language model with the conditional output distribution $P_j(w|\boldsymbol{v})$.

Obviously, an HPM is a straightforward generalization of an ordinary discrete-valued *Hidden Markov Model* (HMM) [Rab88] in that the probabilistic output of the model is made statistically dependent on previous output symbols (word in our application).

The parameters of the HPM can be optimized with respect to a training corpus using a modification of the Baum-Welch algorithm. Note that there are two possibilities to treat the finite state probabilities (π, A). On one hand, they can be kept fixed during training in order to fit a prespecified dialog model; an interesting alternative is to tune the parameters to the training data which amounts to an unsupervised learning of dialog structure.

References

[AMR95]   J. Alexandersson, E. Maier, and N. Reithinger. A robust and efficient three-layered dialogue component for a speech-to-speech translation system. In *EACL 1995*, to appear 1995.

[Fis94]   J. Fischer. Integrierte Erkennung von Phrasengrenzen und Phrasenakzenten mit Klassifikationsbäumen. Diplomarbeit, Lehrstuhl für Mustererkennung (Informatik 5), Universität Erlangen-Nürnberg, 1994.

[GRD91]   S. Gelfand, C. Ravishankar, and E. Delp. An Iterative Growing and Pruning Algorithm for Classification Tree Design. *IEEE Trans. on Pattern Analysis and Machine Intelligence*, 13:302–320, Februar 1991.

[Jel90]   F. Jelinek. Self-Organized Language Modeling for Speech Recognition. In A. Waibel and K.F. Lee, editors, *Readings in Speech Recognition*, pages 450–506. Morgan Kaufmann, San Mateo, CA, 1990.

[JM80]   F. Jelinek and R.L. Mercer. Interpolated Estimation of Markov Source Parameters from Sparse Data. In E.S. Gelsema and L.N. Kanal, editors, *Pattern Recognition in Practice*, pages 381–397. North Holland, 1980.

[Kat87]   S. Katz. Estimation of Probability from Sparse Data for the Language Model Component at a Speech Recognizer. *IEEE Trans. on Acoustics, Speech and Signal Processing*, ASSP-35(3):400–401, 1987.

[KM93]   S. Kameyama and I. Maleck. Konstellation und Szenario von Terminabsprachen, Verbmobil–Report–23–93, Dezember 1993.

[KNST94]   T. Kuhn, H. Niemann, and E.G. Schukat-Talamazzini. Ergodic Hidden Markov Models and Polygrams for Language Modeling. In *Proc. Int. Conf. on Acoustics, Speech and Signal Processing*, volume 1, pages 357–360, Adelaide, Australia, 1994.

[Kuh92]   R. Kuhn. Keyword Classification Trees for Speech Understanding Systems. Technical report, CRIM, Montreal, Canada, 1992.

[Mai94]   E. Maier, editor. *Dialogmodellierung in VERBMOBIL - Festlegung der Sprechhandlungen für den Demonstrator Verbmobil–Memo–31–94*. Juli 1994.

[Rab88]   L.R. Rabiner. Mathematical Foundations of Hidden Markov Models. In H. Niemann, M. Lang, and G. Sagerer, editors, *Recent Advances in Speech Understanding and Dialog Systems*, volume 46 of *NATO ASI Series F*, pages 183–205. Springer–Verlag, Berlin, 1988.

[STHKN95] E.G. Schukat-Talamazzini, R. Hendrych, R. Kompe, and H. Niemann. Permugram language models. In *Proc. European Conf. on Speech Communication and Technology*, volume 3, pages 1773–1776, Madrid, September 1995.

[STKN94] E.G. Schukat-Talamazzini, T. Kuhn, and H. Niemann. Speech Recognition for Spoken Dialogue Systems. In Niemann, de Mori, and Hanrieder, editors, *Progress and Prospects of Speech Research and Technology: Proc. of the CRIM/FORWISS Workshop (München, Sept. 1994)*, pages 110–120, Sankt Augustin, 1994. infix.

Sample Selection
in Natural Language Learning

Sean P. Engelson and Ido Dagan

Department of Mathematics and Computer Science
Bar-Ilan University
52900 Ramat Gan, Israel
{engelson,dagan}@bimacs.cs.biu.ac.il

Abstract. Many corpus-based methods for natural language processing
are based on supervised training, requiring expensive manual annotation
of training corpora. This paper investigates reducing annotation cost by
sample selection. In this approach, the learner examines many unlabeled
examples and selects for labeling only those that are most informative at
each stage of training. In this way it is possible to avoid redundantly annotating examples that contribute little new information. The paper first
analyzes the issues that need to be addressed when constructing a sample selection algorithm, arguing for the attractiveness of *committee-based*
selection methods. We then focus on selection for training probabilistic
classifiers, which are commonly applied to problems in statistical natural language processing. We report experimental results of applying a
specific type of committee-based selection during training of a stochastic
part-of-speech tagger, and demonstrate substantially improved learning
rates over complete training using all of the text.

1 Introduction

Many corpus-based methods for natural language processing (NLP) are based on
supervised training, acquiring information from a manually annotated corpus.
Manual annotation, however, is typically very expensive. As a consequence, only
a few large annotated corpora exist, mainly for the English language, and not
covering many genres of text. This situation makes it difficult to apply supervised learning methods to languages other than English, or to adapt systems to
different genres of text. Furthermore, it is infeasible in many cases to develop
new supervised methods that require annotations different from those which are
currently available.

In some cases, manual annotation can be avoided altogether, using self-
organized methods, such as was shown for part-of-speech tagging of English
by Kupiec (1992). Even in Kupiec's tagger, though, manual (and somewhat un-
principled) biasing of the initial model was necessary to achieve satisfactory
convergence. Elworthy (1994) and Merialdo (1991) have investigated the effect
of self-converging re-estimation for part-of-speech tagging and found that some
initial manual training is needed. More generally, the more supervised training
is provided, the better the results. In fact, fully unsupervised methods are not

applicable for many NLP tasks, and perhaps not even for part-of-speech tagging in some languages.

In this paper we investigate the *active learning* paradigm for reducing annotation cost. There are two types of active learning, in both of which the learner has some control over the choice of the examples which are labeled and used for training. The first type uses *membership queries*, in which the learner constructs examples and asks a teacher to label them (MacKay 1992b; Plutowski & White 1993). While this approach provides proven computational advantages (Anguin 1987), it is usually not applicable to natural language problems, for which it is very difficult to construct synthetically meaningful and informative examples. This difficulty can be overcome when a large corpus of unlabeled training data is available. In this case the second type of active learning, *sample selection*, can be applied: The learner examines many unlabeled examples, and selects only those that are most informative for the learner at each stage of training. This way, it is possible to avoid the redundancy of annotating many examples that contribute roughly the same information to the learner.

The machine learning literature suggests several different approaches for sample selection (Seung, Opper, & Sompolinsky 1992; Freund *et al.* 1993; Cohn, Atlas, & Ladner 1994; Lewis & Catlett 1994; Lewis & Gale 1994). In the first part of the paper, we analyze the different issues that need to be addressed when constructing a sample selection algorithm. These include measuring the utility of an example for the learner, the number of models that will be used for the selection process, the method for selecting examples, and, for the case of the committee-based paradigm, alternative methods for generating committee members.

In the second part of the paper we focus on sample selection for training probabilistic classifiers. In statistical NLP, probabilistic classifiers are often used to select a preferred analysis of the linguistic structure of a text (for example, its syntactic structure (Black *et al.* 1993), word categories (Church 1988), or word senses (Gale, Church, & Yarowsky 1993)). Classification in this framework is performed by a probabilistic model which, given an input example, assigns a probability to each possible classification and selects the most probable one. The parameters of the model are estimated from the statistics of a training corpus.

As a representative case for probabilistic classifiers we have chosen to experiment with sample selection for stochastic part-of-speech tagging. We focus on committee-based methods, which we find particularly attractive for NLP due to their generality and simplicity. The variants of the committee-based method that we have examined have achieved substantially better learning efficiency than complete training on all of the text in the corpus.

2 Issues in Active Learning

In this section, we will discuss the issues that affect the design of active learning methods, and their implications for performance. Our focus is on sample selection methods, though some of our discussion applies to membership query approaches as well.

2.1 Measuring information content

The objective of sample selection is to select those examples which will be most informative in the future. How can we determine the informativeness of an example? One method is to derive an explicit measure of the expected information gained by using the example (Cohn, Ghahramani, & Jordan 1995; MacKay 1992b; 1992a). For example, MacKay (1992b) assesses the informativeness of an example, for a neural network learning task, as the expected decrease in the overall variance of the model's prediction, after training on the example. Explicit measures can be appealing, since they attempt to give a precise characterization of the information content of an example. Also, for membership querying, an explicit formulation of information content sometimes enables finding the most informative examples analytically, saving the cost of searching the example space. The use of explicit methods is limited, however, since explicit measures are generally (a) model-specific, (b) complex, often requiring various approximations to be made practical, and (c) depend on the accuracy of the current hypothesis at any given step.

The alternative to measuring the informativeness of an example explicitly is to measure it implicitly, by quantifying the amount of uncertainty in the classification of the example, given the current training data. The committee-based paradigm (Seung, Opper, & Sompolinsky 1992; Freund *et al.* 1993) does this, for example, by measuring the disagreement among committee members on a classification. The main advantage of the implicit approach is its generality, as it needs no complicated model-specific derivations of expected information gain.

The utility for learning of a given example E depends on the examples we expect to see in the future. Hence, selection must be sensitive to the probability of seeing an example whose correct classification relies on the information contained in E. The *sequential selection* scheme, in which examples are selected sequentially on an individual basis, achieves this goal implicitly, since the training examples examined are drawn from the same distribution as future test examples. Examples may be selected from the input stream if their information content exceeds a threshold (Seung, Opper, & Sompolinsky 1992; Freund *et al.* 1993; Matan 1995). Alternatively, they may be selected randomly, with some probability proportional to information content, as we do in this paper, inspired by Freund's (1990) method for boosting. Another selection scheme that has been used (Lewis & Catlett 1994) is *batch selection*, in which the k most informative examples in a batch of n examples are chosen for training (the process is then repeated on either the same or a new batch). In order for batch selection to properly relate to the distribution of examples, however, an explicit model of the probability distribution must be incorporated into the informativeness measure (this is also true generally for membership querying). Otherwise, the algorithm may concentrate its effort on learning from informative, but highly atypical, examples.

2.2 How many models?

In the implicit approach, the informativeness of an example is evaluated with respect to models derived from the training data at each stage. The key question, then, is how many models to use to evaluate an example. One approach is to use a single model based on the training data seen so far. This approach is taken by Lewis and Gale (1994), for training a binary classifier. They select for training those examples whose classification probability is closest to 0.5, i.e, those examples for which the current model is most uncertain.

There are some difficulties with the single model approach, however (Cohn, Atlas, & Ladner 1994). First is the fact that a single model cannot adequately measure an example's informativeness with respect to the entire set of models allowed by the training data. Instead, what is obtained is a local estimate of the example's informativeness with respect to the single model used for evaluation. Furthermore, the single model approach may conflate two different types of classification uncertainty: (a) uncertainty due to insufficiency of training data, and (b) uncertainty due to inherent classification ambiguity with respect to the model class. We only want to measure the former, since the latter is unavoidable (given a model class). If the best model in the class will be uncertain on the current example no matter how much training is supplied, then the example does not contain useful information, despite current classification uncertainty.

From a practical perspective, it may be difficult to apply the single-model approach to complex or probabilistic classification tasks, such as those typical in natural language applications. Even for a binary classification task, Lewis and Gale (1994) found that reliable estimates of classification uncertainty were not directly available from their model, and so they had to approximate them using logistic regression. In other natural language tasks, obtaining reliable estimates of the uncertainty of a single model may be even more difficult. For example, in part-of-speech tagging, a 'classification' is a sequence of tags assigned to a sentence. Since there are many such tag sequences possible for a given sentence, the single-model approach would somehow have to compare the probability of the best classification with those of alternative classifications.

These difficulties are ameliorated by measuring informativeness as the level of disagreement between multiple models (a *committee*) constructed from the training data. Using several models allows greater coverage of the model space, while measuring disagreement in classification ensures that only uncertainty due to insufficient training (type (a) above) is considered.

2.3 Measuring disagreement

The committee-based approach requires measuring disagreement among the committee members. If two committee members are used, then either they agree, or they don't. If more are used some method must be devised to measure the amount of disagreement. One possibility is to consider the maximum number of votes for any one classification—if this number is low, then the committee members mostly disagree. However, in applications with more than two categories, this method does not adequately measure the spread of committee member classifications. Section 4.3 below describes how we use the entropy of the vote distribution to measure disagreement.

Given a measure of disagreement, we need a method which uses it to select examples for training. In the batch selection scheme, the examples with the highest committee disagreement in each batch would be selected for training (Lewis & Catlett 1994)[1]. The selection decision is somewhat more complicated when sequential selection is used. One option is to select just those examples whose disagreement is above a threshold (Seung, Opper, & Sompolinsky 1992). Another option, which may relate training better to the example distribution, is to use random selection (following the method used by Freund (1990) for boosting). In this method, the probability of an example is given by some function of the committee's disagreement on the example. In our work, we used a linear function of disagreement, as a heuristic for obtaining a selection probability (see Section 4.3 below). Finding an optimal function for this purpose remains an open problem.

2.4 Choosing committee members

There are two main approaches for generating committee-members: The *version space* approach and the *random sampling* approach. The version space approach, advocated by Cohn et al. (1994) seeks to choose committee members on the border of the space of models allowed by the training data (the *version space* (Mitchell 1982)). Hence models are chosen for the committee which are as far from each other as possible, while being consistent with the training data. This ensures that any example on which the committee members disagree will restrict the version space.

The version space approach can be difficult to apply since finding models on the edge of the version space is non-trivial in general. Furthermore, the approach is not directly applicable in the case of probabilistic classification models, where all models are possible, though not equally probable. The alternative is random sampling, in which models are sampled randomly from the set of possible models, given the training data. This approach was first advocated in theoretical work on the Query By Committee algorithm (Seung, Opper, & Sompolinsky 1992; Freund *et al.* 1993), in which they assume a prior distribution on models and choose committee members randomly from the distribution restricted to the version space. In our work, we have applied the random sampling approach to probabilistic classifiers by computing an approximation to the posterior model distribution given the training data, and generating committee members from that distribution (see (Dagan & Engelson 1995) and below for more detail). Matan (1995) presents two other methods for random sampling. In the first, he trains committee members on different subsets of the training data. It remains to be seen how this method compares with explicit generation from the posterior model distribution using the entire training set. For neural network models,

---

[1] Recall, though, the problem of modeling the distribution of input examples when using batch selection.

Matan generates committee members by backpropagation training using different initial weights in the networks so that they reach different local minima.

3 Information gain and probabilistic classifiers

In this section we focus on information gain in the context of probabilistic classifiers, and consider the desirable properties of examples that are selected for training. Generally speaking, a training example contributes data to several statistics, which in turn determine the estimates of several parameter values. An informative example is therefore one whose contribution to the statistics leads to a useful improvement of parameter estimates. We identify three properties of parameters for which acquiring additional statistics is most beneficial:

1. The current estimate of the parameter is uncertain due to insufficient statistics in the training set. An uncertain estimate is likely to be far from the true value of the parameter and can cause incorrect classification. Additional statistics would bring the estimate closer to the true value.
2. Classification is sensitive to changes in the current estimate of the parameter. Otherwise, acquiring additional statistics is unlikely to affect classification and is therefore not beneficial.
3. The parameter takes part in calculating class probabilities for a large proportion of examples. Parameters that are only relevant for classifying few examples, according to the probability distribution of the input examples, have low utility for future classification.

The committee-based selection scheme, as we discussed above, tends to select examples that affect parameters with the above three properties. Property 1 is addressed by randomly picking parameter values for committee members from the posterior distribution of parameter estimates (given the current statistics). When the statistics for a parameter are insufficient the variance of the posterior distribution of the estimates is large, and hence there will be large differences in the values of the parameter picked for different committee members. Note that property 1 is not addressed when uncertainty in classification is only judged relative to a *single* model (Lewis & Gale 1994). Such an approach can capture uncertainty with respect to given parameter values, in the sense of property 2, but it does not model uncertainty about the choice of these values in the first place (the use of a single model is also criticized by Cohn et al. (1994)).

Property 2 is addressed by selecting examples for which committee members highly disagree in classification. Thus, the algorithm tends to acquire statistics where uncertainty in parameter estimates entails uncertainty in actual classification. Finally, property 3 is addressed by independently examining input examples which are drawn from the input distribution. In this way, we implicitly model the expected utility of the statistics in classifying future examples. Such modeling is absent in 'batch' selection schemes, where examples with maximal classification uncertainty are selected from a large batch of examples (see also (Freund *et al.* 1993) for further discussion).

4 Implementation For Part-Of-Speech Tagging

We have currently begun to explore the space of sample selection methods for the application of bigram part-of-speech tagging (cf. (Merialdo 1991))[2]. A bigram model has three types of parameters: *transition probabilities* $P(t_i \rightarrow t_j)$ each giving the probability of a tag t_j occuring after the tag t_i, *lexical probabilities* $P(t|w)$ each giving the probability of a tag t occurring for a word w, and *tag probabilities* $P(t)$ each giving the marginal probability of a tag occurring. We have implemented and tested a committee-based sequential selection scheme, using randomized selection as described in Section 2.1. We generate committee members randomly, by approximating the posterior distributions of the transition and output probabilities, given the training data. Some details of our implementation are given below; the system is more fully described in (Dagan & Engelson 1995).

4.1 Posterior distributions for bigram parameters

In this section, we consider how to approximate the posterior distributions of the parameters for a bigram tagging model.[3] (Our method can also be applied to Hidden Markov Models (HMMs) in general.) Let $\{\alpha_i\}$ be the set of all parameters of the model (i.e, all transition and lexical probabilities). First note that these define a number of multinomial probability distributions. Each multinomial corresponds to a conditioning event and its values are given by the corresponding set of conditioned events. For example, a transition probability parameter $P(t_i \rightarrow t_j)$ has conditioning event t_i and conditioned event t_j.

Let $\{u_i\}$ denote the set of possible values for given multinomial variable, and let $S = \{n_i\}$ denote a set of statistics extracted from the training set, where n_i is the number of times that the value u_i appears in the training set. We denote the total number of appearances of the multinomial variable as $N = \sum_i n_i$. The parameters whose distributions we wish to estimate are $\alpha_i = P(u_i)$.

The maximum likelihood estimate for each of the multinomial's distribution parameters, α_i, is $\hat{\alpha}_i = \frac{n_i}{N}$. In practice, this estimator is usually smoothed in some way to compensate for data sparseness. Such smoothing typically reduces the estimates for values with positive counts and gives small positive estimates for values with a zero count. For simplicity, we describe here the approximation of the posterior probabilities $P(\alpha_i = a_i | S)$ for the unsmoothed estimator[4].

We approximate $P(\alpha_i = a_i | S)$ by first assuming that the multinomial is a collection of independent binomials, each corresponding to a single value u_i of the multinomial; we then separately enforce the constraint that the parameters

---

[2] Bigram models are a subclass of Hidden Markov Models (HMM) (Rabiner 1989).

[3] We do not randomize over tag probability parameters, since the amount of data for tag frequencies is large enough to make their MLEs quite definite.

[4] In the implementation we smooth the MLE by interpolation with a uniform probability distribution, following Merialdo (1991). Adaptation of $P(\alpha_i = a_i | S)$ to the smoothed version of the estimator is simple.

of all these binomials should sum to 1. For each such binomial, we approximate $P(\alpha_i = a_i|S)$ as a truncated normal distribution (restricted to $[0,1]$), with estimated mean $\mu = \frac{n_i}{N}$ and variance $\sigma^2 = \frac{\mu(1-\mu)}{N}$.[5] We found in practice, however, very small differences between parameter values drawn from this distribution, and consequently too few disagreements between committee members to be useful for selection. We therefore also incorporate a 'temperature' parameter, t, which is used as a multiplier for the variance estimate σ^2. In other words, we actually approximate $P(\alpha_i = a_i|S)$ as a truncated normal distribution with mean μ and variance $\sigma^2 t$.

To generate a particular multinomial distribution, we randomly choose values for its parameters α_i from their binomial distributions, and renormalize them so that they sum to 1.

To generate a random model given statistics S, we note that all of its parameters $P(t_i{\rightarrow}t_j)$ and $P(t|w)$ are independent of each other. We thus independently choose values for the model's parameters from their multinomial distributions.

4.2 Examples in bigram training

Typically, concept learning problems are formulated such that there is a set of training examples that are independent of each other. When training a bigram model (indeed, any HMM), however, this is not true, as each word is dependent on that before it. This problem may simply be solved by considering each sentence as an individual example. More generally, we can break the text at any point where tagging is unambiguous. In particular, suppose we have a lexicon which specifies which parts-of-speech are possible for each word (i.e, which of the parameters $P(t|w)$ are positive). In bigram tagging, we can use unambiguous words (those with only one possible part of speech) as example boundaries. This allows us to train on smaller examples, focusing training more on the truly informative parts of the corpus.

4.3 Measuring disagreement

We now consider how to measure disagreement among a set of committee members which each assign a tag sequence to a given word sequence. Since we want to quantify the spread of classification across committee member, we suggest using the entropy of the distribution of classes assigned by committee members to an example. (Other methods might also be useful, eg, variance for real-valued classification.)

Let $V(t, w)$ be the number of committee members (out of k members) 'voting' for tag t for the word w. Then w's *vote entropy* is

$$VE(w) = -\sum_t \frac{V(t, w)}{k} \log \frac{V(t, w)}{k}$$

---

[5] The normal approximation, while convenient, can be avoided. The posterior probability $P(\alpha_i = a_i|S)$ for the multinomial is given exactly by the Dirichlet distribution (Johnson 1972) (which reduces to the Beta distribution in the binomial case).

To measure disagreement over an entire word sequence W, we use the average, $\overline{VE}(W)$, of the voting entropy over all ambiguous words in the sequence.

As a function for translating from average vote entropy to probability, we use a simple linear function of the normalized average vote entropy:

$$P_{\text{label}}(W) = \frac{e}{\log k}\, \overline{VE}(W)$$

where e is an *entropy gain* system parameter, which controls the overall frequency with which examples are selected, and the $\log k$ term normalizes for the number of committee members. Thus examples with higher average entropy are more likely to be selected for training.

5 Experimental Results

In this section, we describe the results of applying the committee-based selection method to bigram part-of-speech tagging, as compared with complete training on all examples in the corpus. Evaluation was performed using the University of Pennsylvania tagged corpus from the ACL/DCI CD-ROM I. For ease of implementation, we used a complete (closed) lexicon which contains all the words in the corpus[6]. Approximately 63% of the tokens (word occurrences) in the corpus were ambiguous in the lexicon.

The committee-based selection algorithm was initialized using the first 1,000 words from the corpus (624 of which were ambiguous), and then sequentially examined the following examples in the corpus for possible labeling. Testing was performed on a separate portion of the corpus consisting of 20,000 words. We compare the amount of training required by the different methods to achieve a given tagging accuracy on the test set, where both the amount of training and tagging accuracy are measured only over ambiguous words. Other work on tagging has measured accuracy over all words, not just ambiguous ones. Complete training of our system on 1,000,000 words gave us an accuracy of 93.5% over ambiguous words, which corresponds to an accuracy of 95.9% over all words in the test set, comparable to other published results on bigram tagging.

In Figure 1, we present plots of training effort versus accuracy achieved, for both complete training and committee-based selection ($k = 10$, $e = 0.3$, and $t = 50$). The curves start together, but the efficiency of committee-based selection begins to be evident when we seek 89% accuracy. Committee-based selection requires less than one-fourth the amount of training that complete training does to reach 90.5% accuracy and less than one-sixth the amount of training that complete training does to reach 92.5% accuracy (as indicated by the vertical dashed lines). We see, therefore, that the efficiency improvement provided by committee-based selection greatly increases with the desired accuracy. This is in

---

[6] We used the lexicon provided with Brill's part-of-speech tagger (Brill 1992). While in an actual application the lexicon would not be complete, our results using a complete lexicon are valid, as our evaluation is comparative.

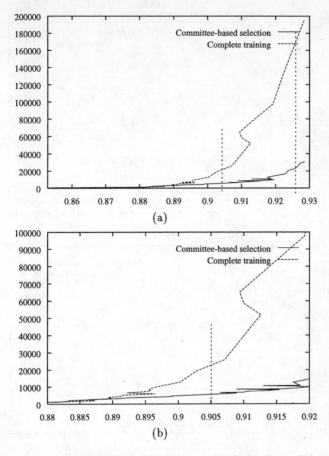

Fig. 1. Amount of training (number of ambiguous words in the training sentences) plotted (y-axis) versus classification accuracy (x-axis). Committee-based selection used $k = 10$ committee members, entropy gain $e = 0.3$, and temperature $t = 50$. (a) Full view. (b) Expanded view for accuracy between 88% and 92%.

line with the results of Freund et al. (1993) on the Query By Committee algorithm, in which they prove exponential speedup (for learning binary concepts) under certain theoretical assumptions.

Figure 2 shows how our results are qualitatively the same for different values of the system parameters. Figure 2(a) shows a plot comparable to Figure 1, for selection using 5 committee members. Results are substantially the same, though the speedup is slightly less and there is more oscillation in accuracy at low training levels, due to the greater coarseness of the evaluation of information content. In Figure 2(b) we show a similar plot on a different test set of 20,000 words, for selection using 10 committee members and an entropy gain of 0.5. Again, we see a similar efficiency gain for committee-based selection as compared with complete training.

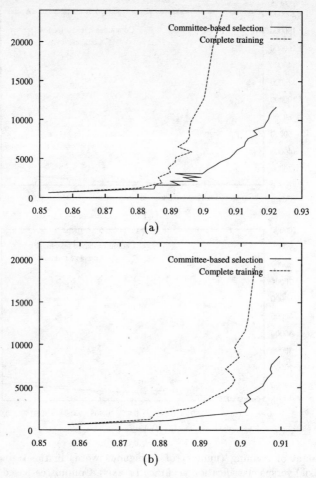

Fig. 2. Further results comparing committee-based and complete training. Amount of training (number of ambiguous words in the training sentences) plotted against desired accuracy. (a) Training vs. accuracy for $k = 5$, $e = 0.3$, and $t = 50$. (b) Training vs. accuracy for $k = 10$, $e = 0.5$ and $t = 50$, for a different test set of 20,000 words.

In the experiments reported above, training was performed by examining (and possibly selecting) examples in the sequence in which they appear in the corpus. This procedure could potentially skew results, due to inhomogeneity in the composition of the corpus. In order to correct for this effect, we ran a comparative experiment, of the type described above, on a version of the training corpus in which sentences were reordered randomly. The results are plotted in Figure 3, together with the results for the non-randomized corpus. First of all, as we would expect, the curves for the randomized corpus are much smoother than those for the non-randomized corpus, due to the greater homogeneity of the text. Second, we do find an increase in efficiency for the randomized corpus, relative

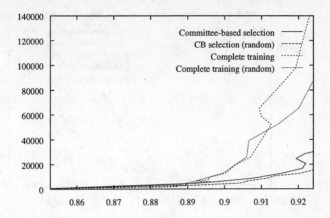

Fig. 3. Committee-based selection and complete training on the randomized corpus. We also show, for comparison, curves for the original corpus (the same as in Figure 1). Again, the committee-based selection used $k = 10$ committee members, entropy gain $e = 0.3$, and temperature $t = 50$.

to our chosen test set. The difference for committee-based selection, however, is quite small.

Figure 4 compares our randomized selection scheme with a batch selection scheme (similar to that of Lewis and Catlett (1994)). In the batch selection scheme a large number of examples are examined (the *batch size*) and the best n examples in the batch are used for training (we call n the *selection size*). As discussed above in Section 2.1, we expect randomized selection to outperform batch selection, since randomized selection also takes into account the frequency with which examples occur. As can be seen in figure 4, this hypothesis appears to be true on average, although the difference is small. As is also evident, different batch and selection sizes in batch selection do not greatly affect results[7]. We are still investigating the relationship between these two selection techniques. Randomized selection does have the clear advantage, though, of computational efficiency; fewer examples must be examined per example selected.

6 Conclusions

Annotating large textual corpora for training natural language models is a costly process. Sample selection methods can be applied to reduce annotation cost, by avoiding redundantly annotating examples that contribute little new information to the learner. Information content may be measured either explicitly, by means of an analytically derived formula, or implicitly, by estimating model classification uncertainty. Implicit methods for measuring information gain tend to be simpler and more general than explicit methods. Sequential selection, unlike

---

[7] Note however, that one of the batch selection runs appears to suddenly reach an asymptotic accuracy at ~91.5%; the cause of this phenomenon is as yet unclear.

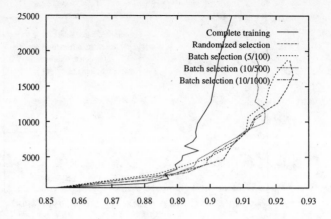

Fig. 4. Comparison of randomized vs. batch committee-based selection. Amount of training (number of ambiguous words in the training sentences) plotted (y-axis) versus classification accuracy (x-axis). Both methods used $k = 5$ committee members and a temperature of $t = 50$. Randomized selection used an entropy gain $e = 0.3$. Batch selection used several batch and selection sizes; we show results for 5 selected from each 100 examples, 10 from each 500, and 10 from each 1000.

batch selection, implicitly measures the expected utility of an example relative to the example distribution.

The number of models used to evaluate informativeness in the implicit approach is crucial. If only one model is used, information gain is only measured relative to a small part of the model space. When multiple models are used, there are different ways to generate them from the training data. The version space approach is applicable to problems where a version space exists and can be efficiently represented. The method is most useful when the probability distribution of models in the version space is uniform. Random sampling is more broadly applicable, however, especially to learning probabilistic classifiers. It is as yet unclear how different random sampling methods compare. In this paper, we have empirically examined two types of committee-based selection methods, and our results suggest the utility of sample selection for natural language learning tasks.

6.1 Further research

As pointed out earlier, the sample selection method of this paper is general, and in principle could be applied to supervised training of any probabilistic classifier. We suggest that the method is thus applicable to many problems in statistical natural language processing which can be handled as probabilistic classification tasks, such as word sense disambiguation, syntactic analysis and text categorization.

Statistical methods for these tasks typically assign a probability estimate, or some other statistical score, to each alternative analysis (a word sense, a category label, a parse tree, etc.), and then select the analysis with the highest score. The score is usually computed as a function of several 'atomic' probability estimates, often binomials or multinomials, such as:

- In word sense disambiguation (Hearst 1991; Gale, Church, & Yarowsky 1993; Yarowsky 1994): $P(s|f)$, where s is a specific sense of the ambiguous word in question w, and f is a feature of occurrences of w. Common features are words in the context of w or morphological attributes of it.
- In prepositional-phrase (PP) attachment (Hindle & Rooth 1993): $P(a|f)$, where a is a possible attachment, such as an attachment to a head verb or noun, and f is a feature, or a combination of features, of the attachment. Common features are the words involved in the attachment, such as the head verb or noun, the preposition, and the head word of the PP.
- In text categorization (Lewis & Gale 1994; Iwayama & Tokunaga 1994; Finch 1994): $P(t|C)$, where t is a term in the document to be categorized, and C is a candidate category label.
- In statistical parsing (Black *et al.* 1993): $P(r|h)$, the probability of applying the rule r at a certain stage of the top down derivation of the parse tree given the history h of the derivation process. Similarly, statistical bottom-up parsing (Briscoe & Carroll 1993) is based on the probability of performing a certain parsing action given the context of the current parse.

Applying committee-based selection to supervised training of such methods can be done analogously to its application in the current paper[8]. At each stage of training, the new example which is considered for annotation would be classified by a committee of classifiers. Each classifier is constructed by generating a variant of the probability estimate for each parameter that participates in the classification of the new example. The variant is drawn randomly from the posterior probability distribution of the parameter estimate given the statistics acquired so far. Depending on the type of this posterior distribution, it might be approximated like in the current paper, or computed by another appropriate method. Finally, the example would be selected for annotation only if there is high disagreement with regard to its analysis[9].

Beyond its use in probabilistic contexts, committee-based selection may be attempted also for training in non-probabilistic contexts, where explicit modeling of information gain is typically impossible. In such contexts, committee members might be generated by randomly varying some of the decisions made in the learning algorithm. This approach might, for example, be profitably applied to learning Hidden Markov Model (HMM) structure (Stolcke & Omohundro 1992), and to transformation-based approaches to learning (e.g. (Brill 1992)).

---

[8] While unsupervised methods exist for some of the problems above, it has been shown in several cases that a certain amount of supervised training makes a significant improvement in performance.

[9] Measuring disagreement in full syntactic parsing is complicated. It might be approached by similar methods to those used for parsing evaluation, measuring the disagreement between the parser's output and the correct parse.

Another important area for future work is in developing sample selection methods which are independent of the eventual learning method to be applied. This would be of considerable advantage in developing selectively annotated corpora for general research use. Recent work on heterogeneous uncertainty sampling (Lewis & Catlett 1994) supports this idea, as it shows positive results for using one type of model for example selection and a different type for classification.

Acknowledgments. Thanks to Yoav Freund and Yishai Mansour for their helpful comments. The first author gratefully acknowledges the support of the Fulbright Foundation.

References

Angluin, D. 1987. Learning regular sets from queries and counterexamples. *Information and Computation* 75(2):87–106.

Black, E.; Jelinek, F.; Lafferty, J.; Magerman, D.; Mercer, R.; and Roukos, S. 1993. Towards history-based grammars: using richer models for probabilistic parsing. In *Proc. of the Annual Meeting of the ACL*, 31–37.

Brill, E. 1992. A simple rule-based part of speech tagger. In *Proc. of ACL Conference on Applied Natural Language Processing*.

Briscoe, T., and Carroll, J. 1993. Generalized probabilistic LR parsing of natural language corpora with unification-based grammars. *Computational Linguistics* 19(1):25–60.

Church, K. W. 1988. A stochastic parts program and noun phrase parser for unrestricted text. In *Proc. of ACL Conference on Applied Natural Language Processing*.

Cohn, D.; Atlas, L.; and Ladner, R. 1994. Improving generalization with active learning. *Machine Learning* 15.

Cohn, D. A.; Ghahramani, Z.; and Jordan, M. I. 1995. Active learning with statistical models. In Tesauro, G.; Touretzky, D.; and Alspector, J., eds., *Advances in Neural Information Processing*, volume 7. Morgan Kaufmann.

Dagan, I., and Engelson, S. 1995. Committee-based sampling for training probabilistic classifiers. In *Proc. Int'l Conference on Machine Learning*.

Elworthy, D. 1994. Does Baum-Welch re-estimation improve taggers? In *Proc. of ACL Conference on Applied Natural Language Processing*, 53–58.

Finch, S. 1994. Exploiting sophisticated representations for document retrieval. In *Proceedings of the 4th Conference on Applied Natural Language Processing*.

Freund, Y.; Seung, H. S.; Shamir, E.; and Tishby, N. 1993. Information, prediction, and query by committee. In *Advances in Neural Information Processing*, volume 5. Morgan Kaufmann.

Freund, Y. 1990. An improved boosting algorithm and its implications on learning complexity. In *Proc. Fifth Workshop on Computational Learning Theory*.

Gale, W.; Church, K.; and Yarowsky, D. 1993. A method for disambiguating word senses in a large corpus. *Computers and the Humanities* 26:415–439.

Hearst, M. 1991. Noun homograph disambiguation using local context in large text corpora. In *Proc. of the Annual Conference of the UW Center for the New OED and Text Research*, 1–22.

Hindle, D., and Rooth, M. 1993. Structural ambiguity and lexical relations. *Computational Linguistics* 19(1):103–120.

Iwayama, M., and Tokunaga, T. 1994. A probabilistic model for text categorization based on a single random variable with multiple values. In *Proceedings of the 4th Conference on Applied Natural Language Processing*.

Johnson, N. L. 1972. *Continuous Multivariate Distributions*. New York: John Wiley & Sons.

Kupiec, J. 1992. Robust part-of-speech tagging using a hidden makov model. *Computer Speech and Language* 6:225–242.

Lewis, D., and Catlett, J. 1994. Heterogeneous uncertainty sampling for supervised learning. In *Machine Learning Proceedings of the 11th International Conference*.

Lewis, D., and Gale, W. 1994. Training text classifiers by uncertainty sampling. In *Proceedings of ACM-SIGIR Conference on Information Retrieval*.

MacKay, D. J. C. 1992a. The evidence framework applied to classification networks. *Neural Computation* 4.

MacKay, D. J. C. 1992b. Information-based objective functions for active data selection. *Neural Computation* 4.

Matan, O. 1995. On-site learning. Technical Report LOGIC-95-4, Stanford University.

Merialdo, B. 1991. Tagging text with a probabilistic model. In *Proc. Int'l Conf. on Acoustics, Speech, and Signal Processing*.

Mitchell, T. 1982. Generalization as search. *Artificial Intelligence* 18.

Plutowski, M., and White, H. 1993. Selecting concise training sets from clean data. *IEEE Trans. on Neural Networks* 4(2).

Rabiner, L. R. 1989. A tutorial on Hidden Markov Models and selected applications in speech recognition. *Proc. of the IEEE* 77(2).

Seung, H. S.; Opper, M.; and Sompolinsky, H. 1992. Query by committee. In *Proc. ACM Workshop on Computational Learning Theory*.

Stolcke, A., and Omohundro, S. 1992. Hidden Markov Model induction by Bayesian model merging. In *Advances in Neural Information Processing*, volume 5. Morgan Kaufmann.

Yarowsky, D. 1994. Decision lists for lexical ambiguity resolution: application to accent restoration in Spanish and French. In *Proc. of the Annual Meeting of the ACL*, 88–95.

Learning Information Extraction Patterns from Examples

Scott B. Huffman

Price Waterhouse Technology Centre, 68 Willow Road, Menlo Park CA 94025, USA

Abstract. A growing population of users want to extract a growing variety of information from on-line texts. Unfortunately, current information extraction systems typically require experts to hand-build dictionaries of extraction patterns for each new type of information to be extracted. This paper presents a system that can learn dictionaries of extraction patterns directly from user-provided examples of texts and events to be extracted from them. The system, called LIEP, learns patterns that recognize relationships between key constituents based on local syntax. Sets of patterns learned by LIEP for a sample extraction task perform nearly at the level of a hand-built dictionary of patterns.

1 Introduction

Information extraction can be defined as the detection and extraction of particular events of interest from text. Although significant progress has been made on information extraction systems in recent years (for instance through the MUC conferences [MUC, 1992; MUC, 1993]), coding the knowledge these systems need to extract new kinds of information and events is an arduous and time-consuming process [Riloff, 1993]. The dictionaries of syntactic and semantic patterns used to recognize each type of event are typically built by hand by a team of highly-trained specialists. As the amount of on-line text (newswires, World Wide Web documents, etc.) and the number of users with access continues to grow, however, there is a need to extract an ever-widening diversity of types of information and events. Having specialists hand-build extraction knowledge for this diversity of extraction tasks is untenable.

This paper examines an alternative: machine learning of dictionaries of information extraction patterns from user-provided examples of events to be extracted. We present a system called LIEP (for Learning Information Extraction Patterns) that learns such a dictionary given example sentences and events. In a sample extraction task (extracting corporate management changes), LIEP learns sets of patterns that achieve performance comparable to a meticulously hand-built dictionary of patterns.

We will begin with a brief description of the information extraction task and the extraction technique that the system uses. Next, we will turn to the learning algorithm and present an example of its operation. Finally, we will describe the system's results on both the management changes extraction task and a corporate acquisitions extraction task, and discuss opportunities for further research.

2 The extraction task

Full-scale extraction systems such as those in the MUC contests typically include a sentence-level extraction phase, followed by a "merging" phase in which information drawn from different sentences is combined. This work focuses on learning to extract information within individual sentences. Soderland and Lehnert [1994] have described one technique for learning to perform the merging process.

Extracting an event from text typically involves recognizing a group of entities of specific types that have particular relationships between them. Entities are generally expressed as noun phrases. To recognize an event in a sentence, a system must identify the entities of interest, and determine that the syntactic and semantic relationships within the sentence indicate the event and the entities' roles in it.

The primary tasks we have applied our system to so far are extracting corporate management changes and corporate acquisitions from newswire texts. In the management changes domain (which we will use to describe the system in this paper) the entities of interest are companies, people, and management titles (e.g., "vp of finance", "CEO", etc.). A variety of syntactic and semantic relationships between these entities in a sentence can indicate a management change event.

NLP-based extraction techniques, as opposed to simple keyword, proximity, or topic/entity searches, are needed for reasonably accurate extraction for this task. Not every combination of person/company/title in close proximity indicates a management change, even when other keyword indicators (e.g., named, announced, appointed, etc.) are nearby. For instance, consider:

> NORTH STONINGTON, Connecticut (Business Wire) – 12/2/94 – Joseph M. Marino and Richard P. Mitchell have been named senior vice presidents of Analysis & Technology Inc. (NASDAQ NMS: AATI), Gary P. Bennett, president and CEO, has announced.

Here, Joseph M. Marino and Richard P. Mitchell participate in management changes, but Gary P. Bennett does not, despite the mention of both a company and a title near his name. LIEP learns patterns that correctly handle examples like this one.

3 The extraction system

The extraction system that uses the extraction patterns learned by LIEP is called ODIE (for "On-Demand Information Extractor"). ODIE processes an input text using a fairly typical set of phases for such systems (as described, e.g., by Hobbs [1993]). It is perhaps closest in design to SRI's FASTUS [Hobbs *et al.*, 1992] and UMass's CIRCUS [Lehnert *et al.*, 1993].

Given an input text, ODIE first tokenizes the text and breaks it into sentences. For each sentence, ODIE first checks whether the sentence contains any of a set of keywords that indicate the possibility that the sentence expresses an event of interest. If no keywords are found, the sentence is thrown away; otherwise, the words in the sentence are tagged with their parts of speech.[1] Next, a set of simple pattern-matchers run over the sentence to identify entities of interest (for management changes, this is people, company names, and management titles) and contiguous syntactic constituents (noun groups, verb groups, and prepositions). The grammars used for identifying noun and verb groups are loosely based on those used by FASTUS [Hobbs *et al.*, 1992].

```
n_was_named_t_by_c:
   noun-group(PNG,head(isa(person-name))),
   noun-group(TNG,head(isa(title))),
   noun-group(CNG,head(isa(company-name))),
   verb-group(VG,type(passive),head(named or elected or appointed)),
   preposition(PREP,head(of or at or by)),

   subject(PNG,VG),
   object(VG,TNG),
   post_nominal_prep(TNG,PREP),
   prep_object(PREP,CNG)
 ==> management_appointment(M,person(PNG),title(TNG),company(CNG)).
```

Fig. 1. An information extraction pattern.

Next, ODIE applies a set of information extraction patterns such as that shown in Figure 1 to identify events. Patterns match syntactic constituents by testing their head words/entities and other simple properties (e.g. `active/passive` for verb groups), and attempt to verify syntactic relationships between the constituents. If all of the syntactic relationships are verified, an event is logged. For instance, the pattern shown in Figure 1 will log a management change event in a sentence like "Sue Smith, 39, of Menlo Park, was appointed president of Foo Inc." Here, `PNG` is "Sue Smith", `VG` is "was appointed", `TNG` is "president", `PREP` is "of", and `CNG` is "Foo Inc."

Rather than construct a complete and consistent parse of the entire sentence, ODIE attempts only to verify the plausibility of specific syntactic relationships between pairs of constituents tested in extraction patterns. A relationship's plausibility is verified using local syntactic constraints. For instance, the relationship `subject(ng,vg)` is considered plausible if `ng` is directly to the left of `vg`, or if `ng` is further to the left, and everything in between `ng` and `vg` could possibly be a right-modifier of `ng` – for instance, prepositional phrases, comma-delimited strings of

---

[1] We are currently using Eric Brill's part-of-speech tagger [Brill, 1994].

words like relative clauses, parentheticals, etc. Similar plausibility judgments are made for other syntactic relationships like object, post-nominal-preposition, preposition-object, etc.[2]

Performing simple, local plausibility verifications "on demand" for only the syntactic relationships in extraction patterns can be contrasted with the "full parsing" of standard NLP systems. The advantage of on-demand parsing, of course, is avoiding the difficult, time-consuming, and semantic knowledge-intensive process of full parsing. The disadvantage is that on-demand parsing's local, non-semantic nature does not provide enough constraint; it can overgenerate. For instance, multiple noun groups can plausibly hold the subject relationship with a given verb group. In a full parsing system such syntactic overgeneration would be constrained by semantics. In on-demand parsing, it is constrained by tests of constituents' heads, properties, and other syntactic relationships within each extraction pattern. For instance, ODIE never generates all possible subject relationships, but rather checks the plausibility of subject(ng,vg) *only* for ng's and vg's that pass the other tests in a specific extraction pattern – such as the tests at the top of Figure 1 on PNG and VG. These tests rule out most ng and vg combinations before any parsing knowledge is even applied. In cases where subject(ng,vg) is checked and found plausible, the relationship is only "accepted" (affects the system's output) if the rest of the relationships in the pattern are also plausible. Essentially, ODIE banks on the likelihood that enough constraint to avoid most false hits comes from the combination of local syntactic relationships between constituents in specific extraction patterns.

4 Learning information extraction patterns

LIEP learns extraction patterns like that shown in Figure 1 from example texts containing events. Most previous work on learning for information extraction has used the large corpus of pre-scored training texts provided for the MUC contests as training input (e.g., [Riloff, 1993; Soderland and Lehnert, 1994]). However, since such a corpus is not available for most extraction tasks, LIEP allows a user to interactively identify events in texts. In the current system, a simple HTML-based interface is used for this. For each sentence of a training text given by the user, entities of interest (e.g. people, companies, and titles) are identified, and the user can then choose which combinations of the entities signify events to be extracted. An event (e.g., a management change) includes a set of roles (e.g., person, title, company) with specific entities filling each role. Each positive example thus consists of a sentence, processed to identify entities and syntactic constituents, and an event that occurs in the sentence.

---

[2] The most recent version of ODIE encodes its extraction pattern dictionary as a finite state machine. Each pattern like the one in Figure 1 takes the form of a path of transitions through the machine, rather than a separate rule; syntactic relationships like subject are recognized by embedded sub-machines. LIEP learns new paths that are added to this finite state machine, rather than new rules. However, the learning algorithm used is very similar to what is presented here.

LIEP tries to build a set of extraction patterns that will maximize the number of extractions of positive examples and minimize spurious extractions. Given a new example that is not already matched by a known pattern, LIEP first attempts to generalize a known pattern to cover the example. If generalization is not possible or fails to produce a high-quality pattern, LIEP attempts to build' a new pattern based on the example. We will first describe how new patterns are built, and then how they are generalized.

4.1 Building new patterns

An extraction pattern matches possible role-filling constituents, and tests for a set of syntactic relationships between those constituents that, if present, indicate an event. Other constituents, such as verb groups, are included in a pattern only when needed to create relationships between the role-filling constituents. LIEP creates potential patterns from an example sentence/event by searching for sets of relationships that relate all of the role-filling constituents in the event to one another. Since our example extraction task has three constituents, LIEP attempts to find paths of relationships between each pair of constituents (three pairs) and then merges those paths to create sets of relationships relating all three.

The relationship between a pair of constituents can either be direct – as between ng and vg if subject(ng,vg) holds – or indirect, where the constituents are the endpoints of a path of relationships that passes through other intermediate constituents. For instance, in (1) "Bob was named CEO of Foo Inc.", Bob and CEO are related by

```
[subject(Bob,named),object(named,CEO)]
```

```
find_relationships(C1,C2) {
    if direct_relationship(C1,C2,R) then return(R)
    else
    while (choose_next_intermediate_constituent(CIntermediate)) {
        Rels1 = find_relationships(C1,CIntermediate)
        Rels2 = find_relationships(C2,CIntermediate)
        return(Rels1 + Rels2)}
    else failure.}
```

Fig. 2. Finding the path of plausible syntactic relationships between two constituents.

To find relationships between pairs of constituents, LIEP uses the recursive, depth-first algorithm shown in Figure 2. It first tries to find a direct relationship between the constituents. If there is none, it chooses another constituent in the sentence and tries to find paths of relationships between each of the original constituents and this intermediate constituent. Choose_next_intermediate_-constituent selects intermediate constituents to use starting from the rightmost constituent between the two being related, and moving left toward the beginning of the sentence.

In some cases, there are multiple paths of relationships between a pair of constituents. The multiple paths very roughly correspond to multiple syntactic parses of the sentence. For instance, in the above sentence, "of Foo Inc." could modify the verb named or the noun CEO. Thus, Bob and Foo Inc. are related by both:

```
[subject(Bob,named),object(named,CEO),
 post_verbal_post_object_prep(named,of),
 prep_object(of,Foo Inc.)]
```

and:

```
[subject(Bob,named),object(named,CEO),
 post_nominal_prep(CEO,of),
 prep_object(of,Foo Inc.)]
```

LIEP does not reason about what "of Foo Inc." modifies; it simply generates both of the possibilities because ODIE's knowledge of plausible syntactic relationships indicates that both post_verbal_post_object_prep(named,of) and post_nominal_prep(CEO,of) are plausible.

In other cases, no path of relationships between a pair of constituents can be found. This indicates that ODIE's set of syntactic relationships (which is very simple) is insufficient to cover the example. A common example of this occurs because ODIE does not understand parallel structure, as in "Foo Inc. named Bob CEO, and *Jane president.*" ODIE cannot relate Foo Inc. to Jane or president because it cannot recognize their relationships to the verb. Thus LIEP cannot create a pattern from the example company(Foo Inc.), person(Jane), title(president) using the built-in relationships. This is not a weakness in the learning algorithm, but in the syntactic vocabulary used to analyze the examples – in machine learning terms, the representation bias.

In the most recent version of LIEP, when a path of relationships cannot be found between the constituents in an example, the system induces a new relationship that connects the smallest unrelatable gap between the constituents – essentially extending the system's vocabulary for analyzing the example. This new relationship allows LIEP to learn a pattern for the example, and the new relationship can also be used in later patterns. This ability to induce new relationships improves LIEP's overall performance, but because it is still being tested, we will not describe the capability in detail in this paper.

Figure 3 shows the routine build_new_pattern(Example,Ptn). The routine Find_relationships_between_role_fillers calls find_relationships for each

```
build_new_pattern(Example) {
    HighestAccuracy = 0, Result = failure
    do 3 times {
        Rels = find_relationships_between_role_fillers(Example)
        if (Rels != failure) then {
            Pattern = create_pattern_from_relationships(Rels)
            Acc = compute_f_score_on_old_examples(Pattern)
            if Acc > HighestAccuracy then {
                HighestAccuracy = Acc
                Result = Pattern }}}
    return(Result).}
```

Fig. 3. Building a new pattern for a positive example.

pair of roles in the example event, and merges the resulting sets of relationships. Calling it multiple times causes find_relationships to backtrack and find multiple paths between constituents if they exist. We have arbitrarily chosen to generate up to three paths of relationships between the role-filler constituents. Create_pattern_from_relationships converts each path of relationships into an extraction pattern like that in Figure 1, in a straightforward way. In addition to the relationships themselves, a test is added to the pattern for each constituent appearing in the set of relationships. The test matches the constituent's head word/entity, and other syntactic properties (e.g. active/passive).

As an example, consider again (1) "Bob was named CEO of Foo Inc." The first set of relationships Find_relationships_between_role_fillers finds relating Bob, CEO, and Foo Inc. is:

```
[subject(Bob,named),object(named,CEO),
 post_verbal_post_object_prep(named,of),
 prep_object(of,Foo Inc.)]
```

From these, create_pattern_from_relationships creates the pattern:

```
LIEP_pattern1:
  noun-group(PNG,head(isa(person-name))),
  noun-group(TNG,head(isa(title))),
  noun-group(CNG,head(isa(company-name))),
  verb-group(VG,type(passive),head(named)),
  preposition(PREP,head(of)),

  subject(PNG,VG),
  object(VG,TNG),
  post_verbal_post_object_prep(VG,PREP),
```

```
   prep_object(PREP,CNG)
==> management_appointment(person(PNG),title(TNG),company(CNG)).
```

After up to three such patterns are constructed, they are compared by running them on all the example sentences LIEP has seen so far. The pattern with the highest F-measure[3] is returned and added to the system's dictionary.

4.2 Generalizing patterns

The new patterns LIEP learns are fairly specific: for non-role-filler constituents, they test for specific properties and head words (e.g., **named**). Often, later training examples have the same syntactic relationships as a previously learned pattern, but with different constituent head words or properties. This indicates that the pattern can be generalized.

LIEP assumes that non-role-filler constituents' head words and properties within a pattern can be generalized, but that constituents' syntactic types and relationships – what might be called the pattern's "syntactic footprint" – should not be generalized. For instance, if LIEP sees a future example which is similar to LIEP_pattern1 except that subject(PNG,VG) is replaced with some other relationship, it will not try to generalize LIEP_pattern1 but rather create a completely new pattern.

In order to recognize when a pattern might be generalized based on a new example, while learning a new pattern LIEP also creates a special version of the pattern that tests only its "syntactic footprint" – that is, the non-generalizable parts of the full pattern. For LIEP_pattern1, this is:

```
LIEP_pattern1(NON-GENERALIZABLE-PORTION):
   noun-group(PNG,head(isa(person-name))),
   noun-group(TNG,head(isa(title))),
   noun-group(CNG,head(isa(company-name))),
   verb-group(VG), preposition(PREP),

   subject(PNG,VG),
   object(VG,TNG),
   post_verbal_post_object_prep(VG,PREP),
   prep_object(PREP,CNG)
==> matches_positive_example(person(PNG),title(TNG),company(CNG)).
```

Consider the example (2) "Joan has been appointed vp, finance, at XYZ Company." Although it uses different head words, this example has the same syntactic relationships between its person, title, and company constituents as the previous example that resulted in LIEP_pattern1. LIEP notices the similarity because LIEP_pattern1(NON-GENERALIZABLE-PORTION) matches the new

---

[3] The F-measure [Chinchor and Sundheim, 1993] balances the recall and precision performance of the pattern being tested. For our tests we used $\beta = 1.0$ (recall and precision equally important).

example. The system forms a generalization of LIEP_pattern1 by inserting disjunctive values within each generalizable test in the pattern. These disjunctive values match the value(s) already in the pattern, plus the value in the new example. The generalized version of LIEP_pattern1 that results is:

```
Gen1_LIEP_pattern1:
    noun-group(PNG,head(isa(person-name))),
    noun-group(TNG,head(isa(title))),
    noun-group(CNG,head(isa(company-name))),
    verb-group(VG, type(passive), head(member(genclass1))),
    preposition(PREP, head(member(genclass2))),

    subject(PNG,VG),
    object(VG,TNG),
    post_verbal_post_object_prep(VG,PREP),
    prep_object(PREP,CNG)
==> management_appointment(person(PNG),title(TNG),company(CNG)).

genclass1 = (named,appointed).
genclass2 = (of,at).
```

This generalized pattern replaces the original pattern in the pattern dictionary.

Later examples can cause further generalizations (further additions to the disjunctive value sets, which LIEP calls genclasses). In addition, for open-class words (nouns and verbs), LIEP re-uses the genclasses it learns across patterns. For instance, if it has learned a genclass containing named, appointed, and elected by generalizing a pattern, when generalizing some other pattern containing named, it will use that genclass instead of creating a new one. For closed-class items like prepositions, LIEP always creates a new genclass for each rule, because those items are often used in a context-specific way.

Since for open-class items, what LIEP is learning is essentially a contextualized set of synonyms, a more aggressive learning strategy would be to use a synonym dictionary like WordNet [Miller, 1990] to propose possible synonyms to the user when a new pattern is first learned. This would reduce the number of training examples needed by the system. We plan to investigate this approach in future work.

5   Results

To test LIEP's performance on the management changes task, we collected a corpus of 300 naturally-occurring texts reporting management changes. The corpus was drawn from newswire articles appearing in the Wall Street Journal, New York Times, Business Wire, PR Newswire, and other newswire services, in January and early February 1995. Each corpus text contains either one or two sentences from a newswire article. Many of the corpus sentences are complex, and contain multiple names and companies. Often, more than one management

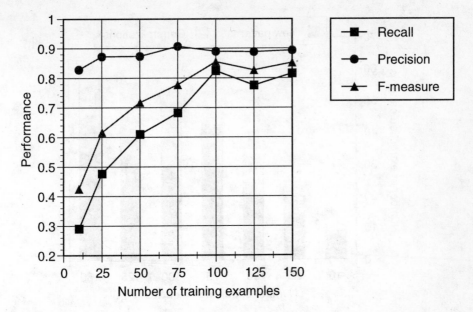

Fig. 4. LIEP's recall, precision, and F-measure on 100 test sentences per number of training examples, on the management changes extraction task.

change is reported in a single sentence, either through multiple complete clauses or parallel structure.

We ran LIEP multiple times over randomly-chosen training sets of different sizes. For each run, LIEP was trained using some number of randomly selected training texts from our 300-text corpus, and then its performance was tested on a disjoint set of 100 randomly selected test texts from the corpus. Figure 4 graphs the system's recall, precision, and F-measure on the test sets for different numbers of training examples. Each point in the graph is averaged over five runs.

ODIE's average F-measure using a hand-built set of patterns on randomly selected sets of 100 test texts from our corpus is 89.4% (recall 85.9%; precision 93.2%; averaged over ten runs). As Figure 4 shows, after 150 training texts, LIEP reaches an average F-measure of 85.2% (recall 81.6%; precision 89.4%) – a difference of less than five percent from the hand-built patterns.

Figure 5 shows the number of patterns LIEP learns and generalizes for given numbers of training texts (again, averaged over five runs). Not surprisingly, as the number of training examples increases, the number of new patterns LIEP has to learn begins to level off, and more of the learning involves generalizing previously learned patterns. Figure 6 emphasizes this point by comparing the percentage of new patterns versus generalized patterns learned. As the number of training examples increases, the percentage of learning by generalized previous patterns grows.

We have also applied LIEP to a corporate acquisitions extraction task – the

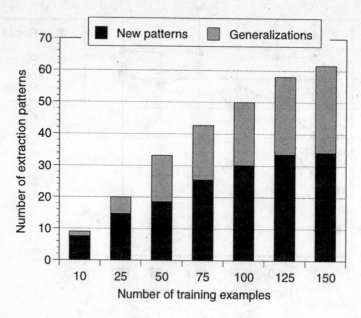

Fig. 5. Number of patterns learned and patterns generalized by LIEP on the management changes task.

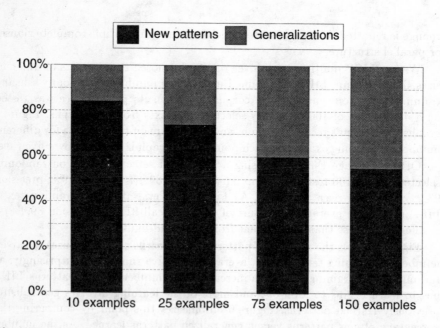

Fig. 6. Percentage of patterns learned and patterns generalized on the management changes task.

event to extract is when one company acquires part or all of another. Similar to management changes, for this task we collected 300 naturally-occurring texts reporting acquisitions from newswire articles of April-July 1995. We followed a similar train/test procedure to that used for the management changes. The resulting learning curves are quite similar to the curves in Figure 4, with the difference that acquisitions performance is a few percent lower overall. After 100 training examples, LIEP achieves an F-measure of 72.6% for acquisitions, compared to 85.4% for management changes. After 150 training examples, the acquisitions F-measure is 75.7%; after 200, it is 76.8%. These results are not surprising, because the language news articles use to report acquisitions is more variable than that used for management changes.

6   Discussion

LIEP is perhaps most closely related to Riloff's AutoSlog system [Riloff, 1993]. AutoSlog is a knowledge acquisition tool that uses a training corpus to generate proposed extraction patterns for the CIRCUS extraction system. A user either verifies or rejects each proposed pattern. AutoSlog does not try to recognize relationships between multiple constituents, as LIEP does; rather, it builds smaller patterns that recognize instances of single role-fillers. Later stages of CIRCUS then combine these instances into larger events.

Recently, Soderland *et al.* [1995] have described CRYSTAL, a system that induces extraction patterns from marked example texts. The general task is similar to LIEP's, but the specific problem and the approaches used are quite different. LIEP learns to extract events with multiple roles, and bases its learning on the relationship between those roles in each example. CRYSTAL, on the other hand, learns to extract single entities in particular categories (e.g. "pre-existing disease"). Thus, rather than relating entities, CRYSTAL's main learning task is to learn what parts of the context around an entity indicate that it is in a category. It uses a specific-to-general induction approach for this, in which it initially includes all the context in each example, and then generalizes by comparing and merging. Because the learning task is less strongly biased than LIEP's, CRYSTAL requires more training examples – on the order of thousands rather than hundreds – to achieve good performance.

One way to view LIEP's learning of new extraction patterns is as explanation-based learning [Mitchell *et al.*, 1986] with an overgeneral and incomplete domain theory. LIEP's "domain theory" is its knowledge about plausible syntactic relationships. LIEP uses this theory to explain the positive examples it is given. The theory is overgeneral in that it generates multiple explanations for some examples, and so LIEP uses an empirical process (computing F-measures on past examples) to choose between explanations. The theory is incomplete in that it cannot form an explanation (a covering set of syntactic relationships) for some examples, because the set of syntactic relationships is insufficient. A number of methods have been proposed for inductively extending domain theories to cover previously unexplainable examples (e.g., [VanLehn, 1987; Hall, 1988; Pazzani,

1991]; many others). As mentioned earlier, LIEP has recently been extended with a simple inductive method for learning new relationships when faced with extraction examples it cannot cover. In this way it extends its domain theory based on those examples, allowing it to learn a pattern dictionary with broader coverage.

Because its domain theory explains the syntactic relationships in each example but does not encompass semantics, LIEP uses the simple inductive process described in the previous section to generalize patterns for varieties of head words that express the same semantics. As mentioned previously, another extension would be to use a dictionary like WordNet as a sort of semantic "domain theory" to allow more active generalization of patterns.

In order to learn quickly (i.e. to learn new patterns from single examples), LIEP makes a strong assumption (in machine learning terms, has a strong bias) about what part of an example sentence is important for recognizing an event. In particular, it assumes that the relationships *between* the role-filling constituents will provide enough context to recognize an event. However, in some cases this assumption fails. For instance, consider this acquisition example:

"Joe Smith announced the acquisition of Foo Co. by Bar Inc."

Here, the role-filling constituents are "Foo Co." and "Bar Inc.", but the context between them provides almost no information. If given this example, LIEP would learn the highly overgeneral pattern (company1) by (company2). Thus, another area of future work on LIEP is to develop a better bias on the amount of context to include from an example. We are hopeful that a fairly small set of heuristics (e.g. always include a verb, include noun groups that are right-modified by role-fillers, etc.) will suffice. In the acquisitions tests described earlier, LIEP was given the simple bias that patterns must include a verb group, to avoid learning highly overgeneral patterns.

Finally, LIEP actively learns patterns from positive examples, but uses negative examples (e.g., the combinations of person/title/company that are *not* to be extracted) only as empirical evidence when comparing positive patterns. Another possibility would be to actively use negative examples, either to specialize positive patterns and/or to learn patterns that reject extractions under certain conditions. For example, in the hand-built pattern dictionary ODIE uses, there is a pattern that rejects a management change if it is preceded or followed by a phrase like "in (non-current-year)," to avoid extracting biographical information about the past positions a new manager has held. LIEP could possibly learn such negative patterns by generalizing across multiple false hits, or even from a single false hit given some simple guidance from the user.

7 Conclusion

In the future, users of on-line text will want the ability to quickly and easily generate information extractors for new events, without having to rely on specialized programmers. LIEP is a step towards that ability. Given only example texts and the events to extract from them, LIEP combines fairly simple learning techniques to learn dictionaries of general information extraction patterns. In a sample extraction task, patterns learned by LIEP perform nearly at the level of a hand-built pattern dictionary.

Acknowledgments

Thanks to David Steier and Scott Waterman for helpful comments on earlier drafts of this chapter.

References

[Brill, 1994] E. Brill. Some advances in transformation-based part of speech tagging. In *Proceedings of the Twelfth National Conference on Artificial Intelligence (AAAI-94)*, pages 722–7. 1994.

[Chinchor and Sundheim, 1993] N. Chinchor and B. Sundheim. MUC-5 evaluation metrics. In *Proceedings of the Fifth Message Understanding Conference (MUC-5)*. Morgan Kaufmann, San Mateo, CA, 1993.

[Hall, 1988] R. J. Hall. Learning by failing to explain. *Machine Learning*, 3(1):45–77, 1988.

[Hobbs *et al.*, 1992] J. R. Hobbs, D. E. Appelt, J. S. Bear, D. J. Israel, and W. Mabry Tyson. FASTUS: A system for extracting information from natural-language text. Technical Report No. 519, SRI International, November 1992.

[Hobbs, 1993] J. R. Hobbs. The generic information extraction system. In *Proceedings of the Fifth Message Understanding Conference (MUC-5)*. Morgan Kaufmann, San Mateo, CA, 1993.

[Lehnert *et al.*, 1993] W. Lehnert, J. McCarthy, S. Soderland, E. Riloff, C. Cardie, J. Peterson, F. Feng, C. Dolan, and S. Goldman. UMass/Hughes: Description of the CIRCUS system used for MUC-5. In *Proceedings of the Fifth Message Understanding Conference (MUC-5)*. Morgan Kaufmann, San Mateo, CA, 1993.

[Miller, 1990] George Miller. Five papers on WordNet. *International Journal of Lexicography*, 3:235–312, 1990.

[Mitchell *et al.*, 1986] T. M. Mitchell, R. M. Keller, and S. T. Kedar-Cabelli. Explanation-based generalization: A unifying view. *Machine Learning*, 1, 1986.

[MUC, 1992] *Proceedings of the Fourth Message Understanding Conference (MUC-4)*. Morgan Kaufmann, San Mateo, CA, 1992.

[MUC, 1993] *Proceedings of the Fifth Message Understanding Conference (MUC-5)*. Morgan Kaufmann, San Mateo, CA, 1993.

[Pazzani, 1991] M. Pazzani. Learning to predict and explain: An integration of similarity-based, theory driven, and explanation-based learning. *Journal of the Learning Sciences*, 1(2):153–199, 1991.

[Riloff, 1993] E. Riloff. Automatically constructing a dictionary for information extraction tasks. In *Proceedings of the Eleventh National Conference on Artificial Intelligence (AAAI-93)*, pages 811–16. 1993.

[Soderland and Lehnert, 1994] S. Soderland and W. Lehnert. Wrap-Up: A trainable discourse module for information extraction. *Journal of Artificial Intelligence Research (JAIR)*, 2:131–158, 1994.

260

[Soderland et al., 1995] S. Soderland, D. Fisher, J. Aseltine, and W. Lehnert. CRYS-TAL: Inducing a conceptual dictionary. In *Proceedings of 14th International Joint Conference on Artificial Intelligence (IJCAI-95)*, pages 1314–9. Morgan Kaufmann, 1995.

[VanLehn, 1987] K. VanLehn. Learning one subprocedure per lesson. *Artificial Intelligence*, 31(1):1–40, 1987.

Implications of an Automatic Lexical Acquisition System

Peter M. Hastings

Artificial Intelligence Lab
The University of Michigan
1101 Beal Avenue
Ann Arbor, MI 48109
peter@umich.edu
(313)763-9297(voice)
(313)763-1260(fax)

Abstract. Camille, the Contextual Acquisition Mechanism for Incremental Lexeme LEarning, was implemented as an addition to Lytinen's LINK parser for use in an information extraction task, automatically inferring the meanings of unknown words from context. Unlike many previous lexical acquisition systems, Camille was thoroughly tested within a complex, real-world domain. The implementation of this system produced many lessons which are applicable to language learning in general. This paper describes Camille's implications for evaluation, for knowledge representation, and for cognitive modeling.

1 Introduction

As reported in [Hastings and Lytinen, 1994b] and [Hastings, 1994], Camille (Contextual Acquisition Mechanism for Incremental Lexical LEarning) implements an algorithm for learning the meanings of words from example sentences without the help of a human trainer. The system was developed to operate on real-world texts as part of an information extraction task. The complexity of the domain and of the sentences created a very demanding environment for the system. Camille was developed with the goal of leveraging all of the available knowledge for learning word meanings — without requiring additional special-purpose knowledge.

The difficulty of this task led to several implications about lexical acquisition in general. A fundamental difference between nouns and verbs was described in [Hastings and Lytinen, 1994b]. Camille relies on argument structure and examples to enable it to learn word meanings. But nouns and verbs play different roles as far as argument structure is concerned. When the semantic representation of a sentence is viewed as a predicate structure, nouns almost always serve as the arguments of the predicate, while verbs denote the predicate itself. The most straightforward way for a language analysis system to represent semantic constraints is by limiting which type of arguments can attach to particular predicates. This principle of NLP results in a fundamental implication for lexical acquisition: verbs and nouns must be treated differently.

This paper begins with a brief description of Camille's lexical acquisition algorithm and the principles that it was based on. The focus of the paper is the set of general implications resulting from Camille's implementation. The structure of the knowledge representation has a profound influence on the types of information that can be inferred and how successful any learning mechanism will be. The following section describes the aspects of knowledge representation that are most important for lexical acquisition. The next section describes the scoring protocol used to evaluate Camille's inferences, making it easier to view the effects of changes on the architecture and to compare it with other systems. Finally, the paper describes the implications of the system for cognitive modeling, and concludes with a general discussion.

2 Camille

As previously mentioned, Camille was implemented as an addition to an information extraction system which was based on Lytinen's LINK parser [Lytinen, 1991]. This particular task had a strong influence on the design decisions for Camille. It also provided the primary motivation. Because an information extraction system must deal with complex, real-world texts, the system requires huge amounts of linguistic knowledge. Although some of this knowledge can be ported to other domains, much of it, especially word definitions, must be tailored for each domain. Thus it is critical to have a learning component in such a knowledge-intensive system. It also limits the amount of additional knowledge which a system can require for a special purpose like lexical acquisition. Camille was designed to use only the knowledge that was necessary for the information extraction task. Because the task involves large corpora and significant computational resources, Camille was designed to learn incrementally and produce its results as a side-effect of parsing. The system is automatic in that it doesn't require the help of a human trainer.

These principles set Camille apart from other lexical acquisition systems. Many early systems were only tested on small sets of data [Salveter, 1979, Granger, 1977, Zernik, 1987]. More recent systems have been applied to real-world texts, but have required the assistance of a trainer [Riloff, 1993, Cardie, 1993]. There have also been statistical approaches which use large corpora but infer little or no information about word meaning [Brent, 1993, Zernik, 1991, for example].

The knowledge representation for LINK consists of an inheritance hierarchy of domain-independent and domain-specific concepts. Figure 1 shows some of LINK's domain-specific object concepts from the Terrorism domain that served as the testing ground for ARPA's third and fourth Message Understanding Conferences [Sundheim, 1992] (the shading will be explained later). The structure of the hierarchy forms an IS-A inheritance tree. Figure 2 shows some of the actions from the domain. Action concepts provide the relational structure that binds together the representation of the meaning of sentences. These concepts also constrain the types of arguments that can be attached as their slot-fillers (also included in fig 2).

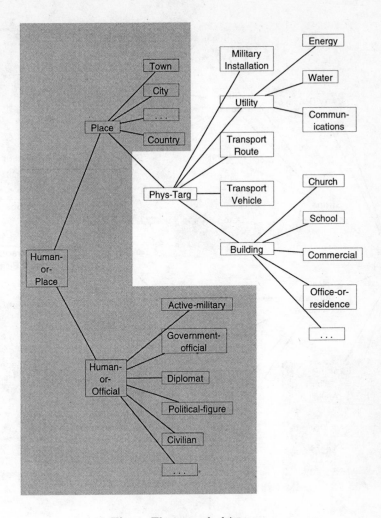

Fig. 1. The pruned object tree

The nodes in LINK's concept hierarchy serve as its basic units of meaning. Learning the meaning of an unknown word reduces to finding the appropriate node in the hierarchy — a graph search problem. To drive the search, the semantic constraints, which are normally used to limit attachment of slot-fillers to the Head verb, interact with the evidence provided by example sentences. But the interaction works in different ways for different classes of words. Nouns (as the Heads of noun phrases) normally serve as the slot-fillers of sentences and thus, as the items which are constrained. For example, in the sentence "Terrorists destroyed a flarge", the word "destroy" refers to the concept **Destroy** which has

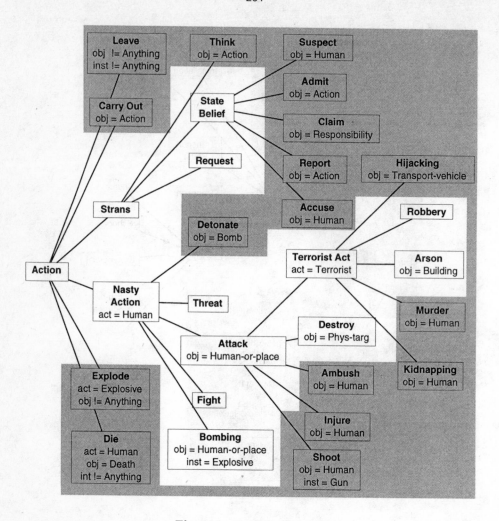

Fig. 2. A pruned action tree

the constraint [Object = Phys-Targ]. When "flarge" is attached as the object of the verb, the constraint places an upper bound on its interpretation as shown in figure 1. The shaded-out nodes cannot be a valid interpretation of the meaning of "flarge".

For unknown verbs, however, the situation is quite different. Because they usually map to the actions in the domain, the verbs *apply* the constraints. Thus, the constraints place an upper bound on the interpretation of unknown verbs.[1]

---

[1] Note that negative examples, for example, "You can't say 'Terrorists froobled the civilians'", would provide the opposing bound (upper for unknown verbs, lower for nouns). Then Mitchell's candidate-elimination approach [Mitchell, 1977] to narrowing the hypothesis set might work. Unfortunately, negative examples are rare in hu-

The shaded areas of figure 2 show the concepts that are ruled out for an example sentence like "Terrorists froobled police headquarters." It is important to note that this is not just an artifact of LINK's knowledge representation structure. It is due to fundamental principle of language. Because actions serve as the relational elements of sentence structure, they are the only logical place for the constraints to reside.

Because of this dichotomy, Camille must have different strategies for learning verbs and learning nouns. They can be stated most succinctly as follows:

```
For nouns, choose the most general consistent hypothesis.
For verbs, choose the most specific hypothesis.
```

The actual process for determining the meanings of unknown words starts out the same for both nouns and verbs. At the beginning of the parse process, LINK creates a data structure in the parse chart for each known word that includes its syntactic category and semantic representation. If the word is polysemous, a data structure will be entered for each definition. For unknown words, Camille enters several "default" definitions into the parse, one for various open lexical classes. As the parsing process proceeds, the extraneous definitions are generally ruled out by syntactic constraints, with only the appropriate lexical class remaining.

At this point, the learning strategies diverge for nouns and for verbs. As mentioned previously, the structure of the knowledge provides an upper bound on the interpretation of unknown nouns. Camille's strategy for learning nouns is to guess that the meaning of an unknown noun is exactly that concept which defines the upper bound, that is, the root of the subtree which is used as the verb's constraint. To take the previous noun example, in the sentence, "Terrorists destroyed a flarge", when the parser attaches "flarge" as the object of the Destroy concept, the knowledge structure dictates that "flarge" must mean Phys-Targ or one of its descendants. Due to the principles stated above, namely to take the most general hypothesis for an unknown noun's meaning, Camille chooses exactly the concept Phys-Targ as the hypothesized meaning for "flarge". Because Camille's learning procedure is incremental, it can revise its definition if a later example conflicts with this hypothesis. For example, Camille might encounter the sentence, "Terrorists were accused of committing arson on a flarge." In this case, Camille would combine the constraint from Arson — that the object is a building — with the previous hypothesis, and infer that "flarge" means Building. In the absence of negative evidence, this most conservative approach to inferring noun meanings is necessary. If Camille chose more specific hypotheses for nouns, those hypotheses would not necessarily be falsifiable by later examples.

In order to learn the meanings of unknown verbs, Camille must take a very different approach. Camille learns verb meanings by searching through the concept hierarchy for an appropriate concept.[2] Because the knowledge representation imposes a lower bound on the interpretation of unknown verbs, the system

---

man speech and non-existent in this and most other information extraction domains.
[2] This is in part necessitated by the tree-like structure of the knowledge representation. The most general node under an upper bound is usually a single node in the tree, but immediately above a lower bound is a set of nodes.

must either settle for an overly general hypothesis (for example Action but not Hijacking or Kidnapping) or inductively set its own upper bound. In order to increase the usability and the falsifiability of its hypotheses, Camille takes the latter approach.

To learn nouns, the system only had to apply the constraints from the actions on the unknown slot fillers. Because verbs refer to the actions, however, the system cannot know which constraints apply. It must therefore infer the meaning of an unknown verb by comparing the slot fillers that are attached to it with the constraints of the various action concepts. Camille does this incrementally, adjusting the definition as each slot filler is attached, and as each example of the word's use is processed.

As when it learns nouns, the system initially places a default definition into the parse structure for an unknown verb and gives it the default meaning Action. As each slot filler is attached, Camille checks which descendants of the current meaning hypothesis have constraints that are compatible with the slot filler. For example, with the sentence, "Terrorist froobled the headquarters", "headquarters" is initially attached as the Object of "froobled". All of the non-shaded nodes in figure 2 have constraints which are consistent with this Object. Because Camille wants to induce an upper bound on this hypothesis set, it eliminates from consideration all but the most specific members of this set. That is, if any node in the set is the parent of another node in the set, the parent is eliminated. To make the set even more specific, the distance in the hierarchy between the slot-filler concept and the constraint concept is computed for each concept, and only the closest matches are kept in the hypothesis set. For example, Arson's Object constraint is Building which is the parent of Headquarters and therefore has a distance of one. Human-or-Place, the Object constraint for Attack has a distance of four from Headquarters, so Attack is removed from consideration. This process is repeated as each slot filler is attached for this and future sentences. After a sentence is processed, Camille's tentative definition is written to the lexicon.

By trimming down the hypothesis set as described, Camille would infer the single concept Arson as the meaning of "frooble". Note that other concepts (Attack and Bombing, for example) are consistent with the evidence, but these concepts would not be as easily disconfirmed. For example if the system encountered the sentence, "Terrorists froobled the pedestrians", the Arson hypothesis would be disconfirmed but not the others. This is a key to Camille's success in learning word meanings. By choosing the most specific concepts, Camille makes the most falsifiable hypotheses. Thus further examples will be more likely to conflict with an initial hypothesis, invoking the generalization procedure. This procedure searches the hierarchy starting at the current hypothesis until a concept is found which has constraints that do not conflict with all of the slot fillers that have been encountered. If another example of the the unknown word does not conflict with the initial hypothesis, the falsifiability of that hypothesis increases the likelihood that it was correct.

3   Evaluation

The choice of evaluation criteria is important for NL learning systems because of the need to compare different algorithms. This section describes the basic testing regime for Camille and the methods used for compiling the results.

The testing concentrated on verb learning because that was the most difficult for Camille. 50 sentences from the domain were chosen at random, and the definitions of all of the domain-specific verbs ("shoot", but not "is", for example) were removed from the lexicon. The sentences were then processed in turn by Camille, and the resulting word definitions written to a file.

The earliest version of Camille hypothesized definitions for each of the 17 target verbs by the end of the test, and 47% of these hypothesis sets included the correct concept. This was fairly encouraging, especially given the complexity of the corpus. Because multiple concepts were allowed for each word definition (and 3.2 concepts per definition hypothesized in this test), however, it became clear that Camille's basic performance was not as good as it initially appeared.

To reflect the need to reduce the size of the hypothesis set, a system of scores was adapted from the MUC conferences [Chinchor, 1992]. These measures, Recall and Precision were originally taken from the field of Information Retrieval and are defined as follows: Recall is the number of words which included a correct concept in their hypothesis set divided by the number of possible words which could have received definitions. Precision is defined as the number of correct hypotheses divided by the total sum of concepts generated.

Two other calculations, Accuracy and Production, describe respectively the system's performance on the hypotheses it made (as reported above), and the percentage of possible verbs for which it produced hypotheses. Accuracy is defined as the number of correct hypotheses divided by the number of words for which definitions were posited. Production is the number of definitions divided by the number of words which could have received definitions.

The test in the terrorism domain produced scores of 33% Recall, 15% Precision, and 67% Production, along with the 47% Accuracy mentioned above. The low Precision scores reflect the fact that Camille was producing a large number of hypotheses per word.

This new style of scoring made explicit the tradeoff between Recall and Precision. By including more concepts in each hypothesis, Camille could increase its Recall scores, but then its Precision scores would fall. Later versions of the system created smaller sets of concepts while maintaining Precision. The final version of Camille produced scores of 41% Recall, 19% Precision, 100% Production, and 47% Accuracy.

The implication for learning systems in general is that evaluation must be taken seriously. It can demonstrate that results which appear to be good on the surface are not so good. The novel use of Recall and Precision measures for evaluating the results of learning is an effective method for making such distinctions.

4 Knowledge Representation

The choice of Knowledge representation is one way that a developer creates a boundary around a task, making an abstract version of a problem and of the information required to solve it. This section describes the abstractions made in the implementation of Camille and how they influence what can be learned.

Where should the knowledge representation lines be drawn? Allen [1981] took a pragmatic approach to answering this question. He considered what it would take to represent the verb "hide", and answer reasonable questions about it. Allen's answer involved a temporal logic that could address "notions of belief, intention, and causality." [Allen, 1981, p. 81]

This work takes the same approach as Allen's, in effect rephrasing the previous question as, "In order to meet the functional requirements of the overall task, what does the NLP system need to know?" Instead of requiring the system to answer all possible questions about the consequences of actions, however, the system is only required to answer a fixed set of questions about a fixed set of actions — in short, the information extraction task.

What is required to successfully perform the information extraction task? In the MUC competitions, systems with greatly varying depths of knowledge representation performed at similar levels of efficiency. Some systems (SRI's FASTUS system [Hobbs *et al.*, 1992], for example) used a simple pattern-matching architecture to process the texts very quickly and rather successfully. They were prone, however, to producing errors in particular situations where a pattern matched a text fragment which was part of a larger context.

The philosophy behind the LINK system is that it is necessary to encode the grammar of the language and the concepts in the domain in order to adequately understand text. (Of course, this implies a need for a larger knowledge base, and therefore, a need for systems like Camille.)

This leads to four basic implications for knowledge representation as it relates to information extraction and lexical acquisition:

Level of atomicity: There is a natural trade-off between the granularity of representation and the amount of knowledge required, for example, Pick-Up versus [Move-Hand, Tighten-Grip, Move-Hand]. LINK makes its atoms at the level of the basic actions and objects that are required by the task (and Camille is pledged to use this granularity). This affects learning in two ways: The system is unable to reason about parts of actions or features of objects. The meanings that it learns are at the same level of granularity as the rest of the domain knowledge.

Compositionality: Although LINK/Camille will not break atomic concepts down to a finer granularity, the system can (and routinely does) combine concepts to create more complex concepts (for example, the meaning of a sentence). The process of combining concepts is critical to Camille's learning task (and to language in general). The word-learning task can be viewed as inferring the missing component of a complex concept.

Inheritance: Conceptual knowledge in LINK forms a standard subsumption hierarchy. This allows parsimonious representation of constraints — they are connected with the concept at the highest level of abstraction to which they apply, and then are inherited, or made more specific, by the descendants. This is important for Camille because the structure that results from organizing the concepts forms the space that is searched for meanings of unknown words.

Concepts vs. Features: Within the knowledge representation, there is a choice of methods for representing "attributes" of the concepts. Attributes are defined as features of the concept which do not affect their set membership. Attributes could be represented by atomic labels, as many syntactic features are. Alternatively, since there is no limit on the number of parents a concept node can have, a separate concept could be created which subsumes the concepts which have that attribute. In keeping with Camille's overall approach to language, attributes are not represented unless they are relevant to the task. This judgment has implications for the choice of representation. If the attribute is relevant, then it is likely that the system would benefit from explicitly knowing its members. For example, the concepts Human and Place are rather dissimilar, but they can both the object of an Attack action. In such cases, the relevancy test leads to the choice of representing attributes as concepts instead of as features.

The importance of making these underlying knowledge representation issues explicit is that by doing so, we can better understand the functional performance limitations of the system. Then, if some additional behavior is desired that lay outside the boundaries, it will be obvious how the system and the underlying knowledge representation must be changed. For example, in order to make inferences about sub-atomic actions like Tighten-Grip, the level of atomicity of the knowledge representation must be changed.

5 Cognitive Modeling

Camille was not developed as a cognitive model. It does, however, perform a task that humans perform, and it shares some striking similarities with psycholinguistic theories for lexical acquisition, as described in [Hastings and Lytinen, 1994a]. An unplanned behavior is inherently more interesting that one that was designed into a system, this section describes some of the implications for cognitive modeling that arose out of this research. Camille makes predictions about the use of constraints, the relation of input to learning, and the relation of conceptual organization to learning.

5.1 Mutual Exclusivity

One fundamental mystery in the field of child language development is how children with limited cognitive abilities conquer such a difficult problem, i.e. learning language. Psycholinguistics researchers have suggested many methods that children might use to reduce the complexity of the task. One of these is called Mutual Exclusivity [Markman, 1991]. This theory posits that when children are first learning the meanings of words, they assume that no two words have overlapping meanings. This simplifies their task by eliminating those possible meanings for a new word that they already know a word for.

Camille has enabled the implementation of a simple form of the Mutual Exclusivity constraint. When Camille is attempting to infer the meaning of a new word, it can simply remove from its hypothesis set any concepts which are already the referent of another word. Despite the fact that most psycholinguistic literature on this subject deals with the application of Mutual Exclusivity to nouns, Camille can apply it to verb-learning as well. This brings up an issue that is not dealt with particularly well by either the psychological literature or by Camille. The difficulty stems from the fact that when learning an unknown verb, the system can entertain multiple hypotheses, all of which are consistent with its experience. So the question becomes, "How certain of a meaning hypothesis must the system be in order for it to rule out that hypothesis for other new words?"

Since there have been no thorough studies of the use of biases in learning labels for actions, this issue has been largely ignored by psychologists. But there is a more general question that subsumes it: "How can children (or computational models, for that matter) choose between several consistent meaning hypotheses?" If the child has a clear preference for one type of meaning over another, the first problem goes away. But there is little evidence for how children might construct such preferences. Behrend's work [1990] suggests one possible mechanism, choosing the most specific hypotheses for verbs and preferring the basic level for objects, but it is clear from Camille's implementation of the Mutual Exclusivity constraint that more work needs to be done to explain these phenomena fully in psychological terms.

Another interesting topic brought up by this addition is the question of when Mutual Exclusivity should be overridden. It is obvious that at some point children realize that both "animal" and "dog" can apply to the same object, but what conditions allow for the constraint to be overridden? This is the topic of current psycholinguistic research, and future research with Camille.

5.2 Input and Learning

Although the testing of Camille was done on input sentences picked randomly from a large corpus, it is clear from the results that there are some important factors that are influenced by the input to the system, and that variation in the input can improve or degrade the system's performance.

One prediction is evident from Camille's use of the hierarchical structure which distinguishes general from specific concepts. Because Camille assumes the most specific meaning for an unknown word, general words will be given overly specific hypotheses unless they are encountered in the input with a variety of slot fillers. Thus if a child were to receive only input sentences like, "Get the string" and "Get the twine", Camille predicts that the child would infer an overly specific meaning for "get" like Tie. In other words, reducing the breadth of input that a child receives should result in overly specific hypotheses.

No psychological tests have been performed that address this prediction directly, but there has been work which more broadly addresses the role of input in learning. First, a study by Fernald and Morikawa [1993] concluded that differences in distributions of nouns and verbs was due to differences in maternal input. Second, Huttenlocher et al. [1991] showed that despite previous predictions that early lexicon size would be dependent on learning capacity, children's lexica are instead related to how talkative their mothers are. In general, children who receive broader input have larger lexica.

5.3 Concept Organization and Learning

The organization of the concept representation is, as mentioned, an important aspect of Camille's implementation. The general framework consists of an IS-A inheritance hierarchy, a type of representation that is widely used in Artificial Intelligence. Various psychological studies support the existence of hierarchical structures in the brain [Keil, 1991, for example]. At the lowest level, this representation is clearly not "brain-like". It is highly unlikely that the brain uses such a rule-like arrangement for representing constraints. But the hierarchical structure has advantages that make it a powerful representation scheme for computers and humans. This format makes it easy to make generalizations, an ability that is a key to learning and reasoning. It also provides efficient storage of information.

These advantages are most easily seen in the case of representing objects. Here, the hierarchical scheme allows for similar objects to be located proximally in the representation, even across different types of objects. Thus for natural kinds like animals, dogs can be stored close to wolves, somewhat further from cats, and rather far from insects. These distinctions can be made based on physical attributes which humans use to delineate natural kinds. For artifacts, the same distance attributes can be found, but the distinctions can be made on functional values, grouping, for example, kitchen appliances together. This type of arrangement allows for the efficient storage of constraints like, "mammals are warm-blooded" and "kitchen appliances are used for food-related activities." Finally, this structure makes it easy to tell when Camille needs further discrimination in the concept representation. Given an input sentence like, "I took my Queensland Blue out for a walk," we can infer that Queensland Blue is a type of dog, even if we've never heard of that particular breed.

For representing actions and relations, the situation is somewhat murkier. As previously pointed out, although some psycholinguistic researchers have postulated a hierarchical scheme for their representation, recently the focus has turned to more "matrix-like" schemes. But the latter approach may be seen to conflict with the observation about the nature of constraints provided by the input and whether an upper bound or lower bound is created on the set of possible meanings for an unknown word. It's just not clear what "lower bound" would mean in a matrix-type organization.

On close inspection, it appears that Camille's representation has the best of both worlds. If the slot-filler constraints are displayed graphically (see figure 3 where the solid lines represent paths in the IS-A hierarchy and the dashed

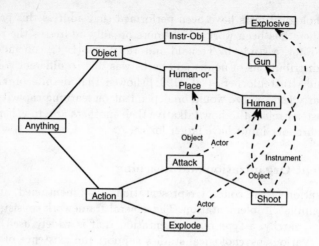

Fig. 3. Matrix-like organization of action concepts

lines represent constraints on the actions), it is apparent that the connections do (as Huttenlocher and Lui put it) cut across the various parts of the hierarchy. This leads to the question, "Does it make sense to have the additional structure imposed by enforcing a hierarchical structure on *actions*?" The answer appears to be yes, for the same reasons given for object representation above. The hierarchy has representational strength — it allows for efficient storage of the attributes and constraints of actions.

The question that remains then is, "What does this imply about human concept organization?" For one thing, it lends support to the idea that there can be multiple organization structures within the brain. There are clear advantages to having both types of concept representation. In addition, it suggests that learning could proceed in one of two ways. If a child realizes that her idea of what a word means is wrong, she should look for concepts that are closely related in the hierarchy. If the child's hypothesized *constraints* for the word are wrong, she should change those constraints based on the structure of the hierarchy that is selected by the matrix links.

6 Conclusion

Life dictates that there are two good ways of learning how to do something: either teach about it, or just do it. Theoretically, there are an infinite number of computer implementations of any algorithm. With a task as difficult as lexical acquisition, however, the behavior of the set of successful solutions must be tightly constrained. The claim of this paper is that Camille is a successful implementation for the task of lexical acquisition. It should be able, therefore, to inform us about some basic constraints on other successful solutions as well as pointing out some interesting questions for future research. This paper describes some of the lessons learned from one lexical acquisition system about evaluation, about knowledge representation, and about cognitive modeling.

References

[Allen, 1981] J. Allen. What's necessary to hide?: Modeling action verbs. In *Proceedings of the 19th Annual Meeting of the ACL*, pages 77–81, 1981.

[Behrend, 1990] D. Behrend. The development of verb concepts: Children's use of verbs to label familiar and novel events. *Child Development*, 61:681–696, 1990.

[Brent, 1993] M. Brent. From grammar to lexicon: Unsupervised learning of lexical syntax. *Computational Linguistics*, 1993.

[Cardie, 1993] C. Cardie. A case-based approach to knowledge acquisition for domain-specific sentence analysis. In *Proceedings of the 11th National Conference on Artificial Intelligence*, pages 798–803, 1993.

[Chinchor, 1992] N. Chinchor. MUC-4 evaluation metrics. In *Proceedings of the Fourth Message Understanding Conference*, San Mateo, CA, 1992. Morgan Kaufmann Publishers, Inc.

[Fernald and Morikawa, 1993] A. Fernald and H. Morikawa. Common themes and cultural variations in Japanese and American mothers' speech to infants. *Child Development*, 64:637–656, 1993.

[Gentner, 1978] D. Gentner. On relational meaning: The acquisition of verb meaning. *Child Development*, 49:988–998, 1978.

[Graesser et al., 1987] A. Graesser, P. Hopkinson, and C. Schmid. Differences in inter-concept organization between nouns and verbs. *Journal of Memory and Language*, 26:242–253, 1987.

[Granger, 1977] R. Granger. Foul-up: A program that figures out meanings of words from context. In *Proceedings of Fifth International Joint Conference on Artificial Intelligence*, 1977.

[Hastings and Lytinen, 1994a] P. Hastings and S. Lytinen. Objects, actions, nouns, and verbs. In A. Ram and K. Eiselt, editors, *Proceedings of the 16th Annual Conference of the Cognitive Science Society*, pages 397–402, Hillsdale, NJ, 1994. Lawrence Erlbaum Associates.

[Hastings and Lytinen, 1994b] P. Hastings and S. Lytinen. The ups and downs of lexical acquisition. In *Proceedings of the 12th National Conference on Artificial Intelligence*, pages 754–759, Cambridge, MA, 1994. MIT Press.

[Hastings, 1994] P. Hastings. *Automatic Acquisition of Word Meaning from Context*. PhD thesis, University of Michigan, Ann Arbor, MI, 1994.

[Hobbs et al., 1992] J. Hobbs, D. Appelt, M. Tyson, J. Bear, and D Israel. SRI International: Description of the FASTUS system used for MUC-4. In *Proceedings of the Fourth Message Understanding Conference*, San Mateo, CA, 1992. Morgan Kaufmann Publishers, Inc.

[Huttenlocher and Lui, 1979] J. Huttenlocher and F. Lui. The semantic organization of some simple nouns and verbs. *Journal of verbal learning and verbal behavior*, 18:141–162, 1979.

[Huttenlocher et al., 1991] J. Huttenlocher, W. Haight, A. Bryk, M. Seltzer, and T. Lyons. Early vocabulary growth: Relation to language input and gender. *Developmental Psychology*, 27(2):236–248, 1991.

[Keil, 1991] F. Keil. Theories, concepts, and the acquisition of word meaning. In J. P. Byrnes and S. A. Gelman, editors, *Perspectives on language and thought: Interrelations in development*. Cambridge University Press, Cambridge, 1991.

[Lytinen, 1991] S. Lytinen. A unification-based, integrated natural language processing system. *Computers and Mathematics with Applications*, 23(6-9):403–418, 1991.

[MacGregor, 1990] R. MacGregor. The evolving technology of classification-based knowledge representation systems. In J. Sowa, editor, *Principles of Semantic Nets: Explorations in the Representation of Knowledge*. Morgan Kaufmann Publishers, San Mateo, CA, 1990.

[Markman, 1991] E. Markman. The whole object, taxonomic, and mutual exclusivity assumptions as initial constraints on word meanings. In J. P. Byrnes and S. A. Gelman, editors, *Perspectives on language and thought: Interrelations in development*. Cambridge University Press, Cambridge, 1991.

[Mitchell, 1977] T. Mitchell. Version spaces: A candidate elimination approach to rule learning. In *Proceedings of the Fifth International Joint Conference on Artificial Intelligence*, pages 305–309, 1977.

[Riloff, 1993] E. Riloff. Automatically constructing a dictionary for information extraction tasks. In *Proceedings of the 11th National Conference on Artificial Intelligence*, pages 811–816, 1993.

[Salveter, 1979] S. Salveter. Inferring conceptual graphs. *Cognitive Science*, 3:141–166, 1979.

[Sundheim, 1992] B. Sundheim. Overview of the fourth message understanding evaluation and conference. In *Proceedings of the Fourth Message Understanding Conference*, San Mateo, CA, 1992. Morgan Kaufmann Publishers, Inc.

[Zernik, 1987] Uri Zernik. How do machine language paradigms fare in language acquisition. In *Proceedings of the Fourth International Workshop on Machine Learning*, Los Altos, CA, 1987. Morgan Kaufmann.

[Zernik, 1991] U. Zernik. Train1 vs. train2: Tagging word senses in corpus. In U. Zernik, editor, *Lexical Acquisition: Exploiting On-line Resources to Build a Lexicon*. Lawrence Erlbaum Associates, Inc, Hillsdale, NJ, 1991.

Using Learned Extraction Patterns for Text Classification

Ellen Riloff

Department of Computer Science
University of Utah
Salt Lake City, UT 84112, USA
riloff@cs.utah.edu

Abstract. A major knowledge-engineering bottleneck for information extraction systems is the process of constructing an appropriate dictionary of extraction patterns. AutoSlog is a dictionary construction system that has been shown to substantially reduce the time required for knowledge engineering by learning extraction patterns automatically. However, an open question was whether these extraction patterns were useful for tasks other than information extraction. We describe a series of experiments that show how the extraction patterns learned by AutoSlog can be used for text classification. Three dictionaries produced by AutoSlog for different domains performed well in our text classification experiments.

1   Introduction

Many researchers in natural language processing have turned their attention recently to a problem called *information extraction* (IE). Information extraction is a natural language processing task that involves extracting predefined types of information from text. Information extraction is essentially a form of text-skimming because only the portions of a text that are relevant to a given domain need to be understood. However, it is crucial for an IE system to have a knowledge base of concepts that provides it with good coverage of the domain.

The challenge for information extraction researchers is to develop methods for acquiring the necessary dictionaries and knowledge bases automatically. To this end, we have developed a system called AutoSlog [Riloff, 1996; Riloff, 1993] that automatically constructs dictionaries of domain-specific extraction patterns. In the domain of Latin American terrorism, a dictionary created by AutoSlog achieved 98% of the performance of a hand-crafted dictionary that took approximately 1500 person-hours to build. We have also used AutoSlog to create dictionaries of extraction patterns for a joint ventures domain and a microelectronics domain.

One of the questions raised by the growing interest in information extraction is whether the methods and resources developed for information extraction will be useful for other natural language processing tasks. We decided to investigate this issue by applying information extraction dictionaries and techniques to the problem of text classification. In a series of experiments, we used an information extraction system and dictionaries produced by AutoSlog to generate *relevancy signatures* [Riloff and Lehnert, 1994] for automatic text classification. The heart of the information extraction system is its dictionary of extraction patterns, so these experiments also served to demonstrate that the AutoSlog dictionaries were useful for making important domain discriminations.

In Section 2, we overview information extraction and the CIRCUS sentence analyzer that was used in these experiments. In Section 3, we describe the AutoSlog dictionary construction system that automatically creates dictionaries of extraction patterns using an annotated training corpus. In Section 4, we describe the relevancy signatures algorithm for text classification and present the results of the text classification experiments. Finally, we discuss related work in machine learning and automated dictionary construction and draw some conclusions.

2   A Brief Introduction to Information Extraction

Information extraction is a natural language processing task that involves automatically extracting predefined types of information from text. In contrast to in-depth understanding, information extraction systems focus only on portions of text that are relevant to a specific domain (e.g., see [Jacobs and Rau, 1990; Lehnert and Sundheim, 1991]). For example, an information extraction system designed for a terrorism domain might extract the names of perpetrators, victims, physical targets, and weapons involved in a terrorist attack. Or an information extraction system designed for a joint ventures domain might extract the names of companies involved in a joint venture and products, facilities, or people associated with those companies.

CIRCUS [Lehnert, 1991] is a conceptual sentence analyzer that performs information extraction. CIRCUS uses a dictionary of *concept nodes* to recognize domain-specific patterns and expressions and to extract relevant information. A concept node is essentially a case frame that is activated by specific linguistic expressions and extracts information from the surrounding context. To illustrate, Figure 1 shows a simple sentence and the resulting instantiated concept node produced by CIRCUS. The concept node $murder-passive$ is activated by passive forms of the verb "murdered", such as "were murdered" in the sample sentence. It then extracts the subject of the verb as the murder victim and the object of the preposition "by" as the perpetrator. In Figure 1, the "three peasants" are extracted as murder victims, and the "guerrillas" are extracted as perpetrators. A similar concept node called $murder-active$ is triggered by active forms of the verb "murdered", and extracts the subject as the perpetrator and the direct object as the victim.

A sentence may activate multiple concept nodes if more than one relevant expression is found, or a sentence may not activate any concept nodes if no relevant expressions are found. All of the information extraction happens through concept nodes, so it is essential for CIRCUS to have a concept node dictionary that provides good coverage of the domain.

> **Sentence:**
> Three peasants were murdered by guerrillas.
>
> **$murder-passive$**
>   victim = "three peasants"
>   perpetrator = "guerrillas"

Fig. 1. An instantiated concept node

3 AutoSlog: Learning Extraction Patterns

CIRCUS was the central component of the UMass/MUC-3[1] system [Lehnert *et al.*, 1991] developed at the University of Massachusetts. The concept node dictionary used by the UMass/MUC-3 system was built by hand. The dictionary performed well[2], but took approximately 1500 person-hours to build [Lehnert *et al.*, 1992]. The dictionary construction process was a major knowledge-engineering bottleneck that limited the scalability and portability of the system.

Subsequently, we developed a system called AutoSlog [Riloff, 1996; Riloff, 1993] that learns domain-specific extraction patterns from an annotated training corpus. As input, AutoSlog needs a text and a set of tagged noun phrases that represent the information that should have been extracted from the text. Each noun phrase needs to be tagged with its semantic type and the event type with which it is associated. Figure 2 shows a sample sentence and annotated noun phrases.

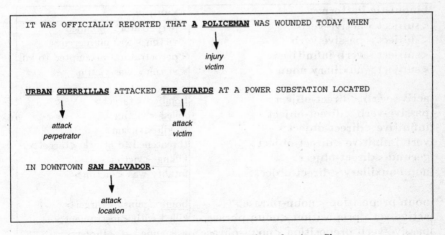

Fig. 2. Example text annotations for AutoSlog

---

[1] The MUCs refer to the message understanding conferences, which are competitive performance evaluations of information extractions systems.

[2] The UMass/MUC-3 system earned the highest combined recall and precision scores of the 15 sites that participated in MUC-3 [MUC-3 Proceedings, 1991].

For each tagged noun phrase, AutoSlog proposes a linguistic pattern that is capable of extracting the noun phrase in an appropriate context. Intuitively, AutoSlog tries to find a pattern that identifies the role of the noun phrase in a relevant event or context. For example, consider the sentence:

(a) <u>John Smith</u> was murdered by <u>armed men</u>.

Suppose "John Smith" is tagged as a murder victim and the phrase "armed men" is tagged as the perpetrator of a murder. AutoSlog will propose that the pattern "<X> was murdered" identifies X as the victim of a murder and should therefore be used to extract John Smith. Since the pattern itself is general, it can be used to extract the names of other murder victims in future texts. Similarly, AutoSlog will propose that the pattern "was murdered by <Y>" identifies Y as a perpetrator and should therefore be used to extract the armed men. Again, the pattern is general so it can be used to extract new perpetrators in the future.

The core of AutoSlog is a simple set of linguistic rules that generate the extraction patterns. Each rule depends solely on the syntactic location of the targeted noun phrase and the surrounding context. The original set of AutoSlog rules[3] is shown in Figure 3. The rules are divided into three sets, depending upon whether the targeted noun phrase was the subject, direct object, or prepositional phrase of a clause. If the noun phrase was the subject, then AutoSlog hypothesizes that the verb determines the role of the noun phrase and should be used as the basis for the pattern. The exact form of the pattern mirrors the syntactic context surrounding the noun phrase.

Linguistic Pattern	Example
<subject> active-verb	<perpetrator> <u>bombed</u>
<subject> passive-verb	<victim> was <u>murdered</u>
<subject> verb infinitive	<perpetrator> attempted to <u>kill</u>
<subject> auxiliary noun	<victim> was <u>victim</u>
active-verb <direct-object>	<u>bombed</u> <target>
passive-verb <direct-object>	<u>killed</u> <victim>
infinitive <direct-object>	to <u>kill</u> <victim>
verb infinitive <direct-object>	threatened to <u>attack</u> <target>
gerund <direct-object>	<u>killing</u> <victim>
noun auxiliary <direct-object>	<u>fatality</u> was <victim>
noun preposition <noun-phrase>	<u>bomb</u> against <target>
active-verb preposition <noun-phrase>	<u>killed</u> with <instrument>
passive-verb preposition <noun-phrase>	was <u>aimed</u> at <target>

Fig. 3. AutoSlog rules and examples in the terrorism domain

---

[3] A slightly different set of rules was used in the joint ventures and microelectronics domains. See [Riloff, 1996] for details.

For example, in sentence (a) AutoSlog determines that "John Smith" is the subject of the sentence so the <subject> rules are activated. Since "murdered" is in the passive voice, the **<subject> passive-verb** rule matches the surrounding context. The rule fires and instantiates its general pattern with the specific verb found in the sentence. The resulting extraction pattern represents expressions such as "X was murdered", "X and Y were murdered", and "X has been murdered." The process is similar for the other two categories of rules. If CIRCUS determines that the targeted noun phrase is a direct object, then those rules are activated. In most cases, the verb is used as the basis for the pattern because the verb usually identifies the conceptual role of the noun phrase. If CIRCUS determines that the targeted noun phrase is in a prepositional phrase, then a simple pp-attachment algorithm is used to attach it to a preceding verb or noun. That verb or noun is then used to create a new extraction pattern.

Figure 4 shows the flow of control in the AutoSlog system. As input, AutoSlog needs texts and tagged noun phrases. For the experiments described here, we used the MUC answer keys as input. It is important to note that the answer keys contain a lot of additional information that AutoSlog does not need and did not use. We used the MUC answer keys because they were readily available, but an annotated corpus would have been sufficient.

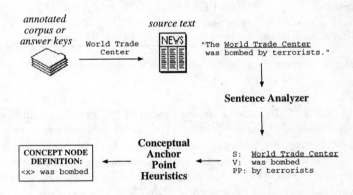

Fig. 4. AutoSlog flowchart

Given the annotated corpus (or answer keys), AutoSlog processes one noun phrase at a time. Given a tagged noun phrase, AutoSlog first finds the sentence from which the noun phrase originated. If there is no pointer from the noun phrase back to the original source text, then AutoSlog uses the first sentence in the text that contains the noun phrase. The sentence is then pushed through CIRCUS, which breaks it up into clauses and identifies the major syntactic constituents of each clause (subject, verb, direct object, and prepositional phrases). The appropriate AutoSlog rules are activated depending upon the syntactic location of the noun phrase. The rules are evaluated in order, and the first rule to recognize its pattern will generate the extraction pattern for the noun phrase.

Figure 5 shows an example of a concept node generated by AutoSlog for the terrorism domain. The targeted noun phrase is "guerrillas", which is tagged as a perpetrator. AutoSlog searches for the first sentence containing the word "guerrillas", shown at the top of Figure 5, and sends it through CIRCUS. CIRCUS determines that the guerrillas are the subject of the first clause in the sentence so AutoSlog's <subject> rules are activated. The **<subject> verb infinitive** rule recognizes its pattern in the sentence and instantiates itself as **<subject> threatened to murder**. The resulting extraction pattern represents the expression "threatened to murder" and will extract the subject of the verb "threatened" as a perpetrator.

Text Id: DEV-MUC4-0071   **Targeted Noun Phrase:** "guerrillas"
Sentence: The Salvadoran guerrillas today threatened to murder
individuals involved in 19 March presidential elections if they do not resign
from their posts.

CONCEPT NODE
Name: perpetrator-subject-verb-infinitive-threatened-to-murder
Trigger: murder
Variable Slots: (perpetrator (*SUBJECT* 1))
Constraints: ((class PERPETRATOR *SUBJECT*))
Constant Slots: (type perpetrator)
Enabling Conditions: ((active) (trigger-preceded-by 'threatened 'to))

Fig. 5. Concept node for "<perpetrator> threatened to murder"

Although many of the concept nodes produced by AutoSlog represent relevant expressions, some of them represent expressions that are too general or do not make much sense (for example, this frequently happens when the sentence analyzer makes a mistake or when the pp-attachment algorithm chooses a bad attachment point). Therefore, we introduced a human in the loop to review all of the concept nodes created by AutoSlog. Using a simple interface, the user can quickly scan each of the extraction patterns (e.g., **"<perpetrator> threatened to murder"**) and determine whether it should be *accepted* for the final dictionary or *rejected* and thrown away.

We have applied AutoSlog to three domains: terrorism, joint ventures, and microelectronics. Since we did not have hand-crafted dictionaries for the joint ventures and microelectronics domains, it was difficult to evaluate the effectiveness of the AutoSlog dictionaries. The experiments described in the next section were done partly to address this issue. Our primary goal was to demonstrate that information extraction systems and resources are useful for natural language processing tasks besides straight information extraction. Our secondary goal was to show that the dictionaries created by AutoSlog are effective at making important domain discriminations. In the next section, we describe the text classification algorithm used in our experiments and present the results.

4 Text Classification Experiments

4.1 The Relevancy Signatures Algorithm

Text classification involves assigning category labels to texts. In these experiments, we focused on a binary classification problem: each text had to be labeled as either relevant or irrelevant to a given domain. The *relevancy signatures algorithm* [Riloff and Lehnert, 1994] was used for this task. Relevancy signatures were motivated by the observation that a single phrase is often enough to classify a text accurately. For example, the phrase "X was bombed" almost always describes a bombing, "X was kidnapped" almost always describes a kidnapping, and "assassination of X" almost always describes a murder. When processing texts in a limited domain, some expressions are reliable enough by themselves to warrant a relevant classification.

The relevancy signatures algorithm represents phrases as *signatures*, which are derived automatically from the concept nodes produced by CIRCUS. A signature is a word paired with a concept node. Together, this pair represents a unique set of linguistic expressions.[4] For example, the word "murdered" can be paired with the $murder-passive$ concept node to recognize passive forms of the verb "murdered", such as "X was murdered", "X and Y were murdered", and "X has been murdered." Similarly, the word "murdered" can be paired with the $murder-active$ concept node to recognize active forms of the verb "murdered", such as "X murdered Y" or "X has murdered Y."

The first step of the algorithm is to collect signatures by applying CIRCUS to a training corpus of preclassified texts. A set of *relevancy signatures* is then separated out using conditional probabilities. For each signature, we estimate the conditional probability that a text is relevant given that it generates the signature (that is, the number of occurrences of the signature in relevant texts divided by the total number of occurrences). Two thresholds are applied to identify the signatures that have the highest conditional probabilities: a relevancy threshold R and a frequency threshold M. A signature is deemed a relevancy signature is its conditional probability is $\geq$ R and its frequency is $\geq$ M. Intuitively, the relevancy signatures are a subset of signatures that were most highly correlated with relevant texts during training. Presumably, if a new text generates a relevancy signature then the text is likely to be relevant.

Although signatures represent only slightly more linguistic information than keywords, we have found that similar signatures can produce dramatically different classification results. Figure 6 shows several signatures, their estimated conditional probabilities (based on a training corpus of 1500 texts from the MUC-4 corpus [MUC-4 Proceedings, 1992]), and example sentences containing phrases represented by each signature. Figure 6 shows that 84% of texts containing the word "assassination" were relevant but only 49% of texts containing the word "assassinations" were relevant. In the MUC-4 terrorism domain, a text

---

[4] Pairing a word with a concept node is not necessary for AutoSlog's concept nodes because they already represent specific expressions. However, the hand-crafted dictionary contains more general concept nodes so this pairing is necessary.

is relevant only if it describes a *specific* terrorist incident. The singular noun, "assassination", usually refers to a specific assassination of a person or group of people, while the plural noun, "assassinations", often refers to assassinations in general (e.g., "The FMLN has claimed responsibility for many assassinations").

Signature	Prob.	Examples
<assassination, $murder$>	.84	the assassination of Hector Oqueli
<assassinations, $murder$>	.49	there were 50 assassinations in 1988
<bombed, $bombing-passive$>	.80	public buildings were bombed
<bombed, $bombing-active$>	.51	terrorists bombed two facilities
<casualties, $no-injury$>	.81	the attack resulted in no casualties
<casualties, $injury$>	.41	the officer reported 17 casualties
<dead, $found-dead-passive$>	1.00	the mayor was found dead
<dead, $left-dead$>	.61	the attack left 9 people dead
<dead, $number-dead$>	.47	the army sustained 9 dead

Fig. 6. Sample signatures and conditional probabilities

Figure 6 also shows that the passive form of "bombed" is more highly correlated with relevant texts than the active form. In the MUC-4 corpus, the active verb form is often used to describe military events but the passive verb form is more commonly used to describe terrorist events. One possible explanation for this phenomenon is that the perpetrator is often unknown in terrorist attacks. The passive verb form may also reflect a sense of victimization being conveyed by the reporters. One advantage of this approach is that these distinctions are identified automatically using statistics generated from a training corpus. It would be difficult, if not impossible, for a person to anticipate these differences.

To classify a new text, CIRCUS processes the text and the concept nodes instantiated during sentence processing are transformed into signatures. If any of the signatures is in the list of relevancy signatures for the domain, then the text is classified as relevant. If not, then the text is classified as irrelevant. We applied the relevancy signatures algorithm to three domains using concept node dictionaries created by AutoSlog. The results for these experiments are presented in the next three sections.

4.2 Results in the Terrorism Domain

Before testing AutoSlog's terrorism dictionary, we first trained the relevancy signatures algorithm using the hand-crafted MUC-3 concept node dictionary. The hand-crafted dictionary serves as a baseline for how well the relevancy signatures algorithm can perform using a manually encoded dictionary. 1500 texts (51% were relevant) from the MUC-4 corpus were used as training input for the relevancy signatures algorithm. After training was completed, testing was done on two blind sets of 100 texts each: TST3 and TST4. We ran the algorithm multiple times using a variety of different threshold settings: R was varied from

70 to 95 in increments of 5, and M was varied from 0 to 20 in increments of 1. Figure 7 shows the scatterplot generated from these runs.

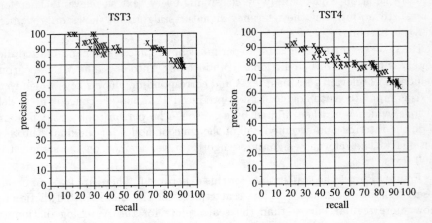

Fig. 7. Terrorism Results for the Hand-crafted Dictionary

Each data point represents a recall/precision pair for one set of threshold values. *Recall* is calculated as the number of texts correctly classified as relevant by the algorithm divided by the number of texts that <u>should</u> have been classified as relevant. *Precision* is defined as the number of texts correctly classified as relevant by the algorithm divided by the total number of texts classified as relevant by the algorithm. Recall and precision are metrics commonly used in the information retrieval community. There is almost always a tradeoff between recall and precision: achieving high recall usually means sacrificing precision and achieving high precision usually means sacrificing recall. Since there are some applications that demand high recall and others that demand high precision, we find it useful to show the spectrum of recall/precision levels that the algorithm can achieve.

Figure 7 shows that the relevancy signatures performed well in the terrorism domain using the hand-crafted dictionary. The relevancy signatures algorithm was designed with high-precision applications in mind, so the data points at the high precision end of the spectrum are the most interesting. If we look closely at a few of these data points, we see that the algorithm could achieve high precision with non-trivial levels of recall on both test sets. On TST3, the algorithm was able to achieve 100% precision with 30% recall and 94% precision with 67% recall. On TST4, the algorithm was able to obtain 93% precision with 24% recall, and 84% precision with 58% recall. In general, the relevancy signatures algorithm performed better on TST3 than TST4 but was able to achieve high precision on both test sets.

At the high recall end of the spectrum, we see one data point with 91% recall and 79% precision on TST3 and another data point with 94% recall and 63%

precision. These numbers should be interpreted with respect to the total number of relevant texts in each test set. TST3 contains 69 relevant texts and TST4 contains 55 relevant texts. So we could easily achieve 69% precision on TST3 and 55% precision on TST4 simply by classifying every text as relevant! Therefore it is worth noting that the relevancy signatures algorithm shows improvement over this baseline.

Next, we performed the same experiment but replaced the hand-crafted dictionary with the terrorism dictionary produced by AutoSlog. The MUC-4 corpus included 772 relevant terrorism texts and corresponding answer keys which were used as input to AutoSlog. AutoSlog produced 1237 unique concept node definitions, which were then filtered by a person. The person took about 5 hours to do the filtering and accepted 450 of the concept nodes for the final AutoSlog dictionary. The relevancy signatures algorithm was trained on the same set of 1500 texts.

Figure 8 shows the scatterplots for this experiment. There are two important observations to be made. (1) The scatterplots for the hand-crafted dictionary show more regular curves than the scatterplots for the AutoSlog dictionary. This is to be expected because the hand-crafted dictionary was built by a person who presumably created only relevant concept nodes. The AutoSlog dictionary, however, was constructed automatically and therefore may contain irrelevant concept nodes. Although the AutoSlog dictionary was manually filtered by a person, it is often difficult for a person to look quickly at an extraction pattern and accurately judge whether it will be useful for the domain. When a person goes to the trouble of defining a pattern by hand, however, presumably the person is motivated to do so because they have reason to believe that it is important.

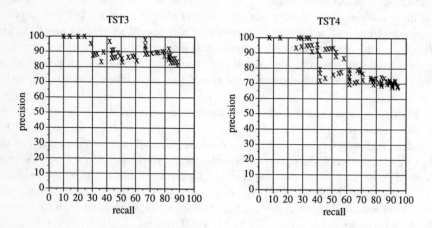

Fig. 8. Terrorism Results for the AutoSlog Dictionary

The second observation (2) is that the AutoSlog dictionary performed at least as well as the hand-crafted dictionary on TST3 and considerably better on TST4. Many of the data points in Figure 7 are paralleled in Figure 8, and improved in several cases. The most notable improvement was on TST4. While the hand-crafted dictionary did not obtain 100% precision at any recall level, the AutoSlog dictionary produced several data points with 100% precision, including one with 35% recall. The AutoSlog dictionary also produced a data point with 93% precision and 51% recall. On TST3, the dictionaries showed similar performance. For example, the Autoslog dictionary also achieved 100% precision but with slightly lower recall of 25%. But it was able to achieve 98% precision with 67% recall which is better than the 94% precision with 67% recall produced by the hand-crafted dictionary.

Overall, the AutoSlog dictionary performed at least as well as the hand-crafted dictionary in the terrorism domain. This result suggests that the AutoSlog dictionary can duplicate most if not all of the functionality of the hand-crafted dictionary (with respect to the problem of text classification). And since the AutoSlog dictionary outperformed the hand-crafted dictionary in some cases, AutoSlog seems to have generated some extraction patterns that were useful for the domain but were not encoded in our hand-crafted dictionary.

4.3   Results in the Joint Ventures Domain

The joint ventures domain was based on the MUC-5 information extraction task, so we used the MUC-5 text corpora and answer keys for our experiments [MUC-5 Proceedings, 1993]. The MUC-5 joint ventures corpus contained 924 relevant texts plus corresponding answer keys, which were used as input to AutoSlog. AutoSlog generated 3167 concept nodes for the joint ventures domain; 944 of these were accepted for the final dictionary after manual filtering. We also automatically generated morphological variants for these concept nodes so the final joint ventures dictionary contained 2515 concept node definitions: the original 944 definitions plus morphological variants (see [Riloff, 1996] for details of this process).

For the text classification task, a text was generally considered to be relevant if it described a joint venture between two or more named entities (companies, governments, or people).[5] We used a corpus of 1200 preclassified texts (54% relevant[6]) to train the relevancy signatures algorithm. However, we did not have separate blind test sets for this domain, so we used a 10-fold cross validation design to evaluate the performance of the algorithm. We also used an empirical method analogous to cross-validation to determine the best threshold values for 7 different recall/precision settings. (The details of this procedure are beyond the scope of this paper but have been discussed elsewhere [Riloff and Lehnert, 1994].) Figure 9 shows the result of this experiment. Each data point represents one of the 7 recall/precision results achieved by the algorithm for the empirically derived threshold values.

---

[5] The official guidelines for relevance are explained in the MUC-5 proceedings [MUC-5 Proceedings, 1993].

[6] Most of the irrelevant texts were drawn from the Tipster detection corpus [Tipster Proceedings, 1993].

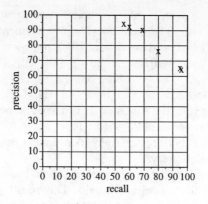

Fig. 9. Joint Venture Results

Figure 9 shows that the relevancy signatures algorithm performed very well in the joint ventures domain using the AutoSlog dictionary. At the high precision end of the spectrum, we see one data point that represents 94% precision with 56% recall and another that represents 92% precision with 60% recall. It is important to keep in mind that these results are based on 1200 texts (using the 10-fold cross-validation design), whereas the terrorism experiments were based on test sets containing a total of 200 texts. Therefore, these results provide strong evidence that AutoSlog produced an effective joint ventures dictionary for the text classification task.

4.4 Results in the Microelectronics Domain

The third text classification experiment involved the MUC-5 microelectronics domain. The MUC-5 microelectronics corpus contained 787 relevant microelectronics texts plus corresponding answer keys that were used as input to AutoSlog. Using this corpus, AutoSlog generated 2952 concept nodes for the microelectronics domain. We manually filtered only some of the concept nodes produced by AutoSlog for this domain (see [Riloff, 1996] for details about this process). After selective filtering and generating morphological variants (as per the joint ventures domain), the final microelectronics dictionary contained 4220 concept node definitions.

In the MUC-5 microelectronics domain, a text was generally defined to be relevant if it mentioned a microelectronics process linked to a specific company or research group. We used 500 texts from the MUC-5 corpus (57% relevant) to train the relevancy signatures algorithm. We then used the same cross-validation design used for the joint ventures domain to evaluate the performance of the dictionary.

Figure 10 shows the results of the microelectronics experiment. The text classification results for this domain were considerably weaker than they were for the other two domains. However, the AutoSlog microelectronics dictionary did

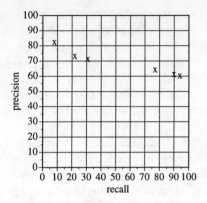

Fig. 10. Microelectronics Results

achieve respectable performance. In particular, we see one data point that represents 82% precision with 8% recall and another data point that represents 73% precision with 22% recall. Since the training corpus contained only 57% relevant texts, these precision results represent a non-trivial improvement over the baseline. Furthermore, the text classification training corpus for the microelectronics domain was much smaller than the corpora used for the terrorism and joint ventures domains (500 microelectronics texts, compared with 1500 terrorism texts and 1200 joint venture texts). Since the relevancy signatures algorithm is based on probability estimates, we expect its performance to be highly dependent on the size of the training corpus.

5 Related Work and Discussion

AutoSlog learns concept node definitions automatically using an annotated training corpus. However, it does not fall neatly into any of the common machine learning pigeonholes. AutoSlog is a one-shot learning system because it generates a complete extraction pattern from a single training instance. Therefore, in one sense, the closest points of comparison in the machine learning community are explanation-based learning (EBL) systems [DeJong and Mooney, 1986; Mitchell *et al.*, 1986] since EBL systems are able to produce complete concept representations from a single training instance. This is in contrast to inductive learning techniques that incrementally build a concept representation in response to multiple training instances (e.g., [Fisher, 1987; Quinlan, 1986; Utgoff, 1988]). AutoSlog does not rely on an explicit domain theory like most EBL systems, but it does use a set of domain-independent rules based on general syntactic properties of natural language. One important feature of AutoSlog is that its input (text and tagged noun phrases) is of a completely different form than its output (extraction patterns).

The one-shot learning aspect of AutoSlog distinguishes it from most other lexical acquisition systems, which build new definitions based on known definitions of other words in the sentence or surrounding context (e.g., [Carbonell, 1979; Granger, 1977; Jacobs and Zernik, 1988]). In contrast, AutoSlog builds new dictionary definitions completely from scratch and depends only on a part-of-speech lexicon, which can be readily obtained from machine-readable dictionaries. AutoSlog is closely related to the PALKA system [Kim and Moldovan, 1993], which also learns structures for information extraction. However, PALKA uses a set of predefined keywords and frame definitions for the domain as a starting point and depends on semantic features associated with words for learning. The CRYSTAL system ([Soderland *et al.*, 1995] and Soderland et al., this volume) and LIEP (Huffman, this volume) also rely on semantic features to learn extraction patterns. AutoSlog discovers the trigger words for case frames on its own and does not require semantic features. Furthermore, a recent extension of AutoSlog, called AutoSlog-TS [Riloff and Shoen, 1995], eliminates the need for detailed text annotations from a user and requires only a training corpus of preclassified texts.

AutoSlog's ability to learn dictionaries of extraction patterns can substantially reduce the time required to build an information extraction system for a new domain. We have also demonstrated that dictionaries created by AutoSlog can be useful for other natural language processing tasks as well. These results suggest that the patterns learned by AutoSlog represent important domain concepts that may be applicable to many different problems, and that information extraction technology may be useful for a variety of language processing tasks.

Acknowledgements

This research was funded by NSF Grant no. EEC-9209623, supporting the Center for Intelligent Information Retrieval at the University of Massachusetts, NSF grant MIP-9023174, and NSF grant IRI-9509820.

References

Carbonell, J. G. 1979. Towards a Self-Extending Parser. In *Proceedings of the 17th Meeting of the Association for Computational Linguistics*. 3–7.

DeJong, Gerald and Mooney, R. 1986. Explanation-Based Learning: An Alternative View. *Machine Learning* 1:145–176.

Fisher, D. H. 1987. Knowledge Acquisition Via Incremental Conceptual Clustering. *Machine Learning* 2:139–172.

Granger, R. H. 1977. FOUL-UP: A Program that Figures Out Meanings of Words from Context. In *Proceedings of the Fifth International Joint Conference on Artificial Intelligence*. 172–178.

Jacobs, Paul and Rau, Lisa 1990. SCISOR: Extracting Information from On-Line News. *Communications of the ACM* 33(11):88–97.

Jacobs, P. and Zernik, U. 1988. Acquiring Lexical Knowledge from Text: A Case Study. In *Proceedings of the Seventh National Conference on Artificial Intelligence*. 739–744.

Kim, J. and Moldovan, D. 1993. Acquisition of Semantic Patterns for Information Extraction from Corpora. In *Proceedings of the Ninth IEEE Conference on Artificial*

Intelligence for Applications, Los Alamitos, CA. IEEE Computer Society Press. 171–176.

Lehnert, W. G. and Sundheim, B. 1991. A Performance Evaluation of Text Analysis Technologies. *AI Magazine* 12(3):81–94.

Lehnert, W.; Cardie, C.; Fisher, D.; Riloff, E.; and Williams, R. 1991. University of Massachusetts: Description of the CIRCUS System as Used for MUC-3. In *Proceedings of the Third Message Understanding Conference (MUC-3)*, San Mateo, CA. Morgan Kaufmann. 223–233.

Lehnert, W.; Cardie, C.; Fisher, D.; McCarthy, J.; Riloff, E.; and Soderland, S. 1992. University of Massachusetts: MUC-4 Test Results and Analysis. In *Proceedings of the Fourth Message Understanding Conference (MUC-4)*, San Mateo, CA. Morgan Kaufmann. 151–158.

Lehnert, W. 1991. Symbolic/Subsymbolic Sentence Analysis: Exploiting the Best of Two Worlds. In Barnden, J. and Pollack, J., editors 1991, *Advances in Connectionist and Neural Computation Theory, Vol. 1*. Ablex Publishers, Norwood, NJ. 135–164.

Mitchell, T. M.; Keller, R.; and Kedar-Cabelli, S. 1986. Explanation-Based Generalization: A Unifying View. *Machine Learning* 1:47–80.

Proceedings of the Third Message Understanding Conference (MUC-3), San Mateo, CA. Morgan Kaufmann.

Proceedings of the Fourth Message Understanding Conference (MUC-4), San Mateo, CA. Morgan Kaufmann.

Proceedings of the Fifth Message Understanding Conference (MUC-5), San Francisco, CA. Morgan Kaufmann.

Quinlan, J. R. 1986. Induction of Decision Trees. *Machine Learning* 1:80–106.

Riloff, E. and Lehnert, W. 1994. Information Extraction as a Basis for High-Precision Text Classification. *ACM Transactions on Information Systems* 12(3):296–333.

Riloff, E. and Shoen, J. 1995. Automatically Acquiring Conceptual Patterns Without an Annotated Corpus. In *Proceedings of the Third Workshop on Very Large Corpora*. 148–161.

Riloff, E. 1993. Automatically Constructing a Dictionary for Information Extraction Tasks. In *Proceedings of the Eleventh National Conference on Artificial Intelligence*. AAAI Press/The MIT Press. 811–816.

Riloff, E. 1996. An Empirical Study of Automated Dictionary Construction for Information Extraction in Three Domains. *Artificial Intelligence*. To appear.

Soderland, S.; Fisher, D.; Aseltine, J.; and Lehnert, W. 1995. CRYSTAL: Inducing a conceptual dictionary. In *Proceedings of the Fourteenth International Joint Conference on Artificial Intelligence*. 1314–1319.

Proceedings of the TIPSTER Text Program (Phase I), San Francisco, CA. Morgan Kaufmann.

Utgoff, P. 1988. ID5: An Incremental ID3. In *Proceedings of the Fifth International Conference on Machine Learning*. 107–120.

Issues in Inductive Learning of Domain-Specific Text Extraction Rules⋆

Stephen Soderland, David Fisher,
Jonathan Aseltine, Wendy Lehnert

Department of Computer Science
University of Massachusetts, Amherst, MA 01003-4610
{soderlan dfisher aseltine lehnert}@cs.umass.edu

Abstract. Domain-specific text analysis requires a dictionary of linguistic patterns that identify references to relevant information in a text. This paper describes CRYSTAL, a fully automated tool that induces such a dictionary of text extraction rules. We discuss some key issues in developing an automatic dictionary induction system, using CRYSTAL as a concrete example. CRYSTAL derives text extraction rules from training instances and generalizes each rule as far as possible, testing the accuracy of each proposed rule on the training corpus. An error tolerance parameter allows CRYSTAL to manipulate a trade-off between recall and precision. We discuss issues involved with creating training data, defining a domain ontology, and allowing a flexible and expressive representation while designing a search control mechanism that avoids intractability.

1 Domain-specific Text Analysis

Considerable domain knowledge is needed by a system that analyzes unrestricted text and identifies information relevant to a particular domain. The text analysis system must consider domain-specific vocabulary and semantics, as well as linguistic patterns typically used in references to domain objects. A system tailored to extracting information from newswire stories about terrorism might identify the subject of the passive verb "kidnapped" as the victim of a kidnapping event. On the other hand, if the system is to analyze medical patient records, it will need a totally different set of rules that identify references to various types of diagnoses and symptoms.

The University of Massachusetts BADGER text analysis system instantiates a set of case frames called "concept nodes" (CN's) to represent information extracted from a document, using a dictionary of rules called CN definitions. BADGER performs selective concept extraction similar to that of its predecessor, the CIRCUS system [1],[2].

Creating CN definitions by hand is a laborious task, which requires both knowledge of the domain and a deep understanding of the text analysis system.

⋆ This research was supported by NSF Grant no. EEC-9209623, State/ Industry/ University Cooperative Research on Intelligent Information Retrieval. Thanks also to David Aronow for help as our medical domain expert.

Researchers at UMass spent about 1500 hours creating a dictionary of CN definitions for the ARPA-sponsored 1991 MUC-3 evaluation, whose domain was Latin American terrorism. The following year a partially automated dictionary construction tool, AutoSlog [8], was developed. AutoSlog automatically created a set of proposed CN definitions which required only 5 hours of review by a "human in the loop". The AutoSlog CN dictionary achieved 98% of the performance of the hand-crafted dictionary.

The CRYSTAL system presented in this paper [9], carries the idea of AutoSlog further. It creates a dictionary of CN definitions with greater expressiveness that that of AutoSlog, and is fully automatic.

2 Concept Node Definitions

A CN definition specifies a set of syntactic and semantic constraints that must be satisfied for the definition to apply to a segment of text. Before the CN definition is applied, BADGER must segment the input text and identify the syntactic constituents of each segment such as subject, verb phrase, direct and indirect object, and prepositional phrases. BADGER looks up the semantic class of each word in a domain-specific semantic lexicon and instantiates a concept node with the extracted information if all constraints are met.

Examples in this paper are from a medical domain, where the task is to analyze hospital discharge reports, and identify references to "diagnosis" and to "sign or symptom". These are further classified with subtypes.

Diagnosis:	Sign or Symptom:
confirmed	present
ruled out	absent
suspected	presumed
pre-existing	unknown
past	history

The example shown in Figure 1 is a CN definition from this domain that identifies references to absent symptoms. This CN definition extracts the phrase in the direct object buffer when the subject buffer has the semantic class <patient>, the verb is "denies" in the active voice, and the direct object has the semantic class <sign_or_symptom>.

This CN definition would extract "any episodes of nausea" from the sentence "The patient denies any episodes of nausea". It would fail to apply to the sentence "The patient denies a history of asthma", since asthma is of semantic class <disease_or_syndrome>, which is not a subclass of <sign_or_symptom>.

In this paper we will describe how CRYSTAL induces a set of CN definitions from training instances. CRYSTAL will be used as a concrete example to ground a discussion of various aspects of using machine learning to generate text extraction rules. We will discuss preparation of a training corpus, definition of a domain ontology, representation of training instances and extraction rules, and designing search control to handle an intractable problem efficiently.

CN-type: sign_or_symptom
Subtype: absent
Extract from Direct Object
Active voice verb
Subject constraints:
    head class <patient>
Verb constraints:
    words include "DENIES"
Direct Object constraints:
    head class <sign_or_symptom>

Fig. 1. A CN definition to identify "sign_or_symptom, absent"

3   Overview of Dictionary Induction

CRYSTAL derives a domain-specific dictionary of text extraction rules from a training corpus, initializing the dictionary with a CN definition for each positive training instance. These initial CN definitions are designed to extract the relevant phrase in the training instance that motivated them, but are too specific to apply broadly to previously unseen sentences.

Figure 2 shows the initial CN definition derived from the sentence fragment "Unremarkable with the exception of mild shortness of breath and chronically swollen ankles." The domain expert has marked "shortness of breath" and "swollen ankles" with CN type "sign_or_symptom" and subtype "present". When BADGER analyzes this sentence, it assigns the complex noun phrase "the exception of mild shortness of breath and chronically swollen ankles" to a single prepositional phrase buffer. When a complex noun phrase has multiple head nouns or multiple modifiers, the class constraint becomes a conjunctive constraint. Class constraints on words such as "unremarkable" that are of class <root_class> are dropped as vacuous.

Before the induction process begins, CRYSTAL cannot predict which characteristics of an instance are essential to the CN definition and which are merely accidental features. So CRYSTAL encodes all the details of the text segment as constraints on the initial CN definition, requiring the exact sequence of words and the exact sets of semantic classes in each syntactic buffer.

The main work of CRYSTAL is to gradually relax the constraints on these initial definitions to broaden their coverage, while merging similar definitions to form a more compact dictionary. Semantic constraints are relaxed by moving up the semantic hierarchy or by dropping the constraint. Exact word constraints are relaxed by dropping all but a subsequence of the words or dropping the constraint. The combinatorics on ways to relax constraints becomes overwhelming. There are over 57,000 possible generalizations of the initial CN definition in Figure 2.

The goal of generalizing is to drop constraints derived from accidental features of the motivating instance while retaining constraints that identify positive instances and constraints that eliminate negative instances. Relaxing constraints

```
CN-type: sign_or_symptom
Subtype: present
Extract from Prepositional Phrase "WITH"
Verb = <NULL>
Subject constraints:
    words include "UNREMARKABLE"
Prepositional Phrase constraints:
    preposition = "WITH"
    words include "THE EXCEPTION OF MILD
                    SHORTNESS OF BREATH
                    AND CHRONICALLY SWOLLEN
                    ANKLES"
    head class <sign_or_symptom>,
                <physiologic_function>,
                <body_part>
    modifier class <sign_or_symptom>
```

Fig. 2. An initial CN definition, including all exact words and classes

enough to unify a CN definition with a similar CN definition tends to accomplish these goals.

CRYSTAL finds useful generalizations of an initial CN definition, D, by locating a highly similar CN definition, D'. A new definition, U, is then created with constraints relaxed just enough to unify D and D'. This involves dropping constraints that the two do not have in common and finding a common ancestor of their semantic constraints. The new CN definition, U, is then tested against the training corpus to make sure that it does not extract phrases that were not marked with the CN type and subtype being learned.

If U is a valid CN definition, CRYSTAL deletes from the dictionary all definitions covered by U, thus reducing the size of the dictionary while still covering all the positive training instances. In particular, D and D' will be deleted. Then U becomes the current CN definition and this process is repeated, using similar CN definitions to guide the further relaxation of constraints. Eventually a point is reached where further relaxation would produce a CN definition that exceeds some pre-specified error tolerance. At that point, CRYSTAL begins the generalization process on another initial CN definition until all initial definitions have been considered for generalization.

CRYSTAL's learning algorithm is similar to the inductive concept learning described by Mitchell [5] and that described by Michalski [4]. Each uses a data-driven search to find the most general rule that covers positive training instances without covering negative instances. CRYSTAL is more robust than Mitchell's version space algorithm, which assumes no noise in the training and searches for a single concept to cover all positive instances. Michalski sees his approach in terms of a minimum covering set problem, where the goal is a minimal set of generalizations that cover all the positive instances. This is exactly the goal of CRYSTAL.

The CRYSTAL algorithm:

```
Initialize Dictionary and Training Instances Database
Do until no more initial CN definitions in Dictionary
    D = an initial CN definition from Dictionary
    Loop
        D' = the most similar CN definition to D
        If D' = NULL, exit loop
        U = the unification of D and D'
        Test the coverage of U in Training Instances
        If the error rate of U > Tolerance
                exit loop
        Delete all CN definitions covered by U
        Set D = U
    Add D to the Dictionary
Return the Dictionary
```

4   Experimental Results

Experiments were conducted with 337 hospital discharge reports, with a total of 13,000 instances, of which 5,100 were "diagnosis" and 1,900 were "sign or symptom". These were partitioned into a training set and a blind test set, then dictionaries of CN definitions were induced from the training set and evaluated on the test set.

Performance is measured here in terms of recall and precision, where recall is the percentage of possible phrases that the dictionary extracts and precision is the percentage correct of the extracted phrases. For instance if there are 5,000 phrases that could possibly be extracted from the test set by a dictionary, but the dictionary extracts only 3,000 of them, recall is 60%. If the dictionary extracts 4,000 phrases, only 3,000 of them correct, precision is 75%.

The setting of an error tolerance parameter can be used to manipulate a trade-off between recall and precision of a dictionary. Figure 3 shows performance of a dictionary of CN definitions that identify "sign_or_symptom" of any subtype, where the error tolerance is varied from 0.0 to 0.4. The results shown here are the averages of 50 random partitions of the corpus into 90% training and 10% test documents for each error tolerance.

To assess the learning curve as training size increases, we chose the partition size for training to be 10%, 30%, 50%, 70%, and 90%. This was done 50 times for each training size and results averaged as before. The number of positive training instances in a partition depends on what CN type and subtype is being learned. Figure 4 shows recall for the most frequent CN type and subtypes as the number of positive training instances increases. The error tolerance is set at .20 for this experiment.

These results are for CN definitions acting in isolation, which explains the different coverage of the subtype "absent" and "present" for "sign_or_symptom". CRYSTAL is able to add a constraint requiring the word "no" for absent symp-

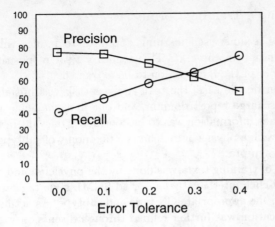

Fig. 3. Effect of the error tolerance setting on performance

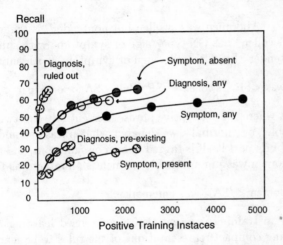

Fig. 4. Learning curve: recall increases with the number of training instances

toms, but has no mechanism to require the absence of "no" for present symptoms. Additional noun phrase analysis rules are needed to handle conjunction, disjunction and the scoping of negation. Future work will address these issues by moving to a granularity of simple noun phrase within syntactic buffers and scoping for negation before applying CRYSTAL's CN definitions.

5 Issues in Automatic Dictionary Induction

With CRYSTAL serving as a concrete example, we now turn to a discussion of some of the design and implementation issues involved in automatic dictionary induction.

5.1 Preparing a Training Corpus

CRYSTAL uses a supervised learning approach to induce rules that identify relevant information in the text. This requires a set of positive and negative training instances of the information to be extracted.

As will often be the case, the text analysis task was initially ill-defined for the hospital discharge report domain, and our first challenge was to specify a taxonomy of what information was to be considered relevant in this domain. We worked closely with a physician to defined a taxonomy of subtypes of "diagnosis" and of "sign or symptom".

Annotation of training texts was done by the physician and three nurses, using a point-and-click interface that inserted SGML style tags around phrases to label them with the appropriate CN type and subtype. As actual tagging began, the task specification was further refined through discussion with the physician who served as our domain expert. The general guidelines were to tag simple phrases, but deciding exactly which phrase to label was not always straightforward.

The sentence "Abdomen was swollen but nontender" is tagged as follows to indicate that "swollen" has CN type "sign or symptom" with subtype "present" and that "nontender" has CN type "sign or symptom" with subtype "absent".

Abdomen was <SP> swollen </SP> but <SA> nontender </SA> .

In sentences where the descriptive phrase is essentially empty of content, such as "unremarkable" or "normal", we debated what phrase should be tagged. In such cases the body part itself is tagged as sign or symptom, absent. An example of this is "Abdomen was unremarkable", which is annotated as follows.

<SA> Abdomen </SA> was unremarkable.

Consistency in training is essential if a supervised learning algorithm is to succeed in finding compact representations of the rules to be learned. In particular, a phrase that is accidentally missed during tagging will become a negative training instance. Coding guidelines and careful quality control are essential.

5.2 Creating a Domain Ontology

Precisely defining a taxonomy of relevant information is only part of creating a domain ontology. CRYSTAL also requires a semantic hierarchy and a semantic lexicon that maps terms into semantic classes in that hierarchy. Early in CRYSTAL's development, we created our own ad hoc semantic hierarchy and semantic lexicon with some assistance from our domain expert. This was replaced by one derived from the Unified Medical Language Systems (UMLS) on-line medical MetaThesaurus and Semantic Network [3]. UMLS is under developement by the National Library of Medicine and represents a knowledge source far superior to our ad hoc efforts, but is itself under development and is still weak in coverage of terms for clinical findings.

Our ad hoc semantic hierarchy grouped together semantic classes that occur in similar contexts for our task. For example the words "patient", "woman", "female", and "she" all belong to the semantic class <human> in the ad hoc hierarchy. In the UMLS hierarchy these have widely scattered semantic classes. A "patient" is of class <patient_or_disabled_group> which is a descendant of <idea_or_concept>. A "woman" is of class <human> (a <physical_object>). A "female" is of class <organism_attribute> (an <idea_or_concept>), and "she" is not even listed in the semantic lexicon.

UMLS also places the class <sign_or_symptom> in a subtree so far removed from <disease_or_syndrome> that their only common ancestor is the root of the entire hierarchy. Our ad hoc hierarchy gave them a common ancestor that at least distinguished them from non-medical terms.

Some rules that can be expressed compactly with our ad hoc semantic hierarchy require a disjunction or several rules using UMLS. We would expect CRYSTAL to require a larger training set when using UMLS than with the task-specific hierarchy. On the other hand, with 134 classes as opposed to 27 in the ad hoc hierarchy, UMLS could be expected to support finer grained distinctions.

For training sizes up to 50 documents, a CN dictionary based on UMLS lagged behind the task-specific ontology in coverage. Figure 5 compares recall of CN dictionaries based on UMLS and on the ad hoc ontology. Both are dictionaries that identify CN type "sign_or_symptom" of any subtype, using error tolerance of 0.20.

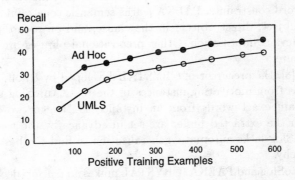

Fig. 5. Comparing recall with UMLS and with an ad hoc ontology

5.3 Expressiveness of Extraction Rules

The representation of training instances and rules is a fundamental design decision, particularly when dealing with a complex phenomenon such as natural language. A richly expressive representation will often cause an unacceptable increase in computational complexity, while a simpler representation glosses over important distinctions.

One issue is the scope of the "local context" to be included in text extraction rules. Shall we include all phrases in the same clause as potentially important to the context or exclude some parts of the clause to make processing more tractable? Another issue is the granularity of representation. Should the representation include exact words, or the semantic classes of words, or a combination of words and classes?

The CN definitions that CRYSTAL generates may include constraints on any or all syntactic buffers in a text segment as analyzed by BADGER. A segment is generally a simple clause with buffers such as subject, verb phrase, direct or indirect object, and prepositional phrases. Each buffer may be constrained to include a sequence of specific words, to have specific semantic classes in the head noun, or to have specific semantic classes in the modifiers. The verb can be further constrained as active or passive voice.

This representation gives CRYSTAL great flexibility in the rules that can be expressed. Identifying relevant information in a prepositional phrase might depend on the semantic class of the phrase itself and the exact word of the verb. In another case the important context may be a sequence of exact words in the subject buffer and the semantic class of the direct object. CRYSTAL has a more expressive representation than other published systems that induce text extraction rules.

PALKA [6], [7], developed by Kim and Moldovan, includes an induction step similar to CRYSTAL's. PALKA constructs an initial "Frame-Phrasal pattern structure" (FP-structure) from each example clause that contains relevant information. The FP-structure constrains the root form of the verb, but allows no other exact word constraints. PALKA learns semantic constraints on each noun group (e.g. subject, direct object) in the clause, and on prepositional phrases containing relevant information. Other prepositional phrases are omitted from the FP-structure.

AutoSlog [8], the precursor of CRYSTAL developed by Riloff, also generates CN definitions from motivating instances in the text. AutoSlog uses heuristics to select certain exact words from an instance as "trigger words". Semantic constraints on the extracted buffer are set in advance by the user rather than learned. AutoSlog lacks automatic generalization to find the best level in a semantic hierarchy.

Unlike AutoSlog and PALKA, CRYSTAL makes no *a priori* decision on which constituents are to be included in its CN definitions. Any constraints including those on the verb may be retained or dropped during CRYSTAL's induction. The following section discusses the search control strategy to handle the large branching factor that results from CRYSTAL's expressive representation.

5.4 Search Control: Avoiding Intractability

Since each CN definition may have several constraints and a variety of ways to relax each constraint, there are an exponential number of generalizations possible for a given CN definition. CRYSTAL has the challenge of producing a near optimal dictionary while avoiding intractability and maintaining a rich expressiveness of its CN definitions.

CRYSTAL reduces the intractable problem of constraint relaxation to the easier problem of finding a similar CN definition. Relaxing the constraints to unify a CN definition with a similar definition has the effect of retaining the constraints shared with another valid definition and dropping accidental features of the current definition. This is also guaranteed to produce a CN definition with greater coverage than either of the definitions being unified.

Finding similar definitions efficiently is achieved by indexing the CN definitions database by verbs and by extraction buffers. In this way, CRYSTAL can retrieve a list of similar CN definitions which is small relative to the entire database. Each of these is tested with a distance metric that counts the number of relaxations required to unify the two definitions.

Testing a generalized CN definition's error rate on the training corpus is actually done on the Training Instances Database, a database of instances which have already been segmented by the BADGER sentence analyzer. This database is indexed on verbs, including the <null> verb for sentence fragments, so only a small percent of training instances are typically tested. CRYSTAL drops the constraint on exact verb only after relaxing all other constraints as far as possible, to take full advantage of the efficiency of indexing by verb.

With this control strategy, CRYSTAL is able to induce a dictionary with all CN types and subtypes from 13,000 instances in about nine minutes of clock time on a DEC ALPHA AXP 3000 using 40 MB of memory.

CRYSTAL's control structure avoids combinatorial explosion and does no back-tracking, but cannot guarantee that CRYSTAL makes optimal choices of which constraints to relax. This does not seem to be a problem in practice. The CN definitions that CRYSTAL generates seems to be generalized as far as possible given the training data.

6 Future Work

Our experience with a variety of domains shows that local context is generally sufficient for identifying relevant information. Sometimes, however, the context of buffers in the same clause is not sufficient. When the documents have section headers or other indications of discourse boundaries, this often influences the meaning of a phrase. A reference in the "Past Medical History" section of a hospital discharge report takes on a different meaning than a similar reference in the "Physical Examination" section.

Consider the following example, where "hypertension" is tagged as a pre-existing diagnosis. CRYSTAL's initial CN definition could be extended to include a constraint that the current section be Past Medical History. If the most similar CN definition was also from that section, this constraint would be retained, otherwise it would be dropped during induction.

PAST MEDICAL HISTORY:
Significant for <DE> hypertension </DE>

In some cases it would be useful to include context from an adjacent text segment in the extraction rule. This is particularly so, given the tendency of the BADGER sentence analyzer to break a sentence into separate segments when it encounters a conjunction. CRYSTAL's initial CN definitions could be extended to include constraints on buffers from neighboring clauses. This more distant context would usually be dropped during the induction process when a CN definition is unified with another that does not have similar constraints on a neighboring text segment.

Another improvement we intend to make to BADGER and CRYSTAL is to use a finer granularity of syntactic analysis. The current version applies CN definitions at the level of syntactic buffer (subject, verb, direct object, prepositional phrase). The CN definition does not pinpoint which simple noun phrase contains the relevant information. The next version of BADGER will segment the syntactic buffers into simple noun (or verb) phrases, also handling the scoping of negation. This will enable CRYSTAL to learn CN definitions that identify simple noun phrases and verb phrases.

Perhaps the most useful enhancement to CRYSTAL would be to add a mechanism that learns exceptions to rules. As it now stands CRYSTAL can only learn positive constraints. There are some cases where the most compact extraction rule has a constraint that a buffer *not* include a certain word or semantic class.

As it relaxes constraints on a CN definition, CRYSTAL reaches a point where there are excessive extraction errors. Rather than abandon the overly generalized CN definition, CRYSTAL could examine the negative training instances covered by the definition. A negative constraint would then be added to exclude some feature in common to several negative instances. If the CN definition is now within error tolerance, generalization would continue as before.

Suppose that training instances with the class <pathologic_function> in the direct object buffer are usually positive instances of "sign or symptom". However, instances with the word "chronic" in the direct object as well as <pathologic_function> are tagged as "diagnosis" and are thus negative training instances for "sign or symptom". If CRYSTAL had the ability to specify a constraint that the direct object *not* contain the word "chronic", it would have a reliable extraction rule for "sign or symptom". Otherwise it would miss out on a useful generalization.

7   Conclusions

CRYSTAL operates as a fully automated knowledge acquisition tool, capable of creating a high quality dictionary of text extraction rules. Because it tests each proposed extraction rule against the training corpus, CRYSTAL is able to generalize each rule as much as possible without creating excessive extraction errors. The error tolerance parameter allows CRYSTAL to operate robustly in the face of noisy training, and allows the user to manipulate a trade-off between recall and precision.

The expressiveness of CRYSTAL's CN definitions causes an enormous branching factor in the search for an optimal level to relax the constraints in each CN definition. CRYSTAL overcomes the intractablility of the search problem by letting unification with a similar CN definition guide the induction process. This search control has worked out well in practice and allows efficient processing, while retaining a flexibility of expression that lets CRYSTAL capture subtle distinctions in its text extraction rules.

References

1. Lehnert, W., McCarthy, J., Soderland, S., Riloff, E., Cardie, C., Peterson, J., Feng, F., Dolan, C., Goldman, S. University of Massachusetts/Hughes: Description of the CIRCUS system as used for MUC-5. In *Proceedings of the Fifth Message Understanding Conference (MUC-5)*. (1993) 277-290
2. Lehnert, W. Symbolic/subsymbolic sentence analysis: Exploiting the best of two worlds. In J. Barnden and J. Pollack, editors, *Advances in Connectionist and Neural Computation Theory, Vol. 1*. Ablex Publishers, Norwood, NJ. (1991) 135-164
3. Lindberg, D., Humphreys, B., McCray, A. Unified Medical Language Systems. *Methods of Information in Medicine, 32(4)*. (1993) 281-291
4. Michalski, R.S. A theory and methodology of inductive learning. *Artificial Intelligence, 20*. (1983) 111-161
5. Mitchell, T.M. Generalization as search. *Artificial Intelligence, 18*. (1982) 203-226
6. Moldovan, D. and Kim, J. PALKA: A system for lingistic knowledge acquisition. Technical Report PKPL 92-8, USC Department of Electrical Engineering Systems. (1992)
7. Moldovan, D., Cha, S., Chung, M., Gallippi, T., Hendrickson, K., Kim, J., Lin, C., and Lin, C. USC: Description of the SNAP system as used for MUC-5. In *Proceedings of the Fifth Message Understanding Conference (MUC-5)*. (1993) 305-319
8. Riloff, E. Automatically constructing a dictionary for information extraction tasks. In *Proceedings of the Eleventh National Conference on Artificial Intelligence*. AAAI Press/ MIT Press. (1993) 811-816
9. Soderland, S., Fisher, D., Aseltine, J., Lehnert, W. CRYSTAL: Inducing a conceptual dictionary. In *Proceedings of the Fourteenth International Joint Conference on Artificial Intelligence*. (1995)

Applying Machine Learning
to Anaphora Resolution

Chinatsu Aone and Scott William Bennett

Systems Research and Applications Corporation (SRA)
2000 15th Street North
Arlington, VA 22201
aonec@sra.com, bennett@sra.com

Abstract. We describe one approach to build an automatically trainable anaphora resolution system. In this approach, we used Japanese newspaper articles tagged with discourse information as training examples for a machine learning algorithm which employs the C4.5 decision tree algorithm by Quinlan [10]. Then, we evaluate and compare the results of several variants of the machine learning-based approach with those of our existing anaphora resolution system which uses manually-designed knowledge sources. Finally, we will compare our algorithms with those in the related work.

1 Motivation

Anaphora resolution is an important but still difficult problem for various large-scale natural language processing (NLP) applications, such as information extraction and machine translation. For instance, in information extraction, it is critical to recognize when two statements made in a text convey information about a single entity. This recognition allows more information to be associated with that entity. In building an anaphora resolution system, a first step might be to examine existing theories of discourse to determine which approach might do the best job of resolving anaphora. Unfortunately, few discourse theories have been tested on an empirical basis, and therefore there is no answer to the "best" anaphora resolution algorithm.[1] Moreover, an anaphora resolution system within an NLP system for real applications must handle:

- degraded or missing input (no NLP system has complete lexicons, grammars or semantic knowledge, and outputs perfect results), and
- different anaphoric phenomena in different domains, languages, and applications.

These requirements have motivated us to develop robust, extensible and trainable anaphora resolution systems. Previously [4], we reported our data-driven multilingual anaphora resolution system, which is robust, extensible and

---

[1] Walker [12] compares Brennan, Friedman and Pollard's centering approach [5] with Hobbs' algorithm [7] on a theoretical basis.

manually trainable. It uses discourse knowledge sources (KS's) which are manually selected and ordered. (Henceforth, we call the system the Manually-Designed
Resolver, or MDR.) We wanted to develop, however, truly automatically trainable systems, hoping to improve resolution performance and reduce the overhead
of manually constructing and arranging such discourse KS's.

In this paper, we first describe one approach we are taking to build an automatically trainable anaphora resolution system. In this approach, we tag corpora
with discourse information, and use them as training examples for a machine
learning algorithm. (Hereafter, we call the system the Machine Learning-based
Resolver, or MLR.) Specifically, we have tagged Japanese newspaper articles
about joint ventures, and used the C4.5 decision tree algorithm by Quinlan [10].
Then, we evaluate and compare the results of the MLR with those produced by
the MDR. Finally, we will compare our algorithms with those in related work.

2 Machine Learning for Anaphora Resolution

In this section, we first discuss corpora which we created for training and testing.
Then, we describe the learning approach chosen, and discuss training features
and training methods that we employed for our current experiments.

2.1 Training and Test Corpora

In order to both train and evaluate an anaphora resolution system, we have been
developing corpora which are tagged with discourse information. The tagging has
been done using a GUI-based tool called the Discourse Tagging Tool (DTTool)
according to "The Discourse Tagging Guidelines" we have developed.[2] The tool
allows a user to link an anaphor with its antecedent and specify the type of the
anaphor (e.g. pronouns, definite NP's, etc.). The tagged result can be written
out to an SGML-marked file, as shown in Fig.1.

For our experiments, we have used a discourse-tagged corpus which consists
of Japanese newspaper articles about joint ventures. The tool lets a user define
types of anaphora as necessary. The anaphoric types used to tag this corpus are
shown in Table 1.

NAME anaphora are tagged when proper names are used anaphorically. For
example, in Fig.1, "Yamaichi (ID=3)" and "Sony-Prudential (ID=5)" referring
back to "Yamaichi Shouken (ID=4)" (Yamaichi Securities) and "Sony-Prudential
Seimeihoken (ID=6)" (Sony-Prudential Life Insurance) respectively are NAME
anaphora. NAME anaphora in Japanese are different from those in English in
that any combination of *characters* in an antecedent can be NAME anaphora
as long as the character order is preserved (e.g. "abe" can be an anaphor of
"abcde").

Japanese definite NPs (i.e. DNP anaphora) are those prefixed by "dou" (literally meaning "the same"), "ryou" (literally meaning "the two"), and deic-
tic determiners like "kono"(this) and "sono" (that). For example, "dou-sha" is

---

[2] Our work on the DTTool and tagged corpora was reported in a recent paper [2].

<COREF ID="1"><COREF ID="4">山一証券</COREF>と<COREF ID="6">ソニー・プルデンシャル生命保険
（平井竜明社長、本社・東京）</COREF></COREF>は、顧客の開拓、情報提供などの分野で業務提携する
ことにし、二日覚書に<COREF ID="0" TYPE="QZPRO-ORG" REF="1"></COREF>調印した。四月中旬から
<COREF ID="2" TYPE="ZPRO-ORG" REF="1"></COREF>実施する。<COREF ID="3" TYPE="NAME-ORG" REF="4">
山一</COREF>が<COREF ID="8">中小企業の節税などに役立つ財産管理情報システム</COREF>を
<COREF ID="5" TYPE="NAME-ORG" REF="6">ソニー・プルデンシャル</COREF>に提供、
<COREF ID="7" TYPE="DNP" REF="8">このシステム</COREF>を<COREF ID="9" TYPE="ZPRO-ORG" REF="5">
</COREF>使って<COREF ID="10" TYPE="QZPRO-ORG" REF="5"></COREF>獲得した顧客の証券運用を
<COREF ID="11" TYPE="NAME-ORG" REF="3">山一</COREF>が担当する。

Fig. 1. Text tagged with discourse information using SGML

Table 1. Summary of anaphoric types

Tags	Meaning
DNP	Definite NP
DNP-F	Definite NP whose referent is a facility
DNP-L	Definite NP whose referent is a location
DNP-ORG	Definite NP whose referent is an organization
DNP-P	Definite NP whose referent is a person
DNP-T	Definite NP whose referent is time
DNP-BOTH	Definite NP whose referent is two entities
DNP-BOTH-ORG	Definite NP whose referent is two organization entities
DNP-BOTH-L	Definite NP whose referent is two location entities
DNP-BOTH-P	Definite NP whose referent is two person entities
REFLEXIVE	Reflexive expressions (e.g. "jisha")
NAME	Proper name
NAME-F	Proper name for facility
NAME-L	Proper name for location
NAME-ORG	Proper name for organization
NAME-P	Proper name for person
DPRO	Deictic pronoun (this, these)
LOCI	Locational indexical (here, there)
TIMEI	Time indexical (now, then, later)
QZPRO	Quasi-zero pronoun
QZPRO-ORG	Quasi-zero pronoun whose referent is an organization
QZPRO-P	Quasi-zero pronoun whose referent is a person
ZPRO	Zero pronoun
ZPRO-IMP	Zero pronoun in an impersonal construction
ZPRO-ORG	Zero pronoun whose referent is an organization
ZPRO-P	Zero pronoun whose referent is a person
JDEL	Dou-ellipsis

equivalent to "the company", and "ryou-koku" to "the two countries". The DNP anaphora with "dou" and "ryou" prefixes are characteristic of written, but not spoken, Japanese texts.

Unlike English, Japanese has so-called zero pronouns, which are not explicit in the text. In these cases, the DTTool lets the user insert a "Z" marker just before the main predicate of the zero pronoun to indicate the existence of the anaphor. We made distinction between QZPRO and ZPRO when tagging zero pronouns. QZPRO ("quasi-zero pronoun") is chosen when a sentence has multiple clauses (subordinate or coordinate), and the zero pronouns in these clauses refer back to the subject of the initial clause in the *same* sentence, as shown in Fig.2.

SONY-wa	RCA-to	teikeishi,	VCR-wo	QZPRO
Sony-subj	*RCA-with*	*joint venture*	*VCR-obj*	*(it)*

kaihatsusuru	to	QZPRO	happyoushita
develop	*that*	*(it)*	*announced*

"(SONY) announced that SONY will form a joint venture with RCA and (it) will develop VCR's."

Fig. 2. QZPRO example

The anaphoric types are sub-divided according to more semantic criteria such as organizations, people, locations, etc. This is because the current application of our multilingual NLP system is information extraction [3], i.e. extracting from texts information about which organizations are forming joint ventures with whom. Thus, resolving certain anaphora (e.g. various ways to refer back to organizations) affects the task performance more than others, as we previously reported [1]. Our goal is to customize and evaluate anaphora resolution systems according to the types of anaphora when necessary.

2.2 Learning Method

While several inductive learning approaches could have been taken for construction of the trainable anaphoric resolution system, we found it useful to be able to observe the resulting classifier in the form of a decision tree. The tree and the features used could most easily be compared to existing theories. Therefore, our initial approach has been to employ Quinlan's C4.5 algorithm at the heart of our classification approach. We discuss the features used for learning below and go on to discuss the training methods and how the resulting tree is used in our anaphora resolution algorithm.

2.3 Training Features

In our current machine learning experiments, we have taken an approach where we train a decision tree using *feature vectors* for pairs of an anaphor and its possible antecedent. Currently we use 66 features, and they include *lexical* (e.g. category), *syntactic* (e.g. grammatical role), *semantic* (e.g. semantic class), and *positional* (e.g. distance between anaphor and antecedent) features. Those features can be either *unary* features (i.e. features of either an anaphor or an antecedent such as syntactic number values) or *binary* features (i.e. features concerning relations between the pairs such as the positional relation between an anaphor and an antecedent.) We started with the features used by the MDR, generalized them, and added new features. The features that we employed are common across domains and languages though the feature values may change in different domains or languages. Examples of training features are shown in Table 2.

Table 2. Examples of training features

	Unary feature	Binary feature
Lexical	category	matching-category
Syntactic	topicalized	matching-topicalized
Semantic	semantic-class	subsuming-semantic-class
Positional		antecedent-precedes-anaphor

The feature values are obtained automatically by processing a set of texts with our NLP system, which performs lexical, syntactic and semantic analysis and then creates *discourse markers* [8] for each NP and S.[3] Since discourse markers store the output of lexical, syntactic and semantic processing, the feature vectors are automatically calculated from them. Because the system output is not always perfect (especially given the complex newspaper articles), however, there is some noise in feature values.

2.4 Training Methods

We have employed different training methods using three parameters: anaphoric chains, anaphoric type identification, and confidence factors.

The anaphoric chain parameter is used in selecting training examples. When this parameter is *on*, we select a set of *positive* training examples and a set of *negative* training examples for each anaphor in a text in the following way:

Positive training examples are those anaphor-antecedent pairs whose anaphor is directly linked to its antecedent in the tagged corpus and also whose anaphor

---

[3] Existence of zero pronouns in sentences is detected by the syntax module, and discourse markers are created for them.

is paired with one of the antecedents on the *anaphoric chain,* i.e. the transitive closure between the anaphor and the first mention of the antecedent. For example, if B refers to A and C refers to B, C-A is a positive training example as well as B-A and C-B.

Negative training examples are chosen by pairing an anaphor with all the possible antecedents in a text except for those on the transitive closure described above. Thus, if there are possible antecedents in the text which are not in the C-B-A transitive closure, say D, C-D and B-D are negative training examples.

When the anaphoric chain parameter is *off,* only those anaphor-antecedent pairs whose anaphora are directly linked to their antecedents in the corpus are considered as positive examples. Because of the way in which the corpus was tagged (according to our tagging guidelines), an anaphor is linked to the most recent antecedent, except for a zero pronoun, which is linked to its most recent *overt* antecedent. In other words, a zero pronoun is never linked to another zero pronoun.

The anaphoric type identification parameter is utilized in training decision trees. With this parameter *on,* a decision tree is trained to answer "no" when a pair of an anaphor and a possible antecedent are not co-referential, or answer the anaphoric type when they are co-referential. If the parameter is *off,* a binary decision tree is trained to answer just "yes" or "no" and does not have to answer the types of anaphora.

The confidence factor parameter (0-100) is used in pruning decision trees. With a higher confidence factor, less pruning of the tree is performed, and thus it tends to overfit the training examples. With a lower confidence factor, more pruning is performed, resulting in a smaller, more generalized tree. We used confidence factors of 25, 50, 75 and 100%.

The anaphoric chain parameter described above was employed because an anaphor may have more than one "correct" antecedent, in which case there is no absolute answer as to whether one antecedent is better than the others. The decision tree approach we have taken may thus predict more than one antecedent to pair with a given anaphor. Currently, confidence values returned from the decision tree are employed when it is desired that a single antecedent be selected for a given anaphor. We are experimenting with techniques to break ties in confidence values from the tree. One approach is to use a particular bias, say, in preferring the antecedent closest to the anaphor among those with the highest confidence (as in the results reported here). Although use of the confidence values from the tree works well in practice, these values were only intended as a heuristic for pruning in Quinlan's C4.5. We have plans to use cross-validation across the training set as a method of determining error-rates by which to prefer one predicted antecedent over another.

Another approach is to use a hybrid method where a preference-trained decision tree is brought in to supplement the decision process. Preference-trained trees, like that discussed in Connolly *et al.* [6], are trained by presenting the learning algorithm with examples of when one anaphor-antecedent pair should be preferred over another. Despite the fact that such trees are learning preferences, they may not produce sufficient preferences to permit selection of a single best anaphor-antecedent combination (see Sect.5 below).

3 Testing

In this section, we first discuss how we configured and developed the MLRs and the MDR for testing. Next, we describe the scoring methods used, and then the testing results of the MLRs and the MDR. In this paper, we report the results of the four types of anaphora, namely NAME-ORG, QZPRO-ORG, DNP-ORG, and ZPRO-ORG, since they are the majority of the anaphora appearing in the texts and most important for the current domain (i.e. joint ventures) and application (i.e. information extraction).

3.1 Testing the MLRs

To build MLRs, we first trained decision trees with 1971 anaphora[4] (of which 929 were NAME-ORG; 546 QZPRO-ORG; 87 DNP-ORG; 282 ZPRO-ORG) in 295 training texts. The six MLRs using decision trees with different parameter combinations are described in Table 3.

Table 3. Six configurations of MLRs

	anaphoric chain	anaphoric type identification	confidence factor
MLR-1	yes	no	100%
MLR-2	yes	no	75%
MLR-3	yes	no	50%
MLR-4	yes	no	25%
MLR-5	yes	yes	75%
MLR-6	no	no	75%

Then, we trained decision trees in the MLR-2 configuration with varied numbers of training texts, namely 50, 100, 150, 200 and 250 texts. This is done to find out the minimum number of training texts to achieve the optimal performance.

3.2 Testing the MDR

The same training texts used by the MLRs served as development data for the MDR. Because the NLP system is used for extracting information about joint ventures, the MDR was configured to handle only the crucial subset of anaphoric

---

[4] In both training and testing, we did not include anaphora which refer to multiple discontinuous antecedents.

types for this experiment, namely all the name anaphora and zero pronouns and the definite NPs referring to organizations (i.e. DNP-ORG). The MDR applies different sets of *generators*, *filters* and *orderers* to resolve different anaphoric types [4]. A generator generates a set of possible antecedent hypotheses for each anaphor, while a filter eliminates unlikely hypotheses from the set. An orderer ranks hypotheses in a preference order if there is more than one hypothesis left in the set after applying all the applicable filters. Table 4 shows KS's employed for the four anaphoric types.

Table 4. KS's used by the MDR

	Generators	Filters	Orderers
NAME-ORG	current-text	syntactic-category-propn name-char-subsequence semantic-class-org	reverse-recency
DNP-ORG	current-text	semantic-class-org semantic-amount-singular	topicalization subject-np recency
QZPRO-ORG	current-paragraph	not-in-the-same-dc semantic-class-from-pred	topicalization subject-np category-np recency
ZPRO-ORG	current-paragraph	not-in-the-same-dc semantic-class-from-pred	topicalization subject-np category-np recency

3.3 Scoring Method

We used *recall* and *precision* metrics, as shown in Table 5, to evaluate the performance of anaphora resolution. It is important to use both measures because one can build a high recall–low precision system or a low recall–high precision system, neither of which may be appropriate in certain situations. The NLP system sometimes fails to create discourse markers exactly corresponding to anaphora in texts due to failures of lexical or syntactic processing. In order to evaluate the performance of the anaphora resolution systems themselves, we only considered anaphora whose discourse markers were identified by the NLP system in our evaluation. Thus, the system performance evaluated against *all* the anaphora in texts could be different.

Table 5. Recall and precision metrics for evaluation

Recall = N_c/I, Precision = N_c/N_h	
I	Number of system-identified anaphora in input
N_c	Number of correct resolutions
N_h	Number of resolutions attempted

3.4 Testing Results

The testing was done using 1359 anaphora (of which 1271 were one of the four anaphoric types) in 200 blind test texts for both the MLRs and the MDR. It should be noted that both the training and testing texts are newspaper articles about joint ventures, and that each article always talks about more than one organization. Thus, finding antecedents of organizational anaphora is not straightforward. Table 6 shows the results of six different MLRs and the MDR for the four types of anaphora, while Table 7 shows the results of the MLR-2 with different sizes of training examples.

Table 6. Recall and precision of the MLRs and the MDR

	NAME-ORG		DNP-ORG		QZPRO-ORG		ZPRO-ORG		Average		F-measure
# exmpls	631		54		383		203		1271		1271
	R	P	R	P	R	P	R	P	R	P	F
MLR-1	84.79	92.24	44.44	50.00	65.62	80.25	40.78	64.62	70.20	83.49	76.27
MLR-2	84.79	93.04	44.44	52.17	64.84	84.69	39.32	73.64	69.73	86.73	77.30
MLR-3	83.20	94.09	37.04	58.82	63.02	84.91	35.92	73.27	67.53	88.04	76.43
MLR-4	83.84	94.30	38.89	60.00	64.06	85.12	37.86	76.47	68.55	88.55	77.28
MLR-5	85.74	92.80	44.44	55.81	56.51	89.67	15.53	78.05	63.84	89.55	74.54
MLR-6	68.30	91.70	29.63	64.00	54.17	90.83	13.11	75.00	53.49	89.74	67.03
MDR	76.39	90.09	35.19	50.00	67.19	67.19	43.20	43.20	66.51	72.91	69.57

Table 7. MLR-2 configuration with varied training data sizes

# texts	NAME-ORG		DNP-ORG		QZPRO-ORG		ZPRO-ORG		Average		F-measure
	R	P	R	P	R	P	R	P	R	P	F
50	81.30	91.94	35.19	48.72	59.38	76.77	29.13	56.07	64.31	81.92	72.06
100	82.09	92.01	38.89	53.85	63.02	85.82	28.64	62.77	65.88	85.89	74.57
150	82.57	91.89	48.15	60.47	55.73	85.60	20.39	70.00	62.98	87.28	73.17
200	83.99	91.70	46.30	60.98	63.02	82.88	36.41	65.22	68.39	84.99	75.79
250	84.79	93.21	44.44	53.33	65.10	83.89	40.78	73.04	70.04	86.53	77.42
295	84.79	93.04	44.44	52.17	64.84	84.69	39.32	73.64	69.73	86.73	77.30
MDR	76.39	90.09	35.19	50.00	67.19	67.19	43.20	43.20	66.51	72.91	69.57

4 Evaluation

4.1 The MLRs vs. the MDR

Using F-measures[5] as an indicator for overall performance, the MLRs with the chain parameters turned on and type identification turned off (i.e. MLR-1, 2, 3, and 4) performed the best. MLR-1, 2, 3, 4, and 5 all exceeded the MDR in overall performance based on F-measure.

Both the MLRs and the MDR used the character subsequence, the proper noun category, and the semantic class feature values for NAME-ORG anaphora (in MLR-5, using anaphoric type identification). It is interesting to see that the MLR additionally uses the topicalization feature before testing the semantic class feature. This indicates that, information theoretically, if the topicalization feature is present, the semantic class feature is not needed for the classification. The performance of NAME-ORG is better than other anaphoric phenomena because the character subsequence feature has very high antecedent predictive power.

Evaluation of the MLRs. Changing the three parameters in the MLRs caused changes in anaphora resolution performance. As Table 6 shows, using anaphoric chains without anaphoric type identification helped improve the MLRs. Our experiments with the confidence factor parameter indicates the trade off between recall and precision. With 100% confidence factor, which means no pruning of the tree, the tree overfits the examples, and leads to spurious uses of features such as the number of sentences between an anaphor and an antecedent near the

---

[5] F-measure is calculated by:

$$F = \frac{(\beta^2 + 1.0) \times P \times R}{\beta^2 \times P + R}$$

where P is precision, R is recall, and β is the relative importance given to recall over precision. In this case, $\beta = 1.0$.

leaves of the generated tree. This causes the system to attempt more anaphor resolutions albeit with lower precision. Conversely, too much pruning can also yield poorer results.

MLR-5 illustrates that when anaphoric type identification is turned on the MLR's performance drops but still exceeds that of the MDR. MLR-6 shows the effect of not training on anaphoric chains. It results in poorer performance than the MLR-1, 2, 3, 4, and 5 configurations and the MDR.

One of the advantages of the MLRs is that due to the number of different anaphoric types present in the training data, they also learned classifiers for several additional anaphoric types beyond what the MDR could handle. While additional coding would have been required for each of these types in the MDR, the MLRs picked them up without additional work. The additional anaphoric types included DPRO, REFLEXIVE, and TIMEI (cf. Table 1). Another advantage is that, unlike the MDR, whose features are hand picked, the MLRs automatically select and use necessary features.

We suspect that the poorer performance of ZPRO-ORG and DNP-ORG may be due to the following deficiency of the current MLR algorithms: Because anaphora resolution is performed in a "batch mode" for the MLRs, there is currently no way to percolate the information on an anaphor-antecedent link found by a system after each resolution. For example, if a zero pronoun (Z-2) refers to another zero pronoun (Z-1), which in turn refers to an overt NP, knowing which is the antecedent of Z-1 may be important for Z-2 to resolve its antecedent correctly. However, such information is not available to the MLRs when resolving Z-2.

Evaluation of the MDR. One advantage of the MDR is that a tagged training corpus is not required for hand-coding the resolution algorithms. Of course, such a tagged corpus is necessary to evaluate system performance quantitatively and is also useful to consult with during algorithm construction.

However, the MLR results seem to indicate the limitation of the MDR in the way it uses orderer KS's. Currently, the MDR uses an ordered list of multiple orderer KS's for each anaphoric type (cf. Table 4), where the first *applicable* orderer KS in the list is used to pick the best antecedent when there is more than one possibility. Such selection ignores the fact that even anaphora of the same type may use different orderers (i.e. have different preferences), depending on the types of possible antecedents and on the context in which the particular anaphor was used in the text.

4.2   Training Data Size vs. Performance

Table 7 indicates that with even 50 training texts, the MLR achieves better performance than the MDR. Performance seems to reach a plateau at about 250 training examples with a F-measure of around 77.4.

5   Related Work

Anaphora resolution systems for English texts based on various machine learning algorithms, including a decision tree algorithm, are reported in Connolly *et al.* [6]. Our approach is different from theirs in that their decision tree identifies which of the two possible antecedents for a given anaphor is "better". The assumption seems to be that the closest antecedent is the "correct" antecedent. However, they note a problem that their decision tree is not guaranteed to return consistent classifications given that the "preference" relationship between two possible antecedents is not transitive.

Zero pronoun resolution for machine translation reported by Nakaiwa and Ikehara [9] used only semantic attributes of verbs in a restricted domain. The small test results (102 sentences from 29 articles) had high success rate of 93%. However, the input was only the first paragraphs of newspaper articles which contained relatively short sentences. Our anaphora resolution systems reported here have the advantages of domain-independence and full-text handling without the need for creating an extensive domain knowledge base.

Soderland and Lehnert's machine learning-based information extraction system [11] is used specifically for filling particular templates from text input. Although a part of its task is to merge multiple referents when they corefer (i.e. anaphora resolution), it is hard to evaluate how their anaphora resolution capability compares with ours, since it is not a separate module. The only evaluation result provided is their extraction result. Our anaphora resolution system is modular, and can be used for other NLP-based applications such as machine translation. Soderland and Lehnert's approach relies on a large set of filled templates used for training. Domain-specific features from those templates are employed for the learning. Consequently, the learned classifiers are very domain-specific and thus the approach relies on the availability of new filled template sets for porting to other domains. While some such template sets exist, such as those assembled for the Message Understanding Conferences, collecting such large amounts of training data for each new domain may be impractical.

6   Future Directions

The work reported in this paper is an encouraging step toward automating acquisition of anaphor resolution strategies. We will further analyze the types of errors which the systems make, and continue to improve system performance. In addition, we will explore the possibility of combining machine learning results with manual encoding of discourse knowledge. This can be accomplished by allowing the user to interact with the produced classifiers, tracing decisions back to particular examples and allowing users to edit features and to evaluate the efficacy of their changes.

We also are pursuing machine learning for developing other modular trainable NLP components. These include trainable extraction, name and phrase recognition, as well as for specific tasks like achieving improved Japanese segmentation. The modular approach offers the advantage of being able to perform more direct comparisons between different learning methods and learning and manually-coded modules through direct swapping in the overall NLP architecture. Also, rather than attempting to perform the overall NLP task through learning or a manually encoded set of techniques it allows the system to be composed of a hybrid of learned and manual techniques as necessary to achieve optimum performance.

References

1. Chinatsu Aone. Customizing and Evaluating a Multilingual Discourse Module. In *Proceedings of the 15th International Conference on Computational Linguistics (COLING)*, 1994.
2. Chinatsu Aone and Scott W. Bennett. Discourse Tagging Tool and Discourse-tagged Multilingual Corpora. In *Proceedings of International Workshop on Sharable Natural Language Resources (SNLR)*, 1994.
3. Chinatsu Aone, Sharon Flank, Paul Krause, and Doug McKee. SRA: Description of the SOLOMON System as Used for MUC-5. In *Proceedings of Fourth Message Understanding Conference (MUC-5)*, 1993.
4. Chinatsu Aone and Douglas McKee. Language-Independent Anaphora Resolution System for Understanding Multilingual Texts. In *Proceedings of 31st Annual Meeting of the ACL*, 1993.
5. Susan Brennan, Marilyn Friedman, and Carl Pollard. A Centering Approach to Pronouns. In *Proceedings of 25th Annual Meeting of the ACL*, 1987.
6. Dennis Connolly, John D. Burger, and David S. Day. A Machine Learning Approach to Anaphoric Reference. In *Proceedings of International Conference on New Methods in Language Processing (NEMLAP)*, 1994.
7. Jerry R. Hobbs. Pronoun Resolution. Technical Report 76-1, Department of Computer Science, City College, City University of New York, 1976.
8. Hans Kamp. A Theory of Truth and Semantic Representation. In J. Groenendijk et al., editors, *Formal Methods in the Study of Language*. Mathematical Centre, Amsterdam, 1981.
9. Hiromi Nakaiwa and Satoru Ikehara. Zero Pronoun Resolution in a Japanese to English Machine Translation Systemby using Verbal Semantic Attribute. In *Proceedings of the Fourth Conference on Applied Natural Language Processing*, 1992.
10. J. Ross Quinlan. *C4.5: Programs for Machine Learning*. Morgan Kaufmann Publishers, 1993.
11. Stephen Soderland and Wendy Lehnert. Corpus-driven Knowledge Acquisition for Discourse Analysis. In *Proceedings of AAAI*, 1994.
12. Marilyn A. Walker. Evaluating Discourse Processing Algorithms. In *Proceedings of 27th Annual Meeting of the ACL*, 1989.

Embedded Machine Learning Systems for Natural Language Processing: A General Framework

Claire Cardie

Department of Computer Science, Cornell University, Ithaca NY 14853, USA

Abstract. This paper presents Kenmore, a general framework for knowledge acquisition for natural language processing (NLP) systems. To ease the acquisition of knowledge in new domains, Kenmore exploits an online corpus using robust sentence analysis and embedded symbolic machine learning techniques while requiring only minimal human intervention. By treating all problems in ambiguity resolution as classification tasks, the framework uniformly addresses a range of subproblems in sentence analysis, each of which traditionally had required a separate computational mechanism. In a series of experiments, we demonstrate the successful use of Kenmore for learning solutions to several problems in lexical and structural ambiguity resolution. We argue that the learning and knowledge acquisition components should be *embedded* components of the NLP system in that (1) learning should take place within the larger natural language understanding system as it processes text, and (2) the learning components should be evaluated in the context of practical language-processing tasks.

1   Introduction

Although current natural language processing (NLP) systems cannot yet perform in-depth text understanding, they *can* read an arbitrary text and summarize its major events provided that those events fall within a particular domain of interest (e.g., stories about natural disasters or terrorist events) [11, 17]. Thus far, among the best-performing and most robust language-processing systems for this type of limited summarization task have been knowledge-based natural language systems — NLP systems that rely heavily on domain-specific, handcrafted knowledge to handle the myriad syntactic, semantic, and pragmatic ambiguities that pervade virtually all aspects of text understanding. Not surprisingly, however, generating this knowledge for new domains is time-consuming, difficult, and error-prone, and requires the expertise of computational linguists familiar with the underlying NLP system. In addition, handcoded lexicons and knowledge bases are generally too rigid to handle the novel language and range of phenomena that occur in real-world text. This *knowledge engineering bottleneck* is one of the biggest problems in designing and building natural language systems and promises only to become worse as natural language systems attempt to understand a wider variety of texts, to produce more complex summaries of the text, and to derive knowledge structures directly from text. On the other hand, much of human knowledge is described in written documents and, as mentioned above, NLP systems can now perform limited understanding of relatively complicated texts. Machine learning techniques for inductive learning have also become increasingly available and offer powerful mechanisms for simplifying the knowledge acquisition process.

As a result of these advances, we believe that it is feasible for NLP systems to begin to bootstrap their own knowledge bases using embedded machine learning components. This paper presents and evaluates a framework within which this bootstrapping process can occur and argues that learning for NLP systems should occur within the NLP system itself as it processes text — the natural language learning components should be directly incorporated into the larger natural language understanding system and should be evaluated in the context of practical language-processing tasks.

The paper is organized as follows. In the next section, we describe the problems encountered by an NLP system as it analyzes a text and describe how standard inductive machine learning algorithms can be used in a general way to help with the associated knowledge acquisition tasks. We then present Kenmore[1], a general framework for the machine learning of natural language and summarize the results of experiments that evaluate the architecture using real-world text in a real-world text-processing application. The experiments demonstrate that the framework offers a promising approach to knowledge acquisition for natural language processing systems. In particular, we show that symbolic inductive machine learning techniques can be used to learn solutions to significant problems in sentence analysis and that these learning mechanisms can be embedded in a working NLP system that has demonstrated success in processing real-world text. The paper concludes with a discussion of the advantages of embedded learning systems for natural language processing and the advances required to make existing machine learning algorithms better equipped for natural language learning tasks.

2 Ambiguity Resolution in Language Understanding

Many of the most difficult problems in natural language understanding can be characterized as problems of *ambiguity resolution*: the NLP system reaches a word or phrase for which it has multiple interpretations, and must decide which interpretation is appropriate in the current context. As an example, consider the following sentence:

BMW plans to build a plant for large machine tools in Eisenach.

First, the sentence contains a number of *part-of-speech ambiguities* that demand adequate resolution before the sentence can be understood. "Plans," for example, can be a noun or a verb; "to" can be an infinitive, a preposition, or an

---

[1] ken (ken), *vi.* 1 [Scot.] to know.

adverb; "plant" can be a noun or a verb. Even if a word's part of speech is known, the intended meaning of the word in a particular context often requires disambiguation. "Plant," for example, exhibits this sort of *word sense ambiguity*. At a minimum, the noun form of "plant" can be used in its "factory" sense or in its "living organism" sense. In addition to these cases of *lexical* ambiguity, disambiguation is required at the constituent, or *structural*, level as well. Consider the prepositional phrase "in Eisenach." Does it modify "tools," "plant," or "build"? All three options are syntactically legal and the NLP system must access semantic knowledge of some sort to make the correct attachment decision. Other structural ambiguities encountered in sentence analysis include: pronoun resolution, compound noun analysis, adjective scoping, and understanding conjunctions and appositives.

Typically, NLP systems treat each of these ambiguities separately along a number of dimensions. First, each type of ambiguity is viewed as a different problem. As a result, each is handled by a separate module of the system. There is often a part-of-speech tagger, for example, that is solely responsible for handling part-of-speech ambiguities. In addition, each ambiguity resolution module has limited access to the system's knowledge. The part-of-speech tagger, for example, may only have access to part-of-speech information for each word in the sentence. Finally, the NLP system may handle each ambiguity using a different computational mechanism (e.g., rule-based processing, context free parsers, regular expression recognizers, Markov models, constraint satisfaction, relaxation networks), each one of which may require access to diverse types of background knowledge. Until fairly recently, for example, a common approach to the problem of ambiguity resolution was to manually design separate sets of disambiguation heuristics to handle each type of ambiguity and to manually create the lexicons on which the heuristics rely.

We take a different approach in the Kenmore framework and, instead, use symbolic machine learning algorithms to support the acquisition and application of heuristics for semantic and syntactic ambiguity resolution at both the lexical and structural levels. The solution depends critically on the following assumption:

> **All problems of ambiguity resolution
> can be recast as classification tasks.**

By viewing disambiguation as a classification task, we can apply any of a number of inductive machine learning techniques to *learn* solutions to problems in ambiguity resolution rather than handcrafting a set of disambiguation rules: we expect the inductive learning algorithms to capture automatically those regularities in the use of language that permit the resolution of ambiguity in sentence analysis. As a result of this uniform view of ambiguity, lexical, structural, syntactic, and semantic ambiguities can be handled within a single architecture. As described below, solutions to these problems can be acquired in the Kenmore framework with minimal human intervention, thus avoiding the knowledge acquisition bottleneck in natural language system design. The next section describes the framework in more detail.

3   The Kenmore Framework

The Kenmore framework for the machine learning of natural language relies on three major components: a **corpus of texts**; a **robust sentence analyzer**, or parser; and an **inductive learning module**. There are two phases to the framework: (1) a partially automated training phase, or **acquisition phase**, in which the solution to a particular problem in sentence analysis is learned, and (2) an **application phase**, in which the learned solution can be applied in novel situations.

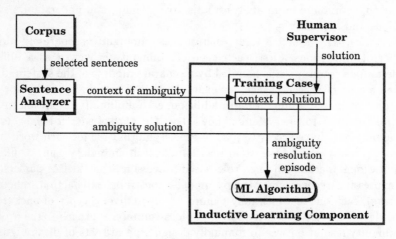

Fig. 1. Kenmore training/acquisition phase. Note that the human supervisor can be replaced by an annotated corpus.

More specifically, the goal of Kenmore's training phase (Fig. 1) is to create a set of ambiguity resolution episodes to be used as training examples for the inductive machine learning (ML) subsystem. To do this, a small set of sentences is first selected randomly from the corpus. Next, the sentence analyzer processes the training sentences and, with a human supervisor or annotated corpus, creates a training case every time an ambiguity occurs. To learn a set of heuristics to handle prepositional phrase attachment, for example, the parser would create a case whenever it recognizes a prepositional phrase. As shown in Fig. 1, each case has two parts. The *context* portion of the case encodes the context in which the ambiguity was encountered — this is an attribute-value pair representation of the state of the parser at the point of the ambiguity. The context part of the case is supplied automatically by the sentence analyzer in both the training and application phases. The *solution* portion of the case describes how the ambiguity was resolved in the current example — it encodes one or more pieces of "class" information. In the training phase, a person supplies this part of the case using a menu-driven interface. Alternatively, the necessary supervisory information can be extracted automatically from an appropriately annotated corpus. For part-of-speech disambiguation, for example, the human supervisor chooses the part of speech that is appropriate for the current word in the current context and this information is encoded as the class value for the training case. Together, the context and solution portions of the case represent a single ambiguity resolution episode. (See [8] for a general discussion of how to convert both lexical and structural ambiguity problems into classification tasks.)

To give a more concrete idea of what training cases look like, we show a portion of a sample training case for part-of-speech and word-sense disambiguation in Fig. 2. In this example, Kenmore was instantiated with the CIRCUS conceptual sentence analyzer [15] as its parser and training sentences were taken from the TIPSTER business joint ventures (JV) corpus.[2] The training case of Fig. 2 contains 15 context features and two solution features and was generated in response to the word "parts" in the sentence:

Daihatsu...has so far been in alliance with Astra Motor in production of auto **parts** *and engines...*

Once a training case is created, it is made available to the machine learning component, which uses the case to update the concept description it derives for the current ambiguity task. In addition, the solution to the ambiguity is forwarded to the parser so that it can resolve the current ambiguity, update its state, and continue processing the training sentence. At the end of the training phase, Kenmore will have created one training case for every instance of the ambiguity that appears in the training sentences.

After training, Kenmore resolves ambiguities in novel sentences from the corpus *without human intervention* (Fig. 3). Whenever the sentence analyzer encounters an ambiguity, it creates a problem case, automatically filling in its context portion based on the state of the natural language system at the point of the ambiguity. The structure of a problem case is identical to that of a training case except that the "solution" is missing. To resolve the current ambiguity, Kenmore presents the problem case to the machine learning system, which uses the concept description derived during training to determine the solution (i.e., class) of the current ambiguity. This information is then used directly by the parser to resolve the ambiguity.

4 Evaluation of the Approach within Practical Text-Processing Tasks

We evaluated Kenmore using corpora from two real-world domains in the context of a practical text summarization task: *information extraction*. Very generally, NLP systems for information extraction process a collection of texts, search for all information related to a predefined domain of interest, and then produce for

---

[2] The JV corpus contains over 1000 documents that describe world-wide activity in the area of joint ventures or "tie-ups" between businesses [21]. Unless otherwise noted, all examples are derived from sentences in this corpus.

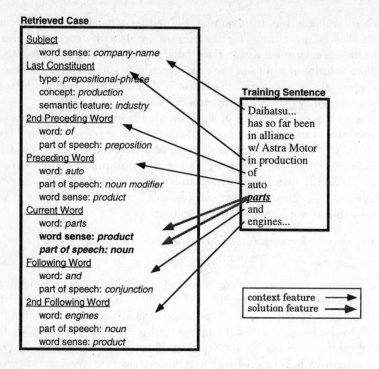

Fig. 2. Training case for "parts": part-of-speech and word-sense disambiguation. (Arrows indicate which parts of the sentence are responsible for which attribute-value pairs.)

each text a summary of this domain-relevant information in a rigid template format. In the experiments below, we tested the ability of the embedded machine learning components to handle a number of difficult problems in sentence analysis within an information extraction task: part-of-speech tagging, word-sense tagging, and relative pronoun disambiguation. Note, however, that Kenmore has been evaluated for additional language learning tasks along a number of dimensions [8] — this section summarizes just a subset of those experiments.

In all experiments, training and test sentences were drawn from the MUC/-TIPSTER corpora [20, 21] and Kenmore was instantiated with the CIRCUS parser. A variety of machine learning algorithms have been used as Kenmore's inductive learning component: a decision tree system (C4.5 [23]), a simple case-based learning algorithm (k-nearest neighbors), a conceptual clustering system (COBWEB [14]), and a hybrid inductive learning system that combines a nearest-neighbor algorithm with a decision tree system for feature selection [7]. In experiments to date, the hybrid algorithm has achieved the highest accuracies and we focus on these results below. Finally, all experiments use a 10-fold cross validation evaluation scheme. A more detailed description of the experiments and an analysis of the results can be found in [8].

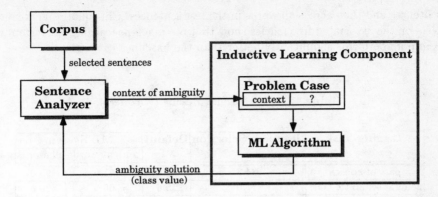

Fig. 3. Kenmore application phase.

4.1 Lexical Ambiguity

We tested Kenmore's ability to handle simultaneously two lexical ambiguity tasks: (1) part-of-speech ambiguity and (2) word sense ambiguity. There were 18 possible parts of speech including: noun, noun modifier, auxiliary, adverb, preposition, verb particle. Word senses were represented in terms of a two-level semantic feature hierarchy that included 14 general semantic classes (e.g., human, facility, joint venture entity) and 42 specific semantic classes (e.g., company name, government, factory). We assume the existence of only a small dictionary of 129 function words (e.g., prepositions, auxiliaries, determiners) — all other words are assumed to be *completely unknown* to the system in that it has no part-of-speech or semantic class information available for them. We then train the machine learning subsystem to predict the part of speech and semantic classes for all non-function words as they appear in an input text.[3] For this task, the machine learning system must deal with: (1) the consequences of making tagging errors on preceding input (as these become part of the "context" that is encoded in a problem/test case), and (2) the fact that little or no information is known about subsequent words since the parser has not yet encountered them in its left-to-right traversal of the sentence. In addition, the system currently assigns all three tags to a word simultaneously: it does not assume, for example, that the part of speech of the word is known when it assigns a semantic class value, and vice versa.

The accuracy of the machine learning subsystem is shown in Table 1 and compared to two baselines. The first baseline (labeled Random Selection) indicates the expected accuracy of a system that randomly guesses a legal tag based on the distribution of values across the training set. The second baseline (labeled Default) shows the performance of a system that always chooses the most frequent value across the training set as a default. The final two columns indicate the performance of the ML system first for the content words in the test

---

[3] Highly ambiguous function words are also excluded from the function word lexicon and instead are disambiguated by the machine learning component.

sentences and then across all words in the test sentences. Chi-square significance tests on the associated frequencies show that the machine learning subsystem in Kenmore performs significantly better than the baselines ($p = .01$).

Table 1. Lexical Tagging Results (% correct).

Tagging Task	Random Selection	Default	ML System	
			content words	all words
part of speech	34.3	81.5	91.0	95.0
general semantic class	17.0	25.6	65.3	80.6
specific semantic class	37.3	58.1	74.0	85.5

In practice, Kenmore performs quite well for the tested lexical ambiguity tasks. When trained on a larger set of examples (see Table 2), the learned heuristics for semantic class tagging performed well enough to be used in the UMass/Hughes CIRCUS system that participated in the the MUC-5 performance evaluation of information extraction systems [16]. In addition, the part-of-speech tagging heuristics match the accuracy of those obtained using the trigram-based tagger of the UMass/Hughes MUC-5 system and are comparable to those achievable using probabilistic taggers which generally reach accuracies in the 95–96% range [9].

In an attempt to determine the impact of the semantic feature tagging component on the overall performance of the information extraction system, we ran two variations of the UMass/Hughes MUC-5 system on test sets from the final MUC-5 performance evaluation.[4] In the first run, the system used the machine learning component to assign semantic features to all content words in the test texts. In the second run, content words were assigned a semantic type based instead on a set of handcrafted default heuristics designed to handle frequently occurring, hopefully clearcut cases (e.g., "Co." almost always indicates the name of a company). Content words that fell outside the domain of the heuristics were given a default value of *nil* as their general and specific semantic class. When compared to the learned heuristics, the handcoded default heuristics produced a 1% increase in precision and a 41% decrease in recall for the information extraction task as measured on the MUC-5 test sets. The significant drop in recall can be explained by the fact that the default heuristics were not designed to handle novel or ambiguous situations (it is too time-consuming and difficult to design such heuristics), but these "special" cases occur rather frequently in the texts. It should be emphasized that this experiment was meant only to give an indication of the extent to which the learned heuristics contributed to the information extraction system. Additional testing would be required to determine more specifically the role played by the machine learning component.

---

[4] Thanks to Jonathan Peterson for running these experiments.

Table 2. Semantic feature tagging using Kenmore with a larger case base (% correct).

Tagging Task	Original Results (2056 cases)	Larger Case Base (3060 cases)
general semantic class	80.6	85.7
specific semantic class	85.5	86.3

4.2 Structural Ambiguity

We have also used the embedded machine learning component to handle a single structural ambiguity task: relative pronoun disambiguation. In this task, the machine learning component acquires heuristics for locating the antecedents of relative pronouns [5, 6]. In the sentence, "I saw Mary and the boy *who* won the contest," for example, the NLP system disambiguates the relative pronoun, "who," by deciding that it refers to "the boy." Here we used texts that describe Latin American terrorist events and concentrated on locating the antecedent of "who." In all experiments, the machine learning system was also responsible for (1) deciding whether or not "who" was actually being used as a relative pronoun, and (2) recognizing antecedents that consisted of conjunctions and appositives. The experiments drew training and test cases from a base set of cases that contained all occurrences of "who" from three sets of 50 texts from the MUC terrorism corpus (241 instances). The results are summarized in Table 3. They indicate that the learned heuristics: (1) perform significantly better than a default strategy that simply chooses the single most recent phrase as the antecedent, and (2) perform as well as a set of hand-coded heuristics developed for use with UMass/MUC-3 system in the terrorism domain.

Table 3. Relative Pronoun Disambiguation Results (% correct).

ML System	Default Strategy	Hand-Coded Heuristics
84.2	74.3	80.5

4.3 Discussion of Results

Results from the experiments above indicate that symbolic inductive machine learning systems can learn solutions to a number of difficult problems in sentence analysis within the proposed Kenmore framework. There are a number of advantages of this approach over traditional methods for knowledge acquisition for natural language systems:

- The concept descriptions derived by the machine learning component implicitly define a set of disambiguation heuristics **as well as** the system lexicon (in the case of lexical ambiguities).
- The approach obviates the need for generating and maintaining explicit, handcrafted lexicons and the associated disambiguation heuristics.
- No hand-coded heuristics are required to drive the acquisition process.
- The machine learning approach to knowledge acquisition provides a flexible control structure for combining multiple sources of knowledge.

Connectionist approaches to classification could also be used as Kenmore's inductive learning component. In fact, a number of existing systems successfully combine traditional parsing techniques and distributed connectionist modules for sentence analysis (e.g., [26, 27, 10]). Symbolic machine learning systems, however, provide at least two advantages. First, there are many incremental symbolic machine learning algorithms (e.g., ID5[24], instance-based learning methods[1]) that would allow the training phase to become progressively easier for the human supervisor: Kenmore can access the existing concept description to suggest solutions to each ambiguity and rely on the supervisor only to override incorrect predictions. This type of incremental learning is generally not feasible in connectionist systems. Second, symbolic learning algorithms offer better explanations of their decisions and allow for easy incorporation of known processing biases and prior knowledge.

In the following section, we summarize the advantages of using *embedded* machine learning components in an NLP system.

5   Advantages of Embedded Machine Learning Mechanisms for NLP Systems

Corpus-based language acquisition methods recently have been the focus of much attention in the natural language processing community [4, 9, 12, 13, 28]. With very few exceptions, however, these systems treat language learning and knowledge acquisition in isolation from the actual natural language system that will use the acquired knowledge and in isolation from any specific natural language understanding task. In Kenmore, however, the learning mechanisms are directly incorporated into the larger NLP system and learning takes place within this system as it processes text. We believe that natural language processing systems can benefit in a number of ways from the use of such embedded machine learning components:

First, parsing knowledge is learned in a form directly usable by the sentence analyzer. Second, because the learning system has access to structural knowledge (from the parser) and class-level knowledge (e.g., syntactic and semantic class information for lexical items) in addition to individual words, less training data may be required when compared with statistical approaches to ambiguity resolution based on lexical cooccurrence data. Hidden Markov Models (HMM) trained using the Viterbi algorithm [25] on the same data as the Kenmore experiments above (Fig. 1, for example, achieved accuracies of 89.0% correct (bigram model) and 73.8% versus Kenmore's 95.0% for the part-of-speech tagging task.

Finally, evaluation of the language learning components can be guided by their performance within the larger natural language processing task. Ultimately, it is the performance of the NLP system in the larger task that matters and some types of errors from the machine learning component undoubtedly will be more grievous than others with respect to this task.[5] In information extraction, for example, part-of-speech tagging errors that mistake non-verbs for verbs and vice versa are the most grievous. In the lexical tagging experiments of Fig. 1, 55% of the errors were of this variety. Similarly, accurate prediction of domain-specific semantic features is more important than that of domain-independent semantic features. This is, in fact, the situation in Kenmore: it achieves 64.2% correct on domain-dependent semantic features in comparison to 71.2% correct for domain-dependent general semantic features. By monitoring the overall performance of the NLP system, we can focus on reducing "important" errors in the machine learning component and can end the training phase as soon as performance on the larger NLP task has reached a plateau.

5.1 The Need for New Learning Algorithms

Thus far, Kenmore has been used only for a relatively small number of natural language learning tasks. Still, however, we have found that the characteristics of the resulting datasets exhibit a number of complications for the embedded learning algorithms:

- *Noisy training (and test) cases.* Some of the noise is in the form of inconsistent and/or incorrect class information provided by the human supervisor or annotated corpus and some of the noise is in the form of incorrect feature values provided by the sentence analyzer. Because the concepts being learned are open-textured concepts that lack distinct boundaries, some portion of the noise is unavoidable.
- *Missing features in training and test cases.*
- *Irrelevant features in the training and test cases.* In the Kenmore framework, at least as described above, the parser always provides the "context" in terms of the same set of features. Intuitively, however, different subsets of features might be important for each ambiguity task.
- *Cases may not include all features necessary for the learning task to succeed.* There are many opportunities to make use of constructive induction algorithms that can add features to a case representation as needed.
- *Concepts to be learned have many classes.* The tasks tackled in the above experiments have a minimum of ten class values.

---

[5] It is also the case that some types of errors will be more or less important with respect to the type of *parser* employed.

- *Some features are better described as relations rather than attribute-value pairs.* Using relational learning systems (e.g., FOIL [22]) will be important here.

While most standard machine learning algorithms handle a subset of the listed problems, it proved difficult to find a single system that simultaneously addressed all of them for the NL datasets. In addition, a number of meta-level learning issues must be addressed before machine learning techniques can be employed as general-purpose learning components in a natural language understanding system: when should we stop learning? which learning algorithms are best for each language learning task? which sentences from the corpus will make the best training examples? should the current case representation evolve over time? how can information that is acquired in one learning task be transferred to another?

6 Conclusions

In summary, we have presented a general framework for the machine learning of natural language that relies on embedded, symbolic, inductive learning components. We have shown that the architecture can be use to acquire solutions to a number of difficult problems in sentence analysis within the context of a practical text-processing task. In related work, symbolic machine learning algorithms, and case-based algorithms in particular, have also been found to work well for a number of low-level language acquisition tasks (e.g., stress acquisition [13] and grapheme-to-phoneme conversion [3]) and discourse-level tasks (e.g., anaphora resolution [2, 19] and segmentation [18]). This work provides additional evidence for the viability of a machine learning approach to natural language learning and knowledge acquisition for natural language processing systems. Finally, we have argued that the language learning components should be directly incorporated into the larger natural language understanding system and should be evaluated in the context of practical language-processing tasks.

References

1. D. Aha, D. Kibler, and M. Albert. Instance-Based Learning Algorithms. *Machine Learning*, 6(1):37–66, 1991.
2. Chinatsu Aone and William Bennett. Evaluating Automated and Manual Acquisition of Anaphora Resolution Strategies. In *Proceedings of the 33rd Annual Meeting of the ACL*, pages 122–129. Association for Computational Linguistics, 1995.
3. A. van den Bosch and W. Daelemans. Data-oriented methods for grapheme-to-phoneme conversion. In *Proceedings of European Chapter of ACL*, pages 45–53, Utrecht, 1993. Also available as ITK Research Report 42.
4. E. Brill. Some Advances in Transformation-Based Part of Speech Tagging. In *Proceedings of the Twelfth National Conference on Artificial Intelligence*, pages 722–727. AAAI Press / MIT Press, 1994.

5. C. Cardie. Corpus-Based Acquisition of Relative Pronoun Disambiguation Heuristics. In *Proceedings of the 30th Annual Meeting of the ACL*, pages 216–223, University of Delaware, Newark, DE, 1992. Association for Computational Linguistics.

6. C. Cardie. Learning to Disambiguate Relative Pronouns. In *Proceedings of the Tenth National Conference on Artificial Intelligence*, pages 38–43, San Jose, CA, 1992. AAAI Press / MIT Press.

7. C. Cardie. Using Decision Trees to Improve Case-Based Learning. In P. Utgoff, editor, *Proceedings of the Tenth International Conference on Machine Learning*, pages 25–32, University of Massachusetts, Amherst, MA, 1993. Morgan Kaufmann.

8. C. Cardie. *Domain-Specific Knowledge Acquisition for Conceptual Sentence Analysis*. PhD thesis, University of Massachusetts, Amherst, MA, 1994. Available as University of Massachusetts, CMPSCI Technical Report 94–74.

9. E. Charniak. Equations for Part-of-Speech Tagging. In *Proceedings of the Eleventh National Conference on Artificial Intelligence*, pages 784–789, Washington, DC, 1993. AAAI Press / MIT Press.

10. T. Chen, V. Soo, and A. Lin. Learning to Parse with Recurrent Neural Networks. In *Proceedings of European Conference on Machine Learning Workshop on Machine Learning and Text Analysis*, pages 63–68, 1993.

11. N. Chinchor, L. Hirschman, and D. Lewis. Evaluating Message Understanding Systems: An Analysis of the Third Message Undestanding Conference (MUC-3). *Computational Linguistics*, 19(3):409–449, 1993.

12. K. Church. A Stochastic Parts Program and Noun Phrase Parser for Unrestricted Text. In *Proceedings of the Second Conference on Applied Natural Language Processing*, pages 136–143. Association for Computational Linguistics, 1988.

13. W. Daelemans, G. Durieux, and S. Gillis. The Acquisition of Stress: A Data-Oriented Approach. *Computational Linguistics*, 20(3):421–451, 1994.

14. D. Fisher. Knowledge Acquisition Via Incremental Conceptual Clustering. *Machine Learning*, 2:139–172, 1987.

15. W. Lehnert. Symbolic/Subsymbolic Sentence Analysis: Exploiting the Best of Two Worlds. In J. Barnden and J. Pollack, editors, *Advances in Connectionist and Neural Computation Theory*, pages 135–164. Ablex Publishers, Norwood, NJ, 1990.

16. W. Lehnert, J. McCarthy, S. Soderland, E. Riloff, C. Cardie, J. Peterson, F. Feng, C. Dolan, and S. Goldman. University of Massachusetts/Hughes: Description of the CIRCUS System as Used in MUC-5. In *Proceedings of the Fifth Message Understanding Conference (MUC-5)*, pages 277–291, San Mateo, CA, 1993. Morgan Kaufmann.

17. W. Lehnert and B. Sundheim. A performance evaluation of text analysis technologies. *Artificial Intelligence Magazine*, 12(3):81–94, 1991.

18. Diane J. Litman and Rebecca J. Passonneau. Combining Multiple Knowledge Sources for Discourse Segmentation. In *Proceedings of the 33rd Annual Meeting of the ACL*, pages 108–115. Association for Computational Linguistics, 1995.

19. Joseph F. McCarthy and Wendy G. Lehnert. Using Decision Trees for Coreference Resolution. In C. Mellish, editor, *Proceedings of the Fourteenth International Conference on Artificial Intelligence*, pages 1050–1055, 1995.

20. *Proceedings of the Third Message Understanding Conference (MUC-3)*. Morgan Kaufmann, San Mateo, CA, 1991.

21. *Proceedings of the Fifth Message Understanding Conference (MUC-5)*. Morgan Kaufmann, San Mateo, CA, 1994.

22. J. R. Quinlan. Learning Logical Definitions from Relations. *Machine Learning*, 5:239–266, 1990.

23. J. R. Quinlan. *C4.5: Programs for Machine Learning.* Morgan Kaufmann, San Mateo, CA, 1992.

24. P. Utgoff. An Improved Algorithm for Incremental Induction of Decision Trees. In W. Cohen and H. Hirsh, editors, *Proceedings of the Eleventh International Conference on Machine Learning*, pages 318–325, Rutgers University, New Brunswick, NJ, 1994. Morgan Kaufmann.

25. A. J. Viterbi. Error bounds for convolutional codes and an asymptotically optimal decoding algorithm. *IEEE Transactions on Information Theory*, 13:260–269, 1967.

26. S. Wermter. Combining Symbolic and Connectionist Techniques for Coordination in Natural Language. In *Proceedings of the 14th German Workshop on Artificial Intelligence*, Eringerfeld, Germany, 1990.

27. S. Wermter and W. Lehnert. A hybrid symbolic/connectionist model for nounphrase understanding. *Connection Science*, 1(3), 1989.

28. David Yarowsky. Decision Lists for Lexical Ambiguity Resolution: Application to Accent Restoration in Spanish and French. In *Proceedings of the 32th Annual Meeting of the ACL*, 1994.

Acquiring and updating hierarchical knowledge for machine translation based on a clustering technique

Takefumi Yamazaki[1] and Michael J. Pazzani[2] and Christopher Merz[2]

[1] NTT Communication Science Laboratories
1-2356 Take, Yokosuka-Shi
Kanagawa-Ken, Japan 238-03
[2] Department of Information and Computer Science,
University of California, Irvine, CA, USA 92717

Abstract. This paper addresses the problem of constructing a semantic hierarchy for a machine translation system. We propose two methods of constructing a hierarchy: acquiring a hierarchy from scratch and updating a hierarchy. When acquiring a hierarchy from scratch, translation rules are learned by an inductive learning algorithm in the first step. A new hierarchy is then generated by applying a clustering method to internal disjunctions of the learned rules and new rules are learned under the bias of this hierarchy. When updating an existing manually-constructed hierarchy, we take advantage of its node structure. We report experimental results showing that the semantic hierarchies generated by our method yield learned translation rules with higher average accuracy.

1 Introduction

Hierarchical knowledge is an important part of many natural language processing tasks such as machine translation, text retrieval, and text summary. This kind of knowledge is essential to capture general linguistic rules that apply in a variety of contexts. For example, the WordNet system [12] contains a lexical inheritance system of approximately 33,400 terms. Similarly, ALT-J/E [8], which is an experimental Japanese-English translation system developed at Nippon Telegraph and Telephone Corporation (NTT), uses a semantic hierarchy to aid in the process of translating texts. The research reported in this paper centers on the important task of automatically acquiring this hierarchical knowledge.

ALT-J/E contains a large collection of translation rules (currently over 10,000) and a large semantic hierarchy (about 3,000 nodes). Each of the translation rules associates one Japanese sentence pattern with an appropriate English pattern. Each rule is expressed in terms of "semantic categories" which are nodes of the semantic hierarchy. To translate a Japanese sentence into English, ALT-J/E looks for the rule whose Japanese pattern matches the sentence best, and then uses the English pattern of that rule for translation.

Creating new translation rules has proven to be extremely difficult and time-consuming because this task requires considering the huge space of possible combinations of nodes in the hierarchy. Previous research investigated the application of inductive learning techniques for the acquisition of translation rules [2, 3]. Experimental results showed that this method was promising in facilitating the construction of rules. However, this method used the semantic hierarchy created by a human expert as it was and did not consider learning this hierarchy. Learning the semantic hierarchy is essential and crucial in the machine translation task because the quality of learned translation rules is determined by the quality of this hierarchy and it is very difficult for a person to create and maintain a useful hierarchy.

In this paper, we propose two methods of learning a semantic hierarchy: learning a hierarchy from scratch and updating an existing hierarchy. In learning a hierarchy from scratch, translation rules are learned without using a hierarchy with an inductive learning tool called FOCL [13] in the first step. Statistical clustering is then used to generate a hierarchy from the learned rules. In updating an existing hierarchy, its node structures are utilized to guide the construction of the new hierarchy. This method uses some of the procedures used in the method of learning a hierarchy from scratch.

In the remainder of this paper, we give a brief description of the machine translation task. We then show how to represent translation rules in FOCL and how to extend FOCL to handle hierarchical knowledge efficiently. We propose a method for creating a semantic hierarchy from scratch. Next we extend the method for creating a semantic hierarchy to update an existing incomplete hierarchy. Finally, we show experimental results and related works.

2 Background

We illustrate the machine translation task by examining an experimental Japanese-English translation system, ALT-J/E [8, 9] as an example. In this work, we are concerned with the following ALT-J/E components: the Semantic Hierarchy, Noun Dictionary, and the Translation Rules.

As shown in Figure 1, the **Semantic Hierarchy** is a sort of concept thesaurus represented as a tree structure in which each node is called a *semantic category*, or a *category* for simplicity. Edges in this structure represent "is-a" relations among the categories. The current version of ALT-J/E's Semantic Hierarchy is 12 levels deep and has 2715 nodes, which consist of 790 intermediate nodes and 1925 leaf nodes.

The **Noun Dictionary** maps each Japanese noun to its appropriate semantic category in the hierarchy. For example, the Noun Dictionary states that the noun "maguro", which means "tuna" in English, is an instance of the category "fish" and also an instance of the category "food".

The **Translation Rules** in ALT-J/E associate Japanese patterns with English patterns. Currently, ALT-J/E holds roughly 10,000 of these rules. As Figure 2 shows, each translation rule has a Japanese pattern as its left-hand side and an English pattern as its right-hand side. For example, the first rule in this figure basically says that if the Japanese verb in a sentence is "TSUKAU", the

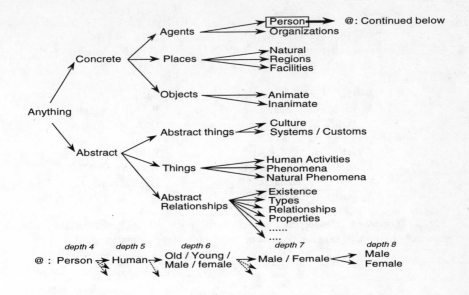

Fig. 1. The upper levels of the Semantic Hierarchy in ALT-J/E

category of its subject is "Agents", and the category of its object is "Time" or "Money", then the following English pattern is to be used:

Subject "spend" Object.

Note that in this case the Japanese verb "TSUKAU" is translated into the English verb "spend". This same Japanese verb can also be translated into the English verbs "employ" or "use", depending on the context. These cases are handled by the two other rules given in Figure 2.

3 Learning Translation Rules with FOCL

3.1 The Learning Task

In this section we describe the task of learning translation rules[3] from examples. Each learning session concentrates on one Japanese verb, where it is desired to construct rules for mapping the verb in a given context to the appropriate English verb.

---

[3] To be strict, the present work is to learn what we call "verb selection rules". A verb selection rule consists of the left-hand side, along with the English verb of the right-hand side of a translation rule. In other words, the only difference between a translation rule and a verb selection rule is that the latter has only an English verb rather than a full English pattern as its right-hand side.

IF		THEN	
J-Verb	= "TSUKAU"	Subj	$= N_1$
N_1 (Subj)	$\equiv$ "Agents"	E-Verb	="spend"
N_2 (Obj)	$\equiv$ "Time" or "Money"	Obj	$= N_2$
IF		THEN	
J-Verb	= "TSUKAU"	Subj	$= N_1$
N_1 (Subj)	$\equiv$ "Agents"	E-Verb	="employ"
N_2 (Obj)	$\equiv$ "People"	Obj	$= N_2$
IF		THEN	
J-Verb	= "TSUKAU"	Subj	$= N_1$
N_1 (Subj)	$\equiv$ "Agents" or	E-Verb	="use"
	"Artificial Objects"	Obj	$= N_2$
N_2 (Obj)	$\equiv$ "Anything"		

Fig. 2. Translation rules for the Japanese verb "TSUKAU". These rules are composed manually by human experts. A symbol " $\equiv$ " indicates "an instance of".

As an example, consider the Japanese verb "Tsukau" in the sentence "Shachou ga kane wo Tsukau", which means "The president spends money". The following pair is given after parsing (which is carried out by ALT-J/E's parser):

$$\langle\,[\text{ J-Verb} = \text{Tsukau}\,,\ \text{Subject} = \text{Shachou},$$
$$\text{Object} = \text{Kane}\,],\ \text{E-Verb} = \text{spend}\,\rangle.$$

It is usually the case that a given Japanese noun has more than one possible meaning. By looking in the Semantic Dictionary of ALT-J/E, the possible semantic categories for "Shachou" are "Manager" and "Chief", and those for "Kane" are "Asset", "Metal", and "Medal". Thus, this example is finally given to the learning algorithm in the following form to create rules for translating "tsukau:"

$$\langle\quad[\text{ Subject} \equiv \{\text{ Manager, Chief }\},$$
$$\text{Object} \equiv \{\text{ Asset, Metal, Medal }\}]\,,$$
$$\text{E-Verb} = \text{spend}\quad),$$

where $N \equiv S$ indicates that sentence component N is an instance of each category $s \in S$. As you can see in the example shown above, this example includes ambiguity in the sense that each of the attributes **Subject** and **Object** is assigned a set of possible values rather than a single value. The general format of the training examples is as follows:

$$\langle[\ N_1 \equiv \{a_1, a_2, \cdots\},$$
$$N_2 \equiv \{b_1, b_2, \cdots\}, \cdots$$
$$N_n \equiv \{c_1, c_2, \cdots\}],\ E\text{-}Verb\rangle$$

where each N_i represents a component of the sentence (subject, object, etc.), and a_i, b_i, and c_i are semantic categories.

The job of the learning algorithm is to find the rules such as those in Figure 2.

3.2 An extension to FOCL

Representation in FOCL We use an inductive learning tool, FOCL [13] to learn translation rules from examples. FOCL inductively learns classification rules by constructing a set of Horn Clauses in terms of a set of background predicates (such as isa). Here we concentrate on describing FOCL's inductive learning component based on FOIL [14]. It creates clauses in a set-covering manner until each positive example is covered by at least one clause. A clause is learned using hill-climbing search by adding the literal yielding the maximum information gain to the clause body.

In this paper, when learning from potentially ambiguous data, we use a predicate "one-isa(TermSet, C)" to represent the fact that one of the terms in TermSet is an instance of category C, such as one-isa({asset, metal, medal}, money). This predicate is very useful when dealing with real world data in which words may have more than one possible meaning. Moreover, we have extended the semantics of the "one-isa" predicate so that the second argument may be a set of categories. In this case, one-isa(TermSet, CategorySet) is true if one term in TermSet is an instance of one of the categories in CategorySet. This extension enables the "one-isa" predicate to allow a form of internal disjunction. For example,

tsukau(Subject, Object, Everb) :-
one-isa(Subject, {agents}),
one-isa(Object, {time, money}), Everb = spend.

indicates that "tsukau" is translated to "spend" when one sense of the subject is a kind of "agents" and one sense of the object is "time" or "money."

An efficient way of handling hierarchical knowledge Hierarchical knowledge is efficiently handled as background knowledge by exploiting the hierarchical relationships among the categories. We extended FOCL to compute the information-gain of literals of the form "one-isa(Role, Categories)" efficiently. This was accomplished by associating counters with each node in the hierarchy where each node describes the number of positive and negative training examples. The training data is traversed once for each variable (e.g., Subject and Object), to set counter values on the leaves of the hierarchy for each possible sense, and these values are propagated up the hierarchy. Care must be taken to insure that a parent node is incremented only once if a word has two senses corresponding to different children of the node. The information gain of only those nodes that satisfy at least one positive example is computed by using the counts stored at that node.

Creation of an internal disjunction based on hill-climbing FOCL was modified to create the internal disjunctions in a greedy, set covering manner. First, the literal with the maximum information gain of the form one-isa(V, c_1) is found. Next, all literals of the form one-isa(V, $\{c_1, c_i\}$) are checked where c_i satisfies at least one positive example, and neither one-isa(c_1, c_i) nor one-isa(c_i, c_1) is true. If the information gain of one of these literals is not greater than that of one-isa(V, c_1), then one-isa(V, c_1) is returned as the literal with the maximum gain. Otherwise, the process of adding constants to the internal disjunction continues until adding another constant to the set does not increase the information gain. Using literals of the form one-isa(V, $\{c_1, ..., c_n\}$) is useful for representing disjunction of nodes in the existing hierarchy (e.g., one-isa(Object, {fish, seafood})). It is also useful when there is no hierarchy. In this case, one-isa represents disjunctions of specific constants (e.g., one-isa(Object, {salmon, swordfish, lobster, shrimp})).

4 Acquiring a Semantic Hierarchy from scratch

As mentioned above, a semantic hierarchy plays an important role from the view of offering the more general terms needed for generating an appropriate level of generalization for translation rules. It is desirable that a semantic hierarchy has general nodes that include a proper group of leaf nodes as the most specific categories. Thus we regard the task of learning a semantic hierarchy as generating the appropriate nodes when leaf nodes are given.

We describe how to create a semantic hierarchy by using the translation rules learned by FOCL. After learning rules without a hierarchy by FOCL, the frequency with which two terms occur together in an internal disjunction of these rules (i.e., in a literal of the form one-isa(V, $\{c_1, ..., c_n\}$)) is used as a measure of the similarity between the terms. In particular, the mutual information gain ratio is used as follows. Let $p(c_i)$ be the probability that the term c_i appears in an internal disjunction of all learned translation rules. This is estimated by dividing the number of times that c_i appears in an internal disjunction by the total number of internal disjunctions. The probability that both c_i and c_j appear in an internal disjunction ($p(c_i \& c_j)$) is estimated in the same manner. The mutual information gain measure $log(p(c_i \& c_j)/p(c_i)p(c_j))$ is used as the measure of the similarity between terms c_i and c_j.

A triangular matrix is created to store the value of the mutual information for all pairs.[4] A standard statistical clustering algorithm, the average-linkage method [1] is then used to create a hierarchy. This method is normally used to create binary hierarchies. We modified the method slightly to create hierarchies in which a node may have any number of children, provided all pairs of the children have the exact same value of the mutual information gain measure. The clustering algorithm is described in Table 1.

The generated semantic hierarchy works well to improve the accuracy of the learned rules in the following case:

---

[4] In the statistical literature, such a matrix is called a dissimilarity matrix, since a value of 0 indicates that two terms are unrelated, and large values indicate a strong relationship between the two terms. A similarity matrix is one in which 0 indicates that the two items are identical and larger values indicate a difference between the two items. A similarity matrix might be formed by taking the Euclidean distance between two feature vectors.

1. Search the dissimilarity matrix to find the pair of categories that has maximum dissimilarity. Find all other categories that have the same maximum value in that column.
2. Combine the categories found in Step 1 to create a new node in the hierarchy.
3. The similarity between this node and the remaining categories is calculated by computing the average of the similarity between each of the categories used to form the new node and all others.
4. Update the matrix by adding the new node, deleting the categories used for creating the node, and assigning the similarity values computed by the previous step, to the new node.
5. If the matrix is empty, stop. Otherwise, go to step 1.

Table 1. The average-linkage clustering method

Suppose that the categories C1, C2, and C3 appear together in several rules learned without a hierarchy and are used to generate a hierarchy. In this case, this proposed method produces new node H1, which consists of C1, C2, and C3.

Next compare the rules learned by using this hierarchy with those learned without it. Suppose that only the categories C1 and C2 appear in the training examples. The form of rules learned without the hierarchy might be C1 or C2, while the form learned with the hierarchy might include generalized node H1. Therefore, when a test example includes C3, the example will be properly classified only if the rules were learned using the semantic hierarchy.

5 Updating an existing hierarchy

The goal here is to take advantage of human supplied knowledge when it proves useful in guiding the translation task, while tolerating omissions or errors in the hierarchy. If a hierarchy has already been developed manually, it is reasonable to utilize the human knowledge invested in the hierarchy by refining it.

The hierarchy updating process will take as input an existing hierarchy, and the set of translation rules learned using that hierarchy. This procedure is as follows.

First, the existing hierarchy is converted into a matrix that represents the similarity among the leaves of the hierarchy. There are an infinite number of matrices that could be constructed from a hierarchy, such that when the average-linkage clustering method were run on that matrix the original hierarchy would be created. We created one such matrix in which the similarity between two leaves is represented by the minimum number of is-a links that need to be traversed to reach the first common ancestor of the two nodes. We will call the matrix E.

Second, general nodes in learned rules are replaced by a disjunction of their children since rules learned with an existing hierarchy may contain general nodes. A similarity matrix is then generated by computing the mutual information

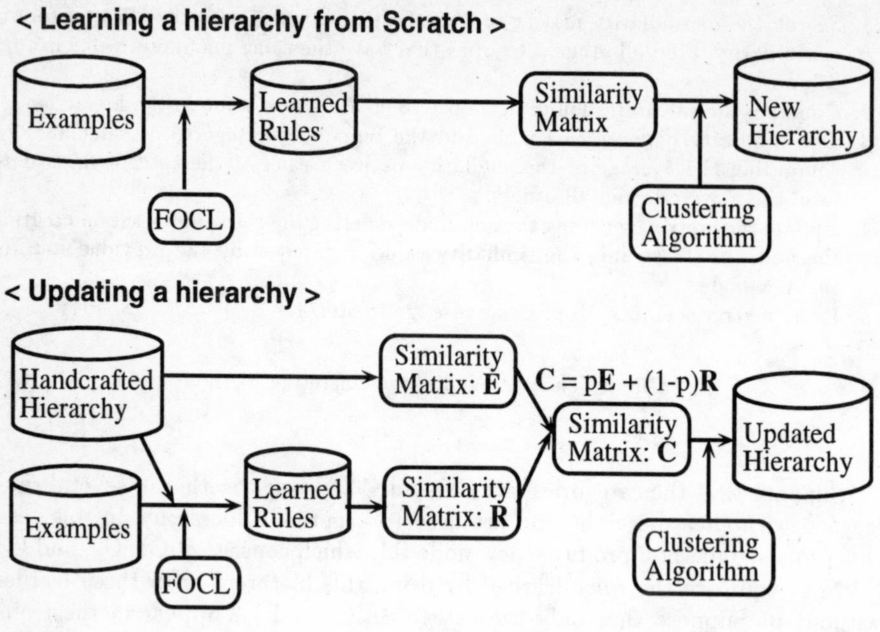

< Learning a hierarchy from Scratch >

< Updating a hierarchy >

Fig. 3. An overview of our proposed methods

between specific nodes used in internal disjunctions in the same way as mentioned in the previous section. This matrix is called R.

Third, these two matrices are combined. To combine these matrices, first each entry in the matrix is normalized to the range [0,1]. The combined similarity matrix C is obtained by the weighted addition of these two matrices: $C_{ij} = pE_{ij} + (1-p)R_{ij}$

where p is a parameter that represents how much weight should be placed upon the existing hierarchy. In our experiments, we set p to 0.5 so that both sources of information are weighed equally. We have obtained good results with this value and have not experimented with other possible values.

Finally, a new hierarchy is formed from this combined matrix by the average-linkage method. An overview of our approach is shown in Figure 3.

6 Experimental results

6.1 Experimental setting

In this experiment, we used two kinds of data set. One used artificially created data.[5] We generated 300 examples for each English verb's rule. We dealt with

---

[5] This data set was generated by using the translation rules and the semantic hierarchy created by human experts that are currently used in the ALT-J/E system. Namely,

24 different Japanese verbs corresponding to about 100 English verbs. A total of approximately 30,000 examples were generated.

The other set consisted of natural data. We collected Japanese-English corpora from example sentence translations in bilingual dictionaries (e.g. [10] etc.), processed these corpora with the parser used in ALT-J/E, and then generated learning data. The total number of collected corpora amounted to approximately 48,000. It included more than 5,000 kinds of Japanese verbs. 30 Japanese verbs were used from among them in this experiment corresponding to 120 English verbs. About 3400 examples were utilized in all. The real data is more complex than the artificial data in a variety of ways. First, the real data typically has several possible values for each subject and object, while the artificial data has one. Second, it's not clear whether the existing hierarchy is adequate for the the real data. Finally, some noise may be introduced into the real training data since it was prepared by using a Japanese parser and no parser is 100% accurate.

6.2 Artificial Data

Learning a hierarchy from scratch The accuracy was estimated by 10 fold cross validation.[6] Table 2 shows the accuracies of rules generated for the artificial data under three conditions: "No Hierarchy", the "Learned Hierarchy" and the "Handcrafted Hierarchy". On average, with no hierarchy, the translations rules are 85.9% accurate, while with the handcrafted hierarchy the rules are 97.4% accurate ($t(23) = 5.19$, $p < .0001$). Moreover, the average accuracy with the learned hierarchy (90.6%) is substantially higher than learning with no hierarchy ($t(23) = 4.13$, $p < .001$). This result indicates the effectiveness of using the handcrafted hierarchy and the learned hierarchy for learning translation rules.

Figure 5 shows a part of the generated semantic hierarchy (where "Hxxx" indicates new nodes). The total number of generated nodes was 415. This hierarchy reproduces a part of the hierarchy created manually. This suggests that semantically reasonable nodes are created by our method. The rules learned with the generated semantic hierarchy are expressed with new nodes. Figure 4 shows a part of the learned rules for the Japanese verbs "Nomu" and "Taku". You can find the new nodes shown in Figure 5 in this rule.

An important limitation of the current approach is that the newly created categories in the hierarchy do not have meaningful names and the rules learned using such terms are not easy for a person to comprehend.

---

first, it searches the hierarchy to find all leaf nodes of categories used in the rule for each variable such as N_1 and N_2. Then, it chooses one leaf node among them randomly as a value for the variable.

[6] First one-tenth of the examples for each verb were set aside for testing. Next we ran FOCL on the remaining nine tenths of the data, learning translation rules for the Japanese verbs without a hierarchy. A hierarchy was created from the learned rules by the clustering method. We then ran FOCL again on the same training data with the learned hierarchy. Finally, we tested the accuracy of the rules learned with this learned hierarchy on the one-tenth of the examples reserved for testing. This process was repeated ten times, each time using a different set of test examples.

Table 2. Accuracy Result : 5 methods : For artificial Data

Japanese Verb	Accuracy				
	NO Hierarchy	Handcrafted Hierarchy	Learned Hierarchy	Incomplete Hierarchy	Update Hierarchy
Yaku	.827	.943	.897	.867	.937
Nomu	1.000	1.000	1.000	1.000	1.000
Okonau	.994	.997	.994	.997	.991
Oujiru	1.000	1.000	1.000	1.000	1.000
Toku	.999	.999	.999	.999	.999
Tsukau	.751	.938	.841	.848	.914
Ataru	.647	.913	.710	.718	.906
Atsumeru	.698	.997	.926	.938	.997
Eru	.996	.992	.992	.996	.996
Karamu	.675	1.000	.859	.897	.998
Kotaeru	.927	.999	.989	.984	.996
Nobiru	.853	1.000	.993	.972	1.000
Noru	.823	.907	.860	.89	.90
Nuru	.998	1.000	.998	1.000	1.000
Osamaru	.867	.999	.880	.995	.999
Oshimu	.738	.968	.797	.911	.963
Sasageru	.831	.997	.931	.830	.997
Soeru	.969	.987	.950	.985	.981
Taku	1.000	1.000	1.000	1.000	1.000
Taosu	.728	.953	.798	.917	.947
Tataku	.893	.875	.872	.89	.866
Umu	.859	.987	.923	.903	.987
Yaburu	.82	.987	.876	.88	.983
Yashinau	.713	.945	.732	.927	.946
Average	.859	.974	.906	.935	.971

Updating a hierarchy To evaluate the procedure for updating a hierarchy with the artificial data, we purposely introduced errors into the handcrafted hierarchy by randomly deleting some of the categories in the current hierarchy. We call this the "Incomplete Hierarchy".

Table 2 contains the results of this experiment. Rules learned with the incomplete hierarchy is less accurate than those learned with the handcrafted hierarchy, showing that deletions affect the learning of translation rules. Rules learned with the updated incomplete hierarchy were on average 97.1% accurate, which is significantly more accurate than the rules learned with the incomplete hierarchy ($t(23) = 3.449$, $p < .005$). Moreover, this accuracy is significantly more accurate than the accuracy with the hierarchy learned from scratch. ($t(23) =$

nomu(Subject, Object, Everb) :-
one-isa(Object, {h294}), Everb = take.
nomu(Subject, Object, Everb) :-
one-isa(Object, {narration, lecture}, Everb = accept.
......
nomu(Subject, Object, Everb) :- Everb = drink.

taku(Subject, Object, Everb) :-
one-isa(Object, {h107, fuel}), Everb = burn.
....

Fig. 4. Part of the Learned rule for the Japanese verbs "Nomu" and "Taku"

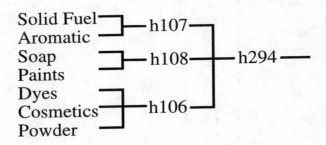

Fig. 5. Part of the Generated Semantic Hierarchy

4.364, p < .001). This result shows that the method of updating an existing hierarchy yields a more useful hierarchy than learning a hierarchy from scratch.

6.3 Real Data

The accuracy was estimated by 10 fold cross validation as in the case of artificial data. Table 3 contains the result for real data. Note that for the real data, we updated the actual hierarchy used by ALT-J/E; no errors were introduced.

With the real data, the hierarchy created by our learning method from scratch resulted in rules that were more accurate than those learned using the hand-crafted hierarchy. This result is marginally significant (t(29) = 1.752, p < .1). In addition, rules learned by updating the handcrafted hierarchy were on average 87.2% accurate, which is significantly more accurate than the accuracy (84.9%) of rules with the original hierarchy (t(29) = 3.796, p < .001). Although these results are promising, the rules learned from real, ambiguous data are not as accurate as those obtained from the artificial data. Note that there are fewer examples of each English verb in the real data and the real data has additional complications because it contains potentially ambiguity. We are going to con-

Table 3. Accuracy Result : 4 methods : 30 J-Verbs For a real data

Japanese Verb	Accuracy			
	NO Hierarchy	Handcrafted Hierarchy	Learned Hierarchy	Update Hierarchy
Agaru	.976	.976	.952	.976
Au	.917	.91	.924	.937
Asobu	.979	.979	.979	1.000
Dasu	.642	.667	.704	.728
Deru	.771	.843	.759	.795
Hairu	.709	.759	.778	.772
Hanasu	.901	.887	.887	.915
Hiku	.878	.919	.811	.851
Huru	1.000	1.000	1.000	1.000
Iku	1.000	1.000	1.000	1.000
Iru	.333	.424	.455	.485
Kaeru	.896	.87	.965	.948
Kaku	.943	.967	.975	.984
Kekkonsuru	.926	.981	.926	.981
Kiku	.725	.739	.773	.749
Kuru	.967	.967	.989	.989
Matsu	.725	.706	.843	.804
Miru	.735	.748	.809	.785
Motsu	.717	.732	.783	.79
Naru	.803	.788	.808	.803
Neru	.969	.99	.979	.979
Nomu	.993	.993	.993	.993
Noru	.843	.843	.863	.882
Okuru	.97	.848	.788	.879
Owaru	.909	.909	.97	.97
Tomeru	.741	.81	.845	.845
Toru	.688	.714	.747	.747
Tsukau	.962	.955	.968	.962
Ukeru	.636	.682	.667	.712
Yaru	.913	.913	.924	.913
Average	.839	.849	.864	.872

tinue collecting real data from other sources such as newspapers to improve the accuracy of rules learned from real data.

7 Limitation

The hierarchy generated by our method experimentally showed similar ability to the original handcrafted hierarchy, however, some problems remain left unsolved.

One important limitation of the current approach is that the categories newly created in the hierarchy do not have meaningful names and the rules learned using such terms are not easy for a person to comprehend. A person has to explicitly give a label to each node so that it is understandable to another human.

Another limitation is that all necessary leaf nodes have to be prepared before learning. Other clustering techniques (e.g., [4]; [7]; [6]) might be useful to find a meaningful group from a set of noun words and regard it as one of leaf nodes.

Moreover, we have not addressed pruning of learned translation rules. With no pruning, too many specific rules may be learned. As a result, the hierarchy that is generated from these rules might contain redundant or incorrect nodes. In contrast, if the rules are pruned too much, fewer categories appear together in rules and it is not possible to create a hierarchy that contains enough nodes to make the needed distinctions when learning translation rules.

8 Related Work

The general topic of clustering has been studied extensively in the artificial intelligence field(e.g., [5]; [11]). However, this work is not directly applicable to our problem. AI clustering methods work by computing some measure between features vectors that describe examples. In our case, examples are not described by such feature vectors but by similarity as represented by mutual information gain.

In natural language processing some approaches have been made to finding similarities among nouns. Hindle [7] uses mutual information between a verb and its object as a measure of degree of the association between the verb and an object. A measure of similarity among two nouns with respect to a single verb is defined to be the minimum noun similarity to the verb, and the overall similarity among two nouns is defined as the sum of similarities over all verbs. Grenfenstette [6] proposed a method of making noun clusters appropriate for each target domain by exploiting the kinds of nouns that appear as noun modifiers in the target domain. Both are intended to identify similar nouns, but they do not use similarity criteria as a metric for forming a hierarchy.

9 Conclusion

This paper reported our work on the acquisition and refinement of a semantic hierarchy through the use of clustering techniques. We extended the function of FOCL, a tool for learning translation rules, to handle the ambiguity of real data. We have shown that the constructive induction of terms representing general categories provides a useful bias for learning translation rules. Furthermore, the results on real and artificial data demonstrate that learning a hierarchy or updating an existing hierarchy can improve the generalization accuracy of systems that learn translation rules.

Acknowledgement

We wish to thank Dr. Shigeo Kaneda, Dr. Satoru Ikehara and Dr. Tsukasa Kawaoka for their continuous encouragement of this research. The research reported here was supported in part by NTT, NSF grant IRI-9310413, ARPA grant F49620-92-J-0430, and AFOSR AASERT grant F49620-93-1-0569.

References

1. Aldenderfer, M., and Blashfield, R.: Cluster Analysis. SAGE University Papers (1984)
2. Almuallim, H., Yamazaki T., AKiba, Y., Yokoo, A., Kaneda, S., and Kawaoka, T.: Acquisition of Machine Translation Rules Using Inductive Learning Techniques. IJCAI-93 Workshop Machine Learning and Knowledge Acquisition (1993)
3. Almuallim, H., Akiba, Y., Yamazaki T., Yokoo, A., and Kaneda, S.: A tool for the Acquisition of Japanese-English Machine Translation Rules Using Inductive Learning Techniques. The 10th Conference of Artificial Intelligence for Applications (1994)
4. Brown, P.F., Della Pietra, P.V., Lai, J.C., and Mercer, R.L.: Class-Based n-gram Models of Natural Language. Computational Linguistics. 18 (1992) 467-479
5. Fisher, D.: Knowledge acquisition via incremental conceptual clustering. Machine Learning 2 (1987) 139-172
6. Grenfenstette, G.: SEXTANT: Exploring unexplored contexts for semantic extraction from syntactic analysis. The 30th Annual Meeting of ACL. (1992) 324-326
7. Hindle, D.: Noun classification from predicate argument structures. The 28th Annual Meeting of ACL. (1990) 268-275
8. Ikehara, S., Miyazaki, M., Shirai, S. and Yokoo, A.: An Approach to Machine Translation Method based on Constructive Process Theory. Review of ECL 37 (1989) 39-44
9. Ikehara, S., Shirai, S., Yokoo, A. and Nakaiwa, H.: Toward an MT System without Pre-Editing—Effects of New Methods in ALT-J/E. MT Summit-3 (1990)
10. Keene, D.: Japanese-English Sentence Equivalents (Revised Version). Asahi Press (1991)
11. Michalski, R., and Stepp, R.: Conceptual clustering of structured objects: A goal-oriented approach. Artificial Intelligence 28 (1986) 43-69
12. Miller, G., Beckwith, R., Felbaum, C., Gross, D., and Miller, K.: Five Papers on Wordnet. CSL Report 43, Cognitive Systems Laboratory, Princeton University (1990)
13. Pazzani, M., and Kibler, D.: 1992. The utility of knowledge in inductive learning. Machine Learning 9 (1992) 57-94.
14. Quinlan, J. R.: 1990. Learning logical definitions from relations. Machine Learning 5 (1990)

Applying an Existing Machine Learning Algorithm to Text Categorization

Isabelle Moulinier and Jean-Gabriel Ganascia

LAFORIA-IBP-CNRS
Université Paris VI
4 place Jussieu
F-75252 Paris Cedex 05 – FRANCE
Ph: +33 (1) 44 27 70 10 Fax: +33 (1) 44 27 70 00
moulinie@laforia.ibp.fr ganascia@laforia.ibp.fr

Abstract. The information retrieval community is becoming increasingly interested in machine learning techniques, of which text categorization is an application. This paper describes how we have applied an existing similarity-based learning algorithm, CHARADE, to the text categorization problem and compares the results with those obtained using decision tree construction algorithms. From a machine learning point of view, this study was motivated by the size of the inspected data in such applications. Using the same representation of documents, CHARADE offers better performance than earlier reported experiments with decision trees on the same corpus. In addition, the way in which learning with redundancy influences categorization performance is also studied.

1 Introduction

Text categorization, which can be defined as the automatic content-based assignment of predefined categories to texts, is a topic of increasing interest. Even though it is a rather simple task, compared to other natural language processing problems, it possesses properties that are inherent to natural language data. Text categorization systems are primarily designed to assign categories to documents in order to support information retrieval, or to provide an aid to human indexers in the assignment task [1]. Other applications of categorization components include document routing to topic-specific processing mechanisms [2, 3].

The manual assignment of categories to documents is a time-consuming and expensive task. The automation of text categorization by knowledge engineers, although very effective, is also time-consuming and expensive [1]. These drawbacks are rather significant, since changes to the set of categories invalidate earlier assignments. Some research in machine learning has focused on the automatic construction of decision means; this research is also relevant to text categorization where the main problem is to decide whether or not to assign a given category to a document. Given a set of documents with assigned categories, inductive learning yields rule-based or probabilistic classifiers that assign categories to new documents. Classifiers do not directly handle raw texts, but rather a set of features such as the words the documents contain. Data sets are needed to train classifiers; these training sets can be artificially constructed or extracted from previous experiments such as indexed databases.

Several of the different systems based on inductive learning have been evaluated on the same data, namely the Reuters corpus [4, 5]. As a result, and owing to its size, this corpus provides an interesting medium of comparison between learning algorithms.

The purpose of this paper is the experimental application of CHARADE, a similarity-based learning algorithm, to the text categorization problem. It was carried out through a comparison of CHARADE with decision tree construction algorithms, using Reuters data, since results on a decision tree approach have already been reported in [4]. The CHARADE system was chosen because certain of its properties, in particular its ability to generate redundant rules and the search technique it uses, differ from other inductive learning approaches.

Section 2 describes text categorization as a challenging application to machine learning. Section 3 gives a brief overview of CHARADE and its potential. Section 4 reports the experimental results obtained with the Reuters corpus and explains the influence of redundancy when learning is performed on textual data. Section 5 presents properties we believe a learning algorithm needs to possess in order to successfully deal with textual data.

2 Text Categorization

Text categorization has been applied to support information retrieval on technical abstracts or newspapers articles for business or research uses. Text categorization is concerned both with parts of documents, like sentences or paragraphs, and entire documents.

Text categorization presents challenging properties when machine learning is confronted with such a task. Only two of the most interesting aspects are described in this paper. First of all, the size of textual data is itself a challenge: a real-size corpus, composed of several thousand texts, may include tens of thousands of words, even more – hundreds of thousands of features – when phrases are considered. Secondly, natural language data have properties, such as synonymy or ambiguity, that existing learning algorithms can hardly handle. Moreover, categorization is context-dependent with regards to documents. Let us consider the story in Fig. 1. The keyword gold was relevant for a human indexer and subsequently assigned to the story, whereas the terms lead and copper were overlooked as meaningless. Retaining this distinction is a hard task for inductive classifiers. However, natural language characteristics are not directly addressed here, but represent future research directions.

In order to make category decisions, a representation of texts must be chosen. Most categorization systems consider documents as sets of words: they ignore the initial ordering of the text and consider the presence or absence of a word in a text as a binary feature. Local frequency of words in texts is sometimes chosen as an alternative to presence/absence. Other approaches rely on spatial and linguistic structures, multi-word phrases and any other information as features.

```
16-MAR-1987 04:09:11.15
TOPICS: gold    END-TOPICS
PLACES: japan   END-PLACES
```

JAPAN'S DOWA MINING TO PRODUCE GOLD FROM APRIL
    TOKYO, March 16 - <Dowa Mining Co Ltd> said
it will start commercial production of gold,
copper, lead and zinc from its Nurukawa Mine in
northern Japan in April.
    A company spokesman said the mine's monthly
output is expected to consist of 1,300 tonnes
of gold ore and 3,700 of black ore, which
consists of copper, lead and zinc ores.
    A company survey shows the gold ore contains
up to 13.3 grams of gold per tonne, he said.
    Proven gold ore reserves amount to 50,000
tonnes while estimated reserves of gold and black
ores total one mln tonnes, he added.
    REUTER

Fig. 1. A categorized story from the Reuters newswire

Text representation is a preliminary step to both artificial intelligence (AI) related approaches and learning-based systems. AI techniques, similar to those used in expert systems dedicated to classification or diagnosis, apply to the text categorization problem. In such categorization systems [1], knowledge engineers introduce one or more intermediate concepts, structured in layers, between the input representation of texts and the output category assignments. They also write rules that involve mapping layers together and determining whether to keep or remove concepts. For instance, in the story from Fig. 1, *gold* is an intermediate concept between the gold ore feature and the gold category.

Several learning techniques have been applied to the text categorization task: they use existing sets of categorized documents in order to construct classifiers by induction. These methods include Bayesian classification [6], neural networks [7], decision tree construction [4, 8], memory-based learning [9] and optimization techniques [5]. Most of these approaches have been proposed by the Information Retrieval community. Experiments on the Reuters corpus, composed of financial news stories from Reuters newswire, have compared Bayesian classification and decision tree construction [4]. The experiments were conducted under the following constraints: text representation was identical; feature extraction (i.e. the means by which words are turned into learning features) was carried out using the same technique. Before reporting the experimental results on the Reuters data set, we present the main outlines of the CHARADE system.

3 An Overview of Charade

Most of the learning techniques used on a categorization task are based on induction, whatever their theoretical basis is. Inductive learning algorithms aim at detecting empirical correlations between examples [10].

Top-down inductive systems (TDIS), such as ID3 [11] or CN2 [12], can be characterized by the use of an attribute-value representation and by a top-down search strategy. Symbolic algorithms furthermore deal with domain or learned knowledge expressed as axioms or graphs. CHARADE [13] belongs to this family. Informally, given a set of training examples, the CHARADE system extracts rules, written as k-DNF expressions, which cover some positive examples in the training set and no negative examples.

3.1 Generating k-DNF Expressions versus Constructing Decision Trees

Some TDIS, ID3-like algorithms, generate decision trees and choose attributes at each step of the decision tree construction, according to heuristic criteria. The building tree method introduces a *bias*, which we intuitively describe below.

Let us consider the learning set given in Table 1. It can be classified using the four production rules in Fig. 2.

Table 1. A toy learning set

	E_1	E_2	E_3	E_4	E_5	E_6	E_7	E_8	E_9
A	a_1	a_1	a_1	a_2	a_3	a_2	a_2	a_2	a_1
B	b_1	b_3	b_1	b_2	b_2	b_1	b_1	b_3	b_4
D	d_1	d_2	d_1	d_2	d_1	d_1	d_2	d_2	d_2
$Class$	c_1	c_1	c_1	c_2	c_2	c_3	c_3	c_1	c_1

$$
\begin{aligned}
R_1 &: \text{if } A = a_1 & &\text{then } Class = c_1 \\
R_2 &: \text{if } B = b_2 & &\text{then } Class = c_2 \\
R_3 &: \text{if } A = a_2 \text{ and } B = b_1 & &\text{then } Class = c_3 \\
R_4 &: \text{if } B = b_3 & &\text{then } Class = c_1
\end{aligned}
$$

Fig. 2. Rule set classifying the learning set from Table 1

These rules are produced by CHARADE or CN2. However, no decision tree technique is able to build this knowledge base; any decision tree will contain *empty, over-specific* and *useless* nodes. Let us examine one such tree (Fig. 3), derived from the learning set with ID3.

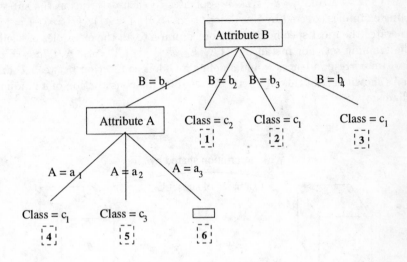

Fig. 3. One of the possible decision trees for the training set in Table 1

It is easy to see that node $\boxed{1}$ corresponds to rule R_2, node $\boxed{2}$ to rule R_4 and node $\boxed{5}$ to rule R_3. Rule R_1 does not itself appear in the tree; it cannot be generated. In fact, node $\boxed{4}$ corresponds to an over-specification of rule R_1: all examples in node $\boxed{4}$ are covered by rule R'_1: if $A = a_1$ and $B = b_1$ then $Class = c_1$, which is more specific than R_1. Lastly, it appears that node $\boxed{6}$ is *empty* and node $\boxed{3}$ *useless*, when R_1 is available.

For the sake of clarity, this inability has been explained through a toy example. The construction bias does not weaken on larger sets of data. CHARADE, which has no such bias, overcomes this inability and enables the production of more concise rules, for instance R_1 instead of R'_1.

3.2 Charade: a Theoretical Framework

The generation of k-DNF expressions conforms to a theoretical framework presented briefly below. CHARADE uses a distributive lattice formalism as a theoretical framework to generate production rule systems. Thanks to the properties of lattices, generalization does not rely on pattern matching. The proposed framework, as claimed in [14], covers classical TDIS.

The formalism is based on the use of two distributive lattices: the description space lattice, $\mathcal{D}$, which contains all possible descriptions[1] and the example lattice, $\mathcal{E}$, which corresponds to the set of parts of the training set. Let us, for instance, consider the small training set given in Table 1. $((A = a_1) \wedge (B = b_3))$ belongs to $\mathcal{D}$, whereas $\{E_1\ E_2\ E_3\}$ belongs to $\mathcal{E}$.

As illustrated in Fig. 4, two functions between these lattices are then introduced: $\delta : \mathcal{D} \rightarrow \mathcal{E}$ and $\gamma : \mathcal{E} \rightarrow \mathcal{D}$. δ associates to each description the subset of training examples covered by this description; so $\delta((A = a_1) \wedge (B = b_3)) = \{E_2\}$. γ generates the most specific description common to all the examples of a subset of the training set. For instance, $\gamma(\{E_1\ E_2\ E_3\}) = ((A = a_1) \wedge (Class = c_1))$. These two correspondences γ and δ define a Galois connection between $\mathcal{D}$ and $\mathcal{E}$ [15]. As shown in [14], this characteristic enables the construction of an inductive mechanism.

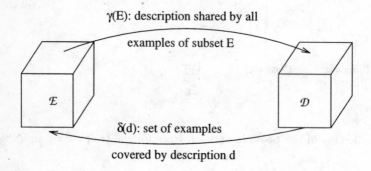

γ(E): description shared by all
examples of subset E

δ(d): set of examples
covered by description d

Fig. 4. δ and γ functions

The inductive mechanism in CHARADE is based on a top-down exploration of the description space $\mathcal{D}$, i.e. from general to specific. The search space can be reduced by two means: properties of rules and properties of the generated knowledge base.

In the theoretical framework of CHARADE, it is established in [14] that once all examples covered by description d_1 are also covered by description d_2, descriptions that are more specific than $d_1 \wedge d_2$ are useless. This consideration allows drastic cuts in the top-down exploration of the description space. A secondary benefit from this property is that CHARADE naturally tends to generate discriminant rules with a minimum number of premises.

In a classification system – categorization systems are related to this kind –, requirements on rule generation may be specified. The minimum percentage of positive examples a rule has to cover may be such a requirement. This constraint, which considerably reduces the search space, may be useful when large numbers of examples and descriptors are studied.

---

[1] A description is a conjunction of descriptors. A descriptor is an attribute-value pair.

Finally, some applications may benefit from redundancy. For instance, when working on a categorization task humans often decide to assign some category to a document according to several criteria. This can be expressed in terms of distinct rules for the same example. CHARADE offers the opportunity to generate redundant rules. This property is discussed next.

3.3 Learning with Redundancy

Redundant learning has the faculty of producing various means to classify a given training example. Redundancy is almost impossible with decision trees, whereas approaches which handle k-DNF expressions have this faculty.

In fact, the bias introduced in decision trees construction methods forbids redundant learning. Once a training example is affected to a leaf (or to a subtree), it cannot be found in any other leaf (or subtree). Let us consider the learning set in Table 1. Given the decision tree in Fig. 3, it is easy to see that example E_8 can only be found in leaf $\lceil 2 \rceil$. On the contrary, the rule set given in Fig. 2, generated by both CHARADE and CN2, is redundant: example E_8 is covered by rule R_1 and rule R_4.

Although it naturally tends to lessen useless redundancy, the CHARADE system emphasizes redundant learning via the redundancy parameter λ. Take the case where λ is set to 2. CHARADE will attempt to generate a rule base in which each training example is covered at least twice.

Gams, in [16], claims that learning may benefit from redundancy. This is illustrated by the previous example. However, redundancy may lead to less accurate prediction on unseen test sets. Since premises of rules are not exclusive, each unseen (testing) example may fire several rules. Yet these rules may have distinct conclusions, i.e. assign the unseen example to different classes, and this may lessen the predictive power of the learned rule base. For instance, let us consider example $E_{10} = (a_1, b_2, d_2, c_1)$ as a testing example. Rule R_1 and rule R_2 from Fig. 2 are used to cover E_{10}. It results in an obviously incorrect prediction for rule R_2. It is worth noticing that the decision tree from Fig. 3 also leads to the incorrect class assignment. Figure 5 illustrates the difference between rule-based and tree-based approaches on the learning set from Table 1.

4 Experimental Results

CHARADE's performance was assessed by measuring its ability to reproduce manual assignments on a given data set. The Reuters data set provides a means of comparison, since it has been investigated using other techniques [1, 4, 5].

4.1 The Reuters Data Set

Over the past few years the Reuters data set has emerged as a benchmark for text categorization. It consists of a set of 21,450 Reuters newswire stories from

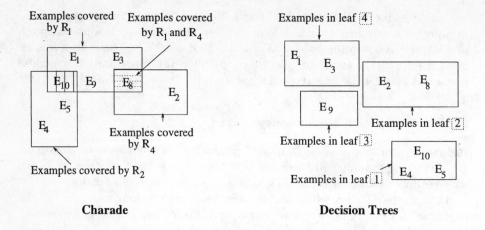

Charade   **Decision Trees**

Fig. 5. Influence of redundancy on learning and testing examples

1987 which have been indexed manually using 135 financial topics to support document routing and retrieval for Reuters customers.

The original corpus is divided into a training set containing 14,704 stories dated from April 7, 1987 and earlier, and a test set, containing all the other 6,746 stories. Several thousand documents in the data set have no topic assignments and we have chosen to ignore them as we cannot possibly learn from them. As a result, the raw data we have worked on has 7,789 training examples and 3,875 testing examples. The examples are described by 22,971 words, using Lewis' representation [4].

4.2 Evaluation Measurements

In order to compare our approach with published work, we use the performance measures *recall* and *precision* as they are defined in information retrieval. Recall is the percentage of times a particular category should have been assigned to a document and was, in fact, assigned. Precision is the percentage of category assignments actually made that were correct.

Recall and precision have been designed to evaluate performance on a single category. Given a set of n documents and k categories, nk assignment decisions are made. Micro-averaging [4] considers all nk decisions as a whole group and synthesizes recall and precision for the group.

Text categorization systems classically have a parameter controlling their willingness to assign categories. The more the system is willing to make decisions, the more recall goes up and precision usually goes down. A *break-even point*, where recall equals precision, is often chosen to summarize the results.

4.3 Overall Performance

Our primary aim was to apply the CHARADE system to a text categorization task and to compare the results obtained using CHARADE with those obtained using DT-min10 [4], an ID3-like algorithm. To do so we conducted a set of experiments.

From Texts to Learning Examples In order to introduce as little bias as possible in our experimental comparison, we used Lewis' preprocessing, which was available with the Reuters corpus. Each document was then turned into a training example using an information gain criterion: for each category, features with the best information measurement were retained as attributes in CHARADE's description language.

We first represented learning examples using binary features, i.e. we were concerned solely with the presence/absence of words in texts. All categories assigned to a document were included in its corresponding learning example description. However, the induction step was considered as a multiple two-class problem: assignment decisions were learned separately for each category.

Experimental Results We ran our experiments with various sizes of attributes per category. The results of our experiments, given in Table 2, show that CHARADE performs better than both of Lewis' approaches, under the same preprocessing constraints. Experiments with 25 attributes will be discussed in the following section.

Table 2. Recall/Precision break-even points for various sizes of attribute set

Method	Representation	Break-even(%)
CHARADE	Bool. (50 att.)	73.8
CHARADE	Bool. (100 att.)	73.4
CHARADE	Bool. (200 att.)	71.5
CHARADE	Bool. (25 att.)	– (cf. Table 3)
Decision Tree	Bool.	67.0
Bayes	Boolean	65.0

Using the learned knowledge base to classify unseen testing examples, we examined the performance of this rule base on the most frequently assigned category. Recall is at 84.4% when precision peaks at 93.2%. The price of this result, however, is the large number of generated rules for this category, around 450 rules. On the other hand, when two categories are semantically related, the stories indexed by these categories may be described with the same subset of attributes. In this case the CHARADE system, like most TDIS, produces classifiers with less outstanding performance.

As a means of further comparison CONSTRUE, a hand-written rule-based text categorization system, achieves a break-even point of 90% [1] on a smaller test set (723 unseen news stories). In [5], results using a different representation of examples have been presented. The difference resides in text representation, i.e. extraction of features and conversion into attributes. Figures of 75.5% for boolean attributes and 80.5% when local frequency of terms is used, are presented. However, a comparison with this approach is inconclusive as it is difficult to assess the quality of learning separately from the quality of preprocessing.

Influence of Redundancy on Text Categorization Earlier reported experiments did not consider the influence of redundancy on performance, whereas the experiments described in this paper have. We investigated this influence on text categorization. No added redundancy ($\lambda = 1$) favors precision over recall, while a higher redundancy favors recall over precision (cf. Table 3). Best performance, when both recall and precision have a high value, is obtained when each training example has been covered 3 or 4 times. This backs up our earlier intuition: there may be several reasons to assign a given category to a document.

Table 3. Influence of redundancy on precision/recall

λ	Nb. of att.	Nb. of rules	Precision	Recall
1	50	1689	82.8%	65.2%
2	50	3227	77.2%	70.5%
3	50	4669	74.8%	73.3%
4	50	6005	72.2%	74.6%
5	50	7269	70.2%	75.6%
8	50	9982	69.1%	76.1%
4	25	3282	78.5%	62.4%
8	25	5442	74%	64.2%
16	25	8617	70.3%	65.3%
∞	25	30570	57.1%	66.4%

Experiments with 25 attributes lead to the following observations. It is not possible to relate redundancy directly to the willingness of assignment presented by Lewis. In addition, high redundancy tends to deteriorate precision considerably, whereas recall reaches an asymptote. However, this last result is correlated with the following major notion: redundant learning cannot be an alternative to example representation, i.e. an inadequate representation will not benefit from redundancy, as is the case with 25 attributes.

5 Discussion

We have shown experimentally that a machine learning algorithm can be successfully applied to the text categorization task, even though some experiments have shown limitations of the CHARADE system where the size of the description space prohibits extensive use of the characteristics of the learning algorithm.

In order to assess whether the question of the size of the description space is peculiar to CHARADE, we have started a series of experiments using the CN2 algorithm. These experiments are still in progress, but preliminary results suggest a salient difference between the two algorithms. Let us consider that n binary features are relevant to a category. Each news story is described by exactly n values in the CN2 formalism. On the other hand, examples in CHARADE are only expressed in terms of the presence of words in a given document, i.e. the description of each example does not need to be complete. This difference in description induces differences in the learned knowledge base. CN2 mostly generates rules in which premises are expressed in terms of the absence of certain features, while CHARADE generates rules based on the presence of terms. In our view, assigning categories with regards to the absence of certain features makes little sense.

However, we have encountered some problems – as yet unsolved – with the description language based on binary features. They can be stated as follows. The basic representation used has the following major drawback, when the corpus is composed of documents of different lengths. Documents are mapped onto the set of all attributes found relevant to some category, on an information basis. Hence shorter documents may be represented by a couple of terms, whereas longer ones may include several dozen attributes. Thus, the representation of short documents may be included in the description of longer ones. Let us consider examples E and E', respectively described by $D \wedge Class = c_1$ and $D \wedge d \wedge Class = c_2$. When CHARADE is faced with E and E', it does not generate rules that cover E, since E' is a negative example to any rule **if** D **then** $Class = c_1$.

Nevertheless, we believe that these problems will be lifted once the full descriptive power of CHARADE is taken into account. CHARADE supports learning using domain knowledge which can, for instance, be expressed using hierarchies. In the context of natural language, synonymy or ambiguity can be considered as additional knowledge that could be provided to enhance learning. We intend to carry out future research in this direction with the help of a knowledge acquisition software program [17] in which CHARADE has been embedded.

To sum up, reducing the search space is one of our research directions, in order to address more complex problems. Several approaches are possible: exploring the description space using new heuristics, reducing the number of training examples and refining the learned rule-base using post-processing. Furthermore, generating rules with exceptions may help in exploring the description space and overcoming the lack of descriptive power of binary representation. Finally, we have studied text categorization as a first approach to text indexing using a controlled vocabulary. We shall now analyze how external knowledge can be represented and how it influences the performance of our learning system.

References

1. P. Hayes and S. Weinstein. CONSTRUE/TIS: a system for content-based index-ing of a database of news stories. In *Second Annual Conference on Innovative Applications of Artificial Intelligence*, 1990.
2. P. Hayes, P. Andersen, I. Nirenburg, and L. Schmandt. TCS: A Shell for Content-Based Text Categorization. In *Proceeding of the Sixth IEEE CAIA*, pages 321–325, 1990.
3. G. DeJong. An Overview of the FRUMP system. In W. H. Lehnert and M.H. Ringle, editors, *Strategies for Natural Language Processing*. Lawrence Erlbaum Associates, Hillsdale, New Jersey, USA, 1982.
4. D. Lewis and M. Ringuette. A comparison of two learning algorithms for text categorization. In *Symposium on Document Analysis and Information Retrieval*, Las Vegas, Nevada, USA, 1994.
5. C. Apté, F. Damerau, and S. Weiss. Automated learning of decision rules for text categorization. *ACM Transactions on Information Systems*, July 1994.
6. M. E. Maron. Automatic indexing: an experimental inquiry. *Journal of the Association for Computing Machinery*, (8):404–417, 1961.
7. Y. Yang. Expert network: Effective and efficient learning from human decisions in text categorization and retrieval. In *Proc. of the 17th SIGIR*, 1994.
8. N. Fuhr, S. Hartmann, G. Lustig, M. Schwantner, and K. Tzeras. AIR/X — a Rule-Based Multistage Indexing System for Large Subject Fields. In *Proc. of RIAO'91*, Barcelona, Spain, 1991.
9. B. Masand, G. Linoff, and D. Waltz. Classifying News Stories using Memory Based Reasoning. In *Proc. of the 15th SIGIR*, Copenhagen, Denmark, 1992.
10. R. S. Michalski, J. G. Carbonell, and T. M. Mitchell, editors. *Machine learning: an artificial intelligence approach (Vol. 2)*. Morgan Kaufmann, Los Altos, California, USA, 1986.
11. J. R. Quinlan. Induction of decision trees. *Machine Learning*, 1:81–106, 1986.
12. P. Clark and T. Niblett. The CN2 induction algorithm. *Machine Learning*, 3:261–284, 1989.
13. J.-G. Ganascia. Deriving the learning bias from rule properties. In J. E. Hayes, D. Mitchie, and E. Tyngu, editors, *Machine Intelligence 12*, pages 151–167. Clarendon Press, Oxford, 1991.
14. J.-G. Ganascia. TDIS: an Algebraic Formalization. In *International Joint Conference on Artificial Intelligence*, Chambéry, France, 1993.
15. G. Birkhoff. *Lattice Theory*. American Mathematical Society, Providence, Rhode Island, third edition, 1967.
16. M. Gams. New measurements that highlight the importance of redundant knowledge. In M. Morik, editor, *Proc. of the Fourth European Working Session on Learning*, Montpellier, France, 1989. Pitman–Morgan Kaufman.
17. J. Thomas, J.-G. Ganascia, and P. Laublet. Model-driven knowledge acquisition and knowledge-based machine learning: an example of a principled association. In *Workshop IJCAI 16*, Chambéry, France, 1993.

Comparative Results on Using Inductive Logic Programming for Corpus-based Parser Construction

John M. Zelle[1], and Raymond J. Mooney[2]

[1] Department of Mathematics and Computer Science, Drake University, Des Moines
IA 50311, USA (jz6011r@dunix.drake.edu)
[2] Department of Computer Sciences, University of Texas, Austin TX 78712, USA
(mooney@cs.utexas.edu)

Abstract. This paper presents results from recent experiments with
CHILL, a corpus-based parser acquisition system. CHILL treats language
acquisition as the learning of search-control rules within a logic program.
Unlike many current corpus-based approaches that use statistical learning algorithms, CHILL uses techniques from inductive logic programming
(ILP) to learn relational representations. CHILL is a very flexible system
and has been used to learn parsers that produce syntactic parse trees,
case-role analyses, and executable database queries. The reported experiments compare CHILL's performance to that of a more naive application
of ILP to parser acquisition. The results show that ILP techniques, as
employed in CHILL, are a viable alternative to statistical methods and
that the control-rule framework is fundamental to CHILL's success.

1 Introduction

Empirical or *corpus-based* methods for constructing natural language systems has
been an area of growing research interest in the last several years. The empirical
approach replaces hand-generated rules with models obtained automatically by
training over language corpora. Corpus-based methods may be used to augment
the knowledge of a traditional parser, for example by acquiring new case-frames
for verbs [13] or acquiring models to resolve lexical or attachment ambiguities
[11, 8]. More radical approaches attempt to replace the hand-crafted components
altogether, constructing complete parsers directly from suitable corpora. Recent
approaches to constructing robust parsers from corpora primarily use statistical
and probabilistic methods such as stochastic grammars [4, 23, 7] or transition
networks [17]. These methods eschew traditional, symbolic parsing in favor of
statistical and probabilistic methods. Although several current methods learn
some symbolic structures such as decision trees [3, 12] and transformations [6],
statistical methods dominate.

A common thread in all of these approaches is that the acquired knowledge
is represented in a *propositional* form (perhaps with associated probabilities).
This means for example, a decision about how to label a node in a parse tree is
made by considering a fixed set of properties (e.g., syntactic category) about a

fixed context of surrounding nodes (e.g., parent and immediate left sibling). The exact conditions of the rule(s) are determined by the acquisition algorithm but the context over which the rules are formed, and the exact properties which may be tested are determined *a priori* by the designer of the acquisition system. In machine learning, such approaches are often called feature-vector representations, as each decision context can be specified by a finite vector of atomic values associated with the various features of interest.

In contrast, the CHILL system [28, 30, 27] uses a framework for learning with structured representations. Relational representations have long been a tool of traditional NLP. Virtually all of this work has utilized hand-crafted grammars as suitable methods for automating the construction of relational knowledge bases had not yet been developed. Now, however, a growing subfield of machine learning research called Inductive Logic Programming (ILP) addresses the problem of learning first-order logic descriptions (Prolog programs). Due to the expressiveness of first-order logic, ILP methods can learn relational and recursive concepts that cannot be represented in the featural languages assumed by most machine-learning algorithms. ILP methods have successfully induced small programs for sorting and list manipulation [24] as well as produced encouraging results on important applications such as predicting protein secondary structure [21]. Our research seeks to apply ILP methods to NLP in a effort to bridge the gap between traditional NLP and empirical approaches.

A major advantage using ILP techniques is the resulting flexibility. Given the power of first-order rules, there is less need to hand-engineer appropriate features and contexts over which the system learns. The induction algorithm can automatically extract the relevant portions of structured contexts and construct new predicates to represent novel syntactic and/or semantic word and phrase categories that are necessary to perform accurate parsing. Furthermore, the combination of traditional and empirical approaches allows the insights of traditional parsing to provide structure or *bias* to the learning component. Stronger biases potentially allow better results from smaller training corpora. Finally, the approach is easily adapted to learn parsers for various types of analyses. CHILL has been used to learn parsers that produce syntactic parse trees, case-role analyses, and actual executable database queries.

This paper considers two methods of applying ILP to the problem of corpus-based parser construction. We present a naive approach based on the direct induction of logic programs to perform parsing, and a more sophisticated system, CHILL, which applies ILP within the context of a fixed parsing framework. Experimental results demonstrate that the bias provided by the parsing framework significantly improves the accuracy of the resulting parsers.

2 Using ILP for Parser Construction

2.1 Introduction to ILP

ILP research considers the problem of inducing a first-order, definite-clause logic program from a set of examples and given background knowledge[10, 22]. As such, it stands at the intersection of the traditional fields of machine learning and logic programming.

As an example ILP task, consider learning the concept of list membership. The input to the learning system consists of a number of positive and negative instances of the predicate, member/2.[3] Some positive instances might be: member(1, [1,2]), member(2, [1,2]), member(1,[3,1]). Instances such as member(1,[]), member(2,[1,3]), would serve as negative examples. Additional information is provided in the form background relations in terms of which the desired concept is to be learned. In the case of list membership, this information might include a definition of the concept, components/3 which decomposes a list into its component head and tail. This type of "constructor" predicate is typically used as many ILP systems learn function-free clauses; using components/3 eliminates the need for list constructions (e.g. [X|Y]) within learned clauses. Given this input, an ILP system attempts to construct a concept definition which entails the positive training examples, but not the negatives. In this case, we hope to learn the correct definition of member, namely:

member(X, List) :- components(List, X, Tail).
member(X, List) :- components(List, Head, Tail), member(X, Tail).

2.2 "Naive" Parser Construction

A straight-forward application of ILP to parser construction would be to simply present a corpus of sentences paired with representations as a set of positive examples to an ILP system. For example, we might try to learn a definition of the concept parse(Sentence,Rep). The induced logic program, might then be used to prove goals having the second argument uninstantiated, effectively producing parses of sentences provided as input. There are a number of difficulties with this approach.

First, it is not clear what the other inputs to the ILP system should be. We do not have a convenient set of negative examples or a good theory of what the background relations should be. Both of these are critical to the success of current ILP algorithms. Clearly, it is intractable to generate all possible sentences paired with incorrect analyses as a set of negative examples. Even selecting a manageable–sized random subset of these negative examples is unlikely to be sufficient, as such a sample is unlikely to include the many "near-miss" examples which are crucial to learning good generalizations. Rather than attempting to generate a set of explicit negative examples, we have developed a technique of quantifying *implicit* negative examples that effectively overcomes this difficulty [31]. The problem of providing appropriate background knowledge has been largely unexplored; in our experiments, we relied on the ability of the ILP algorithm to invent suitable background relations.

---

[3] We use the standard notation ⟨name⟩/⟨number⟩ to indicate the name and arity (number of arguments) for a predicate.

Even given these other inputs, it seems unlikely that an uninformed ILP system could produce a program which generalizes well to new inputs. The space of logic programs is too large, and the learning problem too unconstrained to hope that the results would be useful. In short, the "inductive leap" is simply too great. Evaluating the success of the naive approach is, ultimately, an empirical question. In this paper we compare the naive technique with a more sophisticated alternative, namely CHILL, which addresses these issues by considering language acquisition as a control-rule learning problem.

2.3 Acquisition as Control Rule Learning

Rather than using ILP techniques to directly learn a logic grammar, CHILL begins with a well-defined parsing framework and uses ILP to learn control strategies within this framework. Treating language acquisition as a control-rule learning problem is not in itself a new idea. Berwick [1] used this approach to learn rules for a Marcus-style deterministic parser. When the system came to a parsing impasse, a new rule was created by inferring the correct parsing action and creating a new rule using certain properties of the current parser state as trigger conditions for its application. In a similar vein, Simmons and Yu [26] controlled a simple shift-reduce parser by storing example contexts consisting of the syntactic categories of a fixed number of stack and input buffer locations. New sentences were parsed by matching the current parse state to the stored examples and performing the action corresponding to the best matching previous context. Like the statistical approaches mentioned above, these early control-rule acquisition systems used pre-defined feature-vector representations. CHILL is the first system to use ILP techniques rather than less flexible propositional approaches.

The input to CHILL is a set of training instances consisting of sentences paired with the desired parses. The output is a shift-reduce parser in Prolog which maps sentences into parses. Figure 1 shows the basic components of the system.

CHILL employs a simple deterministic, shift-reduce parser with the current parse state represented by the content of the stack and the remaining portion of the input buffer. Parsing operators are program clauses which take the current stack and input buffer as input arguments and return a modified stack and buffer as outputs. During Parser Operator Generation, the training examples are analyzed to extract all of the general operators which are required to produce the analyses. For example, when producing case-role analyses, an operator to reduce the top two items on the stack by attaching the second item as an agent of the first is represented by the clause op([Top,Second|Rest],In,[NewTop|Rest],In) :- reduce(Top,agt,Second,NewTop) where the arguments to op/4 are, in order, the current stack, current input buffer, new stack, and new input buffer. The reduce/4 predicate simply combines Top and Second using the role agt to produce the new structure for the top of the stack. In general, one such operator clause is constructed for each attachment-role in the training examples. The resulting parser is severely over-general, as the operators contain no conditions specifying when they should be used; any operator may be applied to (virtually) any parse state.

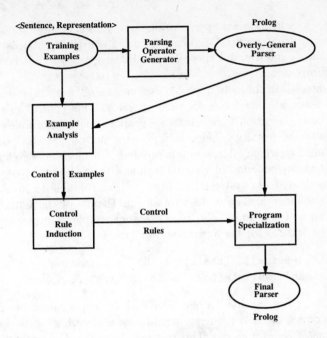

Fig. 1. The CHILL Architecture

In Example Analysis, the overly-general parser is used to parse the training examples to extract contexts in which the various parsing operators should and should not be employed. These contexts form sets of positive and negative *control examples* from which the appropriate control rules can be subsequently induced. A control example is a "snapshot" of the subgoal to which a particular operator clause may be applied in the course of parsing an example. Examples of correct operator applications are generated by finding the first correct parsing of each training pair with the overly-general parser; any subgoal to which an operator is applied in this successful parse becomes a positive control example for that operator.

For the `agent` operator shown above, the sentence "the man ate the pasta," would produce a single positive control example: `op([ate,[man, det:the]], [the,pasta], A, B)`. This is the only subgoal to which this operator is applied in the correct parsing of the sentence. `A` and `B` are uninstantiated variables since they are outputs from the `op/4` clause and are not yet bound at the time the clause is being applied. The sentence generates the following negative control examples for this operator:

```
op([man,the],[ate,the,pasta],A,B)
op([the,[ate,agt:[man,det:the]]],[pasta],A,B)
op([pasta,the,[ate,agt:[man,det:the]]],[],A,B)
op([[pasta,det:the],[ate,agt:[man,det:the]]],[],A,B)
```

Note that there are additional parse states such as `op([], [the,man,ate,the,` pasta], A, B) which do not appear in this list. This is because the agent clause of op/4 requires that its first argument be a list containing at least two items. Since the clause cannot match these other subgoals, they will not be included as negative examples.

The Control-Rule Induction phase uses a general first-order induction algorithm to learn a *control rule* for each operator. This control rule comprises a definite-clause definition that covers the positive control examples for the operator but not the negative. There is a growing body of research in inductive logic programming which addresses this problem. CHILL combines elements from bottom-up techniques found in systems such as CIGOL [19] and GOLEM [20] and top-down methods from systems like FOIL [25], and is able to invent new predicates in a manner analogous to CHAMP [9]. Details of the CHILL induction algorithm can be found in [28, 29, 27]. Given our simple example, a control rule that might be learned for the agent operator is

```
op([X,[Y,det:the]], [the|Z], A, B) :- animate(Y).
animate(man). animate(boy). animate(girl) ....
```

Here the system has invented a new predicate to help explain the parsing decisions. Of course, the new predicate would have a system generated name. It is called "animate" here for clarity. This rule may be roughly interpreted as stating: "the agent reduction applies when the stack contains two items, the second of which is a completed noun phrase whose head is animate." The output of the Control-Rule Induction phase is a suitable control-rule for each clause of op/4. These control rules are then passed on to the Program Specialization phase.

The final step, Program Specialization, "folds" the control information back into the overly-general parser. A control rule is easily incorporated into the overly-general program by unifying the head of an operator clause with the head of the control rule for the clause and adding the induced conditions to the clause body. The definitions of any invented predicates are simply appended to the program. Given the program clause:

```
op([Top,Second|Rest],In,[NewTop|Rest],In) :-
      reduce(Top,agt,Second,NewTop).
```

and the control rule:

```
op([X,[Y,det:the]], [the|Z], A, B) :- animate(Y).
animate(man). animate(boy). animate(girl) ....
```

the resulting clause is

```
op([A,[B,det:the]],[the|C],[D],[the|C]) :-
      animate(B), reduce(A,agt,[B,det:the],D).
animate(boy). animate(girl). animate(man)...
```

The final parser is just the overly-general parser with each operator clause suitably constrained.

3   CHILL vs. Naive ILP

3.1   Experimental Method

In Section 2.2, we noted that the naive application of ILP to parser acquisition would be to induce a program directly from the examples of the parse/2 relation. The advantage gained by the control-rule framework can be assessed by comparing CHILL to the performance achieved by CHILL's ILP component trying to learn the parse/2 relation directly. These two approaches were compared using the standard machine learning paradigm of first choosing a random set of test examples and then learning and evaluating parsers using increasingly larger subsets of the remaining examples.

Since the naive approach requires positive and negative examples of the parse/2 concept, we employed a version of the induction algorithm which exploits the output-completeness assumption to learn in the context of *implicit* negative examples [31, 18]. A complete discussion of this technique is beyond the scope of this paper, but the intuition is straightforward. A developing program is evaluated by using it to construct all possible parses that it can generate from a given training sentence. Since all of the correct parses are supplied for each sentence, any generated outputs which are not present in the training set are considered to be negative examples. Likewise, outputs which are not complete (i.e. contain uninstantiated variables) are considered to cover many negative examples, since there could be a large number of incorrect representations that they could match.

3.2   Results for Case-Role Mapping

In one experiment, CHILL and naive ILP were compared on an artificial data set for case-role mapping that has been used to demonstrate certain language processing abilities of artificial neural networks [16]. This task involves a corpus of 1475 sentence/case-structure pairs originally presented in [15]. The corpus was produced from a set of 19 sentence templates, generating sentences such as "The HUMAN ate the FOOD with the UTENSIL", where the capitalized items are replaced with words of the given category. The sample actually comprises 1390 unique sentences, some of which allow multiple analyses. Since our parser is capable (through backtracking) of generating all legal parses for an input, training was done considering each unique sentence as a single example, and insuring that the training corpus contained all correct parses.

Our results reflect averages over five trials using different testing sets of 740 sentences each. During testing, the parser was used to enumerate all analyses for a given test sentence. Parsing of a sentence can fail in two ways: an incorrect analysis may be generated, or a correct analysis may not be generated. In order to account for both types of inaccuracy, a metric was introduced to calculate the "average correctness" for a given test sentence as follows: $Accuracy = (\frac{C}{P} + \frac{C}{A})/2$ where P is the number of distinct analyses produced, C is the number of the produced analyses which were correct, and A is the number of correct analyses possible for the sentence. This measure can be viewed as an average of the parser's precision and recall for a given sentence.

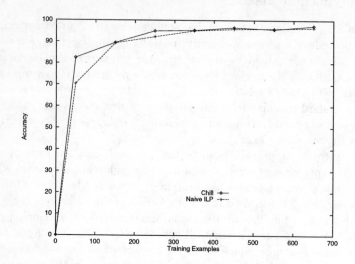

Fig. 2. CHILL vs. Naive ILP on Artificial Case-role Task

Figure 2 shows the average learning curves of these two systems. Both are able to learn this simple task very accurately, significantly outperforming the previous neural network approaches [16]. The results show that the naive approach performs only slightly worse than CHILL for small examples sets, and becomes indistinguishable as the sample grows. Inspection of the resulting programs showed that the induction algorithm was fairly accurately recreating the template-and-filler style of program which was used to generate this corpus. This provides strong evidence of the power of the ILP induction algorithm for inducing programs from examples exhibiting regular structure. The next subsection considers a more realistic task.

3.3 Parsing the Penn Tree-bank

Applying CHILL: A second set of experiments was carried out using a portion of the ATIS dataset from a preliminary version of the Penn Tree-bank (specifically, the sentences in the file `ti_tb`)[14]. We chose this particular data because it represents realistic input from human-computer interaction, and because it has been used in a number of other studies on automated grammar acquisition [6, 23] that can serve as a basis for comparison to CHILL. The corpus contains 729 sentences with an average length of 10.3 words. The experiments reported here were performed using "tagged" strings of lexical categories as input rather than words.

The learning component of CHILL remained exactly the same as in the case-role experiments except that the initial Parsing Operator Generator was modified to produce operators appropriate for the syntactic analyses of the Penn Tree-bank. As in case-role parsing, building an overly-general parser from a set of training examples is accomplished by constructing clauses for the op predicate. For example, an operator to reduce a prepositional phrase might look like: op([S1,S2|Ss], Words, [pp:[S2,S1]|Ss], Words).

Our initial experiments used this simple representation of parsing actions [30]. However, better results were obtained by making the operators more specific, effectively increasing the number of operators, but reducing the complexity of the control-rule induction task for each operator. The basic idea was to index the operators based on some relevant portion of the parsing context. In these experiments, the operators were indexed according to the syntactic category at the front of the input buffer. As an example, the general "shift" operator op(Stack, [Word|Words], [Word|Stack], Words) becomes multiple operators in slightly differing contexts such as:

op(Stack, [det|Ws], [det|Stack], Ws)
op(Stack, [np|Ws], [np|Stack], Ws)

The operators were placed in order of increasing frequency as indicated by the training set. This allows the learning of control rules which take advantage of "default" effects where specific exceptions are learned first before control falls through to the more generally applicable rules.

CHILL **Results:** Obviously, the most stringent measure of accuracy is the proportion of test sentences for which the produced parse tree exactly matches the tree-banked parse for the sentence. Sometimes, however, a parse can be useful even if it is not perfectly accurate; the tree-bank itself is not completely consistent in the handling of various structures.

To better gauge the partial accuracy of the parser, we adopted a procedure for returning and scoring partial parses. If the parser runs into a "dead-end" while parsing a test sentence, the contents of the stack at the time of impasse is returned as a single, flat constituent labeled S. Since the parsing operators are ordered and the shift operator is invariably the most frequently used operator in the training set, shift serves as a sort of default when no reduction action applies. Therefore, at the time of impasse, all of the words of the sentence will be on the stack, and partial constituents will have been built. The contents of stack reflect the partial progress of the parser in finding constituents.

Partial scoring of trees is computed by determining the extent of overlap between the computed parse and the correct parse as recorded in the tree-bank. Two constituents are said to match if they span exactly the same words in the sentence. If constituents match and have the same label, then they are identical. The overlap between the computed parse and the correct parse is computed by trying to match each constituent of the computed parse with some constituent in the correct parse. If an identical constituent is found, the score is 1.0, a matching constituent with an incorrect label scores 0.5. The sum of the scores for all constituents is the overlap score for the parse. The accuracy of the parse is then computed as $Accuracy = (\frac{O}{Found} + \frac{O}{Correct})/2$ where O is the overlap score, $Found$ is the number of constituents in the computed parse, and $Correct$ is the number of constituents in the correct tree. The result is an average of the proportion of the computed parse that is correct and the proportion of the correct parse that was actually found.

Another accuracy measure, which has been used in evaluating systems that bracket the input sentence into unlabeled constituents, is the proportion of constituents in the parse that do not cross any constituent boundaries in the correct tree [2]. We have computed the number of sentences with parses containing no crossing constituents, as well as the proportion of constituents which are non-crossing over all test sentences. This gives a basis of comparison with previous bracketing results, although it should be emphasized that CHILL is designed for the harder task of actually producing labeled parses, and is not optimized for bracketing.

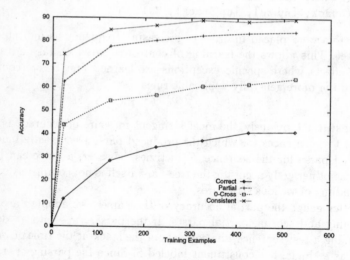

Fig. 3. CHILL ATIS Results

The average learning curves over 5 trials using independent testing sets of 204 sentences are shown in Figure 3. *Correct* is the percentage of test sentences with parses that matched the tree-banked parse exactly. *Partial* is partial correctness using the overlap metric. *0-Cross* is the proportion of test sentences having no constituents that cross constituent boundaries in the correct parsing. Finally, *Consistent* shows the overall percentage of constituents that are consistent with the tree-bank (i.e. cross no constituents in the correct parse).

The results are very encouraging. After training on 525 sentences, CHILL constructed completely correct parses for 41% of the novel testing sentences. Using the partial scoring metric, CHILL's parses garnered an average accuracy of over 84%. The figures for 0-cross and consistent compare very favorably with those reported in studies of automated bracketing for the ATIS corpus. Brill (1993) reports 60% and 91.12%, respectively. CHILL scores higher on the percentage of sentences with no crossing violations (64%) and slightly lower (90%) on the total percentage of non-crossing constituents. This is understandable as Brill's transformation learner tries to optimize the latter value, while CHILL's preference for sentence accuracy might tend to improve the former (since correctly parsed sentences are consistent).

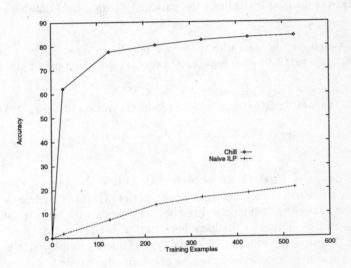

Fig. 4. CHILL vs. Naive ILP on ATIS Corpus

Comparison: On this less-structured, real-world corpora, the advantage of the control-rule framework over the naive approach becomes readily apparent. Figure 4 shows the results for the partial accuracy metric of the two systems in the ATIS experiment. Here CHILL has an overwhelming advantage, achieving 84% accuracy compared to the 20% accuracy of induction with implicit negatives. Clearly, providing the shift-reduce parsing framework significantly eases the task of the inductive component.

4 An Application: Parsing Database Queries

The foregoing experiments demonstrate that ILP techniques as implemented in CHILL can produce results that are comparable to, or better than, previous empirical approaches for constructing syntactic parsers on certain corpora. One of the shortcomings of these experiments is that the target representations were either syntactic or relatively shallow semantic structures. Parsing to this level of representation is only a small part of the larger problem of natural language understanding. Because of this, parsing systems are usually compared on the types of artificial metrics presented here. Unfortunately, it is not clear how well these metrics translate to performance on actual language processing tasks.

As we argued in the introduction, one of the major attractions of an approach based on first-order learning is its flexibility. The type of representation learned by CHILL is controlled only by the type of parsing operators employed. We have already shown that changing the parsing operators allows CHILL to learn parsers for either case-role assignments or syntactic parse-trees. However, CHILL is not restricted to learning syntactic representations. In an effort to assess the utility of CHILL in constructing a complete natural language application, a third operator framework was devised that allows the parsing of logic-based database queries.

What is the capital of the state with the largest population?
```
answer(C, (capital(S,C), largest(P, (state(S), population(S,P))))).
```

What are the major cities in Kansas?
```
answer(C, (major(C), city(C), loc(C,S), equal(S,stateid(kansas)))).
```

Fig. 5. Sample Database Queries

In the db-query task, CHILL is presented with a training set consisting of sentences paired with executable database queries. CHILL then learns a parser which maps subsequent sentences directly into queries with no other intermediate representation. Experiments have been performed using a database on U.S. geography. Figure 5 shows a sample of the type of queries employed. The data for these experiments was gathered by asking uninformed subjects to generate sample questions for the system. An analyst then paired the questions with approriate queries to generate an experimental corpus. Experiments were then performed by training on subsets of the corpus and evaluating the resulting parser on the unseen examples. The parser was judged to have parsed a new sentence correctly when the generated query produced exactly the same result as the query provided by the analyst. Hence, the metric is a true measure of performance in a complete database-query application.

Figure 6 shows the accuracy of CHILL's parsers over a 10 trial average. The line labeled "Geobase" shows the average accuracy of the Geobase system, a natural-language front-end supplied as an example application with a commercial Prolog system (Turbo Prolog 2.0 [5]). The curves show that CHILL outperforms the existing system when trained on 175 or more examples. In the best trial, CHILL's induced parser comprising 1100 lines of Prolog code achieved 84% accuracy in answering novel queries.

5 Future Work

Obviously, there is room for improvement in the results reported here. Improving the accuracy of the resulting parsers requires progress on two fronts. One way

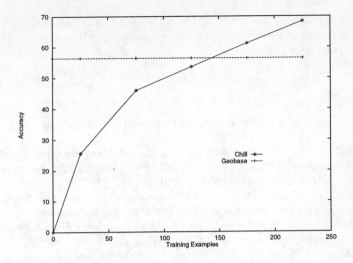

Fig. 6. CHILL Accuracy on Database Query Domain

to improve accuracy is to use larger training sets. Making this practical requires further improvements in the efficiency of the induction algorithm. Another avenue to improvement is the incorporation of more language-specific biases into the induction process. The shift-reduce framework of the current system is a rather weak bias compared to the types of restrictions which might be found in a "principles and parameters" based approach. A tighter integration of linguistic insights with ILP methods could probably create more efficient learning systems for language tasks.

We are also investigating the extension of these methods to deal with a broader range of NLP issues. On the lexical side, we are investigating new methods of parsing operator generation. These operators will allow the creation of deeper semantic representations that replace words with semantic tokens and infer information not explicitly given in the sentence. We also believe that ILP techniques might be usefully applied in learning larger discourse structures and information extraction tasks. We view CHILL as a mere starting point in the investigation of the usefulness of relational learning techniques for NLP in general.

6 Conclusions

In this paper we have argued that ILP techniques offer a more flexible approach to learning in natural language systems than do feature-vector representations. Experimental results with CHILL show that ILP techniques perform as well or better than propositional approaches on some comparable tasks. One of the major attractions of ILP is the ease with which it may be integrated with traditional, symbolic parsing methods. Indeed, the experiments demonstrate that the traditional shift-reduce framework used by CHILL is fundamental to CHILL's success in learning realistic language processing tasks.

Acknowledgments This research was supported by the National Science Foundation under grant IRI-9310819 and the Texas Advanced Research Program under grant ARP-003658-114.

References

1. B. Berwick. *The Acquisition of Syntactic Knowledge*. MIT Press, Cambridge, MA, 1985.
2. E. Black and et. al. A procedure for quantitatively comparing the syntactic coverage of English grammars. In *Proceedings of the Fourth DARPA Speech and Natural Language Workshop*, pages 306–311, 1991.
3. E. Black, F. Jelineck, J. Lafferty, D. Magerman, R. Mercer, and S. Roukos. Towards history-based grammars: Using richer models for probabilistic parsing. In *Proceedings of the 31st Annual Meeting of the Association for Computational Linguistics*, pages 31–37, Columbus, Ohio, 1993.
4. E. Black, J. Lafferty, and S. Roukaos. Development and evaluation of a broad-coverage probabilistic grammar of English-language computer manuals. In *Proceedings of the 30th Annual Meeting of the Association for Computational Linguistics*, pages 185–192, Newark, Delaware, 1992.
5. Borland International. *Turbo Prolog 2.0 Reference Guide*. Borland International, Scotts Valley, CA, 1988.
6. E. Brill. Automatic grammar induction and parsing free text: A transformation-based approach. In *Proceedings of the 31st Annual Meeting of the Association for Computational Linguistics*, pages 259–265, Columbus, Ohio, 1993.
7. Eugene Charniak and Glenn Carroll. Context-sensitive statistics for improved grammatical language models. In *Proceedings of the Twelfth National Conference on Artificial Intelligence*, Seattle, WA, August 1994.
8. D. Hindle and M. Rooth. Structural ambiguity and lexical relations. *Computational Linguistics*, 19(1):103–120, 1993.
9. B. Kijsirikul, M. Numao, and M. Shimura. Discrimination-based constructive induction of logic programs. In *Proceedings of the Tenth National Conference on Artificial Intelligence*, pages 44–49, San Jose, CA, July 1992.
10. N. Lavrač and S. Džeroski, editors. *Inductive Logic Programming: Techniques and Applications*. Ellis Horwood, 1994.
11. Jill Fain Lehman. Toward the essential nature of satistical knowledge in sense resolution. In *Proceedings of the Twelfth National Conference on Artificial Intelligence*, Seattle, WA, August 1994.
12. David M. Magerman. *Natrual Lagnuage Parsing as Statistical Pattern Recognition*. PhD thesis, Stanford University, 1994.
13. Christopher D. Manning. Automatic acquisition of a large subcategorization dictionary from corpora. In *Proceedings of the 31st Annual Meeting of the Association for Computational Linguistics*, pages 235–242, Columbus, Ohio, 1993.
14. M. Marcus, B. Santorini, and M.A. Marcinkiewicz. Building a large annotated corpus of English: The Penn treebank. *Computational Linguistics*, 19(2):313–330, 1993.
15. J. L. McClelland and A. H. Kawamoto. Mechanisms of sentence processing: Assigning roles to constituents of sentences. In D. E. Rumelhart and J. L. McClelland, editors, *Parallel Distributed Processing, Vol. II*, pages 318–362. MIT Press, Cambridge, MA, 1986.

16. R. Miikkulainen and M. G. Dyer. Natural language processing with modular PDP networks and distributed lexicon. *Cognitive Science*, 15:343–399, 1991.

17. Scott Miller, Robert Bobrow, Robert Ingria, and Richard Schwartz. Hidden understanding models of natural language. In *Proceedings of the 32nd Annual Meeting of the Association for Computational Linguistics*, pages 25–32, 1994.

18. R. J. Mooney and M. E. Califf. Induction of first-order decision lists: Results on learning the past tense of English verbs. *Journal of Artificial Intelligence Research*, 3:1–24, 1995.

19. S. Muggleton and W. Buntine. Machine invention of first-order predicates by inverting resolution. In *Proceedings of the Fifth International Conference on Machine Learning*, pages 339–352, Ann Arbor, MI, June 1988.

20. S. Muggleton and C. Feng. Efficient induction of logic programs. In S. Muggleton, editor, *Inductive Logic Programming*, pages 281–297. Academic Press, New York, 1992.

21. S. Muggleton, R. King, and M. Sternberg. Protein secondary structure prediction using logic-based machine learning. *Protein Engineering*, 5(7):647–657, 1992.

22. S. H. Muggleton, editor. *Inductive Logic Programming*. Academic Press, New York, NY, 1992.

23. F. Periera and Y. Shabes. Inside-outside reestimation from partially bracketed corpora. In *Proceedings of the 30th Annual Meeting of the Association for Computational Linguistics*, pages 128–135, Newark, Delaware, 1992.

24. J. R. Quinlan and R. M. Cameron-Jones. FOIL: A midterm report. In *Proceedings of the European Conference on Machine Learning*, pages 3–20, Vienna, 1993.

25. J.R. Quinlan. Learning logical definitions from relations. *Machine Learning*, 5(3):239–266, 1990.

26. R. F. Simmons and Y. Yu. The acquisition and use of context dependent grammars for English. *Computational Linguistics*, 18(4):391–418, 1992.

27. J. M. Zelle. *Using Inductive Logic Programming to Automate the Construction of Natural Language Parsers*. PhD thesis, University of Texas, Austin, TX, August 1995.

28. J. M. Zelle and R. J. Mooney. Learning semantic grammars with constructive inductive logic programming. In *Proceedings of the Eleventh National Conference on Artificial Intelligence*, pages 817–822, Washington, D.C., July 1993.

29. J. M. Zelle and R. J. Mooney. Combining top-down and bottom-up methods in inductive logic programming. In *Proceedings of the Eleventh International Conference on Machine Learning*, pages 343–351, New Brunswick, NJ, July 1994.

30. J. M. Zelle and R. J. Mooney. Inducing deterministic Prolog parsers from treebanks: A machine learning approach. In *Proceedings of the Twelfth National Conference on Artificial Intelligence*, pages 748–753, Seattle, WA, August 1994.

31. John M. Zelle, Cynthia A. Thompson, Mary Elaine Califf, and Raymond J. Mooney. Inducing logic programs without explicit negative examples. In *Proceedings of the Fifth International Workshop on Inductive Logic Programming*, 1995.

Learning the Past Tense of English Verbs Using Inductive Logic Programming

Raymond J. Mooney and Mary Elaine Califf

Department of Computer Sciences, University of Texas
Austin,TX 78712-1188

Abstract. This paper presents results on using a new inductive logic programming method called FOIDL to learn the past tense of English verbs. The past tense task has been widely studied in the context of the symbolic/connectionist debate. Previous papers have presented results using various neural-network and decision-tree learning methods. We have developed a technique for learning a special type of Prolog program called a *first-order decision list*, defined as an ordered list of clauses each ending in a cut. FOIDL is based on FOIL [19] but employs intensional background knowledge and avoids the need for explicit negative examples. It is particularly useful for problems that involve rules with specific exceptions, such as the past-tense task. We present results showing that FOIDL learns a more accurate past-tense generator from significantly fewer examples than all previous methods.

1 Introduction

The problem of learning the past tense of English verbs has been widely studied as an interesting subproblem in language acquisition. Previous research has applied both connectionist and symbolic method to this problem [22, 12, 9]; however, previous efforts used specially-designed feature-based encodings that impose a fixed limit on the length of words and fail to capture the generativity and position-independence of the underlying transformation. We believed that representing the problem as constructing a logic program for the predicate past(X,Y) where X and Y are words represented as lists of letters (e.g past([a,c,t], [a,c,t,e,d]),past([a,c,h,e],[a,c,h,e,d]),past([r,i,s,e],[r,o,s,e])) would produce much better results.

Inductive logic programming (ILP) is a growing subtopic of machine learning that studies the induction of Prolog programs from examples in the presence of background knowledge [15, 8]. Due to the expressiveness of first-order logic, ILP methods can learn relational and recursive concepts that cannot be represented in the attribute/value representations assumed by most machine-learning algorithms. However, current ILP techniques make important assumptions that restrict their application. Many assume that background knowledge is provided *extensionally* as a set of ground literals. However, an adequate extensional representation of background knowledge for some problems is infinite or intractable large. Most techniques assume that explicit negative examples of the target predicate are available or can be computed using a closed-world assumption, but for some problems explicit negative examples are not available, and an adequate set of negative examples computed using a closed-world assumption is infinite or intractably large. A third assumption is that the target program is expressed in "pure" Prolog where clause-order is irrelevant and procedural operators such as cut (!) are disallowed. However, a concise representation of many concepts requires the use of clause-ordering and/or cuts [2]. The currently most well-known and successful ILP systems, GOLEM [14] and FOIL [19], both make all three of these assumptions.

Due to these limitations, we were unable to get reasonable results on learning past tense from either FOIL or GOLEM. This paper presents a new ILP method called FOIDL (First-Order Induction of Decision Lists) which helps overcome these limitations. The system represents background knowledge *intensionally* as a logic program. It does not require explicit negative examples. Instead, an assumption of *output completeness* can be used to implicitly determine whether a hypothesized clause is overly-general and to quantify the degree of over-generality by estimating the number of negative examples covered. Finally, a learned program can be represented as a *first-order decision list*, an ordered set of clauses each ending with a cut. As its name implies, FOIDL is closely related to FOIL and follows a similar top-down, greedy specialization guided by an information-gain heuristic. However, the algorithm is substantially modified to address the three advantages listed above. The resulting system is able to learn the past tense of English more accurately and from fewer examples than any of the previous methods applied to this problem.

The remainder of the paper is organized as follows. Section 2 provides background material on FOIL and on the past-tense learning problem. Section 3 presents the FOIDL algorithm. Section 4 presents our results on learning the past-tense of English verbs. Section 5 discusses some related work, and Section 6 presents directions for future work. Section 7 summarizes and presents our conclusions.

2 Background

2.1 FOIL

Since FOIDL is based on FOIL, this section presents a brief review of this important ILP system; see articles on FOIL for a more complete description [19, 18, 4]. FOIL learns a function-free, first-order, Horn-clause definition of a *target* predicate in terms of itself and other *background* predicates. The input consists of extensional definitions of these predicates as tuples of constants of specified types. FOIL also requires negative examples of the target concept, which can be supplied directly or computed using a closed-world assumption.

Given this input, FOIL learns a program one clause at a time using a greedy-covering algorithm that can be summarized as follows:

Let *positives-to-cover* = positive examples.
While *positives-to-cover* is not empty
        Find a clause, C, that covers a preferably large subset of *positives-to-cover*
            but covers no negative examples.
        Add C to the developing definition.
        Remove examples covered by C from *positives-to-cover*.

The "find a clause" step is implemented by a general-to-specific hill-climbing search that adds antecedents to the developing clause one at a time. At each step, it evaluates possible literals that might be added and selects one that maximizes an information-gain heuristic. The algorithm maintains a set of tuples that satisfy the current clause and includes bindings for any new variables introduced in the body. The gain metric evaluates literals based on the number of positive and negative tuples covered, preferring literals that cover many positives and few negatives. The papers referenced above provide details and information on additional features.

2.2   Learning the Past Tense of English Verbs

The problem of learning the English past tense has been attempted by both connectionist systems [22, 12] and systems based on decision tree induction [11, 9]. The task to be learned in these experiments is: given a phonetic encoding of the base form of an English verb, generate the phonetic encoding of the past tense form of that verb. The task can also be done using the alphabetic forms forms of the verbs, and we use that form of the task for the examples in this paper. All of this work encodes the problem as fixed-length pattern association and fails to capture the generativity and position-independence of the true regular rules such as "add 'ed'," instead producing several position-dependent rules. Each output unit or separate decision tree is used to predict a character in the fixed-length output pattern from all of the input characters.

Although ILP methods seem more appropriate for this problem, our initial attempts to apply FOIL and GOLEM to past-tense learning gave very disappointing results [3]. Below, we discuss how the three problems listed in the introduction contribute to the difficulty of applying current ILP methods to this problem.

In principle, a background predicate for `append` is sufficient for constructing accurate past-tense programs when incorporated with an ability to include constants as arguments or, equivalently, an ability to add literals that bind variables to specific constants (called *theory constants* in FOIL). However, a background predicate that does not allow appending with the empty list is more appropriate. We use a predicate called `split(A, B, C)` which splits a list `A` into two non-empty sublists `B` and `C`. An intensional definition for `split` is:

```
split([X, Y | Z], [X] , [Y | Z]).
split([X | Y], [X | W], Z) :- split(Y,W,Z).
```

Providing an extensional definition of `split` that includes all possible strings of 15 or fewer characters (at least 10^{21} strings) is clearly intractable. However, providing a partial definition that includes all possible splits of strings that actually appear in the training corpus is possible and generally sufficient. Therefore, providing adequate extensional background knowledge is cumbersome and requires careful engineering; however, it is not the major problem.

Supplying an appropriate set of negative examples is more problematic. Accuracy for this domain should be measured by the ability to actually generate correct output for novel inputs, rather than the ability to correctly classify novel ground examples. Using a closed-world assumption to produce all pairs of words in the training set where the second is not the past-tense of the first tends to produce clauses such as:

```
past(A,B) :- split(B,A,C).
```

which is useless for producing the past tense of novel verbs. However, supplying all possible strings of 15 characters or less as negative examples of the past tense of each word is clearly intractable.

When Quinlan applied FOIL to the past tense problem [17], he used a three-place predicate past(X,Y,Z) which is true iff the input word X is transformed into past-tense form by removing its current ending Y and substituting the ending Z; for example: past([a,c,t],[],[e,d]), past([r,i,s,e],[i,s,e],[o,s,e]). This method allows the generation of useful negatives under the closed world assumption, but relies on an understanding of the desired transformation.

Although he solves the problem of providing negatives, Quinlan notes that his results are still hampered by FOIL's inability to exploit clause order [17]. For example, when using normal alphabetic encoding, FOIL quickly learns a clause sufficient for regular verbs:

```
past(A,B,C) :- B=[], C=[e,d].
```

However, since this clause still covers a fair number of negative examples due to many irregular verbs, it continues to add literals. As a result, FOIL creates a number of specialized versions of this clause that together still fail to capture the generality of the underlying default rule.

However, an experienced Prolog programmer would exploit clause order and cuts to write a concise program that first handles the most specific exceptions and falls through to more general default rules if the exceptions fail to apply. Such a program might be:

```
past(A,B) :- split(A,C,[e,e,p]), split(B,C,[e,p,t]), !.
past(A,B) :- split(A,C,[y]), split(B,C,[i,e,d]), !.
past(A,B) :- split(A,C,[e]), split(B,A,[d]), !.
past(A,B) :- split(B,A,[e,d]).
```

FOIDL can directly learn programs of this form, i.e., ordered sets of clauses each ending in a cut. We call such programs first-order decision lists due to the similarity to the propositional *decision lists* introduced by Rivest [21]. FOIDL uses the normal binary target predicate and requires no explicit negative examples. Therefore, we believe it requires *significantly* less representation engineering than all previous work in the area.

3   FOIDL Induction Algorithm

As stated in the introduction, FOIDL adds three major features to FOIL: 1) Intensional specification of background knowledge, 2) Output completeness as a substitute for explicit negative examples, and 3) Support for learning first-order decision lists. We now describe the modifications made to incorporate these features.

As described above, FOIL assumes background predicates are provided with extensional definitions; however, this is burdensome and frequently intractable. Providing an intensional definition in the form of general Prolog clauses is generally preferable. Intentional background definitions are not restricted to function-free pure Prolog and can exploit all features of the language.

Modifying FOIL to use intensional background is straightforward. Instead of matching a literal against a set of tuples to determine whether or not it covers an example, the Prolog interpreter is used in an attempt to prove that the literal can be satisfied using the intensional definitions. Unlike FOIL, expanded tuples are not maintained and positive and negative examples of the target concept are reproved for each alternative specialization of the developing clause.

Learning without explicit negatives requires an alternate method of evaluating the utility of a clause. A mode declaration and an assumption of output completeness together determine a set of implicit negative examples. The output completeness assumption indicates that for every unique input pattern in the training set, the training set includes all of the correct output patterns. Therefore, any other output which a programm produces for a given input pattern must be a negative example.

Consider the predicate, `past(Present,Past)` which holds when `Past` is the past-tense form of a verb whose present tense is `Present`. Providing the mode declaration `past(+,-)` indicates that the predicate should provide the correct past tense when provided with the present tense form. Assuming the past form of a verb is unique, any set of positive examples of this predicate will be output complete. However, output completeness can also be applied to non-functional cases such as `append(-,-,+)`, indicating that all possible pairs of lists that can be appended together to produce a list are included in the training set (e.g., `append([], [a,b], [a,b])`, `append([a], [b], [a,b])`, `append([a,b], [], [a,b])`).

Given an output completeness assumption, determining whether a clause is overly-general is straightforward. For each positive example, an *output query* is made to determine all outputs for the given input (e.g., `past([a,c,t], X)`). If any outputs are generated that are not positive examples, the clause still covers negative examples and requires further specialization. In addition, in order to compute the gain of alternative literals during specialization, the negative coverage of a clause needs to be quantified. Each ground, incorrect answer to an output query clearly counts as a single negative example (e.g., `past([a,c,h,e]`, `[a,c,h,e,e,d])`). However, output queries will frequently produce answers with universally quantified variables. For example, given the overly-general clause `past(A,B) :- split(A,C,D).`, the query `past([a,c,t], X)` generates the answer `past([a,c,t], Y)`. This implicitly represents coverage of an infinite number of negative examples.

In order to quantify negative coverage, FOIDL uses a parameter u to represent a bound on the number of possible terms in the universe. The negative coverage represented by a non-ground answer to an output query is then estimated as $u^v - p$, where v is the number of variable arguments in the answer and p is the number of positive examples with which the answer unifies. The u^v term stands for the number of unique ground outputs represented by the answer (e.g., the answer `append(X,Y,[a,b])` stands for u^2 different ground outputs) and the p term stands for the number of these that represent positive examples. This allows FOIDL to quantify coverage of large numbers of implicit negative examples without ever explicitly constructing them. It is generally sufficient to estimate u as a fairly large constant (e.g., 1000), and empirically the method is not very sensitive to its exact value as long as it is significantly greater than the number of ground outputs ever generated by a clause.

Unfortunately, this estimate is not sensitive enough. For example, both clauses

```
past(A,B) :- split(A,C,D).
past(A,B) :- split(B,A,C).
```

cover u implicit negative examples for the output query `past([a,c,t], X)` since the first produces the answer `past([a,c,t], Y)` and the second produces the answer `past([a,c,t], [a,c,t | Y])`. However, the second clause is clearly better since it at least requires the output to be the input with some suffix added. Since there are presumably more words than there are words that start with "a-c-t" (assuming the total number of words is finite), the first clause should be considered to cover more negative examples. Therefore, arguments that are partially instantiated, such as `[a,c,t | Y]`, are counted as only a fraction of a variable when calculating v. Specifically, a partially instantiated output argument is scored as the fraction of its subterms that are variables, e.g., `[a,c,t | Y]` counts as only 1/4 of a variable argument. Therefore, the first clause above is scored as covering u implicit negatives and the second as covering only $u^{1/4}$. Given reasonable values for u and the number of positives covered by each clause, the literal `split(B,A,C)` will be preferred.

As described above, first-order decision lists are ordered sets of clauses each ending in a cut. When answering an output query, the cuts simply eliminate all but the first answer produced when trying the clauses in order. Therefore, this representation is similar to propositional decision lists [21], which are ordered lists of pairs (rules) of the form (t_i, c_i) where the test t_i is a conjunction of features and c_i is a category label and an example is assigned to the category of the first pair whose test it satisfies.

In the original algorithm of Rivest [21] and in CN2 [5], rules are learned in the order they appear in the final decision list (i.e., new rules are appended to the end of the list as they are learned). However, Webb and Brkic [23] argue for learning decision lists in the reverse order since most preference functions tend to learn more general rules first, and these are best positioned as default cases towards the end. They introduce an algorithm, *prepend*, that learns decision lists in reverse order and present results indicating that in most cases it learns simpler decision lists with superior predictive accuracy. FOIDL can be seen as generalizing *prepend* to the first-order case for target predicates representing functions. It learns an ordered sequence of clauses in reverse order, resulting in a program which produces only the first output generated by the first satisfied clause.

The basic operation of the algorithm is best illustrated by a concrete example. For alphabetic past-tense, the current algorithm easily learns the partial clause:

```
past(A,B) :- split(B,A,C), C = [e,d].
```

This clause still covers negative examples due to irregular verbs. However, it produces correct ground output for a subset of the examples. Therefore, it is best to terminate this clause to handle these examples, and add earlier clauses in the decision list to handle the remaining examples. The fact that it produces incorrect answers for other output queries can be safely ignored in the decision-list framework. The examples correctly covered by this clause are removed from *positives-to-cover* and a new clause is begun. The literals that now provide the best gain are:

```
past(A,B) :- split(B,A,C), C = [d].
```

covering the verbs that just add "d" since they end in "e". This clause also produces correct ground output for a subset of the examples; however, it is not complete since it produces incorrect output for examples correctly covered by a previously learned clause (e.g., past([a,c,t], [a,c,t,d])). Therefore, specialization continues until all of these cases are also eliminated, resulting in the clause:

```
past(A,B) :- split(B,A,C), C = [d], split(A,D,E), E = [e].
```

which is added to the front of the decision list. This approach ensures that every new clause produces correct outputs for some new subset of the examples but doesn't result in incorrect output for examples already correctly covered by previously learned clauses. This process continues adding clauses to the front of the decision list until all of the exceptions are handled and *positives-to-cover* is empty.

The resulting clause-specialization algorithm can now be summarized as follows:

Initialize C to $R(V_1, V_2, ..., V_k)$:-. where R is the target predicate with arity k.
Initialize T to contain the examples in *positives-to-cover* and output queries for a all positive examples.
While T contains output queries
    Find the best literal L to add to the clause.
    Let T' be the subset of positive examples in T whose output query still produces a first answer that unifies with the correct answer, plus the output queries in T that either

> 1) Produce a non-ground first answer that unifies with the correct answer, or
>
> 2) Produce an incorrect answer but produce a correct answer using a previously learned clause.

Replace T by T'.

In many cases, this algorithm is able to learn accurate, compact, first-order decision lists for past tense, like the "expert" program shown in section 2.2. However, the algorithm can encounter local-minima in which it is unable to find any literals that provide positive gain while still covering the required minimum number of examples.[1] This was originally handled by terminating search and memorizing any remaining uncovered examples as specific exceptions at the top of the decision list. However, this can result in premature termination that prevents the algorithm from finding low-frequency regularities. For example, in the alphabetic version, the system can get stuck trying to learn the complex rule for when to double a final consonant (e.g., grab → grabbed) and fail to learn the rule for changing "y" to "ied" since this is actually less frequent.

The current version, like FOIL, tests if the learned clause meets a minimum-accuracy threshold, but only counts as errors incorrect outputs for queries correctly answered by previously learned clauses. If it does not meet the threshold, the clause is thrown out and the positive examples it covers are memorized at the top of the decision list. The algorithm then continues to learn clauses for any remaining positive examples.

When the minimum-accuracy threshold is met, the decision-list property is exploited in a final attempt to still learn a completely accurate program. If the negatives covered by the clause are all examples correctly covered by previously learned clauses, FOIDL treats them as "exceptions to the exception to the rule" and returns them to *positives-to-cover* to be covered correctly again by subsequently learned clauses. With the minimum clause-accuracy threshold set to 50%, FOIDL only applies this *uncovering* technique when it results in covering more examples than it uncovers, thereby guaranteeing progress towards fitting all of the training examples.

An implementation of FOIDL in Quintus Prolog is available by anonymous FTP from `ftp.cs.utexas.edu`.

4 Experimental Results

To test FOIDL's performance on the English past tense task, we ran experiments using data from Ling [9] which consist of 1390 pairs of base and past tense verb forms in alphabetic and UNIBET phonemic form. We ran three different experiments. In one we used the phonetic forms of all verbs. In the second we used the phonetic forms of the regular verbs only, because this is the easiest form of the task and because this is the only problem for which Ling provides

---

[1] Like FOIL, FOIDL includes a parameter for the minimum number of examples that a clause must cover (normally set to 2).

learning curves. Finally, we ran trials using the alphabetic forms of all verbs. The training and testing followed the standard paradigm of splitting the data into testing and training sets and training on progressively larger samples of the training set. All results were averaged over 10 trials, and the testing set for each trial contained 500 verbs.

In order to better separate the contribution of using implicit negatives from the contribution of the decision list representation, we also ran experiments with IFOIL, a variant of the system which uses intensional background and the output completeness assumption, but does not build decision lists.

We ran our own experiments with FOIL, FOIDL, and IFOIL and compared those with the results from Ling. The FOIL experiments were run using Quinlan's representation described above. As in Quinlan [17], negative examples were provided by using a randomly-selected 25% of those which could be generated using the closed world assumption.[2] All experiments with FOIDL and IFOIL used the standard default values for the various numeric parameters. The differences among FOIL, IFOIL, and FOIDL were tested for significance using a two-tailed paired t-test.

4.1 Results

The results for the phonetic task using all verbs are presented in Figure 1. The graph shows our results with FOIL, IFOIL, and FOIDL along with the best results from Ling, who did not provide a learning curve for this task. As expected, FOIDL out-performed the other systems on this task, surpassing Ling's best results with 500 examples with only 100 examples. IFOIL performed quite poorly, barely beating the neural network results despite effectively having 100% of the negatives as opposed to FOIL's 25%. This poor performance is due at least in part to overfitting the training data, because IFOIL lacks the noise-handling techniques of FOIL6. FOIL also has the advantage of the three-place predicate, which gives it a bias toward learning suffixes. IFOIL's poor performance on this task shows that the implicit negatives by themselves are not sufficient, and that some other bias such as decision lists or the three-place predicate and noise-handling is needed. The differences between FOIL and FOIDL are significant at the 0.01 level. Those between FOIDL and IFOIL are significant at the 0.001 level. The differences between FOIL and IFOIL are not significant with 100 training examples or less, but are significant at the 0.001 level with 250 and 500 examples.

Figure 2 presents accuracy results on the phonetic task using regulars only. The curves for SPA and the neural net are the results reported by Ling. Here again, FOIDL out-performed the other systems. This particular task demonstrated one of the problems with using closed-world negatives. In the regular past tense task, the second argument of Quinlan's 3-place predicate is always the same: an empty list. Therefore, if the constants are generated from the positive examples, FOIL will never produce rules which ground the second argument,

---

[2] We replicated Quinlan's approach since memory limitations prevented us from using 100% of the generated negatives with larger training sets.

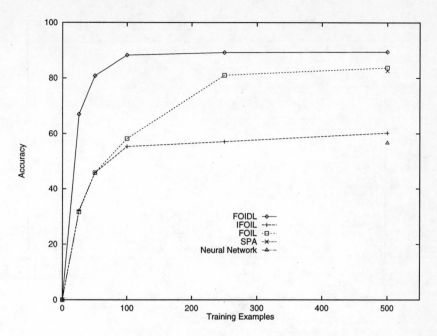

Fig. 1. Accuracy on phonetic past tense task using all verbs

since it cannot create negative examples with other constants in the second argument. This prevents the system from learning a rule to generate the past tense. In order to obtain the results reported here, we introduced extra constants for the second argument (specifically the constants for the third argument), enabling the closed world assumption to generate appropriate negatives. On this task, IFOIL does seem to gain some advantage over FOIL from being able to effectively use all of the negatives. The regularity of the data allows both IFOIL and FOIL to achieve over 90% accuracy at 500 examples. The differences between FOIL and FOIDL are significant at the 0.001 level, as are those between IFOIL and FOIDL. The differences between IFOIL and FOIL are not significant with 25 examples, and are significant at the 0.02 level with 500 examples, but are significant at the 0.001 level with 50-250 training examples.

Results for the alphabetic version appear in Figure 3. This is a task which has not typically been considered in the literature, but it is of interest to those concerned with incorporating morphology into natural language understanding systems which deal with text. It is also the most difficult task, primarily because of consonant doubling. Here we have results only for FOIDL, IFOIL, and FOIL. Because the alphabetic task is even more irregular than the full phonetic task, IFOIL again overfits the data and performs quite poorly. The differences between FOIL and FOIDL are significant at the 0.001 level with 25, 50, 250, and 500 examples, but only at the 0.1 level with 100 examples. The differences between IFOIL and FOIDL are all significant at the 0.001 level. Those between FOIL and IFOIL are not significant with 25 training examples and are significant only at

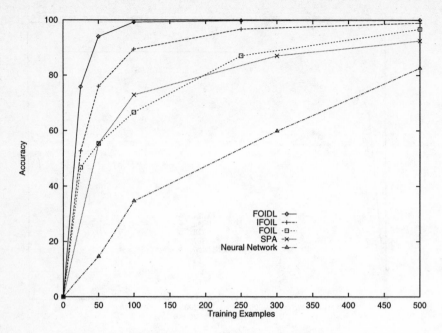

Fig. 2. Accuracy on phonetic past tense task using regulars only

the 0.01 level with 50 training examples, but are significant at the 0.001 level with 100 or more examples.

For all three of these tasks, FOIDL clearly outperforms the other systems. A sufficient set of negatives is necessary, and all five of these systems provide them in some way: the neural network and SPA both learn multiple-class classification tasks (which phoneme belongs in each position); FOIL uses the three-place predicate with closed world negatives; and IFOIL and FOIDL, of course, use the output completeness assumption. The primary importance of the implicit negatives is not that they provide an advantage over propositional and neural network systems, but that they enable first order systems to perform this task at all. Without them, some knowledge of the task is required. FOIDL's decision lists give it a significant added advantage, though this advantage is less apparent in the regular phonetic task, where there are no exceptions.

FOIDL also generates very comprehensible programs. The following is an example program generated for the alphabetic version of the task using 250 examples (excluding the memorized examples).

```
past(A,B) :- split(A,C,[e,p]), split(B,C,[p,t]),!.
past(A,B) :- split(A,C,[y]), split(B,C,[i,e,d]),
             split(A,D,[r,y]),!.
past(A,B) :- split(A,C,[y]), split(B,C,[i,e,d]),
             split(A,D,[l,y]),!.
past(A,B) :- split(B,A,[m,e,d]), split(A,C,[m]),
```

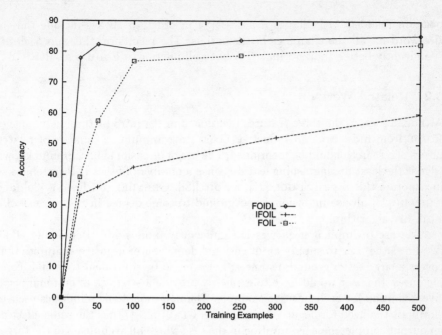

Fig. 3. Accuracy on alphabetic past tense task

```
                split(A,[s],D),!.
past(A,B) :- split(B,A,[r,e,d]), split(A,C,[u,r]),!.
past(A,B) :- split(B,A,[d]), split(A,C,[e]),!.
past(A,B) :- split(B,A,[e,d]),!.
```

5 Related Work

5.1 Related Work on Past-Tense Learning

The shortcomings of most previous work on past-tense learning were reviewed in section 2.2, and the results in section 4 clearly demonstrate the generalization advantage FOIDL exhibits on this problem.

Most of the previous work on this problem has concerned the modelling of various psychological phenomenon, such as the U-shaped learning curve that children exhibit for irregular verbs when acquiring language. This paper has not addressed the issue of psychological validity, and we make no specific psychological claims based on our current results.

However, humans can obviously produce the correct past tense of arbitrarily-long novel words, which FOIDL can easily model while fixed-length feature-based representations clearly cannot. Ling also developed a version of SPA that eliminates position dependence and fixed word-length [10] by using a sliding window. A large window is used which includes 15 letters on either side of the current position (padded with blanks if necessary) in order to always include the entire word for all the examples in the corpus. The results on this approach are significantly better than normal SPA but still inferior to FOIDL's results.

5.2 Related Work on ILP

Although each of the three features mentioned in the introduction distinguishes FOIDL from most work in Inductive Logic Programming, a number of related pieces of research should be mentioned. The use of intensional background knowledge is the least distinguishing feature, since a number of other ILP systems also incorporate this aspect. FOCL [16], MFOIL [[8]], GRENDEL [6], FORTE [20], and CHILLIN [25] all use intensional background to some degree in the context of a FOIL-like algorithm.

The use of implicit negatives is significantly more novel. Bergadano et al. [2] allows the user to supply an intensional definition of negative examples that covers a large set of ground instances; however, to be equivalent to output completeness, the user would have to explicitly provide a separate intensional negative definition for each positive example. The non-monotonic semantics used to eliminate the need for negative examples in CLAUDIEN [7] has the same effect as an output completeness assumption in the case where all arguments of the target relation are outputs. However, output completeness permits more flexibility by allowing some arguments to be specified as inputs and only counting as negative examples those extra outputs generated for specific inputs in the training set. FLIP [1] provides a method for learning functional programs without negative examples by making an assumption equivalent to output completeness for the functional case only.

The notion of a first-order decision list is unique to FOIDL. The only other ILP system that attempts to learn programs that exploit clause-order and cuts is that of Bergadano et al. [2]. Their paper discusses learning arbitrary programs with cuts, and the brute-force search used in their approach is intractable for most realistic problems. FOIDL is tailored to the specific problem of learning first-order decision lists, which use cuts in a very stylized manner that is particularly useful for functional problems that involve rules with exceptions.

6 Future Work

One obvious topic for future research is FOIDL's cognitive modelling abilities in the context of the past-tense task. Incorporating over-fitting avoidance methods may allow the system to model the U-shaped learning curve in a manner analogous to that demonstrated by Ling and Marinov [11]. Its ability to model human results on generating the past tense of novel psuedo-verbs (e.g., spling → splang) could also be examined and compared to SPA and connectionist methods.

Although first-order decision lists represent a fairly general class of programs, currently our only convincing experimental results are on the past-tense problem. The decision list mechanism in general should be applicable to other language problems (as evidenced by the use of propositional decision lists for problems such as lexical disambiguation [24]. Many realistic problems consist of rules with exceptions, and experimental results on additional applications are needed to support the general utility of this representation.

7 Conclusions

Learning the past tense of English is a small by interesting subproblem in language acquisition which captures some of the fundamental problems such as the generative ability to handle arbitrarily long input and the ability to learn exceptions as well as underlying regularities. Compared to feature-based approaches such as neural-network, decision tree, and statistical methods, inductive logic programming offers the advantage of generativity in being able to handle arbitrarily long input. In addition, the use of first-order decision lists allow one to easily represent exceptions as well as general default rules. Our results clearly demonstrate that an ILP system for learning first-order decision lists can outprerform both the symbolic and the neural-network systems previously applied to the past-tense task. Since the issues of generativity and exceptions and defaults are ubiquitous in language acquisition, we believe this approach will also be useful for other language learning problems.

Acknowledgements Most of the basic research for this paper was conducted while the first author was on leave at the University of Sydney supported by a grant to Prof. J.R. Quinlan from the Australian Research Council. Thanks to Ross Quinlan for providing this enjoyable and productive opportunity and to both Ross and Mike Cameron-Jones for very important discussions and pointers that greatly aided the development of FOIDL. Partial support was also provided by grant IRI-9310819 from the National Science Foundation and an MCD fellowship from the University of Texas awarded to the second author. A fuller discussion of this research appears in [13].

References

1. F. Bergadano and D. Gunetti. An interactive system to learn functional logic programs. In *Proceedings of the Thirteenth International Joint Conference on Artificial Intelligence*, pages 1044–1049, Chambery, France, 1993.
2. F. Bergadano, D. Gunetti, and U. Trinchero. The difficulties of learning logic programs with cut. *Journal of Artificial Intelligence Research*, 1:91–107, 1993.
3. M. E. Califf. Learning the past tense of English verbs: An inductive logic programming approach. Unpublished project report, 1994.
4. R. Mike Cameron-Jones and J. Ross Quinlan. Efficient top-down induction of logic programs. *SIGART Bulletin*, 5(1):33–42, Jan 1994.
5. P. Clark and T. Niblett. The CN2 induction algorithm. *Machine Learning*, 3:261–284, 1989.

6. W.W. Cohen. Compiling prior knowledge into an explicit bias. In *Proceedings of the Ninth International Conference on Machine Learning*, pages 102–110, Aberdeen, Scotland, July 1992.

7. L. De Raedt and M. Bruynooghe. A theory of clausal discovery. In *Proceedings of the Thirteenth International Joint Conference on Artificial Intelligence*, pages 1058–1063, Chambery, France, 1993.

8. N. Lavrač and S. Džeroski, editors. *Inductive Logic Programming: Techniques and Applications*. Ellis Horwood, 1994.

9. C. X. Ling. Learning the past tense of English verbs: The symbolic pattern associator vs. connectionist models. *Journal of Artificial Intelligence Research*, 1:209–229, 1994.

10. C. X. Ling, 1995. Personal communication.

11. C. X. Ling and M. Marinov. Answering the connectionist challenge: A symbolic model of learning the past tense of English verbs. *Cognition*, 49(3):235–290, 1993.

12. B. MacWhinney and J. Leinbach. Implementations are not conceptualizations: Revising the verb model. *Cognition*, 40:291–296, 1991.

13. R. J. Mooney and M. E. Califf. Induction of first-order decision lists: Results on learning the past tense of English verbs. *Journal of Artificial Intelligence Research*, 3:1–24, 1995.

14. S. Muggleton and C. Feng. Efficient induction of logic programs. In *Proceedings of the First Conference on Algorithmic Learning Theory*, Tokyo, Japan, 1990. Ohmsha.

15. S. H. Muggleton, editor. *Inductive Logic Programming*. Academic Press, New York, NY, 1992.

16. M. Pazzani and D. Kibler. The utility of background knowledge in inductive learning. *Machine Learning*, 9:57–94, 1992.

17. J. R. Quinlan. Past tenses of verbs and first-order learning. In C. Zhang, J. Debenham, and D. Lukose, editors, *Proceedings of the Seventh Australian Joint Conference on Artificial Intelligence*, pages 13–20, Singapore, 1994. World Scientific.

18. J. R. Quinlan and R. M. Cameron-Jones. FOIL: A midterm report. In *Proceedings of the European Conference on Machine Learning*, pages 3–20, Vienna, 1993.

19. J.R. Quinlan. Learning logical definitions from relations. *Machine Learning*, 5(3):239–266, 1990.

20. B. L. Richards and R. J. Mooney. Automated refinement of first-order Horn-clause domain theories. *Machine Learning*, 19(2):95–131, 1995.

21. R. L . Rivest. Learning decision lists. *Machine Learning*, 2(3):229–246, 1987.

22. D. E. Rumelhart and J. McClelland. On learning the past tense of English verbs. In D. E. Rumelhart and J. L. McClelland, editors, *Parallel Distributed Processing, Vol. II*, pages 216–271. MIT Press, Cambridge, MA, 1986.

23. G. I. Webb and N. Brkič. Learning decision lists by prepending inferred rules. In *Proceedings of the Australian Workshop on Machine Learning and Hybrid Systems*, pages 6–10, Melbourne, Australia, 1993.

24. David Yarowsky. Decision lists for lexical ambiguity resolution: Application to accent restoration in Spanish and French. In *Proceedings of the 32nd Annual Meeting of the Association for Computational Linguistics*, pages 88–95, Las Cruces, NM, 1994.

25. J. M. Zelle and R. J. Mooney. Combining top-down and bottom-up methods in inductive logic programming. In *Proceedings of the Eleventh International Conference on Machine Learning*, pages 343–351, New Brunswick, NJ, July 1994.

A Dynamic Approach to Paradigm-driven Analogy*

Stefano Federici[1], Vito Pirrelli[2], François Yvon[3]

[1] Parola s.a.s., via del Borghetto 35 , 56100 Pisa
[2] ILC-CNR Pisa, Via Della Faggiola 32, 56216 Pisa
[3] ENST-Paris, 46 rue Barrault 75013 Paris

Abstract. When looked at from a multilingual perspective, grapheme-to-phoneme conversion is a challenging task, fraught with most of the classical NLP "vexed questions": bottle-neck problem of data acquisition, pervasiveness of exceptions, difficulty to state range and order of rule application, proper treatment of context-sensitive phenomena and long-distance dependencies, and so on. The hand-crafting of transcription rules by a human expert is onerous and time-consuming, and yet, for some European languages, still stops short of a level of correctness and accuracy acceptable for practical applications. We illustrate here a self-learning multilingual system for analogy-based pronunciation which was tested on Italian, English and French, and whose performances are assessed against the output of both statistically and rule-based transcribers. The general point is made that analogy-based self-learning techniques are no longer just psycholinguistically-plausible models, but competitive tools, combining the advantages of using language-independent, self-learning, tractable algorithms, with the welcome bonus of being more reliable for applications than traditional text-to-speech systems.

1 Analogy and Grapheme-to-Phoneme Conversion

In Computational Linguistics, generalization by analogy is defined as the inferential process by which an unfamiliar linguistic object O (the *target object*) is seen as an analogue of more familiar objects (the *base objects*), so that whatever piece of knowledge is acquired about the latter can be used to deal with the former too [13]. For the present purposes this means that a written unknown word can be read aloud on the basis of its analogy to known words whose spelling and pronunciation are already familiar to the reader. In Fig. 1 overleaf, the pronunciation of the (target) Italian name 'bellini' is inferred from the pronunciation of the known 'bellomo' and 'martini', based on their orthographic overlap (shared letters) with the input string. The approach is conceptually close to both instance-based [5, 12] and case-based [11, 18] learning, although in analogy-based pronunciation more emphasis is laid on the cognitive plausibility

---

* This paper is the outcome of a cooperative effort. However, for the specific concern of the Italian Academy only, S. Federici is responsible for sections 6 and 7, V. Pirrelli for sections 1, 2 and 3, and F. Yvon for sections 4 and 5

of base retrieval and the role of analogizing factors, rather than on automatic data clustering and extraction of statistically-grounded grapheme-to-phoneme regularities.

Several proposals have been put forward in psycholinguistic circles as to what counts as an analogically relevant factor, that is as a clue to a true analogy between words [7]. Here, we will not go into this issue: for the sake of simplicity, orthographic similarity is the only relevant analogizing factor. Moreover, it is assumed that knowing how a written word is to be read aloud implies knowledge of its spelling, its transcription and the way orthographic characters are aligned with phonological segments. Information about alignment is by no means a necessary condition for analogized transcription [16, 2], but certainly helps to simplify the learning problem considerably. Finally, although it was shown that more sophisticated linguistic knowledge than raw alignment can profitably be used for the task at hand [8], we intended to see how far one can go with a somewhat linguistically-impoverished dataset of base objects.

In what follows, we will give a precise characterization of the sort of learning involved in the process of reading words aloud by analogy in a computer simulation, with particular emphasis on the nature of the internal architecture of the dataset of base objects, the way it changes through exposure to more and more data, and the way this incremental change affects the accuracy of analogy. This emphasis differentiates our model from other well-known analogy-based systems [4, 19], whose exclusive focus is on base retrieval by analogical mapping. Finally, we will show that automatic pronunciation by analogy is not just cognitively more plausible, but also more accurate than statistically-based or rule-based transcription, a point which, together with the self-learning capabilities of analogy-based generalization, gives further credit to its potential for applications.

2 Basics

In this section, we introduce and discuss the essential ingredients of our procedural definition of pronunciation by analogy: namely, *analogical mapping, structure of the dataset of base objects, search space* and *recombination*.

In analogy-based transcription *analogical mapping* is the core algorithmic procedure through which, for a target word to be pronounced (say the Italian name 'bellini'), a subset of its closest analogues is extracted from the dataset (say 'bellomo' and 'martini'). As pointed out before, analogues are found on the basis of the number of characters they share with the target word: the more characters are shared, the more reliable the overlapping analogue is likely to be.

Given a dataset and a target word W, a simple way of implementing the notion of analogical mapping is to look for two best analogues at a time: first, the base object which shares with the target the longest chunk of running characters, starting from the leftmost character rightwards (the *longest head*); second, the base object which shares the longest continuous chunk starting from W's rightmost character backwards (the *longest tail*). The strategy is illustrated in

Fig. 1, where the chunks corresponding to the longest head and tail are simply concatenated one after the other.

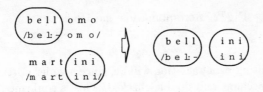

Fig. 1. Pronunciation of 'bellini' by Analogy

An interesting related issue here is whether analogical mapping presupposes the existence of some *search space*, and, if so, how this search space should be defined. If one responds affirmatively, then it is assumed that some candidate analogues should be given precedence over other base objects, and that this precedence should reflect some underlying structure of the *dataset of base objects* (hereafter dataset for short). In our view of things, the assumption that there exists a linguistic structure underlying the dataset of base objects is correct: moreover, we claim that this structure has an analogical nature (see further below).

Once mapping candidates are found, it remains to be seen how they are best *recombined* for the pronunciation of the target word. It is not always possible to obtain a correct pronunciation by aligning analogical chunks one after the other at recombination. There is a trivial element of context-sensitivity that simple chunk concatenation fails to account for. Assume that the Italian dataset contains the names 'bacco' (/bak:o/) and 'martini' (/martini/), which are candidate analogues of the target word 'baccini'. The concatenation of their respective head and tail would yield the transcription */bak:ini/, while in Italian the character 'c' reads always /tʃ/ before 'i' and 'e' (/batʃ:ini/), and /k/ otherwise.

What analogy fails to capture in this case is that one cannot consider the pronunciation of Italian 'c' independently of its right context, and some look-ahead is needed. We say that 'c' starts a phonological discontinuity, which can be got around by taking into account more context . If this context is included, we say that 'c' and its neighbourood form an *island of reliability* [3], that is an orthographic span which is read safely when taken as a whole. This means, in practice, that 'c'-ending chunks like 'bacc-' are not reliable candidates for pronunciation by analogy, as they fail to include the relevant island of reliability.

A mild form of context-sensitivity at recombination can be ensured by enforcing the condition that the final part of the longest head be also shared by the longest tail (see Fig. 2): only chunks whose overlapping parts are pronounced in the same way are recombined.

Hereafter, we will refer to a compatible overlap between consecutive chunks as a *hook*. Hooks can be of various length. Intuitively, the longer a hook is, the more

Fig. 2. Recombination and Hook Length

accurate the resulting pronunciation will be, since a wider portion of context has been taken into account and double-checked. This is confirmed by the evidence collected on Italian names, shown in Table 1 below, where *accuracy* varies as a function of hook length, while remaining comparatively constant as the size of the dataset increases [16]. At one end of the scale, Q1 (Quality 1) transcriptions make use of hooks which are more than one character long, while, at the opposite end of the scale, Q3 (Quality 3) transcriptions use no hooks. By *contribution* we mean here the ratio between the number of Quality *i* pronunciations and the total number of pronunciations provided by the system: note that, as the training set grows, Q1 contribution goes up while Q2 and Q3 contribution go down; accordingly, the overall accuracy rate of the system steadily increases.

Table 1. Accuracy and Hook Length

Training set: 5,000 names	Contribution	Accuracy
Q1	15.86%	99.75%
Q2	42.46%	97.79%
Q1+Q2	58.32%	98.31%
Q3	40.64%	40.64%
Training set: 40,000 names	Contribution	Accuracy
Q1	78.70%	99.60%
Q2	16.22%	97.64%
Q1+Q2	94.92%	99.05%
Q3	5.04%	35.32%
Training set: 85,000 names	Contribution	Accuracy
Q1	83.62%	99.22%
Q2	14.62%	97.27%
Q1+Q2	98.24%	98.92%
Q3	1.74%	32.19%

Surely, there are cases (averaging at about 6.40% for ordinary words and 1% for proper names) where the best head and tail are not long enough to cover the target entirely. Then, no pronunciation is provided (silence), with interesting consequences on overall performances (see conclusion). For the time being, attention is focused on thornier cases, which seem to elude the grasp of analogy-based inference in a more principled way.

3 False Friends and Sheer Exceptions: the "Liaisons Dangereuses" between Martine and Martin

One of the striking advantages of analogy-based inference is that good performances can be obtained by means of a fairly basic algorithm (see also final section), where recombination is constrained at chunk boundaries, and analogical mapping is limited to extraction of the longest heads and tails. Still, there remains a non-negligible amount of grapheme-to-phoneme regularities that the machinery described so far fails to capture.

Suppose that the French 'martin' is the target word whose pronunciation is to be analogized. Suppose further that 'martine' is already known, i.e. it is already a base object. Trivially, no other base object will possibly match the target object 'martin' better than 'martine' itself, as the former is completely contained in the latter. Thus, 'martin' is pronounced like 'martine', /martin/, if a suitable best tail is found which hooks the candidate head. In a French dataset of proper names, 'in'-ending Arabic names such as 'amin' (/amin/) provide an easy hook for /martin/. Unfortunately, the transcription /martin/, although analogically well-grounded, clashes with a powerful regularity in the French pronunciation system, according to which every 'in'-ending word reads with a final /ɛ̃/. In our view, this example is indicative of a general weakness of the strategy delineated so far, mainly due to a difficulty for such an analogy-based model to tell the analogical pressure of an exception from that of a regularity: it appears that the relation between 'martine' and 'martin' goes beyond the pairwise analogical mapping between them, to fit in with a general alternation /in/↔/ɛ̃/, which defines a systematic *paradigm* in French, as illustrated in Fig. 3 (more on this in the following section).

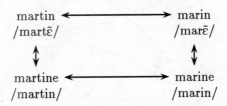

Fig. 3. A Phonological Paradigm

4 Paradigmatic Slots and Analogical Islands

There is a straightforward analogy-based way of expressing the paradigmatic proportion of Fig. 3. The analogy between 'marine' and 'marin' can be represented (Fig. 4) as a common *core* which contains what the two names share at both the orthographic and phonological level. What is not shared gives rise to two separate nodes, linked to their common core. These nodes are in parallel distribution relative to the same context (i.e. relative to their common core), meaning that either appears in that context when the other does not. Hereafter we will refer to distinct nodes in parallel distribution as *paradigmatic nodes*, or, interchangeably, *paradigmatic slots*. By the same token, the links between a core and its paradigmatic slots will be called *paradigmatic links*.

Note further that cores can be in their turn in parallel distribution with some other node relative to a different context: so, analogical cores themselves can be paradigmatic slots. For example, 'martine' shares with 'marine', among other things, word-final 'ine' (together with its pronunciation /in/). Again, this is expressed through a common core from which two distinct links depart. Paradigmatic links define the relationship between distinct paradigmatic slots and their common cores, and can be used for making predictions about the most likely pronunciation of an unknown word whose orthographic string fits in with (a portion of) the network.

Paradigmatic nodes are often analogical islands of reliability (hereafter analogical islands for short) in their own right. For our purposes, a phonological alternation can be seen as a phonological discontinuity in an orthographic string: in spite of their similarity, two strings such as 'marine' (/marin/) and 'marin' (/marẽ/) are pronounced differently; thus their endings are in parallel distribution and represented as independent nodes (see Fig. 4).

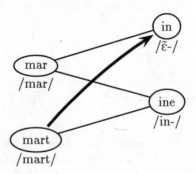

Fig. 4. A Paradigmatic Network and Paradigm Extension

5   Paradigm-Driven Analogy

Suppose now that analogical mapping does no longer operate blindly on an unstructured dataset but is somehow paradigmatically-harnessed, i.e. that it explores a dataset which in fact consists of a network of nodes and their paradigmatic links. To be more concrete, assume that 'marine', 'marin' and 'martine' form an analogical paradigm in the system's dataset, and that 'martin' is the unknown word to be analogized. However new, 'martin' can be reconstructed through the continuous path of paradigmatic links which goes from the slot 'mart'-/mart/ to the slot 'in'-/ɛ̃/ (shown by the arrow in Fig. 4), hereafter referred to as *paradigm extension*. The recombination of /mart/ and /ɛ̃/ gives the desired pronunciation.

This idea can be given a more formal attire as follows. Let A_1 and A_2 be two alphabets of symbols, and $S_1 = A_1^*$ and $S_2 = A_2^*$ the free monoids on these alphabets. Let $\Pi : S_1 \to S_2$ be the pronunciation function to be induced. Let $E_1 \subset S_1$ be the set of base objects' orthographic strings, and $\Pi(E_1) \subset S_2$ the set of their related pronunciations. For all $(x, y) \in E_i \times E_i$, we call $lch(x, y)$ and $lct(x, y)$ respectively the *longest common head* and *longest common tail* of x and y. Conversely, let $lch(x, y)^{-1}(z)$ be the *remaining part* of z once $lch(x, y)$ has been stripped off z. For x in E_i, let $L(x)$ be its length. Finally, λ is the empty string and $+$ the *string concatenation operator*. For all $(x, y) \in E_i \times E_i$, we define $TT_{xy} : S_i \to S_i$ (*Tail Transformation*) as follows:

if $\exists h$ such that $z = h + lch(x, y)^{-1}(x)$ then $TT_{xy}(z) = h + lch(x, y)^{-1}(y)$; otherwise: $TT_{xy}(z) = \lambda$. Thus:

Algorithm 1 *A Paradigm-Driven Algorithm*
> **forall** $x \notin E_1$
> $\Pi(x) \leftarrow \lambda$
> Build $H(x) = \{y \in E_1 / (z = lch(x, y)) \neq \lambda\}$, *(common head subset) sorted by decreasing value of* $L(z)$.
> **foreach** $y \in H(x)$
>> Build $P(x, y) = \{(z, t) \in E_1 \times E_1$ *such that:*
>> $-i$ $z = TT_{xy}(t)$ *and*
>> $-ii$ $L(lch(z, t)) \leq L(lch(\Pi(z), \Pi(t)))$ *and*
>> $-iii$ $L(lct(y, z)) \leq L(lct(\Pi(y), \Pi(z)))\}$
>> *sorted by decreasing value of* $L(lct(y, z))$
>> **foreach** $(z, t) \in P(x, y)$
>>> **if** $TT_{\Pi(z)\Pi(t)}(\Pi(y)) \neq \lambda$ **then do**
>>>> $\Pi(x) \leftarrow TT_{\Pi(z)\Pi(t)}(\Pi(y))$
>>>> **break**
>>> **end**
>> **end**
>> **if** $\Pi(x) \neq \lambda$ **then break**
> **end**

More concretely, let $x = martin$ be the target object, and $y = martine$ a candidate head-analogue of x, that is a base object sharing with x a (non-empty) word-initial string, as shown in Fig.4. Then the following equations obtain:

- $lch(x,y) = mart$ (clearly, this is true under the assumption that equations 1, 2 and 3 below hold as well)
- $lch(x,y)^{-1}(x) = in$
- $lch(x,y)^{-1}(y) = ine$
- $TT_{xy}(a) = b$ defines the orthographic tail transformation by which a string ending as x does is turned into another string ending as y does (so that $x : y = a : b$)
- $TT_{xy}(x) = y$ by changing in into ine (trivially, $x : y = x : y$)

The system looks then for the pair of base objects which stand with y in the best paradigmatic proportion relative to x. Accordingly, the following equations must hold:

- $(z,t) = (marine, marin)$
- $(\Pi(z), \Pi(t)) = (\ /marin\text{-}/, /mar\tilde{\varepsilon}\text{-}/\ )$

The formal justification for this particular choice goes through the following steps:

1. $TT_{xy}(t) = TT_{xy}(marin) = marine$
2. $L(lch(z,t)) = L(lch(marine, marin)) = L(mar) = 3 \leq L(/mar/) = L(lch(/marin\text{-}/, /mar\tilde{\ }\varepsilon\text{-}/)) = L(lch(\Pi(z), \Pi(t)))$
3. $L(lct(y,z)) = L(lct(martine, marine)) = L(ine) = 3 \leq L(/in\text{-}/) = L(lct(/martin\text{-}/, /marin\text{-}/)) = L(lct(\Pi(y), \Pi(z)))$

where, informally, 1) states that z is to t as y is to x; 2) states that the common orthographic head that (as a consequence of 1) is shared by z and t is paired with a phonological head of equal length; and 3) that the common orthographic tail which y and z have in common (due to 1) is paired with a phonological tail of equal length. Once z and t are found, the following functions are further defined:

- $TT_{\Pi(z)\Pi(t)}$, i.e. the phonological transformation which applies to a (rhyming with $\Pi(z)$) to turn it into something rhyming with $\Pi(t)$; its application to $\Pi(y)$ yields the following:
$TT_{\Pi(z)\Pi(t)}(\Pi(y)) = TT_{\Pi(z)\Pi(t)}(/martin\text{-}/) = /mart\tilde{\varepsilon}\text{-}/$

by changing $/in\text{-}/$ into $/\tilde{\varepsilon}\text{-}/$. Finally, we assign x the pronunciation thus obtained:

- $\Pi(x) = TT_{\Pi(z)\Pi(t)}(/martin\text{-}/) = /mart\tilde{\varepsilon}\text{-}/$.

By doing this way, the target object is no longer mapped onto an unstructured list of base objects, but onto the paradigmatic nodes (analogical islands) into which base objects can be chopped up. Once a paradigmatic node is mapped onto the head of the target word, the paradigmatic links departing from that node tell the system where to go next for mapping the tail: only paradigmatically-related analogical islands are considered as suitable candidate analogues.

A further point worth stressing in this context is that such a network of paradigmatically-related nodes is not created once and for all, but is dynamically built up at response time, relative to the particular target word at hand. As an alternative to this conception, Pirrelli and Federici [15] illustrate a strategy for the automatic incremental learning of morphonological paradigms where progressively finer analogical islands are extracted and bigger paradigmatic alternations are discovered during training, as new data enter the dataset of base objects. In this latter approach, contrary to what is proposed here, paradigms are actually stored in the dataset. Extraction and storage of paradigms during training, however, takes considerable computational overhead and, generally speaking, achieves the intended degree of flexibility only at the considerably high price of extracting and storing all possible paradigmatic alternations, independently of the target word to be pronounced. Thus care must be taken for the whole architecture to be able to accomodate and use rival paradigmatic portions of the network. The solution suggested in these pages is more practical, as it combines a fairly simple learning routine with a parsimonious use of storage resources, with no degradation in the system's flexibility in response.

6 Unextendable and False Paradigms

Turning back to our previous illustrative example, the analogical pressure of 'martine' on 'martin' is now weakened in a principled, non ad-hoc way. The target 'martin' can no longer be mapped onto 'martine', since the resulting match 'martin' is not a suitable paradigmatic node and hence a valid analogical island (see Fig. 5a) and 5b). According to the dynamic strategy sketched in this section, this is a consequence of the fact that in the dataset there exists no word 'X+ine' (i.e. any word ending in 'ine') whose resulting transformed 'X+in' (TT_{xy}('X+ine')) is such that: $L(lch('X+ine','X+in')) \leq L(lch(\Pi('X+ine'), \Pi('X+in')))$ (informally, there is no 'X+in' which is pronounced in the same way as 'X+ine' is). In other words, the match 'martin', although a potential paradigmatic node, cannot be extended paradigmatically either to 'marin' (in the dataset there exists no 'marin' pronounced like 'marine', (see Fig. 5a), nor to 'amin' (due to the non-existence of 'amine' in the dataset (see Fig. 5b).

Eventually, it should be noted here that cases of false friendship are by no means limited to a few idiosyncratic proper names, as witnessed, in Italian, by word-pairs such as 'uccelli'-/u'tʃ:el:i/ and 'uccelliera'-/utʃ:e'l:jera/, where derivational suffixation and accent shift turn the segment /i/ into a glide /j/, and, in English, by well-known triples of morphonological alternation such as 'marginal'⇔'marginality'⇔'marginalia', where the vowel in bold is pronounced respectively as /ə/, /æ/, and /eɪ/. For all such cases, any blind analogical routine would miss the correct, systematic alternation, while paradigmatic links get analogy off the hook.

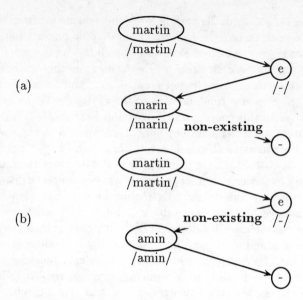

(a)

(b)

Fig. 5. Unextendable nodes

To sum up, in our view of things, analogy is not just a matter of pairwise similarity between target and base, but a general association principle governing the dataset in its entirety. Analogical paradigms capture the network of analogical relationships of the dataset and their structure changes as the size of the dataset increases. As finer paradigms emerge, the system's accuracy improves. For example, the pronunciation of 'vanity' would be */veɪnɪtɪ/ (instead of /vænɪtɪ/) if analogized, for lack of a better example, to the paradigm between 'immune', 'immunity' and 'vane' in Fig. 6.

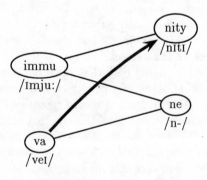

Fig. 6. A Case of False Paradigm

However, learning one more example of the alternation 'ane'⇔ 'anity', e.g. by adding the pair 'sane'⇔'sanity' to the dataset, would suffice to construe the appropriate analogical paradigm. The new paradigm would override the analogizing pressure of 'immune'⇔'immunity' on 'vanity', since 'vane' shares with 'sane' one more character than the string 'immune' does (see Fig. 7). In our algorithm, this constraint is enforced when the function $L(lct(y, z))$ is evaluated, since, for $y =$ 'vane', $L(lct(\text{'vane'},\text{'immune'})) \leq L(lct(\text{'vane'},\text{'sane'}))$.

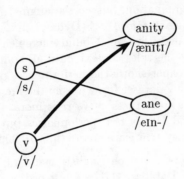

Fig. 7. The Correct Alternation

7 Analogy and Accuracy

Unlike most of the systems we are aware of, an analogy-based transcriber fails to provide any output if the input word cannot possibly be split into admissible orthographic chunks. In analogy-based transcription, there is nothing like a minimum context for rule application. If a particular (sub)string is not already available, it will never be pronounced: i.e., the system will remain silent. To give but a trivial example, consider the following set of Italian grapheme-to-phoneme rules for the transcription of the character 'c', ranked for context length, from the most specific context to the most generic one:

cci → [t ʃ :] /_ {a, o, u, e}
cci → [t ʃ :] /_ {i, e}
cc → [k :] / otherwise
ci → [t ʃ] /_ {a, o, u, e}
ci → [t ʃ] /_ {i, e}
c → [k] / otherwise

Assume now that the non Italian name 'charles' is input to a transcriber which contains, among others, the rules listed above. This is not an unlikely event if one wishes to transcribe a set of names randomly drawn from the Italian telephone directory. The improbable transcription /karles/ would thus be yielded, thanks to the built-in default enforced by the otherwise conditions. This is not the case of the analogy-based algorithm illustrated here though. Under the assumption that the set of base objects consists of Italian names only, 1) 'cha' cannot be found as such (being an impossible orthographic sequence of Italian), 2) neither 'ch' and 'a', nor 'c' and 'ha' can be paradigmatically-related nodes with a suitable hook. Hence, both 1) and 2) force the system to remain silent.

Arguably, this is a very weak and conservative attitude, which nonetheless pays off in the long run. Yvon [20] proves this claim for French by comparing the performances of JUPA (an analogy-based transcriber with head-and-tail mapping and hook-recombination, but no paradigms) to the performances of an alternative self-learning system: DEC (Dynamic Expanding Context) [9], an instance-based learning algorithm which builds incrementally the (decision) tree by iteratively expanding the rules context until all training words can be correctly transcribed. The paper shows the performances of the three systems by increasing size of a training dataset (drawn from the French Onomastica Proper Names Dataset): JUPA's correctness curve rises more slowly at early stages of training, but goes beyond DEC's best perfomances (up to 90.25% correctness per word) as soon as the system learns more than 70,000 names.

A similar experiment was run on English, using 2,000 words randomly selected from the NETtalk Database [17] as a test-bed, and the remaining 18,000 words of the Database for training.

In table 2, accuracy performances of DEC, JUPA and SELEGRAPH, an instance-based transcriber which makes use of mutual information scores and a look-up table [1], are shown and compared.

Table 2. Comparison of three transcription systems using NETtalk database

SELEGRAPH		DEC		JUPA	
words	segments	words	segments	words	segments
54.25	90.28	55.30	90.71	62.00	92.16

A paradigm-driven version of JUPA, implementing the strategy described above, tested on the same data yields 62% correctness, and improves considerably on accuracy: 70%.

Finally, results of paradigmatically-driven analogy are even more striking in Italian, where an instance-based approach implemented in the SELEGRAPH software [1], scores 94% correctness/accuracy, a rule-based [14] transcriber is 97% correct/accurate, while analogy-based trancription is 98% correct, and 99% accurate.

8 Outstanding Problems, Future Work and Conclusion

To sum up, a relatively crude form of orthographic analogy is effective enough to outperform fairly sophisticated techniques of grapheme-to-phoneme conversion, whether statistically- or rule-based. Paradoxically, the power of analogy hinges on its weak and rather conservative inferential routine, so that an unfamiliar target (say a foreign word) is more often not pronounced than tentatively mispronounced.

Furthermore, analogy is more at easy with exceptions. First, hapaxes elude the grasp of statistical methods (which treat them as dispensable noise), and are dealt with rather clumsily by rules: to the contrary, once learned by route, they are never missed through analogy. Secondly, less isolated exceptions are a further complication for both rule writing and rule ordering, and are often too sparse to be captured statistically. With paradigm-driven analogy, groups of exceptions enter their own fine grained paradigm and exert their analogical pressure accordingly. All of this makes analogy more accurate than both statistically- and rule-based transcribers, where default rules are always available to provide often unreliable transcriptions, as, in R.W. Langacker's words, "a rule says always something less than its array of conventional instantiations" [10].

Certainly, more could be done if analogical factors other than sheer orthography were considered [8]. Furthermore, there are interesting phonological alternations that the routine of analogical mapping illustrated in this paper fails to capture: consider a word pair like 'seraph'⇔'seraphic', and assume that 'seraphic' and its transcription /səræfɪk/ are stored in the dataset. Analogizing the correct pronunciation of 'seraph' (/serəf/) by analogy to 'seraphic' is by no means trivial, as two alternations take place simultaneously: one in the head 'ser' (/sər/ is turned into /ser/), the other in the tail 'aph' (with /æf/ turned into /əf/). If analogical mapping is carried out in two stages, by mapping the head of the target first and then its tail (or the other way round), either alternation is likely to be missed, as the two are interdependent.

For lack of the alternation 'eraph'⇔'eraphic', the only principled solution is to allow the extraction of discontinuous chunks [6], that is chunks with some characters missing in the middle, and to define a more sophisticated routine of recombination, by which holes in discontinuous chunks can be filled out. We are currently working on this.

To conclude, paradigm-driven analogy offers interesting solutions to old and less old NLP cruxes: data acquisition is directly performed through self-learning; exceptions are no longer fastidious noise but steadily contribute to the system's performances; context sensitivity is tackled through paradigms and analogical islands; finally, discontinuous analogical mapping promises to be an effective tool for dealing with long- distance (phonological) dependencies.

References

1. Ove Andersen and Paul Dalsgaard. A self-learning approach to transcription of proper names. Draft research paper from the LRE project ONOMASTICA, 1993.

2. John A. Bullinaria. Neural networks models of reading without wickelfeatures. In *Proceedings of the second Neural Computation and Psychology Workshop*, Edinburgh, 1993.

3. T. Carr and A. Pollatsek. Recognizing printed words: a look at current models. In Besner et al., editor, *Reading Research: advances in theory and practice*. Academic Press, 1985.

4. Michael J. Dedina and Howard C. Nusbaum. Pronounce: a program for pronunciation by analogy. *Computer Speech and Langage*, 5:55–64, 1991.

5. Thomas G. Dietterich, Hermann Hild, and Ghulum Bakiri. A comparative study of id3 and back-propagation for english text-to-speech mapping. In Morgan Kaufman, editor, *Proceedings of the 7th International Machine Learning Workshop*, Austin, 1990.

6. Stefano Federici and Vito Pirrelli. Analogy as a computable process. In *Proceeding of Nemlap*, Manchester, 1994. Umist.

7. J. R. Glushko. The organization and activation of orthographic knowledge in reading aloud. *Journal of experimental psychology : Human perception and performance*, 5:674–691, 1979.

8. Andrew R. Golding. *Pronouncing Names by a Combination of Rule-Based and Case-Based Reasoning*. PhD thesis, Stanford University, Stanford, CA, oct 1991.

9. Teuvo Kohonen. Dynamically expanding context with application to the correction of symbol strings in the recognition of continuous speech. In *Proceedings of the 8th International Conference on Pattern Recognition*, volume 2, pages 1148–1151, Paris, France, oct. 1986.

10. R. W. Langacker. *Concept, Image and Symbol: the cognitive basis of grammar*. Berlin, Berlin, 1991.

11. Wendy G. Lehnert. Case-based problem solving with a large knowledge base of learned cases. In *Proceedings of the meeting of the American Association for Artificial Intelligence (AAAI)*, pages 301–306, Seattle, WA, 1987.

12. J.M. Lucassen and R.L. Mercer. An information theoretic approach to the automatic determination of phonemic baseforms. In *Proceedings of the International Conference on Acoustics, Speech and Signal Processing (ICASSP)*, volume 3, pages 45.5.1–42.5.4, San Diego, 1984.

13. S. Owen. *Analogy for Automated Reasoning*. Academic Press, 1990.

14. Vito Pirrelli. Evaluation of italian transcription rules in onomastica. Onomastica technical report, 1994.

15. Vito Pirrelli and Stefano Federici. "derivational" paradigms in morphonology. In *Proceedings of COLING*, Kyoto, Japan, 1994.

16. Vito Pirrelli and Stefano Federici. On the pronunciation of unknown words by analogy in text-to-speech systems: an evaluation. In *Proceeding of the 2nd Onomastica Research Colloquium*, London, Nov 1994.

17. Terrence J. Sejnowski and Charles R. Rosenberg. Parrallel network that learn to pronounce english text. *Complex Systems*, 1:145–168, 1987.

18. Craig W. Stanfill. Memory-based reasonning applied to english pronunciation. In *Proceedings of the meeting of the American Association for Artificial Intelligence (AAAI)*, pages 577–581, Seattle, WA, 1987.

19. K.P.H Sullivan and Robert .I Damper. Novel-word pronunciation within a text-to-speech system. In Gérard Bailly and Eric Moulines, editors, *Talking Machines*, pages 183–195. North Holland, 1992.

20. François Yvon. Self-learning techniques for grapheme-to-phoneme conversion. In *Proceeding of the 2nd Onomastica Research Colloquium*, London, Nov 1994.

Can Punctuation Help Learning?

Miles Osborne

Department of Computer Science, University of York, Heslington,
York YO1 5DD, U. K.
miles@minster.york.ac.uk

Abstract. The quality of learnt natural language grammars can be enhanced by exploiting the linguistic devices that comprise a corpus. This paper considers one such device, namely *punctuation*. After briefly considering the linguistics of punctuation, a model capturing some of these properties is presented. Following this, a series of experiments learning unification-based natural language grammars, using the Spoken English Corpus as data, demonstrate that even a simple model of punctuation increases the plausibility of learnt grammars over grammars learnt without the use of punctuation.

1 Introduction

Natural Language Processing (NLP) systems have for many years suffered from what Magerman terms "the toy problem syndrome" [20]. Systems are built, often with a small lexicon or modest grammar, that are usually demonstrational rather than being operational. That is, there has been little work in developing systems capable of dealing with unrestricted, naturally occurring language. Since the mid-80s, this has begun to change. Systems such as SRI's Core Language Engine have emerged that have been designed to deal with unrestricted language [1]. However, achieving such coverage requires extensive amounts of linguistic knowledge. For example, the NLP system will need, if it is to process naturally occurring language successfully, a grammar capable of generating all of the grammatical sentences that the system is expected to deal with. Creating wide covering grammars is a major undertaking, requiring many months of skilled labour. One recent approach to this logistical problem has been to adopt *learning* strategies capable of automatically creating the necessary linguistic knowledge.

Broadly speaking, there are two main approaches at grammar learning: approaches that use data-driven learning, and approaches that use model-based learning.

Data-driven (or inductive) approaches (for example [5, 3, 29]) are by far the most popular learning style, and roughly speaking, identify constituents in sentences by searching for 'regularities' in the input stream. For example, in the sentences:

1 Sam chases the cat

2 The cat ran down the road

a determiner precedes a noun three times, and hence constitutes a regularity. Such regularities can then be recorded to form a grammar.

The other approach at grammar learning is model-based (for example [2]). Model-based (or deductive) learners are far less frequently used in NLP systems than data-driven approaches. However, they are used by language acquisition theorists (for example [28]). Roughly speaking, these methods consist of trying to determine if a specific training example satisfies some domain knowledge. This knowledge is called a *model*. After using the model to analyse an example, these methods produce a generalisation of the example, along with a justification of the generalisation in terms of the model [21]. In the context of grammar learning, the training examples will be sentences, and the generalisation will be a grammar generating that sentence. For example, using sentence 1, a model might contain a statement to the effect that languages such as English are determiner-initial, and so a model-based learner would consider the phrase *the cat* to be a constituent.

Both learning styles have their respective strengths and weaknesses. Data-driven learning, for example, is 'complete' in the sense that such a learner is always capable of making a decision, but inadequate at learning natural language grammars [11]. Model-based learning is capable of learning such grammars, but in practice suffers from incompleteness. In previous work [25, 24, 23] we have shown how using both learners together produces qualitatively better grammars than are produced when using either learner in isolation. Model-based learning compensated for the inadequacy of data-driven learning, whilst data-driven learning reduced the incompleteness problem facing the model-based learner.

The quality of learnt grammars can also be enhanced by enriching the model of grammaticality. Enriching a model reduces that model's incompleteness. For example, researchers have used bracketing information [26], or linguistic theories [23] to construct a model. One neglected source of grammatical knowledge that might be used to enrich a model is *punctuation*. By neglected, we mean that to our knowledge, no other researchers have looked at using punctuation to help in grammar learning. In this paper, we show how punctuation can enhance the quality of learnt grammars. In particular, we are interested in enhancing the linguistical plausibility of parses produced by the learnt grammar. However, we shall also consider other aspects of the grammar. Section 2 outlines some of the uses of punctuation. Section 3 sketches our learner, concentrating mainly on its model-based component. Section 4 draws upon the previous two sections and presents a model of punctuation that the learner can use. To test the effects of punctuation, we report on a series of experiments in sections 5 and 6. Finally, section 7 discusses the results.

2 Punctuation

Following Jones [16], we define punctuation to be those non-lexical marks found in written texts. This includes commas, colons, semi-colons, full-stops, question marks, exclamation marks, open and close brackets and parentheses, quotation marks, speech marks, and hyphens. Also following Jones [16], we exclude structural 'punctation' as found in mark-up languages such as SGML.

Punctuation has three roles to play [22]:

- To delimit modifiers:

  3 John, my best friend, laughed.

  4 John (my best friend) laughed.

  5 John -my best friend- laughed.

  6 John, 'my best friend', laughed.

- To separate a list of similar, conjoined phrases:

  7 John, Mary and Bill laughed.

  8 John laughed; Bill shouted; Mary smiled.

  9 John laughed: Bill shouted: Mary smiled.

- To disambiguate:

  10 Earlier, work was halted.

  11 I do not think -this is false.

  12 John and Bill, or Bill and Ted, will clean the road.

These roles can be described as being 'intra-punctual' (in the sense that they relate to non-punctuation material). Punctuation also has an 'inter-punctual' role (in the sense that marks relate to other marks). In this paper we are more concerned with the former and not the latter. Consequently, we are not interested in having our learner acquire knowledge of (for example) the use of commas.

We now give an overview of our learner. After this, we shall make explicit our model of punctuation. The model of punctuation is designed to capture some of the intra-punctual roles previously outlined.

3 The learner

3.1 The grammar formalism

The learning system is designed to overcome the undergeneration of grammar G. Undergeneration is the term used to describe the case when a grammar fails to generate a sentence that a human would judge to be grammatically well-formed. Although G may be empty, usually, it will contain some rules.

An important aspect of G is the *formalism* used to encode it. *Unification-based* formalisms are widely used in computational linguistics. This is in contrast to other formalisms, used in grammar learning, such as a context free grammars

(CFG), which might be computationally effective but do not capture all gener-alisations a linguist might want to make. The grammars learnt in our system are therefore unification-based. A consequence of using such a formalism is that we can express our model of punctuation succinctly.

The formalism we use is a variant of the PATR-II formalism [27]. PATR-II is intended to be a tool formalism and so can be used to simulate most other unification-based formalisms.

3.2 Architecture

We assume that the system has some initial grammar fragment, G, from the outset. Presented with an input string, W, an attempt is made to parse W using G. If this fails, the learning system is invoked. Learning takes place through the interleaved operation of a parse completion process and a parse rejection process.

In the parse completion process, the learning system tries to generate rules that, had they been members of G, would have enabled a derivation sequence for W to be found. This is done by trying to extend incomplete derivations using what we call *super rules*. Super rules are the following unification-based grammar rules:

$$[\,] \rightarrow [\,]\,[\,] \text{ (binary)}$$
$$[\,] \rightarrow [\,] \quad \text{(unary)}$$

The binary rule says (roughly) that any category rewrites as any two other categories, and the unary rule says (roughly) that any category rewrites as any other category. The categories in unification grammars are expressed by sets of feature-value pairs; as the three categories in the binary super rule and two categories in the unary super rule specify no values for any of the grammar's features, these rules are the most general (or vacuous) binary and unary rules possible. These rules thus enable constituents found in an incomplete analysis of W to be formed into a larger constituent. In unifying with these constituents, the categories on the right-hand side of the super rules become partially instantiated with feature-value pairs. Hence, these rules ensure that at least one derivation sequence will be found for W. Note that using unary and binary super rules means that the system will not learn rules such as $VP \rightarrow V\,NP\,NP$. As most rules in manually written grammars (for example the Alvey Tools Grammar [12]) are either unary or binary, this is a plausible constraint to make.

Many instantiations of the super rules may be produced by the parse com-pletion process described above. Linguistically implausible instantiations must be rejected and we interleave this rejection process with the parse completion process. Rejection of rules is carried out by the model-driven and data-driven learning processes described below.[1] Note that both of these processes are mod-ular in design, and it would be straightforward to add other constraints, such

---

[1] It should be stressed that in this paper only the model-driven component was used. We mention the data-driven component for completeness.

as lexical co-occurrence statistics or a theory of textuality, to help select correct analyses.

If all instantiations are rejected, then the input string W is deemed ungrammatical. Otherwise, surviving instantiations of the super rules are regarded as being linguistically plausible and may be added to G for future use.

The system is implemented to make use of the Grammar Development Environment (GDE) [6] and it augments the GDE with 3300 lines of Common Lisp. A chart parser drive the learning process.

3.3   Model-driven learning

A grammatical *model* is a high-level theory of syntax. In principle, if the model is complete, an 'object' grammar could be produced by computing the 'deductive closure' of the model (e.g. a 'meta'-rule can be applied to those 'object' rules that account for active sentences to produce 'object' rules for passive sentences). An example of purely model-based language learning is given by Berwick [2]. More usually, though, the model is incomplete and this leads us to give it a different rôle in our architecture.

Our model currently consists of GPSG Linear Precedence (LP) rules [10], semantic types [7], a Head Feature Convention [10] and X-bar syntax [14].

- *LP rules* are restrictions upon *local trees*. A local tree is a (sub)tree of depth one. An example of an LP rule might be [10, p.50]:

$$[\text{SUBCAT}] \prec \sim [\text{SUBCAT}]$$

   This rule should be read as 'if the SUBCAT feature is instantiated (in a category of a local tree) then the SUBCAT feature of the linearly preceding category should not be instantiated'. The SUBCAT feature is used to help indicate minor lexical categories, and so this rule states that verbs will be initial in VPs, determiners will be initial in NPs, and so on. In our learning system, any putative rule that violates an LP rule is rejected.
- We construct our syntax and semantics in tandem, adhering to the *principle of compositionality*, and pair a semantic rule to each syntactic rule [9]. Our semantics uses the typed λ-calculus with extensional typing. For example, the syntactic rule:

$$S \rightarrow NP\ VP$$

   is paired with the following semantic rule:

$$\textbf{VP(NP)}$$

   which should be read as 'the functor **VP** takes the argument **NP**'[2]. The functor **VP** is of type[3]:

$$<<< e, t >, t >, t >$$

---

[2] Syntactic categories are written in a normal font and semantic functors and arguments are written in a **bold** font.

[3] The exact details of these types is not important to understanding the thrust of this section and so they are not given any detailed justification.

and the argument **NP** is of type:

$$<< e, t >, t >$$

The result of functionally applying **VP(NP)** has the type:

$$t$$

For many newly-learnt rules, we are able to check whether the semantic types of the categories can be functionally applied. If they cannot, then the syntactic rule can be rejected. For example, the syntactic rule:

$$VP \rightarrow VP\ VP$$

has the semantic rule **VP(VP)**, which is ill-formed because the type

$$<<< e, t >, t >, t >$$

cannot be functionally applied with itself.

- Head Feature Conventions (HFCs) help instantiate the mother of a local tree with respect to immediately dominated daughters. For example, the verb phrase dominating a third person verb is itself third person.
- X-bar syntax specifies a restriction upon the space of possible grammar rules. Roughly speaking, the RHS of a rule contains a distinguished category called the *head* that characterises the rule. The LHS of the rule is then a *projection* of the head. Projecting the head category results in a phrasal category of the same syntactic class as that of the head. For example, the rule *NP → Det N1* has a nominal head and a NP projection. A head can only be projected a finite number of times. The LHS of a rule whose head can no longer be projected is termed a *maximal projection*. Often, the learner (through model incompleteness) is unable to determine which category should be used to construct the RHS. For such cases, the learner creates a disjunction of the possible candidate categories. At a later stage, the learner has the opportunity to refine such disjunctive categories into non-disjunctive categories. We use curly braces to represent a disjunctive category.

Model-based learning consists of filtering out instantiations of the super rules that violate any aspect of the model, or refining instantiation of a super rule such that they comply with some aspect of the model. LP rules and semantic types filter instantiations, whilst the Head Feature Convention and X-bar syntax refine instantiations.

3.4 Data-driven learning

This aspect of the learner is not relevant for the purposes of this paper. For completeness however, this component prefers learnt rules that are 'similar' to rules previously seen by the parser. The data-driven learner is trained by recording the frequencies of *mother-daughter pairs* found in parses of sentences taken from the training corpus [18]. For example, the tree :

$$(S \; (NP \; Sam) \; (VP \; (V \; smiles)))$$

has the following mother-daughter pairs:

$$< S, NP >$$
$$< S, VP >$$
$$< VP, V >$$

The frequencies of these mother-daughter pairs in the parses of the corpus are noted. From these frequencies, the probability of each distinct pair can be computed. During learning, after parse completion by the super rules, local trees in completed parses can be scored. After scoring, instantiations of the super rule that have daughters whose scores exceed some threshold can be accepted. Other instantiations can be rejected.

The approach we have described is a generalisation of the work of Leech, who uses a simple phrase structure grammar, whereas we use a unification-based grammar [17].

4 The punctuation model

We wish to consider how punctuation relates to grammar learning. But, we have a choice of ways of representing punctuation. One possibility, due to Numberg [22], is to represent punctuation separately from the grammar. Another, more common possibility, is to weave punctuation into the grammar rules. This approach requires no extra machinery in our learner, other than extending the feature space of the grammar. We therefore take this latter approach.

We treat punctuation as follows. Firstly, the feature space is extended with the binary valued feature PUNCT:

$$PUNCT : \{+, -\}$$

Secondly, each category in the grammar, other than the lexical categories of the punctuation marks, carries the feature:

$$[PUNCT \; -]$$

while the lexical categories of the punctuation marks carry the feature:

$$[PUNCT \; +]$$

Punctuation marks do not have a bar level and so are treated similarly to minor categories such as determiners. As PUNCT is not a head feature, we do not have 'punctuation' phrases. The final step is to determine how punctuation interacts with syntax. From the list of roles that punctuation plays, we take the simplifying stance that punctuation marks, of all kinds, attach to maximal projection phrases. This means we treat a sentence such as

13 Earlier, work was halted

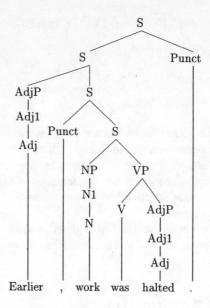

Fig. 1.

as in figure 1. Our punctuation constraint blocks implausible parses, as for example figure 2, being generated. Blocking implausible parses means that the learner does not acquire linguistically dubious rules. For example, our constraint would prevent the comma after the word *earlier* in figure 2 from attaching to the nominal category. Consequently, punctuation as a constraint would prevent rules such as *NP → Adj N* from being acquired.

As should be evident, our constraint will at times be overly strong. For example, it is possible to have non-maximal bar level phrases conjoined:

14 The ball, bat, whicket, and stumps were in the trunk.

Nevertheless, our stance is sufficiently useful to demonstrate that this constraint enhances learning.

The model of punctuation is simply the set of LP rules:

$$[\text{BAR m}] \prec [\text{PUNCT }+]$$
$$[\text{PUNCT }+] \prec [\text{BAR m}]$$

Here, m is a bar level that is one less than the maximal bar level of the grammar. These rules are intended to mean that a local tree can only contain a daughter node marked as being $[PUNCT +]$ if the other daughter nodes are of a bar level greater than m.

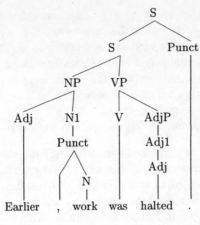

Fig. 2.

5 Experiments

To determine the effect of the punctuation model, we need a set of metrics measuring grammar 'quality'. We measure a grammar's *undergeneration, overgeneration* and *plausibility*. In general, measuring just undergeneration is insufficient. For example, a grammar might not overgenerate, but might vacuously achieve this by hugely overgenerating; a grammar might not undergenerate, but might instead assign implausible, linguistically worthless parses to sentences. We therefore measure all three aspects of a grammar. Undergeneration is measured by determining how many sentences a grammar generates from some unseen corpus; overgeneration in turn is measured as how many ungrammatical strings a grammar generates from some unseen corpus; plausibility is defined as parse conformity to a set of manually produced parses.

The model of punctuation is designed primarily to deal with plausibility. We therefore predicted that the plausibility of grammars learnt using a model containing knowledge of punctuation would be better than the plausibility of grammars obtained by using a model without knowledge of punctuation.

To test this hypothesis requires a corpus of naturally occurring language. We used the Spoken English Corpus (SEC) as data. The SEC is a collection of monologues for public broadcast and is small (*circa* 50,000 words) in comparison to other corpora, such as the Lancaster-Oslo-Bergen Corpus [15], but sufficiently large to demonstrate the capabilities of the learning system. Furthermore, the SEC is tagged and parsed, thus side-stepping the problems of constructing a suitable lexicon and of creating an evaluation corpus to determine the plausibility of the learnt grammars.

Plausibility is defined as how closely a parse produced by the grammar for some sentence exactly matches a parse, for the same sentence, that was produced manually. We refer the reader to our other work for details of the algorithm use (for example [23]). It should be noted that this algorithm is stricter than other tree matching metrics such as the crossing rate [13]. This strictness, along with the effects of normalising the steep, feature-based parse trees to the shallow, atomic labelled parse trees, and the unevenness of the SEC manual parses, means that the numeric matching values will all be lower than comparable results reported using the crossing rate metric.

To test the prediction, the following steps were taken:

- Two disjoint sets of sentences were selected from the SEC. These were *train* (466 sentences) and *test* (60 sentences). 100 ungrammatical strings (called *bad*) were constructed to test how much the grammar overgenerates. Each string in *bad* consisted of the random concatenation of 6 terminals. These strings are highly unlikely to be grammatically well-formed.
- A grammar, G, was used as the initial grammar. This was manually constructed and consisted of 97 unification-based rules with a terminal set of the CLAWS2 tagset [3]. We used this grammar as it has been used in other research (for example [4, 16]) and is realistically large, being a good test of our system. Also, we are more interested in the task of grammar engineering than in the area of machine learning of grammar per se. As such, we are not interested in having our learner re-invent for itself a grammar such as G from scratch.
- The Base Model (M_B) was configured to consist of 4 LP rules, 32 pairings of semantic types and corresponding syntactic categories, and a Head Feature Convention. The Punctuation Model (M_P) consisted of the Base Model, along with the LP rules stated in section 4.
- *Train* was then processed using interleaved parsing and learning with the following configurations of the learner:

Config.	Grammar produced
(A) No learning	G
(B) M_B	G1
(C) M_P	G2

- The set of sentences *plausible* was created as being 48 sentences in *test* that could be generated by grammars G1 and G2.
- *Plausible* was then parsed using grammars G1 and G2 and the first 10 parses produced for each sentence was sampled. Out of these 10 parses, the score of the most plausible parse was noted. We sample the first 10 parses because our system lacks a parse selection mechanism. As most sentences will have more than 10 parses, and since we never examine all of these parses, we do not benefit from overgeneration.
- Finally, *bad* was parsed with all of the grammars.

Learning grammars is computationally intractable. For example, using the binary super rule may lead to a number of parses equal (at least) to the Catalan series with respect to sentence length. This is because, as a worst case, the binary super rule will create all possible binary branching parses for some sentence [8]. In order to generate results therefore, steps were taken to place resource bounds upon the learning process. These bounds were to halt when n parses or m edges had been generated ($n=1$, $m=3000$) for some sentence. Increasing n leads to more ambiguous attachments being learnt. The motivation for the m limit follows from Magerman and Weir who suggest that large numbers of edges being generated might correlate with ungrammaticality [19]. In effect, the parser spends a lot of time searching unsuccessfully for a parse and this is reflected in the large number of edges generated. The other constraint upon the system was that we only used the binary super rule during interleaved parsing and learning. This is because use of the unary rule greatly increases the search space that needs to be explored. The effect of only learning binary rules, however, will be to decrease the plausibility of the parses produced.

6 Results

In the following table, showing some characteristics of the various grammars, the size column is the number of rules in the grammar, coverage is the percentage of sentences in *test* generated by each grammar, overgeneration (abbreviated to *overgen.*) is the percentage of strings in *bad* parsed, and plausibility is the arithmetic mean of the closeness scores of *plausible* with G1 and G2.

Config.	Size	Coverage	Overgen.	Plausibility
A	97	0.0	2	-
B	152	98.3	31	0.102
C	171	90.0	31	0.125

As can be seen, the learnt grammars have a greater coverage than that of the original grammar. However, these grammars also overgenerate more than grammar G. Note that the data-driven component of our learner does have the ability to reduce this overgeneration. This was not attempted. The plausibility results are as expected: using a model of punctuation when learning produces a more plausible grammar than when learning without such a model.

These tests do not allow plausibility or coverage comparisons between the learnt grammars and the original grammar. Also, the tests measure both inter and intra-punctuation roles (that is, *test*, *bad* and *plausible* contained punctuation marks). As was stated previously, we are more interested in intra-punctuation roles. Consequently, we repeated the previous tests, but this time using depunctuated versions of the testing material. This gave the following results:

Config.	Coverage	Overgen.	Plausibility
A	31.6	2	0.179
B	81.7	25	0.165
C	83.3	29	0.176

Again, the results are similar to before: the learnt grammars have a greater coverage than the original grammar, but they also overgenerate more than the original grammar. The grammar learnt using the punctuation model is more plausible than the grammar learnt without the model, whilst he manually constructed grammar is the most plausible of all. It is difficult to explain the changes in coverage and overgeneration of the learnt grammars when tested with punctuated material and without punctuated material.

7 Discussion

In this paper, we briefly considered the linguistics of punctuation, presented a grammar learner, formalised some of the roles of punctuation in terms of a punctuation model, and finally reported on a series of experiments that investigated the utility of our punctuation model.

To answer the question in this paper's title, punctuation can help in (grammar) learning. This should be expected given the roles that punctuation plays and the fact that a model of grammaticality enables our learner to exploit such knowledge. Furthermore, this help was achieved with only an approximately correct punctuation model.

We believe that the process of automated grammar engineering can only be successful when the learner has access to a rich model of grammaticality. Our use of punctuation is one attempt at creating such a model. Future work will consider those other aspects of language that can aid in grammar learning.

Acknowledgements

I wish to thank Derek Bridge for reading versions of this paper. The author was funded by the DSS.

References

1. Hiyan Alshawi, editor. *The CORE Language Engine*. The MIT Press, 1992.
2. Robert C. Berwick. *The acquisition of syntactic knowledge*. MIT Press, 1985.
3. Ezra Black, Roger Garside, and Geoffrey Leech, editors. *Statistically driven computer grammars of English the IBM-Lancaster approach*. Rodopi, 1993.
4. Ted Briscoe and Nick Waegner. Robust Stochastic Parsing Using the Inside-Outside Algorithm. In *Proceedings of the AAAI Workshop on Statistically-based Techniques in Natural Language Processing*, 1992.
5. Glenn Carroll and Eugene Charniak. Two Experiments on Learning Probabilistic Dependency Grammars from Corpora. In *AAAI-92 Workshop Program: Statistically-Based NLP Techniques, San Jose, California*, 1992.
6. John Carroll, Claire Grover, Ted Briscoe, and Bran Boguraev. A Development Environment for Large Natural Language Grammars. Technical report number 127, University of Cambridge Computer Laboratory, 1988.
7. Claudia Casadio. Semantic Categories and the Development of Categorial Grammars. In Richard T. Oehrle, editor, *Categorial Grammars and Natural Language Structures*, pages 95–123. D. Reidel, 1988.

8. K. Church and R. Patil. Coping with syntactic ambiguity or how to put the block in the box on the table. *Computational Linguistics*, 8:139–49, 1982.

9. D.R. Dowty, R.E. Wall, and S. Peters. *Introduction to Montague Semantics*. D. Reidel Publishing Company, 1981.

10. G. Gadzar, E. Klein, G.K. Pullum, and I.A. Sag. *Generalized Phrase Structure Grammar*. Harvard University Press, 1985.

11. E. M. Gold. Language Identification to the Limit. *Information and Control*, 10:447–474, 1967.

12. Claire Grover, Ted Briscoe, John Carroll, and Bran Boguraev. The Alvey Natural Language Tools Grammar (Second Release). Technical report number 162, University of Cambridge Computer Laboratory, 1989.

13. Philip Harrison, Steven Abney, Ezra Black, Dan Flickinger, Ralph Grishman Claudia Gdaniec, Donald Hindle, Robert Ingria, Mitch Marcus, Beatrice Santorini, and Tomek Strzalkowski. Natural Language Processing Systems Evaluation Workshop, Technical Report rl-tr-91-362. In Jeannette G. Neal and Sharon M. Walter, editors, *Evaluating Syntax Performance of Parser/Grammars of English*, 1991.

14. Ray S. Jackendoff. *X-Bar Syntax: A Study of Phrase Structure*. The M.I.T Press, 1977.

15. S. Johansson, G. Leech, and H. Goodluck. Manual of Information to Accompany the Lancaster-Oslo/Bergen Corpus of British English, for Use with Digital Computers. Technical report, Department of English, University of Oslo, 1978.

16. Bernard E. M. Jones. Can Punctuation Help Parsing? In 15th *International Conference on Computational Linguistics, Kyoto, Japan*, 1994.

17. Fanny Leech. *An approach to probabilistic parsing*. MPhil Dissertation, 1987. University of Lancaster.

18. Geoffrey Leech and Roger Garside. Running a grammar factory: The production of syntactically analysed corpora or "treebanks". In Stig Johansson and Anna-Brita Stenström, editors, *English Computer Corpora: Selected Papers and Research Guide*. Mouten de Gruyter, 1991.

19. David Magerman and Carl Weir. Efficiency, Robustness and Accuracy in Picky Chart Parsing. In *Proceedings of the 30th ACL, University of Delaware, Newark, Delaware*, pages 40–47, 1992.

20. David M. Magerman. *Natural Language Parsing as Statistical Pattern Recognition*. PhD thesis, Stanford University, February 1994.

21. T. Mitchell, R. Keller, and S. Kedar-Cabelli. Explanation-based generalization: A unifying view. *Machine Learning*, 1.1:47–80, 1986.

22. G. Nunberg. *The linguistics of punctuation*. Center for the Study of Language and Information, 1990.

23. Miles Osborne. *Learning Unification-based Natural Language Grammars*. PhD thesis, University of York, September 1994.

24. Miles Osborne and Derek Bridge. Learning unification-based grammars using the Spoken English Corpus. In *Grammatical Inference and Applications*, pages 260–270. Springer Verlag, 1994.

25. Miles Osborne and Derek Bridge. More for Less: Learning a Wide Coverage Grammar from a Small Training Set. In *International Conference on New Methods in Language Processing*. Centre for Computational Linguistics, UMIST, Manchester, 1994.

26. Fernando Pereira and Yves Schabes. Inside-outside reestimation from partially bracketed corpora. In *Proceedings of the 30th ACL, University of Delaware, Newark, Delaware*, pages 128–135, 1992.

27. S. M. Shieber, H. Uszkoreit, F. C. N. Pereira, and M. Tyson. The Formalism and Implementation of PATR-II. In *Research on Interactive Aquisition and Use of Knowledge*. SRI International, Menlo Park, California, 1983.
28. Lydia White. *Universal Grammar and second language acquisition*. John Benjamins Publishing Company, 1989.
29. S. J. Young and H. H. Shih. Computer Assisted Grammar Construction. In *Grammatical Inference and Applications*, pages 282–290. Springer Verlag, 1994.

Using Parsed Corpora for Circumventing Parsing*

Aravind K. Joshi and B. Srinivas

Department of Computer and Information Science
University of Pennsylvania
Philadelphia, PA 19104-6228
{joshi, srini}@linc.cis.upenn.edu

Abstract. Corpora tagged with part-of-speech and phrase structure information have been used for both exploratory data analysis as well as unsupervised learning of language models. These corpora have proved invaluable resources for research activities such as training part-of-speech taggers, disambiguating word-senses, detecting noun-phrases, inducing selectional restrictions, extracting argument structure and inducing probabilistic grammars.

In this paper, we present some new techniques that use parsed corpora, not for inducing grammars but for circumventing parsing as much as possible. In particular, we will describe how a parsed corpus using a wide-coverage Lexicalized Tree Adjoining Grammar (LTAG) is used for this purpose. The first technique exploits the fact that LTAGs represent dependency and constituency information in a uniform way. The second technique uses Explanation-Based Learning methodology to view parsing as Finite State Transduction. Both the techniques exploit the central notions of LTAGs – lexicalization, extended domain of locality and factoring of recursion from the domain over which dependencies are specified.

1 Introduction

Corpora tagged with part-of-speech and phrase structure information [8, 9, 15] have been used for both exploratory data analysis as well as unsupervised learning of language models. These corpora have proved invaluable resources for research activities such as training part-of-speech taggers [4], disambiguating word-senses, detecting noun-phrases [3, 23], inducing selectional restrictions [14], extracting argument structure [2] and inducing probabilistic grammars [1, 6, 18]. Although there have been a number of corpora annotated for various purposes, there is a significant lack of corpora that have been annotated with any kind of dependency information among the words in a sentence. We have collected a modest sized parsed corpus using a wide-coverage English LTAG grammar that not only includes the phrase structure information but also provides dependency information for each sentence. This is made possible due to the fact that LTAGs represent both the constituent structure and dependency information in the same elementary tree. In this paper, we show that a corpus that combines the dependency and

---

* We would like to thank R. Chandrasekhar, Christine Doran, Mitch Marcus and Martha Palmer for their valuable comments.

phrase structure information can be exploited to perform Supertagging [7], a technique that provides an 'almost parse' for a sentence.

Another novel use of parsed corpora is to improve the efficiency of parsing LTAGs for restricted domains using Explanation-Based learning (EBL) methodology. EBL techniques were originally introduced in the AI literature by [10, 11, 22]. Rayner [13] was the first to investigate this technique in the context of natural language parsing. Some other recent work is presented in [12] and [16]. In Section 4, we will take a closer look at these other approaches.

Although our work can be considered to be in this general direction, it is distinguished by the following novel aspects that exploit some of the key properties of LTAG to achieve certain straightforward generalizations that are not possible in other approaches. We represent the set of generalized parses as a finite state transducer (FST) which is the first such use of FST in the context of EBL, to the best of our knowledge. We also introduce a device called "stapler", a very significantly impoverished parser, whose only job is to do term unification and compute alternate attachments for modifiers. We achieve substantial speed-up by the use of "stapler" together with the output of the FST.

The structure of this paper is as follows. In Section 2, we provide a brief introduction to LTAGs using an example. In Section 3, we present the technique of Supertagging and a dependency based model for supertagging. We also present performance results of this model on the Wall Street Journal corpus. In Section 4, we present the application of Explanation Based Learning techniques to parsing LTAGs and illustrate the Finite State Transducer representation with an example. We also present experimental results on the performance improvement gained by using the EBL component in the context of a wide coverage grammar.

2 Lexicalized Tree-Adjoining Grammars

Lexicalized Tree-Adjoining Grammar[2] (LTAG) [19, 20] consists of ELEMENTARY TREES, where each elementary tree has a lexical item (anchor) on its frontier. An elementary tree localizes agreement dependencies, filler-gap dependencies and predicate-argument dependencies and serves as a complex description of the anchor. Elementary trees are of two kinds – (a) INITIAL TREES and (b) AUXILIARY TREES.

Examples of initial trees (αs) and auxiliary trees (βs) are shown in Figure 1. Nodes on the frontier of initial trees are marked as substitution sites by a '$\downarrow$', while exactly one node on the frontier of an auxiliary tree, whose label matches the label of the root of the tree, is marked as a foot node by a '$*$'. The other nodes on the frontier of an auxiliary tree are marked as substitution sites. Each node of an elementary tree is associated with two feature structures (FS), the top and the bottom. Elementary trees are combined by *Substitution* and *Adjunction* operations. A parse for the sentence *the company is being acquired* proceeds as follows:

1. α_4 substitutes at the DetP node in α_2, the result of which is substituted at the NP_1 node in α_3.

---

[2] See [5] for a description of XTAG system, a wide-coverage grammar for English based on LTAGs.

415

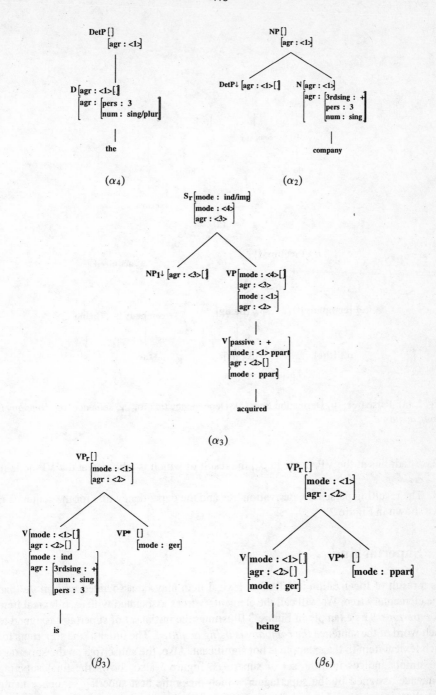

Fig. 1. (αs) and (βs): Elementary trees for the sentence: *the company is being acquired*

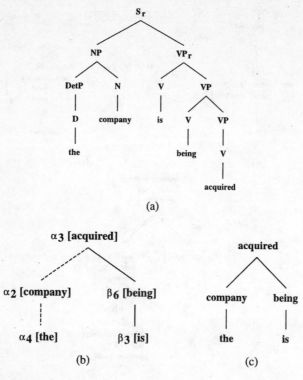

Fig. 2. (a): Parse tree, (b):Derivation tree, (c): Dependency tree for the sentence: *the company is being acquired*

2. β_3 adjoins at the VP_r node in β_6, the result of which is adjoined at the VP node in α_3.
3. The resulting parse tree, derivation tree and the dependency tree for the sentence is shown in Figure 2.

3 Supertagging

As a result of localization in LTAG, a lexical item may be associated with more than one elementary tree. We will call the elementary trees associated with each lexical item as *supertags*. The example in Figure 3 illustrates the initial set of supertags assigned to each word of the sentence *the company is being acquired*. The order of the supertags for each lexical item in the example is not significant. Also, the subscripts on the supertags are simply indices into the set of supertags. Figure 3 also shows the final supertag sequence assigned by the supertagger, which picks the best supertag sequence using statistical information (as described in Section 3.1) about individual supertags and their dependencies on other supertags. The chosen supertags are combined to derive a parse, as explained in Section 2.

Without the supertagger, the parser would have to process combinations of the entire set of trees; with it the parser must only processes combinations of n trees (where n is the length of the sentence) since the supertagger selects one supertag for each lexical item.

Sentence: the company is being acquired

Initial α_1 α_2 β_1 β_2 α_3
Assignment: α_4 α_5 β_3 β_4 α_6
                  α_7 α_8 β_5 β_6 α_9
                    $\vdots$ $\vdots$ $\vdots$ $\vdots$ $\vdots$

Final
Assignment: α_4 α_2 β_3 β_6 α_3

Fig. 3. Initial lattice and the final disambiguated assignment

3.1 Dependency Model of Supertagging

To summarize, given a set of supertags for each lexical item of a sentence, the task of a supertagger is to select the best supertag for each lexical item. Owing to the close similarity of supertagging to POS tagging, we have experimented with the n-gram models that perform extremely well for POS tagging. However, in an n-gram model for standard POS tagging, dependencies between parts-of-speech of words that appear beyond the n-word window cannot be incorporated into the model. This limitation does not have a significant effect on the performance of a standard trigram POS tagger, since it is rare for dependencies to occur between POS tags beyond a three-word window.

In contrast, dependencies between supertags do not occur in a fixed sized window. A supertag is *dependent* on another supertag if the former substitutes or adjoins into the latter. Therefore the n-gram model is inadequate for supertagging. This limitation can be overcome if no a priori bound is set on the size of the window, but instead a probability distribution of the distances of the dependent supertags for each supertag is maintained.

Experiments and Results Table 1 shows a few sample entries from the data[3] required for the dependency model of supertag disambiguation. Ideally, each entry would be indexed by a (word, supertag) pair but, due to sparseness of data, we have backed-off to a (POS, supertag) pair. Each entry contains the following information.

– The POS and Supertag pair.
– A list of + and − signs, representing the direction of the dependent supertags with respect to the indexed supertag. (The size of this list indicates the total number of dependent supertags required, e.g. $(-) = 1$.)

---

[3] Data has been collected from parses of Wall Street Journal, IBM-manual and ATIS corpora using the XTAG system.

(P.O.S,Supertag)	Direction of Dependent Supertag	Dependent Supertag	Ordinal position	Occurrence Probability
(D,α_4)	()	-	-	-
(N,α_2)	(−)	α_4	−1	0.975
(V,α_3)	(−)	α_2	−1	0.620
(V,β_3)	(+)	α_3	1	0.130
(V,β_3)	(+)	β_3	1	0.448
(V,β_6)	(+)	α_3	1	0.420

Table 1. Dependency Data

- The "id" of the dependent supertag.
- A signed number representing the direction and the ordinal position of the particular dependent supertag mentioned in the entry from the position of the indexed supertag.
- A probability of occurrence of such a dependency. The sum of the probabilities over all the dependent supertags at all ordinal positions in the same direction is one[4].

For example, the third entry in the Table 1 reads that the tree α_3, anchored by a verb (V), has a left dependent (−) and the first word to the left (−1) with the tree α_2 serves as a dependent of the current word. The strength of this association is represented by the probability 0.600.

The dependency model of disambiguation finds the most probable sequence of supertags with non-crossing dependency links among them using the information shown in Table 1. The output of this model consists of supertag assignment for each word (POS) and dependency arcs between the supertags. From this, the nature of the combining operation between supertags (adjunction or substitution) can be inferred directly, since the names of the supertags directly encode the type of the supertags (α for initial and β for auxiliary). However, the location of the combining operation in a supertag cannot always be uniquely determined. Thus the output of this model of supertagging can be regarded as an *almost parse*.

Table 2 shows results on 100 Wall Street Journal sentences. The table shows two measures of evaluation. In the first, the dependency link measure, the test sentences were independently hand-tagged with dependency links and then were used to match the links output by the dependency model. The columns show the total number of dependency links in the hand-tagged set, the number of matched links output by this model and the percentage correctness. The second measure, supertags, shows the total number of correct supertags assigned to the words in the corpus by this model.

We believe that the performance of this model can be improved further by including lexical sensitivity into the model. This, however, requires a large corpus that is annotated with LTAG derivation trees. We are currently collecting the parses resulting from the XTAG system on some of the available on-line corpora for this purpose.

---

[4] This is not seen in Table 1 as only a few sample entries are shown here.

	Total	Number	%
Criterion	number	correct	correct
Dependency links	815	620	76.07%
Supertags	915	707	77.26%

Table 2. Results of Dependency model

4 Explanation Based Learning

In this section, we present some novel applications of the so-called Explanation-Based Learning technique (EBL) to parsing Lexicalized Tree-Adjoining grammars (LTAG). EBL techniques were originally introduced in the AI literature by [10, 11, 22]. The main idea of EBL in the AI domain is to keep track of problems solved in the past and to replay those solutions to solve new but somewhat similar problems in the future. Although, when phrased in these general terms, the approach sounds attractive, it is by no means clear whether it would actually improve the performance of the system.

Rayner [13] was the first to investigate this technique in the context of natural language parsing. Rayner and Samuelsson [17] attempt to specialize a grammar for the ATIS domain using a treebank of a large set of parsed training examples. The idea is to redo the derivation for each of the training examples by letting the parse tree drive the rule expansion process and aborting the expansion of a specialized rule if the current node meets the 'tree-cutting' criteria. However, the problem of specifying the optimal 'tree-cutting' criteria was not addressed in this work. Samuelsson [16] used information-theoretic measure of entropy to derive the appropriate sized tree chunks automatically. Neumann [12] also attempts to specialize a grammar given a training corpus of parsed examples by generalizing the parse for each sentence and storing the generalized phrasal derivations under a suitable index. We use the term generalization and Explanation-Based Learning in the same sense as used in [12, 13].

Although our work can be considered to be in this general direction, it is distinguished by the following novel aspects. We exploit some of the key properties of LTAG to (a) achieve an *immediate* generalization of parses in the training set of sentences, (b) represent the set of generalized parses as a finite state transducer (FST), which is the first such use of FST in the context of EBL, to the best of our knowledge, (c) achieve an additional level of generalization of the parses in the training set, not possible in other approaches, thereby being able to directly deal with test sentences which are not necessarily of the same length as one of the training sentences. In addition to these special aspects of our work, we will present experimental results evaluating the effectiveness of our approach on more than one kind of corpus. These results are far more detailed and comprehensive than results reported so far. We also introduce a device called "stapler", a very significantly impoverished parser, whose only job is to do term unification and compute alternate attachments for modifiers. We achieve substantial speed-up by the use of "stapler" together with the output of the FST.

4.1 Implications of LTAG Representation for EBL

An LTAG parse of a sentence can be seen as a sequence of elementary trees associated with the lexical items of the sentence along with substitution and adjunction links among the elementary trees. Given an LTAG parse, the generalization of the parse is truly *immediate* in that a generalized parse is obtained by (a) uninstantiating the particular lexical items that anchor the individual elementary trees in the parse and (b) uninstantiating the feature values contributed by the morphology of the anchor and the derivation process. In other EBL approaches [12, 16, 13], it is necessary to walk up and down the parse tree to determine the appropriate subtrees to generalize on, and to suppress the feature values. In LTAG, the subtrees to generalize on are the elementary trees that each lexical item anchors, and the generalized parse is a proof tree represented by the derivation tree.

We would like to reiterate that it might appear at first sight that all we are doing is deleting the lexical anchor and uninstantiating the feature values for the elementary trees. This impression is incorrect. A parse in LTAG can be viewed as a sequence of elementary trees with feature values instantiated along with the links among trees showing the adjunction and substitution operations. Owing to the special nature of the LTAG representation deleting the anchor and uninstantiating the feature values achieves an *immediate* generalization of the parse.

The generalized parse of a sentence is stored under a suitable index computed from the sentence, such as, part-of-speech (POS) sequence of the sentence. In the application phase, the POS sequence of the input sentence is used to retrieve a generalized parse(s) which is then instantiated to the features of the sentence. If the retrieval fails to yield any generalized parse then the input sentence is parsed using the full parser. However, if the retrieval succeeds then the generalized parses are input to the "stapler".

This method of retrieving a generalized parse allows for parsing of sentences of the same lengths and the same POS sequence as those in the training corpus. However, in our approach there is another generalization that falls out of the LTAG representation; this allows for flexible matching of the index and thus the system is able to parse sentences that are not necessarily of the same length as sentences in the training corpus.

Auxiliary trees in LTAG represent recursive structures. So if there is an auxiliary tree that is used in an LTAG parse, then that tree along with the trees for its arguments can be repeated any number of times, or possibly omitted altogether, to get parses of sentences that differ from the sentences of the training corpus only in the number of modifiers. This type of generalization can be called *modifier-generalization*. This type of generalization is not possible in other EBL approaches.

This implies that the POS sequence covered by the auxiliary tree and its arguments can be repeated zero or more times. As a result, the index of a generalized parse of a sentence with modifiers is no longer a string but a regular expression pattern on the POS sequence and retrieval of a generalized parse involves regular expression pattern matching on the indices. If, for example, the training example was

Show/V me/N the/D flights/N from/P Boston/N to/P Philadelphia/N.

then, the index of this sentence is

V N D N (P N)*

since the prepositions in the parse of this sentence would anchor auxiliary trees.

The *Finite State Transducer (FST)* representation shown in Figure 4 combines the generalized parse with the POS sequence (regular expression) that it is indexed by. The idea is to annotate each of the finite state arcs of the regular expression matcher with the elementary tree associated with that POS and also indicate which elementary tree it would be dependent on (adjoined or substituted into). The 4-tuple associated with each word is as follows:

this_tree : the elementary tree that the word anchors

head_word : the word on which the current word is dependent on; "−" if the current word does not depend on any other word.

head_tree : the tree anchored by the head word; "−" if the current word does not depend on any other word.

number : a signed number that indicates the direction and the ordinal position of the particular head elementary tree from the position of the current word
OR
: an unsigned number that indicates the node address in the derivation tree to which the word attaches *OR*
: "−" if the current word does not depend on any other word.

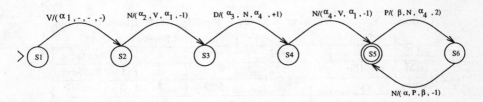

Fig. 4. Finite State Transducer Representation for the sentences: *show me the flights from Boston to Philadelphia, show me the flights from Boston to Philadelphia on Monday, . . .*

The FST representation exploits the key notions of LTAGs as explained below.

- *Lexicalization* allows for immediate generalization of parses by defining the elementary trees to generalize over.
- *Extended domain of locality* allows for the dependency information and phrase structure information to be represented in one structure – an elementary tree. This feature allows the phrase structure parse tree to be represented in terms of dependency information.
- *Factoring of recursion from the domain of dependencies* allows for an additional level of generalization not possible in other approaches – modifier generalization.

It must be noted that the FST representation makes a distinction between dependencies between modifiers and complements. The number in the tuple associated with each word is a signed number if a complement dependency is being expressed and is an unsigned number if a modifier dependency is being expressed. This distinction is essential for yielding correct dependencies since we assume that the additional modifiers that result from modifier-generalization modify the same head (i.e. the same node in the derivation tree).

4.2 Experiments and Results

We now present experimental results from two different sets of experiments performed to show the effectiveness of our approach. The first set of experiments are intended to measure the coverage of the FST representation of the parses of sentences from a range of corpora: the ATIS, IBM-Manual and Alvey corpora. For each of the training sentences, the parses were ranked using heuristics [21] and the top three derivations were generalized and stored as an FST. The results of these experiments provide a measure of repetitiveness of patterns as described in this paper, at the sentence level, in each of these corpora.

Results of these experiments are summarized in Table 3. The size of the FST obtained for each corpus, the coverage of the FST and the traversal time per input are shown in this table. The coverage of the FST is the number of inputs that were assigned a correct generalized parse among the parses retrieved by traversing the FST. Since these experiments measure the performance of the EBL component on various corpora we will refer to these results as the 'EBL-Lookup times'.

Corpus	Size of Training set	Number of States	% Recall	Av. # of parses	Response Time (secs)
ATIS	300	1000	80%	2	0.35 sec/sent
IBM	1500	9000	47%	4	3.00 sec/sent
Alvey	80	500	50%	2	0.20 sec/NP

Table 3. Coverage and Retrieval times for various corpora

System	Number of sentences	Coverage %	Average time (in secs)
XTAG	100	100%	125.18
Morph. Analysis+EBL lookup	100	80%	1.78
Morph. Analysis+EBL+XTAG parser	100	90%	62.93
Morph. Analysis+EBL+Stapler	100	70%	8.00

Table 4. Performance comparison of XTAG with and without EBL component

The second set of experiments measure the performance improvement obtained by using EBL in the XTAG system on the ATIS corpus on the same set of training and test material as used in the previous experiment on the ATIS corpora.

Table 4 summarizes the results of this experiment under various configuration scenarios. The coverage represents the percentage of sentences that were assigned a parse. The first row indicates the performance of XTAG on the test sentences. The second row shows the coverage and response times for the EBL component along with the times for morphological analysis and POS tagging. As before, 80% of the sentences were assigned a generalized parse. However, the speed-up when compared to the XTAG system is a factor of about 60. The third row shows the performance in a scenario in which the output from the EBL lookup is input to the full parser of the XTAG system. The speed-up is due to the reduced ambiguity of assigning elementary trees. The fourth row shows the performance of the "stapler" in conjunction with the EBL component. The "stapler" uses both the elementary tree assignment information and the dependency information present in the *almost parse* and speeds up the performance even further, by a factor of about 15.

5 Summary

In this paper, we have presented some novel approaches of using parsed corpora to circumvent parsing as far as possible. We have demonstrated two techniques that exploit some of the key notions of LTAGs such as lexicalization, extended domain of locality and factoring of recursion from the domain of dependencies. We have also introduced an impoverished parser called "stapler" whose only task is to perform term unification and provide alternate attachments of modifiers. We have shown that using these techniques can provide up to 60 times speed-up in the performance of the parser.

References

1. Eric Brill. Automatic grammar induction and parsing free text: A transformation-based approach. In *Proceedings of the 31st Annual Meeting of the Association for Computational Linguistics*, Columbus, Ohio, 1993.
2. Ted Briscoe. Prospects for Practical Parsing of Unrestricted Text: Robust Statistical Parsing Techniques. In *Corpus-based Research into Language*. Rodopi, 1994.
3. Kuang-Hua Chen and Hsin-Hsi Chen. Extracting noun phrases from large-scale texts: A hybrid approach and its automatic evaluation. In *Proceedings of the 32nd Annual Meeting of the Association for Computational Linguistics*, Las Cruces, New Mexico, 1994.
4. Kenneth Ward Church. A Stochastic Parts Program and Noun Phrase Parser for Unrestricted Text. In *2nd Applied Natural Language Processing Conference*, Austin, Texas, 1988.
5. Christy Doran, Dania Egedi, Beth Ann Hockey, B. Srinivas, and Martin Zaidel. XTAG System - A Wide Coverage Grammar for English. In *Proceedings of the 17th International Conference on Computational Linguistics (COLING '94)*, Kyoto, Japan, August 1994.
6. F. Jelinek, J. Lafferty, D. Magerman, R. Mercer, A. Ratnaparkhi, and S. Roukos. Decision Tree Parsing using a Hidden Derivation Model. *ARPA Workshop on Human Language Technology*, pages 260–265, 1994.
7. Aravind K. Joshi and B. Srinivas. Disambiguation of Super Parts of Speech (or Supertags): Almost Parsing. In *Proceedings of the 17th International Conference on Computational Linguistics (COLING '94)*, Kyoto, Japan, August 1994.

8. R. Leech, G. & Garside. *Computer Corpora: Selected Papers and Bibliography*, chapter Running a grammar factory:the production of syntactically analysed corpora or 'treebanks'. Berlin, 1991.

9. Mitchell M. Marcus, Beatrice Santorini, and Mary Ann Marcinkiewicz. Building a Large Annotated Corpus of English: The Penn Treebank. *Computational Linguistics*, 19.2:313–330, June 1993.

10. Steve Minton. Quantitative Results concerning the utility of Explanation-Based Learning. In *Proceedings of 7th AAAI Conference*, pages 564–569, Saint Paul, Minnesota, 1988.

11. Tom M. Mitchell, Richard M. Keller, and Smadar T. Kedar-Carbelli. Explanation-Based Generalization: A Unifying View. *Machine Learning 1*, 1:47–80, 1986.

12. Günter Neumann. Application of Explanation-based Learning for Efficient Processing of Constraint-based Grammars. In 10th *IEEE Conference on Artificial Intelligence for Applications*, San Antonio, Texas, 1994.

13. Manny Rayner. Applying Explanation-Based Generalization to Natural Language Processing. In *Proceedings of the International Conference on Fifth Generation Computer Systems*, Tokyo, 1988.

14. Francesc Ribas. On learning more appropriate selectional restrictions. In *Proceedings of the Seventh Conference of the European Chapter of the Association for Computational Linguistics*, Dublin, Ireland, 1995.

15. G. Sampson. Susanne: a Doomsday book of English Grammar. In *Corpus-based Research into Language*. Rodopi, Amsterdam, 1994.

16. Chister Samuelsson. Grammar Specialization through Entropy Thresholds. In *32nd Meeting of the Association for Computational Linguistics*, Las Cruces, New Mexico, 1994.

17. Christer Samuelsson and Manny Rayner. Quantitative Evaluation of Explanation-Based Learning as an Optimization Tool for Large-Scale Natural Language System. In *Proceedings of the 12th International Joint Conference on Artificial Intelligence*, Sydney,Australia, 1991.

18. Y. Schabes, M. Roth, and R. Osborne. Parsing the Wall Street Journal with the Inside-Outside Algorithm. In *Proceedings of the European ACL*, 1993.

19. Yves Schabes. *Mathematical and Computational Aspects of Lexicalized Grammars*. PhD thesis, Computer Science Department, University of Pennsylvania, 1990.

20. Yves Schabes, Anne Abeillé, and Aravind K. Joshi. Parsing strategies with 'lexicalized' grammars: Application to Tree Adjoining Grammars. In *Proceedings of the 12th International Conference on Computational Linguistics (COLING'88)*, Budapest, Hungary, August 1988.

21. B. Srinivas, Christine Doran, and Seth Kulick. Heuristics and parse ranking. In *Proceedings of the 4th Annual International Workshop on Parsing Technologies*, Prague, September 1995.

22. Frank van Harmelen and Allan Bundy. Explanation-Based Generalization = Partial Evaluation. *Artificial Intelligence*, 36:401–412, 1988.

23. Atro Voutilainen. NPtool, a Detector of English Noun Phrases. In *Proceedings of the Seventh Conference of the European Chapter of the Association for Computational Linguistics*, Dublin, Ireland, 1995.

A Symbolic and Surgical Acquisition of Terms Through Variation*

Christian Jacquemin

Institut de Recherches en Informatique de Nantes (IRIN)
IUT de Nantes, 3 rue Joffre, F-44041 Nantes, France
Email: jacquemin@irin.univ-nantes.fr

Abstract. Terminological acquisition is an important issue in learning for Natural Language Processing (NLP) due to the constant terminological renewal through technological changes. Terms play a key role in several NLP-activities such as machine translation, automatic indexing or text understanding. In opposition to classical once-and-for-all approaches, this paper proposes an incremental process for terminological enrichment which operates on existing reference lists and large corpora. Candidate terms are acquired by extracting variants of reference terms through *FASTR* (FAst Syntactic Term Recognizer), a unification-based partial parser. As acquisition is performed within specific morpho-syntactic contexts (coordinations, insertions or permutations of complex nominals), rich conceptual links are learned together with candidate terms. A clustering of terms related through coordinations yields classes of conceptually close terms while graphs resulting from insertions denote generic/specific relations. A graceful degradation of the volume of acquisition on partial initial lists confirms the robustness of the method to incomplete data.

1 Aims

Multi-word terms and compounds play an increasing role in language analysis for the following reasons: their interpretation is rarely transparent, they generally denote a specific class of mental or real-world objects and the words composing them are strongly related. Therefore, a correct processing of terms ensures a higher quality in several applications of Natural Language Processing (NLP). In Machine Translation, their lack of transparency makes word-for-word translation fail and calls for specific descriptions. In Information Retrieval, their high informational content makes them good descriptors (Lewis & Croft 1990). In parsing,

---

* All the experiments reported in this paper have been performed on [Pascal] a list of 71,623 multi-domain terms and [Medic] a 1.56-million word medical corpus composed of abstracts of scientific papers owned by the French documentation center *INIST/CNRS*. This work has benefited from the helpful and friendly collaboration of Jean Royauté (*INIST*) and from rich discussions in the research group *Terminologie et Intelligence Artificielle* (*PRC IA*). This research was partially funded by the *GRAAL* project grant to Nantes University.

the selectional restrictions found between head words and their arguments within a term give important clues for structural noun phrase disambiguation (Resnik 1993).

As terms mirror the concepts of the domain to which they belong, a constant knowledge evolution leads to a constant term renewal. Thus terminological acquisition is a necessary companion to NLP, specifically when dealing with technical texts.

Tools for terminological acquisition, whether statistical, such as (Church & Hanks 1989), or symbolic, such as (Bourigault 1993), acquire terms from large corpora through a once-and-for-all process without consideration for any prior terminological knowledge. This lack of incrementality in acquisition has the following drawbacks:

- Acquired terms must be merged with the initial ones with consideration of eventual variants.
- Acquired terms are neither conceptually nor linguistically related to the original ones.
- The set of original terms is ignored although it could be a useful source of knowledge for acquisition.

It is possible to conceive a finer approach to term acquisition by considering existing term lists and the local variants of these terms within corpora. As term variants generally involve more than one term, they can be exploited in a process of non massive incremental acquisition. For example, if *viral hepatitis* is a known term, *viral and autoimmune hepatitis* is a variant of this term (a coordination) which displays *autoimmune hepatitis* as a candidate term. Moreover, this coordination indicates a strong closeness between the interpretation of both terms which can be associated to a link within a thesaurus. Henceforth, potential terms discovered through acquisition techniques will be called *candidate terms*. A formal definition of this notion is given by Definition 2 in section 5. The decision whether to include a candidate term into a terminology is outside the scope of my work.

2 Acquiring with a Concern for Prior Knowledge

Tools for acquiring terms generally operate on large corpora using various techniques to detect term occurrences. There are mainly two families of tools for term acquisition: statistical measures and NLP symbolic techniques.

The first family which comprises most of the tools is composed of statistical analyzers which have little or no linguistic knowledge. These applications take advantage of the specific statistical behavior of words composing terms: words which are lexically related tend to be found simultaneously more frequently than they would be just by chance. Pure statistical methods such as (Church & Hanks 1989) are rare. Generally some linguistic knowledge is associated to the statistical measures through a prior (Daille 1994) or a posterior (Smadja 1993) filtering of correct syntactic patterns. The assumption implicitly stated by statistical works, and which is backed up by my study, is that it is more likely to find a term in the neighborhood of another one than anywhere else in a text. More specifically, I assume that the best way of combining two terms syntactically and semantically is to build a specific structure, a *variant*, which is either a term or a restricted noun phrase and which is observed within a small span of words.

The second approach to term acquisition consists of knowledge-based methods which rely on local grammars of noun phrases and compounds (Bourigault 1993). Word sequences accepted by these grammars are extracted through a more or less shallow parse of corpora and are good candidate terms.

The counterpart of both statistical and knowledge-based acquisitions is to provide the user with large lists of candidates which have to be manually filtered out. For example, *LEXTER* (Bourigault 1993) extracts 20,000 occurrences from a 200,000-word corpus which represent 10,000 candidate terms. It is due to a lack of initial terminological knowledge along with a lack of consideration for terminological variation that such methods propose too large sets of terms. In order to reduce the volume of acquisition and also to propose candidates which are more likely to be terms, this paper presents a method based on an initial list of terms called *reference terms*. The acquisition procedure starts from this supposed comprehensive set of reference terms. It decomposes variations of these terms found in corpora and is then able to detect candidate terms.

Updating Rather Than Acquiring

Is it realistic to suppose that lists of terms exist for technical domains? The ever-growing mass of electronic documents calls for tools for accessing these data which have to make extensive use of term lists as sources of indexes. For this purpose, and for other activities related to textual databases, more and more thesauri exist. Some of them, such as the *Unified Medical Language System* meta-thesaurus, carry conceptual and/or linguistic information about the terms they contain. In my experiments I have used the [Pascal] terminological list composed of 71,623 multi-domain terms without conceptual links, provided by the documentation center *INIST/CNRS*.

Because of the availability of large term lists, it is natural to lay a greater stress on the updating of such data than on their acquisition from scratch. Therefore, my approach to acquisition focuses on how to improve a list of terms through the observation of corpora. My approach also differs from previous experiments on term acquisition because it yields conceptual links between candidate and reference terms. It can be used to check or to enhance the conceptual knowledge of thesauri in a way complementary to automatic semantic clustering of terms through an observation of their syntactic contexts (Grefenstette 1994).

3   A Micro-syntax for an Accurate Extraction

The first step in my approach to terminological acquisition is the extraction of term variants from large corpora. The tool used is *FASTR*, a unification-based partial parser. *FASTR* recycles lists of reference terms by transforming them into grammar rules. Then, it dynamically builds term variant rules from these term rules. The parser is described in (Jacquemin 1994) and, here, it will just be sketched out, by focusing on the features that are relevant for terminological acquisition. More specifically, I will omit the aspects of the parser concerning its optimization and the feature structures associated with rules and meta-rules.

In such a simplified framework, each reference term corresponds to a *PATR-II*-like rule (Shieber 1986) comprising a context free skeleton and lexical items. For example, rule (1) denotes the term *serum albumin* with a $\langle Noun \rangle \langle Noun \rangle$ structure:

$$
\begin{aligned}
&\text{Rule } N_1 \rightarrow N_2 \ N_3 \ : \\
&\quad < N_2 \ lemma > \doteq \text{ 'serum'} \\
&\quad < N_3 \ lemma > \doteq \text{ 'albumin'}.
\end{aligned}
\tag{1}
$$

At a higher level, a set of meta-rules operates on the term rules and produces new rules describing potential variations. Each meta-rule is dedicated to a specific term structure and to a specific type of variation. For the sake of clarity, meta-rules are divided into two sets – meta-rules for two-word terms and meta-rules for three-word terms – and each set is subdivided into three subsets – meta-rules for coordination, insertion and permutation. Meta-rules for terms of four words or more are ignored because they produce very few variants (approximately 1 % of the variants). Meta-rule (2) applies to rule (1) and yields a new rule (3):

$$
\text{Meta-rule } Coor(X_1 \rightarrow X_2 \ X_3) \ \equiv \ X_1 \rightarrow X_2 \ C_4 \ X_5 \ X_3 \ : .
\tag{2}
$$

$$
\begin{aligned}
&\text{Rule } N_1 \rightarrow N_2 \ C_4 \ X_5 \ N_3 \ : \\
&\quad < N_2 \ lemma > \doteq \text{ 'serum'} \\
&\quad < N_3 \ lemma > \doteq \text{ 'albumin'}.
\end{aligned}
\tag{3}
$$

This transformed rule accepts any sequence *serum C_4 X_5 albumin* as a variant of *serum albumin* where C_4 is any coordinating conjunction and X_5 any single word. For example, it correctly recognizes *serum and egg albumin* as a variant of *serum albumin*. The second column of Table 1 presents some other meta-rules for two-word terms together with examples of pairs composed of a term and one of its variants. Currently, the meta-grammar of *FASTR* for English includes 73 meta-rules for 2- and 3-word terms: 25 coordination meta-rules, 17 insertion meta-rules and 31 permutation meta-rules (plus 66 meta-rules for 4-word terms which are not used for acquisition).

When term variations are described through meta-rules as in *FASTR*, it is very simple to devise a process for term acquisition: each paradigmatic meta-rule (or skeleton of a filtering meta-rule) is linked to a pattern extractor, yielding a candidate term. As no further analysis of the variants is required, such an acquisition is extremely fast. The acquisition of terms by extracting patterns from variants is processed as follows for the different categories of variants:

– *Coordination.* The candidate is the term coordinated with the original one.

- *Insertion.* The candidate is the term which has replaced the head of the original term through substitution.
- *Permutation.* In a permutation of a 2-word term, the argument of the original term is shifted from the left of the head to its right and is transformed into a prepositional phrase. The candidate term is the noun phrase inside this prepositional phrase. This definition is extended to terms of 3 words or more where one of the arguments is permuted.

The third column of Table 1 exemplifies patterns of acquisition for each of the three categories of term variants.

Table 1. Acquisition through pattern extraction from variants. (Examples are from the [Medic] corpus.)

Variation	Meta-rule and associated variant	Acquisition
Coordination (25 meta-rules)	$X_2\ X_3 \mapsto X_2\ X_4\ C_5\ X_3$ *surgical closure* $\mapsto$ *surgical exploration and closure*	$X_2\ X_4$ *surgical exploration*
Insertion (17 meta-rules)	$X_2\ X_3 \mapsto X_2\ X_4\ X_3$ *medullary carcinoma* $\mapsto$ *medullary thyroid carcinoma*	$X_4\ X_3$ *thyroid carcinoma*
Permutation (31 meta-rules)	$X_2\ X_3 \mapsto X_3\ P_4\ X_5\ X_2$ *control center* $\mapsto$ *center for disease control*	$X_5\ X_2$ *disease control*

This method for term acquisition does not systematically succeed for each encountered term variant. Firstly, some correct variants involve only one term instead of two or more and cannot produce new candidates. For example, *cells and their subpopulations* is a coordination variant of *cell subpopulation* which is unproductive in comparison with the variant *surgical exploration and closure* exemplified for coordination in Table 1. Secondly, some of the terms acquired through variations may already be reference terms (see the non-underlined candidates in Tables 2, 3 and 4). For the reference list to be sufficiently comprehensive, it is expected and even desirable that some of the acquired terms are already known. Moreover, "acquisitions" of known terms are not useless because they reveal conceptual links between these terms.

4   Acquiring Conceptual Classes

Tables 2, 3 and 4 exemplify some terms acquired through the three main kinds of variations observed for English: coordinations, insertions and permutations. The terms acquired through permutations are not conceptually related to the original ones due to the syntagmatic nature of this transformation. On the contrary, coordination and insertion variations relate semantically close terms. In 4.1 and 4.2, I examine in turn the decomposition of these two kinds of variations in the aim of acquiring conceptual links.

Table 2. Examples of term acquisition through coordination from the [Medic] corpus. Terms which do not belong to the reference list are underlined.

Candidate term	Reference Term
abdominal aorta	Thoracic aorta
acidic lipid	Neutral lipid
active phase	Latent phase
adrenal gland	Thyroid gland
affective disorder	Cognitive disorder
aged animal	Young animal
agonist bromocriptine	Agonist antagonist
air conduction	Bone conduction
amniotic fluid estimation	Ratio estimation
aortic arch	Aortic coarctation
aortic valve	Mitral valve
arterial acid base	Arterial blood

4.1 Coordination

Two terms are coordinated only if they share the same semantic scheme. For example, the variant *surgical exploration and closure* (see the first example of Table 1) indicates that the two terms *surgical exploration* and *surgical closure* are semantically close. They both denote a surgical act. This fact is interesting because some of the terms with a *surgical⟨Noun⟩* structure such as *surgical shock* do not belong to the same conceptual class and could not be coordinated with any of the *surgical⟨Noun⟩* terms from this class: *a surgical shock and closure* is incorrect. Thus, when heads are coordinated (approximately 15 % of the coordinations) the head nouns of the terms must belong to the same semantic class (with respect to their entry selected by their argument). On the other hand, when arguments are coordinated, they must select the same entry of the head noun. For example, *dorsal spine* and *cervical spine* can be coordinated as both being a part of the *(nervous) spine* but neither of them can be coordinated with a *hedgehog* or a *fish spine*. Such coordinations are useful indicators for the disambiguation of a head word by its arguments:

– For its classification with other related words through head coordination.

Table 3. Examples of term acquisition through insertion from the [Medic] corpus. Terms which do not belong to the reference list are underlined.

Candidate term	Reference Term
abdominal spear injury	Penetrating injury
ablating tool	Cutting tool
absorbed dose	Radiation dose
access pressure	Blood pressure
accessory nerve	Spinal nerve
acetylcholine receptor	Muscarinic receptor
acetylcholine receptor	Nicotinic receptor
acid analysis	Organic analysis
acid base disorder	Metabolic disorder
action potential	Evoked potential
action potential	Membrane potential
activity curve	Time curve

Table 4. Examples of term acquisition through permutation from the [Medic] corpus. Terms which do not belong to the reference list are underlined.

Candidate term	Reference Term
accessory cell	Cell proliferation
acetabular growth	Growth factor
activated b cell	Cell differentiation
acute phase protein	Protein synthesis
adipose tissue	Tissue extract
adult cell	Cell function
agarose gel	Gel electrophoresis
airway control	Control method
anaphylatoxin level	Level measurement
aneuploid tumor cell	Cell population
animal tolerance	Tolerance limit
arterial pressure	Pressure control

– For the definition of its subsenses depending on its arguments through argument coordination.

The fine-grained selectional restrictions revealed by coordinations take advantage of the preexisting knowledge embodied in lists of reference terms. They complement the lexical relationships acquired from statistical measures on the results of a shallow syntactic analysis where words have semantic tags, whether manually assigned (Basili, Pazienza, & Velardi 1993) or deduced from a thesaurus (Resnik 1993).

The acquisition from variants, illustrated for one step in Table 1, is repeated on candidate terms as long as new candidates are discovered. Then *conceptual classes* of compatible sense restrictions are built from terms related through constructions of coordination according to the following definition:

Definition 1 Conceptual class. Two terms t and t' are placed in the same conceptual class if and only if there exists a chain of coordination variants from t to t': a set of n terms $t_1 = t$, $t_2, \ldots, t_{n-1}$, $t_n = t'$ such that for each pair $(t_i, t_{i+1})_{i \in \{1,2,\ldots,n-1\}}$ either t_i is acquired from a coordination variant of t_{i+1} or t_{i+1} is acquired from a coordination variant of t_i.

Figure 1 is a planar representation of the graph constructed from one of the conceptual classes observed in the [Medic] corpus. Each arrow from a term t to a term t' indicates that t' has been acquired from a coordination variant of t.

Leaving apart the only head coordination in the figure that holds between *cirrhotic control* and *cirrhotic patient*, all the terms have a ⟨*Modifier*⟩ *control* structure [2] and can be coordinated through a head coordination. Conceptually, the terms of Figure 1 are related to a common hypernym whose linguistic utterance is *medical control*.

Moreover, the spatial organization of the graph outlines the central role played by *normal control* and *disease control*. These two terms are the most generic ones. Their root position in this acyclic graph (except for the two symmetric links) mirrors the linguistic fact that an argument coordination between two terms tends to place first the most generic argument and then the most specific one. Thus, although placed at a similar conceptual level in the taxonomy, these terms are ordered from the most generic to the most specific along the coordination links. This two-level observation reveals that linguistic clues, when precisely observed, are good indications of the conceptual organization.

4.2 Insertion

The meta-rules accounting for insertions insert one or more words inside a term string. The following meta-rule (4) denotes an insertion of one word inside a two-word term:

$$\text{Meta-rule } Ins(X_1 \rightarrow X_2 \, X_3) \equiv X_1 \rightarrow X_2 \, X_4 \, X_3 \; : . \tag{4}$$

The resulting structure is ambiguous depending on whether the leftmost word of the term is still an argument of the head noun in the variation (e.g. [*inflammatory* [*bowel disease*]]) or an argument of the inserted word (e.g. [[*sunflower seed*] *oil*]). The second structure is quite rare and does not correspond to a genuine variant

---

[2] *Matched control* is a partial term with a missing noun argument which is not ruled out by my acquisition process. With a proper acquisition, this term would not appear as a candidate and the links issuing from this term would issue from one of the correct terms ⟨*Noun*⟩ *matched control*.

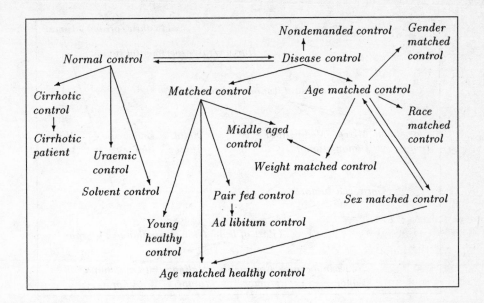

Fig. 1. Network of coordination links from the [Medic] corpus.

of the original term because it has a different argument structure. However, most of these possibly incorrect variants are correct. It happens every time when the reference term (here *sunflower oil*) corresponds to an elided denomination of the variant which is in fact the reference term. In this case, the non-ambiguity of the elided form relies on pragmatic knowledge, because everyone knows that the *seed* is the part of the *sunflower* used to make *sunflower oil*.

Whatever the structure of the variant, either $((X_3\ X_2)\ X_1)$ or $(X_3\ (X_2\ X_1))$, the extraction of the sequence $X_2\ X_1$ as candidate term (see Tables 1 and 3) yields a correct term. When extracted from the latter structure, the candidate term is more specific than the original one because modifiers in the noun phrase tend to be ordered from the most generic to the most specific.

As stated for coordination, an iteration of acquisition on candidates terms yields conceptual relations. However, the construction of the graph linking terms acquired through insertion is not as straightforward as it is for coordination. The reason is that one must first conflate conceptually close terms that are likely to be in the same conceptual class (Definition 1) before constructing the hierarchy resulting from insertion variants. Figure 2 has been constructed by grouping together *malignant tumor/benign tumor*, *metastatic tumor/primary tumor* and *human tumor/experimental tumor* which have been observed in coordinated constructions. A further grouping of *rat tumor* with *human tumor* was necessary but was not indicated by a coordination in the [Medic] corpus. Similarly, a general class labeled ⟨*Part of body*⟩ *tumors* has been created although only some coordinations were observed among the possible ones: *mammary/skin tumors*, *cutaneous/corneal tumors*, *bone/soft tissue tumors*...

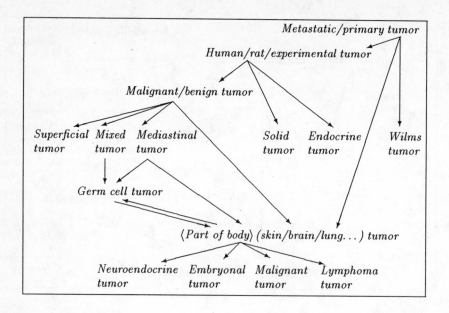

Fig. 2. Network of insertion links from the [Medic] corpus.

Due to the parallel between insertion constructions and generic/specific links, there is a good similarity between the observed graph and the taxonomy of this part of the terminology. An exception to this rule is the link from the class labeled ⟨*Part of body*⟩ *tumor* to *malignant tumor* coming from the variant *ovarian malignant tumor*. It is indeed an exceptional link: there are fifteen different links from *malignant tumor* to more specific terms but only one link from a more specific term (*ovarian tumor*) to *malignant tumor*. The utterance *ovarian malignant tumor* which is responsible for this surprising link is extracted from *react with a surface antigen present on the majority of nonmucinous ovarian malignant tumors tested but not with normal adult tissue*. It occurs in the abstract of a paper on cancerology where the type of tumor (*malignant* vs. *benign*) is surely more salient than its location. Therefore the modifier *malignant* stands closer to the head word *tumor* than the location *ovarian*.

5   Incrementality and Robustness

Definition 1 has introduced the incremental repetition of coordinations for the construction of conceptual classes. This definition can be generalized to the three types of variation in order to give a formal definition of *candidate terms*. As indicated by the following definition, candidate terms are acquired from candidate terms of the preceding step until no new term is discovered:

Definition 2 Candidate term. A term t_n is a candidate if and only if there exists a chain of couples $(t_i, t_{i+1})_{i \in \{1,2,\ldots,n-1\}}$ where t_{i+1} is acquired from a variant of t_i and where t_1 is a reference term. That is to say that the set of candidates is the closure of the set of reference terms through the relation of acquisition.

Due to the finite corpus, due to the finite length of terms and due to the non circularity of the definition, the incremental acquisition reaches a fixed point after a finite number of iterations. It takes fifteen cycles to complete an acquisition of 5,080 terms when starting from the 71,623 terms of the [Pascal] list.[3]

Table 5 shows five sequences of acquisition obtained from term variants in [Médic] starting from a reference term in [Pascal]. For example, the first sequence indicates the acquisition of *tumour tissue* from *tissue extract* through a permutation variant (*extract of tumour tissue*) followed by the acquisition of *normal tissue* from a coordination (*tumour or normal tissue*), and so on. This sequence mixes the three kinds of variations while the last three sequences are restricted to insertions and/or coordinations. When not using permutations, the acquisition process yields smaller sets of terms: it produces 2,998 terms in fourteen steps through coordinations and insertions, 2,193 terms in seven steps through insertions and 357 terms in six steps through coordinations.

Table 5. Examples of sequences of acquisition.

Var.	Acquired terms		
P-C	*Tissue extract*	→ *tumour tissue*	→ *normal tissue*
I-P-I	→ *rat tissue*	→ *sprague dawley rat*	→ *female rat*
I-I-P	→ *F344 rat*	→ *strain rat*	→ *milan strain*
I-I	→ *normotens. strain*	→ *control strain*	
I-C	*Blood cell*	→ *leukemic cell*	→ *normal cell*
C-I-I	→ *CF cell*	→ *pancreatic cell*	→ *beta cell*
C-I	→ *alpha cell*	→ *activated NK cell*	
I-I	*Cell line*	→ *tumor line*	→ *derived cell line*
I-I-I	→ *T cell line*	→ *leukemia cell line*	→ *U937 cell line*
I	→ *histiocytic cell line*		
C-C	*Experimental study*	→ *clinical study*	→ *echocardiograph. study*
C-C	→ *doppler study*	→ *angiography study*	
C-C	*Pigment. disorder*	→ *nail disorder*	→ *nail change*
C	→ *palmar change*		

As my method is based on the observation of rare occurrences, the number of acquired terms depends on the set of reference terms. As indicated in (Engue-

---

[3] Among these 71,623 terms, only 12,717 are found in the [Medic] corpus under their basic form or one of its correct variants.

hard 1994), such a correlation does not exist in her statistical approach to term acquisition because she observes larger sets of (co-)occurrences. Figure 3 exemplifies acquisition curves for different values of the volume of reference terms. It shows that the size of the acquisition gradually degrades when the size of the bootstrap decreases: 5,080 terms are acquired when starting from the total list of 12,717 terms, 3,833 terms are still acquired from a bootstrap of 6,000 terms and 2,329 terms from a bootstrap of 1,000 terms. Thus, with only a twelfth of the initial bootstrap, almost half the terms are still acquired. Although a serious degradation of the results is observed under this lower limit, these values suggest that acquisition depends more on the size of the corpora than on the initial terminology. As a partial initial list of terms is easily compensated by larger corpora, the completeness of the reference list is not a crucial issue for the quality of the acquisition in my framework.

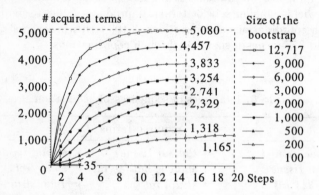

Fig. 3. Acquisition volumes for different sizes of bootstrap on the [Medic] corpus.

6   Precision

The precision of the first step of the acquisition process has been evaluated on the [Medic] corpus. Incorrect acquisitions correspond to candidates with an unacceptable linguistic structure such as *for the expression* or to candidates with an obvious lack of informative content such as *related proteins*. The former kind of error is due mainly to incorrect variations produced by *FASTR*. Hence, the occurrence *gene and for the expression*, extracted from *... mouse lung tumors* (...) *were analyzed for the presence of mutations at codon 61 of the Ki-ras gene and for the expression of the surfactant protein...* is incorrectly extracted by *FASTR* as a coordination variant of *gene expression*. This spurious variant yields the unacceptable candidate *for the expression*.

The second kind of incorrect acquisition is more difficult to detect because it relies on the "terminologization" of a phrase. Although extracted from the correct variation *heat shock and related proteins* (a variant of *heat shock proteins*), the candidate *related proteins* is unlikely to be a term because the modifier *related* assigns an occasional characteristic to the noun *protein*. *Related proteins* does not name a specific type of protein with its own inherent properties, it denotes an occasional group of proteins. Therefore, it is probably not the linguistic label of a concept in the medical domain. It is difficult to discard automatically this kind of spurious candidate, mostly because its structure, a past participle followed by a noun, is a possible term structure and cannot be used as a correct criterion to reject it. For example, *controlled delivery*, *compressed air* or *prolonged apnea* are terms of the [Pascal] list with this syntactic structure. In most cases, human expertise or, at least, intensive lexical semantics knowledge is required to confirm the terminological status of such candidate terms.

The precision of acquisition on the [Medic] corpus is 84.6 % and is distributed as follows: 92.6 % for coordination-based acquisition, 88.7 % for insertion-based acquisition and 72.4 % for permutation-based acquisition. The low rate of garbage (15.4 %) is due to the high precision of variant extraction in *FASTR*. In this application, high precision rate (94.5 %) is preferred to high recall (84.7 %). Incorrect occurrences are intentionally filtered out, arguing that human selection of incorrect variants is tedious and that recall can be improved by increasing the size of the corpora used for extraction and acquisition.

To conclude, the candidates obtained from coordinations and insertions are "better" than the ones obtained from permutation because the first two types of transformations yield compounds. Conversely, permutations, which transform compounds into syntactic noun phrases, tend to produce candidates of a lower quality.

7   Conclusion and Future Work

This study has proposed a novel approach to terminological acquisition that differs from the two main trends in this domain: morpho-syntactic filtering or statistical extraction. The main feature of my approach is accounting for existing lists of terms by observing their variants and yielding conceptual links as well as candidate terms. As long as they are accessible through morpho-syntactic dependencies in a corpus, these links can be used to automatically construct parts of the taxonomy representing the knowledge in this domain. Among the applications of this method are lexical acquisition, thesaurus discovery and technological survey. More generally, terminological enrichment is necessary for NLP activities dealing with technical sublanguages because their efficiency and their quality depend on the completeness of their lexicons of terms and compounds.

References

Basili, R.; Pazienza, M. T.; and Velardi, P. 1993. Acquisition of selectional patterns in sublanguages. *Machine Translation* 8:175–201.

Bourigault, D. 1993. An endogeneous corpus-based method for structural noun phrase disambiguation. In *Proceedings, 6th European Chapter of the Association for Computational Linguistics (EACL'93)*, 81–86.

Church, K. W., and Hanks, P. 1989. Word association norms, mutual information and lexicography. In *Proceedings, 27th Annual Meeting of the Association for Computational Linguistics (ACL'89)*, 76–83.

Daille, B. 1994. Study and implementation of combined techniques for automatic extraction of terminology. In *Proceedings, The Balancing Act : Combining Symbolic and Statistical Approaches to Language, Workshop at the 32nd Annual Meeting of the Association for Computational Linguistics*, 29–36.

Enguehard, C. 1994. Automatic Natural Acquisition of a terminology. In *Proceedings, 2nd International Conference on Quantitative Linguistics (QUALICO'94)*, 83–88.

Grefenstette, G. 1994. *Explorations in Automatic Thesaurus Discovery*. Dordrecht, The Netherlands: Kluwer Academic Publisher.

Jacquemin, C. 1994. Recycling terms into a partial parser. In *Proceedings, 4th Conference on Applied Natural Language Processing (ANLP'94)*, 113–118.

Lewis, D. D., and Croft, W. B. 1990. Term clustering of syntactic phrasess. In *Proceedings, 13th Annual International ACM SIGIR Conference on Research and Development in Information Retrieval (SIGIR'90)*, 385–404.

Resnik, P. 1993. *Selection and Information : A Class-Based Approach to Lexical Relationships*. Ph.D. thesis, University of Pennsylvania, Institute for Research in Cognitive Science.

Shieber, S. N. 1986. *An Introduction to Unification-Based Approaches to Grammar*. CSLI Lecture Notes 4. Stanford, CA: CSLI.

Smadja, F. 1993. Xtract : An overview. *Computer and the Humanities* 26:399–413.

A Revision Learner to Acquire Verb Selection Rules from Human-made Rules and Examples *

Shigeo KANEDA[1] and Hussein ALMUALLIM[2] and Yasuhiro AKIBA[1] and
Megumi ISHII[1] and Tsukasa KAWAOKA[3]

[1] NTT Communication Science Laboratories,
1-2356 Take, Yokosuka-Shi,
Kanagawa-Ken, 238-03, Japan
[2] King Fahd University of Petroleum and Minerals,
PO BOX 801, Dhahran 31261, Saudi Arabia
[3] Doshisha University
1-3, Tatara-miyakodani, Tanabe-cho,
Tuzuki-gun, Kyoto-fu, 610-03, Japan

Abstract. This paper proposes a learning method that automatically acquires English verb selection rules for machine translation using a machine learning technique. When learning from real translation examples alone, many examples are needed to achieve good translation quality. It is, however, difficult to gather a sufficiently large number of real translation examples. The main causes are verbs of low frequency and the frequent usage of the same sentences. To resolve this problem, the proposed method learns English verb selection rules from hand-made translation rules and a small number of real translation examples. The proposed method has two steps: generating artificial examples from the hand-made rules, and then putting those artificial examples and real examples into an internal learner as the training set. The internal learner outputs the final rules with improved verb selection accuracy. The most notable feature of the proposed learner is that any attribute-type learning algorithm can be adopted as the internal learner. To evaluate the validity of the proposed learner, English verb selection rules of NTT's Japanese-English Machine Translation System ALT-J/E are experimentally learned from hand-made rules and real examples. The resultant rules have better accuracy than either those constructed from the real examples or those that are hand-made.

1 Introduction

This work aims at the automatic acquisition of semantic analysis rules for rule-based Japanese-English Machine Translation (MT) systems. To realize this aim, this paper proposes a learning method to acquire English verb selection rules.

The rule-based Japanese-English MT system called *"ALT-J/E"* is being developed at Nippon Telegraph and Telephone Corporation (NTT) [6, 7]. In its

---

* An earlier version of this paper has been published in the Proceedings of the Sixth International Conference on Theoretical and Methodological Issues in Machine Translation (TMI95)

Japanese-English translation knowledge base, ALT-J/E has about fifteen thousand hand-made English verb selection and semantic analysis rules.

To improve the translation quality of ALT-J/E, it needs more English verb selection rules and more specific English verb selection rules for each translation domain. Unfortunately, this would require excessive effort using the conventional manual approach. Thus, rules should be acquired automatically.

In [3], two algorithms were introduced that learn English verb selection rules from Japanese-English translation examples. These algorithms need many translation examples to develop good rules. It is very difficult, however, to gather a sufficient number of real translation examples from existing documents because some sentences are used repeatedly while a large number of verbs occur infrequently.

Thus, some kind of information should be extracted from human knowledge to overcome this scarcity of real examples in existing documents. One practical way to extract human knowledge is to write hand-made English verb selection rules. These hand-made rules are, however, not complete nor sufficient for practical use. If these rules and real examples could be integrated, better translation performance would be obtained automatically.

```
IF                                        THEN
    J-Verb  = "焼く (yaku)"
    N_1 (Subj) ≡ "People"                     E-Verb = "bake"
    N_2 (Obj) ≡ "Bread" or "Cake"
IF                                        THEN
    J-Verb  = "焼く (yaku)"
    N_1 (Subj) ≡ "People"                     E-Verb = "roast"
    N_2 (Obj) ≡ "Meat"
IF                                        THEN
    J-Verb  = "焼く (yaku)"
    N_1 (Subj) ≡ "People"                     E-Verb = "broil"
    N_2 (Obj) ≡ "Fish" or "Seafood"
IF                                        THEN
    J-Verb  = "焼く (yaku)"
    N_1 (Subj) ≡ "Agents"                     E-Verb = "cremate"
    N_2 (Obj) ≡ "People" or "Animals"
IF                                        THEN
    J-Verb  = "焼く (yaku)"
    N_1 (Subj) ≡ "Agents" or "Machines"       E-Verb = "burn"
    N_2 (Obj) ≡ "Places" or "Objects" or
               "Locations"
```

Fig. 1. English verb selection rules for the Japanese verb 焼く (yaku). " ≡ " indicates "an instance of".

This paper proposes a learning method that learns English verb selection rules with high accuracy from hand-made rules and sparse real examples. The proposed method generates examples from hand-made English verb selection rules. These examples are called *"artificial examples"* hereafter. The artificial examples and "real examples" are given to an internal learner as the training data. The internal learner can be any attribute-based learner. The output of the internal learner is the final output of the proposed method.

To represent the importance of artificial examples and real examples, each example is assigned a weight in the proposed method. If a hand-made rule is very accurate, the artificial examples generated from it are assigned a large weight. On the other hand, if the hand-made rule is inaccurate, only a small weight is assigned. The proposed method determines the best weights by cross validation.

To estimate the validity of the proposed method, English verb selection rules of ALT-J/E system are experimentally learned from hand-made rules and real examples gathered from existing documents. In this experiment, we used, as the internal learner, the learning algorithm reported in [3] which is a modification of the ID3 (C4.5) algorithm. The English verb selection rules learned by the proposed method have better accuracy than either those constructed from only real examples or those that are hand-made.

First, a brief explanation of English verb selection rules is given in the following section. Second, a previous method and its shortcomings are discussed. Third, the new learning method is proposed. Forth, experimental results and related works are shown. Finally, conclusions of this paper are described.

2 English Verb Selection Rules

This section describes ALT-J/E's English verb selection rules and discusses the difficulties encountered in the acquisition of these rules.

2.1 English Verb Selection Rules

This paper defines an English verb selection rule as having a Japanese pattern as its left-hand side and an English verb as its right-hand side, as shown in Figure 1. Such rules associate a Japanese pattern with an English verb. Here, a Japanese pattern consists of only one Japanese verb and the variables N_1, N_2, etc., which represent various Japanese sentence components, such as the Subject and the Object; "Fish", "Seafood", etc. are semantic categories. ALT-J/E has about 3,000 semantic categories that constitute a semantic hierarchy with 12 levels. Figure 2 shows a part of the semantic hierarchy.

ALT-J/E has a semantic dictionary with 400,000 words that are nouns or proper nouns. The semantic dictionary maps each Japanese noun to its appropriate semantic categories. Note that a noun usually has more than one semantic category. For example, the semantic dictionary states that the noun 鶏 (niwatori), which means "chicken" or "hen" in English, is an instance of the categories "Meat" and "Birds".

2.2 Difficulty of Acquiring English Verb Selection Rules

Matching a Japanese sentence to English verb selection rules is described below. For example, when the Japanese sentence "コックがアップルパイを焼く[4](Kokku

---

[4] This Japanese sentence means "A cook bakes an apple-pie.".

ga appurupai wo yaku.)" is input, ALT-J/E runs morphological analysis and syntactic analysis and analyzes the sentence into the Japanese verb "焼く (yaku)", the noun "コック (kokku)", and the noun "アップルパイ (appurupai)". ALT-J/E states that "コック (kokku)" has 3 semantic categories, "tools", "people", and "jobs", while "アップルパイ (appurupai)" has only one semantic category "confectionery".

Matching succeeds when each noun in the sentence has a descendant, on the semantic hierarchy, of one case element in the rule. In this example, the Object in the sentence (appurupai) matches only with the first rule in Figure 1, while the Subject in the sentence (kokku) matches only those rules that contain semantic category "people". Therefore, only the first rule for the English verb "bake" satisfies both Subject (N_1) and Object (N_2). Thus the noun "コック (kokku)" means "people" not "tools".

The most difficult task in acquiring English verb selection rules is the selection of semantic categories for each case element in the rules because this involves a huge number of combinations of the nearly 3,000 semantic categories of ALT-J/E. Therefore, English verb selection rules should be acquired automatically—a task which we believe can be achieved using suitable machine learning techniques.

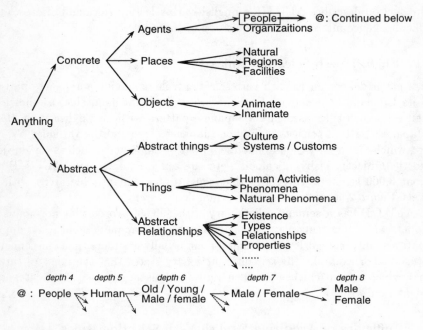

Fig. 2. The upper levels of the Semantic Hierarchy in ALT-J/E.

3 A Former Work and its Problem

In [3], two algorithms for learning English verb selection rules from Japanese-English translation examples were proposed. In that work, training examples are prepared through the following process:

(1) Preparing pairs of a simple sentence and an appropriate English verb like the following: ("コックがアップルパイを焼く" "bake"),

(2) Parsing the Japanese sentence in each pair,

(3) Picking up head nouns,

(4) Making training examples like the following from the nouns as in step (3):
⟨ N1(Subj) = "tools", "people", or "jobs", N2(Obj) = "confectionery", "bake" ⟩,
where " =" indicates "a semantic category of".

The approach of [3] needs many training examples to construct English verb selection rules with satisfactorily high accuracy. To investigate whether or not it is possible to get enough training examples to construct English verb selection rules with high accuracy, a corpus with about 50,000 Japanese-English translation entries was formed from existing documents [8, 4]. The 50,000 Japanese simple sentences contain about 5,000 different Japanese verbs. Only 1% of all Japanese verbs were used in 100 or more Japanese sentences. Also, the translation examples contain repeated sentences.

Because approximately 100 sentences are needed per verb to ensure sufficient accuracy and 95% of all the Japanese verbs were used in 2 or more Japanese sentences, the analysis shows that, at least, about 2.5 million translation examples are required to construct good English verb selection rules for 95% of the 5,000 verbs. This number of translation examples is clearly hard to collect.

In our opinion, it is too optimistic to think that any learning algorithm can construct English verb selection rules from corpora extracted from just existing documents. That is, we need a new algorithm to construct English verb selection rules from hand-made English verb selection rules and real translation examples. The algorithm must offer adequate performance even if the number of examples is not enough to construct good rules and the hand-made rules don't have enough quality for practical use. In the next section, a revision learner will be proposed that realizes this approach.

4 Revision Learner

This section proposes the new method called *"Revision Learner"* that composes English verb selection rules from hand-made rules and real translation examples. Before talking about Revision Learner, we will clarify the learning task.

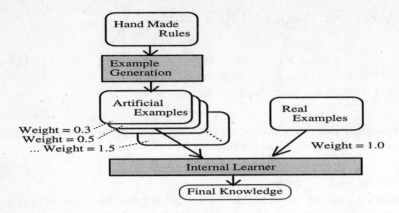

Fig. 3. Block Diagram of The Proposed Revision Learner.

4.1 Learning Task

For a given Japanese verb *J-verb* and a possible English translation *E-verb$_i$* of that verb, the algorithm has to find the appropriate condition(s) that should hold in the context in order to map *J-verb* to *E-verb$_i$*. The task of learning English verb selection rules for a Japanese verb, for example the Japanese verb 焼く (yaku), is described as follows:

【Learning Task】

Step-I Making English verb selection rules by hand, as shown in Figure 1,
Step-II Gathering real examples, as in Step (4) of the previous section, and
Step-III Automatically constructing the final rules from the above examples
  and rules by Revision Learner as described in the next subsection.

4.2 Outline of Revision Learner

Revision Learner gets information from hand-made English verb selection rules and real examples. The influence of a hand-made rule depends on its level of accuracy. If the provided rule is a highly accurate one, it would then be emphasized during the learning process. On the other hand, a hade-made rule with low accuracy would have very limited influence on the final result. The balance between hand-made rules and real examples is expressed by assigning numerical values, called *weights*, to the artificial and real examples. In general, these weights are not known when the human-made rules and real examples are given. Assuming that the number of candidate such weights N, the Revision Learner determines the best weights based on cross-validation as described in the following procedure:

【Revision Learner】

Step-i Generate artificial examples from the hand-made English verb selection rules—details are described in the following subsection,

Step-ii Form a family of example sets $\{Data_i; i = 1 \cdots N\}$, where $Data_i$ is the union set of the artificial examples, with the ith candidate weighting values, and the real examples.

Step-iii For each $Data_i$, calculate average accuracy A_i of the rule learned from $Data_i$, by using cross validation[5], which is described in subsection 4.4,

Step-iv Finally, output the rule that has the best average accuracy in $A_i (i = 1 \cdots N)$.

Figure 3 shows a block diagram of the proposed method. One notable feature of the proposed Revision Learner is that we can select any attribute-based learning algorithm as the internal learner.

4.3 Artificial Example Generation Method

This section details Step-i in the previous subsection.

Step-A Decompose the hand-made English verb selection rules into unit rules. A typical unit rule has the following format: [6]

$$\text{IF } (N_1 \equiv V_1) \ \& \ (N_2 \equiv V_2) \ \& \ \cdots \qquad \text{THEN Class} = \text{CV},$$

where " $\equiv$ " indicates "an instance of", N_1, N_2 etc. are case elements, V_1, V_2 etc. are semantic categories, and CV is an English verb,

Step-B From the above unit rules, generate artificial examples in the following form:

$$\langle N_1 = v_1, N_2 = v_2, \cdots, CV \rangle$$

where N_1, N_2 etc. are case elements, v_i is randomly selected from the descendants of V_i on the semantic hierarchy and V_i is a semantic category in the unit rule, and

Step-C Repeat Step-B until the desired number of examples are generated.

---

[5] When cross-validation is executed, the weight of each test examples is set to 1.0.

[6] Negation in the condition part is expressed like the following form: $N_1 = \text{not } V_1$.

4.4 Cross Validation

Cross validation is a widely used method for estimating the accuracy of learning algorithms. In this work, we use cross validation in Step-iii of our Revision Learner to tune the weight values.

For clarity, let us denote each $Data_i$ of Step-iii of the Revision Learner simply as D. Given integer m and data set D, m-fold cross validation is outlined below:

Step-a Partition D into m disjoint subsets $S_1 \cdots S_m$ of equal size,

Step-b From each difference set $D \setminus S_k (k = 1 \cdots m)$, learn a rule $rule_k$ by using the internal learner,

Step-c For each $rule_k (k = 1 \cdots m)$, calculate the accuracy $accuracy_k$ by using S_k as test examples, and

Step-d Calculate the average of the accuracies $accuracy_k (k = 1 \cdots m)$.

A wide practice in machine learning research to let m be either 10, or $|D|$ to well-estimate the accuracy of learned rules.

5 Experimental results

The proposed Revision Learner was tested in experiments. As the internal learner, we used the learning method reported in [3] which uses the ID3 (C4.5) learning algorithm [10, 11].

5.1 The Experiment

Evaluation Data In this evaluation, hand-made rules were selected from English verb selection rules in ALT-J/E. Real examples were made with reference to an existing document [5] and they were expressed using only essential case elements. The target rules were English verb selection rules for four Japanese verbs "入る (hairu)", "見える (mieru)" ," 見る (miru)", and" 取る (toru)". The semantic hierarchy is the semantic hierarchy in ALT-J/E and the cross validation used was 10-fold cross validation.

Case element values of artificial examples Usually, high level nodes on the Semantic hierarchy are used in the hand-made rules. On the other hand, example sentences have leaf categories of the semantic hierarchy in the head noun. Thus, when a rule is converted into artificial examples (see Step-B in the artificial example generation procedure), we can select

(1) A *leaf* that is a descendant of the category in the rule, or

(2) Any *descendant* of the category in the rule.

These two ways of category selection will be evaluated in the following subsection.

Case element values of learned rules It is well known that ID3 employs "information gain" for attribute selection. In this paper, attributes are case elements. In this domain, we noticed that quite often, many case elements score equally under the information gain criterion. We have experimented with the following two ways to resolve such ties:

(1) Selecting the upper-most category, or

(2) Selecting the lower-most category, in the semantic hierarchy.

Type (1) is called *Upper selection* and type (2) is called *Lower selection* in this evaluation.

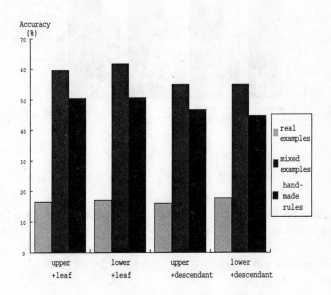

Fig. 4. Japanese verb 入る (hairu)

5.2   Result (1)

Figure 4 – Figure 7 show the experimental results. In these figures, *real examples* and *hand-made rules* indicate respectively the accuracy of the rules generated from the real examples alone and from the artificial examples alone, while *mixed examples* indicate the accuracy of the rules learned from the artificial and real examples together.

In the mixed examples case, candidate weight pairs (used in Step-ii of the Revision Learner) are selected from the following set:

$\{(0.01, 9.99), (0.1, 9.9), (1, 9), (2, 8), (3, 7), (4, 8), (5, 5),$
$(6, 4), (7, 3), (8, 2), (9, 1), (9.9, 0.1), (9.99, 0.01)\}$

where, in each ordered pair, the two numbers indicate the weight of a real example and of an artificial example, respectively.

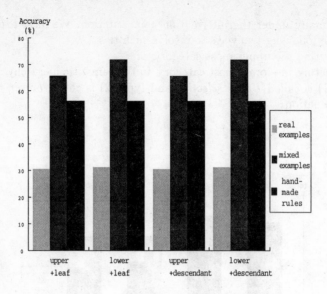

Fig. 5. Japanese verb 見える (mieru)

The accuracy of the mixed examples shown in Figure 4 – Figure 7 is the best accuracy achieved by these candidate weight values. Please note that the sum of the weights of real examples and artificial examples is exactly 10 in each of the candidate weight pairs. Other total values will be examined in the following subsection.

In these figures, *Upper (Lower) + Descendant* means that (1) the case element values of the learned rules are selected with upper (lower) node prior in the internal learner, and (2) in the Artificial Example Generation step in Section 4.3, any descendant nodes are randomly selected. Also, *Upper (Lower) + Leaf* means that (1) the case element values of the learned rules are selected with upper (lower) node priori, and (2) in the Artificial Example Generation step, the selection of a descendant is restricted to only a leaf.

As shown in Figure 4 – Figure 7, for every Japanese verb, regardless of the method used to resolve ties between case elements, as well as of the method of chosing random values during artificial examples generation, English verb selection rules generated by our approach, i.e. "mixed examples" have better accuracy than "real examples" or "hand-made rules". Therefore, the proposed approach using real examples and hand-made rules at the same time, makes up for the shortage of real examples.

The best application of our approach is "lower + leaf" in the case of three Japanese verbs "入る (hairu)", "見える (mieru)", and "取る (toru)", and "upper + leaf" in the case of one Japanese verb "見る (miru)". This difference among Japanese verbs depends on the number of real examples. That is, when many real examples can be gathered as for the Japanese verb "見る (miru)", English verb selection rules should be expressed using the upper semantic category. The reason is that the confidence level of the generalization using training examples increases when many real examples can be gathered [7]. For all the four Japanese verbs, the best selection of descendant at step-B of Artificial Example Generation Method, is to restrict a descendant to a leaf.

The accuracy of the constructed English verb selection rules for Japanese verb "見る (miru)" is much better than that for any other Japanese verb. This phenomenon is due to the fact that English verbs in the hand-made rules nearly equal those in the real examples. When constructing English verb selection rules using our approach, the hand-made rules should be prepared using English verbs similar to those in the real examples. This means that good hand-made rules bring good machine-translation quality.

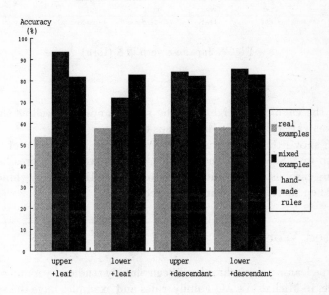

Fig. 6. Japanese verb 見る (miru)

5.3 Result (2)

In the above subsection, the sum of the weights of the an artificial example and a real example was always 10. Figure 8 shows the accuracy of the rules constructed from real examples and hand-made rules for the Japanese verb "取る (toru)". In

---

[7] The number of real examples used was 95, 130, 33, and 385 for the verbs "Hairu", "Mieru", "Toru", and "Miru", respectively.

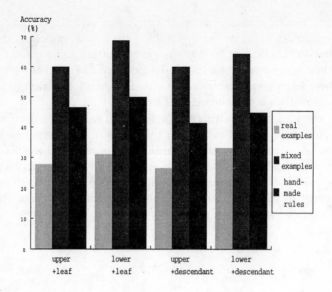

Fig. 7. Japanese verb 取る (toru)

this figure, the candidate weights for the real examples as well as the artificial examples was varied from 1 to 49 in steps of two.

Figure 8 shows that more thorough search through the space of weight values can help in achieving higher accuracy. This, however, requires longer CPU times. In any case, using efficient algorithms such as ID3[8], this technique can be employed when more accurate rules are necessary.

6 Related Works

Revision-type leaning algorithms have been already studied by many researchers. For example, in Michalski's AQ Family, rules and examples have the same representation [9]. Thus, AQ is a kind of revision-type learner. Though the expression of hand-made rules is restricted, Tsujino et al. proposed a kind of revision-type learner for ID3[13]. Also, in Inductive Logic Programming, revision-type learners have been studied in "Theory Revision"[12].

A major difficulty in the task of learning English verb selection rules addressed in this paper is the presence of ambiguity in the training examples. Another difficulty stems from the need to utilize the background knowledge represented by the semantic hierarchy. Existing revision-type learning algorithms cannot be employed in such a situation. On the other hand, our proposed Revision Learner can employ any attribute-based learning algorithm as the internal

---

[8] The learning time of ID3 is nearly proportion to the number of training examples.

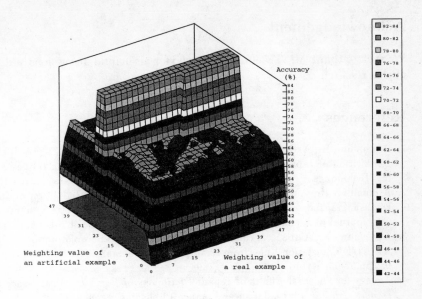

Fig. 8. Result of Cross Validation

learner. This important feature of our approach allowed the use of the learning algorithm of [1][3] which is capable of handling the ambiguity and the utilization of the background hierarchy.

7 Conclusion

In this paper, a new learning method has been proposed that constructs English verb selection rules with high accuracy from hand-made English verb selection rules and sparse real examples. First, "artificial examples" are generated from hand-made English verb selection rules. Second, the artificial examples and the real examples are used as training examples for an internal learner. Finally, an internal learner outputs English verb selection rules having improved translation quality. Determining the relative contribution of the hand-made rules and the real examples to the final rules is the most difficult issue in this work and was handled using cross validation.

In order to estimate the proposed method's performance, it was applied to hand-made English verb selection rules and real examples generated from existing documents using the learning algorithm of [1] as the internal learner. The English verb selection rules constructed by the proposed method have better accuracy than either those constructed from the real examples or those that were hand-made.

Acknowledgement

We wish to thank Mr. Takefumi Yamazaki for his helpful discussions and support of this research.

References

1. Almuallim, H., Akiba, Y., Yamazaki, T., Yokoo, A., and Kaneda, S.,: A Tool for the Acquisition of Japanese-English Machine Translation Rules using Inductive Learning Techniques. *Proc. CAIA-94*, PP.194-201, San Antonio, Texas, March 1-4, 1994
2. Almuallim, H., Akiba, Y., Yamazaki, T., and Kaneda, S.: Induction of Japanese-English Translation Rules from ambiguous Examples and a Large Semantic Hierarchy. Journal of Japanese Society for Artificial Intelligence, Vol.9, No.5, (Sept, 1994)
3. Almuallim, H., Akiba, Y., Yamazaki, T., and Kaneda, S.: Two Methods for Learning ALT-J/E Translation Rules from Examples and A Semantic Hierarchy. *Proc. Coling-94*, pp.57-63, Kyoto, August, 5-9, 1994
4. Agency for Cultural Affairs of Japan: *Dictionary of Basic Japanese Usage for Foreigners, (in Japanese)*, Japanese Finance Publishing Agency, 1990.
5. Horiguchi,T.: *A handbook of illustrative sentences of English*, Nihon Tosho Library, 1989.
6. Ikehara, S., Miyazaki, M.,Shirai,S. and Yokoo,A.: An Approach to Machine Translation Method based on Constructive Process Theory. *Review of ECL*, vol.37, No., 39-44,1989.
7. Ikehara,S.,Shirai, S., Yokoo, A. and Nakaiwa, H.: Toward an MT System without Pre-Editing-Effects of New Methods in ALT-J/E. *Proc. MT Summit-3*, 1990.
8. Donald Keene: *Japanese-English Sentence Equivalents (Revised Version)*, Asahi Press, 1991.
9. Michalski,R.S., Carbonell,J.G., and Mitchell, T.M.(Eds.), Machine Learning : An Artificial Intelligence Approach. Tioga, Palo Alto, Calif.,1983.
10. Quinlan, J.R.: Induction of Decision Trees. *Machine Learning*, 1(1), 81-106, 1986.
11. Quinlan, J.R.: *C4.5: Programming for Machine Learning*. Morgan Kaufmann, San Mateo, California, 1992
12. Raedt,L.,: Interactive Theory Revision. Academic Press, London, 1992.
13. Tsujino,K.,Nishida,S.,: Inductive Generation of Classification Knowledge from Examples and Correlation Tables. Proc. of JKAW94, PP.183-195,1994

Learning from Texts - A Terminological Metareasoning Perspective

Udo Hahn, Manfred Klenner & Klemens Schnattinger

Freiburg University
Computational Linguistics Group Ⓒ🄵
Europaplatz 1, D-79085 Freiburg, Germany
{hahn,klenner,schnattinger}@coling.uni-freiburg.de

Abstract We introduce a methodology for concept learning from texts that relies upon second-order reasoning about statements expressed in a (first-order) terminological representation language. This metareasoning approach allows for quality-based evaluation and selection of alternative concept hypotheses.

1 Introduction

In this paper, we consider the problem of concept learning from a new methodological perspective, viz. one based on second-order reasoning about statements expressed in a (first-order) terminological representation language. This metareasoning approach is motivated by requirements which emerged from our work in the overlapping fields of natural language parsing and learning from texts — both tasks are characterized by the common need to evaluate alternative representation structures, either reflecting parsing ambiguities or multiple concept hypotheses. For instance, in the course of concept learning from texts, various and often conflicting concept hypotheses for a single item are formed as the learning environment usually provides only inconclusive evidence for exactly determining the properties of the concept to be learned. At least for "realistic" natural language understanding (NLU) systems working with large text corpora the underdetermination of results can often be attributed to incomplete knowledge provided for that concept in the data (source texts), but it may also be due to imperfect parsing results (originating from lacking lexical, grammatical, conceptual specifications, or ungrammatical input).

We view the problem of choosing from among several alternatives as a *quality-based decision task* which can be decomposed into three constituent parts: the continuous generation of quality labels for single hypotheses (reflecting the *reasons* for their formation and their significance in the light of other hypotheses), the estimation of the overall *credibility* of single hypotheses (taking the available set of quality labels for each hypothesis into account), and the computation of a *preference order* for the entire set of competing hypotheses, which is based on these accumulated quality judgments. As we will be dealing with second-order rules about basic (first-order) terminological statements for quality-based reasoning, we have to provide a formal mapping between the two language layers. This is achieved by reification (see Section 4.2) yielding different contexts for encapsulating reasoning processes and by various translation rules mediating between those contexts under truth-preserving conditions (see Section 4.3). As second-order reasoning can thus be reduced to first-order, we gain the full-blown classification mechanism from standard (first-order) terminological systems for our metareasoning approach.

2 Framework for Concept Learning from Texts

Two major approaches to concept learning in an NLU framework can currently be distinguished – a resource-oriented and a context-oriented one (Wilensky, 1993). Advocates of resource orientation claim that it is often more promising to look up an unknown word in a machine-readable dictionary (MRD) than to infer its meaning from a sparse textual context. Given, e.g., the sentence "a car struck an abutment", where "abutment" is unknown, all that can be contextually derived from the sample text is that "abutment" is a kind of physical object. Clearly, any reasonably sized MRD is capable of providing at least the same kind of information (or even a much more specific word sense description). However, we have good reasons to rely on context information rather than on MRDs. First of all, many domain-specific, e.g., technical usages of a word are not contained in MRDs, even if they are highly specialized. Therefore, the only strategy left to recover from incomplete dictionaries is to infer the meaning of unknown lexical items from the original texts in which they actually occur. Second, many words simply cannot be found in an MRD due to reasons of timeliness or lexicographic irrelevance. In the information technology domain we deal with, lexical innovations play a rather prominent role, i.e., the names of new products, new companies and – at least for the critical time period from their invention to their wider acceptance as an integral part of the domain's jargon – terms denoting new technologies. Thus, text understanding becomes a sheer necessity to properly account for the concept learning problem posed by the processing of realistic expository texts.

In the architecture we propose, text parsing and concept learning from texts are tightly coupled. For instance, whenever two nominals or a nominal and a verb are supposed to be syntactically related the semantic interpreter simultaneously evaluates the conceptual compatibility of the items involved (incompatibility excludes a structural relation from being established). Since these reasoning processes are fully embedded into a KL-ONE-style knowledge representation system, checks are made whether a concept denoted by one of these objects can fill a role of the other one (permitted role filler). If one of the items involved is unknown, i.e., a lexical or conceptual gap is encountered, this interpretation mode generates initial concept hypotheses about the class membership of the unknown object based on a single, yet very powerful rule:

IF parser queries : $permitted\text{-}role\text{-}filler(X, OBJ) \land X$ ISA unknown-object $\implies$
  FORALL $Role_i$ of OBJ **DO**
    generate : $hypothesis(OBJ, Role_i, X)$ as $Hypo_i$

The basic assumption is that the unknown object (*target concept*) fills (exactly) one of the n roles of the known object (*base concept*). Since it cannot be decided on the correct role yet, n alternative hypotheses are opened and the target concept is assigned as a potential filler of the i-th role in its corresponding hypothesis space. The classifier thus derives a suitable concept hypothesis by specializing the initial hypothesis on the target concept according to the value restriction of the base concept's i-th role. Consider the occurrence of a base and a target concept in a sentence fragment such as "computers ... OS/2", and let "OS/2" be the target concept. The base concept "computer" has multiple attributes encoded in the domain's knowledge base, e.g., relating it to conceptual representations of a motherboard, hard disks, a monitor, and software. Each of these roles must be taken into account as a provisionally valid hypothesis for the correct integration of "OS/2". We thus get at least four initial hypotheses: OS/2 INST-OF MOTHERBOARD, OS/2 INST-OF HARDDISK, OS/2 INST-OF MONITOR, OS/2 INST-OF SOFTWARE.

There are two sources of evidence to further discriminate the initial hypothesis set: First, facts about the target concept that can be acquired from subsequent utterances in the same text or facts that can be accessed from previously analyzed texts, remotely stored in particular text knowledge bases. Second, the evaluation of the remaining hypotheses with the aid of specialized metaknowledge and domain-specific background knowledge. In this paper, we will mainly elaborate on the second mode of hypothesis refinement.

3 Architecture for Concept Learning from Texts

The concept learning methodology we propose is heavily based on the representation and reasoning facilities provided by terminological knowledge representation languages. As the representation of alternative hypotheses and their subsequent evaluation turn out to be major requirements of that approach, provisions have to be made to reflect these design decisions by an appropriate architecture of the learner (cf. Fig. 1). In particular, mechanisms should be provided for:

- Expressing *quality-based assertions* about propositions in a terminological language; these metastatements capture the ascription of belief to these propositions, the reasons why they came into existence, the support/weakening they may have received from other propositions, etc.

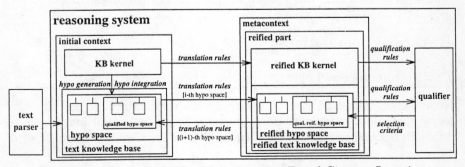

Figure 1: Architecture for Metareasoning-Based Concept Learning

– *Metareasoning* in a terminological knowledge base about properties and relations that certain propositions may have; the corresponding *second-order expressions* refer to factual propositions (ABox elements) as well as concept and role definitions (TBox elements).

The notion of context we use as a formal foundation for metaknowledge and metareasoning is based on McCarthy's context model (McCarthy, 1993). We here distinguish two types of contexts, viz. the initial context and the metacontext. The *initial context* contains the original terminological knowledge base (KB kernel) and the text knowledge base reflecting the knowledge acquired from the underlying text by the text parser (Hahn et al., 1994). Knowledge in the initial context is represented without any explicit qualifications, attachments, provisos, etc. Note that in the course of text understanding – due to the working of the basic *hypothesis generation* rule (cf. Section 2) – a hypothesis space is created which contains alternative subspaces for each concept to be learned, each one holding a different or a further specialized concept hypothesis. According to various structural constraints inherent in the KB kernel some rearrangements might occur (*hypothesis integration*), slightly altering the structure of the initial hypothesis space. Various translation rules map the description of the initial context to the *metacontext* which consists of the reified knowledge of the initial context. By *reification*, we mean a common reflective mechanism (Friedman & Wand, 1984), which splits up a predicative expression into its constituent parts and introduces a unique anchor term, the *reificator*, on which *reasoning about* this expression, e.g., the annotation of qualifying assertions, can be based (cf. also MacGregor (1993)). Among the reified structures in the metacontext there is a subcontext embedded, the *reified hypothesis space*, the elements of which carry several qualifications, e.g., reasons to believe a proposition, indications of consistency, strength of support, etc. These quality labels are the result of the mechanisms underlying hypothesis evaluation and subsequent hypothesis selection, thus reflecting the operation of several second-order qualification rules in the *qualifier* (*quality*-based classifier). The derived labels are the basis for the selection of those representation structures that are assigned a high degree of plausibility – only those *qualified hypotheses* will be remapped to the hypothesis space of the initial context by way of (inverse) translation rules. Thus, the circle is closed. In particular, at the end of each quality-based reasoning cycle the entire original i-th hypothesis space is replaced by its $(i+1)$-th successor in order to reflect the qualifications computed in the metacontext. The $(i+1)$-th hypothesis space is then the input of the next quality assessment round.

4 Formal Foundations

4.1 Terminological Logic

We use a fairly standard concept description language, referred to as $\mathcal{TL}$, which has several constructors combining *atomic* concepts, roles and individuals to define the terminological theory of a domain (for a subset, see Table 1; a survey of

Syntax	Semantics
C_{atom}	$\{d \in \Delta^{\mathcal{I}} \mid C_{atom} \text{ is atomic}, \mathcal{I}(C_{atom}) = d\}$
$C \sqcap D$	$C^{\mathcal{I}} \cap D^{\mathcal{I}}$
$C \sqcup D$	$C^{\mathcal{I}} \cup D^{\mathcal{I}}$
$\neg C$	$\Delta^{\mathcal{I}} \setminus C^{\mathcal{I}}$
$\exists R.C$	$\{d \in \Delta^{\mathcal{I}} \mid R^{\mathcal{I}}(d) \cap C^{\mathcal{I}} \neq \emptyset\}$
$\forall R.C$	$\{d \in \Delta^{\mathcal{I}} \mid R^{\mathcal{I}}(d) \subseteq C^{\mathcal{I}}\}$
$\exists_{\geq n} R$	$\{d \in \Delta^{\mathcal{I}} \mid \|R^{\mathcal{I}}(d)\| \geq n\}$
$\exists_{\leq n} R$	$\{d \in \Delta^{\mathcal{I}} \mid \|R^{\mathcal{I}}(d)\| \leq n\}$
R_{atom}	$\{(d,e) \in \Delta^{\mathcal{I}} \times \Delta^{\mathcal{I}} \mid$ $R_{atom} \text{ is atomic}, \mathcal{I}(R_{atom}) = (d,e)\}$
$R \sqcap S$	$R^{\mathcal{I}} \cap S^{\mathcal{I}}$

Table 1: Syntax and Semantics for a Subset of $\mathcal{TL}$

Terminological Axioms

Axiom	Semantics
$A \doteq C$	$A^{\mathcal{I}} = C^{\mathcal{I}}$
$A \sqsubseteq C$	$A^{\mathcal{I}} \subseteq C^{\mathcal{I}}$
$Q \doteq R$	$Q^{\mathcal{I}} = R^{\mathcal{I}}$
$Q \sqsubseteq R$	$Q^{\mathcal{I}} \subseteq R^{\mathcal{I}}$

Assertional Axioms

Axiom	Semantics
$a : C$	$a^{\mathcal{I}} \in C^{\mathcal{I}}$
$a \, R \, b$	$(a^{\mathcal{I}}, b^{\mathcal{I}}) \in R^{\mathcal{I}}$

Table 2: $\mathcal{TL}$ Axioms

the major properties of terminological languages is given by Woods & Schmolze (1992)). *Concepts* are unary predicates, *roles* are binary predicates over a domain Δ, with *individuals* being the elements of Δ. We assume a common set-theoretical semantics for $\mathcal{TL}$ — an interpretation $\mathcal{I}$ is a function that assigns to each concept symbol (the set $\mathbf{A}$) a subset of the domain Δ, $\mathcal{I} : \mathbf{A} \to 2^{\Delta}$, to each role symbol (the set $\mathbf{P}$) a binary relation of Δ, $\mathcal{I} : \mathbf{P} \to 2^{\Delta \times \Delta}$, and to each individual symbol (the set $\mathbf{I}$) an element of Δ, $\mathcal{I} : \mathbf{I} \to \Delta$.

Concept terms and *role terms* are defined inductively. Table 1 states some useful constructors and their semantics. Each constructor defines a concept term. C and D denote concept terms, R and S denote roles and n stands for a natural number. $R^{\mathcal{I}}(d)$ represents the set of role fillers of the individual d, i.e., the set of individuals e with $(d,e) \in R^{\mathcal{I}}$. $\|R^{\mathcal{I}}(d)\|$ denotes the number of role fillers.

By means of *terminological axioms* (for a subset, see Table 2) a symbolic name can be defined for each concept and role term. We may also supply sufficient and necessary constraints (using $\doteq$) or only necessary constraints (using $\sqsubseteq$) for concepts and roles. A finite set of such axioms is called the *terminology* or *TBox*.

Concepts and roles are associated with concrete individuals by *assertional axioms* (see Table 2; a, b denote individuals). A finite set of such axioms is called the *world description* or *ABox*. An interpretation $\mathcal{I}$ is a model of an ABox with regard to a TBox, iff $\mathcal{I}$ satisfies the assertional and terminological axioms. Terminology and world description together constitute a *terminological theory*.

4.2 Reification

We here restrict ourselves to the reification of the assertional and terminological axioms and the constructors $\sqcap$ and $\forall$ in $\mathcal{TL}$. The remaining constructors can be reified in a straightforward way based on the scheme outlined below (for a more detailed account, cf. Schnattinger et al. (1995)). In our running example the symbolic names COMPANY, PRODUCER, PRODUCT, etc. represent concepts, while DEVELOPS, PRODUCES, etc. stand for roles. Using terminological notation we introduce a hypothesis space H with the following terminological theory:

(P1)   *Compaq* PRODUCES *LTE-Lite*

(P2)   *Compaq* : PRODUCER

(P3)   PRODUCER $\doteq$ COMPANY $\sqcap$ $\forall$DEVELOPS.PRODUCT

REIF	$\doteq$	$\forall \text{BINARY-REL}.\mathbf{P}^{ext} \ \sqcap \ \forall \text{DOMAIN}.\mathbf{A} \ \sqcap \ \forall \text{RANGE}.\mathbf{A} \ \sqcap \ \forall \text{HYPO}.\mathbf{H}$

Table 3: General Data Structure for Reification

$\Re(a : C)$	$r : \text{REIF} \ \sqcap \ r \ \text{BINARY-REL INST-OF} \ \sqcap$
	$r \ \text{DOMAIN} \ a \ \sqcap \ r \ \text{RANGE} \ C \ \sqcap \ r \ \text{HYPO} \ H$
$\Re(a \ R \ b)$	$r : \text{REIF} \ \sqcap \ r \ \text{BINARY-REL} \ R \ \sqcap$
	$r \ \text{DOMAIN} \ a \ \sqcap \ r \ \text{RANGE} \ b \ \sqcap \ r \ \text{HYPO} \ H$
$\Re(A \doteq C)$	$\Re^*(A, C)$
$\Re^*(A, C_{atom})$	$r : \text{REIF} \ \sqcap \ r \ \text{BINARY-REL ISA} \ \sqcap$
	$r \ \text{DOMAIN} \ A \ \sqcap \ r \ \text{RANGE} \ C_{atom} \ \sqcap \ r \ \text{HYPO} \ H$
$\Re^*(A, \forall R.C_{atom})$	$r : \text{REIF} \ \sqcap \ r \ \text{BINARY-REL} \ R \ \sqcap$
	$r \ \text{DOMAIN} \ A \ \sqcap \ r \ \text{RANGE} \ C_{atom} \ \sqcap \ r \ \text{HYPO} \ H$
$\Re^*(A, \forall R.C \sqcap D)$	$\Re^*(A, \forall R.C) \ \sqcap \ \Re^*(A, \forall R.D)$
$\Re^*(A, C \sqcap D)$	$\Re^*(A, C) \ \sqcap \ \Re^*(A, D)$

Table 4: Reification Functions $\Re$ and $\Re^*$

We equate the proposition P1 with the reification of the tuple $\langle Compaq,$ $LTE\text{-}Lite \rangle$ which belongs to PRODUCES, P2 with the reification of $\langle Compaq,$ PRODUCER$\rangle$ which belongs to the relation INST-OF, and P3 with the reification of $\langle$PRODUCER,COMPANY$\rangle$ which belongs to the relation ISA as well as the reification of $\langle$PRODUCER,PRODUCT$\rangle$ which belongs to DEVELOPS. Additionally, our reification mechanism is sensitive to hypothesis spaces, i.e., each reified proposition must be true in at least one hypothesis space H. Assertions about tuples are represented by making assertions about their reified form (e.g., P1 QUALI-FIED $q \ \sqcap \ q :$ INCONSISTENT).

We have chosen a particular 'data structure', itself expressed in $\mathcal{TL}$ (see Table 3), to make the reification format explicit. It provides the common ground for making qualitative assertions and serves as the foundation for the evaluation of second-order expressions with which various degrees of plausibility or credibility can be determined. $\mathbf{H}$ is the set of all hypothesis spaces and $\mathbf{P}^{ext}$ the set $\mathbf{P} \cup \{$INST-OF, ISA$\}$. The symbol REIF denotes a concept and BINARY-REL, DOMAIN, RANGE and HYPO denote roles. With these conventions, we are able to define the (bijective) reification function $\Re : t.term_H \to r.term$, where $t.term_H$ is a terminological term known to be true in hypothesis space H and $r.term$ is its corresponding reified term (see Table 4). By analogy, we may also define the function $\Re^{-1}$ with the corresponding inverse mapping. The following expressions provide the reified terms for the above examples (in hypothesis space H):

$\Re(Compaq$ PRODUCES $LTE\text{-}Lite) = \ \ p_1 : \text{REIF} \ \sqcap \ p_1 \ \text{BINARY-REL PRODUCES} \ \sqcap$
p_1 DOMAIN $Compaq \ \sqcap \ p_1$ RANGE $LTE\text{-}Lite \ \sqcap \ p_1$ HYPO H

$\Re(Compaq : $ PRODUCER$) = \ \ \ \ \ \ \ \ p_2 : \text{REIF} \ \sqcap \ p_2 \ \text{BINARY-REL INST-OF} \ \sqcap$
p_2 DOMAIN $Compaq \ \sqcap \ p_2$ RANGE PRODUCER $\sqcap \ p_2$ HYPO H

$\Re($PRODUCER $\doteq$ COMPANY $\sqcap \ \forall$DEVELOPS.PRODUCT$) = \ \ p_{3_1} : \text{REIF} \ \sqcap$
p_{3_1} BINARY-REL ISA $\sqcap \ p_{3_1}$ DOMAIN PRODUCER $\sqcap \ p_{3_1}$ RANGE COMPANY $\sqcap$
p_{3_1} HYPO $H \ \sqcap \ \ \ \ \ \ \ \ \ \ \ \ \ p_{3_2} : \text{REIF} \ \sqcap \ p_{3_2}$ BINARY-REL DEVELOPS $\sqcap$
p_{3_2} DOMAIN PRODUCER $\sqcap \ p_{3_2}$ RANGE PRODUCT $\sqcap \ p_{3_2}$ HYPO H

4.3 Contexts and Translation Rules

According to McCarthy (1993) and McCarthy and Buvač (1995), a context is an object in a first-order language which has an associated vocabulary (we use that of $\mathcal{TL}$) and therefore denotes a set of models. $\text{ist}(\kappa, \phi)$ holds iff formula ϕ is true in all the models denoted by context κ. For finitely axiomatizable theories T and the theorems Th derived from a finite set of axioms A we require $T = Th(A)$. We then stipulate that $\text{ist}(\kappa, T)$ holds iff $\text{ist}(\kappa, \sqcap A)$, i.e., the conjunction of the axioms is true in context κ.

Translation rules are syntactic transformations which derive sentences in the metacontext that are equivalent to sentences in the initial context. A *translation rule* from context κ to context κ' is any axiom of the form $\text{ist}(\kappa, \phi) \leftrightarrow \text{ist}(\kappa', \phi')$.

Given the set $\mathcal{R}$ which denotes all $\Re(x \ R \ y)$ and the set $\mathcal{P}$ of all instances p of the class REIF (i.e., $p : \text{REIF}$), the function $\pi : \mathcal{R} \to \mathcal{P}$ maps each reified term to its corresponding reificator:

$$\pi\left(\Re\left(x \ R \ y\right)\right) \ \equiv \ \pi\left(p : \text{REIF} \ \sqcap \ p \ \text{BINARY-REL} \ R \ \sqcap \right.$$
$$\left. p \ \text{DOMAIN} \ x \ \sqcap \ p \ \text{RANGE} \ y \ \sqcap \ p \ \text{HYPO} \ H\right) = \quad p$$

According to these conventions, we have to supply a translation rule for mapping each relation from the initial context to the metacontext including the attachment of a quality relation (QUALIFIED). Instead of enumerating each of these rules we here provide a shorthand second-order rule schema:

$$\forall R : R \in \mathbf{P}^{ext} \ \to$$
$$(\forall d, r \ \exists q : \text{ist}\left(initial, d \ R \ r\right) \leftrightarrow \text{ist}\left(meta, \pi\left(\Re\left(d \ R \ r\right)\right) \ \text{QUALIFIED} \ q\right))$$

In a similar way, we may construct translation rules which retranslate qualified portions of the metacontext back to the initial context using the inverse of $\Re$. These rules pick up those reified elements that fulfil a certain quality threshold:

$$\forall R : R \in \mathbf{P}^{ext} \ \to \ (\forall p, d, r, H \ \exists q :$$
$$\text{ist}(meta, p : \text{REIF} \ \sqcap \ p \ \text{BINARY-REL} \ R \ \sqcap \ p \ \text{DOMAIN} \ d \ \sqcap \ p \ \text{RANGE} \ r \ \sqcap$$
$$p \ \text{HYPO} \ H \ \sqcap \ p \ \text{QUALIFIED} \ q) \qquad \leftrightarrow$$
$$\text{ist}(initial, \Re^{-1}(p : \text{REIF} \ \sqcap \cdot p \ \text{BINARY-REL} \ R \ \sqcap \ p \ \text{DOMAIN} \ d \ \sqcap$$
$$p \ \text{RANGE} \ r \ \sqcap \ p \ \text{HYPO} \ H)))$$

5 Quality-based Reasoning with Qualification Rules

Within second-order logic we may quantify over relations of first-order terms, e.g., $\forall R : a \ R \ b$ quantifies over all roles R which relate a and b. Our intention is to use second-order expressions in order to reason about the properties of terminological descriptions and, thus, to determine the credibility of various concept hypotheses. Such expressions can be integrated into the condition part of production rules in order to generate qualifying assertions for concept hypotheses. These qualifying assertions link the reificator of a terminological term via a role QUALIFIED to a qualifying proposition. Qualifying assertions are the raw data for the computation of quality labels by the classifier which asserts INST-OF relations to the corresponding quality labels (we here only deal with simple quality labels that are associated with exactly one qualifying role, though more complex conditions can be envisaged). Combining the evidences collected this way in terms of a quality ranking of concept hypotheses, only those reified terms that have reached a certain credibility threshold after each quality assessment cycle are transferred from the metacontext back to the initial context (cf. Fig.1; qualified hypothesis space in the initial context).

Next, we will describe some of our production rules for quality-based reasoning (the symbol $\Longrightarrow$ separates the condition from the action part). Note that these rules are tested in the metacontext immediately after the reification function $\Re$ has been applied to some proposition in the initial context. In addition, the operator **TELL** is used to initiate the assertion of terminological terms. The procedural semantics of the operator **EXISTS** should be intuitively clear. We also define a function $\hbar$ that retrieves the role filler of the role HYPO, which refers to the relevant hypothesis space, for a given reificator, i.e. $\hbar : \mathcal{P} \to \mathbf{H}$:

$$\hbar(p) \equiv \hbar\left(\pi(p : \text{REIF} \sqcap p \text{ BINARY-REL } R \sqcap \right.$$
$$\left. p \text{ DOMAIN } x \sqcap p \text{ RANGE } y \sqcap p \text{ HYPO } H)\right) = H$$

In the remainder of this section we supply verbal, graphical and formal descriptions of four qualification rules. The bold portions in the figures indicate the terminological terms to be qualified, while the lighter ones depict the qualifying instance. A detailed example of the working of these rules will be provided in Section 6.

Rule I: Cross-Supported. A relation, $R1$, between two instances, o_1 and o_2, can independently be confirmed by another relation, $R2$, involving the same two instances, but where the role fillers occur in "inverted" order (note that $R1$ and $R2$ need not necessarily be conceptually inverse relations in the strict sense, such as with *"buy"* and *"sell"*). This causes the role CROSS-SUPPORTED-BY of the qualifying instance q to be filled with the reificator of the inverted relation. As a consequence, the classifier deduces the *positive* quality label CROSS-SUPPORTED.

This rule captures the inherent symmetry between concepts related via quasi-inverse relations.

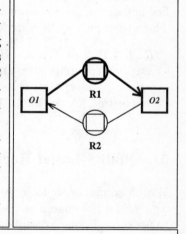

EXISTS o_1, o_2, q, R_1, R_2 :
$\Re(o_1 \ R_1 \ o_2) \ \sqcap \ \Re(o_2 \ R_2 \ o_1) \ \sqcap \ R_1 \neq R_2 \ \sqcap$
$\hbar(\pi(\Re(o_1 \ R_1 \ o_2))) = \hbar(\pi(\Re(o_2 \ R_2 \ o_1))) \ \sqcap$
$\pi(\Re(o_1 \ R_1 \ o_2)) \text{ QUALIFIED } q \ \Longrightarrow$
TELL q CROSS-SUPPORTED-BY $\pi(\Re(o_2 \ R_2 \ o_1))$

Rule II: Supported. An INST-OF relation between o_1 and C can independently be confirmed by another INST-OF relation between o_2 and C iff an instance o_3 (not being an ACTION) exists which is itself related to o_1 and o_2 via some role R. This causes the role SUPPORTED-BY of the qualifying instance q to be filled with a triple of reificators including that of the INST-OF relation between o_2 and C and the role R linking o_3 and o_1 and o_3 and o_2, resp. As a consequence, the classifier deduces the *positive* quality label SUPPORTED.

This rule reflects the conceptual proximity a relation induces on its component fillers, provided that they share a common concept class.

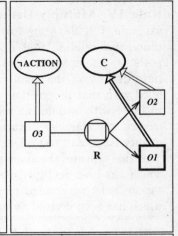

EXISTS o_1, o_2, o_3, q, R, C :
$$\Re(o_1 : C) \ \sqcap \ \Re(o_2 : C) \ \sqcap \ \Re(o_3 \ R \ o_1) \ \sqcap \ \Re(o_3 \ R \ o_2) \ \sqcap \ o_3 : \neg\text{ACTION} \ \sqcap$$
$$\hbar(\pi(\Re(o_1 : C))) = \hbar(\pi(\Re(o_2 : C))) = \hbar(\pi(\Re(o_3 \ R \ o_1))) = \hbar(\pi(\Re(o_3 \ R \ o_2))) \ \sqcap$$
$$\pi(\Re(o_1 : C)) \ \text{QUALIFIED} \ q \implies$$
TELL q SUPPORTED-BY $(\pi(\Re(o_2 : C)), \pi(\Re(o_3 \ R \ o_1)), \pi(\Re(o_3 \ R \ o_2)))$

Rule III: Additional-Role-Filler. Whenever an already filled conceptual relation receives an additional, yet <u>different</u> role filler the role ADDITIONALLY-FILLED-BY of the qualifying instance q is filled with the reificator of the already available proposition(s). As a consequence, the classifier deduces the *negative* quality label ADDITIONAL-ROLE-FILLER.

This application-specific rule is particularly suited to our NLU task and has its roots in the distinction between mandatory and optional case roles for verbs. Roughly, it yields a negative assessment for any attempt to fill the same mandatory case role more than once (this is not expressed in the formal term below). Note also that rule II and rule III differ in that they address two non-overlapping portions of the KB kernel, viz. rule III exclusively refers to ACTIONs, while rule II relates to objects (denoted by ¬ACTION).

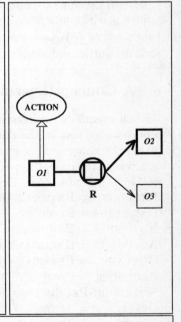

EXISTS o_1, o_2, o_3, q, R :
$$\Re(o_1 \ R \ o_2) \ \sqcap \ \Re(o_1 \ R \ o_3) \ \sqcap \ o_2 \neq o_3 \ \sqcap \ o_1 : \text{ACTION} \ \sqcap$$
$$\hbar(\pi(\Re(o_1 \ R \ o_2))) = \hbar(\pi(\Re(o_1 \ R \ o_3))) \ \sqcap$$
$$\pi(\Re(o_1 \ R \ o_2)) \ \text{QUALIFIED} \ q \implies$$
TELL q ADDITIONALLY-FILLED-BY $\pi(\Re(o_1 \ R \ o_3))$

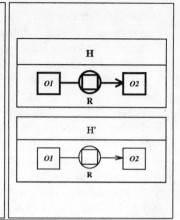

Rule IV: Multiply-Deduced. Any repetitive assignment of the <u>same</u> role filler to one specific conceptual relation that occurs in different hypothesis (sub)spaces causes the role MULTIPLY-DEDUCED-BY of the qualifying instance q to be filled with that proposition, but one which is associated with a different reificator. As a consequence, the classifier deduces the *(very) positive* quality label MULTIPLY-DEDUCED.

This rule captures the assumption that a role filler which has been multiply derived at different occasions must be granted more strength than one which has been derived at a single occasion only.

EXISTS $o_1, o_2, p_1, p_2, R, H, H'$:
$\Re(o_1 \ R \ o_2)_H \ \sqcap \ \Re(o_1 \ R \ o_2)_{H'} \ \sqcap$
$\pi(\Re(o_1 \ R \ o_2)_H) = p_1 \ \sqcap \ \pi(\Re(o_1 \ R \ o_2)_{H'}) = p_2 \ \sqcap \ p_1 \neq p_2 \ \sqcap \ \hbar(p_1) \neq \hbar(p_2) \ \sqcap$
$\pi(\Re(o_1 \ R \ o_2)_H)$ QUALIFIED $q \ \implies$
TELL q MULTIPLY-DEDUCED-BY $\pi(\Re(o_1 \ R \ o_2)_{H'})$

Taking the direction (positive/negative) and the individual 'strength' of each label into account, we might, e.g., prefer labels such as MULTIPLY-DEDUCED, or (CROSS-)SUPPORTED over others such as ADDITIONAL-ROLE-FILLER or even INCONSISTENT. We are currently investigating reasonable combinations and associated partial orderings of various labels in terms of a *qualification calculus*.

6   A Concept Learning Example

We will exemplify quality-based terminological reasoning by considering a concept learning task in the domain of information technology. As a result of applying the above qualification rules different degrees of credibility are assigned to alternative concept hypotheses and, finally, one hypothesis may be selected as the most credible one. Let us assume the following terminological axioms:

PRODUCT $\doteq$ PHYSICAL-OBJECT $\sqcap$ ∀HAS-DEVELOPER.PRODUCER
HARDWARE $\doteq$ PRODUCT
NOTEBOOK $\doteq$ HARDWARE
ACCU $\doteq$ HARDWARE $\sqcap$ ∀ENERGY-FOR.NOTEBOOK
COMPANY $\doteq$ PHYSICAL-OBJECT
PRODUCER $\doteq$ COMPANY $\sqcap$ ∀PRODUCES.HARDWARE
NOTEBOOK-PRODUCER $\doteq$ PRODUCER $\sqcap$ ∃PRODUCES.(NOTEBOOK $\sqcup$ ACCU)
OFFER $\doteq$ ACTION $\sqcap$ ∀AGENT.PRODUCER $\sqcap$ ∀PATIENT.PRODUCT
DEVELOP $\doteq$ ACTION $\sqcap$ ∀AGENT.PRODUCER $\sqcap$ ∀PATIENT.HARDWARE

Furthermore, the following reified assertional axioms are stipulated:
$p_1 = \pi(\Re(Compaq : \text{NOTEBOOK-PRODUCER})) \ \sqcap \ p_1$ QUALIFIED q_1
$p_2 = \pi(\Re(Compaq : \text{PRODUCER})) \ \sqcap \ p_2$ QUALIFIED q_2
$p_3 = \pi(\Re(Compaq : \text{COMPANY})) \ \sqcap \ p_3$ QUALIFIED q_3

$$p_4 = \pi(\Re(Compaq : \text{PHYSICAL-OBJECT})) \; \sqcap \; p_4 \text{ QUALIFIED } q_4$$

$$p_5 = \pi(\Re(Compaq \text{ PRODUCES } LTE\text{-}Lite)) \; \sqcap \; p_5 \text{ QUALIFIED } q_5$$

$$p_6 = \pi(\Re(LTE\text{-}Lite \text{ HAS-DEVELOPER } Compaq)) \; \sqcap \; p_6 \text{ QUALIFIED } q_6$$

$$p_7 = \pi(\Re(LTE\text{-}Lite : \text{NOTEBOOK})) \; \sqcap \; p_7 \text{ QUALIFIED } q_7$$

$$p_8 = \pi(\Re(LTE\text{-}Lite : \text{HARDWARE})) \; \sqcap \; p_8 \text{ QUALIFIED } q_8$$

$$p_9 = \pi(\Re(LTE\text{-}Lite : \text{PRODUCT})) \; \sqcap \; p_9 \text{ QUALIFIED } q_9$$

$$p_{10} = \pi(\Re(LTE\text{-}Lite : \text{PHYSICAL-OBJECT})) \; \sqcap \; p_{10} \text{ QUALIFIED } q_{10}$$

$$p_{11} = \pi(\Re(NiMH\text{-}Accu \text{ ENERGY-FOR } LTE\text{-}Lite)) \; \sqcap \; p_{11} \text{ QUALIFIED } q_{11}$$

$$p_{12} = \pi(\Re(NiMH\text{-}Accu : \text{ACCU})) \; \sqcap \; p_{12} \text{ QUALIFIED } q_{12}$$

$$p_{13} = \pi(\Re(NiMH\text{-}Accu : \text{HARDWARE})) \; \sqcap \; p_{13} \text{ QUALIFIED } q_{13}$$

$$p_{14} = \pi(\Re(NiMH\text{-}Accu : \text{PRODUCT})) \; \sqcap \; p_{14} \text{ QUALIFIED } q_{14}$$

$$p_{15} = \pi(\Re(NiMH\text{-}Accu : \text{PHYSICAL-OBJECT})) \; \sqcap \; p_{15} \text{ QUALIFIED } q_{15}$$

Finally, two (simplified) verb interpretation rules are supplied mapping lexical items onto "conceptually entailed" propositions of the text knowledge base:

EXISTS v, a, p : $v : \text{DEVELOP} \; \sqcap \; v \text{ AGENT } a \; \sqcap \; v \text{ PATIENT } p \implies$
TELL p HAS-DEVELOPER a

EXISTS v, a, p : $v : \text{OFFER} \; \sqcap \; v \text{ AGENT } a \; \sqcap \; v \text{ PATIENT } p \implies$
TELL a PRODUCES p

Consider the phrase "Marktanalytiker bestätigen, daß **Compaq** seit Jahren erfolgreich **LTE-Lites anbietet** und seit kurzem auch **Venturas**." Assuming *Venturas* to be the target concept two ambiguities arise (these are rephrased in English terms): (1) "Market analysts say that Compaq has been successfully offering LTE-Lites for many years and Venturas [AGENT] has recently begun to do so as well." *vs.* (2) "Market analysts say that Compaq has been successfully offering LTE-Lites for many years and has recently begun to offer Venturas [PATIENT] as well.". The parser incrementally generates a new instance of OFFER, assigns *Compaq* as AGENT and *LTE-Lite* as PATIENT of that instance (it has not yet encountered the unknown item, viz. *Venturas*). Thus, we get:

$$p_{16} = \pi(\Re(offer\text{-}01 : \text{OFFER})) \; \sqcap \; p_{16} \text{ QUALIFIED } q_{16}$$

$$p_{17} = \pi(\Re(offer\text{-}01 \text{ AGENT } Compaq)) \; \sqcap \; p_{17} \text{ QUALIFIED } q_{17}$$

$$p_{18} = \pi(\Re(offer\text{-}01 \text{ PATIENT } LTE\text{-}Lite)) \; \sqcap \; p_{18} \text{ QUALIFIED } q_{18}$$

The verb interpretation rule for OFFER has no effects, since $\langle Compaq \text{ PRODUCES } LTE\text{-}Lite \rangle$ is already true (p_5). As already mentioned, the unknown item *Venturas* can either be related to *LTE-Lite* via the AGENT role or to *Compaq* via the PATIENT role of OFFER. Thus, two hypothesis subspaces, **H1** and **H2**, are opened, one for each interpretation of *Venturas*; for both spaces the propositions p_1 to p_{18} are assumed to hold. **H1** (p_{19} to p_{23}) covers the AGENT interpretation. The creation of p_{19} (together with p_{17}) triggers the generation of an ADDITIONALLY-FILLED-BY role according to rule III. p_{19}, p_{18} and p_{16} cause the verb interpretation rule for OFFER to fire yielding p_{20}. Applying the terminological axioms for OFFER leads to the deduction of p_{21} (the AGENT role of OFFER restricts any of its fillers to PRODUCER and its taxonomic superconcepts, viz. COMPANY (p_{22}) and PHYSICAL-OBJECT (p_{23}), by way of transitive closure).

$p_{19} = \pi(\Re(offer\text{-}01 \text{ AGENT } Venturas)) \sqcap p_{19} \text{ QUALIFIED } q_{19} \sqcap$
   $q_{19} \text{ ADDITIONALLY-FILLED-BY } p_{17} \sqcap q_{17} \text{ ADDITIONALLY-FILLED-BY } p_{19}$
$p_{20} = \pi(\Re(Venturas \text{ PRODUCES } LTE\text{-}Lite)) \sqcap p_{20} \text{ QUALIFIED } q_{20}$
$p_{21} = \pi(\Re(Venturas : \text{PRODUCER})) \sqcap p_{21} \text{ QUALIFIED } q_{21}$
$p_{22} = \pi(\Re(Venturas : \text{COMPANY})) \sqcap p_{22} \text{ QUALIFIED } q_{22}$
$p_{23} = \pi(\Re(Venturas : \text{PHYSICAL-OBJECT})) \sqcap p_{23} \text{ QUALIFIED } q_{23} \sqcap$
   $q_{23} \text{ MULTIPLY-DEDUCED-BY } p_{27}$

On the other hand, **H2** (p_{24} to p_{28}) covers the PATIENT interpretation:

$p_{24} = \pi(\Re(offer\text{-}01 \text{ PATIENT } Venturas)) \sqcap p_{24} \text{ QUALIFIED } q_{24} \sqcap$
   $q_{24} \text{ ADDITIONALLY-FILLED-BY } p_{18} \sqcap q_{18} \text{ ADDITIONALLY-FILLED-BY } p_{24}$
$p_{25} = \pi(\Re(Compaq \text{ PRODUCES } Venturas)) \sqcap p_{25} \text{ QUALIFIED } q_{25}$
$p_{26} = \pi(\Re(Venturas : \text{PRODUCT})) \sqcap p_{26} \text{ QUALIFIED } q_{26} \sqcap$
   $q_{26} \text{ SUPPORTED-BY } (p_9, p_5, p_{25})$
$p_{27} = \pi(\Re(Venturas : \text{PHYSICAL-OBJECT})) \sqcap p_{27} \text{ QUALIFIED } q_{27} \sqcap$
   $q_{27} \text{ SUPPORTED-BY } (p_{10}, p_5, p_{25}) \sqcap q_{27} \text{ MULTIPLY-DEDUCED-BY } p_{23}$
$p_{28} = \pi(\Re(Venturas : \text{HARDWARE})) \sqcap p_{28} \text{ QUALIFIED } q_{28} \sqcap$
   $q_{28} \text{ SUPPORTED-BY } (p_8, p_5, p_{25})$

In **H2** all hypotheses generated for $Venturas$ (p_{26} to p_{28}) receive the quality label SUPPORTED, in **H1** none. This support (cf. rule II) is derived from p_{25} and p_5 and the taxonomic implications p_5 has (e.g., p_9 corresponds to p_{26}). Since both hypothesis spaces, **H1** and **H2**, imply that $Venturas$ is at least a PHYSICAL-OBJECT the label MULTIPLY-DEDUCED (rule IV) is derived for both spaces. Rule III also triggers in both hypothesis spaces, so it does not contribute to any further discrimination.[1]

H2, however, can further be refined. According to the terminological axioms, $Compaq$ – a NOTEBOOK-PRODUCER (p_1) – produces NOTEBOOKs or ACCUs. Thus, $Venturas$, the filler of the PRODUCES role of $Compaq$ (p_{25}) must either be a NOTEBOOK (**H2$_1$**)

   $p_{29} = \pi(\Re(Venturas : \text{NOTEBOOK})) \sqcap p_{29} \text{ QUALIFIED } q_{29} \sqcap$
      $q_{29} \text{ SUPPORTED-BY } (p_7, p_5, p_{25})$

or an ACCU (**H2$_2$**)

   $p_{30} = \pi(\Re(Venturas : \text{ACCU})) \sqcap p_{30} \text{ QUALIFIED } q_{30}$

Finally, **H2$_1$** (but not **H2$_2$**) is supported by $\langle Compaq \text{ PRODUCES } LTE\text{-}Lite \rangle$, $\langle LTE\text{-}Lite : \text{NOTEBOOK} \rangle$ and $\langle Compaq \text{ PRODUCES } Venturas \rangle$; cf. rule II.

Since we operate with a partial parser, the linguistic analyses may remain incomplete due to extra- or ungrammatical input. Assume such a scenario as in: "... **Venturas** ... **entwickelt** ... **Compaq**."[2] Due to the value restrictions that hold for DEVELOP, $Compaq$ may only fill the AGENT role (in **H1** and in **H2**):

---

[1] We only consider the derivation of quality labels referring to the target concept and leave away those labels that support propositions already contained in the KB kernel.
[2] "... **Venturas** ... **develops** ... **Compaq**."

$$p_{31} = \pi(\Re(develop\text{-}02 : \text{DEVELOP})) \sqcap p_{31} \text{ QUALIFIED } q_{31} \sqcap$$
$$p_{32} = \pi(\Re(develop\text{-}02 \text{ AGENT } Compaq)) \sqcap p_{32} \text{ QUALIFIED } q_{32}$$

In **H1**, where *Venturas* is assumed to be a PRODUCER, *Venturas* (additionally to *Compaq*) may fill the AGENT role of DEVELOP:

$$p_{33} = \pi(\Re(develop\text{-}02 \text{ AGENT } Venturas)) \sqcap p_{33} \text{ QUALIFIED } q_{33} \sqcap$$
$$q_{33} \text{ ADDITIONALLY-FILLED-BY } p_{32} \sqcap q_{32} \text{ ADDITIONALLY-FILLED-BY } p_{33}$$

In **H2** and the spaces it subsumes, viz. **H2$_1$** and **H2$_2$**, *Venturas* may only fill the PATIENT role. Given the occurrences of p_{31}, p_{32} and p_{34} the verb interpretation rule for DEVELOP fires and produces p_{35}. This immediately leads to the generation of a CROSS-SUPPORT label (rule I) from proposition (p_{25}):

$$p_{34} = \pi(\Re(develop\text{-}02 \text{ PATIENT } Venturas)) \sqcap p_{34} \text{ QUALIFIED } q_{34} \sqcap$$
$$p_{35} = \pi(\Re(Venturas \text{ HAS-DEVELOPER } Compaq)) \sqcap p_{35} \text{ QUALIFIED } q_{35} \sqcap$$
$$q_{35} \text{ CROSS-SUPPORTED-BY } p_{25} \sqcap q_{25} \text{ CROSS-SUPPORTED-BY } p_{35}$$

Finally, one of the interpretations of an ambiguous phrase such as "Die **NiMH-Akkus** von **Venturas** ..."[3] invalidates context **H2$_2$** (ACCU hypothesis). The inconsistency is due to the fact that an accumulator cannot be part of another accumulator. For the hypothesis space **H1** we get

$$p_{36} = \pi(\Re(Venturas \text{ PRODUCES } NiMH\text{-}Accu)) \sqcap p_{36} \text{ QUALIFIED } q_{36}$$

and for **H2$_1$**

$$p_{37} = \pi(\Re(NiMHAccu \text{ ENERGY-FOR } Venturas)) \sqcap p_{37} \text{ QUALIFIED } q_{37} \sqcap$$
$$q_{27} \text{ SUPPORTED-BY } (p_{10}, p_{11}, p_{37}) \sqcap q_{28} \text{ SUPPORTED-BY } (p_8, p_{11}, p_{37}) \sqcap$$
$$q_{26} \text{ SUPPORTED-BY } (p_9, p_{11}, p_{37}) \sqcap q_{29} \text{ SUPPORTED-BY } (p_7, p_{11}, p_{37})$$

Summing up that discussion, the most promising hypothesis space is **H2$_1$** (covering the NOTEBOOK reading) which holds 10 positive labels: MULTIPLY-DEDUCED (1), CROSS-SUPPORTED (1), SUPPORTED (8), but only one negative label (ADDITIONAL-ROLE-FILLER). In contrast, **H2$_2$** is ruled out, since an inconsistency has been detected by the classifier. Finally, **H1** (holding the PRODUCER interpretation) has received only little confirmation – MULTIPLY-DEDUCED (1) and ADDITIONAL-ROLE-FILLER (2) – and is, therefore, less plausible than **H2$_1$**.

From the example above, it should be quite evident that the learning procedure we propose is heavily knowledge-based and thus bears strong similarities with analytical learning approaches. It requires a significant stock of deep *a priori* knowledge of the underlying domain (TBox level), as evidenced by rule I (CROSS-SUPPORTED) and the general rule excluding inconsistent information. It also expects large volumes of explicit factual background knowledge (ABox level) acquired from whatever sources, as evidenced by rule II (SUPPORTED) and rule IV (MULTIPLY-DEDUCED).

---

[3] "The **NiMH accus** contained in the **Venturas**..." provokes the inconsistency; this reading is opposed to "The **NiMH accus** supplied by **Venturas**..."

We have run a first round of experiments to empirically test our approach, still suffering from the lack of sufficiently sized knowledge bases (the current test site contains approximately 650 concepts and 350 roles). The preliminary results we have achieved are far from being conclusive to judge the relative merits of the entire approach or its component parts (e.g., the validity of single qualification rules). We have, nevertheless, gathered some experience, in particular, relating to the effects the (non-)availability of knowledge structures has on the proper discrimination of concept hypotheses. Under conditions of poor knowledge coverage, the potential for quality assessment diminishes more and more and results in low reduction rates for the number of hypotheses. The total size of hypothesis spaces in our experiments ranged from 3 to 50. Under *worst-case* conditions (unconstrained generation of hypothesis spaces, on the order of 40 to 50) the mean reduction rate drops to approximately 10%, since only few qualification rules can fire due to insufficient knowledge structures. Under *quasi-optimal* conditions (generation of few hypothesis spaces, on the order of 3 to 5) reduction rates rise to almost perfect values singling out one valid hypothesis. The successful discrimination of concept hypotheses is thus a direct reflection of sufficiently rich knowledge structures which enable most or all qualification rules to fire.

7 Related Work

In this section, we will briefly locate our approach in the intersecting fields of NLU and concept learning. We are not engaged in learning word definitions from machine-readable dictionaries like work reported in Alshawi (1987) or Slator (1989), since the lexical gaps encountered in texts, at least in our technical domain, cannot be satisfactorily closed by MRDs. We are also not concerned with lexical acquisition from *very large* corpora using sentence level collocational data as proposed in Zernik (1989) or Velardi et al. (1991), although our learning scheme would allow for such an extension. However, our approach bears a much closer relationship to the work of Mooney (1987), Riloff (1993), Hastings & Lytinen (1994), and Soderland et al. (1995), who aim at the automated learning of *word meanings* from context. But there is a main difference between their work and ours — the need to cope with *several competing* concept hypotheses is not an issue in these studies. Considering, however, the apparent limitations almost any parser available for realistic text understanding tasks currently suffers from, usually more than one concept hypothesis can be derived from a given natural language input. Therefore, we stress the need for a hypothesis generation and evaluation component as an integral part of any robust NLU system that learns in tandem with such restricted parsing devices.

On the other hand, concept learning which is deeply rooted in the framework of terminological logics is just beginning to attract the machine learning community. For instance, KLUSTER (Kietz & Morik, 1994) is a system that builds a TBox from a given ABox by way of constructive induction. To keep the learning task tractable several restrictions on the expressiveness of the language are introduced (e.g., disjunctions are not allowed). Cohen and Hirsh (1994) take a similar induction-oriented perspective. The main difference to our work lies in the overall learning task: We start with an already specified TBox and plenty of hypotheses concerning a new concept. The immediate goal is to build up concept hypotheses for that concept and to evaluate and rank these tentative concept descriptions in quality-based terms according to a credibility scale. Such a quality-based evaluation of competing hypotheses in a learning system has also been suggested by Clark (1988). However, the resolution strategy he proposes is not flexible enough, as it crucially depends on a pre-specified *stronger-than* relation between sets of hypotheses. This requirement seems untenable for our application, since unrestricted combinations of quality assessments cannot be reasonably specified in advance.

8 Conclusion

In this paper, we have introduced a methodology for concept learning from texts that relies upon second-order reasoning about statements expressed in a (first-order) terminological representation language. Metareasoning, as we conceive it, is based on the reification of terminological expressions, the assignment of qualifications to these reified structures, and the reasoning about degrees of credibility these qualifications give rise to based on the evaluation of second-order qualification rules. A major constraint underlying our work is that this kind of quality-based metareasoning is completely embedded in the homogeneous framework of standard (first-order) terminological reasoning systems using multiple contexts, so that we may profit from their full-blown classification mechanisms.

The applicability of this terminological metareasoning framework (cf. Schnattinger et al. (1995) for a more detailed account) has been shown for a concept learning task in the framework of realistic text understanding. We are currently focusing on the formulation of additional qualification rules and the formalization of a qualification calculus which captures the evaluation logic of multiple qualification labels within a terminological framework. The learning system described in this paper has been fully implemented in LOOM (MacGregor, 1994).

Acknowledgments. This work was supported by a grant from DFG under the account Ha2097/2-1. We like to thank the members of our group for fruitful discussions. We also gratefully acknowledge the provision of the LOOM system from USC/ISI; in particular, we appreciate the valuable, constant support from Thomas A. Russ.

References

Alshawi, H. (1987). Processing dictionary definitions with phrasal pattern hierarchies. *Computational Linguistics*, 13(3-4):195–202.

Buvač, S., Buvač, V., & Mason, I. (1995). Metamathematics of contexts. *Fundamenta Informaticae*, 23(3).

Clark, P. (1988). Representing arguments as background knowledge for constraining generalisation. In *EWSL'88 - Proc. of the 3rd European Working Session on Learning*, pages 37–44. London: Pitman.

Cohen, W. & Hirsh, H. (1994). The learnability of description logics with equality constraints. *Machine Learning*, 17(2-3):169–199.

Friedman, D. & Wand, M. (1984). Reification: Reflection without metaphysics. In *Proc. of the 1984 ACM Symposium on Lisp and Functional Programming*, pages 348–355. Austin, Texas, August 1984.

Hahn, U., Schacht, S., & Bröker, N. (1994). Concurrent, object-oriented dependency parsing: The PARSETALK model. *International Journal of Human-Computer Studies*, 41(1-2):179–222.

Hastings, P. & Lytinen, S. (1994). The ups and downs of lexical acquisition. In *AAAI'94 - Proc. of the 12th National Conf. on Artificial Intelligence. Vol. 2*, pages 754–759. Seattle, Wash., July 31 - August 4, 1994. Menlo Park: AAAI Press/MIT Press.

Kietz, J. & Morik, K. (1994). A polynomial approach to the constructive induction of structural knowledge. *Machine Learning*, 14(2):193–217.

MacGregor, R. (1993). Representing reified relations in LOOM. *Journal of Experimental and Theoretical Artificial Intelligence*, 5:179–183.

MacGregor, R. (1994). A description classifier for the predicate calculus. In *AAAI'94 - Proc. of the 12th National Conf. on Artificial Intelligence. Vol. 1*, pages 213–220. Seattle, Wash., July 31 - August 4, 1994. Menlo Park: AAAI Press/MIT Press.

McCarthy, J. (1993). Notes on formalizing context. In *IJCAI'93 - Proc. of the 13th Intl. Joint Conf. on Artificial Intelligence. Vol. 1*, pages 555–560. Chambery, France, August 28 - September 3, 1993. San Mateo, CA: Morgan Kaufmann.

Mooney, R. (1987). Integrated learning of words and their underlying concepts. In *Proc. of the 9th Annual Conf. of the Cognitive Science Society*, pages 974–978. Seattle, Wash.,16-18 July 1987. Hillsdale, NJ: L. Erlbaum.

Riloff, E. (1993). Automatically constructing a dictionary for information extraction tasks. In *AAAI'93 - Proc. of the 11th National Conf. on Artificial Intelligence*, pages 811–816. Washington, D.C., July 11-15, 1993. Menlo Park: AAAI Press/MIT Press.

Schnattinger, K., Hahn, U., & Klenner, M. (1995). Terminological meta-reasoning by reification and multiple contexts. In *Progress in Artificial Intelligence. EPIA'95 - Proc. of the 7th Portuguese Conf. on Artificial Intelligence*, pages 1–16. Funchal, Madeira Island, Portugal, October 3-6, 1995. Berlin: Springer.

Slator, B. (1989). Extracting lexical knowledge from dictionary text. *Knowledge Acquisition*, 1:89–112.

Soderland, S., Fisher, D., Aseltine, J., & Lehnert, W. (1995). CRYSTAL: Inducing a conceptual dictionary. In *IJCAI'95 - Proc. of the 14th Intl. Joint Conf. on Artificial Intelligence. Vol. 2*, pages 1314–1319. Montreal, Quebec, Canada, August 19-25, 1995. San Mateo, CA: Morgan Kaufmann.

Velardi, P., Pazienza, M., & Fasolo, M. (1991). How to encode semantic knowledge: A method for meaning representation and computer-aided acquisition. *Computational Linguistics*, 17(2):153–170.

Wilensky, R. (1993). Knowledge acquisition and natural language processing. In Chipman, S. & Meyrowitz, A. (Eds.), *Foundations of knowledge acquisition: Cognitive models of complex learning*, pages 309–336. Boston: Kluwer.

Woods, W. & Schmolze, J. (1992). The KL-ONE family. *Computers & Mathematics with Applications*, 23(2-5):133–177.

Zernik, U. (1989). Lexicon acquisition: Learning from corpus by capitalizing on lexical categories. In *IJCAI'89 - Proc. of the 11th Intl. Joint Conf. on Artificial Intelligence. Vol. 2*, pages 1556–1562. Detroit, Michigan, USA, 20-25 August, 1989. San Mateo, CA: Morgan Kaufmann.

Lecture Notes in Artificial Intelligence (LNAI)

Lecture Notes in Computer Science